MASTERPLOTS II

DRAMA SERIES
REVISED EDITION

MASTERPLOTS II

DRAMA SERIES
REVISED EDITION

4

Sev–Z

Indexes

Editor, Revised Edition
CHRISTIAN H. MOE
Southern Illinois University

Editor, First Edition
FRANK N. MAGILL

SALEM PRESS

Pasadena, California   Hackensack, New Jersey

Editor in Chief: Dawn P. Dawson

Managing Editor: Christina J. Moose *Assistant Editor:* Andrea E. Miller
Project Editor: R. Kent Rasmussen *Research Supervisor:* Jeffry Jensen
Production Editor: Joyce I. Buchea *Acquisitions Editor:* Mark Rehn
Copy Editor: Sarah Hilbert *Layout:* William Zimmerman

Library of Congress Cataloging-in-Publication Data
Masterplots II : drama series / editor Christian H. Moe. — Rev.
    p. cm.
    ISBN 1-58765-116-5 (set : alk. paper) — ISBN 1-58765-117-3 (vol. 1 : alk. paper) —
ISBN 1-58765-118-1 (vol. 2 : alk. paper) — ISBN 1-58765-119-X (vol. 3 : alk. paper) —
ISBN 1-58765-120-3 (vol. 4 : alk. paper)
    1. Drama—20th century—Stories, plots, etc. I. Moe, Christian Hollis, 1929-
PN6112.5 .M37 2003
809.2′04—dc21

                                                                        2003012651

Second Printing

PRINTED IN THE UNITED STATES OF AMERICA

TABLE OF CONTENTS

TABLE OF CONTENTS

COMPLETE LIST OF TITLES IN ALL VOLUMES

Volume 1

Volume 2

Volume 3

MASTERPLOTS II

Volume 4

MASTERPLOTS II

DRAMA SERIES
REVISED EDITION

A SEVERED HEAD

Authors: Iris Murdoch (1919-1999) and J. B. Priestley (1894-1984)
Type of plot: Psychological
Time of plot: The early 1960's
Locale: London
First produced: 1963, at the Theatre Royal, Bristol, England
First published: 1964

> *Principal characters:*
> MARTIN LYNCH-GIBBON, the owner of a family winery
> GEORGIE HANDS, Martin's mistress, a junior lecturer
> ANTONIA, Martin's wife
> PALMER ANDERSON, a psychoanalyst
> ROSEMARY, Martin's sister
> ALEXANDER, Martin's brother, a sculptor
> HONOR KLEIN, Palmer's half sister, an anthropologist

The Play

A *Severed Head* is a play in three acts, the first two of which contain seven scenes each; the shorter third act contains four scenes. The play opens in late December in Georgie Hands's untidy bed-sitting-room near Covent Garden and moves back and forth between there, the sitting room of the Lynch-Gibbons' house in Hereford Square, and Palmer Anderson's house in Chester Square. The play is about the passionate entanglements between the Lynch-Gibbon family and Palmer and his half sister Honor Klein. Georgie is involved with both families.

Georgie's room is a candlelit nest where Georgie and Martin lie half-entwined in front of the fire. The dialogue begins with Georgie's anxious questions about Martin's wife, and her fear of being dropped if Antonia discovers the affair. The relationship between Martin and Georgie is much more important to her than it is to him.

The second scene occurs in Martin's elegant, lavishly decorated home after he leaves Georgie. Antonia returns from a visit with Palmer Anderson, her therapist, and announces that she is desperately in love with him and wants her freedom. Martin, incredulous, tries to talk her out of it, then lets her lead him to Palmer's house. Palmer tries to convince Martin that he and Antonia will continue to care for Martin in a loving way.

Martin's sister, Rosemary, and his brother, Alexander, visit him at home to try to cheer him. Martin writes to Georgie about his marital problems, imploring her to be patient. The next day Martin and Honor converse, and Honor berates Martin for giving in so readily to Palmer and Antonia's demands.

Martin visits Georgie and begs her to remain his "secret" for the time being. He takes her to his home in Hereford Square, hears someone making an entrance, and shoos Georgie out the back entrance. Honor enters and notices Georgie's scarf.

Act 2 takes place in Palmer's house, where Martin has been summoned. Palmer announces that he and Antonia have found out about Georgie. Although Martin begs to be left alone, the couple demands to meet Georgie. Martin rushes to Georgie's apartment, and Georgie confesses that she told Honor about their affair. The next day Martin goes to Georgie's empty apartment. Georgie and Alexander arrive together. Furious, Martin demands that Alexander leave and then asks Georgie to marry him. Georgie mocks him, and Martin leaves. That night he goes to Palmer's house to deliver a case of wine he has promised Antonia. The three have a glass of wine together. On his way out, Martin meets Honor, who berates him. He turns rude and grabs her wrist as she tries to leave. They exchange blows, wrestle, and he overpowers her, striking her face. Dazed, he releases her and returns home. At home, Martin realizes he must see Honor. He goes to Palmer's house, finds no one downstairs, and ascends to the bedroom in a mental fog. He finds Honor and Palmer embracing in bed.

Act 3 opens in Martin's drawing room, thirty-six hours later. Martin is sleeping when Antonia arrives, demanding to know what has changed Palmer. Palmer arrives, and a scuffle between him and Martin occurs when Palmer tries to force Antonia to return to him. Palmer leaves, defeated. Alexander calls and announces he will marry Georgie. Martin receives a parcel with Georgie's hair. The next scene opens in Palmer's bedroom, where Georgie is convalescing after a suicide attempt. Martin visits her and then runs into Honor downstairs. Martin announces his love for her, but Honor says he is dreaming and that she and Palmer are leaving London shortly. The play ends in Martin's home, where Antonia breezes in to announce she is off to Rome with Alexander, with whom she had a previous affair. She leaves. Honor arrives unexpectedly to announce that Georgie is flying off to the United States with Palmer. Martin and Honor try to imagine what their own future together will be.

Themes and Meanings

The title of this play, *A Severed Head*, is a key clue to the underlying themes. The "head" theme appears in the first act, when Alexander, after stopping at a gallery to pick up one of his sculptures, stops in at Martin's house to offer condolence. Martin asks to see the sculpture, and Alexander unpacks a head of Antonia. Martin protests that it cannot be Antonia without her body, but Alexander answers that "heads are us most of all; they are the apex of our incarnation." Further, he adds, "the head can represent the female genitals, feared not desired."

Martin introduces the associated theme of power in his reply: "You're a magician too, you know. You gain power over people by making images of them." Power is an important issue in this play. Martin seems to have less power than the other men: He loses Antonia, then Georgie, and he is under Antonia and Palmer's power through most of the play.

As the play progresses it is apparent that Honor also has a great deal of power. She is the one who discovers the affair between Martin and Georgie and tells Palmer and Antonia. She is also the one who introduces Alexander and Georgie, which leads to their affair. She is a catalyst in the affairs of the others and does not hesitate to use her power. In act 3, when Martin professes his love and apprehension of her, which he believes is deeper than ordinary knowledge, she defines herself in mythic terms.

> I have become a terrible object of fascination for you. I am a severed head such as primitive tribes and old alchemists used, when they put a piece of gold on the tongue to make the head utter prophecies. And perhaps long acquaintance with such an object might lead one to a very strange knowledge indeed.

Honor, the anthropologist who has lived in many lands and acquired occult knowledge, as she demonstrates earlier with her Japanese sword trick, has also acquired power, which comes with this knowledge.

Yet, once he discovers the incestuous relationship between Palmer and Honor, Martin also gains power. Antonia returns to him. When Palmer comes to Martin's home to retrieve Antonia and she resists, he strikes Palmer, who then backs off. This is the first time he fights Palmer's power and wins. When Antonia confesses that she has been involved in an affair with Alexander, the scales fall from Martin's eyes and he realizes that his comfortable life has been based on illusion. Finally able to see the truth, Martin is a changed man, a man worthy to be Honor's mate. She returns to him and reminds him of a myth in which a king's friend, having seen the queen naked, finds out he must either die or kill the king and marry her. Martin, having seen the real Honor, must now be her consort.

Dramatic Devices

Most of the characters in the play are introduced in the first scene of the first act through Martin and Georgie's conversation. The audience learns much about Antonia, who is the main topic of the conversation, and by extension, about Palmer and Honor. The audience learns that Georgie met Palmer and Honor at a party in Cambridge once. Martin remarks about Palmer, "I feel he has real power in him," and by saying so, forecasts the plot of the play, which involves a power struggle. Georgie describes Honor as somewhat formidable: "Well, she's spent a lot of time in weird places—living with tribes. . . . My God—she used to terrify me," a comment that provides a context for the strange emotions Honor evokes in Martin later in the play.

The action takes place in three interiors, and each of them is a reflection of the people who inhabit them. Georgie's bed-sitting-room is untidy, cluttered, and ripe with cigarette, wine, and presumably lovemaking scents. By contrast, Martin's drawing room is lavish, elegantly paneled, and finely furnished, with a cheery fire in the grate and Christmas cards on the piano. Yet, as Martin's life unravels during the first act, his home also deteriorates. By the last scene the audience finds his drawing room dusty, bleak, and uninhabited, with a cold hearth. Palmer Anderson's home is different: His study is bright, hygienic, and modernly furnished, decorated with Asian objects. His bedroom, where part of the action takes place, contains a huge, golden, double bed.

There is a great deal of rushing back and forth between residences, which lends a certain comic effect to the shifting allegiances between characters. The rushing back and forth is not as obvious in the novel from which the play was adapted, but the required cutting for stage presentation emphasizes it.

Irony is the device that provides the play with dramatic tension and excitement. The audience is as uninformed as Martin about the alliances of the characters, but since new revelations are foreshadowed in previous acts, when they do occur they seem both inevitable and shocking. For example, Martin is surprised to discover that Antonia has notified Alexander of the breakup of her marriage by letter, yet later, when Martin discovers that Antonia has had a previous affair with Alexander, the audience realizes that the letter was a clue.

Critical Context

The novel, *A Severed Head*, was adapted as a play in a collaboration between Iris Murdoch and J. B. Priestley. The play had a trial run in Bristol, England, in 1963, then ran to critical acclaim in London for two and one-half years. Columbia Pictures released a film version in 1970. The play is seldom staged, but the film still runs occasionally in museums and art houses. It is the only internationally successful play that Murdoch, one of the foremost British novelists of her generation, ever wrote.

Although the play was a collaboration, it is apparent that Priestley's main role was in structuring it for the stage. Many of Murdoch's stock characters and her novelistic devices are immediately recognizable. Significantly, Honor is Jewish, a member of an ethnic group often used in Murdoch's novels to indicate special powers, such as the memorable Julius King in *A Fairly Honorable Defeat* (1970). Martin is one of Murdoch's typical male protagonists, a self-deceived man who must undergo several painful experiences before he accepts the reality of other people. Only after Antonia leaves him for Palmer does he understand he has been living in a dream world.

Symmetrical pairing of lovers is also one of Murdoch's favorite plot devices, one that has long been a staple of playwrights. This device drives the plot of her novel *Nuns and Soldiers* (1980), which has no fewer than six romantic pairings, as well as the plot of *A Severed Head*, in which the couplings and separations of the three pairs of lovers are handled with irony, wit, and a certain amount of irrationality.

Sources for Further Study

Baldanza, Frank. *Iris Murdoch*. New York: Twayne, 1974.

Bove, Cheryl K. *Understanding Iris Murdoch*. Columbia: University of South Carolina Press, 1993.

Conradi, Peter J. *Iris Murdoch: The Saint and the Artist*. New York: St. Martin's Press, 1986.

Johnson, Deborah. *Iris Murdoch*. Bloomington: Indiana University Press, 1987.

Sage, Lorna. *Women in the House of Fiction: Post-war Women Novelists*. New York: Routledge, 1992.

Sheila Golburgh Johnson

SEXUAL PERVERSITY IN CHICAGO

Author: David Mamet (1947-   )
Type of plot: Comedy
Time of plot: The 1970's
Locale: Chicago, Illinois
First produced: 1974, at the Organic Theatre, Chicago, Illinois
First published: 1977

> *Principal characters:*
> DAN SHAPIRO, an inexperienced young man
> BERNARD LITKO, his cynical friend
> DEBORAH, an inexperienced young woman
> JOAN, her cynical friend

The Play

Sexual Perversity in Chicago opens as Bernard is telling his best friend Dan about a recent sexual adventure. Bernard's story is unrelated to the play's plot, but it does establish the play's thematic motif: men, women, and sex. This first scene also presents Bernard and Dan's relationship as that of experienced man-of-the-world to relative neophyte and establishes some of David Mamet's stylistic trademarks—a discovery of the poetic rhythms of everyday speech, an abundance of obscenities, and a non-reflective, give-and-take dialogue. The next scene introduces the play's two female characters, Joan and Deborah. Their relationship is similar to the Bernard and Dan relationship. Joan is jaded, bitter, and full of advice concerning men, while Deborah by comparison seems naïve and hopeful. Their first scene is only five lines long and portrays their confusion as to what it is men really want. The audience, however, has been given the answer to that question in the preceding scene—men want wild sexual adventures with no commitment.

Thus begins a montage of scenes involving Bernard, Dan, Joan, and Deborah, singularly and in various combinations. Plot—what there is of it—is subservient to character and thematic explorations. Mamet is not as interested in his story as he is in why the story happens. What one might perceive as the play's plot—Deborah and Dan meet, sleep together, move in together, fall in love, fall out of love, and separate— takes only seven of the play's thirty-four scenes. Fully twice as many scenes are exclusively male, as Bernard and Dan talk about women, and Deborah has as many scenes with Joan as she does with Dan. The play's story seems really to be about the relationship between the male characters and how it affects Deborah and Dan's romance, with a second story being about how the female relationship is affected by the romance. The least important (though catalytic) story seems to be the romance itself. The progression that this romance takes, from sex to love to hate, and the fact that more than half of the Deborah and Dan scenes take place in bed lead the audience to believe that romance is equated with sexual conquest and gratification, even though Deborah and Dan want to believe otherwise.

Bernard emerges as the play's most interesting character. His audacious language and reactionary attitudes toward women make him outrageously humorous, while his boundless energy and intensity make him a very compelling—if not a laudable— personality. The implausibility of his introductory anecdote makes the audience doubt his truthfulness at the same time they are enjoying his imagination; while Bernard says and does funny things, however, he is a serious character. The play reveals that for all of his machismo and the fatherly advice that he constantly offers Dan concerning women, Bernard fails in his own efforts to establish contact with the opposite sex. Mamet gives him only two scenes with women. In the first, Joan rebuffs his advances in a singles bar, and he reacts with extreme hostility. In the second, he treats Deborah and Dan in such a condescending manner that he manages to alienate both of them.

Late in the play, the audience is given a glimpse of why Bernard is the way he is. The scene is set in the toy department of Marshall Field's Department Store, a locale rich with connotations of family, childhood, and innocence. Here Bernard feels secure enough to admit to an early childhood homosexual experience, whose impact he has not yet fully resolved. Mamet is strongly suggesting that Bernard's compulsive womanizing and woman-baiting is masking (and revealing) latent homosexual tendencies. It becomes clear that Bernard's hostility toward Deborah and Dan's relationship is the hostility of a spurned lover, however platonic the love may have been.

Joan balances Bernard. She hates men, disparages relationships, and is probably herself in love with Deborah. She and Bernard together form a kind of antagonistic Greek chorus, commenting on the progress of Deborah and Dan's affair, interjecting their own viewpoints, and fashioning morals from the affair's dismal conclusion. Joan and Bernard represent the social/sexual reality with which Deborah and Dan's attempts at contact must contend. It is ironic that this couple's best friends become their worst enemies, ridiculing and trivializing the emotions that Deborah and Dan are experiencing. At the play's end the women are with the women and the men are with the men. Deborah and Dan have learned the hard way that Joan was right when she described relations between the sexes as "physical and mental mutilations we perpetrate on each other, day in, day out. . . . It's a dirty joke, Deborah, the whole god-forsaken business."

Themes and Meanings

Sexual Perversity in Chicago examines why it is so difficult to find and express heterosexual love. Deborah and Dan are attracted to each other and move in together, hoping to create a long-term, loving relationship. Their efforts to communicate, however, are thwarted by the very language that they use. As critic Robert Storey has pointed out, "It is not so much Bernie as it is his language that forbids all real intimacy with women." Men and women are at a barely concealed, all-out war, treating each other with a casual hostility. Vulgarities are a part of the courting ritual and are used as substitutes for the expression of real thought or emotion.

Mamet has stated that he wrote this play to show "how what we say influences what we think." When the characters in *Sexual Perversity in Chicago* refer to each other as bodily parts, bodily functions, or as unhuman beings, they are thinking of each other and relating each other as if these words were factual descriptions. For Mamet, vulgarity is not casual—it represents a dehumanization, a destruction of the communication process in the same way as do more obvious words such as "nigger," "kike," or "spick." The play's final scene clearly demonstrates this process and its results.

Bernard and Dan are relaxing on a Lake Michigan beach, becoming angry at women's behavior and simultaneously admiring women's bodies. Dan has the play's last words, which describe women as unhuman beings who cannot meet his expectations or demands. His word choice succinctly demonstrates that the very words he uses block the communication he seems to want so badly. His words, as an attractive woman ignores his advances, are simply "deaf *bitch*." It is possible to consider Bernard and Dan as innocents, to believe that they do not realize what they are doing; it is more to the point, however, that they are continually contributing to the destruction of their own ability to communicate.

That language creates perception and resultant behavior is the play's main idea: Developed in the context of relationships among young, unmarried urbanites, it leads to other concepts as well. The first is that true communication can only be established with members of one's own sex. Bernard and Dan can talk to each other, but not to Deborah or Joan; the reverse is also the case. For better or worse, Mamet's observation is that humans' relationships with members of their own sex are more important to them than their relationships with members of the opposite gender, largely because they find comfort in being understood and being able to understand. Language has created a division between genders, a rift more potentially dangerous to basic human interactions than those between nations, races, or even species.

Both men and women in the play see themselves as victims, but the primarily male focus of the play clearly indicts them as the major cause for this dilemma. Bernard may blame the women's movement for his problems and Dan may blame Deborah, but in actuality they themselves are the cause of their—and women's—unhappiness. The primarily male focus of the play within the context of a heterosexual love story also supports the play's third main thematic motif: Were it not for sex, men would prefer not to have anything to do with women at all.

Dramatic Devices

Sexual Perversity in Chicago has a running time of approximately fifty-five minutes. Despite this relatively short length, the play has thirty-four separate scenes which make use of thirteen different settings in the city of Chicago, including a health club, a library, an art museum, a restaurant, and a pornographic movie theater. Mamet does not make linear time connections between most of the scenes. For example, the scene in which Dan moves Deborah's belongings out of Joan's apartment is followed not by a scene in which he moves Deborah's belongings into his apartment, but rather by a totally unrelated monologue by Bernard concerning the Equal Rights Amendment. Emotional or thematic connections take place in the psyche of the individual audience member, but are not apparent in the psyches of the characters.

Twenty of the play's scenes are self-contained; that is, they do not advance the play's plot because they make no reference to what occurred in previous scenes, nor do they provide information used or repeated in scenes that follow. Most of the play's scenes, then, could be placed anywhere in the script—the play does not have a logical structure, save for the seven scenes which present Dan and Deborah's relationship from first meeting to final dissolution. Mamet clearly uses a dramatic device— structure—to support the play's content. The multitude of scenes juxtaposed in alogical ways in unrelated settings creates a fast-paced, disjointed montage—an appropriate background for distrust and hate among unmarried young people living in an urban environment.

Mamet's use of another basic device, language, further adds to this feeling of hostility and also singles out the male characters for particular criticism. If one accepts the argument that the habitual use of scatological and sexual expletives dehumanizes both user and listener, that it exposes the lack of ability or the lack of desire to communicate, then language usage in this play exposes Dan and Bernard as insensitive and uncaring. Of the more than 170 scatological or sexual expletives in the script, the male characters speak nearly 160 of them. (Significantly, female use of the terminology increases in their scenes with the male characters.) Two scenes in particular are notable for the way that Mamet shows how men use vulgarities in their relationships with women. In the first, when Joan rejects Bernard's attempt to pick her up in a singles' bar, he responds with a torrent of abusive language. He uses such language as a weapon, in an attempt to destroy Joan's self-respect as she has destroyed his by spurning his advances. When she does not respond in kind, does not dehumanize herself by using Bernard's obscene, dehumanizing language, he is rendered impotent and angrily leaves the bar.

In the second example, Deborah lets Dan know that his language protects him from self-expression and self-exposure; she demands more of their relationship than Dan's reductive language allows him to commit. It is significant that Deborah's final judgment on Dan ("jerk") is neither scatological nor sexual—she, like Joan, refuses to lower herself to the male language level.

Critical Context

Sexual Perversity in Chicago, along with its companion play, *Duck Variations* (pr. 1972, pb. 1977), was Mamet's first critical and popular success. *Sexual Perversity in Chicago* won the Joseph Jefferson Award in 1975; in 1976, along with *American Buffalo* (pr. 1975, pb. 1977), it won the Obie Award for best new American play. While later plays did not return to the sexual battleground in any significant way, Mamet continued his exploration of how characters speak to one another, and how language exposes and hides feelings and intentions. Many critics have compared him to Harold Pinter because of these efforts; Mamet paid the British author homage by dedicating the published version (1984) of the Pulitzer Prize-winning *Glengarry Glen Ross* (pr. 1983) to him.

Mamet has continued to focus on male characters, but *Sexual Perversity in Chicago* is unusual in that the main topic of male conversation is women. With *American Buffalo*, Mamet shifts from women and what they represent to money and what it means. His major plays are plays about deals—what they are, how they are made, who wins, who loses, and why. All the plays establish bonds of friendship and trust which are then ignored or destroyed for personal gain or power. These plays include *American Buffalo*, *Glengarry Glen Ross*, and *Speed-the-Plow* (pr., pb. 1988). Corruption and betrayal are Mamet's main concerns, although a children's play, *The Revenge of the Space Pandas: Or, Binky Rudich and the Two-Speed Clock* (pr. 1977, pb. 1978) is more light-hearted, and *A Life in the Theater* (pr., pb. 1977) depicts a supportive male relationship as two actors, one older than the other, discuss life and art.

With the exception of *The Revenge of the Space Pandas*, and to an extent *Speed-the-Plow*, women characters are nonexistent or do not figure prominently in the plays' dramatic action. Several one-acts followed closely on the heels of *Sexual Perversity in Chicago*, and although they also exhibited Mamet's facility with language, most critics think they lack the dramatic tension and focus found in *Sexual Perversity in Chicago*. These plays include *The Woods* (pr. 1977, pb. 1978), *The Water Engine* (pr. 1977, pb. 1979), *Reunion* (pr. 1976, pb. 1979), and *Dark Pony* (pr. 1977, pb. 1979). The last decade of the twentieth century was a prolific one for Mamet. His play titles from this period included *Oleanna* (pr. 1992, pb. 1993), *The Cryptogram* (pr., pb. 1994), *An Interview* (pr., pb. 1995), and *Boston Marriage* (pr. 1999, pb. 2001), while his screenplays included *Glengarry Glen Ross* (1992; adaptation of his play), *Hoffa* (1992), *Vanya on 42nd Street* (1994), *Wag the Dog* (1997), and *The Winslow Boy* (1999), among many others.

Sources for Further Study
Bigsby, C. W. E. *David Mamet.* London: Methuen, 1985.
Carroll, Dennis. *David Mamet.* New York: St. Martin's Press, 1987.
Dean, Anne. *David Mamet: Language as Dramatic Action.* Teaneck, N.J.: Fairleigh Dickinson University Press, 1990.
Duberman, Martin. "The Great Gray Way." *Harper's Magazine*, May, 1978, 79-80, 83-87.
Kane, Leslie, ed. *David Mamet: A Casebook.* New York: Garland, 1991.
Lahr, John. "David Mamet." In *Show and Tell.* Woodstock, New York: Overlook, 2000.
Savran, David. "David Mamet." In *In Their Own Words: Contemporary American Playwrights.* New York: Theatre Communications Group, 1988.
Storey, Robert. "The Making of David Mamet." *Hollin's Critic* 16 (October, 1979): 1-11.

Alan Kreizenbeck

THE SHADOW BOX

Author: Michael Cristofer (1945-   )
Type of plot: Psychological
Time of plot: The late twentieth century
Locale: The grounds of a large hospital
First produced: 1975, at the Mark Taper Forum, Los Angeles
First published: 1977

> *Principal characters:*
> JOE, a terminally ill patient
> MAGGIE, his wife
> STEVE, his son
> BRIAN, a terminally ill patient
> MARK, his partner
> BEVERLY, his ex-wife
> FELICITY, a terminally ill patient
> AGNES, her grown daughter
> A DOCTOR/INTERVIEWER, voice only

The Play

The Shadow Box is actually three one-act plays intertwined together around a common theme. Since the play is set in three cottages that are connected to a large hospital and contain a terminally ill patient in each, the assumption is that this is a hospice or experimental program for dying patients and their families. Michael Cristofer never specifies the illness, but most critics have assumed the characters all have cancer. Tying the three plots together are interviews conducted by an unseen doctor, who questions the patients and their loved ones about having to confront death and their reactions to the process of dying. The time is linear with occasional lapses, covering one twenty-four-hour period. Scenes switch rapidly from one cottage to another, and sometimes lines alternate from character to character without regard to scene. The cottage inhabitants, however, never show an awareness of one another. At the end of the play, the characters speak directly to the audience in an almost chantlike delivery of similar lines, reminding the audience that "this moment" is all anyone has for certain.

In cottage one, Joe, a former factory worker and bar owner, awaits the arrival of his wife and son from New York City. The setting is the front porch of Joe's cottage. When they arrive, he learns that his wife, Maggie, has not told their son Steve that Joe is dying. This one-act focuses mainly on Maggie's inability to come to terms with the reality of Joe's situation. She keeps insisting that he will get better and come home, and he gently assures her that he will not. Her resistance to enter the cottage parallels her refusal to acknowledge that Joe's illness is terminal. He hopes she will accept his condition so they can enjoy what time they have left together. In an outburst of anger, Maggie finally faces the truth and they enter the cottage to break the news to Steve.

The setting for the second one-act is the living room of Brian's cottage. He and Mark, his homosexual partner, are surprised by the unannounced arrival of Brian's ex-wife, Beverly. Beverly is an outrageous and cynical drunk, who shows off her sexual trophies for Brian's amusement and to Mark's chagrin. Beverly's mission is to make sure Brian forgives her for past injuries, to say good-bye to him, and to ensure Mark will take care of him. Mark and Beverly make insulting comments about each other throughout the play to a point where Brian scolds them for wasting precious time. The confrontation drains Brian's energy and Mark puts him to bed. In Brian's absence, the tension between Mark and Beverly builds to a dramatic climax when Mark slaps Beverly across the face and then falls into her arms sobbing. They both realize that neither of them feels equipped to deal with Brian's death, but Mark vows to stay with him. Beverly escapes into the night in a drunken stupor, and Mark is left to take care of Brian.

The third one-act is set in the kitchen and dining area of the cottage and focuses on a feisty elderly woman named Felicity and her daughter, Agnes. Felicity mentally fades in and out with no regard to reality, sometimes reverting back to her days as a wife and mother on a farm. She waits for her daughter Claire to return. In one of her interviews with the doctor, Agnes explains that Felicity and Claire had a bitter argument, and Claire left home. Felicity has a deep need to make peace with her younger daughter before she dies. The play focuses more, however, on Agnes, who takes care of Felicity and puts up with her cantankerous outbursts and lapses into the past. Agnes tells the interviewer about Claire running away and getting killed in a car accident. Claire's death triggered Felicity's decline, and in her delusional state, Felicity believes that Claire is alive and coming for a visit. Because of Felicity's illness, Agnes helps her maintain this illusion by writing letters to her as if they were from Claire. Near death, Felicity lives for the next letter and a visit from her deceased daughter. Agnes is tired and hopes that Felicity will surrender to death soon but discovers through her interview that she has unwittingly prolonged Felicity's suffering by giving her something for which to live. Over and over again, Felicity asks Agnes what time it is, hoping that the mail has come and that there will be another letter from Claire.

Themes and Meanings

In describing *The Shadow Box*, one might say it is a play about death, as anyone might suspect of a play focusing on three terminally ill patients. Michael Cristofer, however, never reveals the illness from which his characters suffer because the play is not about their disease; it is about people and human emotions. Although there is a lot of conversation about dying and what it feels like to face impending death, most of the dialogue is about the joy of living.

The play's title indicates the meaning of the play. A shadow box is a picture frame in front of a recessed box on which shadows of objects can be displayed for viewing. The patients in *The Shadow Box* are not only on display for the doctors, who are studying them, but also for the audience. Even though the play is set in an experimental program, it does not focus on the program or the doctors involved. Cristofer's device of making the doctor a faceless voice reinforces the focus on the families and their responses to the dying process.

The final moments of the play affirm more than any other part its basic message, however, that every moment should be treasured. As Brian says near the end: "They tell you you're dying, and you say all right. But if I am dying . . . I must still be alive." The play is sad but never depressing. The characters continually reaffirm the gift of life, and in the antiphonal chanting at the end, they remind the audience that "This living. This life. This lifetime. This air. This earth. This smile. This pain. It doesn't last forever. It was never supposed to last forever. This breath. Yes. Yes. Yes. This moment," is all anyone can truly count on.

Dramatic Devices

Most of the play's critics concede that *The Shadow Box* uses many unique theatrical devices that increase its emotional power in performance. The first and most obvious is Cristofer's intertwining of three short plots into one cohesive play. This episodic structure allows the audience to concentrate on all three "families" without being overly drawn to one character. Scenes switch effortlessly from one cottage to the next and also to the interview area. Often dialogue from one area is overlapped with or punctuated by lines coming from another area. In a lesser play, this technique could blur the focus of the play, confusing and confounding the audience. However, Cristofer's mastery is in the flow of the play from one conversation to the next without any appreciable transitions needed. Although most episodic plays translate well to the screen, the television version of the play lacked the simultaneous impact of seeing all three families at the same time, even when the attention shifts from one to the other, making it flat and not as interesting on television. The beauty of the last two pages of the script had to be omitted, which robbed the play of its most powerful moments. This technique of having the characters walk through the fourth wall and become actors speaking directly to the audience is highly theatrical and most effective in emphasizing the play's theme.

Another interesting theatrical device used in this play is the set, which is basically one cottage seen from three different angles. This device implies that all the cottages are alike, and by setting each family in a different area of the cottage, the audience sees the commonality as well as the individuality of the characters' experiences reflected in the setting.

As in most plays, dramatic dialogue contains the action of the play so there is no need for a narrator that prose requires. Unlike novels that present the entirety of a character's story, plays usually begin very close to the climax so that the most dramatic part of the story is told through the action of the play. It is important to note that dramatic action is different from physical activity. The term "dramatic action" refers to the action that characters carry out in the play, usually related to another character. For example, when Beverly is showing Brian her "medals," she is "entertaining" him.

Likewise, Agnes comforts Felicity, and Maggie resists Joe. The dramatic action is contained in the dialogue of the play and comes through vividly in *The Shadow Box*, even though the characters do very little physical movement or activity. Cristofer handles exposition, the part of the characters' stories that is not presented onstage, in a purely dramatic way, finding present motivation to reveal past history between the characters. For example, Maggie and Joe's reminiscing about their younger days does not feel artificial or didactic, but quite natural for a couple facing the end of their time together.

Critical Context

With the rise of AIDS (acquired immunodeficiency syndrome) and the popularity of television talk shows in the late twentieth century, frank discussion about intimate issues such as terminal illness became commonplace. Plays from this period, such as Tony Kushner's *Angels in America, Parts One and Two* (pr. 1991, pb. 1992; pr. 1992, pb. 1993), deal honestly and openly with death and dying in a way that overshadows this sometimes sentimental play by Michael Cristofer. However, when Cristofer first wrote *The Shadow Box* in 1975, the idea of a hospice was still experimental and no prior play had dealt with this topic in such an unapologetic manner. Perhaps that is why it was awarded the Pulitzer Prize in 1977 and became an unexpected success for its author.

The play also experienced a great deal of controversy, primarily as a result of some of the language and the openly homosexual couple. The play continues to be banned from production in some high school and community theaters. Many educators and theater artists recognize the power of the life-affirming message of the play and the challenging roles it offers to actors, but pressure from parents and community members has forced many productions to close and teachers to be dismissed from their jobs.

Although most would call *The Shadow Box* a critical success since it garnered the Pulitzer Prize in drama and the Tony Award for best play in 1977, many critics originally found the play sentimental and condescending. A stellar 1994 cast revival at Circle in the Square Theatre in New York received a similar mix of reviews. Some critics contend the play is just as moving and affecting as it was originally, while others call it dated and contrived by twenty-first century standards. In his 1978 review of the play in *The Hudson Review*, John Simon likened it to playwriting by numbers with stereotypical characters and garish dialogue. On the other hand, noted critics such as Clive Barnes and Walter Kerr of *The New York Times* recognized the sentimentality of the play but praised Cristofer for its intensely realistic characters and identified it as a moving and courageous play.

Cristofer subsequently did not enjoy the same level of theatrical success that he received for *The Shadow Box*. His later plays, such as *Ice* (pr. 1976) and *Black Angel* (pr. 1978, pb. 1984), suffered from mostly negative reviews calling them, at best, unfocused and at worst, obscene. His *The Lady and the Clarinet* (pr. 1980, pb. 1985) received better reviews, but none equaled the success of *The Shadow Box*.

Cristofer also received praise for his acting and especially for his screenwriting. He played several leading roles in original productions of plays such as *The Tooth of Crime* (1974) and *Ashes* (1976) and won the Los Angeles Drama Critics Award for Acting in 1973 and the Theatre World Award for Performance in 1977. Cristofer has also written the screenplays for many films, including *The Witches of Eastwick* (1987), *Bonfire of the Vanities* (1990), and *Breaking Up* (1997). He wrote and directed a Home Box Office (HBO) movie titled *Gia* (1998) and a feature film, *Original Sin* (2001), both of which received mixed reviews.

Sources for Further Study

Kelley, Margot A. "Life Near Death: Art of Dying in Recent American Drama." In *Text and Presentation*, edited by Karelisa Hartigan. Lanham, Md.: University Press of America, 1988.

Kryhoski, Laura. "Critical Essay on *The Shadow Box*." In *Drama for Students*. Vol. 15. Detroit: Gale, 2002.

Wallace, Carey. "Critical Essay on *The Shadow Box*." In *Drama for Students*. Vol. 15. Detroit: Gale, 2002.

Jill Stapleton-Bergeron

THE SHADOW OF A GUNMAN

Author: Sean O'Casey (John Casey, 1880-1964)
Type of plot: Tragicomedy; history
Time of plot: 1920
Locale: Dublin
First produced: 1923, at the Abbey Theatre, Dublin, Ireland
First published: 1925

> *Principal characters:*
> DONAL DAVOREN, a poet and false gunman
> MINNIE POWELL, a romantic rebel who protects Donal
> SEUMAS SHIELDS, a peddler and former rebel

The Play

    The Shadow of a Gunman takes place amid the disruptions of the Troubles caused by the Irish Rebellion of 1916 and the subsequent war between the Irish and British in the country. Its focus is not the battlefield, however, but the tenement, and the characters are not conventionally heroic but very human and flawed. The most important character is Donal Davoren, a poet who has no interest in the social or political life of his country. He exists, instead, in a world of words and dreams, as he struggles to create beauty in a Dublin tenement. He shares an apartment with Seumas Shields, a former Republican who still has a few friends in the Irish Republican Army (IRA) and now makes a precarious living selling suspenders and buttons. He is no poet, although he knows a substantial amount of poetry; he believes, instead, in the Roman Catholic Church as a means of finding security and peace in a troubled time. He is also superstitious and constantly reading meaning into signs.

    The last major character, Minnie Powell, is perhaps less well developed than the others. She is an enthusiastic Republican and a romantic. She seems to have an independence that the others lack, but her romantic dreams are fed by the same patriotic illusions that animate most of the minor characters in the play. She is attracted to Davoren because she thinks that he is a gunman on the run. When she reveals this perception to Davoren, he allows her to continue thinking of him in this heroic manner because it enables him to have a relationship with an attractive young woman, but this irresponsible furthering of an illusion ends up producing the tragedy at the end of the play.

    The middle section of the play is taken up with comic demands by Davoren's neighbors and the news of the death of Seumas's friend Maguire in an IRA action. To the neighbors, the war is nothing more than a patriotic game they can play; they do not see it as a part of their real daily lives. As Davoren says, "The Irish people are very fond of turning a serious thing into a joke." They want Davoren to get the help of the

IRA against the landlord or to certify their own expressions of patriotism. The death of Maguire, a compatriot of Seumas, intrudes upon this farcical behavior, and it leads Davoren and Seumas to discuss more seriously the political situation in the Ireland of 1920. Seumas describes the country as "mad," since the rebels have sworn allegiance to a religion of the gun. The result, however, is ironic: "It's the people that are dyin' for the gunmen." The rhetoric of revolution and heroism produces sorrow and suffering for the people for whom the rebels are fighting.

The climax of the play comes out of a comic situation. Mrs. Grigson is worried that her husband will be shot while he is drinking after curfew, so she seeks the help of the gunman, Davoren. She is more worried about her husband's insurance than about his survival, but she does reveal that Tommy Owens has been bragging about an IRA general in his building. This clowning is followed by the serious action of a British raid of the tenement and the discovery that the satchel left by Maguire contains bombs. Davoren and Seumas are befuddled and afraid until Minnie runs in and volunteers to take the bag to her room and hide it. Arrested by the British, she dies in the midst of explosions and shots. The two main characters react to this tragedy according to their nature: Seumas appeals to superstition, and Davoren sees it as further evidence of his suffering. However, his suffering is not transformed into awareness or action. He can only lapse into the romantic clichés of suffering in the poetry he is always quoting and trying to write. Most significant of all is the fact that he avoids any real responsibility for the tragedy. He and Seumas both escape the demands of history and the commitments they have to others and hide from reality.

Themes and Meanings

One important theme of *The Shadow of a Gunman* is the criticism of any claims to the ideal. The Irish Republican ideal seems to have little relevance in the world of the tenement. It ignores the social evils that are present and honors violence and destruction; the inevitable result is that those for whom the rebellion was begun are slaughtered and impoverished in the chaos. In addition, it tends to bring out the worst in the people; instead of transforming them into heroes it leads them to use idealism as an escape from the dreary lives they are living. Instead of working for specific and practical social change, they indulge themselves with writing letters to the IRA and bragging at pubs. Moreover, the ideals of the IRA, as Seumas makes clear, lead inevitably to civilian deaths; the people are dying for the gunmen, not the other way around.

Another theme is the necessity of accepting responsibility. Sean O'Casey consistently portrays the female characters in the play as nurturing, brave, and oriented to life, while the men are caught in vanity and evasion. Minnie Powell is unconcerned about conventions and gossip while Davoren is still bound to them, even though he is supposed to be a bohemian poet. Davoren and Seumas, as well as Tommy Owens, create shadow worlds of illusion, while Minnie can and does deal with immediate and practical matters, such as the bag of bombs. She is willing to sacrifice herself in order to preserve Davoren, while the men are irresponsible and unwilling to meet the commitment demanded by their positions as poets or supporters of the rebellion.

Another important theme for O'Casey is the intrusion of historical events upon the lives of ordinary people. History—here seen as the war between the Irish and the British—manifests itself in a sudden, surprising, and destructive manner. It shows the characters that they live in a world subject to outside, uncontrollable forces; their fate cannot be determined or put off by their words or games. It is a destructive and clarifying force, even though it seems to change only a few of the characters.

Dramatic Devices

One of Sean O'Casey's most important devices is the special and noticeable styles he gives to the characters. For example, Seumas always repeats phrases, a speech pattern that indicates his obsessed and nervous character. Davoren's language is full of high-flown romantic imagery and expressions: "Ah me! alas, pain, pain ever, for ever!" This language makes it clear that he is distanced from the real world of the tenements. Seumas says that the job of a poet is "to put passion in the common people," but Davoren replies that the poet "lives on the mountain-top." The florid Republican style of Tommy Owens ("It's 'Up the Republic' all the time—eh, Mr. Davoren?") is also amusing and helps define his character by showing the distance between his rhetoric and his actions. In contrast, Minnie's language is straightforward, without the verbal quirks that abound in the style of everyone else in the play.

Another device is the mixture of the comic and the tragic. The play would be a comic farce without the historical context and the sudden intrusion of death. The characters tend to be absurd and dominated by mannerisms; but one, Minnie, rises to the occasion and acts heroically in the changed circumstances. She may not be a tragic heroine, since she lacks full awareness of herself and her world, but by her actions she defines herself as a caring and serious human being. The others, especially Davoren and Seumas, show, in the end, that they are simply ridiculous posturers, incapable of change.

Critical Context

The Shadow of a Gunman was the first important play by Sean O'Casey. He was to continue that success and improve upon the elements of the early play in his two other Dublin plays, *Juno and the Paycock* (pr. 1924, pb. 1925) and *The Plough and the Stars* (pr., pb. 1926). In *Juno and the Paycock*, male irresponsibility is portrayed as more consciously malign and destructive than in *The Shadow of a Gunman*. The main character, Captain Boyle, has brought his family down to shame and destitution, but when he discovers that his daughter is pregnant out of wedlock, he rejects her insult to his pride and honor. Mrs. Boyle tells her daughter that the child will be better off, since it will have two mothers in place of the absent father.

In his greatest play, *The Plough and the Stars*, O'Casey intensified the historical force, depicting the day-to-day social problems that end in the death of children by consumption. In the destruction of the 1916 Uprising, the common people of the tenement help one another, while the heroes of the IRA are selfish and destructive. All the elements of the later plays can be found in *The Shadow of a Gunman*, but O'Casey was able to strengthen and intensify them and their dramatic effect. O'Casey's later plays became more expressionistic, beginning with his World War I play *The Silver Tassie* (pb. 1928, pr. 1929), as his settings moved out of Dublin tenements into larger worlds. These later plays were not, however, as successful. Once he moved out of the narrow, intimate world he knew so well, he lost the language and characters that made the early plays so important to their Irish audiences.

The Shadow of a Gunman was a radical departure for the Abbey Theatre. It had achieved fame by presenting the plays of William Butler Yeats, John Millington Synge, and Lady Augusta Gregory, but these plays celebrated a rural or heroic vision of Ireland. The playwrights' aim was to create myths to justify the claim of Ireland's spiritual and cultural importance. O'Casey brought the slums of Dublin into the Abbey Theatre and thus changed it forever. He not only brought a new language and subject but also showed the Irish how they were actually living at the time and how they might change things. When audiences rejected *The Silver Tassie*, however, he left the Abbey and Ireland; both playwright and theater were to suffer from this break. The Abbey never found another playwright of O'Casey's force and popularity, and O'Casey lost his roots in the Irish tenements.

Sources for Further Study
Brustein, Robert. Review in *The New Republic* 206 (January 27, 1992): 28-30.
Donoghue, Denis. *We Irish: Essays on Irish Literature and Society.* New York: Knopf, 1986.
Hogan, Robert. *"Since O'Casey" and Other Essays on Irish Drama.* Totowa, N.J.: Barnes and Noble Books, 1983.
Hunt, Hugh. *Sean O'Casey.* 2d ed. Minneapolis: Irish Books Media, 1998.
Krause, David. *Sean O'Casey: The Man and His Work.* New York: Macmillan, 1960.
Malone, Maureen. *The Plays of Sean O'Casey.* Carbondale: Southern Illinois University Press, 1969.
O'Riordan, John. *A Guide to O'Casey's Plays.* New York: St. Martin's Press, 1984.
Schrank, Bernice W. *Sean O'Casey: A Research and Production Handbook.* Westport, Conn.: Greenwood Press, 1996.

James Sullivan

SHORT EYES

Author: Miguel Piñero (1946-1988)
Type of plot: Realism
Time of plot: The 1970's
Locale: House of Detention, New York Prison
First produced: 1974, at the Theater of the Riverside Church, New York City
First published: 1975

Principal characters:

JUAN, a Puerto Rican man in his early thirties

JULIO "CUPCAKES," a twenty-one-year-old Puerto Rican man who appears younger

PACO, a Puerto Rican man in his early thirties who appears to be on drugs

ICE, an African American man in his late twenties who appears older

OMAR, a strong, African American amateur boxer

EL RAHEEM, a militant and regal African American man in his mid-twenties

LONGSHOE, a tough Irishman in his mid-twenties

CLARK DAVIS, a frightened white man in his early twenties whom fellow prisoners dub "short eyes"

MR. NETT, a prison guard in his late forties

CAPTAIN ALLARD and

MR. BROWN, officers in the House of Detention

The Play

A two-act play with an epilogue, *Short Eyes* takes place in a New York prison. The play's action covers the course of one day in a cell-block dayroom of the prison, and the audience is introduced to the grind of prison life, the characters sharing the dayroom, and the relationships among these prisoners. The play opens with a traditional roll call, as the prisoners' disembodied voices call out their locations for dayroom assignments. As Ice, Omar, Longshoe, El Raheem, Paco, Juan, and Cupcakes enter the "B" side of the dayroom, the play begins to distinguish among their characters and establishes their relationships with one another. The inmates alternatively argue, play cards, fight, "jam," cajole one another, and familiarize the audience with prison slang, such as "plexes" (psychological complexes) and "on the help" (a prison job).

Such an apparently "normal" day is interrupted as Clark Davis enters, a white man with whom Longshoe initially attempts a connection based on race. Longshoe explains the complex "protection" network among white, black, and Hispanic prisoners, attempting to advise Davis about survival. However, he is horrified and nearly violent when he discovers that Davis is a "short eyes," prison slang for a pedophile. All the inmates exit and return to their cells for the count, while Juan remains behind, cleaning, with Davis. Left with Juan, Davis makes a full confession of his pedophilia, and Juan responds with disgust. The others return to harass Davis, and the act closes as they force Davis's head into the toilet while he screams.

Act 2 opens thirty minutes later, with the same group of inmates reading, writing, playing chess, and exercising. Davis is not in the dayroom but has been called for a lineup. The clowning and discussion continues as Longshoe shares "heist" (drugs) with several of his fellow inmates. As Cupcakes leaves to shower, Mr. Nett arrives "on the gate" to announce visitors for Longshoe and Juan; Longshoe refuses his visitor, while Mr. Brown announces religious services and El Raheem exits. After arguing with Juan, Longshoe vomits in the toilet and is taken to the infirmary by Omar, Ice, and Mr. Nett, leaving only Paco and the young, beautiful Cupcakes in the dayroom. Their solitude gives Paco the opportunity to seduce Cupcakes, who refuses despite the promise of protection it provides.

Omar returns and tries to advise Cupcakes on survival against predators such as Paco, while Cupcakes informs Omar of the plan to kill "short eyes," Clark Davis. Juan and Ice return, and the appearance of two drag queens leads Ice to tell the tale of his stay in Clinton, an "old school" prison with strictly segregated race rules among prisoners. He then details a night when he masturbated to the image of Jane Fonda, loud enough for the entire cell-block to cheer him on, only to be severely beaten for "pulling his pecker on a white woman."

Mr. Brown announces sick call, and several inmates leave, as Davis and Juan are again alone onstage. Davis describes the lineup to Juan and reveals the possibility that he may get off, generally attempting to befriend Juan once more. As Davis describes the "abuse" he has suffered from the police, journalists, and the staff of the mental hospital he was in prior to prison, Juan will not excuse his behavior, claiming, "In this time and place I am your judge." The other prisoners' return sparks a discussion about killing Davis. Juan advises mercy, and the council falters as Ice, too, expresses doubts, but when Davis, in his terror, begins to threaten to tell Captain Allard, he enrages the inmates. Mr. Nett, his would-be protector as the prison guard, turns away.

Paco gives El Raheem the knife as the others (excluding Juan) egg him on. El Raheem falters at killing a defenseless man, and Longshoe takes the knife, slitting Davis's throat, despite his pleas for mercy. Longshoe taunts El Raheem with racial slurs and tries to kill Ice, and the act ends amid near anarchy.

The epilogue opens the evening of the same day with roll call, as in the opening of act 1. Mr. Brown attempts an investigation of the murder to no avail, as the inmates have their story straight and will not "rat out" their fellows. Despite the hole in their story—they claim to have been watching a broken television—he closes the investigation to protect "the department." As the guards leave, Captain Allard claims that Davis was not in fact a "short eyes" but only mistaken for one, planting the seed of guilt in those who have taken part in the murder. Ice notes than only "Juan is free" and all the rest share in the responsibility of the murder. As Cupcakes exits on bail, Juan reminds him that he will always carry a part of prison with him.

Themes and Meanings

With its claustrophobic atmosphere, *Short Eyes* emphasizes a theme of inside versus outside: Inmates come and go only by the power of others, and their attempts to create structure and power systems strangely mirror those of the outer world. The repetitive use of "on the gate" drives the point home: Each man is isolated and must make community from the unsavory characters around him. Such a confined state forces alliances, as it threatens characters' sense of ownership and identity.

Establishing a stance or an alliance becomes paramount to survival, both literally and psychologically. Each character must navigate and interact across ethnic and racial boundaries, and each must assert an identity to survive the horror and violence of prison life. The audience witnesses the inmates devolve from the friendly, if often violent, gathering of the play's opening to participants in the violent assault on Davis at the end of act 2. The counsel that meets to decide Davis's fate also points to the inmates' need to form structures and hierarchies that mirror the outside and are as ineffective as the system that contains them.

Davis's entrance and his crime—the lowest crime in the inmates' eyes—stand as the catalyst of the play. His detailed confession to Juan suggests a need for connection to another human being, even if such a connection may be dangerous. Although Juan rejects Davis and does not condone his aberrant sexual crime, he does recognize Davis's humanity and thus pleads for his life and then absents himself from Davis's murder. Juan thus stands as a kind of moral center, a man who chooses an alternative to violence despite the violence he himself has experienced.

Only the narrowest reading would label this play solely a "prison play," as the literal setting merely highlights the dangerous, shifting, and confusing human relationships encountered by everyone daily. However, Miguel Piñero uses this setting well to invert racial power and to give voice to the multiple racial identities the world so often smooths over. Longshoe, the tough Irish white man, is alone to negotiate with Hispanics and African Americans on an equal footing, and each man represents not an entire race but an individual struggling to create a self within that race.

Dramatic Devices

The staging and setting of *Short Eyes* contributes to its message of a trapped and devolving society, as the audience sees the gate, a table and chairs, the toilet center stage, and the catwalk above. The prisoners are constantly observed and observing, and their "cage" allows for no privacy and only brief escape. Piñero uses the catwalk well for movement and important "ad lib" moments, such as roll call and sick call. The toilet becomes the focal point of the play several times: for example, in Davis's first violation or in Longshoe's illness.

Piñero's personal experience with prison life allows the play to re-create prison dialogue accurately, again contributing to the sense that the play stages both "another world" and our own world. Phrases such as "short eyes," and "stuff" (a homosexual) not only add verisimilitude but also suggest the need the inmates have to control their confined space through their own particular language. In addition, the play unblinkingly stages the profanity and violent sexual language that even the most realistic dramas usually avoid. The result is a powerful window into a disturbing world far too similar to the "outside" world for audiences to ignore.

Even as it clearly stages a modern experience, the play adheres to dramatic unities of time and place and thus evokes the oldest Greek dramas of Aeschylus and Sophocles. The final act, with its counsel, its performance of mob mentality in the killing of Davis, and the unsatisfying purgation of the cell-block through Davis's murder evokes classical Greek works such as *Oedipus* and *Agamemnon*. Indeed, as the inmates turn on one another following Davis's murder, Cupcakes cries out in choric desperation: "Oh, my God . . . is this really us?"

With the single set, Piñero makes clever use of the guard's repetitive "on the gate" call to move characters in and out of scenes. Most notably, the sick call, religious call, and visitor call in both acts leave Juan and Davis alone for Davis's confession and later confrontation with Juan. Such solitary moments not only underline the overall lack of privacy in the prison system but also build effective suspense (will Juan tell the other prisoners?). Significantly, Davis's confession also allows for either dramatic irony, as only Juan and the audience realize that Captain Allard's final claim of Davis's innocence may be false, or audience doubt: Has Davis been convicted based solely on his fantasies?

Critical Context

Critics initially responded to the "raw" qualities of the play's actors (who were former convicts) and to its unblinking realism. Although critics compared the play to playwright Jean Genet and his portrayal of prison experience, critics also focused on the racial and ethnic lines Piñero drew in his work, as well as on Piñero's savvy political staging of power and violence both in and out of prison. Piñero's treatment of sexuality consistently intertwined with violence raises disturbing questions about the inmates' treatment of Davis, who may be no more depraved than they, and prison life's lasting effects on men.

As a "Nuyorican" (American and Caribbean) poet and playwright, Piñero explores the bleak worlds of the dispossessed: the poor, the outcast, the homosexual, the "other." His works, however, also call for personal responsibility even in the face of often overwhelming social odds. Through Juan's choice to show Davis mercy, as well as El Raheem's last-minute realization that he cannot kill Davis, the play underlines the ability of each individual, no matter the violence, poverty, or horror he or she has experienced, to choose to end the cycle of violence. As such, the play evokes existentialist questions about humanity's ability to create meaning through action, or in this case, inaction.

Sources for Further Study
Hentoff, Nat. "Piñero: 'I Wanted to Survive.'" *New York Times*, May 5, 1974, p. 8.
Maffi, Mario. "The Nuyorican Experience in the Plays of Pedro Pietri and Miguel Piñero." In *Cross-Cultural Studies: American, Canadian, and European Literatures, 1945-1985*, edited by Mirko Jurak. Bled, Slovenia, Yugoslavia: Symposium on Contemporary Literatures and Cultures of the United States of America and Canada, 1988.
Piñero, Miguel. *Outrageous One-Act Plays by Miguel Piñero*. Houston: Arte Público Press, 1986.
Platizky, Roger S. "Humane Vision in Miguel Piñero's *Short Eyes*." *Americas Review* 19, no. 1 (1991): 83-91.

Cami D. Agan

THE SHOW-OFF

Author: George Kelly (1887-1974)
Type of plot: Comedy
Time of plot: 1924
Locale: Philadelphia
First produced: 1924, at the Playhouse Theatre, New York City
First published: 1924

Principal characters:
CLARA HYLAND, a wealthy married woman
MRS. FISHER, the mother of Clara, Joe, and Amy
AMY FISHER PIPER, a spoiled young woman
AUBREY PIPER, a braggart who courts and marries Amy
JOE FISHER, an inventor
FRANK HYLAND, Clara's husband
MR. FISHER, father of Clara, Joe, and Amy
MR. ROGERS, an insurance agent

The Play

The setting of *The Show-Off* is the Philadelphia home of Mr. and Mrs. Fisher. Clara, their oldest daughter and wife of Frank Hyland, stops by one evening to bring her mother some candy. They discuss younger sister Amy's infatuation with Aubrey Piper, a young man who visits to court Amy. Mrs. Fisher says, "It looks like a steady thing. And you never in your life heard anybody talk so much, Clara—I don't know how she stands him."

Clara reveals that Frank knows Aubrey, who has misrepresented himself to Amy. Aubrey claims that he is the head of the Pennsylvania Railroad freight department, but he is merely a clerk there. Aubrey is also not wealthy: Frank says that a clerk earns no more than one hundred fifty dollars per month. However, they all agree that Amy will ignore their warnings that Aubrey is a deceitful show-off. When Amy enters the room, the audience soon sees that she is bratty, headstrong, and interested only in making herself attractive for the evening. By contrast, Clara is sensible, Frank is dreamy and preoccupied, and Mrs. Fisher is a tart-tongued but warmhearted gossip.

Aubrey arrives and soon manages to irritate everybody. For instance, since Joe Fisher is an inventor, Aubrey claims to have invented a formula to prevent rust but says the industrialists refused to pay him the millions he deserved for it. Joe says later that in fact the antirust formula was his own idea. When Aubrey finally leaves, Mrs. Fisher sternly talks with Amy, advising her to look for a man who will be able to support her, but Amy defiantly says that she will marry whom she chooses.

In act 2, six months later, Amy and Aubrey are married. Aubrey arrives with the news that they need to buy a house but laughs off Mrs. Fisher's advice that he should buy one that he can afford. Aubrey departs, saying that he wants to go look at automobiles. Mr. Fisher has a stroke on the job and goes to the hospital. As the family prepares to visit him, Aubrey returns with his head bandaged and evasively admits that he had "borrowed" a car and had "a little misunderstanding on the part of the traffic-officer." Actually, he broke the policeman's arm. Aubrey says he spoke with the police and will not be fined; in fact, he is expected in court the following Monday to pay a one-thousand-dollar fine. Clara is appalled when Aubrey reveals that it was Frank who bailed him out of jail for three hundred dollars. A friend of Mr. Fisher comes by, to whom Aubrey implies that he owns the Fisher house and allows the family to live with him. Meanwhile, Amy learns that her father has died. As she cries, Aubrey holds her and promises he will always take care of her.

Act 3 opens on a Monday. Mrs. Fisher speaks with an insurance agent, Mr. Rogers, who gives her a life insurance check for one thousand dollars and divulges that Aubrey wants to purchase a fifty-thousand-dollar policy. Mrs. Fisher sets Mr. Rogers straight on Aubrey's financial situation, but when the agent is gone, Clara tells her mother that "you can never change a man like Aubrey." When Mrs. Fisher protests that her problem with Aubrey is that her daughter is married to him, Clara explains, "She's in love with him, Mom—she doesn't see him through the same eyes that other people do." Clara confesses that Frank is not in love with her but pines for another girl he had known once and that she envies Amy and Aubrey even if they are exasperating. Amy enters and confides to Clara that she is pregnant. Amy has learned to worry about Aubrey's irresponsible behavior.

Aubrey and Frank enter; Frank has paid Aubrey's fine. Clara speaks privately to Aubrey, warning him that she will see him out on the street if he tells any more lies. Aubrey takes this quietly but is still cocky enough to ask whether the newspaper article about his traffic accident carries a good picture of him. Mrs. Fisher decides that she will allow Aubrey and Amy to live with her, though she resents Aubrey. The play concludes happily when Joe comes in to report that he sold his rust-proofing formula for one hundred thousand dollars. Aubrey reveals that he spoke to the industrial executives and bluffed them from a fifty-thousand-dollar payment up to one hundred thousand; Joe acknowledges that he must be telling the truth for once and offers to give Aubrey a "present" out of the money.

Themes and Meanings

Aubrey, braggart and freeloader, is an antihero difficult to like and impossible to admire. However, his opportunistic bluffing earns Joe a great deal of money, and Amy's adoration of him allows the family to forgive him—at least in part—for his flaws. Of the family members, cheerful Joe is the most likable but also appears on-stage the least. Amy is gullible; Mrs. Fisher is an intrusive, eavesdropping busybody; Clara seems joyless; and her husband Frank is willing to pay for Aubrey's mistakes and irresponsible behavior because he regrets having married Clara when he loves another woman.

George Kelly likes to create characters who are blind to their own flaws. As a writer of comedies, he ridicules vain, self-centered incompetents, who never realize what fools they make of themselves. His satire addresses not social problems but rather individual follies. He considers responsible behavior a great virtue, and therefore his comedy focuses on characters who behave selfishly and without care for the future.

Kelly was a writer of the theater of ideas, not a great character developer: His characters usually behave the same at the end of the play as they appear at the beginning. Aubrey has not learned, in the end, that he should stop lying and boasting: It is evident that the Fishers will have to accept him as he is.

Kelly's comedy, especially in his early plays (*The Show-Off* is his second produced drama), focuses on the subjects of career and family. Written and set in the prosperous 1920's, the play could safely poke fun at a swaggering clerk, who pretends to be a railroad baron, and at the pomposity of the American business world in a way that would have been too painful during the Great Depression of the 1930's. Aubrey struts through life as someone convinced that he holds a winning lottery ticket, believing that at any moment he will become rich and that he can talk his way out of any social or legal problem. He is the total opposite of Mrs. Fisher, who believes in earning a paycheck through hard work and who demands that her daughters work as well as her son. It is, however, suggested that Mr. Fisher dies because he has worked too hard, which makes it look as though the Fishers have spent too much of their lives with nose to the grindstone, forgetting that dreams are important too. Unquestionably, whenever Aubrey walks onstage, he steals the scene. Although he tells lies and constantly admires his reflection in the mirror, his loud laughter at his own jokes and his theatricality make him more colorful than the Fishers, whose talk centers boringly on clothing and furniture.

It is difficult to be sure of Kelly's attitude toward romantic love. Clara and Frank have a financially comfortable marriage, which is devoid of passion. Mrs. Fisher barely mourns the passing of Mr. Fisher. Meanwhile, Amy can see no fault in Aubrey, and they will certainly always love each other, though their blind love is expensive for their friends and family, who must support them. Each of Kelly's four plays deals with the problem of marriage; Kelly himself never married, though he had a long relationship with actress Tallulah Bankhead.

Although the action in the play mostly focuses on the trials and accomplishments of the Fisher family, Kelly highlights how Aubrey takes advantage of each event to display his vanity and braggadocio. Kelly's work presents problems from which the audience will learn a moral lesson, even though the principal characters therein may never gain insight into their own best and worst qualities.

Dramatic Devices

George Kelly's sets reflected his dramatic realism. Unlike the beautiful stages designed by other playwrights of his time, he described an urban, working-class, garish home in which the props and furniture, such as candy boxes, cups and glasses, or junk-filled cabinets, are heavily used in the action. He preferred to stage an entire play in a single set. In *The Show-Off* only the living room is ever seen, though characters use many doors to enter the parlor, basement, kitchen, and other rooms. The result is to produce a familiarity with this room, which may come to seem confining, especially when Aubrey sweeps through it speaking of his grandiose dreams. It also means that actions occurring elsewhere must be reported by characters, who enter and exit the single room, and these actions are described in different manners by the different characters, revealing much about their personalities.

The Show-Off is an expansion of Kelly's one-act play *Poor Aubrey* (pr. 1922). Since Kelly was limited to this single set, the characters are always moving around it, calling offstage to each other, slamming doors, listening at doors, hiding behind doors, running up the stairs or down into the basement. Because his work is realistic rather than experimental, Kelly does not provide spectacle: The action is entirely dialogue-based. A lesser playwright would run the risk of boring the audience, but Kelly's characters are so amusing that his "talky" drama seems busy and kinetic, even frantic, rather than tedious.

Kelly gave specific directions about the color scheme for the set, which included silver-green furniture with tones of orchid and green blended into walls and ceilings. It is the sort of room that a working-class family of the 1920's would consider tasteful, though its poverty cannot be ignored. Many plays of his time featured the adventures of upper-class or aristocratic characters, but Kelly greatly pleased his audiences with his depictions of people much like themselves.

Critical Context

In his preface to the 1924 hardcover edition of *The Show-Off*, Heywood Broun called it "the best play that has yet been written by an American." In the early 1920's, American drama took a turn toward realism, and Kelly has been called a realist representative, even if less known than many of his contemporaries.

The Show-Off was recommended by the Pulitzer committee for the prize in drama. Kelly would win the Pulitzer Prize for his next drama, *Craig's Wife* (pr., pb. 1925). The play was so popular that it ran on Broadway for 567 performances and was adapted into film on three separate occasions. The first, a silent film, was released in 1926, directed by Malcolm St. Clair, and starred Ford Sterling; the second, premiering in 1934, was directed by Charles Reisner and starred Spencer Tracy; the third and most successful version appeared in 1946 and was directed by Harry Beaumont and starred Red Skelton.

Sources for Further Study

Graves, Mark A. *George Kelly: A Research and Production Sourcebook*. Westport, Conn.: Greenwood Press, 1999.

Hirsch, Foster. *George Kelly*. New York: Twayne, 1975.

Hornby, Richard. "*The Show-Off*." *Hudson Review* 44 (Winter, 1992): 636-638.

Kaufman, Alvin S., and Franklin Case. *Modern Drama in America: Realism from Provincetown to Broadway, 1915-1929.* Vol. 1. New York: Washington Square Press, 1982.

Kissane, Joseph. "Brandered by Matthews: The 1924 Pulitzer Prize." *Theatre History Studies* 19 (1999): 43-62.

Maisel, Edward. "The Theatre of George Kelly." *Theatre Arts Monthly* 31 (February, 1947): 39-43.

Moses, Montrose Jonas, and Joseph Wood Krutch. *Representative American Dramas, National and Local.* Boston: D. C. Heath, 1941.

Wills, Arthur. "The Kelly Play." *Modern Drama* 6 (1963): 245-255.

Fiona Kelleghan

THE SIGN IN SIDNEY BRUSTEIN'S WINDOW

Author: Lorraine Hansberry (1930-1965)
Type of plot: Problem play
Time of plot: The early 1960's
Locale: Greenwich Village in New York City
First produced: 1964, at the Longacre Theatre, New York City
First published: 1965

> *Principal characters:*
> SIDNEY BRUSTEIN, a disillusioned intellectual
> IRIS, his wife, an aspiring but unsuccessful actor
> MAVIS PARODUS BRYSON, Iris's older sister
> GLORIA PARODUS, their younger sister
> ALTON SCALES, a black friend of Sidney
> DAVID RAGIN, a homosexual playwright, the Brusteins' neighbor
> WALLY O'HARA, a local politician

The Play

All the action in *The Sign in Sidney Brustein's Window* occurs in the Brustein apartment. Act 1 opens on a late spring evening as Sidney Brustein and Alton Scales return to the apartment carrying cases of restaurant glasses, the remains of Sidney's venture into the nightclub business. The failure of his nightclub/coffeehouse, however, does not deter Sidney from planning another venture—publishing a weekly community newspaper. Sidney has not yet informed his wife, Iris, of his plans, knowing that the revelation will create tension.

Sidney and Iris love each other, but their marital conflict animates half of scene 1. Alton exits, avoiding an impending argument, as Iris enters. Upon noting the cases of glassware, she immediately declares that the "residue" of Sidney's "failures" is not to accumulate in their living room. When the conversation turns to news of a casting call which Iris plans to attend, Sidney counterattacks, singling out her inability to go to an audition. Their interaction intensifies, becoming scathing before it returns to safer channels. Iris defends herself with methods learned in therapy; Sidney discounts psychoanalysis, declaring that although she has seen an analyst for two years, "the only real difference is that you used to cry all the time and now you *scream* before you cry." The tension gradually subsides until Iris discovers the sketch of the masthead for the newspaper. She demands to know how Sidney, with no financial resources, plans to support his latest endeavor.

The scene shifts when Alton returns, bringing with him Wally O'Hara, a politician running for office as the "reform" candidate. They have come seeking an endorsement of O'Hara's platform by Sidney's newspaper and appealing to him to become involved once again. Declaring his intention to abstain from "*any* kind of politics" because he no longer has such interests, Sidney rejects their appeal.

Scene 2 occurs one week later. A sign supporting O'Hara now hangs from Sidney's window, showing his capitulation. While the sign frames the play's developing conflicts, the action of the scene shifts from external political involvement to family politics and aesthetic arguments. The audience meets David Ragin, the avant-garde homosexual playwright living upstairs, and Mavis Parodus Bryson, Iris's conservative older sister. Mavis does not understand the bohemian lifestyle of her sister and Jewish brother-in-law or their various Greenwich Village friends, nor can she acknowledge the extent of her own parochialism. Her limitations make her an object of ridicule in this setting; she does not know what "gay" signifies, and she is stunned upon learning that Alton, a fair-skinned African American, plans to marry her youngest sister, Gloria.

Act 1, the longest segment of the play, introduces most of the characters and establishes underlying conflicts and themes. It closes on an intense note, underscored by the Joan Baez recording of "All My Trials" filling a darkening stage. Mavis, Alton, and David having all left the apartment insulted or angry, Iris and Sidney return to bickering, each recognizing that something is leaving their marriage.

Act 2 has three scenes. Scene 1 opens just before dawn, the next day. Sidney has created an idyllic fantasy; skillful use of lighting and music transport him from New York to a rustic mountain retreat. The background noise changes to mimic country sounds. The Iris of his imagination, a barefoot Appalachian peasant girl with long flowing hair, appears in his fantasy to dance for him as he plays the banjo. With the dance finished, a light comes on in the apartment and a realistic Iris emerges to find Sidney on the outside stairway landing. The scene closes with the reappearance of the city and its noises.

Scene 2 shifts to an evening in late summer, several months later. Sidney has become more involved with the political campaign, but his relationship with Iris is increasingly strained. Desperately wanting "something to happen" in her life, she has begun to follow her own path. Attempting to assist her, Sidney approaches David, who has just received rave reviews of his latest work, about including a part for Iris in one of his plays. This breach of integrity offends David, and his stinging rebuff humiliates Sidney. Wally O'Hara enters on the heels of the previous exchange, excited by the possibility of winning the election and insensitive to Sidney's emotional crisis. The scene closes with Sidney taking a tranquilizer for his ulcer, a task he describes as the modern way of confronting and coping with evil in the world. There is a quick fadeout.

Scene 3 opens on election night, in early fall. The sounds of a crowd can be heard celebrating O'Hara's having won the election. An exhilarated Sidney also celebrates. The "impossible" and the "illogical" have occurred: The community has seemingly elected a responsive man who will take office and institute reform. Alton enters, his mood diametrically opposite that of Sidney. He has discovered that Gloria is not a model but a prostitute, and he is coming to Sidney to verify the fact and to question why he was not told. Unable to accept her past or to face her in person, Alton leaves Gloria a note and exits. Mavis then enters, congratulates Sidney for successfully sponsoring O'Hara, then discusses her childhood and the state of her marriage. For the first time, Sidney realizes that Mavis is a woman of depth who copes realistically within the boundaries of her own world. Mavis also reveals the truth about the Parodus family's background, a truth Iris had been concealing. Shortly after Mavis leaves, Iris returns to the apartment.

She is radically altered: Her long dark hair is now short, blonde, and stiff from a salon beauty treatment. Her appearance reflects her dramatically changed and hardened values. She now performs in television commercials, touting Golden Curl Home Permanents to the gullible. Recognizing that her new job is causing conflict within her, Sidney attempts to soothe her, but she screams, "I DON'T WANT TO PLAY APPALACHIAN ANY MORE!" His response is that she is "learning the cynicism bit at the wrong time" in their relationship because the election shows that they "won something today," and that "just a tiny bit of the world turned right side up." A distraught but more politically sophisticated Iris points out Sidney's naïveté:

> You haven't won anything, Sid, they're all the same people! . . . Don't you hear me? I tried to tell you . . . They *own* Wally . . . The people you've been fighting . . . Own him completely: the house he lives in, the clothes on his back, the toothpaste he uses. *They own* him, utterly, completely, entirely. . . . There it is, Sid, the real world!

Shocked, Sidney does not want to believe that he has been betrayed. However, he must accept this bitter reality, just as he must accept the dissolution of their marriage. Upon her exit, Iris begs Sidney to remove the O'Hara sign from the window because "*It's like spit in your face!*" He cannot. The scene closes on Sidney holding a yardstick, his imaginary sword, saluting the sign as a foe that has beaten him. The audience sees the sign start pulsing with its own life and hears the crowd roar loudly as Sidney snaps his "sword" in half.

Act 3, the shortest act, comprises two brief scenes. The first occurs the same night, several hours later. The audience finally meets Gloria Parodus, who arrives to find Sidney suffering from disillusionment, his ulcer, and too much alcohol. She also meets David, who, when introduced, immediately presumes a kinship ("Isn't it the great tradition for writers and whores to share the world's truths?"). Angrily, Gloria asks him to leave. Upon his exit, she announces that she has quit prostitution, has stopped taking drugs, and plans to tell Alton the truth before they marry. When Sidney then gives her Alton's letter, the rejection hits her hard. Gloria's response is to lose herself in drugs and alcohol, then darkness and music. Disorienting shifts of light and music and disjointed, highly stylized dialogue are key to the mood of the scene, which illustrates disintegration. By the close of the scene, Sidney, lost in his private stupor, will not have noticed that Gloria has killed herself in the bathroom.

The final scene, early the following day, opens with a restrained Iris answering a police detective's questions when Sidney returns from having placed Mavis and her husband in a cab. The detective leaves, and Wally O'Hara enters. He has come ostensibly to offer condolences but more to justify his betrayal. In his world, acquisition of power means compromise; the Brusteins "reek of innocence" because they will not accept this truth. No longer a gullible idealist, and goaded by Gloria's death, Sidney vows to fight the corrupt world that Wally represents, the threat against his newspaper notwithstanding. Finally alone, Iris and Sidney begin to talk, and Iris is at last able to cry. The curtain falls as Sidney vows that "tomorrow, we shall make something strong of this sorrow."

Themes and Meanings

The central themes of *The Sign in Sidney Brustein's Window* concern the obligation of individuals to become involved and to take responsible action; withdrawal or detachment from the community leads to disintegration and failure. At the start of the play, Sidney is disconnected from the world around him. Alton labels Sidney's detachment "*ostrich*-ism" and calls this the "great disease of the modern bourgeois intellectual." Sidney considers his withdrawal an earned right; since his youth he has been involved in various causes and served on assorted committees trying to change the world—all to little avail. One of his intellectual mentors has been Henry David Thoreau, but Alton accuses Sidney of reading the "wrong" portions of Thoreau, those emphasizing the solace and strength the solitary individual can gain from communing with nature. Sidney's mountaintop retreat, where he goes to find innocence, is his version of Thoreau's Walden Pond. Thoreau, however, was also noted for his acute social consciousness, and Sidney stands charged with letting his political and social conscience atrophy.

Commitment to responsible political action represents only the outer level where Lorraine Hansberry's characters engage one another. The personal interaction between Sidney and Iris and the social relationships among members of the Brustein extended family (not only Iris's sisters but also the friends and neighbors wandering in and out of the apartment) are all part of Hansberry's exploration of compassionate involvement. Despite their love, Sidney and Iris grow steadily apart because there is no meaningful communication between them. They fail to ask the crucial questions about the cause of the changes in their relationship. Because Sidney has always assumed the leadership in their marriage, more of the responsibility belongs to him. His mask of cynical detachment dramatically affects his perception of Iris. Not until he really listens to Mavis is he made aware that his wife has lied to him continually about her background. Contrary to his cherished image of her as an uncultured, unsophisticated, rustic girl whom he educated, she grew up in a home presided over by a father who read Greek tragedy to his daughters. For her part, Iris has been trying to fit Sidney's image until finally that image chokes her.

Mavis's social status makes it difficult for her to establish a comfortable relationship with the Greenwich Village intellectuals. An ordinary woman, on their turf she is an alienated outsider. Stung by their callous disregard for her humanity, Mavis challenges their intellectual smugness, suggesting that their lack of compassion, their egocentrism, is not part of any solution to society's ills but in fact is part of the problem.

While Wally, with his sign, symbolizes corruption, Alton and David permit the discussion to range into the areas of the function of art, homophobia, and racism while still treating the themes of individual responsibility and integrity. After confronting Sidney, an angry, disappointed, and disillusioned Alton disappears from the play; David, however, remains a pivotal character, partially responsible for Gloria's death. The themes of David's plays, cynical pieces about guilt, futility, the uselessness of innocence, and the emptiness of modern life, underscore the dilemma faced by the Brusteins; discussion of his work also permits Hansberry to show the paralysis affecting white intellectuals at this juncture of American social history. The dynamic activism of the late 1960's had not yet begun; Sidney and David's arguments represent the problem of "the Western intellectual poised in hesitation before the flames of involvement." Gloria's death forces Sidney to drop that stance.

Dramatic Devices

The Sign in Sidney Brustein's Window is primarily a realistic play that uses traditional dramatic devices to help the audience understand its intentions. Hansberry establishes a credible setting, viable characters, and crisp interaction between them to dramatize the examination of ideas. Production notes specify set design. At rear stage are the "recognizable sight symbols" of New York; in the foreground are facades indicating the Greenwich Village locale—tenement buildings, old farmhouses, a stable, and converted brownstone buildings. There are no extensive special effects, although lighting changes and shifts of music suggest both mood and imagery. Finally, the audience must heed the sign highlighted in the window as it emphasizes various turns in the action.

The play's complex characterization allows all the characters to function as people, neither types nor stereotypes. Sidney is an intellectual who neither looks nor acts the part; he engages fully in whatever he undertakes. His view of Iris as an unspoiled Appalachian princess (his habit of pulling the pins from her bound-up hair infuriates her) shows both tenderness and tension in their marriage. When Iris has her hair cut, curled, and dyed, it becomes a visual cue that she is a new and different woman.

Mavis undergoes no physical change, but the audience, like Sidney, becomes more aware of her depth as she shares her family's background and the emotional pain she endures. The family name was changed from Parodopoulos to Parodus (literally, Greek chorus) because their father wanted a "symbolic" name and saw his family functioning the way a chorus works ("no matter what is happening in the main action of the play—the chorus is always there, commenting, watching"). Ironically, even as Mavis recalls her past, it becomes apparent that she still functions as a chorus and is perhaps a parody of the role, standing at the edge of the action, not changing anything, just watching.

Though concerned with more than race relations, Hansberry uses Alton, a black political radical, to frame delicate racial issues. His very appearance is a subtle dramatic device because he is so light in color that he can be mistaken for white by the audience (and Mavis) until he speaks or until race becomes the subject. In act 1, when Mavis believes that Alton is white, she accepts him as a suitor for Gloria; the moment Sidney reveals Alton's race she is repulsed. In act 2, the irony develops further. While Alton can love a white woman, he cannot marry a white prostitute, a "commodity." For him, that is an issue entangled in American social history: "Man like I am spawned from commodities . . . and their purchasers. I am running from being a commodity. I got this color from my grandmother being used as a commodity, man."

Tone and mood, as noted above, are clearly indicated by changes in lighting and music. Act 1 closes with soothing guitar music and a folksong. Act 2 begins with contrast between dark and light; then, stage directions call for the lighting to "shift magically to an eerie blue of fantasy" as Sidney plays his banjo. The third act begins in moonlight and darkness. As the scene progresses, lighting and sound are employed to move the action from the realistic world to the "denaturalized" world which the characters have entered. Their descent is accompanied by modern jazz, which, as the dialogue becomes more fragmented, becomes progressively more strident.

The most obvious dramatic device is the sign itself. Initially, it is a proud banner that the audience sees in dim or sharp light. By the close of act 2, however, the sign underscores the fact that Sidney has been betrayed. After Iris tells him to take it down, the sign becomes a malevolent object pulsing with its own power and corrupt energy. Several hours later, when act 3 opens, half of the sign has been ripped down, yet it still radiates force and power. During the final scene, as Iris responds to the police detective, stage directions specify that "the Sign seems more naked now, more assertive, more dominating, and for all of its unnoticed presence, necessary."

Critical Context

The Sign in Sidney Brustein's Window opened on October 15, 1964, and closed on January 12, 1965, hours after Lorraine Hansberry died of cancer. There were 101 Broadway performances, each of them virtually the last show because of production problems (both the original star and the director were replaced a week before the opening; Hansberry was too ill to work on script revisions) and a mixed, largely hostile, critical reception. Despite the obstacles, actors and audience members donated money and energy to keep the play alive.

The Sign in Sidney Brustein's Window differs considerably from Hansberry's most acclaimed work, *A Raisin in the Sun* (pr., pb. 1959). Perhaps critics were confounded because an African American playwright had turned away from an expected focus on black American family life and its struggles in white America, instead directing her attention to white characters confronting issues of moral responsibility, political corruption, anti-Semitism, sexuality, and commitment—the necessity not merely to survive but to become involved. Some reviewers found the play too didactic; others were bothered by what they saw as a lack of "concision and cohesion." While one critic argued that *The Sign in Sidney Brustein's Window* works within the tradition of the well-made play (orderly plot development, balanced scenes, smooth introduction of complications, clear climax and resolution), others noted the subordination of plot to character.

In this play, Hansberry dared to mix genres, fusing fantasy with realism, comedy with tragedy. She also dared to move outside the world of racial protest or "problem" drama, showing her concern for all people, whatever their racial, ethnic, social, or religious background. For this she was accused of being an "unadulterated integrationist" who would not examine the alienated black intellectual. *The Sign in Sidney Brustein's Window* is unabashedly a play of ideas whose principal thrust is that unless people learn to care about individuals, unless people learn that standing by merely to witness is not enough, until people learn about commitment and meaningful involvement, society will remain fragmented and limited, unable to reach its full potential. In his introduction to *Les Blancs: The Collected Last Plays of Lorraine Hansberry* (1972), Julius Lester saw *The Sign in Sidney Brustein's Window* as a "call to arms," a "conscious warning, a plea to her white intellectual counterparts to pick up the gauntlet and return to the field."

Despite its flaws, *The Sign in Sidney Brustein's Window* has aged well. It was included in the 1969 anthology *Stages: The Fifty-year Childhood of the American Theater* because it "captured so vividly the fervor and Angst" of American intellectuals; it was included in a 1971 anthology, *Best American Plays*; it had a brief revival in 1972 as a musical. Notwithstanding its lack of commercial success, the play was described by one critic in 1980 as Hansberry's "greatest triumph."

Sources for Further Study

Carter, Steven. *Hansberry's Drama: Commitment and Complexity.* Champaign-Urbana: University of Illinois Press, 1991.

Cheney, Anne. *Lorraine Hansberry.* Boston: Twayne, 1994.

Cruse, Harold. "Lorraine Hansberry." In *The Crisis of the Negro Intellectual.* New York: Morrow, 1967.

Davis, Ossie. "The Significance of Lorraine Hansberry." *Freedomways* 5 (Summer, 1965): 396-402.

Leeson, Richard M. *Lorraine Hansberry: A Research and Production Sourcebook.* Westport, Conn.: Greenwood Press, 1997.

Lester, Julius. *Introduction to Les Blancs: The Collected Last Plays of Lorraine Hansberry.* New York: Random House, 1972.

McKissack, Patricia C., and Frederick L. McKissack. *Young, Black, and Determined: A Biography of Lorraine Hansberry.* New York: Holiday, 1998.

Nemiroff, Robert. "The 101 'Final' Performances of *Sidney Brustein:* Portrait of a Play and Its Author." In *A Raisin in the Sun and The Sign in Sidney Brustein's Window.* New York: New American Library, 1966.

Scheader, Catherine. *Lorraine Hansberry: Playwright and the Voice of Justice.* Berkeley Heights, N.J.: Enslow, 1998.

Sandra Y. Govan

THE SILVER TASSIE

Author: Sean O'Casey (John Casey, 1880-1964)
Type of plot: Tragicomedy; war
Time of plot: World War I
Locale: Dublin, Ireland, and the front lines in France
First produced: 1929, at the Apollo Theatre, London
First published: 1928

> *Principal characters:*
> HARRY HEEGAN, a star player for the Avondale Football Club, a
>   young working man recently inducted into the British Army
> JESSICA "JESSIE" TAITE, a charming flirt whom Harry loves
> SUSIE MONICAN, a pretty girl in love with Harry but intensely
>   devoted to evangelical Christianity
> MRS. FORAN, a gossip and busybody
> TEDDY FORAN, her husband, an abrasive drunkard
> THE CROUCHER, an unidentified soldier, leader of a chorus of
>   soldiers

The Play

    The Silver Tassie unfolds in four relatively long acts. Act 1 opens in the home of the Heegans; as Mrs. Heegan gets Harry's clothes ready for his return to his army unit, Mr. Heegan and his friend exchange stories about Harry's strength and athletic prowess. Meanwhile, Susie Monican, a friend of the family and a young woman with a crush on Harry, attempts to get attention by uttering constant dour predictions and prophecies of doom prompted by her narrow fundamentalist piety. This domestic scene is disturbed by noise from the flat upstairs, where the Forans are having another row. Mrs. Foran comes in hastily to hide from her drunken husband, Teddy, who follows shortly, clearly inebriated and looking for his wife and Mr. Heegan—both of whom have hidden under the bed. General disapproval and Mrs. Foran's scolding force Teddy to leave, but he can be heard smashing furniture and dishes above.

    The mood changes when cheers and concertina music can be heard, and Harry enters with his arms around his favorite girlfriend, Jessica Taite. They bring the silver trophy cup, or silver tassie, that the Avondale Football Club has won by Harry's decisive goal, the "odd goal in five." While Harry exults in his victory and the strength of his youth, Jessie, a beautiful girl of twenty-two who is attracted to winners, and Barney, a young man who admires Harry's superior strength and skill, join Harry in drinking wine from the silver cup, which Harry calls a "sign of youth, sign of strength, sign of victory." Even Susie abandons her preaching and quoting of scripture to put her arm around Harry and flirt with him, though she has just bitterly repulsed an advance from Barney. Under Mrs. Heegan's constant urging, Harry gathers up his belongings, and he, Barney, and Teddy Foran depart to catch the boat that will take them back to their army unit. At their departure, Mrs. Heegan breathes a sigh of relief.

Act 2 shifts to a frontline combat zone in France, where a ravaged monastery has been converted into a makeshift Red Cross station. Barney is the only main character to appear, although one of the anonymous soldiers seems to be Teddy. Inside the station, unnamed soldiers await an uncertain fate while recuperating from trauma, wounds, and exhaustion. They are led in various laments and litanies by a wounded soldier called simply The Croucher, who begins the scene with a lamentation in biblical cadences about the surrealist landscape. In a series of poetic complaints, the soldiers voice their disillusionment with the war and express their sense of the futility of fighting. A visiting civilian dignitary arrives and utters absurd clichés about the significance of war. Finding Barney under restraint for the crime of stealing a chicken, the civilian voices his approval of such discipline. The civilian dignitary disappears for a while into a dugout, and a "staff-wallah" appears. This officer from headquarters arrives full of pomp and circumstance, and he tries to raise the men's morale while enforcing petty regulations to the very letter of the law. His efforts are unsuccessful. Receiving warning that an enemy attack is imminent, a corporal leads the soldiers in a series of rhymed chants, deifying the gun as one of the two gods in whom the men trust (the other being the Creator). While making their ritualistic prayers to the steel god, the men seem to gain renewed strength. An assault begins.

Act 3 takes place in a hospital ward an indefinite time later. Harry's father lies in a bed, receiving a visit from his friend. They comment on the change in Susie Monican, who, as a nurse, now wears rather daring clothes and relishes her role as a person of responsibility. Moreover, her evangelical piety has been abandoned; she now behaves in a decidedly secular manner and carries on a flirtation with Surgeon Maxwell. Among the other patients are Teddy Foran, who has been blinded, and Harry, who, having been shot in his spine and paralyzed from the waist down, enters in a wheelchair. Harry expresses hope that an operation tomorrow will help him, although Surgeon Maxwell expresses skepticism when Harry is out of earshot. Harry also worries because Jessie has not come to visit him, and he expresses bitterness and self-pity, which is heightened when he learns that his friend Barney will receive the Victoria Cross for removing him from danger.

From his mother and Mrs. Foran, who have come to visit, Harry learns that Jessie is on the hospital grounds with Barney but that she is clearly unwilling to come to visit him. Harry's agitation forces Susie to send the visitors away. Barney enters awkwardly to deliver flowers and a ukelele from Jessie, but her absence is painfully conspicuous. Barney makes a quick exit; he is obviously aiding Jessie in her betrayal. Harry cries out in despair.

Act 4 opens some weeks later at the dance hall of the Avondale Football Club, where a dance is being held to celebrate the retiring of the Silver Tassie because the Avondale team has won it three times, twice with Harry's help. Barney and Jessie have come together and are now obviously constant companions, but in their conversation they complain of Harry's constant shadowing of their movements. Mrs. Heegan and Mr. Foran express concern that Harry has come, but Mrs. Heegan says that Harry wants to stay until the ceremony over the cup: He wants to drink from the Silver Tassie since he did so much to win it. Harry appears, but is seen to be rather drawn and faint when he enters in a wheelchair pushed by Susie. Surgeon Maxwell decides that Harry should leave as soon as he drinks from the cup. Harry is joined by Teddy Foran, now blind, and they engage in a litany of lament about their losses.

Susie brings Harry his ukelele, and he plays the spiritual "Swing Low Sweet Chariot," drinks some wine from the cup, and wheels himself outside into the garden dispiritedly. Barney and Jessie enter; one strap of her gown is broken. Despite her protests, he takes advantage of their concealment behind the curtains of an alcove to embrace her and break the other strap, allowing her gown to collapse to her waist. Harry appears and makes a scene, denouncing Barney for his disloyalty and Jessie for her fickleness. He then tells Barney to go on and make love to Jessie there at the club as he himself had done before his wound. Jessie denies losing her virginity to Harry, although not very convincingly. Surgeon Maxwell and the others arrive to break up the quarrel, which has turned ugly with Barney attacking Harry and beating him.

Coming to his senses, Harry realizes that his wound has removed him irrevocably from the normal course of life, and he calls on Teddy to join him on a bitter journey homeward, for "what's in front we'll face like men!" Susie pronounces the judgment of the others: Life must go on, and Harry must accept his tragic fate.

Themes and Meanings

The Silver Tassie is an uncompromising antiwar play, focusing on the tragic wound of Harry Heegan, a common soldier who goes to war as mindlessly as he goes to a football match. Sean O'Casey concentrates so intensely on his theme that one wonders how William Butler Yeats or anyone else could have considered the play to lack unity, although this was one of the alleged reasons for Yeats's rejection of the play when O'Casey offered it to the Abbey Theatre in Dublin.

The four acts all show the folly of Harry's involvement in World War I. In act 1, the play presents Harry in the prime of life, as an athletic hero at the peak of his strength, though completely unaware of the possibilities and values of life. Act 2, a controversial experiment with expressionist and symbolic theater, shows the cynicism and despair of the common soldier at the front lines. Act 3 portrays the bitterness of the veterans in a veterans' hospital, and act 4 contrasts the grim plight of the disabled Harry Heegan with the vitality of those who were not combatants and have normal lives and futures to anticipate. In its study of Harry's loss of many of his life's hopes during and after the war, the play is quite unusual: Few modern dramas cover such an extended period of time. The constant reiteration of the antiwar theme is obvious.

Had Harry been portrayed as a more thoughtful man, his disabling wound and the loss of a normal life might have been considered tragic. However, even when Harry's lack of self-awareness is taken into account, *The Silver Tassie* is a strong work, more tragic than comic. The antiwar theme is not confined to Harry's experience: The effects of the war on Teddy Foran and on Susie Monican are equally strong. Susie, for example, at first appears to be an extremely pious and otherworldly woman, but in the uninhibited atmosphere of the veterans' hospital, Susie has become a rather worldly woman, perhaps even a little coarse. Thus, O'Casey not only implies that common soldiers like Harry go to war without reflecting on the meaning of the conflict or on the price that they may have to pay, but also that the general effect of war is destructive of ideals and values.

The major symbol of the play is the cup that gives the drama its title, the "Silver Tassie," which is a symbol of youth and strength and the joy of living. Harry calls attention to this point rather obviously early in the play, and a later reference in the fourth act reiterates the cup's importance. Harry's prowess as a soccer player is emblematic of his virility, and his use of the ukelele provides evidence of poetic feeling, despite the fact that Harry is not one of O'Casey's more sensitive or thoughtful protagonists.

Dramatic Devices

Sean O'Casey's major break with the realistic tradition, and his chief innovation, is his experimental and poetic portrayal of the battlefront in act 2. This act is largely impressionistic and symbolic in its theatrical design, with a chorus of soldiers uttering their lamentations about the war, a symbolic civilian voicing platitudes about honor, and a stylized backdrop. In its conception and its poetic refrains, the act foreshadows much of the later O'Casey works, especially the visionary transformation of Dublin in act 3 of *Red Roses for Me* (pb. 1942, pr. 1943). The staging of act 2 is not especially difficult, although it does make demands of a theatrical company with limited personnel and resources. The act is not particularly difficult for an audience to understand or accept. It is curious that Yeats, in rejecting *The Silver Tassie* for the Abbey Theatre, accused the play of a lack of unity. In large part, it may be suspected that the reason was the diversion of this act from the story of Harry Heegan, yet most sophisticated modern audiences, especially those familiar with the conventions of American musical comedy, would find the act quite easy to accept.

The action of the rest of the play is fairly close to conventional realism, although the action is rather episodic, covering an indefinite period—roughly a year. The use of the festival dance at the Avondale Football Club in the final act adds a particular irony and poignancy to Harry's tragedy. A man in a wheelchair cannot join in the victory dance, or, symbolically, in the dance of life. Barney's sexual aggressiveness at the dance may seem to be somewhat unrealistic. Certainly a more experienced seducer would wait until Jessie was in a more private situation before breaking the second strap of her gown, but Barney is not necessarily experienced, and he is, perhaps, as excited by his betrayal of Harry as he is by Jessie's charms. Barney's assault on Jessie's gown is a bold theatrical stroke for the dramatist, and it helps create a sympathetic context for Harry's savage denunciation of the pair.

Critical Context

The Silver Tassie is a pivotal work in Sean O'Casey's career; it provoked the bitter quarrel with Yeats which led to O'Casey's decisive break with the Abbey Theatre.

The play also clearly marks the direction that O'Casey's subsequent work was to take, with its attempt to go beyond realism by venturing into the stylized poetic expressionism of the second act. Although there are those who continue to insist that some of Yeats's criticisms were accurate, and that O'Casey's stubborn championing of the play was a mistake, which led to an unwise exile in England, the majority opinion of O'Casey scholars seems to be that *The Silver Tassie* is a solid and powerful work. Indeed, the play is only one of many antiwar novels and plays that emerged in print in the late 1920's, and it should be viewed in the context of the decade's disillusionment with war and patriotism. The bitter and ironic tone of the work is comparable to that found in Robert Graves's *Goodbye to All That* (1929), Ernest Hemingway's *A Farewell to Arms* (1928), and much of the modernist poetry of the time, especially that by Graves, W. H. Auden, T. S. Eliot, and E. E. Cummings.

As for the negative views of O'Casey's later career, which often begin with disparagement of *The Silver Tassie*, O'Casey's sympathetic critics reply that his dramatic ambitions and vision were moving beyond the realism of his early masterpieces. In his later work, O'Casey attempts to become a spokesman for the visionary and romantic imagination and to comment on themes of world significance. In other words, he moved beyond the somewhat provincial concerns to Irish poverty and Irish nationalism, though this growth did not please those who wanted him to remain a realistic dramatist, fusing Ibsenist dramaturgy with Dickensian humor.

The problem of evaluating *The Silver Tassie* as a work of art remains; there are still differences of opinion. While the antiwar theme is handled effectively, for example, it may be contended that O'Casey's play tends to become obsessively didactic. Moreover, the controversial second act may seem too strident and obvious, now that the shock impact of the antiwar rhetoric has worn off.

More important than these considerations, the major problem of the play for some may be the limited nature of the protagonist, Harry Heegan. Harry is not a very reflective hero before being wounded: As the author comments, he has gone to war "as unthinkingly as he would go to the polling booth." O'Casey apparently created Heegan as a symbol of the working-class victims of all nations, who were duped and manipulated by nationalist rhetoric and cynical political leaders, but by giving Harry so little self-awareness, the author ran the risk of developing a character who could gain only a limited degree of sympathy.

After Harry sustains his tragic wound, he does grow in moral stature and self-consciousness, but the increase is not extraordinary. Perhaps it is somewhat difficult for sophisticated audiences to identify with a hero whose chief distinction has been his athletic ability. At any rate, Harry's limited vision and moral awareness prevent him from becoming an authentic tragic hero. Unlike O'Casey's later working-class hero, Ayamonn Breydon in *Red Roses for Me*, Harry is not an original thinker, nor is he very poetic, except at second hand. *The Silver Tassie* is a harsh and durable play, but it remains a tragicomedy, rather than the tragic masterpiece some of O'Casey's most ardent admirers claim it to be.

Sources for Further Study

Hogan, Robert T., and Richard Burnham. *The Years of O'Casey, 1921-1926: A Documentary History*. Newark: University of Delaware Press, 1992.

Krause, David. *Sean O'Casey: The Man and His Work*. New York: Macmillan, 1960.

Malone, Maureen. *The Plays of Sean O'Casey*. Carbondale: Southern Illinois University Press, 1969.

Mikhail, E. H. *O'Casey and His Critics: An Annotated Bibliography*. Landham, Md.: Scarecrow, 1985.

Mitchell, Jack. *The Essential O'Casey: A Study of the Twelve Major Plays of Sean O'Casey*. New York: International, 1980.

O'Riordan, John. *A Guide to O'Casey's Plays*. New York: St. Martin's Press, 1984.

Rollins, Ronald Gene. *Sean O'Casey's Drama: Verisimilitude and Vision*. Tuscaloosa: University of Alabama Press, 1981.

Schrank, Bernice W. *Sean O'Casey: A Research and Production Handbook*. Westport, Conn.: Greenwood Press, 1996.

Edgar L. Chapman
Diane Happ

SISTER MARY IGNATIUS EXPLAINS IT ALL FOR YOU

Author: Christopher Durang (1949-   )
Type of plot: Satire; psychological
Time of plot: 1979
Locale: United States
First produced: 1979, at the Ensemble Studio Theatre, New York City
First published: 1980

> *Principal characters:*
> SISTER MARY IGNATIUS, a parochial-school teacher
> THOMAS, a parochial-school pupil
> DIANE SYMONDS,
> GARY SULLAVAN,
> PHILOMENA ROSTOVITCH, and
> ALOYSIUS BUSICCIO, former pupils, now adults

The Play

The play unfolds in a single setting: a simple stage containing a lectern, a potted palm, a few chairs, and an easel. Standing at the lectern and addressing her remarks directly to the audience, Sister Mary Ignatius, an old-fashioned nun and parochial-school teacher, begins a loosely structured lecture on Roman Catholic principles concerning the proper conduct of life and the ways in which such conduct will earn one eternal reward or punishment after death. Illustrating her points with drawings on the easel, she speaks first of the nature and purpose of the divinely ordained regions that lie beyond the physical universe—heaven, hell, purgatory, and limbo—and then of doctrinal matters, including the meaning of the Immaculate Conception and the question of papal infallibility. This monologue is not completely coherent, however, and Sister Mary Ignatius digresses frequently, weaving into her prepared remarks autobiographical reflections and abrupt requests for water and cookies. These requests are satisfied by Thomas, a second-grader at Our Lady of Perpetual Sorrows School. The opening lecture concludes with a vivid description of Christ's suffering on the Cross and a final digression, in this case involving bitter memories of her parents and her oppressive childhood.

In the play's second scene, Sister Mary Ignatius answers questions on Roman Catholic theory and practice. Reading wide-ranging questions from file cards supposedly submitted to her by the audience, she responds in a variety of ways or not at all, depending on how the questions strike her. Asked, for example, whether nuns go to the bathroom and whether Jesus was effeminate, she answers tersely, "Yes." On the other hand, she refuses to answer questions that call into doubt God's goodness in view of the great suffering in the world and that ask her to detail the exact nature of the sins committed at Sodom. Her most detailed responses come when she is asked about situ-

ational ethics and about her own life. Her speeches on the former reveal a strict, morally simplistic, even outmoded, orthodoxy; on the latter, a nightmarish childhood
spent with twenty-six siblings, an alcoholic and abusive father, and a mentally unstable mother. This question-and-answer session ends with Sister Mary Ignatius, bathed
in blue light, singing the "Ave Maria."

As she sings, four people enter, all of them former pupils whom she taught in 1959.
Though now adults, they are costumed to perform a Nativity pageant, a play that was
written by a pious student of hers in 1948 and which she has had her students stage
every Christmas since. Beginning as a conventional juvenile enactment of the Nativity story, the play comes to reveal the same strict, eccentric, and egocentric theology
reflected in Sister's earlier remarks, thus suggesting why she enjoys the presentation
so much. Delighted with their little performance, Sister proceeds to question the four
adults, first on catechismal matters, much as she did with young Thomas in his brief
appearances earlier, and then about their lives since she taught them. While their answers on Catholic dogma are more or less satisfactory to her, their revelations about
how they have lived are far from acceptable. Diane Symonds claims to have had two
abortions; Philomena Rostovitch is an unwed mother; Aloysius Busiccio is an alcoholic and a wife abuser with suicidal tendencies; and Gary Sullavan admits to being a
homosexual, having first been seduced when he was studying to become a priest. Although she is very disappointed with her former charges, Sister nevertheless tries to
reform them by lecturing on proper Catholic values and practices.

A major turn in the play occurs at the end of this lecture. Sister Mary Ignatius concludes by asking rhetorically, "Are you insane?" and Diane Symonds delivers a direct
rejoinder to the question: "You're insane." With this frontal verbal assault, Diane, the
group's leader, stridently accuses their former teacher of deception, of lying to children about what life is really like. Using her own experiences as examples of this deception, Diane tells of her unanswered prayers as she watched her mother's agonizing
death from cancer, of being raped one day after visiting her mother in the hospital, and
of her seduction by the psychiatrist to whom she had gone after her mother's death
and her own rape. Essentially Diane's diatribe raises the issue that Sister refused to
address during the earlier question-and-answer period—namely, why a benevolent
God would allow bad things to happen to faithful and innocent people. Far from encountering a world governed by Divine Providence, as Sister promised, she has found
herself lost in incomprehensible suffering, and, as she says, "this randomness seemed
intolerable." Insisting now that Sister admit openly to deceptive teachings, Diane
takes out a gun and threatens her life, at which point Sister immediately assents to Diane's demands.

Before long, however, Sister Mary Ignatius distracts Diane, pulls out her own gun,
and shoots her former pupil dead. She also shoots the homosexual, Gary Sullavan, her
excuse for this action being that, since Gary had gone to confession that morning, she
has sent his cleansed soul to heaven. As for the others, Philomena is warned to reform
her sinful life and released, and Aloysius is held at gunpoint, his urgent requests to go
to the bathroom denied. Exhausted now, Sister Mary Ignatius decides to take a nap,

leaving young Thomas in charge. The play ends with Thomas obediently holding the gun on the frightened Aloysius and reciting "some nice catechism questions."

Themes and Meanings

As a Roman Catholic play, *Sister Mary Ignatius Explains It All for You* satirically examines the psychological problems associated with parochialism—the sort of parochialism that concerns both educational practice and the view of life that education engenders. Thus, there are at least two thematic levels at which the play operates, one of these levels immediate, the other more general.

On the most obvious level, the play is about the harmful effects of misguided authority. Christopher Durang takes pains to show that the rigidly moralistic Sister Mary Ignatius, herself the product of a troubled family, possesses little insight or sensitivity toward people and life and even religion itself and, as Diane Symonds suggests, should never have been given the authority to teach children. Psychologically abusive, ignorantly pietistic, and often self-indulgent, Sister has sought to make her young charges over not in her image, for she regards her position as all too exalted, but rather in the image that she, in accordance with selected and harshly interpreted Catholic teachings, deems appropriate. Parodoxically, even as she professes authority, she makes clear that she is in no position psychologically to make such determinations about other people's lives. In her repeated requests for displays of her pupils' rote knowledge of the catechism, she encourages uncritical acceptance, even though she herself is not quite so yielding, as seen when she shows her resentment toward Pope John XXIII for instituting changes in the Church; she insists that her charges restrain their own physical and mental needs while she yields to ego demands at every turn. This authoritarian egotism is evident, for example, when, in answer to the question "How do we know" that "Christ loves us an infinite amount . . .?" Thomas answers, "Because you tell us," and when her name and her restrictive moral visions are heard in dramatic lines spoken by the Virgin Mary in the juvenile Nativity pageant.

On the larger level, the play is concerned with much more than the excesses of the central character. *Sister Mary Ignatius Explains It All for You* is also about guilt—the mental struggle brought about by the sharp conflict between narrow-minded acceptance of parochial principles and the demands experienced by the individual in the wider arena of life. Durang explores this theme by incorporating, so to speak, "before and after" portraits of people nurtured on such principles. On one hand, there is the obliging young pupil, Thomas, appearing on demand to serve up cookies or catechismal theology, as Sister requires. On the other hand, there are Sister's four former students, each of them a sorely troubled adult, each of them struggling with a conscience that she has programmed to recognize only sin and purity, with no moral middle ground. The parochial educational system, through the agency of Sister Mary Ignatius, has offered these pathetic individuals fear of divine retribution rather than Christian compassion, self-loathing rather than moral fortitude. Although Sister Mary Ignatius is not the Roman Catholic Church in its complex entirety, the effects of her work can be regarded as an indictment of the system that she serves.

Dramatic Devices

Although, like all drama, *Sister Mary Ignatius Explains It All for You* reveals its themes through the playwright's manipulation of language and spectacle, the emphasis here is decidedly on the former. The only physical action in the play occurs near the end, when Diane Symonds pulls her gun on Sister Mary Ignatius and when Sister pulls her own gun and shoots Diane and Gary Sullavan. That the self-righteous nun should have a concealed weapon is ironic and bitingly amusing; that she should use it is also ironic and quite shocking. This surprising scene provides a sudden and effective climax to the relatively flat action that precedes it.

Christopher Durang's technique is far more reliant on language, particularly verbal irony, than on physical movement. Sister Mary Ignatius's commentaries on life and religion are especially noteworthy in this regard, continually revealing as they do her insensitivity about the human condition (thus supporting Diane Symonds's accusations) and her ignorance. That ignorance is especially acute when it comes to the matter she professes to know best—religion—and this is where Durang's subtle satiric thrusts are most evident. In one speech, for example, she twice alludes to biblical passages. In the first, she says that Christ wanted the little children brought to him, but then adds, "I don't remember in reference to what." In like manner, quoting Christ's exclamation, "Oh ye of little faith," Sister expresses doubt regarding the audience he was addressing at the time. Her lapses undermine her credibility as a religious authority and render ironic her professions of knowledge and righteousness.

Moreover, Sister Mary Ignatius's applications of Christian principles are suspect. When, for example, Philomena insists that Jesus forgives sinners, citing, with particular bearing upon her own "sin," the woman taken in adultery, Sister denies Christ's moral intervention. She then goes on to maintain that his protection of the adulteress was merely a "political gesture," and that, in private, Christ himself stoned many women taken in adultery. When Philomena will not accept that answer and presses her to admit that Jesus was forgiving, Sister grudgingly gives up a little ground, but only a little: "Yes, of course, He forgives sins, but He's *tricky*," she asserts.

Such inadvertently self-revealing statements as these by the central character demonstrate the degree to which Durang's satiric method is dependent upon language. In fact, his technique is perhaps best summed up in the author's notes appended to printed editions of the play. Durang suggests there that the actor playing Sister Mary Ignatius should avoid self-consciousness in her portrayal of the character. Sister thinks there is nothing wrong with her statements and actions, Durang maintains, and, whenever she does or says something that is outrageous or horrifying, it is up to the audience to recognize her excesses. The subtle discovery of such excesses through word and gesture is precisely what Durang's dramatic method involves.

Critical Context

The Obie Award-winning *Sister Mary Ignatius Explains It All for You* is the best known of the satiric comedies that constitute Christopher Durang's dramatic canon. Although none of his other plays is as overtly critical of Catholicism as is this one, religion as a satiric target is not far below the surface in many of the other plays. In *The Nature and Purpose of the Universe* (pr. 1979), for example, he explores the existential question of human suffering and the ways in which religion, notably Christianity, tries to rationalize its meaning in the divine scheme of things, avoiding, as Sister Mary Ignatius so often does, the issue of God's intentions in making innocent people suffer, and masochistically asserting that pain and anguish are somehow redemptive. Similarly, in *The Marriage of Bette and Boo* (pr. 1973, pb. 1976), people confronted with horrible physical and emotional pain are disabused of the notion that God punishes people for specific sins. Rather, God punishes everyone and for no particular reason, says one of the play's main characters, Matt. (Durang himself played Matt in Joseph Papp's 1985 production of the admittedly autobiographical play, and the dramatist's performance earned for him another Obie, this one for acting.)

Placed within this context, the importance of *Sister Mary Ignatius Explains It All for You* becomes apparent, for it is here that Durang focuses his haunting interest in the matter of religion and its effects upon people. The difference between Diane and other suffering human beings in Durang's plays is that, rather than accuse God, she tries to take direct action against her misinformant, her elementary school teacher. That she loses in the struggle to get Sister to admit to her "lies," however, places her squarely in the company of the other helpless and emotionally wounded victims whom Durang so often depicts in his plays.

The importance of the play is also attributable in part to the controversy it has generated. Appreciated by many for its satiric authenticity, the play also has been severely denounced by critics for its jokes in bad taste and "excessive spleen" and by religious authorities for its distortions and misconceptions. Not surprisingly, its most vocal detractors have been representatives of the Catholic Church, who, in several American cities, have demonstrated to have performances canceled and in some cases have succeeded. Nevertheless, Durang's reputation rests largely upon *Sister Mary Ignatius Explains It All for You*, which has been reprinted several times in anthologies of the most important plays of the late 1970's and early 1980's.

Sources for Further Study

Brustein, Robert. "The Naked and the Dressed." *The New Republic*, December 9, 1981, 21, 24-25.

Durang, Christopher. "Day by Day with Christopher Durang." *Dramatist*, Spring, 1997, 34.

Lauder, Robert. "Theatrical Catholics." *America* 145 (December 26, 1981): 417-418.

Savran, David. "Christopher Durang." In *In Their Own Words: Contemporary American Playwrights*. New York: Theatre Communications Group, 1988.

Weales, Gerald. "Father Tim, Sister Sade: Anguish and Anger." *Commonweal* 109 (January 29, 1982): 50-51.

Leonard Mustazza

SLEUTH

Author: Anthony Shaffer (1926-2001)
Type of plot: Mystery and detective
Time of plot: The 1970's
Locale: England
First produced: 1970, at St. Martin's Theatre, London
First published: 1970

> *Principal characters:*
> ANDREW WYKE, a successful mystery author
> MILO TINDLE, a travel agent and the lover of Andrew's wife
> INSPECTOR DOPPLER, a police detective

The Play

Sleuth is presented in two acts, with all the action taking place in the country-home interior of famous mystery writer Andrew Wyke. It is a summer evening; a solitary Andrew is absorbed in finishing his latest manuscript featuring his famous fictional creation, the eccentric and brilliant amateur sleuth, St. John Lord Merridew. Andrew, middle-aged and dressed casually in his smoking jacket, is obviously pleased with his latest work and begins to recite it aloud as he strolls around his living room decorated with a variety of games, puzzles, and toys.

The doorbell rings and Andrew invites Milo Tindle in. Milo is a young, handsome travel agent whom Andrew has invited over this evening to discuss Milo's involvement with Andrew's wife, Marguerite. Milo is at first taken aback by Andrew's civil openness about the situation, but Andrew insists that he has no animosity against Milo, that he only wants to make sure Milo knows what he is getting into. Andrew claims he does not love Marguerite and is perfectly willing to divorce her so he can more fully enjoy his mistress, Teya. He wants to make sure, however, that Milo can take care of Marguerite in the comfort and luxury to which she is accustomed in order to prevent her from becoming dissatisfied with Milo in a few months and trying to reconcile with Andrew. Milo admits that his travel agency business, although successful, is still somewhat financially insecure.

Andrew, smug and aggressive, filled with devilish energy and cunning, proposes a scheme to Milo in an effort to keep Marguerite happy and lavishly content and therefore permanently out of Andrew's life. Andrew suggests that Milo rob the estate of some valuable jewelry along with the receipts, and sell the jewels on the black market, enabling Milo to garner a sizable amount of cash and giving Andrew the opportunity to collect on the insurance. Andrew then outlines an elaborate burglary plan involving Milo breaking into the home, ransacking various rooms and ultimately taking the gems.

Milo is quite suspicious at first. He cannot believe Andrew would be so obliging in his efforts to free himself of Marguerite. Andrew insists, however, that his motives are free from malice and the scheme is foolproof. Finally, to Andrew's delight, Milo agrees to the plan. Andrew insists that Milo disguise himself using one of Andrew's old theatrical costumes and break into the estate through an upstairs window. Milo begins to catch Andrew's enthusiastic, flamboyant fever and ends up dressing like a clown. He follows Andrew's orders and while he is busy breaking into the home, Andrew rigs the safe containing the jewels with explosives and blows it open. Both men then indulge in a frenzied ransacking of the home, throwing papers, overturning furniture, disemboweling drawers and closets, until the house is in sufficient disarray.

Andrew then announces that they must make it appear as if Andrew walked in on the crime and that Milo subdued Andrew before escaping with the jewels. First Andrew proposes that Milo strike him so it will appear as if the two had struggled. Then Andrew produces a gun, however, and says that the plan should be that Andrew at first held the gun on Milo but after a struggle in which shots were fired, Milo escaped. Andrew then fires two shots from the gun, breaking various objects in the living room. Then he turns to Milo and says that he is going to kill him. Milo thinks that Andrew is joking. Andrew then reveals the real reason for inviting Milo over for the evening. Andrew is outraged that a young, unaristocratic upstart could even contemplate running off with the wife of a respected nobleman. Andrew has set up the mock crime in order to make it appear as if he merely shot an anonymous burglar instead of his wife's lover. He then tells Milo to put on his clown mask and prepare to die. Milo pleads for his life but to no avail. Andrew puts the gun to Milo's head and shoots him. The curtain falls, ending act 1.

Act 2 begins two days later. Andrew, alone again, is preparing a small supper for himself when the doorbell brings. It is Detective Inspector Doppler of the local county constabulary investigating the disappearance of Milo. Andrew insists that he knows nothing about Milo's disappearance until Doppler produces a note written two days ago by Andrew inviting Milo over for the evening. Doppler says the note was found in Milo's cottage. Andrew then admits to having Milo visit him two nights ago but states that Milo had left later in the evening. Doppler mentions that reports of gunshots coming from Andrew's home had been made by a neighbor passing by that evening. Doppler also mentions that, after talking to other neighbors, he learned that Milo and Andrew's wife were having an affair.

Andrew, visibly agitated, begins to relate the events of Milo's visit. He tells Doppler of the elaborate burglary scheme, of Milo agreeing to the plan, dressing up like a clown, and breaking into the home. Andrew also explains how he shot Milo. He then confesses that the real purpose of the scheme was to invite Milo over and humiliate him, to teach him a lesson for trying to run off with Andrew's wife. Andrew insists that he shot Milo with a blank and that Milo, after recovering from the shock, left for the evening. Doppler is horrified at Andrew's callousness, unnerved that anyone could go to such elaborate and sadistic extremes to humiliate a person. He also does not believe that Milo left the house alive. Andrew insists that it was merely a game to teach Milo a lesson. Doppler suggests that it might have started out as a game but that it had ended up as murder.

Doppler begins to investigate the premises. At first, Andrew is amused by Doppler's plodding techniques but then becomes horrified when Doppler finds fresh bloodstains on the carpet and clothes hidden in a closet with Milo's name sewn into the lining. Andrew is dumbfounded and cannot explain how the bloodstains or the clothes got there. Doppler then announces that Andrew is under arrest for murder. Andrew shrieks and attempts to evade Doppler. As they scuffle, Doppler suddenly reveals to Andrew that he, Detective Inspector Doppler, is actually Milo in disguise.

After the shock of the revelation wears off and Andrew grudgingly congratulates Milo on his clever masquerade, Milo also confesses his admiration for Andrew's bogus crime. Milo also states that he feels his own game has hardly settled the score. Milo is still shaken by Andrew's mock murder and announces that, unlike Andrew, he has committed a real murder. He tells Andrew that while he had been planting the fake evidence for his own game the previous day when Andrew had been away, Andrew's mistress, Teya, had shown up, and that after seducing her, Milo killed her. Andrew does not believe him and calls Teya, only to learn from Teya's roommate that Teya has indeed been murdered. Milo then tells Andrew that he has informed the police, who are on their way at the moment. Milo also tells Andrew that he has left incriminating evidence around the living room that will implicate Andrew as the murderer. Milo then gives clues to Andrew to help him find the evidence so he can destroy it before the police arrive.

Andrew becomes frantic as he begins tearing around the living room, looking for the evidence. With Milo's cryptic clues, he is able to find all the evidence only moments before the police arrive. It turns out, however, that the police are merely voices coming from the doorway, impersonated by Milo. Milo then tells Andrew that Teya is alive and that she had enthusiastically agreed to help Milo fake her murder by lending him some of her personal items as the phony evidence. Milo also tells Andrew that Teya is not really his mistress because Andrew is impotent. Milo then reconfirms his plans to run off with Marguerite and goes to collect some of Marguerite's belongings.

Andrew sits, slumped and defeated. As Milo rummages through Marguerite's room, Andrew retrieves his gun and begins plotting a new scheme. When Milo returns, Andrew announces that if Milo tries to leave, Andrew will shoot him as a burglar, and this time he will use real bullets. Milo laughs and says that he would not be able to get away with the murder because Milo did in fact tell the police all about Andrew's mock crime and that if Andrew were to shoot him now, the police would not believe the burglary story. Andrew, dismissing Milo's news as just another charade, shoots Milo. As Milo slumps to the floor, the sound of an approaching car is heard and a flashing police car light shines through the window. Andrew screams in anguish as the curtain falls, ending the play.

Themes and Meanings

Sleuth, like its own Milo Tindle, disguises itself and purports to disapprove of the old-fashioned parlor room murder mysteries popularized by such masters of the genre as Agatha Christie, Dorothy L. Sayers, and Sir Arthur Conan Doyle. Also like Milo, the play indulges in flamboyant and elaborate tricks used so successfully by the past masters. In so doing, *Sleuth* unmasks itself for what it really is: Anthony Shaffer's backhanded, revitalized homage to the supposed outdated parlor room puzzler. While it is lambasting the genre for being sterile, overly intellectual, and bloodless, *Sleuth* is also lauding the genre for its playful plot twists, elaborate deceptions, and unabashed ability to entertain.

Andrew Wyke is the personification of the genre itself. He is quick-witted, theatrical, and obsessed with elaborate plot schemes. His speech is lively and rich with horrible puns and allusions to his beloved literary compatriots as well as his own works. He is also, like the genre, extremely class-conscious, intolerant of people whom he deems not part of his insulated, aristocratic world. Milo, young, vigorous, and handsome, the son of an Italian immigrant, is a threat to Andrew. He represents everything that Andrew is not. As he tells Milo just before he shoots him in act 1:

> I hate your smarmy, good-looking Latin face and your easy manner. . . . I hate you because you are a culling spick. A wop—a not one-of-me. Come, little man, did you really believe I would give up my wife and jewels to you? That I would make myself *that* ridiculous?

Milo represents the world of flesh and blood reality. His world is in direct conflict with Andrew's universe of intellectual games, contrivances, and manipulation. However, both worlds are potent ones. It is obvious that Milo is at first awed by Andrew's passionate love for games-playing. Although Milo does not agree with Andrew's assertion that the world of detective fiction is superior to detective fact, and that the detective story is "the normal recreation of noble minds," he still cannot resist becoming caught up in Andrew's frenzied enthusiasm for games-playing. After the games turn deadly, however, Milo's admiration turns to revulsion. In the end, after he has taken his revenge on Andrew by beating him at his own manipulative games of deceit and humiliation, he tells Andrew:

> Take a look at yourself, Andrew, and ask yourself a few simple questions about your attachment to the English detective story. Perhaps you might come to realize that the only place you can inhabit is a dead world. . . . It's a world of coldness and class hatred, and two-dimensional characters who are not expected to communicate; it's a world where only amateurs win, and where foreigners are automatically figures of fun. To put it shortly, the detective story is the normal recreation of snobbish, outdated, life-hating, ignoble minds.

In the end, it is Milo's world of facts, of real police detectives and real death, that destroys Andrew's world of charades and betrayal. Or so it seems. For the main, overriding theme of *Sleuth* is the beguiling fascination this artificial world of games has on the world of fact. The audience is held spellbound by the play's string of deceits, fake murders, disguises, and manipulative acts. *Sleuth* therefore proves that Andrew's world is hardly dead, and that with a few modifications the old-fashioned parlor room puzzler can still pack quite a dramatic punch.

Dramatic Devices

The two acts of *Sleuth* are presented to illustrate the contrast as well as the interrelationships that exist between the world of detective fact and detective fiction. In act 1, Andrew is clearly in control of the proceedings as he manipulates Milo into first believing he is helping to assure his successful future with Marguerite by playing Andrew's games, and then into believing that Andrew has actually shot him dead.

In act 2, it is the plodding and methodical Inspector Doppler and his world of detective fact that manipulates Andrew. In this world, Andrew's flamboyance, his gift for mimicry and his allusions to his literary heroes, so charming and appropriate in act 1, now fail to impress the serious Doppler. Even the canned laughter from one of Andrew's most innocent props, a life-size doll dressed as a sea captain, sounds hollow and ironic in Doppler's presence.

Milo avenges himself in act 2 by using all the tricks Andrew used to humiliate him in act 1: disguises, deceit, horrible puns, literary allusions, and a chilling disregard for human life. Throughout both acts, the setting remains the same, the traditional country estate interior, as if it were a huge game board itself, unchanging except for its human game pieces. The two characters, with their theatrical disguises and repertoire of voices, create the illusion of a houseful of eccentric caricatures, all of whom would be found in the traditional drawing room whodunit: maids and butlers, police detectives, tantalizing mistresses, frivolous wives, and the infallible amateur supersleuth.

Probably the most effective device used to illustrate the ironic relationship that exists between flesh and blood, fact and fiction, is the staging of Milo's two deaths. Milo's first "death" is the more shocking and unsettling of the two. It is set up so the audience believes right along with Milo that he has been shot in the head and killed. Milo's second death, although now in deadly earnest, does not have as much emotional impact. At this point, the audience, having been manipulated time and again, feels as Andrew must, so caught up in the deceitful world of games-playing that it cannot feel remorse over the death of another person. Death has been rendered merely another bloodless, intellectual preoccupation. Milo's final words, a parody of Andrew's comment which ended act 1, echo with bloodless irony and typify the world he supposedly despises: "Game, set and match!"

Critical Context

When *Sleuth* premiered in London in 1970, it was called the play that critics could not review. Indeed, critics found it next to impossible to say anything about the subject of the play for fear of slipping up and revealing one of the many devious plot twists, and thus earning the wrath of those who had not yet seen it. Certainly *Sleuth*'s effectiveness depends to a large degree on its shocking plot devices. There is no denying, however, that the play's two characters are more than two-dimensional plot foils. Both are strong, dynamic individuals who go far beyond the stereotypical stick figures found in plays which rely heavily on plot trickery as opposed to character development for their effectiveness. The language is especially lively and rich with witticisms, in keeping with the flamboyant nature of the characters themselves.

Sleuth was Anthony Shaffer's first play. He had previously written detective novels with his brother Peter (also a successful playwright) under the pseudonym Peter Antony and worked on several television projects. Shaffer admitted that the inspiration for *Sleuth* came after learning that Agatha Christie, the undisputed queen of the parlor room style of murder mystery, was the most-published author in the world. Shaffer wanted both to send up Christie and the genre in which she excelled, and at the same time to use the elements inherent in this most popular genre. The result was an extremely commercially successful entertainment, a spellbinding crowd pleaser.

Like *Sleuth*, Shaffer's other plays are playful and cunning variations on the traditional murder mystery. In *Murderer* (pr. 1975), the protagonist, like *Sleuth*'s Andrew Wyke, is obsessed with games-playing and likes to graphically reenact the crimes of celebrated murderers of the past. In *The Case of the Oily Levantine* (pr. 1977; also known as *Whodunnit*, pr. 1979), the play begins as a hilarious burlesque of the traditional drawing room mystery, complete with all the stock, stuffy, aristocratic characters, but then turns into a wild variation of the genre as all the characters suddenly reveal their true identities. Shaffer was enamored of the old "cozy crime" genre. In all of his works (which include the original screenplay for Alfred Hitchcock's *Frenzy*, in 1972, and screen adaptations of some of Christie's books featuring Hercule Poirot), Shaffer's intent was both to honor and to harass the genre. However, his main concern was to entertain, to breathe new life into one of the most popular genres of all and enthrall his audience with the elements that have made the genre so successful and well loved.

Sources for Further Study

Gill, Brendan. "Things Going Wrong." *The New Yorker*, November 21, 1970, 103.

Glenn, Jules. "Twins in the Theater: A Study of Plays by Peter and Anthony Shaffer." *Blood Brothers: Siblings as Writers*, edited by Norman Kiell. New York: International University Press, 1983.

Gussow, Mel. "With *Sleuth*, Another Shaffer Catches Public Eye." *New York Times*, November 18, 1970, p. 38.

Hewes, Henry. "Two Can Play at a Game." *Saturday Review*, November 28, 1970.

Klein, Dennis A. *Peter and Anthony Shaffer: A Reference Guide*. Boston: G. K. Hall, 1982.

Morley, Sheridan. "The Whodunit That Did It Right: *Sleuth* Still Offers More than the Genre's Usual Suspects." *International Herald Tribune*, July 24, 2002, p. 9.

Newsweek. Review of *Sleuth*. November 23, 1970, 138.

Time. Review of *Sleuth*. March 30, 1970, 77.

James Kline

A SOLDIER'S PLAY

Author: Charles Fuller (1939-   )
Type of plot: Mystery and detective
Time of plot: 1944
Locale: Fort Neal, Louisiana
First produced: 1981, at Theatre Four, New York City
First published: 1981

> *Principal characters:*
> TECH/SERGEANT VERNON C. WATERS, a black murder victim
> CAPTAIN CHARLES TAYLOR, a liberal white company
>   commanding officer (C.O.)
> CORPORAL BERNARD COBB, an African American officer
> PRIVATE FIRST CLASS MELVIN PETERSON, an African American
>   soldier and murderer
> CORPORAL ELLIS and
> PRIVATE LOUIS HENSON, African American soldiers
> PRIVATE JAMES WILKIE and
> PRIVATE TONY SMALLS, African American career soldiers
> CAPTAIN RICHARD DAVENPORT, an African American army
>   lawyer
> PRIVATE C. J. MEMPHIS, an African American soldier and
>   talented baseball player and blues singer
> LIEUTENANT BYRD and
> CAPTAIN WILCOX, racist white officers

The Play

The first act opens on a darkened stage with the murder of Sergeant Waters by a mysterious man holding a .45-caliber pistol. Drunk and trying to stand, Waters is mumbling "They'll still hate you! They still hate you. . . !" when he is shot twice. His last words are symbolic of the play's theme of the effects of the institutional racism rampant in the United States Army in the 1940's and the self-hatred it often created in people living under its oppression.

The scene immediately shifts to the Company B barracks, where five African American enlisted men are being searched by Corporal Ellis, a black "spit-and-polish" soldier. Captain Charles Taylor, a white officer in his mid- to late thirties, watches the policelike search for weapons, worried that the murder of Waters might incite severe racial confrontations between members of Company B and local whites in the nearby town of Tynin. Those being searched are Corporal Bernard Cobb, a man in his mid- to late twenties; career soldier Private James Wilkie, a soldier in his early forties who has lost his stripes; Private Louis Henson, a thin man in his late twenties or early thirties; the angelic-looking Private First Class Melvin Peterson, a soldier in his late twenties who wears eyeglasses and has the most polished appearance; and Private Tony Smalls, a career soldier in his late thirties who "is as small as his name feels."

Finding no weapons, Captain Taylor and Ellis then exit the barracks, leaving the men to discuss how, instead of being allowed to fight alongside white soldiers overseas, they have been stationed in the Deep South, essentially doing custodial work. They also discuss the Ku Klux Klan and Waters's murder. Henson says, "I just hope we get lucky enough to get shipped outta' this hell hole to the War": A cutting commentary not only on the life of a black man in the American South at this time, but also on the reality of black American soldiers who will eventually be allowed to fight overseas for a freedom that they cannot experience at home.

Captain Taylor then meets Captain Richard Davenport, who will be investigating Waters's murder. Captain Davenport is a very confident African American man with a degree in law from Howard University and the first "colored officer" that Captain Taylor has ever met. Even though he believes himself to be a liberal man who is concerned about his black troops even to the peril of his own career, Captain Taylor is very threatened by Captain Davenport's rank, composure, and confidence.

As Captain Davenport begins to interview each soldier (with flashbacks accompanying each interview), the many facets of Waters's character are revealed. From Private Wilkie, Captain Davenport learns about Waters's unyielding standards as he demotes Wilkie for being drunk on duty and lectures him that his behavior provides ammunition for racist claims that blacks are untrustworthy.

The next interview with Private First Class Melvin Peterson begins to reveal Waters's internalization of the racism he has dealt with all of his life, and how this racism created both a self-hatred and hatred of members of his own race. For instance, after winning another baseball game against the white soldiers, Waters tries to make the company paint the lobby of the Officers Club, a club they are not allowed to enter under normal circumstances. In response to his men's protests, especially Peterson's, Waters responds that he is the "kinda' colored man that don't like lazy, shiftless Negroes!" When Peterson later attempts to defend C. J. Memphis from Waters's rage, he and Waters almost get into a physical fight just as Captain Taylor enters. It is apparent that C. J.'s boyish mentality, ball playing, and musical abilities bring out a violent response from Waters. Despite Waters's request to the contrary, Captain Taylor relieves the men from painting duty and gives them some time off. Yet, after Captain Taylor leaves, Waters insists on fighting Peterson and beats him badly.

Peterson leaves and Captain Davenport then meets Captain Taylor. Taylor tells Captain Davenport that two racist officers, Byrd and Wilcox, were seen fighting with Waters outside the club for "colored" soldiers. He also tells Captain Davenport that he is working to get him off the case because he believes that only he, a white liberal officer, has a chance to bring these two to trial for murdering a black officer. In the flashback of Byrd and Wilcox's interview with Captain Taylor, a drunken Waters mocks them, telling them that he is not going to listen to white people, do what they tell him to do, or try to be like them any more. Waters tells them, "Look what it's done to me!—I hate myself!" and divulges a clue about what really happened when he says, "I've killed for you!"

In act 2, Captain Davenport interviews Private Louis Henson, who reveals that Waters was after C. J. Memphis, especially after the incident at the pay phone that resulted in two dead black soldiers and one dead white M.P. (military police). Wilkie finds the gun under C. J.'s bunk; Waters accuses C. J. of the crime, and C. J. denies any involvement in it. When he realizes what the consequences of being arrested for this could be, C. J. attempts to break free from the other soldiers, lunges at Waters, and knocks him down. He is restrained and put in the stockade.

In his next interview with Corporal Bernard Cobb, Captain Davenport learns that C. J. had relayed to Cobb that Waters had come to his cell and told him that he and Wilkie had caught the real murderer, but that Waters was going to let C. J. take the rap. The audience learns that Waters has developed his own plan to cleanse his race of black men like C. J., men whom he describes as "singin', clownin'—yas-sah-bossin'" types who make white people believe "the whole race is unfit." Distraught at what lies ahead of him, C. J. commits suicide. His suicide, though, impacts Waters on a deep psychological level and awakens him to what he has been willing to do to himself and others in his efforts to integrate into a racist white society.

Captain Davenport dismisses Cobb, and he and Captain Taylor begin talking about the case. Captain Davenport tells Captain Taylor he believes that Waters goaded C. J. into attacking him. They both arrive in Captain Taylor's office where Captain Davenport interviews Byrd and Wilcox. After the interrogation, Captain Taylor wants to arrest the two, but Captain Davenport overrules him. He realizes that Waters's earlier claim to have killed for white people was really about his "killing" of C. J.

Captain Davenport then returns to talk with Wilkie, where he learns about a racist incident that happened to Waters in France in World War I. This incident helped to develop the self-loathing and hatred of his own race that Waters carried with him to the end. During his talk with Wilkie, a celebration breaks out as the black troops learn they are finally going to be sent overseas to fight the Germans.

Captain Davenport goes on to meet Private Tony Smalls in the stockade, where he was placed for going absent without leave with Peterson. Smalls admits that they were running because they knew Davenport would figure out that Peterson had killed Waters while they were both on guard duty. Meeting with the drunken Waters after he was beaten by Byrd and Wilcox, Peterson had compared Waters to Adolf Hitler and Japanese war general Hideki Tojo, the racists they were supposed to be fighting overseas. In response, Waters tells the two that in order to succeed, they have to be like white people, even to sacrifice their own. Yet, he admits that despite his efforts, he could never fit in because the "rules are fixed." No matter what he did, in the end, he says, "They still hate you!" Peterson then shoots Waters twice, killing him.

In the denouement, Captain Davenport describes how Peterson is caught and sent to prison, Waters is incorrectly reported as the first colored soldier killed in action, which elevates him to a hometown hero, and the rest of the outfit gets killed in a surprise German advance.

Themes and Meanings

Like many of his other works, Charles Fuller's *A Soldier's Play* shows the devastating effect racism has both psychologically and physically on its victims and perpetrators. Fuller's goal is to expose both overt racist behaviors and beliefs, and those that are so ingrained in the culture that they are taken for granted.

In an interview with George Goodman of *The New York Times*, Fuller describes how the themes in his work (and the work of other African American writers in the early 1980's) were shifting from "focusing on our problems with whites, to matters involving blacks as human beings." Instead of depicting simple confrontations between blacks and whites, Fuller was "concerned about how racism affects blacks in their dealing with each other rather than as victims of a larger plot by whites. I want to explore the internal psychological effects of racism."

Fuller is also concerned about showing black men as complex humans instead of simplistic stereotypes. As the audience sees from the various interviews with the other characters, Waters is a black man with a Messiah complex, determined to save blacks from a racist American society; yet he is willing to sacrifice some of them to accomplish this goal. In the process he denies his own culture and loses his identity. C. J. is a threat to him because, by maintaining strong connections to his cultural traditions and music, C. J. maintains his identity in the face of adversity. As C. J. says about Waters, "I feel kinda' sorry for him myself. Any man ain't sure where he belongs, must be in a whole lotta' of pain." Fuller, in a 1999 interview with N. Graham Nesmith, notes that

> My concern throughout my work has been to depict African-Americans, especially African-American men, not as the stereotypes we have seen for years, but as we see ourselves. We live lives that are interesting, exciting. My struggle all these years has been to do nothing more than to change how people see us, and in doing so perhaps change how we see ourselves.

Dramatic Devices

Creating this play as a mystery was an important strategy that allowed Fuller to use the interviews with the other characters as a means of slowly unraveling the complex Sergeant Waters. It also allowed the author to comment on American society and racism. Gary Storhoff, an African American literary critic, notes that the detective genre generally represents crime as an anomaly in a well-ordered society and that the solution of the crime therefore restores the proper social order and gives the audience a sense that justice has been restored. Yet in Fuller's case, the typical detective-story pattern is reversed since Waters's murder is, in fact, a logical extension of a society that is itself corrupt and unjust.

Another important element is the entire stage set, which Fuller designed to resemble a courtroom with several platforms at varying levels. On the right side of the stage near the barracks arrangement is a poster of boxing champion Joe Louis in military uniform. As Storhoff notes, this arrangement is symbolic not only of American society and justice on trial, but also is effective in demonstrating how a black superstar in the public world can become literally and figuratively a lowly private in the army.

Critical Context

Drawing from his own experiences with racism in college, his enlistment in the U.S. Army, and later work in minority neighborhoods and local theaters in Philadelphia, Fuller wrote plays that explore relationships between blacks and whites and relationships within the black community. His plays have been praised by critics for their realism and complex characters.

Fuller's first major play was *The Village: A Party*, produced in 1968. Renamed *The Perfect Party* with the 1969 production, this play about interracial relationships then moved to New York City where it played Off-Broadway for several weeks. While not the best work of his career, it garnered Fuller enough attention and encouragement to persuade him to move to New York, where he wrote several more plays. In 1976 he wrote *The Brownsville Raid* (pr. 1976), based on the real-life story of a U.S. Army regiment dishonorably discharged after black soldiers in it were falsely accused of starting a riot in Brownsville, Texas, in 1906. It ran for more than one hundred performances. In 1980 he wrote *Zooman and the Sign* (pr. 1980, pb. 1982) about violence in black communities. It won two Obie Awards and an Audelco Award for best playwright.

Building upon his previous work and continuing to hone his talents, Fuller wrote *A Soldier's Play* in 1981 and won a Pulitzer Prize for it in 1982, along with several other awards, including the New York Drama Critics Circle Award for best American play. In 1984 Fuller wrote the screenplay for *A Soldier's Story*, an adaptation that starred many of the original cast members of the play, including Denzel Washington.

Fuller went on to write *We* (pr. 1989), a series of plays featuring characters from the Civil War and postwar periods. In addition to plays, Fuller has written short stories and television and movie scripts that continue to focus on the black experience in the United States.

Sources for Further Study

Andrews, William L., Frances Smith Foster, and Trudier Harris, eds. *The Oxford Companion to African American Literature*. Oxford, England: Oxford University Press, 1997.

Fuller, Charles. "Charles Fuller: Steadfast." Interview by N. Graham Nesmith. *American Theatre* 16 (October, 1999): 99.

Goodman, George. "Black Theater: Must It Appeal to Whites?" *New York Times*, January 10, 1982, p. 1.

Magill, Frank N., ed. *Masterpieces of African-American Literature*. New York: HarperCollins, 1992.

Lisa-Anne Culp

SONG OF A GOAT

Author: John Pepper Clark-Bekederemo (1935-   )
Type of plot: Tragedy; folk
Time of plot: 1960
Locale: Deinogbo, Delta Province, Nigeria
First produced: 1961, at Ibadan University, Ibadan, Nigeria
First published: 1961

> *Principal characters:*
> ZIFA, a fisherman and part-time ship pilot on the Niger Estuary
> TONYÁ, his younger brother and assistant
> THE MASSEUR, the village doctor, confessor, and oracle
> EBIERE, Zifa's wife
> ORUKORERE, Zifa's half-possessed aunt
> DODE, Zifa's child
> NEIGHBORS, as the chorus

The Play

John Pepper Clark-Bekederemo's first drama, *Song of a Goat*, is a one-act play with four scenes. The play contains a ritual sacrifice of a goat at its climax, which echoes the early Old Testament as well as classical Greek dramas in that it shares with them a blood ritualism. The play is akin to a classical tragedy; its language is often in parable and riddle form and its characters, although common people, are depicted with dignity.

The setting is Delta Province, Nigeria, in a small village where the hero, Zifa, a man of property, is cursed by impotence, a familiar African dramatic theme. The first "movement" introduces the masseur, who is questioning Zifa's wife, Ebiere, about her barren state. The masseur asks if Zifa has a mistress. When Ebiere says he does not, the masseur realizes Zifa's sexual deficiency and suggests that Ebiere have a child by Zifa's younger brother, Tonyá, an act that traditionally has been acceptable to Nigerian people. Ebiere cannot accept this advice, however, and Zifa is even more strongly opposed. He intends to wait and see if his condition will improve. Zifa's aunt, Orukorere, prophesies tragic consequences were the masseur's advice to be followed.

Eventually Tonyá does seduce the frustrated Ebiere; Orukorere's warning goes as unheeded as did the classical Cassandra's. Zifa discovers the infidelity and, in a rage, ritually slaughters a goat, forcing Tonyá to put the goat's head into a pot that is too small for it—symbolizing his illicit act with Ebiere. The furious Zifa thinks of killing Tonyá, but Tonyá, in shame, hangs himself. Soon after, a neighbor (messenger) tells of Zifa's sleeplike walk to the sea to drown himself in atonement for his own shame. It is also said that Ebiere miscarried. In an alternative closing of the play, the masseur returns to act as the choral leader (as would happen in classical tragedy); his final words provide an epitaph on the disaster.

Themes and Meanings

Song of a Goat is almost a classical tragedy. Added to the mode of classic Greek tragedy are the traditions, myths, riddles and metaphors, indigenous to African folk drama. In African drama, these characteristics are both classic and modern. The play has most of the techniques of classic drama: foreshadowing (Orukorere's prophecy in the first movement); sacrifice (Zifa's ironic sacrifice of the goat); heroism (Tonyá's atonement by his suicide); metaphor (the use of the word "house" for Ebiere's womb); gods (the divinity of the sea and its spokesperson, Orukorere); pride (Zifa's refusal to accept his infertility); and redemption (Zifa's sacrificing himself to the sea gods).

The classical theme of women's supposed infertility is displayed in the person of Ebiere, who, like Caesar's wife, Calpurnia, appears unable to bear children. Like Julius Caesar, Zifa refuses to acknowledge his own impotence. Zifa states, "Meanwhile I may regain my power. . . . Is it my fault I cannot lift up my lifeless hand?" In reference to Ebiere's womb, Zifa declares, "I will not give up my piece of land."

The masseur, a natural confidant of the people of the village, and a parental figure, attempts without success to convince Zifa that he must be a mature person and accept his failure to procreate: "One learns to do without the masks he no longer wears. They pass on to those behind." The masseur's advice foreshadows Tonyá's surrogate fatherhood. Like Oedipus, Zifa has consulted all the other "experts," but to no avail. Zifa's hubris will not allow him to admit that he has been drained of his manhood, for that admission can rob him of his masculinity and thus kill his spirit. As a classic tragic hero, he contributes to his own destruction.

Many other themes of African drama are revealed in this play. Among them are the conflict between the young and the old, rejection by oneself and others, symbolism taken from folklore, and the problem of sterility.

Dramatic Devices

Clark-Bekederemo's drama is built upon the tenets of classical drama. Aside from Zifa's curse of impotence, the play describes the curse on Zifa's family, but the scope of the play limits the cause of the curse. Zifa's aunt, Orukorere, who is half-possessed, reinforces the family curse. A neighbor tells the audience that Orukorere's father knowingly killed clansmen, a terrible sin, and he was indifferent to the fate of his daughter, who has remained unmarried. The sacrifice of the goat, usually a cleansing, is, in this drama, a defiling of classical sacrifice. Zifa has insulted the gods with his ceremony, which he uses to parody the illicit relationship between Ebiere and Tonyá.

The chief linguistic device used by Clark-Bekederemo is his use of metaphor and riddle; the language is vigorous but elevated diction. The masseur speaks of infertility in metaphorical terms: "An empty house, my daughter, is a thing of danger. If men will not live in it, bats or grass will, and that is enough signal for worse things to come." The masseur introduces the subject of Zifa's impotence with a riddle: "you have allowed the piece of fertile ground made over to you to run fallow with elephant grass."

During the four movements of the drama, the plot reveals the theme of impotence, followed by prophecy, which is highlighted by the sacrifice of the goat, Tonyá's suicide and Zifa's final act of atonement. Throughout, the neighbors in the village act as chorus. The role of the masseur is a central one. He, as the most important person in the community, acts as the sage. His appearance in the alternate closing attests his paramount importance as a symbol of strength. The people of the village will survive the losses and learn to endure. They are more self-reliant than they were at the outset of the play; they have witnessed the fall of Zifa's household stoically.

Critical Context

Song of a Goat is Clark-Bekederemo's first play. An outstanding African dramatist, Clark-Bekederemo is also a major poet. *Song of a Goat* has received divergent criticism. Its use of rhetorical control, symbolism, and language in general has been praised by numerous critics. As a play for the stage, however, *Song of a Goat* has a mixed history. The sacrifice of the goat onstage, for example, was not well received, and many of the riddles and African allusions are lost to non-African audiences. Further, the success of this play onstage depends to a large degree on the ability of the actor who plays the masseur. John Pepper Clark-Bekederemo wrote a sequel to this play, *The Masquerade* (pb. 1964), in which he continued the story of the family—similar to the continuing stories about great families in Greek tragedy. In this play, Clark-Bekederemo diverges from the ending of *Song of a Goat:* Ebiere has died in childbirth, and her son, Tufa, survives. Tufa also meets a tragic end when the father of the girl he loves shoots both his daughter and Tufa rather than allow Tufa's family curse to endanger his family.

Sources for Further Study

Astrachan, Anthony. "Like Goats to the Slaughter: Three Plays by John Pepper Clark."*Black Orpheus* 16 (October, 1964): 21-24.

Banham, Martin. *A Critical View of John Pepper Clark's Three Plays*. London: Collins, 1985.

Cartey, Wilfred. *Whispers from a Continent: The Literature of Contemporary Black Africa*. New York: Random House, 1969.

Ferguson, John. "Nigerian Drama in English." *Modern Drama* 11 (May, 1969): 10-26.

Graham-White, Anthony. "John Pepper Clark-Bekederemo." In *Contemporary Dramatists*. 6th ed. Detroit: St. James, 1999.

O'Malley, Patrick. "J. P. Clark and *The Example of Shakespeare*." *Odi* 3, no. 1 (1978): 4-14.

Wren, Robert M. *J. P. Clark*. Boston: Twayne, 1984.

Robert J. Willis

SOUTH PACIFIC

Authors: Oscar Hammerstein II (1895-1960) and Joshua Logan (1908-1988)
Type of plot: Musical; war
Time of plot: World War II
Locale: Two islands in the South Pacific
First produced: 1949, at the Majestic Theatre, New York City
First published: 1949

> *Principal characters:*
> ENSIGN NELLIE FORBUSH, a U.S. Navy nurse
> EMILE DE BECQUE, a French planter
> LIEUTENANT JOSEPH CABLE, a young Marine
> BLOODY MARY, a Tonkinese entrepreneur
> LIAT, Bloody Mary's daughter
> LUTHER BILLIS, a Seabee
> CAPTAIN GEORGE BRACKETT, a naval commander of the island
> COMMANDER WILLIAM HARBISON, Captain Brackett's executive
> officer
> NGANA and
> JEROME, Emile de Becque's young children

The Play

A two-act musical play containing twelve scenes in each act, *South Pacific* is set during World War II on an unnamed Pacific island and the nearby island Bali Ha'i. The curtain opens on Emile de Becque's plantation home, revealing Ngana, age about eleven, and Jerome, age about eight, his children of European and Asian descent. Emile de Becque is entertaining Nellie Forbush, an attractive Navy nurse much younger than he, at his home for the first time. The children have left the stage before Emile and Nellie enter. She will not learn of the children's existence for a while and will not learn until later still that they belong to Emile. The lovers met at a dinner at the Officers' Club and were instantly attracted to each other. Many years earlier, Emile fled France after killing the village bully. Nellie fled her small-town life in Little Rock, Arkansas, by joining the Navy. However, their differences in age and background furnish the central conflict in the play. Their age differences are exacerbated when Nellie finally learns that Emile lived for a long period with a "native" woman, now dead, and fathered two children by her.

The conflict between Nellie and Emile is mirrored by a subplot featuring Marine Lieutenant Joseph Cable, a well-to-do native of Philadelphia and Princeton graduate, and Liat, a Tonkinese girl of perhaps seventeen. Liat's mother is Bloody Mary, a coarse crone, who earns a nice living selling grass skirts, boar's teeth, and spurious shrunken heads (oranges painted with shoe polish) to American servicemen. Bloody

Mary encourages the young couple to rendezvous on Bali Ha'i, a nearby island viewed as extremely exotic by the Americans because it is the site of the ceremony of the boar's tooth (and because, rumor has it, the French planters have hidden their young women there). Despite the fact that Liat speaks no English, she and Cable fall in love. He eventually breaks off their affair, however, concluding that a future life together is an impossible dream. This is a decision he comes bitterly to regret.

Captain Brackett and Commander Harbison, who head up naval operations on the island, earlier attempted to recruit Emile for a dangerous mission to Marie Louise Island, a place the Frenchman knows very well. Their plan calls for Emile to act as Cable's guide. From there, Emile and Cable would spy on Japanese shipping and would direct American aircraft to enemy targets by radio. After initially declining, Emile agrees to go once Nellie rejects him. Cable is also eager to risk his life after his own rejection—for what he has come to believe is no good reason—of Liat. Emile and Cable are transported by seaplane and submarine to Marie Louise Island, where they do excellent work and are responsible for derailing several lines of Japanese shipping. During Emile's absence, Nellie realizes that her love for him is all that matters and that her reservations were small-minded and silly. Sadly, Cable is wounded during the mission and dies three days later.

The play's dramatic and occasionally grim action is lightened throughout by the antics of Luther Billis, an irrepressible Seabee (a member of the Navy Construction Battalion). Billis flouts authority, competes with Bloody Mary in the grass skirt and shrunken head business, and gets into one outrageous scrape after another.

In the final scenes of the play, the men and some of the nurses undertake a mass exodus from the island, no longer a backwater locale in the war. The tide of battle has turned, Operation Alligator is under way, and the Americans are on the move. Nellie remains behind with the island hospital. As the play ends, Nellie and Emile are reunited on the terrace of his home, where act 1, scene 1 began. The play concludes with the same song that introduced it, and there are fifteen musical numbers throughout.

Themes and Meanings

South Pacific is adapted from *Tales of the South Pacific* (1947), a collection of stories by James A. Michener. The book won a Pulitzer Prize in 1948, as did the play in 1950. *South Pacific* is a play about wartime, but it is neither a pro-war nor an antiwar play. Its themes are racial and class prejudice and their pernicious effect upon human behavior. World War II sent Americans to remote islands thousands of miles from home, where they were exposed to people and cultures that, under normal circumstances, they would never have encountered in their lives. The conflicts that arise from this literal and figurative dislocation are numerous. Nellie decides that she cannot marry a man who has lived with a woman of another race and fathered children of mixed race, even though she loves him and the children. Nellie also feels unworthy of Emile and his friends because they seem more cultivated than she. For example, she observes that they have read French novelist Marcel Proust while she has read nothing. Cable loves Liat, but he cannot conceive of taking her home to Philadelphia after the war or remaining with her on Bali Ha'i. He is also repelled by the prospect of having Bloody Mary—who has, from the first, played the role of procurer—as his mother-in-law.

Racial prejudice is a recurrent subject in Michener's writing, especially in his early works. It should be noted that when Michener's book and Hammerstein and Logan's play appeared, public schools in the American South were still racially segregated, as were many public and private accommodations. A number of states enforced miscegenation laws. The Civil Rights movement would not occur for another decade or more. After nine black students were initially barred from attending Central High School in Little Rock, Arkansas, in 1957, there were reports that some performances of South Pacific were interrupted by boos and catcalls each time Nellie mentioned her home in Little Rock. The play's most overt indictment of racial prejudice occurs in act 2, scene 4, when Cable sings "You've Got to Be Taught." The song laments the fact that racial prejudice is a learned behavior and has been taught to children.

In the decades since *South Pacific* was first produced, race relations have been central to political and social debates in the United States, and a great deal of literature has grappled with the subject as it has evolved. For this reason, some critics feel that the play's handling of the theme is somewhat old-fashioned and dates the play for contemporary audiences. Nevertheless, *South Pacific* is regularly performed by professional and amateur companies throughout the United States and elsewhere.

Dramatic Devices

The collaborative creation of *South Pacific* illustrates well the differences between drama and prose fiction. The dramatic version of *South Pacific* was created by several people: Michener wrote the work of fiction, Hammerstein and Logan wrote the book (the text of the play), Richard Rodgers wrote the music, and Hammerstein wrote the lyrics. Logan coproduced and directed the play. In his musical collaborations with Rodgers, Hammerstein typically wrote the words first, although the effort always was to integrate words and music into a single expression. Prior to the 1920's, the American custom in musical theater had been to borrow the music from outside sources and fit lyrics to the score.

South Pacific skillfully combines comedy with the development of a serious theme, but it is, foremost, a musical play. No musical, despite what other elements it might possess, can succeed if its music is unmemorable. Fortunately, *South Pacific* contains some of the most memorable songs in the history of musical theater, including "Some Enchanted Evening," "There Is Nothin' Like a Dame," "Bali Ha'i," and "Younger than Springtime," among others. The staging is elaborate, imaginatively using lighting and a transparent curtain to represent twenty-four separate scenes on two different islands. The cast is huge: thirty-five speaking parts and additional singers and dancers.

One bit of stage business has become legendary. In act 1, while Nellie sings "I'm Gonna Wash That Man Right Outa My Hair," the actor playing the part, Mary Martin, actually shampooed her hair onstage in every one of the roughly two thousand Broadway performances.

Critical Context

South Pacific played almost as long on Broadway as *Oklahoma!* (1943), one of Rodgers and Hammerstein's earlier plays. *South Pacific* won the Drama Critics Circle Award for best musical play of 1948-1949 and nine Tony Awards. Within three years of its opening in New York, the play was produced in London, Australia, and Sweden. A successful motion-picture version was released in 1958.

In 1942, Rodgers and Hammerstein began a successful collaboration that ended only with Hammerstein's death in 1960. Together they wrote the hit musicals *The King and I* (pr. 1951), *Flower Drum Song* (pr. 1958), and *The Sound of Music* (pr. 1959). Beginning in 1949, Rodgers and Hammerstein acted as theatrical producers for their own works as well as for the works of others. They also formed Williamson Music, a music publishing firm. The collaborators combined bright tunes with more sophisticated stories than had been previously employed in musical comedy. This blend was widely imitated, however, following their successes. From the beginning of his career, Hammerstein followed the tradition of the light operas of Sir W. S. Gilbert and Sir Arthur Sullivan, wherein the words were written first and the music was composed to reflect the character and the situation.

Joshua Logan, the other creator of the play, also had a distinguished theatrical career both before and after *South Pacific*. He directed *Annie Get Your Gun* (pr. 1946) and cowrote and directed *Mister Roberts* (pr. 1948), both highly successful Broadway plays. He directed many other popular plays, as well as several major motion pictures: *Bus Stop* (1956), *Sayonara* (1957), *Fanny* (1961), *Camelot* (1967), and *Paint Your Wagon* (1969). Logan directed *South Pacific* again in 1958, when the play was adapted as a motion picture.

Sources for Further Study

Block, Geoffrey Holden. *Enchanted Evenings: The Broadway Musical from "Show Boat" to Sondheim*. New York: Oxford University Press, 1997.

Green, Stanley. *Broadway Musicals: Show by Show*. 3d ed. Milwaukee, Wis.: Hal Leonard Publishing, 1990.

_____, ed. *Rodgers and Hammerstein Fact Book: A Record of Their Works Together and with Other Collaborators*. New York: Lynn Farnol Group, 1980.

Hischak, Thomas S. *Word Crazy: Broadway Lyricists from Cohan to Sondheim*. New York: Praeger, 1991.

Logan, Joshua. *Josh: My Up and Down, In and Out Life*. New York: Delacorte, 1976.

Michener, James A. *The World Is My Home: A Memoir*. New York: Random House, 1992.

Patrick Adcock

SPEED-THE-PLOW

Author: David Mamet (1947-   )
Type of plot: Comedy
Time of plot: The late 1980's
Locale: A Hollywood film studio office
First produced: 1988, at the Royale Theatre, New York City
First published: 1988

> *Principal characters:*
> BOBBY GOULD, a film executive, around forty years of age
> CHARLIE FOX, a lesser film executive, around forty
> KAREN, Gould's temporary secretary, in her twenties

The Play

Scene 1 of *Speed-the-Plow* opens with Bobby Gould in his new but as yet undecorated office, debunking the prose of a heavy-sounding book about radiation. His old friend and right-hand man Charlie Fox walks in unannounced. Gould, who has attained a new position at a Hollywood studio only two days before, continues mocking the book, aware that Fox will shortly let him know why he came. Fox asks Gould how close he is to his boss, the head man in Gould's Hollywood studio, whose name is Ross.

When Gould tells Fox that he can approve ("greenlight") a picture, Fox tells Gould that the actor Doug Brown is willing to "cross the street" to do a script that Fox has procured for him. Without answering, Gould tells his temporary secretary to get Ross on the telephone. At this point, the quality of the script is not mentioned. It is clear, however, that Doug Brown means money at the box office.

Fox acquaints Gould with the events leading to this lucky break. Only a few moments before Fox entered Gould's office, Doug Brown drove to Fox's house and said that he would settle the deal the next morning at ten. Gould tells his temporary secretary to hold all calls except those from Ross; then he asks her to fetch coffee.

Gould and Fox learn that Ross will see them in ten minutes, during which time Fox briefly describes the plot of the script, using the jargon of the film industry: The film is "a buddy film, a prison film, Douggie Brown, blah blah, some girl. . . ." Gould, thankful for Fox's loyalty in bringing in a major star, promises that Fox will be co-producer. Protocol will still be observed, however, with Gould doing the talking in Ross's office: "We get in, get out and we give it to him in one sentence." Unfortunately, Ross must go to New York, and the meeting is rescheduled for ten the next morning. Fox, nervous that ten will be too late, since Brown has given him only a twenty-four-hour option, is reassured by Gould that it is important to see Ross in person to "forge that bond." Gould convinces Fox not to worry, promising, "It's done."

To pass the time, Fox and Gould ecstatically count their as yet unearned money: Gould plans to hire "someone just to figure out the things we want to buy." It is clear, however, that Gould feels ambivalent about the impending deal when he says—hypocritically denying the capitalistic nature of his position as well as its moral vacuity—"Money is not gold." Fox comments on the appearance of the secretary, whom he calls "the broad," but Gould denigrates her: "Baby, she's nothing. You wait 'til we make this film."

Fox reads a few lines from the radiation book that Gould was examining when the play opened, sarcastically noting that it is by an "Eastern sissy writer" and suggesting that Gould make it into a film instead of the buddy film. Gould indicates that he could. Then Karen, Gould's temporary secretary, enters with coffee. Fox happily informs her, to her astonishment, that the two buddies consider themselves a pair of prostitutes.

Karen is told to cancel everything except Gould's meeting with Ross the next morning. When Fox asks her if she would be willing to stay on with Gould, Karen indicates that she is only a temporary and does not even know what to do. Gould tells her to call the Coventry, a restaurant, and order a table for two at one o'clock.

Fox bets Gould five hundred dollars that Gould cannot get Karen to go to bed with him and then leaves. Karen reenters to say that the Coventry does not have a table—immediately realizing her naïvete in not having mentioned Gould's name, which would have secured a reservation. Gould, who clearly has been thinking of his bet with Fox, kindly insists that she has made no grave mistake and proceeds to explain the film business to Karen, including what it means to give a "courtesy read" to the radiation book. Karen agrees to read the book and report her opinion of it to Gould at his home that evening. Without blinking, Gould tells Karen to phone Fox, tell him that he (Gould) will be late for lunch, and that Fox owes him five hundred dollars.

Scene 2 occurs later that evening, in Gould's apartment. Karen tries to convince Gould that the confusing, philosophical radiation book will make a worthwhile film by appealing to his conscience, believing that he wants "to do good." Convinced that Fox's prison script is not the basis for a good film, she goes on to explain, unconvincingly, the excellent qualities she finds in the radiation book.

Scene 3 begins as scene 1 did. Gould is sitting behind his desk when Fox walks in optimistically promising more deals. Gould interrupts with "I'm not going to do the film." Fox thinks that Gould, whom he now calls Bobby, must be joking and says agreeably that the buddy film is worthless. He then intimates that Gould has changed his mind as a result of having slept with Karen. Gould announces that he is going to see Ross himself, leading Fox to believe that Gould is cutting him out of their deal. Fox reminds Gould of his promise. Gould tells Fox that he has decided to use the radiation book as the basis for his next film. Fox, sure that Gould has lost his mind, tries to persuade him that Karen does not "understand" Gould, that she must have ulterior motives. Gould, to convince Fox of the soundness of his decision, allows him to question Karen, who firmly tells Fox that she and Gould, the previous evening, had talked about "the ability to make a difference." Her position weakens, however, when Fox asks her if she would have slept with Gould had he not decided to make the radiation book into a film. She hesitatingly admits that she would not have slept with him. Gould immediately says, "Oh, God, now I'm lost." As both Fox and Karen argue—

Fox maintaining that she is an ambitious nobody willing to do anything to get ahead and Karen pleading with Gould to remember their "perfect love" and their decision of the night before—Gould fights to maintain objectivity: "I have to *think* now."

In the closing lines of the play, Karen reminds Gould, "we have a meeting"—presumably with Ross to seal the deal. Instead, she succeeds in convincing Gould of her ulterior motives, for Gould asks Fox to show her the door. Fox tells her that her idea to make a film out of the radiation book was stupid, because it would never have become a "movie": "the people wouldn't come." Gould regretfully laments that he "wanted to do good" but that he was instead "foolish," and he and Fox agree that, after all is said and done, they were put on earth to make a movie, so "how bad can life be?"

Themes and Meanings

There is a subtle moral fabric to *Speed-the-Plow*, as there is to all David Mamet's plays. In *Speed-the-Plow*, Mamet casts a person at the lowest level of the totem pole—a temporary secretary and a woman—to be the one who attempts to make a difference, to "do good," to create a film with ethical values instead of one designed to make money.

Within Mamet's scheme, Charlie Fox emerges as the victorious antihero because Fox has no confusing, contradictory scruples and no self-defeating desire to "do good." Uncomplicated in his desire for money and power, he will do whatever it takes to get to the top. Since Fox does not seem to possess one admirable quality, moral confusion confronts an intelligent audience which finds itself rooting for this disreputable person's victory, validating his "money above art" credo, and cheering for his shoddy way of life.

Gould submerges whatever urges he has to "do good" in order to be successful in his dog-eat-dog world. He believes himself to be loyal, but he honors that loyalty only until a better deal comes along. Gould is a happy, self-proclaimed "secure whore" until Karen reawakens his slumbering ideals. Karen's own idealism, however, is seen to be impure, inspired by her desire for power (unacceptable for women in Mamet's male world). When Karen consciously uses sex to achieve her goal, she becomes the play's real whore. Her methods are the worse because she thinks herself better. She, like most Mamet characters, not "knowing herself," proves herself to be a fake idealist and a hypocrite. In Mamet's moral world, there can be nothing worse.

The audience is never meant to assume that the theoretical "radiation book," full of ideas about the meaning of existence, would make a good film. It is confusing; its plot cannot be explained, as the buddy film can, in one simple sentence. Karen's explication of people's fears in scene 2 is intentionally turgid and unconvincing, forcing the observation that people's deepest fears cannot perhaps be intelligibly or honestly expressed.

Dramatic Devices

Much has been written about the nature of Mamet's dialogue, his special ear for the dialogue of the street with its short, often foul, staccato one-liners. Mamet often has his characters subvert important truths by muttering clichéd truisms. Moreover, in *Speed-the-Plow* Fox and Gould take shortcuts in their speech, speaking in a kind of shorthand that is native to their situation but strange to the uninitiated. Karen's attempt to become an insider cannot succeed because she misuses the argot. Her attempt to become a part of the team, to penetrate the insider's world, is seen by Gould and Fox as a hostile take-over bid.

Further, Karen's unsuccessful explication of people's fears forces the observation that what people most fear cannot be intelligibly expressed. Unable to communicate their feelings, the characters use words which are not the right signifiers; their words mask their feelings even to themselves. Mamet's specialized and lean dialogue is enhanced by stage gestures that demonstrate the relationship between the power holder and the power seeker: Critic Brent Staples notes, "While Gould telephones the head of the studio to arrange for Fox to go before the altar of power, Fox pantomimes pretending to perform fellatio on him. Elsewhere he trails Gould across the stage, burying his face in his buttocks." At one point Gould starts smoking a cigarette while he is already smoking his cigar; the gesture indicates the frantic nature of that particular character at that particular moment.

Perhaps the most intense dramatic moment occurs in act 3. Fox, seeing his twenty-year career going up in smoke, physically knocks sense into Gould, beating him into the recognition that his previously sound mind was worked over, roughed-up, by a "whore." Fox proves that actions-of-the-street speak louder than words. Gould listens; he does not effect a change. He does not make the film that might better its audience. The only change he makes—in full view of the audience—is to remove his roughed-up shirt and don a clean one. Gould and Fox become, once again, professional white-collar businessmen.

Critical Context

There has been much speculation about the significance of the title *Speed-the-Plow*, with its flow-through hyphenation. Researchers have uncovered its agrarian good luck phraseology from eighteenth century England; it means roughly, "Hope your ploughing gets finished swiftly and profitably." If this is what Mamet had in mind, he is using the title subtly to suggest that the fast-paced movie industry has had many forebears. *Speed-the-Plow*'s business-as-usual realistic ending wins out over its possible romantic counterpart.

One ironic aspect to *Speed-the-Plow* is that the buddy movie that the men are going to make is contained within a buddy play. Mamet, too, has had to wrestle with the fact that art for art's sake does not sell tickets. If his characters seem to practice an "honor among thieves" (with the buzzword in *Speed-the-Plow* being "loyalty"), we see much the same characters in his dramas as in his screenplays: *The Postman Always Rings Twice* (1981), *The Verdict* (1982), *The Untouchables* (1987), *House of Games* (1987), and *Things Change* (1988).

Mamet's misogynistic and immature male characters, Bobby and Charlie, are like the others in his canon. Pascale Hubert-Liebler states that "the rare heterosexual relationships, doomed from the start by male misogyny and the mutual incomprehension of the sexes, usually end in disaster." In *Speed-the-Plow*, Karen is objectified, as Mamet's women often are. She is regarded as a body, not as an individual to be taken seriously. Like a commodity, she is a trophy to be won in bed and conned into submission.

The audience cannot assume that the values and relationships found in *Speed-the-Plow* apply only to Hollywood. The characters in *Speed-the-Plow* seem no different in psychological make-up from the thieving salesmen found in *Glengarry Glen Ross* (pr. 1983) or the unsuccessful schemers of *American Buffalo* (pr. 1975). One cannot assume that these psychological cripples are any different from the rest of the world.

The roundness of structure found in *Speed-the-Plow*, the careful matching of form to content, is also found in other Mamet plays. Mamet's repeated themes are also here: that humans are all alone; that their friends are only their business associates; that business implies money; that people like a person for what he or she can do for them. Worthy of note is the thematic similarity between this play and Mamet's earlier *The Disappearance of the Jews* (in his *Three Jewish Plays*, pb. 1987), which contains a character named Bobby Gould who has fantasies about Hollywood.

Sources for Further Study

Bigsby, C. W. E. *David Mamet.* London: Methuen, 1985.

Carroll, Dennis. *David Mamet.* New York: St. Martin's Press, 1987.

Friedman, Samuel G. "The Gritty Eloquence of David Mamet." *New York Times Magazine*, April 21, 1985, 32-38.

Hubert-Liebler, Pascale. "Dominance and Anguish: The Teacher-Student Relationship in the Plays of David Mamet." *Modern Drama* 31 (December, 1988): 557-570.

Kane, Leslie, ed. *David Mamet: A Casebook.* New York: Garland, 1991.

Lieberson, Jonathan. "The Prophet of Broadway." *New York Review of Books*, July 21, 1988, 3-5.

Radavich, David. "Man Among Men: David Mamet's Homosocial Order." In *Fictions of Masculinity: Crossing Cultures, Crossing Sexualities*, edited by Peter F. Murphy. New York: New York University Press, 1994.

Savran, David. "David Mamet." In *In Their Own Words: Contemporary American Playwrights.* New York: Theatre Communications Group, 1988.

Staples, Brent. "Mamet's House of Word Games." *New York Times*, May 29, 1988, sec. 2, p. 1.

Marjorie J. Oberlander

STEAMBATH

Author: Bruce Jay Friedman (1930-   )
Type of plot: Dark comedy
Time of plot: The late twentieth century
Locale: A steambath
First produced: 1970, at the Truck and Warehouse Theatre, New York City
First published: 1971

> *Principal characters:*
> OLDTIMER, a steambath user
> TANDY, a charity worker
> MEREDITH, a young woman of loose morals
> GOTTLIEB, a stockbroker
> MORTY, God in the guise of a Puerto Rican steambath attendant

The Play

   Steambath is set in a nondescript steambath that serves as a metaphor for Sheol, Purgatory, or Limbo. Characters are clothed in towels and sit on benches. The curtain opens on Tandy and the Oldtimer discussing how the hot benches cause one to develop tough bottoms. Tandy, who taught art appreciation in a prison and works for a charity for brain-damaged welders, meets a series of characters, who help him to realize that he has died. Among these characters is Meredith, a beautiful young blonde woman, who appears to be a prostitute or, at the very least, a woman of "low" morals. Tandy is attracted to Meredith, calling her the first yellow-haired girl to whom he can speak. Meredith, however, does not want to be involved because she feels she just does not have the strength for another affair. Tandy and Meredith begin comparing their last memories and come to the conclusion that they must, indeed, be dead.

   Tandy decides to explore the steambath, at which time the Oldtimer tells Tandy that there is a Puerto Rican attendant, named Morty, who appears to be in charge. Morty appears watching a console and a large screen from which he doles out punishments and miracles. At first Tandy is not convinced that Morty is God, despite Morty's enacting a card trick, a spectacular drinking trick, and a Houdini-style trunk escape. Act 1 ends when Morty reverts to thundering organ music and Old Testament poetry, which brings the entire cast to their knees.

   Act 2 begins with small talk among the characters. Tandy continues to look for a way out and flirts with Meredith. Suddenly, Morty appears and gathers the steambath inhabitants around a campfire for Mounds candy bars and the chance to tell their stories. Beginning with Gottlieb, the stockbroker, they all tell the stories of their deaths, and Morty grades these stories in order to determine their destinations. The stories progress to full-blown skits and, at the conclusion of each, a character is sent to his or her final reward through one of the two exit doors.

In desperation, Tandy protests that the attendant is merely requiring the damned to perform for some ghoulish enjoyment. He refuses to accept that he is in Limbo and about to be judged. Tandy explains that he worked too hard during his life to accept a judgment as absurd as this. He tells Morty and Gottlieb how he overcame having an unfaithful wife and rescued his bitter mother from Appalachia. He tells of his new happiness with his life and his work on a historical novel about Charlemagne, an eighth century emperor of the Franks. Morty tells Tandy that a film will be made post-humously from his novel. He explains that even though Tandy is a nice person, neither his death nor Meredith's can be postponed. Tandy, in return, calls Morty a "putz." Feigning horror, Morty allows Tandy to tell him that as he was about to die, he prayed, asking for his life to be saved.

Gottlieb confirms Tandy's confession. Taken aback, Morty assures Tandy that he heard him, faintly, and that prayer was why he had come here instead of going straight to Hell. Morty then delivers the play's dark punch line, when he explains that not all dead come to the steambath, only "Neurotics, freaks . . . (*contemptuously*). Those with stories to tell." Tandy panics and assaults Gottlieb with a handful of stolen carpet tacks. Gottlieb tells Tandy to shine a mirror in Morty's face because he cannot stand to see his own reflection. After a moment of struggle with Gottlieb and his own con-science, Tandy cannot bring himself to hurt Morty.

Meredith is then instructed to leave. Tandy continues to talk about why he should return to life, focusing his reasons mainly on women, writing, and cigars. Morty be-gins a game of solitaire as Tandy's monologue continues. The stage fades to black to the sound of the steady flipping of Morty/God's deck of cards.

Themes and Meanings

Steambath is a play that focuses on the apparent absurdity and randomness of life, death, and love. The play also focuses on the personal narrative that those in the steambath create not only to tell their own story but also to justify their choices, ac-tions, and outcomes. Indeed, in the play, one's ability to weave a good story is a deter-mining factor in one's eventual destination upon leaving the steambath.

Much of this work examines the modern urban psyche. The tapestry of each charac-ter's life is woven with threads of hang-ups, desires, and dreams. Friedman unravels this tapestry as each of the characters tell the stories of their lives as a means both of getting acquainted with their fellow travelers and of justifying their lives before the ultimate judgment. Within each of these stories is a series of seemingly contradictory revelations. Tandy, for instance, teaches art appreciation to police officers. Meredith, despite being very sexually active, just had her first orgasm. Friedman leaves the audi-ence with an understanding that it is people's neuroses and dysfunctions that make them human and therefore they are the very plotline of one's individual story.

Steambath also examines the apparent randomness of fortune and failure. God is seen looking into a monitor and then ordering seemingly random miracles and pun-ishments. When Tandy challenges him, he claims, "Half the things I do are good, maybe even a little more. . . . Nobody notices them." Morty's actions serve to remind the audience that the universe is indifferent to the absurd journey that makes up an individual's existence.

Setting Purgatory in a steambath is the central allegory of this work. In Judeo-Christian mythology, most postlife destinations are very formal, allegorical versions of life. The steambath, while fitting the description of the mist-filled caverns of some depictions of Limbo, is an informal setting that allows for an informal view of God. At one point God orders a sandwich, threatens to "smite you with my terrible swift sword" if the toast is burned, and claims he is saving his grandeur and majesty for the next group of patrons because they "got some terrific broads."

Dramatic Devices

Steambath is a prime example of black humor, a fact not surprising since Friedman is credited with coining the term in his 1965 anthology *Black Humor*. The work is dark and disturbing, focusing on the scatological, grotesque, and morbid aspects of humanity. Friedman uses humor to explore those subjects that are generally taboo and that most Americans find uncomfortable to address in public. His use of humor lessens the impact of the discussion, yet he forces the audience to confront many of the taboo issues from which people build their own hang-ups. Friedman's world is markedly cynical. It is populated with characters who, except for Tandy, have given up any hope and are resigned to their fate. These characters enable Friedman to display clearly his disillusionment with traditional values and mores.

Steambath's tone is pessimistic, at best. The viewer is shown a worldview in which many of the dead are still concerned with sex and their bodily functions rather than what lies beyond the pale. This type of gallows humor does not use fiction to escape reality, but rather it uses fiction to examine reality with a harsh, piercing light.

Although this is a play with little action, the device that keeps the plot moving is Friedman's use of confession. Each character tells his or her story before going into "the great beyond." It is these vignettes, which are loaded with the despair and dysfunction of urban life—unpaid bills, lack of sexual fulfillment, charity work with brain damaged welders, stalkers, and unfinished novels—which provides the spirit of the work.

Friedman illustrates the duality of life by showing how individuals must balance desires with social norms. This balancing act is at the center of the neuroses with which he afflicts many of his characters. Meredith's request to know exactly "where to kick someone so that he's temporarily paralyzed and cannot rape you—yet doesn't feel you are an insensitive person" is a prime example of this type of internal conflict. In fact, by depicting God as a member of a culturally voiceless minority (Puerto Ricans), Friedman illustrates that the status quo, represented by Tandy, has a difficult time recognizing and respecting a god who is not of the "appropriate" ethnicity.

Friedman also demonstrates an ear for idioms and wordplay. A prime example is the name of the Puerto Rican steambath attendant: "Morty" a homonym for *muerte*, the Spanish word for death.

At the time of the play's debut, frank sexual humor was shocking. Friedman, a former editor of men's magazines, also proves his mastery of sexual humor with such lines as this: "All the men you meet here insist on dressing you up in something before they make love to you—garter belts, stiletto heels, earmuffs, *Luftwaffe* costumes. Right in the middle of this cultural wonderland I spend all my time dressing up for weirdos. I don't need that." Although such humor has become less shocking, it nonetheless remains a challenge to standard views of morality.

Critical Context

Bruce Jay Friedman is frequently mentioned as the master of the "funny horror story." *Steambath* was less of a financial success than his early play, *Scuba Duba: A Tense Comedy* (pr. 1967, pb. 1968), but *Steambath* proved to be a darling of the critics. Critics praised Friedman's "wild and original" ideas and called him a comic genius.

Friedman's body of work, which ranges from novels (*Stern: A Mother's Kisses*, 1966) to short stories, essays, dramatic works and screenplays (*Splash!*, 1984), are difficult to distill into one leitmotif. His *Black Humor* collection is frequently cited as the cornerstone of the American Black Humor movement. His history as an editor of pulp fiction for men's magazines can be seen in his love for absurdist and shocking endings, which are a staple of the pulp genre. At the same time, the cultural groundings of the Jewish schlemiel story are equally evident in his focus upon the struggles of a young man in an urban setting. These elements of his literary career are clearly evident in *Steambath*.

Friedman's style is frequently described as an extension of the world around him or an evocation of his worldview. He is quoted as seeing a "fading line between fantasy and reality, a very fading line, a goddamned, almost invisible line." Friedman uses *Steambath* as a means of questioning many of the mores of modern society. In 1973, when the play was produced for television by the Public Broadcasting System (PBS) only nineteen stations televised it. Brief nudity, blatant depictions of homosexual characters, frank sexual discussions, and heretical religious themes proved to be too controversial for most local PBS affiliates. Despite this censorship, the PBS production of *Steambath* was nominated for two Emmy Awards in 1974.

Sources for Further Study

Friedman, Bruce Jay. *Even the Rhinos Were Nymphos: Best Nonfiction*. Chicago: University of Chicago Press, 2000.

_____, ed. *Black Humor*. New York: Bantam, 1965.

Schulz, Max F. *Bruce Jay Friedman*. New York: Twayne, 1972.

Seed, David. "Bruce Jay Friedman's Fiction: *Black Humor* and After." *Thalia: Studies in Literary Humor* 10, no. 1 (Spring/Summer, 1988): 14-22.

B. Keith Murphy

THE STICK WIFE

Author: Darrah Cloud (1955-   )
Type of plot: Social realism; symbolist
Time of plot: 1963
Locale: Birmingham, Alabama
First produced: 1987, at the Los Angeles Theatre Center, Los Angeles
First published: 1987

> *Principal characters:*
> JESSIE BLISS, a middle-aged housewife
> ED BLISS, her husband, a mechanic
> MARGUERITE PULLET, a housewife, younger than Jessie
> TOM PULLET, her husband, a truck driver
> BETTY CONNER, a middle-aged housewife
> BIG ALBERT CONNER, her husband, a mechanic

The Play

The Stick Wife is a two-act play set behind the Bliss home in Birmingham, Ala-bama, during the autumn of 1963. Clotheslines haphazardly crisscross the stage, which is littered with what Cloud terms "the junk of marriage." Rusting upturned tubs substitute for patio furniture and a rifle box serves as the back step. Such a set is ap-propriate for the debris of human lives that fall under examination throughout the play. In act 1 the play interweaves the lives of three unemployed working-class white men and their wives as they respond to the news of the Birmingham church bombing, which killed four young black girls. In Cloud's backyard perspective of historical events, the most unremarkable of characters become the key figures: housewives, who passively watch the unfolding events on television, and their husbands, members of the Ku Klux Klan, who clandestinely participate.

The title character and protagonist is Jessie Bliss, a housewife married to Ed Bliss, an out-of-work mechanic, who insists her place is in the home. While Ed roams the city on Klan business, Jessie remains in a backyard that is more prison than play-ground. "You always gonna be right where you are," Ed insists when Jessie threatens to leave. His words prove eerily accurate when he returns, after a prolonged absence, to reunite with her in the same place. In his absence she reclaimed the yard as her ref-uge and her body as her own, but upon his return, both the land and, by extension, her personhood are instantly relinquished to him. Two additional stick wives and their controlling husbands complete the cast of characters. Shadows of light appear at inter-vals during the play to indicate moments of insight or haunting, but these ghosts are technologically produced, not enacted. Thoughts of her grown children, who fled the very home that she cannot leave, equally haunt Jessie.

Act 1 opens with Ed and Jessie engaged in a verbal battle. Jessie wants to know where Ed is going and when he will return, but her repetitive questions about space and time are deflected. Ed's reticence drives Jessie to consider following her husband, an idea he prohibits. She cannot accompany him on his secret mission because, according to Ed, as a woman she cannot protect herself from attack, and he refuses to be her bodyguard. Jessie is commanded to keep quiet and stay put, while Ed is free to speak and to leave. In a monologue Jessie reveals her fantasy of having a former life in which she was a makeup artist to the Hollywood stars. Though this past is obviously a creation, Jessie's confession that she has "dreams that don't come from sleep" is followed by the appearance of the first ghostly shadow of light, signifying that her last admission is true. Echoing Dr. Martin Luther King's "I Have a Dream" speech given in Washington, D.C., Jessie's unfulfilled desires link women's rights and civil rights, a connection maintained throughout the play.

During Ed's absence, Jessie is visited by her girlfriends, Marguerite Pullet, a cola addict, and Betty Conner, who numbs herself with stronger spirits. Unlike these other stick wives, Jessie does not imbibe: Her respite will not be found in a bottle, but in rebellion. While the women gossip at the clothesline, news of the bombing is revealed. "Who would be so hateful as to bomb a church?" asks Marguerite, while certitude of their husbands' connections remains unvoiced. The last words spoken by Ed to his wife in act 1 are "You don't know nothing." Yet Jessie does know something, and it is knowledge that she will leak to the Federal Bureau of Investigation (FBI) once Ed, arrested on suspicion of committing the heinous act, is safely ensconced in a jail far from home. Big Albert Conner enters the Bliss backyard to warn Jessie to stay put and maintain her silence, announcing, "We gonna be watchin' out for you," implying that the Klan will fulfill the patriarchal role of watchdog in Ed's absence.

As act 2 begins, Jessie has exchanged her tattered robe for a diaphanous nightgown, indicating her transformation from housewife to free spirit. She avoids entering the house, which neighbors fear hides FBI agents. Jessie denies this interpretation, offering instead the possibility of ghost dogs, whose whines she hears at night. Reminiscent of her own phantasms of desire in act 1, the ghosts have multiplied into the unfulfilled desires of white society in general, people who "stay too long at the all-white lunch counters." Bright red dresses replace the white sheets on the lines that bisect the yard, emblems of her newfound sexuality and social activism. When she is caught masturbating against the clothesline pole by a shocked Marguerite, Jessie is ordered into the house and out of public view, but she stands her ground.

Exacerbating the local political turmoil caused by the bombing in act 1, act 2 brings the news of President John F. Kennedy's assassination. The violence has spread from the city of Birmingham across the United States and to the national capital. The violence returns to Jessie's backyard when Big Albert Conner and Tom Pullet, attired in Klan robes, come to silence her with a litany of punishments for independent women: Denied a job, she will starve; without the mechanical aptitude of her husband, she will be stranded; unprotected, she will be raped. Before the latter can happen, Marguerite and Betty intervene, hurling an accusation of their own at their husbands: "You cheatin' on us?" The men's anger is now directed at their own wives, who, inspired by Jessie's independence, drive them off with the revelation that "Nobody understands you!" The three women establish their own matriarchy free of male dominance, but it is short-lived. Big Albert and Tom return bearing news of Ed's imminent release. Jessie resumes her subservient role with ease, again asking a wandering Ed where he is going, but not before revealing "I know who you are."

Themes and Meanings

Birmingham in the turbulent 1960's becomes the stage upon which issues of social significance are played out. Incidents of personal, local, and national importance are compounded as are issues of gender, class, and race. The overarching premise of the play is that the personal is the political. Cloud examines the search for an authentic and autonomous female identity and the need for equal rights for women. This search occurs in tandem with the bloody fight for civil rights for African American citizens, suggesting that legally mandated rights are necessitated by gender inequality as well as racial prejudice.

The role of the wife is narrowly defined in this play: It suggests that the ideal wife is submissive, silent, and stationary. Spatially, Jessie is "kept" in her backyard "pen." She abandons the house of her husband to take refuge outdoors, a movement which, in the end, does not make her any freer. The red dresses she hangs from her clothesline attract the attention of her neighbors. In the microcosm of their neighborhood, her declaration of independence is perceived as an act of defiance, the formation of a renegade state: the erstwhile emancipated woman. Outfitted in KKK attire, the militia arrives to subdue this woman. The fact that she is rescued by other stick women is no victory, only a reprieve. Big Albert and Tom's wrath is unleashed on their wives, who simultaneously suffer for Jessie and appease their husbands. When Ed returns to his former kingdom, signs of rebellion have been squelched. Jessie, through her own accord, becomes once more his stick wife.

The title bears consideration as it applies to all three women characters. Stick connotes dead wood and connotes an object devoid of life, attributes that pertain to the women characters in this play. They are fragile objects easily broken by their aggressive and more physically powerful husbands, whose threats of violence are repeated in the play and nearly realized in the KKK scene in which a thinly disguised Tom and Big Albert attempt to beat and rape Jessie for her "treason." Similar to children's drawings, in which a head appears on a pole with pencil-thin arms and legs, the women are stick figures denied the flesh of authentic identity. In one scene Marguerite fantasizes about a catalog dress; dreams of external adornment substitute for authentic self-realization, a paper doll mentality. Jessie, Marguerite, and Betty are stick wives, women who adhere to their husbands despite threatened and real abuse.

Dramatic Devices

The Stick Wife calls on both realist and Symbolist dramatic genres. Domestic concerns about the prescribed social roles of women and men are enacted beneath a cat's cradle of clothesline, representative of divisions that separate and entangle wives and husbands, blacks and whites, poor and rich. The minimalist set is static with no location shifts and few props. The scene is always the Bliss backyard. While other characters enter and depart, Jessie remains onstage throughout both acts, a woman firmly rooted in place. The play employs special effects of light and sound to project the disembodied spirits of deferred dreams and unrealized lives central to the play's main theme: the quest for self-realization.

The play relies on symbolism to convey the complex interrelationships of women and men confronting racial, class, and gender stereotypes. Symbolism is carried into the characters' names. The ironic last name for Ed and Jessie Bliss is obvious in their joyless marriage. Marguerite Pullet acts as a pullet, or young hen: She is a coward, afraid to defy the berating and belittling Tom. A model of submission, she clucks around Jessie's backyard until called home to roost by her husband. The Conners are self-conning artists. Numbed by alcohol, Betty endures being Big Albert's diminutive possession. Big Albert's nominal adjective enhances his stature as a man, but he is still a little man, unimportant, unemployed, and invisible. The men's racial intolerance stems in part from their own working-class insecurities and sense of inferiority, as Ed reveals to Jessie before leaving to bomb the church: "You see me marchin'. . . through the rich people's neighborhood, just to prove I'm equal as them? No you don't. I admit myself. I accept what I am." Ed's self-loathing seeks release in a hate crime enacted against people he deems low on the social ladder.

Critical Context

Cloud first debuted her work on the American stage with *The House Across the Street* (pr. 1982). The success of her second produced play, *The Stick Wife*, secured for her a place among such notable feminist American playwrights as Marsha Norman, Megan Terry, and Beth Henley. Much of Cloud's work for the stage and screen, whether original or adapted, focuses on the social concerns of women's lives. Her plays are a product of and for feminist theater and its goals of providing insight into the lives of women otherwise unrecorded, its exposure of patriarchy through which women are subject to male dominance, and its mission of promoting gender rights.

Her plays in the 1970's and 1980's depict women's struggles to gain autonomy within a culture of socially prescribed and oppressive roles, as well as their efforts to find and employ authentic voices to break the silence of sexual repression. Her works in the 1990's and early twenty-first century, including her 1990 adaptation of Willa Cather's *O Pioneers!* (1913), depict strong, intelligent, self-emancipated women, who defy traditional stereotypes and succeed on their own merits and efforts. After writing *The Stick Wife*, Cloud focused on ongoing racial injustice in *Honor Song for Crazy Horse* (pr. 1993) and surviving physical and sexual abuse in *The Sirens* (pr. 1992), two issues originally confronted in *The Stick Wife*. Cloud continues to be on the cutting edge of social issue drama.

Sources for Further Study

Arkatov, Janice. "Cloud's New Play: The Tough Life of a Klansman's Wife." *Los Angeles Times*, January, 14, 1987, p. 2.

Brown, Janet. *Taking Center Stage: Feminism in Contemporary U.S. Drama*. Metuchen, N.J.: Scarecrow Press, 1991.

Miles, Julia, ed. *Playwriting Women: Seven Plays from the Women's Project*. Portsmouth, N.H.: Heinemann, 1993.

Richards, David. "The Demons Next Door." *Washington Post*, April 29, 1989, p. C1.

Dorothy Dodge Robbins

STORM

Author: August Strindberg (1849-1912)
Type of plot: Naturalistic
Time of plot: The early twentieth century
Locale: A residential district of Stockholm, Sweden
First produced: 1907, at the Intimate Theater, Stockholm, Sweden
First published: Oväder, 1907 (English translation, 1913)

> *Principal characters:*
> THE GENTLEMAN, a pensioned civil servant
> KARL FREDRIK, his brother, a consul (lawyer)
> STARCK, a confectioner
> AGNES, Starck's daughter
> LOUISE, the Gentleman's domestic
> GERDA, the Gentleman's former wife

The Play

 Storm begins on a warm evening in late summer in a quiet, residential district of Stockholm. The set consists of the facade of a large apartment building called "The Silent House" by its tenants, who make it their business to avoid one another. Karl Fredrik attempts to solicit information from Starck about his brother, the Gentleman, who, along with Starck, has lived in the building for ten years. Starck is evasive in answering Karl Fredrik, noting only that new tenants have moved in.

 The Gentleman comes to the window of his apartment to greet Karl Fredrik. Fond memories bind him to the Silent House, and he feels calm and serene and wants only peace in his old age. He believes that loneliness is the price that one must pay for freedom. The conversation shifts to Louise, the Gentleman's young domestic. Karl Fredrik wonders if perhaps his brother is interested in her, but the Gentleman claims to be too old for that sort of thing. He does not want another "boss" to rule him in his home, his first marriage having failed. Karl Fredrik informs him that Gerda, the Gentleman's former wife, has slandered him. The Gentleman explains that he was fifty-five years old when he married the relatively young Gerda; he had promised to set her free when his advancing age became too burdensome, and he believes that his abandonment of her saved rather than destroyed his honor. For five years he has suffered, missing the wife and child he loved.

 A disheveled Gerda suddenly rushes out of the Silent House. The audience learns that the new tenants are Gerda, her daughter Anne-Charlotte, and her new husband Fischer. She has run out because Fischer struck her; Karl Fredrik pledges his help. Gerda wants to know if the Gentleman, now offstage, hates her, and Karl Fredrik assures her that his brother seems to subsist on fond memories. Karl Fredrik asks Gerda why she dishonored his brother with slanderous rumors—Karl himself having believed these rumors and defended her. Gerda claims that the Gentleman's desertion insulted her honor. The Gentleman catches a glimpse of Gerda in a flash of heat lightning. Dismissing it as a hallucination, he invites Karl Fredrik in for a game of chess. Karl Fredrik, however, has exited with Gerda to help her save Anne-Charlotte (the Gentleman and Gerda's daughter) from Fischer.

Scene 2 shifts to the interior of the Gentleman's apartment, where he and Louise are playing chess. Starck enters the room. The Gentleman tells him that it is best to avoid the complexities of love and friendship. However, later the Gentleman confides to Karl Fredrik that perhaps he has grown a little tired of peace. He reminisces about his marriage and love for his daughter, Anne-Charlotte. He fears that he would not recognize her if he saw her, and doubts that he could survive such an encounter.

Karl Fredrik encourages Gerda to reacquaint herself with her former husband. The Gentleman returns, but he mistakes Gerda for Louise. When he finally recognizes her, he is at first stunned, then calm. Gerda, angered by his indifference, asks if he has read her charges against him. He says that he is aware that she lured away his friends, even his own brother, in a conspiracy against him. Worse, he charges, she has raised doubts about the legitimacy of his child. He reveals that he has just run into Anne-Charlotte on the stairwell, and that she called him "uncle." The meeting has disturbed him so thoroughly that he resolves to erase it from his mind.

A telephone caller informs him that Fischer has run off with Starck's eighteen-year-old daughter, Agnes. The Gentleman tells Gerda that now the tables have turned. She begs him to help her find Anne-Charlotte; he refuses. Once again Karl Fredrik and Gerda go off after Fischer. The Gentleman invites Louise to play chess with him.

Scene 3 returns to the exterior of the Silent House. Louise comforts the Gentleman as they wait for news about Anne-Charlotte and Agnes. The reappearance of Gerda, he complains, has destroyed his fond memories. Louise contends that Gerda's reappearance has, in fact, set him free. She urges him to think about Anne-Charlotte's welfare. Agnes returns, unharmed, and reconciles with her parents. The Gentleman's real feelings about his brother erupt in a tirade to Louise. They all hated my independence, he fumes, and took sides with Gerda. Louise assures the Gentleman that this stormy weather will pass.

Karl Fredrik relates the events that occurred at the train station, where he found Fischer. During the commotion, Gerda seized Anne-Charlotte and rushed off with her to her mother's house. The Gentleman is relieved that no one will again impose upon him, that the stormy weather has subsided. He announces that he will soon leave the Silent House.

Themes and Meanings

Storm is an intimate study of human loneliness and solitude. In the play, August Strindberg universalizes and objectifies what is essentially autobiographical material. The Gentleman, for example, defends the attitude of resignation that Strindberg himself suffered during a difficult period following his divorce. The Gentleman insists that one can find peace only by isolating oneself from others and their oppressive passions. He resorts to living in and for his happy memories of his former wife and child. He has, in effect, engineered calm weather for himself. Even his relationships with Louise and Karl Fredrik are aloof and detached.

The "stormy weather" of the title is represented by Gerda, Fischer, and Anne-Charlotte. These new tenants—associated with heat lightning throughout the play—disturb the Gentleman's tranquillity and upset his plan for a peaceful old age. However, they also serve to resolve some loose ends: The Gentleman's suppressed emotions about Gerda and Karl Fredrik finally emerge. Rage, it seems, simmers beneath his calm facade; thus, as Louise recognizes, he is not as free as he thinks. Genuine freedom would mean release from the past rather than imprisonment within it.

Ironically, Gerda's reappearance liberates the Gentleman from his fossilized memories and ghosts. Strindberg leaves the matter of who abandoned whom unclear. Gerda apparently left her husband—and took Anne-Charlotte with her—only after he had in effect abandoned her by "setting her free." For five years he has remained alone in the apartment where his family once resided. He has converted it into a kind of shrine, which Karl Fredrik and Louise find unhealthy. When he meets Gerda again, he finds her so changed that she almost seems to be a complete stranger. He is not interested in restoring his father/daughter relationship with Anne-Charlotte, since he believes that the child's mind has been poisoned against him. It is impossible, he contends, to start over again at his age.

The Gentleman's feeling of betrayal by Karl Fredrik also surfaces during this spell of stormy weather. He accuses his brother of conspiring with Gerda, of taking sides with an enemy who has maligned him. He concludes that Gerda, Karl Fredrik, and others who defected from his life could not bear his independence from the common conventions and mores of bourgeois society. His sole option has been to withdraw from entangling alliances which, he concludes, lead only to grief.

Once the storm has passed, the Gentleman feels only relief; he refuses to become a part of Gerda's and Anne-Charlotte's lives. His peace is restored. Indeed, he plans to move out of the Silent House—which can be taken as a premonition or foreshadowing of his death.

Dramatic Devices

In *Öppna brev till Intima Teatern* (1911-1912; *Open Letters to the Intimate Theater,* 1959), Strindberg articulated aesthetic principles which, he hoped, would inform a new, intimate, and more natural drama. He employed these principles in his chamber plays with the ultimate aim of transferring the virtues of chamber music to drama. Strindberg was particularly interested in "intimate action," the "highly significant motif," avoidance of "frivolity" and "calculated effort," and dynamic interaction among all characters.

Storm, the second chamber play, well illustrates Strindberg's modus operandi. In place of a well-developed, linear and narrative plot, the playwright explores the "highly significant motif" of human loneliness through a field of interrelationships rather than through a star protagonist to whom all other characters defer. The Gentleman only seems more important than other characters because he has more lines and echoes Strindberg's point of view. Frivolity and calculated effort are also avoided— every line of dialogue, every nuance and metaphor, contribute to the unfolding of the meaning of the play.

The mode of *Storm* is the same lyrical naturalism that characterizes *Fröken Julie* (pb. 1888; *Miss Julie*, 1912) and other early plays. Naturalism is an inaccurate term for Strindberg's work, which, even at its most realistic, relies upon symbolism and, to a lesser extent, mysticism. Indeed, the mode of *Storm* might best be described as "symbolic naturalism."

Strindberg advances the "highly significant motif" of human loneliness through both character interaction and the strategic placement of poignant symbols and metaphors. The heat lightning flashing throughout the play at critical moments serves two purposes: First, it suggests moments of revelation, and second, it figuratively "heats" up the situation. It is a multipurpose and ambiguous symbol, however, because heat lightning is false lightning. Thus Strindberg suggests that the storm introduced by Gerda and Fischer cannot in the end disturb the Gentleman. Conversely, what such heat lightning illuminates may prove false as well.

Other significant, evocative symbols include the music issuing from Gerda's apartment, the chess games that the Gentleman plays with various characters, and the thermometer kept in the Gentleman's drawer. Gerda's music, which the Gentleman knows well, signifies the lingering life in an otherwise dead marriage. The chess games signify both life and nonlife. Games can be enjoyable when played with a committed and loving partner, but in the end they remain games, artificial constructs subject to strict rules. The Gentleman plays chess with Louise rather than relate to her in a more loving, meaningful way; in this way he can manipulate, control, and, unfortunately, deaden life. The Gentleman's thermometer is still another relic from his marriage. Its reading never varies while in the drawer, as the Gentleman's life never varies while he entombs himself in the past.

The ambivalence of Strindberg's symbols and metaphors exposes a worrisome flaw in the Gentleman's worldview. His quest for peace and quiet is tantamount to searching out death in life. The play can thus be read as a conflict between the harrowing vitality of Eros and the numb sedation of Thanatos.

Critical Context

Storm is one of Strindberg's late chamber plays. Only four plays in his canon are so designated, each of which was designed to be staged at the Intimate Theater, which Strindberg and an associate founded. However, even a cursory examination of Strindberg's work reveals that he was experimenting with theatrical intimacy from the beginning. The methods, style, and feel of the relatively early *Miss Julie* are remarkably similar to those of *Storm*.

It is generally assumed, however, that Strindberg began as a naturalist of sorts and progressed toward both expressionism—*Ett drömspel* (pb. 1902, pr. 1907; *A Dream Play*, 1912) and *Spöksonaten* (pb. 1907, pr. 1908; *The Ghost Sonata*, 1916)—and mythic-historical drama—the three *Till Damaskus* plays (pb. 1898, 1904; *To Damascus*, 1913) and *Gustav Adolf* (pb. 1900, pr. 1903; English translation, 1957). The work can also be divided into four distinct chronological periods that reflect varied life circumstances of the playwright.

The first period (pre-1891) includes apprenticeship pieces reflecting the influence of Henrik Ibsen and William Shakespeare. Their subject matter is largely restricted to historical concerns and the conflicts of youthful artists. From 1886 to 1892 Strindberg's work matured considerably. He experimented with naturalism, as well as with comedies and pilgrimage plays. The third phase (1898-1903) was largely influenced by personal events in Strindberg's life. Divorce, poverty, and bouts of madness prompted his interest in atonement and salvation; he wrote chronicle and historical plays. The final phase of Strindberg's work is astonishingly varied and experimental. It includes expressionistic work and the four chamber plays, including *Storm*. Once again the thematic emphasis is on atonement and refuge from life's miseries.

Given the breadth and variety of Strindberg's achievement, and the fact that he was able to produce work of radically different modes and forms at virtually the same time, it is probably most productive to categorize his work by dramatic genre. Considered to be the most important of these genres are the naturalistic plays in contemporary settings, the period plays related to Swedish history, the pilgrimage plays, and the expressionistic plays. *Storm* is a late naturalist play in a contemporary setting, with the added distinction of being one of the four experimental chamber plays.

Sources for Further Study

Adler, Stella. *Stella Adler on Ibsen, Strindberg, and Chekhov.* New York: Knopf, 1999.

Carlson, Harry G. *Out of the Inferno: Strindberg's Reawakening as an Artist.* Seattle: University of Washington Press, 1996.

Johnson, Walter. *August Strindberg.* Boston: Twayne, 1978.

_____. Introduction to *Stormy Weather.* In *A Dream Play and Four Chamber Plays.* Seattle: University of Washington Press, 1973.

Lagercrantz, Olof. *August Strindberg.* Translated by Anselm Hollo. New York: Farrar, Straus, Giroux, 1983.

Robinson, Michael, ed. and trans. *Strindberg and Genre.* Chester Springs, Pa.: Dufour-Novik, 1991.

Sprigge, Elizabeth. *The Strange Life of August Strindberg.* New York: Macmillan, 1949.

Sprinchorn, Evert. *Strindberg as Dramatist.* New Haven, Conn.: Yale University Press, 1982.

Steene, Birgitta. *The Greatest Fire: A Study of August Strindberg.* 2d rev. ed. Atlantic Highlands, N.J.: Humanities Press, 1982.

Louis Gallo

STREAMERS

Author: David Rabe (1940-   )
Type of plot: Psychological; war
Time of plot: The late 1960's
Locale: An army barracks in the United States
First produced: 1976, at the Long Wharf Theater, New Haven, Connecticut
First published: 1977

>*Principal characters:*
>MARTIN, a suicidal young soldier
>RICHIE, a homosexual soldier
>CARLYLE, a belligerent black soldier
>BILLY, a restless young soldier
>ROGER, a likable black soldier
>SERGEANT COKES, a Vietnam veteran
>SERGEANT ROONEY, a career soldier

The Play

Streamers is set in an army barracks somewhere in the United States. The three young soldiers who occupy it have finished training and are awaiting orders, which they fear will send them to the war in Vietnam. Richie jokes about his homosexuality and makes teasing advances toward Billy. Billy and Roger try to behave like "good soldiers": They relieve stress by cleaning their area to make it "stand tall" and by dropping to the floor to do push-ups. Occasionally they lapse into half-believed horror stories about Vietnam.

The play opens with Richie trying to comfort Martin, a young soldier who has slit one of his wrists in an unconvincing suicide attempt. They are interrupted by Carlyle, a black soldier who has heard that another black man is quartered there. Wary and suspicious, Carlyle soon leaves, and Billy enters and tries to examine Martin's bloody-towel-wrapped wrist but is prevented by Richie. Later Martin is discharged from the army.

Later, Carlyle's friendly approach to Roger has an uncomfortable undertone: "C'mon. C'mon. I think you a Tom you don't drink outa my bottle." He bursts into a frantic admission of his fear of being sent to Vietnam, his hatred of army life, his feelings of being an outsider. Carlyle is still assigned to the processing company, which has no special mission and requires a disproportionate amount of menial work, such as daily kitchen duty. Roger refuses Carlyle's invitation to go out drinking.

Later in act 1, annoyed by Richie's flirtatious insinuations, Billy angrily tells him to stop or be ostracized. They have mentioned an alcoholic old sergeant named Rooney, a career soldier since World War II, who has just received orders to go to Vietnam. Now Rooney makes a boisterous, intoxicated entrance, introducing an old pal, Sergeant Cokes, a decorated Vietnam veteran whom he is delighted to have found newly assigned to the base. Cokes is fearful because he has been told that he has leukemia.

Cokes tells a story of trapping a Korean enemy in a "spider hole." Cokes threw a grenade into the hole, sat on its lid, and heard him screaming and struggling to get out until the grenade exploded. "He was probably singin' it," Rooney says. Explaining that "this is what a man sings, he's goin' down through the air, his chute don't open," the two former airborne soldiers sing about a parachute, or "beautiful streamer," which does not open, plunging the parachutist to a death he is able to anticipate.

After the sergeants leave and turn out the lights, Billy explains from his bed that he had a buddy, Frankie, with whom he teased "queers" into buying them drinks, until one night Frankie went home with one of the men. Later, Frankie dropped his girlfriend and became a "faggot." Carlyle enters drunk and disturbed and passes out on their floor. Richie covers him and pats his arm, to the expressed annoyance of Billy. The lights dim as taps is played.

Act 2 begins in the late afternoon as Roger talks the restless Billy into going to the gym to work out. Richie lies down to read, and Carlyle enters seeking Roger. Richie closes the door and offers Carlyle a cigarette. Carlyle, unsure of what signals he is getting, advances on Richie, asking him whether he wants to play with his "rope." Attracted and repelled, Richie is finally insulted by Carlyle's nasty manner and runs out. Carlyle lies on Richie's bed. When Billy enters, Carlyle asks him if Richie is the only "punk" in the room and whether Richie "takes care of" Roger and Billy. Upset, Billy protests that Richie is normal.

When Richie returns, hostile, Carlyle apologizes, indicates that he is simply looking for friendship, and saunters out. Billy is furious, more so when Richie asks whether his story about Frankie was really about himself. Roger enters and asks for a loan to join Carlyle to go drinking. He invites Richie, who declines; Roger then encourages Billy to go with him, quieting Billy's fears about Carlyle. They leave Richie alone.

Scene 2 finds all four men lying about after taps. Richie tells of seeing his father walk out on the family when Richie was only six years old; Carlyle says that his father lived nearby but refused to acknowledge him. Richie flirts with Carlyle to annoy Billy, who refuses to leave the room or turn away, as Roger suggests, so that Richie can have sex with Carlyle. Aroused and angered, Carlyle orders Richie to perform sexual acts with him. Roger, now convinced of Richie's homosexuality, says that Richie wants a black man as an "animal," then walks out. Carlyle turns out the light. Billy turns it on again to see Richie kneeling before Carlyle, who sits on Richie's bed. Billy hurls his sneaker at them.

Challenged, Carlyle pulls a knife and orders the frightened Billy to hold out his hand, cuts him, then, anguished, explains that he did not want to hurt anyone. Out of control, Billy admits how ridiculous his sudden fury, his racial hatred, his impulse to strike back are. He nevertheless advances on the cringing Richie and verbally attacks him; then he turns on the weary Carlyle, calling him "SAMBO!" Carlyle instinctively stabs Billy in the stomach.

At first Richie does not notice the stabbing; then he becomes hysterical. Covering his wound, Billy denies that it is serious. Terrified, on the floor, he tries to cover himself with a blanket. Roger runs for help. Carlyle mutters that Billy's crazed talk of razors and revenge unsettled him. Like a frightened little boy, Billy pats Carlyle's hand, apologizes and begs not to be stabbed again.

Sergeant Rooney staggers in looking for Sergeant Cokes. Alternatingly attempting to calm and threaten Carlyle, Rooney futilely brandishes his bottle as a weapon. Carlyle lunges at him and stabs Rooney repeatedly. Rooney calls out, "WHAT ARE YOU DOING? WAIT! WAIT!" then "No fair. No fair!" Then he whimpers, crawls along the floor, stops under Billy's bed, and dies.

Carlyle runs out. Roger cradles the dying Billy, who is deliriously begging Carlyle not to stab him anymore and threatening to get his dog after him, when an officious military police lieutenant comes running in, leveling his gun at Roger. Richie rushes in with another military policeman, explaining that Roger was not the attacker. A third policeman shoves Carlyle into the room. He rants about being innocently covered with chicken blood. The military policemen quickly ascertain what happened, remove both dead bodies, give Roger and Richie forms to fill out, and leave. Weeping, Roger mops the floor.

Roger accuses Richie of causing the tragedy by not being honest about his homosexuality. Sergeant Cokes, grinning and waving a wine bottle, comes in with affectionate ramblings about his day with Rooney. They were playing hide-and-seek, and he lost Rooney downtown. Roger tells Richie not to tell Cokes about Rooney. Disgustedly, he explains that Richie is crying because he is "queer." The hardened old combat veteran gently questions Richie about being homosexual and explains that there are worse things, such as leukemia.

Cokes is haunted by the vision of the Korean he trapped in a hole with a grenade and says that now he would release him. His sad, gentle manner quiets the less experienced, tormented young soldiers. In the dim light Roger asks Cokes whether he thought that Korean "was singin' it." Cokes says that he was; then, at first mockingly, finally very quietly, he sings an imitation of Korean-language sounds to the tune of "Beautiful Dreamer" (the same tune to which the song about the "beautiful streamer" was sung). It becomes, the playscript says, "a dream, a lullaby, a farewell, a lament." Then there is silence. The play ends in dim light and a calm atmosphere after Cokes "makes the soft, whispering sound of a child imitating an explosion, and his entwined fingers come apart."

Themes and Meanings

Despite its shocking subject matter—homosexuality, racism, and murder in a military installation—*Streamers* is clearly about larger human concerns. The subjects of racism and homosexuality allow playwright David Rabe to examine realistically human imperfection and sources of inner and overt conflict. In one sense, the barracks horror is a microcosm for the larger battlefield, specifically the Vietnam War, which hovers over this American scene like a curse.

Violence, moral laxity, and intolerance are simply the soldiers' responses to a threatening situation and confusion about their fate, what roles they are expected to play, and why they are in this situation. The two boozy sergeants can be seen as the traditional military's corruption of values: They are alcoholic, self-indulgent, amoral breakers of rules, and they are, or at least were in the past, killers. Cokes's tired acceptance of war, killing, others' homosexuality, and his own dazed irresponsibility can be seen as a moral decay. His role, however, ultimately seems a resolution, however temporary, of the opposing forces he has encountered: Americans versus Vietnamese; homosexuals versus heterosexuals; whites versus African Americans; career soldiers versus draftees; military versus civilian; camaraderie versus antagonism. The world around him has become unclear, more reminiscence and fantasy than immediate event. Though he cannot understand, he can forgive and let live.

That this image of war-making ardor and professionalism can emerge worn but accepting, is—at least in the dramatic emotional effect of the ending—reassuring. Perhaps he is merely evading a comprehension of human conditions which should inspire despair, but of all the characters in the play, he is the most direct and honest in his response. It is, notably, his response that concludes the play.

Perhaps too much has been made of the role of Carlyle as evil exploiter of the weaknesses of the other men. He does taunt the other soldiers. Surly and morose and potentially vicious though he may be, however, Carlyle is not malevolent. He is frightened about being sent to Vietnam, insecure in his role as black man in a white man's army, and wary of others' response to him, and he feels persecuted because he is still assigned to a unit of transients with menial daily tasks. He feels himself to be an outsider among this threesome, about whose exact relationship he is not sure. His role is certainly that of a catalyst, but not that of a villain.

In dramatic terms, *Streamers* is about human fear, weakness, and misunderstanding. Thematically, it is about evasions of moral responsibility, the limits of tolerance, sexual role-playing, and—in a limited sense—the war in Vietnam. Symbolically, it presents the military as a microcosm of all society; its viewpoint, though realistically seen in the confines of a single room of a military installation, is clearly more encompassing in suggestion. It has also been pointed out that Billy's interfering and inability to understand the behavior of Richie and Carlyle or the violence within himself could be a metaphor for Americans in Vietnam; the unopened parachute has been noted as a possible metaphor for the fate awaiting all of Rabe's characters. Above all, however, *Streamers* is an entirely involving drama that seems complete in its complex dramatic statement.

Dramatic Devices

A theatrical tour de force, *Streamers* eventually erupts into almost unbearable stage violence, but just when it threatens to become melodrama, it is saved by an unexpectedly touching view of humanity on the part of a formerly ridiculous minor character. Theatrically, the two minor roles of Sergeant Rooney and especially of Sergeant Cokes eventually steal the play. Their transformation from buffoonlike stereotypes into vulnerable, empathetic characters in the last scene is so unexpected that the roles loom larger in final effect than they are in proportion.

The play keeps shifting the audience's center of attention. For most of the first act, Billy seems the central hero—decent, likable, educated but unassuming, virile, seemingly an ideal average boy. Richie's mockery, even when directed at himself, and his game-playing refusal to admit or deny his homosexuality seem to relegate him to a tangential point of view. Roger does not have enough to do to seem central. Carlyle's role seems to be solely that of the antagonist. In act 2, however, their interactions flesh out the characters, creating an ensemble piece in which one can see flaws and values in all roles. The ending, in which the two clownlike intruders provide ultimate horror and a kind of resolution, respectively, pulls *Streamers* together into a piece that emerges as an evocative slice of life.

The setting is deliberately claustrophobic; one feels as trapped in this one room as the soldiers are in their situation. As the characters behave naturally there, a sense of authenticity is established. The script's requirement that the young men continually dress and undress and lie about on their own and one another's bunks reinforces the homoerotic overtones of the play. When the three comrades—Billy, Richie, and Roger—sit on one another's beds, put a foot on another's footlocker, or move another's possessions, that action reinforces their intimacy. When Rooney or Cokes, or, most important, Carlyle, does any such thing, it seems an intrusion. That invasion of property thus precedes the invasion of personal rights, and it is a characterizing device as well as a foreshadowing one. The set is used naturalistically to reflect what such an environment looks like. The dimming of lights at the end of each scene is justified realistically by oncoming night, but it also functions traditionally to bring down the emotional level and indicate an ending.

Critical Context

Streamers was generally regarded as the last and best of a trilogy of plays by David Rabe about the Vietnam War, though the author denied any such intention. *The Basic Training of Pavlo Hummel* (pr. 1971, pb. 1973), which earned for Rabe an Obie Award, a Drama Desk Award, and a Drama Guild Award in 1971, presents a surrealistic picture of a soldier's life. Shifting between time periods, realism and fantasy, civilian and military life, this dark play shows an innocent, good-natured young soldier who becomes a crude, bitter, nasty veteran before dying pointlessly from a grenade thrown into a bar where he is drinking. The military is seen as an entity entirely separate from civilian experience and the Vietnam War as a meaningless horror.

Although the play's form is unrealistic, its contents are seen in almost reportorial balance: None of the experiences is admirable, but no side is seen to be the more virtuous. Rabe's next play, clearly related, was performed at New York's Public Theatre while *The Basic Training of Pavlo Hummel* was still playing there, before it moved to a Broadway theater. *Sticks and Bones* (pr. 1969, pb. 1972), which won for Rabe honors from the Drama Guild and Variety Critics Poll, an Outer Circle Critics Award, and a Tony Award, is an ugly satire about a Vietnam veteran's return to an unaccepting, horrified family. The caricatured members of the family have the same names as the Nelson family of the television show *Ozzie and Harriet*. Using this image of stereotypical, sentimentalized American life, Rabe presents an embittered, guilt-ridden, blinded Vietnam veteran, David, who comes home to find that his family is embarrassed and horrified by his presence. Haunted by memories of an Asian girl he loved (who appears onstage but is apparently unseen by the family) and his terrible actions in Vietnam, David is uncommunicative, unlikable, and a general annoyance to a homefront anxious to ignore what he has seen and what he symbolizes. Eventually, the family solves their problem by arranging for David's "suicide." This shocking play strikes out evenhandedly at military and civilian life. Rabe further explored the Vietnam war in his 1989 screenplay *Casualties of War*.

Streamers makes the playwright's anger that of his characters. The deadly accuracy of *The Basic Training of Pavlo Hummel* and the vicious satire of *Sticks and Bones* are enriched with the compassion of *Streamers*. The war may be setting, symbol, and catalyst, but the play is about humanity, seen now as an integration of civilian background and military experience. None of what happens in *Streamers* is the result of military or civilian influences alone. In all three plays Rabe seems to be picturing facets of his own experience in Vietnam, showing the events in unpleasant detail but unwilling to make final judgments about what so repulsed and horrified him. The tone of the first two plays, however, is clearly angry. *Streamers* seems more focused in its overview and much more humane.

Rabe's other plays, *In the Boom Boom Room* (pr. 1974, pb. 1975) and *Hurlyburly* (pr. 1984, pb. 1985), attack American moral decay in settings other than war. The self-despising go-go dancer in the Boom Boom Room is seen as a victim of family, friends, lovers, patrons, and employers. *Hurlyburly*'s drug- and sex-addicted Hollywood denizens are almost equally full of self-loathing, but they are Rabe's most articulate characters. The dialogue consists of self-delusive and meaningless jargon and therefore in its very style is an indictment of a morally and intellectually bankrupt society. *Hurlyburly* is a bleak, if glossy, evocation of an overprivileged society empty and neurotically despairing beneath its glamorous exterior. In comparison, *Streamers* plays as Rabe's most accepting and generous view of his world, among a series of vividly engrossing, often darkly comic, and always unpleasant dramas. In the 1990's Rabe brought forth several more plays, including *Those the River Keeps* (pr. 1991, pb. 1994), *The Vietnam Plays* (pb. 1993), *A Question of Mercy* (pr. 1997, pb. 1998), and, in 2000, *The Dog Problem*.

Sources for Further Study

Asahina, Robert. "The Basic Training of American Playwrights: Theater and the Vietnam War." *Theater* 9 (Spring, 1978): 30-37.

Beidler, Philip D. *American Literature and the Experience of Vietnam*. Athens: University of Georgia Press, 1982.

Hertzbach, Janet S. "The Plays of David Rabe: A World of *Streamers.*" In *Essays on Contemporary American Drama*, edited by Hedwig Bock. Munich: M. Hueber, 1981.

Homan, Richard L. "American Playwrights in the 1970s: Rabe and Shepard." *Critical Quarterly* 24 (Spring, 1982): 73-82.

Kolin, Philip C. *David Rabe: A Stage History and a Primary and Secondary Bibliography.* New York: Garland, 1988.

McDonough, Carla J. *Staging Masculinity: Male Identity in Contemporary American Drama.* Jefferson, Mo.: McFarland, 1996.

Marranca, Bonnie. "David Rabe's Vietnam Trilogy." *Canadian Theatre Review* 14 (1977): 86-92.

Mohr, Hans Ulrich. "David Rabe's *Streamers:* Vietnam and Postmodernism." In *Modern War on Stage and Screen.* Lewiston, New York: Mellen, 1997.

Herbert M. Simpson

THE SUBJECT WAS ROSES

Author: Frank D. Gilroy (1925-   )
Type of plot: Coming of age
Time of plot: May, 1946
Locale: Bronx, New York
First produced: 1964, at the Royale Theatre, New York City
First published: 1962

> *Principal characters:*
> JOHN CLEARY, a businessman
> NETTIE CLEARY, his wife
> TIMMY CLEARY, their twenty-one-year-old son

The Play

The Subject Was Roses begins on Saturday morning after a welcome-home party for Timmy Cleary. The year is 1946, and twenty-one-year-old Timmy is home after fighting in World War II.

One by one, the three members of the family appear for breakfast. Though they try to hide their differences, it is clear from their conversation that John and Nettie Cleary are uncomfortable with each other and that Timmy is aware of their problems. They discuss last night's party, which was a success, although Timmy drank too much and was sick during the night.

Nettie and John exchange accusations over Timmy's drinking, with references to their ongoing disagreements. Money is part of the continuing argument, and the quest for more money sends John out to a business appointment on this Saturday morning, instead of going to a ball game with his son.

Left alone with his mother, Timmy muses about how his father has aged. He is oblivious to his mother's attempts to change the subject and turn his attention to his favorite breakfast. When Timmy fails to appreciate the waffles and then recoils from a possessive touch, Nettie is hurt. When the waffles stick in the waffle iron, she breaks down. This long-anticipated homecoming is not turning out as she had planned.

Timmy breaks the mood by turning on the radio and dancing with his mother. He promises to go with her to visit her mother and cousin. They are still dancing when John returns to go to the ball game after all, and the two men leave.

Scene 2 begins that afternoon, after the ball game. John and Timmy enter, drunk, carrying a bouquet of roses. Timmy insists that his father tell Nettie that the roses are from him; then he asks, half jokingly, how much money his father has. When John reacts angrily, Timmy asks to hear the story of how his parents met. John is in the midst of a sentimental memory when Nettie enters and again the tensions emerge.

Nettie sees the roses, accepts them as a gift from John, and tries to express her pleasure. The more grateful she seems, however, the more uncomfortable John becomes.

He changes the subject, and to keep the mood light, he proposes dinner and a night on the town; the three prepare to leave.

In scene 3 the family returns after their night out. John and Timmy are drunkenly discussing Timmy's plans to become a writer. When John looks for more to drink, Nettie follows him into the kitchen, where they reminisce briefly, and touchingly, about their courtship. Alone in the living room, Timmy amuses himself with snippets of various vaudeville acts. His retreat to bed leads Nettie to remonstrate with John for letting him get drunk again.

When her attention turns again to the roses, John attempts a clumsy seduction. Nettie, however, will have none of it: "One nice evening doesn't make everything different." They fight, and Nettie smashes the vase of roses on the floor. In his frustration and anger, John closes the scene and the act with the revelation that Timmy, not he, bought the roses.

Act 2 opens, like act 1, with breakfast. It is Sunday morning, and John is complaining about the coffee. When Timmy enters, he becomes the object of John's irritation. He insists that Timmy come to church with him, but Timmy refuses. John leaves alone, giving mother and son another opportunity to talk. Once again, the talk is of John; with his father gone, Timmy is ready to defend him. He blames Nettie for caring more for her retarded cousin than for her husband. Angry, Nettie gathers up her large store of coins and leaves the house.

As the next scene opens, Nettie has not returned. It is now ten o'clock at night, and John and Timmy are worried. Timmy is, however, hiding his feeling by drinking. The two argue, until Timmy reveals that Nettie had fought with him before leaving. John uses this information to absolve himself of blame, but Timmy keeps the argument going until John hits him. At that moment Nettie enters.

She refuses to give a straight answer when John asks where she has been. She does claim, however, that "in all my life, the past twelve hours are the only real freedom I've ever known." Timmy rushes from the room to be sick, and the scene ends with Nettie's explanation of the argument that morning. She tells John of Timmy's admiration for him.

Scene 3 is set in the middle of the night. Timmy enters to find his mother sitting in the dark. He tells her that he has decided to leave home the next day. Then, at his prompting, Nettie reveals that she had been thinking about the time she was hit in the eye with an apple core. Embarrassed by her black eye, she had failed to return to her new job and so lost it. The next job she found led to her meeting with John.

Again prompted by Timmy, she recalls what drew her to John: his energy, his determination, his ability to provide her with a good life. Left alone by Timmy, Nettie descends deeper into memory, recalling her need for love from her much-admired father.

The final scene occurs once again at the breakfast table. Nettie tells John that Timmy will leave, and John prepares to argue him out of it. Faced with Timmy's obstinate insistence, he promises concessions. He even answers the earlier question of how much money he has. Finally he reverts to his usual posture of anger, to which Timmy responds by telling of a dream: "Someone would stop me and ask me why I was cry-ing and I'd say, 'My father's dead and he never said he loved me.'" He then speaks the words himself to his father, telling him that he loves him. They embrace.

When Nettie enters, Timmy announces that he has changed his mind and will stay. His father intervenes, however, to tell Timmy that he must leave. Then he turns his at-tention to his coffee, complaining about it as the curtain falls.

Themes and Meanings

The plot of *The Subject Was Roses* takes on different meanings depending on which character appears as the major focus. This deliberate ambiguity emerges as a central theme of the play, as the three balanced characters intertwine their conflicting con-cerns. Each character sees himself or herself as the main character in his or her own story, and the different perceptions that result lead to their failures to understand one another and to their estrangement.

For Timmy, the central concern is coming of age. He had been protected, even spoiled, as an only child; at eighteen, he had left home to go to war. While he had, by his own admission, no significant adventures in the army, his experience away from home made it impossible for him to reenter his parents' life and meet their expecta-tions. Timmy's play is, like Neil Simon's *Broadway Bound* (pr. 1986) and Brian Friel's *Philadelphia, Here I Come!* (pr. 1964), about the struggle for independence from his parents.

For Nettie, the central focus is loss: loss of her son and loss of her hopes for regain-ing John's affection. All had seemed possible. Timmy had come home, and the roses had briefly rekindled her romantic feelings; then both were gone again, along with her expectations for a good life, the life she imagines had existed in her father's house.

For John, the play is a story of frustration. His first frustration had occurred long ago: The stock market crash and his failure to go to South America kept him from making a fortune. Now his marriage is clearly failing, and he has no prospects for a better future. He is at once jealous of his son for his experiences and prospects and frustrated that Timmy is not going to be the person he had hoped.

With each of the three characters caught in a different view of reality, the family falls apart. Each blames the other two for all the family's problems, much as the char-acters in Eugene O'Neill's *Long Day's Journey into Night* (pr., pb. 1956) blame one another. Some learning occurs, as Timmy speaks of his love and John lets Timmy leave home. It is only the audience, however, that can view the three different realities of the three characters, recognize the hopelessness of their estrangement, and pity and forgive all three.

Dramatic Devices

The Subject Was Roses is a realistic play, thoroughgoing and consistent in its use of the devices of realism. It takes place in a Bronx apartment, and the stage set is meant to be completely functional. The toaster and waffle iron must work; the radio must play; the kitchen cabinets must be fully stocked. The play is probably more successful in an arena theater than on a proscenium stage, where the intimacy of the apartment is harder to achieve.

Within the realistic set, Frank Gilroy provides realistic characters, plot, and dialogue. The three characters are very ordinary, so much so that John Chapman, reviewing the Broadway opening for *The Daily News*, found them "uninteresting." There is nothing exceptional about the Clearys; their conflicts, ambitions, and disappointments are all very normal. In them, audiences see people whom they know very well.

The plot is similarly low-keyed: small, ordinary, familiar. The dialogue is realistic. Chapman complained of the "naturalistic exchanges," citing lines such as "I couldn't sleep last night." "Neither could I." However, it is Gilroy's ear for real speech, along with his refusal to write artificially "dramatic" scenes, that gives the play its strength. *The Subject Was Roses* stands as a model of realism, combining all the techniques of realism in a single play.

Significantly, this realistic play includes a substantial element of symbolism. The apple core that Nettie remembers in act 2, scene 3, comes to stand for the accidents that led her to her present condition. The waffles that stick during Timmy's first breakfast at home symbolize the failure of all Nettie's plans for their new life together. The "Welcome Home" banner sags. Nettie hoards coins, and she cannot make good coffee for her husband, a coffee salesman. Objects, actions, and words take on significance beyond themselves, yet they acquire this significance naturally and realistically, as they do in everyday life.

Even the roses do not become an obtrusive symbol. Like any object that carries emotional significance because of past associations, the roses are valued. As a gift to Nettie from John, they may stand for a renewal of their relationship. When John violates that new relationship with a crude pass, the roses, the symbol of her hopes, must be destroyed. Then with the revelation that it was Timmy who bought them, they again take on value. Nettie's relationship with Timmy still seems possible. She forgets that the flowers will fade.

Critical Context

The Subject Was Roses was Frank Gilroy's only major success, winning the Pulitzer Prize in 1965. Gilroy attracted considerable attention with his first Off-Broadway play, *Who'll Save the Plowboy?*, in 1962. He followed *The Subject Was Roses* with plays such as *That Summer—That Fall* (pr., pb. 1967) and *The Only Game in Town* (pr., pb. 1968).

Gilroy came to the theater from television, where he had written for early dramatic series such as *Playhouse 90, U.S. Steel Hour,* and *Kraft Theatre.* Some reviewers of *The Subject Was Roses* commented on the author's connection with television, as though that fact needed noting. It may be, in fact, that Gilroy's experience writing dramas for the small screen gave him the skill and confidence to concentrate on the small details of an ordinary family's life.

In so doing, Gilroy placed himself within the tradition of the classic realistic dramatists. The revolution from nineteenth century spectacle and melodrama was achieved through attention to the ordinary lives of ordinary people. Nora and Torvald Helmer in Henrik Ibsen's *Et dukkehjem* (pr., pb. 1879; *A Doll's House*, 1880) and the Ranevskaya family in Anton Chekhov's *Vishnyovy sad* (pr., pb. 1904; *The Cherry Orchard*, 1908) are such ordinary people whose lives are examined in careful detail. Still, the plot events of the early masterpieces of realism could be extraordinary—for example, Nora's revolutionary departure, the loss of the Ranevskaya estate, or the suicides in *Vildanden* (pb. 1884; *The Wild Duck*, 1891) and *Hedda Gabler* (pb. 1890; English translation, 1891). It was for later realists, such as William Inge in *Come Back, Little Sheba* (pr., pb. 1950), to bring the ordinary to the plot structure of a play. It is from within this "slice of life" tradition that Gilroy wrote *The Subject Was Roses*, and it is this tradition that the play exemplifies.

Sources for Further Study

Adler, Thomas P. "'Over There' and Over Here." In *Mirror on the Stage: The Pulitzer Plays as an Approach to American Drama*. West Lafayette, Ind.: Purdue University Press, 1987.

Ellis, Ted R., III. "Frank D. Gilroy." In *Critical Survey of Drama*, edited by Carl Rollyson. 2d rev. ed. Pasadena, Calif.: Salem Press, 2003.

Gilroy, Frank. *About Those Roses: Or, How Not to Do a Play and Succeed*. New York: Random House, 1965.

Laufe, Abe. *Anatomy of a Hit: Long Run Plays on Broadway from 1900 to the Present Day*. New York: Hawthorn Books, 1966.

Weales, Gerald. *The Jumping-Off Place: American Drama in the 1960's*. New York: Macmillan, 1969.

Bruce H. Leland

THE SUBSTANCE OF FIRE

Author: Jon Robin Baitz (1961-   )
Type of plot: Social realism
Time of plot: 1987-1990
Locale: New York City
First produced: 1991, at the Playwrights Horizon Theater, New York City
First published: 1991

Principal characters:
> ISAAC GELDHART, a publisher and Jewish Holocaust survivor
> AARON GELDHART, his oldest son and publishing partner
> MARTIN GELDHART, his younger son, a professor
> SARAH GELDHART, his daughter, an actress
> MARGE HACKETT, a social worker

The Play

A two-act play, *The Substance of Fire* opens in spring, 1987, in a conference room of Kreeger/Geldhart Publishers in Manhattan. Sarah Geldhart, a woman in her mid-twenties, sits reading among many books and filing cabinets. Her brother Martin, in his late twenties, enters and greets her. Their conversation makes it clear that neither of them wishes to be present for the stockholders' meeting for which their older brother has called them into town. Sarah, a television actress, had to leave in the middle of her scheduled shows, and Martin, who teaches landscape architecture at Vassar College, expresses his impatience by saying, "Let them sort it all out because I just don't care."

The other members of the family enter: Isaac Geldhart, a Holocaust survivor, whose publishing firm is on the verge of bankruptcy, and his eldest child, Aaron, vice president of the company, who at one time had a homosexual affair with the author of a book that he wishes to publish. Isaac is a powerful character—tyrannical, witty, insulting, and constantly belittling his children, who among them own sixty percent of the company stock. The four family members argue bitterly. Aaron, Sarah, and Martin do not approve of the way Isaac is running the publishing house. They feel he must publish more popular books and not merely the works that obsess him: books about the Jewish Holocaust.

Isaac displays both his nastiness and his integrity in his caustic and often funny monologues. He declares his unshakable intention to "publish Louis Fuchold's six volumes on the Nazi medical experiments" and utterly rejects the sensational manuscript written by Aaron's one-time lover; Isaac calls it "some trashy novel by a slicko-hipster." He reminds his children that Abraham Kreeger, their mother's father, started the firm to publish "serious work that was valuable in the larger world." Isaac feels he has already injured that mandate by publishing best-sellers in the past and has no intention of doing so again. His children are alarmed that Isaac has purchased, at great price, a postcard painted by Adolf Hitler, which he finds "not without a certain basic, rudimentary talent."

The arguments grow more personal as Isaac refuses to consider a compromise to keep his firm afloat financially. Isaac calls Aaron pushy, paranoid, and arrogant; refers to Martin as a "gardener" and considers Sarah a television "clown." Aaron replies that Isaac has become humorless and obsessive, while Sarah calls him a thug, and Martin tells him that he has become unapproachable and self-destructive. Isaac threatens to fire Aaron, but Sarah and Martin give their stock shares to Aaron so that he can take over the company. The scene ends with Sarah and Aaron walking out; Martin, always trying to be the peacemaker, suggests that he and Isaac go out to dinner, but Isaac replies, "That is not possible."

Act 2 opens in an old apartment in Gramercy Park in Manhattan. Isaac is sitting in a chair staring out the window, where a snowstorm whirls. The room is filled to the ceiling with books and framed letters. Martin comes in, and as Isaac complains about waiting for the cleaning woman to arrive, it becomes clear that he is increasingly befuddled. He does not know what day of the week it is, and their dialogue reveals that Aaron has taken over the company and intends to have Isaac declared incompetent to manage his own affairs. Marge Hackett, a woman from Social Services, arrives to interview Isaac in order to begin proceedings that will determine his competence. Isaac is rude to her and, in his confusion, occasionally mistakes her for "the Sotheby woman" and tries to sell her his collection of books. Isaac brings out Hitler's postcard again to show her: "You would certainly hope that he had been utterly devoid of talent. I mean, it would at least shed some tiny glimmer of light on the subsequent years, on all that came after. But no. . . ."

During their talk, he discusses the horrors of his experience during the war and his grief for his deceased wife. Marge finds Isaac by turns offensive and fascinating. After his initial rage, Isaac is amused and charmed by Marge and asks her out to dinner; she refuses, but as he reminisces, she realizes that Isaac feels lonely and is capable of love. Finally she agrees that she might have dinner with him some day. When she leaves, Isaac burns the Hitler postcard. He speaks to Martin with surprising tenderness and decides to walk with him toward the train station in the snow.

Themes and Meanings

The Substance of Fire examines the dynamics of a dysfunctional family. Baitz sets this small social unit against the larger unit of a business—one that is falling apart due to inner conflicts—and to the European Jews, who fled the Holocaust and must cope with survivor's guilt in the New World. This parallel between microcosms demonstrates that at each level or grouping of society, people can behave with extraordinary cruelty toward one another.

Isaac's family was destroyed during the Holocaust, and he feels enormous guilt that he was able to escape and come to the United States rather than end up tattooed and dead in a concentration camp. To atone for the atrocities done in the past, he devotes himself to publishing book volumes about the Nazis. He does not realize that his focus on the past is blinding him to the needs of the present and the future, most important of which are his relationship with his children and the stability and success of the publishing firm created by his father-in-law.

Isaac's children are different enough from one another that the presence of their father can cause them to strengthen as well as to forgo their affections and alliances. Aaron is homosexual, though neither Isaac nor Baitz emphasizes the fact. However, Aaron's need for his father's approval is crippling, as is proved by the fact that he is not able to save the company when he ousts his father. Sarah hosts a children's television show and says repeatedly that she does not understand her father's obsessions; her refrain is, "Hey. It's just books." Her loving nature can easily be enraged by Isaac's insults. Martin is a survivor, like his father, but of cancer, which is in remission; however, he drinks and smokes, which shows that he is also self-destructive like his father.

Isaac's obstinate, arrogant personality is at the center of the play, yet Baitz allows the audience to feel sympathy toward him. Certainly Isaac's love of great literature— his speeches show how well read he is—demonstrates an artistic sensibility that only Martin truly shares. Isaac suggests that the "substance of fire" is the printed word; at one point he says, "There used to be some silence to life. There is now none. Just static, white noise, fireworks, and boredom all around you. We lose money because we do something that is no longer held to be vital, we're a side-thought to life." Isaac's own power with words allows him power over his adult children. However, Isaac's life story is primarily one of fighting his awareness of his own human frailties.

Dramatic Devices

The stage sets in both acts are dominated by books, symbolizing the importance of literature to Isaac. His guilt at having survived, when his family was murdered by the Germans, so saturates his soul that he publishes works about Nazi atrocities in the hope that they will find readers and will not compromise by publishing a novel that may be a best-seller. His doggedness is admirable but makes him inflexible. The walls of books that surround him in both office and home symbolize his rigidity; without them, he is afraid he will weaken and crumble.

However, it is the family drama that really commands the audience's attention. Baitz has based his play, in part, upon William Shakespeare's *King Lear* (pr. c. 1605-1606, pb. 1608), in which Lear decides to divide his kingdom among his three daughters but angrily disinherits Cordelia when she will not lavishly flatter him as do Goneril and Regan. The two daughters who take over the kingdom soon show their ingratitude and even force Lear outside in a storm, where, in the course of a wild night, he realizes how selfishly he has behaved. Like Lear, Isaac appears to be slowly losing his mind, though it is unclear to what extent he realizes that he has destroyed his family. Like Lear, Isaac gives too much responsibility to his children while wanting to retain all authority and finds himself losing control because of his inflexible standards and demands. However, after a night stormy in snow and in argument, he shows gentleness to Martin, who exclaims that he cannot "write people off" the way his brother and sister do, and who is most like Shakespeare's Cordelia. The conclusion suggests that Isaac has won an emotional victory, if not the moral one. His obsession with the postcard painted by Hitler is a symptom of his Lear-like madness, and his burning it symbolizes his readiness to change, if only a little, in his remaining years.

Baitz's decision to emphasize Isaac's obsession with the Hitler postcard is not intended to draw a parallel between Isaac and Hitler. Rather, it shows that Isaac seeks a moral compass, tries to fathom how the man who created so much evil could also have created art. Isaac is not irredeemably cynical; he searches for something that can shine out as good in a world he sees as filthy. He can see the good in his son Martin and in Marge Hackett, and his interest in Marge is based on the fact that she, too, has experienced hardships yet has retained her sense of humor.

Critical Context

Jon Robin Baitz is one of the most-often produced dramatists of his generation, his plays having appeared around the United States and abroad. In his introduction to *The Substance of Fire and Other Plays*, Andre Bishop of Lincoln Center Theater characterizes Baitz's works as "bold, stylistically audacious, occasionally disheveled and out to dazzle," and adds, "If Arthur Miller had married Noël Coward, their son would have been Robbie Baitz." Baitz is a recipient of Rockefeller and Revson fellowships, as well as the New York *Newsday* Oppenheimer Award and a National Endowment for the Arts grant. Baitz's plays have been described as classically structured meditations on morality and are popular with both audiences and theater critics.

By 1992, when he had proven his success with two Off-Broadway productions, *The End of the Day* (pr. 1990, pb. 1993) and *The Substance of Fire*, *The New York Times* critic Frank Rich hailed Baitz as "a mature artist with a complete vision." Four years later, he was one of three finalists for the 1996 Pulitzer Prize for his semiautobiographical *A Fair Country* (pb. 1996, pr. 1997). Well established as a promising and challenging playwright, Baitz began to explore other media. He has written and directed television plays, acted, and served in 1996 as both screenwriter and producer of the film version of *The Substance of Fire*.

Sources for Further Study

Guernsey, Otis L., and Jeffrey Sweet. *The Applause/Best Plays Theater Yearbook of 1990-1991: Featuring the Ten Best Plays of the Season*. New York: Applause Theatre Books, 1992.

Guthmann, Edward. "Cast Ignites the Fire in *Substance*." *San Francisco Chronicle*, March 14, 1997, p. D3.

Isenberg, Barbara. *State of the Arts: California Artists Talk About Their Work*. New York: Morrow, 2000.

Marks, Peter. "Two Wrenching Dramas Find Unexpected New Lives." *New York Times*, December 8, 1996, pp. 2, 15.

Millar, Jeff. "*The Substance of Fire* Is Powerful." *Houston Chronicle*, March 21, 1997, p. F5.

Savran, David. *The Playwright's Voice: American Dramatists on Memory, Writing, and the Politics of Culture*. New York: Theatre Communications Group, 1999.

Schiff, Ellen, ed. *Fruitful and Multiplying: Nine Contemporary Plays from the American Jewish Repertoire*. New York: Mentor Penguin Books, 1996.

Smith, Sid. "Nuclear Implosions Playwright Uses Families to Examine Society's Truths." *Chicago Tribune*, July 22, 1997, p. 5.

Fiona Kelleghan

SUBURBIA

Author: Eric Bogosian (1953-   )
Type of plot: Social realism
Time of plot: The 1990's
Locale: Burnfield, a small Massachusetts town near Boston
First produced: 1994, at the Mitzi E. Newhouse Theater of Lincoln Center, New York City
First published: 1995

> *Principal characters:*
> TIM MITCHUM, a twenty-one-year-old alcoholic, honorably discharged from the Air Force
> BUFF MACLEOD, a twenty-one-year-old man who makes videos on a camcorder he stole
> JEFF GALLAGHER, a would-be intellectual about to turn twenty-one
> NORMAN CHAUDRY, the Pakistani manager of a 7-Eleven convenience store, probably in his thirties
> PAKEEZA, Norman's sister, in her thirties
> BEE-BEE, a twenty-one-year-old woman recently released from a drug rehabilitation facility
> SOOZE, a twenty-one-year-old would-be artist who dreams of escaping to New York City
> PONY, a twenty-one-year-old fledgling rock star
> ERICA, his publicist, in her late twenties or early thirties

The Play

The headline of Janet Maslin's review of the film version of *subUrbia* in *The New York Times* reads, "Seeking the Meaningful in a Store's Parking Lot." This description essentially sums up Eric Bogosian's play. The author presents six people in their twenties whose major tie is that they attended high school together. Five of the six are aimless and unmotivated. Still in the process of finding themselves, they congregate in the parking lot of a 7-Eleven convenience store run by a brother-sister team from Pakistan, Norman and Pakeeza. They litter the parking lot with trash that reaches monumental proportions as the action of the play mounts. They play boom boxes at ear-shattering volume. Their xenophobia and racism become apparent as their relationship with Norman deteriorates. The men are unrepentant male chauvinists.

The sixth youth, Pony, is making a name for himself as a rock music artist whose recently released album sold more than ninety thousand copies. Another album is planned. In contrast to Buff Macleod, who arrives on the scene on rollerblades, Pony and his publicist, Erica, a pampered, oversexed Californian from Bel Air, arrive in a chauffeur-driven, black stretch limousine. Pony is in town briefly for a gig that his former classmates choose not to attend.

In his review of *subUrbia*, David Richards calls it a play in which "a lot goes on but nothing happens," an apt assessment. The play is noisy and active, but Bogosian has purposely and appropriately deprived it of forward thrust. The principals are aimless: drinking, littering the area outside the 7-Eleven with their trash, slinking behind it to the decrepit van they use for their frequent assignations, but always returning to where they were. There is a sense of eternal recurrence in their lives. At times they dream dreams: Sooze of going to New York and of possibly creating the cover for Pony's next album; Buff of making videos with his stolen camcorder; Jeff of cultivating his intellect even though he has dropped out of college and is now keeping his oar in the academic pond by taking one community college course on the history of Nicaragua.

Juxtaposed to these static characters is Norman, the Pakistani who owns the 7-Eleven outside of which they gather. Norman has his own problems. He does not like black people and has fled from England because the black residents in his neighborhood burned down his store. Still, Norman has ambition and realistic plans: He will soon have a degree in engineering, his passport to leaving behind the tumult that makes his life difficult. His sister is terrified of the situation in which she finds the two of them and, mouthing dialogue in her native Urdu language, begs to get out of what she calls a horrible place.

Bogosian skillfully allows the play to meander about quite aimlessly. Some of the assembled gang go out with Pony in the limousine to get food at a Chinese take-out that stays open late. Others, resentful of Pony's success, reject the opportunity to ride in the black limousine. When it returns, Buff, who is drunk, has vomited all over the side of it. Cardboard containers in which the Chinese take-out is held accumulate in the already littered parking lot.

The play's confined setting and slow pace creates the atmosphere of a controlled burn. The tensions present from the beginning escalate substantially with Pony's arrival because Pony represents what most of the others would like to be. He is successful, even though he is clearly a moderately large fish in rather a small pond. The physical evidence of his success—the stretch limousine and the publicist—put the static status of the others in a perspective that is difficult for them to acknowledge or accept. As the tension grows, the play becomes increasingly dramatic, not through action so much as through the psychological involvement of the principal characters. What Bogosian achieves dramatically is worthy of Anton Chekhov or Franz Kafka at their best.

He ends the play with a conundrum by leading his audience to think that Erica has been murdered. It appears that Tim has killed her, although in actuality Tim spent the night with her in her hotel. Jeff and Buff cannot bring themselves to look in the van, where they expect to find her lifeless body, reflecting their inability to accept reality.

When Erica finally enters, sexually fulfilled and alive enough to grope Buff, they are astounded. Then the real tragedy is revealed: Tim finds Bee-Bee dead on the roof of the 7-Eleven, the victim of a drug overdose.

Themes and Meanings

SubUrbia is a nihilistic play that in some particulars is reminiscent of Clifford Odets's *Waiting for Lefty* (pr., pb. 1935), John Paul Sartre's *Huis clos* (pr. 1944, pb. 1945; *In Camera*, 1946; better known as *No Exit*, 1947), or Samuel Beckett's *En attendant Godot* (pb. 1952, pr. 1953; *Waiting for Godot*, 1954). The Nietzschean theme of eternal recurrence pervades this play. The five high school buddies—Pony excluded—live drab, hopeless existences, despite their unrealistic dreams of what they might become. For them, each day is like its predecessor. Bogosian uses Pony not to suggest what any of the others might achieve but to emphasize what they have not achieved and are unlikely to achieve.

This thematic thread is strengthened by Norman, who has realistic plans, a well-defined notion of where he wants to go and of how he expects to get there. He is by no means an admirable character. His racist views are repugnant. He is, however, motivated and will likely achieve his ends, the reward for which, as he clearly states, will be material, notably a house with a swimming pool. One can admire his resourcefulness, which has resulted in his owning the 7-Eleven.

Pony's publicist, Erica, whom David Richards describes as "California cool and Bel Air spoiled," is not much better than the drifters in the parking lot, but she has had advantages that have propelled her into her cushy job. A strong libido motivates her more than any other factor. She is something of a zero, but a zero from a moneyed background: She got a new Porsche as a graduation gift.

Less of a zero is Tim, who, after high school, joined the Air Force, not realizing that his lack of a college education would keep him at the bottom of the Air Force totem pole with little hope of advancement. In this depiction, Bogosian comments obliquely on class distinctions. Rather than face the daily humiliation of the lowly status in which Tim's background places him, he gives up, first getting a transfer to kitchen duty, then chopping off the end of his little finger, which earns him an honorable discharge, proclaiming him disabled while serving and entitling him to a small monthly pension.

Bogosian likens Burnfield to Woburn, Massachusetts, where he grew up. Burnfield developed into one of the reaches of suburbia. Connected to Boston by I-95, it has become a bedroom community. Bogosian's name for this new community is calculated. The fields of Woburn are burned, metaphorically, at least—cleared for development. The principals in the play are caught in the middle of the town's transformation from a small industrial community into a suburb.

Dramatic Devices

Bogosian uses confinement as a major device, much as Sartre uses it in *No Exit*. His principals, unlike Sartre's, are physically able to leave the parking lot, but they are stuck there just as they are stuck in their town and stuck in their situations. There is no exit for them. The Dumpster that is prominently displayed at the edge of the set is scarcely used. The parking lot gang just throws its trash on the ground, but the Dumpster looms as a symbol of their futility.

In the directions at the beginning of act 1, Bogosian is explicit in indicating every detail of the area outside the 7-Eleven and some details of the inside that are visible through the windows. He states in a production note that the music and clothing styles, because styles frequently change, should be left up to the producer, designer, and actors so that each performance will be as contemporary as possible.

Bogosian's ensemble approach in this play is reminiscent of most Group Theatre productions of the 1930's. These plays shunned the star system; instead, seven or eight characters had parts of nearly equal length and importance, as is the case in *sub-Urbia*.

This play emphasizes the emptiness and futility of the American suburban lifestyle, particularly for young people. The set is extremely important because, although it is quite open, it simultaneously imprisons. The principals can leave, but where would they go? They live with their families, but they rebel against their living arrangements. The parking lot becomes home to them. The hopelessness of their situations engenders the intense feelings of frustration that erupt into the outbursts that pepper the drama. When these outbursts are over, one might ask, "Was anybody listening? Does anybody care?"

In act 2, Buff tells Bee-Bee how one night he turned on his tape recorder and taped everyone talking. He plans to use some of this dialogue in his video. Actually, the dialogue in *subUrbia* might have been gleaned in exactly this way. Bogosian captures the precise ways in which his principals speak, which results in strings of profane and obscene utterances that may offend some sensibilities. The dialogue, however, is unfailingly authentic.

Critical Context

SubUrbia was among several new plays produced in 1994 for the Festival of American Plays. An underlying theme of these plays is the futility that was facing youth in the final decade before the millennium. Howard Korder's *The Lights* casts an unrelenting beam upon the moral degradation of the city. Michael John La Chiusa's musical, *Hello Again*, presents a frenzy of sexuality, reflecting the desperation rather than the joy of sex.

The overwhelming sense of desperation and hopelessness portrayed in *subUrbia* is akin to much of the substance of such earlier twentieth century plays as Edward Albee's *The Zoo Story* (pr. 1959, pb. 1960) and *Who's Afraid of Virginia Woolf?* (pr., pb. 1962); Arthur Miller's *All My Sons* (pr., pb. 1947) and *Death of a Salesman* (pr., pb. 1949); William Inge's *Come Back, Little Sheba* (pr., pb. 1950), *Picnic* (pr., pb. 1953), and *Bus Stop* (pr., pb. 1955); and nearly the entire body of Tennessee Williams's major dramatic productions.

The 1990's were a time of reflection as both the century and the millennium drew to a close. Society was advancing at breakneck speed, but not everyone could keep pace with it. Much of modern society is closed to people like the five drifters in *subUrbia*. If there is any doubt about this social exclusion, Bogosian reemphasizes it by recounting Tim's humiliation during his service in the Air Force.

Sources for Further Study

Brustein, Robert. *"subUrbia."* *New Republic* 210 (June 27, 1994): 28-30.

Guthmann, Edward. "Shooting Straight from Eric Bogosian." *Advocate*, December 17, 1991, 86-87.

Kaplan, Eliot. "A Couple of White Guys Sitting Around Talking." *Gentlemen's Quarterly* 60 (July, 1990): 137-141.

McGee, Celia. "The 7-Eleven Philosopher Bogosian Had in Mind." *New York Times*, June 26, 1994, p. H-5.

Richards, David. "Aimless Youth, Shouting out Its Angst." *New York Times*, May 23, 1994, pp. C-11, C-15.

Simon, John. *"subUrbia."* *New York* 27 (June 6, 1994): 58-59.

R. Baird Shuman

SUMMER AND SMOKE

Author: Tennessee Williams (1911-1983)
Type of plot: Psychological
Time of plot: The early twentieth century
Locale: Glorious Hill, Mississippi
First produced: 1947, at the Gulf Oil Playhouse, Dallas, Texas
First published: 1948

Principal characters:
THE REVEREND WINEMILLER, a minister
MRS. WINEMILLER, his demented wife
ALMA, their daughter
JOHN BUCHANAN, JR., a physician
JOHN BUCHANAN, SR., also a physician
ROSA GONZALES, the daughter of the owner of Moon Lake
   Casino
NELLIE EWELL, Alma's pupil
ROGER DOREMUS, Alma's friend
ARCHIE KRAMER, a traveling shoe salesman

The Play

Summer and Smoke calls for a fixed set. On the viewer's left is the interior of a rectory, in the center a fountain with a kneeling stone angel, and on the right the interior of a doctor's office. A sky cyclorama, always visible, records afternoon, evening, and night, and together with music and lighting indicates changes of scene and time of day.

In the prologue, John Buchanan, the doctor's son, startles ten-year-old Alma, daughter of the Episcopal minister, with a peashooter. He wants to return her gift of handkerchiefs, which evidently embarrassed him, but she mollifies him and shows him the angel's name on the fountain, "Eternity," which she says is "what people's souls live in when they have left their bodies." Her own name, she explains, means "soul" in Spanish, and he admits that he has been called "devil" at home. The scene ends as John kisses her roughly and runs off, snatching her hair ribbon.

Part 1, "A Summer," begins on July 4, 1916, about fifteen years later. Band music is heard in the background, and fireworks light up the sky. Alma, now a music teacher about to sing at the town's celebration, is announced offstage as "The Nightingale of the Delta."

While John has become a restless young physician with "the fresh and shining look of an epic hero," Alma is prematurely spinsterish, with a nervous laugh and gestures. Her social life seems to be confined to a pathetically small literary group that meets

Wednesdays, whereas John is one of the "wasters, drunkards and lechers" for whom, according to his father, the medical profession has no room. John's affair with Rosa Gonzales, the provocatively sensual daughter of the owner of the gambling casino at Moon Lake, soon becomes an object of town gossip.

John still teases and embarrasses Alma as he did when they were children, but now he also gives his professional opinion. Her frequent attacks of "heart trouble," he believes, are caused by her nervous swallowing of air, a symptom of her "doppelgänger," a term he refuses to explain. When he hurts her by telling her that some people find her speech and manner affected, Alma explains that she was forced at too early an age to assume many of the duties of a minister's wife because of her mother's incompetence. Her demented, perversely childish mother has deprived her of her youth, and she grew up surrounded more by older people than those of her own age.

When Alma reminds John of his forgotten promise to take her riding in his automobile, he makes amends by reluctantly accepting her invitation to a meeting of her club, but he makes his escape as soon as he can. When she consequently has one of her attacks late that night and goes to consult his father, she finds John with Rosa. John is sympathetic, gives her sleeping pills, and arranges to pick her up Saturday for the long-promised ride.

That Saturday, at the Moon Lake Casino, he tells her of his desire to go to South America to escape the depressing life of a doctor, and they discuss the nature of life and love. John denies the existence of the soul, while to Alma love is a matter of the heart as well as the body. When John invites her to a room above the casino, Alma, appalled, calls for a taxi, and he lets her go home alone.

Part 2, "A Winter," has the town gossiping about the orgiastic goings-on at the doctor's house while the elder Buchanan is in Lyon fighting an epidemic. John and Rosa have been celebrating their imminent departure for South America, and Rosa and her father are both in the doctor's office when Dr. Buchanan returns and tries to drive them out. The drunken Gonzales shoots him, and John blames Alma, who telephoned the elder Buchanan and prompted his return. Furious, he confronts her with the life-size anatomical chart in his office, challenging her to show him the location of the soul. Nevertheless, he confesses that he could not have made love to her at the casino, because he is even more afraid of her soul than she is of his body.

John's behavior changes abruptly after his father's death. He finishes his father's work abroad, while Alma gives up music and becomes a sickly recluse. When he returns, now a town hero, she refuses to see him. When she finally does call on him, she at last confesses her lifelong love for him and offers him the physical love she has previously withheld. She has learned that "*Doppelgänger*" means another person who lives within her, one she now acknowledges. The girl who said "no" to him at the casino "died last summer—suffocated in smoke from something on fire inside her." Tormented by her confession, John tells her that she has won their argument; he now believes, as she once did, in "an immaterial something—as thin as smoke" that adds value to this "unfathomable experience of ours." Alma recognizes that "the tables have turned with a vengeance": John has become a "gentleman" just as she is ready to give up being a "lady." He has also, meanwhile, chosen Nellie Ewell, the youngest, prettiest, and least gifted of Alma's former pupils, who has none of Alma's ambivalence. Blinded by tears, Alma bids him farewell as Nellie bursts in happily to announce the engagement.

In the final scene, Alma flirts with a young traveling salesman at the fountain. She takes one of the pills John gave her for her nerves, and when the young man asks her why she is nervous, she explains that she won an argument that afternoon that she had not wanted to win. They exchange some banter in Spanish before hailing a taxi to take them to Moon Lake Casino. The background music turns grave, and Alma gives the stone angel a valedictory salute as they exit.

Themes and Meanings

Summer and Smoke examines the frustrated love of a soulful, faded southern belle for a handsome, virile young physician. On the most obvious allegorical level, it is a play about the eternal conflict between body and soul. John, like his father, ministers to the needs of the body, and Alma, whose very name means "soul," is the daughter of a minister, who attends to the needs of the soul.

Alma's spiritual preoccupation is evident as early as the play's prologue. At the age of ten she already knows that the name of the fountain's prominent angel means "something that goes on and on when life and death and everything else is all through with." Even as a child, John deals with the physical, the visible. He struck his dying mother because her appearance had changed so much that she no longer looked like his mother, and it was this act that earned for him the appellation of "devil." As an adult, John still fails to recognize the existence of the soul, for it is not visible on his chart of the human anatomy. What he does recognize in Alma is her repressed sexuality, that part of her *Doppelgänger* nature which she fears to acknowledge.

The duality of body and soul is seen also as that of the sacred and profane. The soul is associated with the sacred through Alma's church affiliation. She uses the image of a Gothic cathedral to symbolize "the everlasting struggle and aspiration for more than our human limits have placed in our reach," a struggle that she sees as "the principle back of existence." The devil in John, the profane, survives in the dissipation of his adulthood and in his inability to recognize the divine soul.

The play also touches upon the artist as outsider, subject to lack of understanding and to derision. Alma is a musician; her friend Roger Doremus plays the French horn, and her bizarre little club of comically pathetic town characters meets to discuss poetry. Failures and amateurs, they are artists by inclination; their status as outsiders provides them the distance to see the world clearly. John, a quintessential philistine whose amusements are limited to gambling, drinking, sex, and cock fighting, has no patience with the club's interests and does not recognize his own decline until his father's death. The club members are caricatures whose eccentricity sets them apart from the world and the worldly. They, who for all of their ineffectuality nevertheless have the sensibilities of the artist, are seen by the world as impotent and ludicrous and provide some comic relief in this often painful play.

The strong impact of the play, however, is less upon the intellect than upon the emotions. More striking than his use of allegory is Tennessee Williams's compassionate portrayal of an unhappy woman who fails to win the love of the one man she has adored since childhood. Audience members feel her pain even as they smile at her eccentricities and those of her friends.

Dramatic Devices

Tennessee Williams's stage directions for *Summer and Smoke* emphasize production details. The interiors of the symbolic set are suggested as minimally as possible, and the dominant sky is always visible through the mere indications of walls.

Central to the set, the angel seems to preside or brood over the ironically named town of Glorious Hill and over the crucial opening and closing scenes. The soul/body dichotomy is also reflected in the set itself. There is a suggestion of the Gothic, which Alma associates with cathedrals, around the rectory. In the doctor's office, the most prominent feature is the chart that portrays the human anatomy, in which the soul is not visible. The external action of the play shifts back and forth between the two interiors at the opposite sides of the stage, just as its interior action emphasizes the polarity of the physical and the spiritual.

Williams explains that the set and lighting effects should evoke a mood; they are emphatically not to appear realistic. Lighting is also used symbolically, as when the light lingers on the anatomical chart after John puts out the office lights to embrace Rosa. When the reformed John returns from Lyon and passes the rectory, Alma, at the window, is struck by a shaft of light so intense that she staggers back and collapses on the sofa.

Another mood-enhancing device is the intermittent use of background music, a device routinely associated with film. Indeed, the episodic structure of the play is more cinematic or novelistic than conventionally dramatic.

Despite his insistence that this is neither a realistic nor a naturalistic play, Williams is extremely sensitive to nuances of speech and gesture. Consequently, his characters sometimes appear to act almost naturalistically within the confines of the highly symbolic, stylized set.

Minor characters as well as the principal ones serve symbolic functions and underline the play's dualities. The Mexican Rosa, the flashily dressed foil to Alma, exudes sensuality and entirely lacks Alma's reticence and cultivation. Young Nellie combines characteristics of both: Once a singing pupil of Alma, whom she still much admires, she resembles Rosa in her acceptance of her own sexuality. Unlike Alma, who seems to belong to a former, more elegant time, she retains all the freshness and boldness of her youth. Her mother, "the merry widow of Glorious Hill," has a reputation for picking up traveling salesmen, just as Alma does in the final scene. Alma, who initially shares the town's shocked reaction both to Nellie's mother and to Rosa, ends up imitating the actions of the former and speaking the language of the latter, both literally and figuratively.

Contrasts are seen also in the male characters. Dr. Buchanan, Sr., the gentlemanly, nonviolent healer, is killed by the violent Gonzales, who has become rich from the gambling, sex, and cock fighting in his casino and by using his gun; and the powerfully built, physically oriented John is contrasted to the "sparrow-like," intellectual, and ineffectual Bernard.

Critical Context

Summer and Smoke was the first of Tennessee Williams's two dramatic treatments of Alma's story. A substantial revision, *The Eccentricities of a Nightingale*, was written in 1951 but not performed or published until 1964. Williams preferred it as less melodramatic than the earlier work, but what it gained in simplicity it lost in subtlety and the poignancy of Alma's ambivalent torment in *Summer and Smoke*.

Summer and Smoke was a failure on Broadway in 1947 but became the hit of the season in 1952 in its Off-Broadway revival on an arena stage, when it made the reputations both of its director, José Quintero, and its star, Geraldine Page, who also played Alma in the film version. Such themes as that of the outsider and of a poorly integrated sexuality, both prominent in *Summer and Smoke*, inform many of Williams's numerous plays. There is a particularly close connection, however, between three of them.

Virtually every critic commented on the kinship between Alma and Blanche DuBois of *A Streetcar Named Desire* (pr., pb. 1947), both begun in 1945 and first produced in 1947. Both women desperately cling to notions of their own gentility that seems curiously, sometimes comically, outmoded. Each is disgusted at the Moon Lake Casino by a man she loves. Blanche's loss of her love happened a long time ago; she has already lived the promiscuous life on which Alma is just embarking. Both encounter strong, virile men who ultimately destroy them, and both have made tormented attempts to suppress their own strong sexuality.

Alma's other kindred spirits in Williams's plays include Amanda and Laura Wingfield of *The Glass Menagerie* (pr. 1944, pb. 1945). Like Alma and Blanche, Amanda is eccentrically old-fashioned, a faded southern belle, while her daughter, Laura, shares Alma's and Blanche's sensitivity and psychological frailty. Finally, Alma, Blanche, and Laura are all both outsiders and artists, not because of what they create but by temperament and taste. Alma sings, Blanche loves literature, and Laura collects delicate glass animal sculptures.

Summer and Smoke defies classification in a conventional critical category. Williams's reality is a subjective one, so that a realistic treatment is anathema to his intent. To call the play an allegory or parable is to overlook the powerful individuality of its characters. Williams himself used the term "drama of sensibility" to describe the unique blend of the novelistic, psychological, subjective, poetic, and dramatic in his work.

Sources for Further Study

Bloom, Harold. *Tennessee Williams*. Broomall, Pa.: Chelsea House, 1999.
Boxill, Roger. *Tennessee Williams*. New York: St. Martin's Press, 1987.

Crandele, George W. *The Critical Response to Tennessee Williams*. Westport, Conn.: Greenwood Press, 1996.

Falk, Signi. *Tennessee Williams*. Boston: Twayne, 1978.

Griffin, Alice. *Understanding Tennessee Williams*. Columbia: University of South Carolina Press, 1994.

Gunn, Drewey Wayne. *Tennessee Williams: A Bibliography*. 2d ed. Metuchen, N.J.: Scarecrow Press, 1991.

Kolin, Philip G. *Tennessee Williams: A Guide to Research and Performance*. Westport, Conn.: Greenwood Press, 1998.

Spoto, Donald. *The Kindness of Strangers: The Life of Tennessee Williams*. Boston: Little, Brown, 1985.

Weales, Gerald. *Tennessee Williams*. Minneapolis: University of Minnesota Press, 1985.

Maria S. Rost

SUMMER OF THE SEVENTEENTH DOLL

Author: Ray Lawler (1921-   )
Type of plot: Naturalistic
Time of plot: The 1950's
Locale: Australia
First produced: 1955, at the Union Theatre, Melbourne, Australia
First published: 1957

> *Principal characters:*
> OLIVE LEECH, a barmaid
> PEARL CUNNINGHAM, a widow and a barmaid
> BARNEY IBBOTT, a canecutter
> ROO WEBBER, a canecutter

The Play

Anyone not familiar with Australian culture and geography may find it difficult to understand aspects of *Summer of the Seventeenth Doll*. For one thing, in Australia a sharp division has long existed between attitudes toward the city and toward the country—or "the bush." The bush is thought to represent the true Australia, and city life is considered a betrayal of bush values. A masculine world, the bush has bred a mythical man: strong, brave, silent, faithful, self-reliant. These men from the bush—where women are scarce and play a secondary role—take care of one another, share burdens, remain steadfast through all adversities, and form a distinctive alliance called "mateship." The two leading male characters in *Summer of the Seventeenth Doll* are "mates," who work as canecutters in tropical Queensland, a state about one-fifth the size of the United States. Finally, in contrast to the vast and sparsely populated bush where the men in the play spend most of the year, Melbourne is a cosmopolitan city of a million or more people and is located in southern Australia—more than two thousand miles from northern Queensland.

All the play's action takes place in the living room of a house in one of Melbourne's working-class neighborhoods. The drama opens by revealing the events of the past sixteen summers and introducing what will unfold during the seventeenth. (It should be noted that the Southern Hemisphere's summer begins in December.) Barney and Roo, the canecutter mates from Queensland, have spent their past "lay-offs" with two Melbourne barmaids, Nancy and Olive, but since the men last returned to the cane-fields, Barney's longtime lover, Nancy, has married a city man who works in a bookstore. Determined that this summer will be as pleasant as the previous ones, Olive, Roo's faithful part-time lover, has recruited a replacement for Nancy, another barmaid named Pearl.

The men arrive, and everyone works to reestablish the past enchantment. As always, Roo has brought Olive a cheap carnival doll, which symbolizes their seasonal romance; the other sixteen dolls hang on the wall above the piano. No matter how much they try, circumstances are now working against them. Nancy's absence creates a vacuum, because Barney fails to impress her substitute. Roo reveals that he has not worked steadily during the past season and is broke.

As the play unfolds, the seventeenth summer crumbles, and as it does so it undermines the illusions built during the days long gone. The first scene in act 2 depicts a dreary New Year's Eve party that contrasts sharply with the remembered pleasure of such celebrations in the past. After all, the participants in the charade are aging, and what transpires reveals not only their weaknesses but also their failures. Olive holds stubbornly to a lie; Barney emerges a loud and vulgar braggart; Roo, the archetypal bushman, has in fact lost his status as champion canecutter to a younger man and, broke, has taken a factory job in the much-hated city. Pearl, the stand-in for Nancy, places herself above such tawdry relationships and refuses to play a part in the fantasy.

In the second scene of act 2, Barney brings home Roo's competitor from the canefields, a young man named Dowd. Forced to face in Dowd the image of his lost youth, Roo turns on Barney. The "mates" argue bitterly and reveal the truth about one another. Barney had failed with the women he had supposedly seduced; Roo had lost his canecutting job, not because of a bad back, but because of his inability to perform. They begin to fight, and when Olive and her mother intervene, Roo says of the women: "Well, it's about time they knew what they was dealin' with anyway, a coupla lousy no-hopers!" As the scene concludes, Roo smashes a vase containing the seventeenth doll, which lands on the floor; then, in a pathetic gesture, Olive picks up the doll and holds it close to her.

In act 3, Pearl tries to make Olive accept the truth about the fabled summers, but Olive refuses, just as she refuses Roo's offer of marriage, screaming at him in horror: "You think I'll let it all end up in marriage—every day—a paint factory—you think I'll marry you?" Defeated, Roo replies: "This is the dust we're in and we're gunna walk through it like everyone else for the rest of our lives!" Barney then begs to reaffirm their mateship, but Roo reveals without words the futility of such a move when he picks up the seventeenth doll and beats it against the piano, smashes and tears at it "until it is nothing but a litter of broken cane, tinsel and celluloid." The men exit.

Themes and Meanings

Summer of the Seventeenth Doll tells how life's illusions—both public and private—inevitably shatter. First, in the Australian context, the play debunks the bush myth and the corollary idea of mateship. Roo and Barney are in truth "no-hopers," as Roo admits, not heroic figures. While Barney is a paunchy, loud-mouthed sort, Roo is a forty-one-year-old canecutter who can no longer compete with the younger men. Barney fails to see the truth about himself; even at the end of the play he reasserts his optimism, long fed by the belief that the bush offers limitless opportunity, indeed the only real life: "And there's a whole bloody country out there," he tells Roo, "—wide open before us." Roo, however, cursed or blessed with self-awareness, only looks at Barney, and, as the stage directions indicate, "in this brief meeting of eyes there is no bravado or questing hope, it is a completely open acknowledgment of what they have lost." Like Barney, Olive refuses to accept defeat, for she ignores Roo when he tells her that "it's gone—can't you understand? Every last little scrap of it—gone."

The public myth is inextricably bound with the private, for national illusions translate into personal ones. Australia has been called by its inhabitants "the lucky country," a place where all things are deemed possible, where irresponsibility and a carefree existence are within reach. The two couples had lived this myth for sixteen summers, never allowing it to face the reality of winter. Once it started to wither, Nancy—whose presence hangs over the play—escaped into a respectable marriage; Olive clung to the shreds of romance and retreated from reality; Roo admitted the truth; Barney set out to prove that such dreams need not be forsaken. Because the play is open-ended, no one solution receives sanction.

In some ways, *Summer of the Seventeenth Doll* is intrinsically Australian. It did receive acclaim in London, but perhaps, as some critics have pointed out, for the wrong reasons. The British, always condescending toward their former colonists, may have viewed the play as an amusing depiction of dreary, parochial Australian life, rather than as a serious work about the erosion of national and personal myth. On Broadway in 1958 it ran for a mere twenty-nine performances; at that time Australia was largely unknown to Americans, so the play's national peculiarities may have mystified audiences. Still, there remains nothing purely Australian about disillusionment, whether it be personal or national.

Dramatic Devices

Ray Lawler followed the dictates of the traditional well-made play in *Summer of the Seventeenth Doll*. It is reminiscent both of a drama such as Henrik Ibsen's *Et dukkehjem* (pr., pb. 1879; *A Doll's House*, 1880) and of work from the American theater such as Arthur Miller's *Death of a Salesman* (pr., pb. 1949). Lawler worked out his theme through the traditional three-act structure, maintained fidelity to real life, and set ordinary people on a course that takes them to some kind of realization. Each scene is marked by a beginning, middle, and end, with the action rising steadily toward a climax that will lead the characters to their moments of recognition. Lawler avoids didacticism by letting these characters express through their words, actions, and reactions the ideas that inform the play's theme. Finally, because of the ironic denouement, no single interpretation emerges—just as there are no absolutes in life.

Even if, from the standpoint of world theater, *Summer of the Seventeenth Doll* is somewhat imitative and mundane in its dramatics, the play did introduce new devices to the Australian theater. Scant though they were, earlier Australian plays either portrayed comical country life or the epic grandeur that the bush myth engendered. For the first time, Lawler placed down-to-earth, urban Australians on the stage; making full use of the vernacular, he let them sound like Australians. Even in the 1950's, more than 70 percent of the population lived in cities, but as a result of the bush myth's strength—it had been largely ignored in the country's literature, which still promoted the ideals by which the characters in *Summer of the Seventeenth Doll* attempted to live. The dramatic devices Lawler employed revolutionized Australian theater.

Critical Context

Although Lawler has written other plays, his reputation rests on *Summer of the Seventeenth Doll. The Piccadilly Bushman* (pr. 1959, pb. 1961) satirized English-aping Australians, but it received a cool reception when produced. Two more plays appeared during the 1970's, *Kid Stakes* (pr. 1975, pb. 1978) and *Other Times* (pr. 1976, pb. 1978); they also treat the characters from *Summer of the Seventeenth Doll.* The first work concerns their meeting in 1937, the second depicts their adjustments to a changing Australia after World War II. Known collectively as *The Doll Trilogy*, the three plays have been performed together in Australian theaters.

Summer of the Seventeenth Doll, or *The Doll*, as it is most often called, outshines the other two plays in the trilogy and remains one of the most-loved and best-known works in Australian theater, which it has been credited with setting on a new course. First, a number of similar plays—some good, some not—by other writers soon appeared. Then younger playwrights in the 1960's rebelled against what they considered "The Doll's" outdated dramatic structure and the hold that theatrical convention had on the play. They began to direct the Australian theater into an experimental phase, drawing heavily on European and American absurdists. At the same time, though, these playwrights also took much of their material from urban life in Australia, questioned the country's private and public myths, and wrote dialogue that depended on the vernacular—in short, though structurally dissimilar, their work owed a large debt to that of Lawler. Whatever directions the Australian theater has taken or will take in the future, *Summer of the Seventeenth Doll*, dated though it is in some respects, will not be forgotten.

Sources for Further Study

Carroll, Dennis. "Ray Lawler." In *Australian Contemporary Drama.* 1985. Rev. ed. Sydney, Australia: Currency Press, 1995.

Fitzpatrick, Peter. "Ray Lawler." In *After "The Doll": Australian Drama Since 1955.* Melbourne, Australia: Edward Arnold, 1979.

Goldsmith, Kerryn. "Is It a Boy or a Girl? Gendering the *Seventeenth Doll.*" *Southerly: A Review of Australian Literature*, Autumn, 1995, 89-105.

Hibberd, Jack. "After Many a Summer: The *Doll* Trilogy." *Meanjin* 36 (Summer, 1977): 106-109.

Hooton, Joy. "Lawler's Demythologising of *The Doll: Kid Stakes* and *Other Times.*" *Australian Literary Studies* 12 (October, 1986): 335-346.

McCallum, John. "Ray Lawler." In *Contemporary Dramatists.* 4th ed. Chicago: St. James, 1988.

Rees, Leslie. *The Making of Australian Drama.* Sydney, Australia: Angus and Robertson, 1973.

Robert L. Ross

SUNRISE AT CAMPOBELLO

Author: Dore Schary (1905-1980)
Type of plot: Biographical; history
Time of plot: 1921-1924
Locale: Campobello, New Brunswick, and Madison Square Garden, New York City
First produced: 1958, at the Cort Theatre, New York City
First published: 1958

> *Principal characters:*
> FRANKLIN DELANO ROOSEVELT, the future American president
> ELEANOR ROOSEVELT, his wife
> ANNA,
> FRANKLIN JR.,
> JAMES,
> JOHN, and
> ELLIOTT, his children
> SARA DELANO ROOSEVELT, his mother
> LOUIS HOWE, his friend and political adviser
> AL SMITH, the governor of New York

The Play

Sunrise at Campobello chronicles the life of future American president Franklin Delano Roosevelt from the brutal onset of his infantile paralysis (polio) to his triumphant return to political life three years later. The curtain rises on the large living room of his summer home at Campobello in Canada's New Brunswick province. Several of the Roosevelt children run in and report the day's outdoor activities to their mother, Eleanor. Soon Franklin bounds in behind them. He is a forty-year-old man, fit, strong, and in the prime of life. The pleasant family chatter continues with some good-natured bickering among the children.

With Eleanor and Franklin momentarily alone, he reveals that the swim did not refresh him as it usually does. Franklin unexpectedly stumbles and grabs his back. He dismisses it as a spot of lumbago.

Scene 2 opens three weeks later to a changed world for the Roosevelts. The normally robust Franklin has fallen seriously ill and has been diagnosed with polio. His legs are paralyzed, he cannot sit up unsupported, and for a time, cannot even hold a spoon. Sara, Franklin's mother, and Louis Howe, his friend and political adviser, have joined the family to assist with Franklin's care. Sara, Eleanor, and Louis discuss Franklin's condition and their interrelationships become clear. Sara, an indomitable matriarch, disapproves of the chain-smoking Howe, who she thinks enjoys riding on Franklin's coattails. Eleanor, who respects Howe's abilities, carefully defends him to her overpowering mother-in-law. Nevertheless, they all seem united in their love and devotion to the stricken Franklin.

Scene 3 takes place one month later, when preparations are under way for Franklin's trip home to New York City. The journey begins with townsfolk carrying him downstairs into the living room on a stretcher. Though weakened from his illness, he still displays good humor and banters with Louis. Always the political mastermind, Howe discloses that he has diverted the press from Roosevelt's true route and plans for their first glimpse of Franklin to be from the train. Pleased with Louis's shenanigans, Franklin dons his familiar fedora hat, his favorite cigarette holder, and his Scottie dog Duffy, and is carried out of the home.

Act 2 is set in the Roosevelt home in New York City eight months later. Franklin is now quite adept at maneuvering his wheelchair and can crawl up the stairs to his bedroom. However, his usual high spirits have begun to wear thin, and at times he is grumpy, rude, and short-tempered.

Franklin reveals to Eleanor that the illness has created within him a deep loneliness and episodes of despair. He explains that in the beginning only his faith gave him the strength to endure. In the intervening months, Louis Howe has been busy promoting Eleanor as a political speaker to keep the Roosevelt name in the public eye. Eleanor lacks natural ability, but she gamely makes her best effort. However, the situation has taken its toll on everyone. Later, while reading to the children, Eleanor uncharacteristically breaks down crying.

While Howe works toward a political career for Franklin, Sara attempts to persuade him to retire to the family home at Hyde Park, where he can administer the estate and retire from public life. Franklin firmly states that he refuses to surrender to invalidism.

In the final act, Eleanor and Howe encourage Franklin to nominate Governor Al Smith for president at the Democratic National Convention. Reportedly, the governor has been considering asking Franklin to do the honors. Franklin understands that he will need to walk (in his heavy braces and crutches) from his wheelchair to the podium and then speak standing upright for forty-five minutes. Yet he and Howe realize that this speech will make or break Franklin's political future. As anticipated, Smith arrives and asks Franklin to give the nomination speech. Franklin accepts.

The final scenes are at the Democratic National Convention in Madison Square Garden. After being introduced, Franklin rises from his wheelchair and walks the ten painful steps to the podium. The cheering swells while the band plays "Sidewalks of New York." He reaches and holds onto the lectern, hands the crutches to his son, and waves to the crowd, smiling broadly. The roar continues as the curtain falls.

Themes and Meanings

Sunrise at Campobello reveals a side of Franklin Delano Roosevelt that few witnessed or saw publicly portrayed—his affliction with polio. Major themes of the play demonstrate his courage in dealing with this crippling disease and how the ordeal shaped his character as a future president.

Playwright Dore Schary was a longtime supporter and admirer of Roosevelt, having served as chair of the Hollywood for Roosevelt Committee. While reading a book on the president, Schary decided to write the play, hoping that Roosevelt's courage would convey an inspirational message for contemporary audiences.

Roosevelt's courage is vividly characterized through his flamboyant optimism, revealed soon after being stricken by polio. Unable to walk, he needs to be transported by stretcher. He transforms a potentially embarrassing and humiliating situation into a triumphant departure. He jokingly banters with Louis Howe and remarks that he feels like the caliph of Baghdad. Then he dons his favorite fedora, pokes his familiar cigarette holder jauntily in his mouth, and gets his Scottie dog to sit in his lap. This pose was so remarkable that it wound up on the cover of the popular *Life* magazine.

During the period of Roosevelt's convalescence, Louis Howe, his friend and adviser, provided a great deal of humor, which played a significant role in Roosevelt's recuperation. Whether it is reading aloud William Ernest Henley's poem "Invictus" (1875) in a comical, burlesque Dutch accent, gleefully describing the clever schemes he has devised to outwit meddling reporters, or making countless wisecracks, Howe's dry and sometimes caustic humor greatly contributes to buoying Roosevelt's spirits.

The loving support of Roosevelt's family is of prime importance as well. Eleanor especially shows deep compassion and understanding, and Roosevelt confides in her when he experiences the inevitable periods of gloom and depression, as when he describes how physical activity helps overcome what he sees as the loneliness of being disabled. She supports his occasional crawling as a means of locomotion because it affords him independence. The theme of family support culminates in eldest son Jimmy's assisting Roosevelt with his crutches in order to get to the convention podium in the final scene.

Roosevelt was a vigorous athlete and sportsman before his disability, and physical activity plays a major role in his recuperation. In the play, he insists to his mother that the dumbwaiter he uses to travel among floors should remain manually operated, because he values the exercise for his arms and shoulders. When he has an impromptu wrestling match with his sons, as he did before the onset of polio, it suggests that the old Franklin is still present, strong as ever.

While Roosevelt was always an effective politician, in the play his overcoming his disability raises him to a higher level of character and self-awareness. He confides in Eleanor that not being able to rush things has given him a greater sense of patience, and being stricken has taught him humility. He reveals that he has relied on his religious faith for support. Though already politically progressive (he once sold his mining stock because of the cruel treatment of the miners), he reaffirms more strongly than before his compassion for others and desire for global peace. His decision to pursue those goals in the political arena, in spite of his mother's plea for him to retire to Hyde Park and become a country squire, demonstrates how his disability caused him to redouble his resolve to work for a better world.

Dramatic Devices

Roosevelt's wheelchair is a prop of major symbolic importance and visual impact in *Sunrise at Campobello*. When he appears onstage sitting in the wheelchair, it is a startling moment for the audience. Although the general public was aware of his disability, the discreet contemporary press did not publish photographs of him in the wheelchair. To see the president, who had bravely led the country through two crises, the Great Depression and World War II, humbled by disability historically made a huge impression upon Americans, and, in the theater, conveyed a sense of intimacy with the audience.

Additional props related to Roosevelt's illness take on similar significance, including his crutches and braces and the difficulties he experiences adapting to their use. Yet his proudest moments come when he rises above the constraints of these props, as in the stretcher scene, where he manages to emerge resplendent, optimistic, and cocky despite being crippled and unable to walk. The scene in which he crawls across the stage, demonstrating the extent of his helplessness and boundless determination to overcome his disability, is deeply poignant. Finally, the podium in Madison Square Garden represents the difficult challenges ahead for Roosevelt, and his ultimate success in overcoming them.

The stage lighting accomplished by oil lamps during hours of darkness not only conveys the cozy atmosphere of a summer cottage on an island but also suggests that this is an earlier era, when the medical profession was less advanced.

Sunrise at Campobello is a historically accurate play, as opposed to plays based on historical events or persons, which invent situations and characterizations, such as Peter Shaffer's *Amadeus* (pr. 1979, pb. 1980). In addition to conducting considerable research into Roosevelt's life, Dore Schary took special pains to portray accurately Roosevelt's manner of speech at this time and consulted with Eleanor Roosevelt in order to depict it correctly. The dialogue effectively characterizes an aristocratic family, where French is spoken and taught by a governess, William Shakespeare is read aloud, cultured conversation is valued, and courtesy and noblesse oblige are observed.

Critical Context

Before writing *Sunrise at Campobello*, Dore Schary made his reputation in Hollywood as a studio executive, first as vice president of production for RKO (Radio-Keith-Orpheum) Studios, and later at MGM (Metro-Goldwyn-Mayer) Studios as head of all production. He supervised the production of more than 250 motion pictures, and wrote scripts for more than 40, including *Boys Town* (1938) for which he shared an Academy Award. When he was dismissed from MGM in 1956 as a result of company restructuring, he turned his talents to playwriting.

Sunrise at Campobello, his first playwriting effort, was a hit on Broadway, earning four Tony Awards, including awards for best play, best director, and best actor to Ralph Bellamy as Roosevelt (who repeated the role in the popular 1960 film version). Eleanor Roosevelt, with whom Schary had conferred while writing the play, was in the audience on opening night.

Schary's subsequent theatrical works were considerably less successful, most receiving a harsh critical reception and closing within a few weeks. His *Brightower* (pr. 1970), about a suicidal writer, closed after one performance. He seemed to focus on themes from *Sunrise at Campobello* but with unconvincing results. *The Highest Tree* (pr. 1959, pb. 1960), about an atomic scientist opposed to nuclear proliferation, featured an aristocratic family who was supposed to be cohesive and supportive but came across as profoundly dull and tedious. *One by One* (pr. 1964) explored the romantic relationship of a couple, both of whom are disabled, one as a result of polio. Despite potentially engrossing subject matter, the failure of these plays lends some credence to the assertion by some critics that *Sunrise at Campobello* was not necessarily a great play, but rather a great story, populated with characters cherished by the audience.

Sources for Further Study
Atkinson, Brooks. "The Theatre: *Sunrise at Campobello*—Bellamy as Roosevelt Scores at the Cort." *New York Times*, January 25, 1958, p. 25.
Eells, George. "*Sunrise at Campobello:* The Story of Two Comebacks." *Look* 22 (April 1, 1958): 98-101, 103, 105.
Schary, Dore. "F. D. R. in Dramatic Focus." *Theatre Arts* 42 (February, 1958): 62-64, 93, 94.
_____. *Heyday: An Autobiography*. Boston: Little, Brown, 1979.
Schlesinger, Arthur, Jr. "F. D. R. on the Stage." *The New Republic* 138 (February 10, 1958): 20.
"A Time of Ordeal for Young F. D. R.: Eleanor Roosevelt Helps Actors Prepare New Play." *Life* 44 (February 10, 1958): 91-94.

Richard W. Grefrath

SUSAN AND GOD

Author: Rachel Crothers (1878-1958)
Type of plot: Problem play; women's
Time of plot: A late 1930's summer
Locale: The country homes of Irene Burroughs and Susan Trexel
First produced: 1937, at the Plymouth Theatre, New York City
First published: 1938

> *Principal characters:*
> SUSAN TREXEL, a charming but controlling thirty-five-year-old
>   woman
> BARRIE TREXEL, her forty-year-old alcoholic husband
> BLOSSOM TREXEL, their fifteen-year-old daughter
> IRENE BURROUGHS, an attractive, almost divorced woman in her
>   late thirties
> MICHAEL O'HARA, her lover in his late thirties
> CHARLOTTE MARLEY, an unmarried, vital outdoors woman in her
>   mid-thirties
> LEONORA STUBBS, a tall, beautiful former actor in her late twenties
> HUTCHINS "STUBBIE" STUBBS, her wealthy husband
> CLYDE ROCHESTER, a handsome actor in his late twenties

The Play

Act 1 opens in the glass-enclosed terrace of Irene Burroughs's country house. As the curtain rises, Irene and Michael O'Hara enter. Concerned about the arrival of Susan Trexel and how she will react if she learns that Michael and Irene are living together, Irene warns Michael to be careful about what he tells Susan. He is annoyed at Irene's lack of openness. They are interrupted by the arrival of Charlotte Marley, Leonora Stubbs, her husband Stubbie, and Clyde Rochester. It is soon clear that the group is not happy: Stubbie is jealous of the attention Clyde pays to Leonora, Leonora makes fun of Stubbie, and all focus nervously on Susan's impending arrival. They dissect Susan's troubled marriage to the alcoholic Barrie Trexel, and Charlotte criticizes Susan's neglect of her teenage daughter, Blossom.

However, when the charming Susan appears, her friends respond immediately. They are fascinated by Susan's story of meeting Lady Wiggam, a British woman who has begun a "movement" that emphasizes spiritual contact and a "practical" God. Leonora takes Susan to get settled, and the rest scatter when Susan's husband, Barrie, arrives with Blossom, whom he has rescued from her lonely boarding school. While Barrie and Blossom wait to see Susan, they talk about Blossom's dislike of the camp where Susan has sent her every summer. They discuss staying together as a family for the summer, using their own country house. It is clear that this can happen only if Susan agrees. The first scene ends when Irene's butler lies for Irene, telling Barrie that Susan will not come until the next day. Barrie and Blossom leave together.

Scene 2 opens after dinner, with the group feeling guilty about their treatment of Barrie. Susan is expounding on the importance of being "God conscious." She creates a problem by urging Clyde to confess his love for Leonora and make something "fine" of it. This sends Stubbie into a jealous rage. Barrie returns, a bit drunk, wanting to talk to Susan. The group distracts him, and Michael and Stubbie take him away just before Susan returns and tries to get her friends to confess their problems to her. Annoyed with her attitude, Michael, Charlotte, and Irene decide to stage a "confession" scene. Michael is in the middle of this when Barrie returns and hears Susan tell Michael that if he asks God for help, he can be "made over." Barrie challenges her to help him change if she really believes what she is saying.

Act 2 opens the next morning in the guest room where Susan is staying. Barrie confronts Susan about the failure of their marriage and Blossom's unhappiness. He persuades her to spend the summer as a family in their own country house. When Blossom enters, Barrie gives the reluctant Susan credit for the plan, which thrills their daughter.

In the second scene of act 2 Susan and her friends wonder where Barrie has gone, certain that he is drinking. When he returns, sober, he happily tells Susan that he has been making plans for opening their house. As the Trexels leave, Irene tells Susan that what she is doing is "magnificent"; Susan is less enthusiastic.

Act 3 opens three months later, in Susan's sitting room in her country house. Irene finds Susan unhappy in spite of the success of the experiment—Barrie has stopped drinking, and Blossom has become a beautiful, sociable, happy young woman. Susan has been organizing two events: a meeting for Lady Wiggam and her movement and a party for Blossom. Having decided that her work is still more important than her marriage, Susan confronts Barrie, trying to push him toward Charlotte and away from their "spiritual" relationship. When she realizes that Blossom's party conflicts with Lady Wiggam's meeting, she tells Barrie the movement is more important. Barrie finally stands up to her, telling her she does not know anything about God and is only interested in "the show" and her own selfish excitement.

The final scene opens two days later. Barrie has disappeared; Irene blames Susan for this as well as for Irene's loss of Michael. She tells Susan to leave others alone and to attend to her own growing problems. Charlotte returns. She has been nursing Barrie, who got drunk after his fight with Susan, and she tells Susan she will go after Barrie if Susan gives him up. Barrie returns, and he and Susan finally reconcile. A contrite Susan recognizes that God is inside them and will help only if they work on their own problems.

Themes and Meanings

The overriding concern of *Susan and God* is a concern that Rachel Crothers examined throughout her playwriting career: How can the newly independent woman deal with conflicting interests and make a place for herself in the new society? Crothers examines the complexity of women's opportunities, choices, and limitations with both seriousness and humor and considers the problems that come with choice.

Much critical attention has been given to Crothers's protagonist, Susan Trexel, who is shown as shallow and selfish, more interested in excitement and her own aggrandizement than in the real needs of her family and friends. Some see Susan's return to her family as an antifeminist statement; however, this view fails to take into account the complexity of the women characters in the play, beginning with Susan.

Susan is clearly lacking in real commitment in either the public or private sphere. Lady Wiggam's "movement" lacks seriousness, and Susan's "God" is a superficial one. In contrast to this, Susan and Barrie accept each other at the end in a clear-eyed discussion, recognizing each other's faults and making a commitment to a working relationship. This will not be a traditional marriage but a partnership based on a love that is realistic. Susan has clearly grown in the course of the play.

The importance of Susan as mother and mentor for Blossom is painfully clear, and Susan's superficial advice to her daughter—to get rid of her glasses and braces and hold in her stomach—is woefully inadequate. However, in the final act, Susan confesses to Irene that she has developed a real emotional bond with Blossom, and the audience can hope at the end that Susan's relationship with her daughter will also grow stronger.

Susan's friends are also foils, whose circumstances and values contrast with those of Susan. Irene, who depends on her relationship with a man for fulfillment, loses Michael to another woman and will have to rethink her choices. Leonora, who has married Stubbie for financial security, rejects this troubled marriage and returns to her theater career, which she loves and in which she finds fulfillment. Finally, Charlotte, who is portrayed as healthy, vital, and "outdoorsy," is clearly strong enough to do well with or without Barrie.

Dramatic Devices

Susan and God is a problem play, a realistic drama focused on social issues in the tradition of Henrik Ibsen. It follows the conventions of a well-made play, with complex plot development and characters who are realistically developed both physically and psychologically.

The characters are upper middle class, with enough leisure time to have choices about how they live their lives. The portrayal is sometimes depressingly, and sometimes humorously, realistic—they bicker, whine, play mind games, and mock one another. Yet, they also have genuine friendships and can support one another when the need arises—for example, Charlotte nurses Barrie, and Barrie, when he understands Blossom's real feelings, works hard to be the kind of supportive parent that she needs. He also recognizes Susan's importance to Blossom and is careful to portray Susan's actions in the most positive light possible.

The settings are realistic but also serve a symbolic function. For example, Irene's terrace room, which features long, wide windows, wooden tubs of ivy, and chintz-covered garden furniture, seems like a part of the outdoors, an ironic point, given the claustrophobic atmosphere of the first scene. The characters are always seen indoors, in the terrace or sitting rooms, and rarely venture out, except to play tennis, ride horses, or drink on the terrace. The settings emphasize their artificial, shallow lifestyle. Even Blossom's name is ironically symbolic. At first she is ugly and neglected but she later "blossoms" in the company of her parents.

Crothers also enriches the problem aspect of the play by examining religious fraud and alcoholism in addition to women's issues. She clearly demonstrates that her characters' problems come from a variety of sources, and she portrays them in a sympathetic light.

Critical Context

Rachel Crothers wrote, directed, and produced plays for almost forty years. *Susan and God* was her final play. Crothers was interested from her early life in social problem plays, including Ibsen's *Et dukkehjem* (pr., pb. 1879; *A Doll's House*, 1880; also known as *A Doll House*). In spite of her family's objections, she studied acting and taught at New York's Stanhope-Wheatcroft School, where she began writing plays for her students to perform. Believing in the importance of being trained in stagecraft, she directed, designed, and produced most of the professional productions of her own plays—unusual for any playwright, but astonishing for a woman working in American theater in the first half of the twentieth century. She credited other women in theater for helping her get these opportunities.

Her own experiences led her to focus on feminist heroines throughout her career. Her early plays portray women as reformers. *He and She* (1920) is the best known of these plays, featuring protagonist Ann Herford beating her husband in an important competition for an artistic commission, then being forced to choose between her child and her work.

From 1914 to 1919, Crothers wrote a series of sentimental plays with more conventional women characters. In the 1920's, she returned to a feminist perspective, but with comic rather than dramatic protagonists. Her last four plays, including *Susan and God*, are more complicated, as was the status of the feminist heroine in the 1930's. These final plays focus on the new challenges for women, who had more choices but still found fulfillment difficult to achieve. Crothers's heroines of this period take a long-needed look at the idealized man and consider more honestly the relationships they have with men, with children, and with their careers. Crothers also examined the importance of women's relationships with other women.

Rachel Crothers's examination of the double standard and of the independent woman's search for her place in society remain timely. Crothers understood these were complex issues without easy answers, and her best plays reflect that understanding.

Sources for Further Study

Abramson, Doris. "Rachel Crothers: Broadway Feminist." In *Modern American Drama: The Female Canon*, edited by June Schleuter. London: Associated University Presses, 1990.

Friedman, Sharon. "Feminism as Theme in Twentieth-Century Women's Drama." *American Studies* 25 (1984): 69-89.

Gottlieb, Lois. "Looking to Women: Rachel Crothers and the Feminist Heroine." In *Women in American Theatre*, edited by Helen Krich Chinoy and Linda Walsh Jenkins. New York: Theatre Communications Group, 1987.

————. *Rachel Crothers*. Boston: Twayne, 1979.

Lindroth, Colette, and James Lindroth. *Rachel Crothers: A Research and Production Sourcebook*. New York: Greenwood Publishing Group, 1995.

Sutherland, Cynthia. "American Women Playwrights as Mediators of the 'Woman Problem.'" *Modern Drama* 21 (1978): 319-336.

Elsie Galbreath Haley

SWEET BIRD OF YOUTH

Author: Tennessee Williams (1911-1983)
Type of plot: Realism
Time of plot: The 1950's
Locale: A fictional Gulf coast town called St. Cloud
First produced: 1956, in Coral Gables, Florida (early version); 1959, at the Martin
   Beck Theatre, New York City
First published: 1959

> *Principal characters:*
> CHANCE WAYNE, an unsuccessful actor, a gigolo
> PRINCESS KOSMONOPOLIS, an aging actor
> BOSS FINLEY, the local political boss
> TOM JUNIOR, his son
> HEAVENLY FINLEY, the daughter of Boss Finley
> AUNT NONNIE, her aunt
> MISS LUCY, the mistress of Boss Finley
> SCUDDER, a young doctor, ally of Boss Finley
> THE HECKLER, a protester against Boss Finley
> FLY, a waiter at the hotel

The Play

Sweet Bird of Youth opens on Easter morning in the bedroom of an old-fashioned grand hotel, the Royal Palms. Chance Wayne rises from bed, where Princess Kosmonopolis (the alias of actor Alexandra Del Lago) is sleeping uneasily. Fly comes to the door with coffee and recognizes Chance, who has just returned to his native St. Cloud. Fly leaves, but immediately another voice is heard outside the door; it is Scudder, who enters and warns Chance that he is unwelcome in St. Cloud because he disgraced Heavenly Finley. Chance says he will stay until he can get Heavenly to leave with him.

Scudder leaves as Princess awakes from a stupor of alcohol and drugs. She does not remember how she got to St. Cloud or who Chance is. As she struggles to her senses Chance explains that he accompanied her as she fled from another state, where she had attended the disastrous premiere of a film with which she had hoped to make a comeback. As they talk, they resume drinking and smoking hashish. Unbeknownst to Princess, Chance is tape-recording their conversation, and he soon lets her know that he intends to blackmail her. She has the power to put him in films—his dream—and with the recording he has the power to ruin her. Princess, acquiescing, now wants Chance to make love to her; that is how she forgets pain and time and shame.

After Chance has made love to Princess, she gives him a mock screen test: He is to tell his life story. He describes a youth of frustration, without money or fame. All he had was beauty and erotic power. By the time he was discharged from the Army, he was past his prime, he explains, and that is when he found real love with Heavenly. Now that love for Heavenly has brought him back to St. Cloud.

Heavenly is forbidden to Chance; at their last meeting she warned him away. He has returned to St. Cloud to find her, and (with Princess's cash and expensive car) he wants to take her away in style to a film career in Hollywood. As act 1 ends, Chance leaves Princess at the hotel and goes in search of Heavenly.

Act 2 opens at Boss Finley's seaside mansion. Boss knows that Chance is back in St. Cloud. He is incensed because earlier Chance had infected Heavenly with venereal disease, and this led to a hushed-up hysterectomy that cost her emotionally and Boss politically. Boss and his henchmen are discussing how to get Chance out of town just as he arrives at the driveway of the house.

Chance has come to see Aunt Nonnie, who knows where Heavenly is. Aunt Nonnie feels tenderly about Chance and his romance with Heavenly. She promises Boss that she is trying to get Chance out of town so that violence can be avoided. As Boss talks with Tom Junior and other supporters, it becomes clear that Boss has his own guilty secrets to hide. Chance leaves without Heavenly learning that he is in town.

Boss Finley summons Heavenly. He wants her to appear alongside him at a political rally that night wearing a white dress to symbolize purity. Heavenly refuses; she is cynical and bitter, recalling how Boss forced her away from Chance earlier, when they wanted to marry. She confronts Boss with his duplicity, and he tells her that Chance is back in town but will be removed. The curtain falls.

The next scene takes place in the hotel lounge shortly before Boss's rally. In the complicated choreography a number of characters move in and out—Aunt Nonnie, the heckler, Princess, Miss Lucy (Boss's mistress), and other townspeople. Chance, drinking and taking pep pills, swears his love for Heavenly and proclaims his grandiose dreams of escape with her to a better life. He knows what Boss Finley will be discussing at the rally—the recent castration of a black man—but he is heedless of the danger of staying in town through the night. Princess appears, dazed and drugged, to swear her faith in Chance.

As Boss Finley's entourage arrives at the hotel for the rally, Chance and Heavenly come face to face for a moment just before Boss takes her onstage with him. Tom Junior confronts Chance with the story of Heavenly's health problems. Tom exits without hurting Chance, who is left alone onstage briefly with the heckler. As Miss Lucy reenters the cocktail lounge, the heckler leaves and goes to the hall where the rally is, intending to confront Boss Finley about his hypocrisy. The television in the lounge shows the heckler's questions and how he is beaten. The scene ends as Heavenly collapses at the rally.

The third act opens in the hotel bedroom at midnight. Boss's henchmen have come to remove Princess from the hotel and to find Chance, who has been waiting out of sight outside. He enters as they leave and has Princess talk by telephone to a Hollywood entertainment reporter, who tells her that the film in which she made her comeback was a success after all; her confidence bolstered, she refuses to mention Chance and Heavenly to the reporter. Princess and Chance talk wistfully about the futility of trying to beat time. A state trooper comes to escort her away from town. Boss's henchmen enter the room for Chance. The play ends as Chance addresses the audience to ask for understanding.

Themes and Meanings

Sweet Bird of Youth is about desperate people clinging to the vain hope that the ravages of time will not touch them, will not take their youth, hopes, and dreams. With Chance and Princess, as with Heavenly and to some extent Boss Finley, the loss of sexual functioning symbolizes this challenge.

The play also contains subplots about racial and sexual purity, expressed crudely by Boss Finley and his cronies. The castration of the black man before the play begins is balanced with the impending castration of Chance. These events in turn hinge on the quasi-castration of Heavenly by way of her hysterectomy; even Boss Finley experiences a kind of castration as his mistress publicly ridicules him. This emphasis on the brutality of sexual imperfection as an important theme of the play earned for Tennessee Williams savage reviews.

Some early critics believed that the lack of emotional content in the relationships overshadowed the use of sex as a metaphor for youth. Despite frequent references to the deep and long-lasting love between Chance and Heavenly, when they do cross paths they do not exchange any word or touch. Moreover, Chance has come to town somehow not knowing that his mother has died and been buried; nor does he know of Heavenly's infection and operation, although he was not prevented from communicating with Aunt Nonnie, for example.

The invective of Boss Finley as he crusades for purity, the viciousness of the sexual relationships, and the violence among the men all play into the symbolism of Easter, with its promise of resurrection. The play opens on Easter morning, and the tension— the promise of violence—builds toward a deceptively peaceful ending. Boss Finley states to his faithful that on Good Friday he saw an effigy of himself burned, and on Easter he returns with his message of purity to St. Cloud.

The heckler is distinctive in this play as the only voice of conscience. He alone protests the hypocrisy and shame all around him. Notably, when he is beaten the action proceeds without protest.

Dramatic Devices

One of the striking parallels between the themes of *Sweet Bird of Youth* and its stage appearance is the bareness of the sets. The stage directions call for a number of special effects that are used to accentuate the starkness of the themes. While the dialogue is at times flowery and rich, the sets are minimalist.

The action in different scenes is unified by one cyclorama specified by Williams. Projections of abstract images occur throughout. The most important of these, and the most constant, is a grove of palm trees. Wind plays through the palms, with the sound rising and falling according to the mood of the action, at times interspersed with a musical lament. The images on the cyclorama change somewhat according to the time of day.

During the first act, the stage is dominated by a large double bed. There is little else but several incidental props to enrich the Moorish style of the bedroom, and only the suggestion of walls. Thus, the bed, the focal point of the stage, also sets the central theme of sexual interaction. In the first scene of act 2 as well, the action is played against the suggestion of walls, this time on the veranda of Boss Finley's mansion. Williams strongly guides the lighting to a specific paleness—the colors of a Georgia O'Keeffe canvas, he says—as a backdrop to the sinister machinations of Boss Finley. Boss fancies himself a savior, and so all the characters here are instructed to wear white. The telephone ringing, ringing, ringing for Heavenly breaks in to bring the discussion back from the general to the specific.

During the cocktail-lounge scene—arranged, again, with the suggestion of a room—Williams specifies that the heckler is to be portrayed as El Greco would portray a saint. The heckler is given a certain pallor, a lanky build, that contrasts with the fullness of build and conventional clothing of the other characters. The others are morally bankrupt, whereas the heckler is constant in his denunciation of Boss Finley's style of rule.

During the rally scene, which takes place offstage, the action can still be followed through a curious device: The rally is carried on the television in the cocktail lounge, but the television is larger than life, the projected image taking up an entire wall of the stage set. Although the volume is adjusted up and down, the image of Boss Finley as a *deus ex machina* is unavoidable. At the climax of the scene, as the heckler is beaten, the action is split: The heckler has fallen into the lounge, but the television image contains Heavenly's reaction.

Sweet Bird of Youth was met with derision because of its surfeit of brutality and its alleged sexual perversion, but the integrity of the sets as they reflected the vision of the story only served to reinforce Tennessee Williams's reputation as a dramatic poet.

Critical Context

Tennessee Williams readily admitted that the sometimes repellent and warped lives portrayed in *Sweet Bird of Youth* contained much of his own experience. Drugs, alcohol, and promiscuous sex were part of his makeup, and they grew out of the darkly hypocritical society of his native Deep South. This was by no means the first of his plays to expose the hyperbolic vice that had grown into him. The 1959 production of *Sweet Bird of Youth* came soon after two of his most violent plays, *Orpheus Descending* (pr. 1957, pb. 1958) and *Suddenly Last Summer* (pr., pb. 1958). They, too, feature unusual, violent death scenes and bear the theme of personal atonement for social ills.

Despite the morbid aspect of much of Williams's theatrical work, *Sweet Bird of Youth* carries the mark of his early poetic gift. His authentic ear for the language of the South, as well as his innate grasp of the region's rich and complex social fabric, gave each of his plays an appealing glint, no matter how difficult the subject matter. In this respect, *Sweet Bird of Youth* does not stand out particularly from his other works. Conspicuously missing from this and other late works, however, is the more genteel presentation of plays such as *The Glass Menagerie* (pr. 1944, pb. 1945).

By the time *Sweet Bird of Youth* was produced, it was clear that Williams drew his characters from a closetful of symbolic figures who appeared repeatedly throughout his literary life—the sexually ungrounded middle-aged woman and the pure young girl, the sinister political boss, the sensitive young man, and so on—each of whom carried his or her heavy emotional baggage. Although Williams's plays seldom intersect the everyday world, his characters inhabit a real world of theatricality.

Sources for Further Study
Bloom, Harold. *Tennessee Williams*. Broomall, Pa.: Chelsea House, 1999.
Clurman, Harold. "Theatre." *Nation*, March 28, 1959, 281-282.
Devlin, Albert J., ed. *Conversations with Tennessee Williams*. Jackson: University of Mississippi Press, 1986.
Falk, Signi. *Tennessee Williams*. Boston: Twayne, 1978.
Hayman, Ronald. *Tennessee Williams: Everyone Else Is an Audience*. New Haven, Conn.: Yale University Press, 1994.
Kolin, Philip C. *Tennessee Williams: A Guide to Research and Performance*. Westport, Conn.: Greenwood Press, 1998.
Londre, Felicia Hardison. *Tennessee Williams: Life, Work, and Criticism*. Fredericton, England: York Press, 1989.
Stanton, Stephen S., ed. *Tennessee Williams: A Collection of Critical Essays*. Englewood Cliffs, N.J.: Prentice-Hall, 1977.

Nan Chase

TALES OF THE LOST FORMICANS

Author: Constance S. Congdon (1944-   )
Type of plot: Comedy; science fiction
Time of plot: The late twentieth century
Locale: Suburban Midwest America
First produced: 1988, at the Byrdcliffe Theater, Woodstock, New York
First published: 1989

> *Principal characters:*
> CATHY, a recently divorced single mother
> ERIC, her teenage son
> JIM, her father, a former construction worker
> EVELYN, her mother
> JUDY and
> JERRY, her friends
> ALIENS, creatures from far into the future

The Play

The curtain rises on Jerry lying on his back staring at the night sky through binoculars. Two people in sunglasses enter and unroll a large star map. One points to a spot on the map and tells the audience "You are here." These three characters exit, leaving the stage empty except for a kitchen table and chair. A disembodied voice begins describing the chair as though it were an ancient and mysterious object, while one of the people in sunglasses enters and points to various parts of the chair. Thus, with a minimum of explanation, Congdon telegraphs the play's general structure: It is a documentary about contemporary Earth civilization presented by aliens from far into the future.

Throughout the play the aliens continue to deliver a running commentary on the human action. This commentary is a source of comic irony, since the aliens often misinterpret human activities yet also offer off-kilter insight into human nature. In general, the human action, the play-within-a-play, is presented in an impressionistic manner, with many abrupt changes in time and place and very little exposition.

Cathy, the central character in the human story, is recently divorced and has just moved, with her teenage son Eric, to live with her parents, Evelyn and Jim. Moving from New York to a suburban neighborhood in the Midwest has angered Eric and, during the first act, he vents his frustration in a variety of ways. Moreover, Cathy discovers that things are not all well with her parents. Jim has become forgetful, and Evelyn is worried that he may be seriously ill. Adding to Cathy's feelings of displacement are the changes that have overtaken the neighborhood where she grew up. Her childhood friend Judy is all that remains of those days, and the two women bond over discussions of wayward children and former husbands. The story arc of the first act traces the increasing severity of Jim's symptoms. At first he is almost comical—he mistakes lipstick for chapstick, for instance—but it is soon apparent that he is suffering from Alzheimer's disease. Jim's story climaxes midway through the act when he becomes confused at his job on a construction site and is fired. Afterward, Cathy has a brief encounter with Jerry, who happens to be a conspiracy theorist and is the only character aware of the aliens. Jerry becomes infatuated with Cathy, but she finds him disturbing. As the act comes to a close, Eric announces that he is returning to New York. A brief scene follows in which Judy sings a nonsense lullaby to her two children, while aliens abduct Jerry.

Act 2 opens with Jim lucidly describing his experiences as a builder. However, Cathy reveals that this image of Jim is only a dream she recently had. Evelyn then decides that driving Jim out West will somehow cure him. Evelyn, Cathy, and Jim set out but get lost and must return home, where Jim is soon institutionalized. Shortly afterward, Cathy learns that Eric, instead of being with his father, is actually lost without a trace. Cathy then visits Jim at a nursing home and learns that Jerry is a caregiver there. Jerry, in his official role, has lost his nervous, suspicious demeanor, and his compassion for the patients charms Cathy. She later visits him, but at the point of becoming intimate, Jerry reverts to his paranoid fantasies and Cathy leaves. The play then climaxes with the simultaneous return of Eric and the announcement of Jim's death. At this point, it is also announced that a group of teenagers has set fire to the local mall. Cathy, Judy, Evelyn, and Eric gather to watch the blaze. Suddenly, Evelyn and Cathy put on sunglasses, taking on the identity of aliens. They explain to the audience that they were both, long ago, part of an earth race called the Formicans. Cathy and Evelyn then sing Judy's lullaby, as Jerry walks onstage with a gun. He lies on his back and prepares to shoot himself but is lulled to sleep by the song.

Themes and Meanings

As its title suggests, this is a play about loss. The catalog of loss to which Congdon subjects Cathy to is staggering. Cathy has lost her marriage and her childhood home, is losing her father, and is in danger of losing her son. Besides experiencing these personal losses, Cathy also feels that certain institutions and values are missing from the culture in which she lives. The cumulative effect of all these losses is that Cathy has become alienated from the past (symbolized by her parents), the present (symbolized by her culture), and the future (symbolized by her son). Cathy is, indeed, "lost" herself, a point that Congdon drives home by having Cathy become literally and physically lost at two points in the play.

All of the characters, in fact, experience the loss of something they hold dear, and they experiment with various strategies for dealing with these losses. Judy takes revenge on her estranged husband by burning his Corvette. Evelyn tries to save Jim by escaping into the past. Eric runs away to live with his father. The neighborhood children flirt with rebellion and crime. Jerry finds solace in delusional beliefs but also by helping people in his job at the nursing home. Yet, all of these strategies fail. Judy vandalizes the wrong car. Evelyn's trip is a disaster. Eric gets lost and ends up sleeping in a mall. The children's rebellion is unfocused and ultimately pointless. Even Jerry's dual strategies fail. Neither his humane acts nor his odd on-target worldview can save him from despair, and his suicide is thwarted only because he falls asleep before he can pull the trigger.

Yet the view Congdon puts forth in the play is hardly despairing, because her comic flair tempers the play's darker themes. This darkness is also alleviated, at least somewhat, by two other things: the presence of the aliens and the nonsense lullaby.

By making it clear that the aliens are really humans from the future, Congdon implies that it is possible, even certain, that humanity can persist—and that humans can persevere—despite lives filled with loss and pain. However, the comfort the aliens provide is rather cold. As the audience learns in the dialogue that precedes the transformation of Cathy and Evelyn, the aliens are emotionless creatures. Congdon seems to be suggesting that people may indeed survive, but only at the price of losing those qualities that make them fully human.

The nonsense lullaby stands as an alternative to the emotionless rationality of the aliens. Congdon draws attention to it by placing it at the end of each of the play's two acts. It also draws attention to itself by lyrically having absolutely nothing to do with the play. It exists purely as rhyme and melody, as art for its own sake, and that would seem to be Congdon's point: By showing that this song can tame restless children and ease troubled minds, she implies that art itself may be the only true balm for humanity, even if the relief it provides is only temporary.

However, the two possible escapes from despair—the aliens and the lullaby—are mutually exclusive. Although the alien Cathy and Evelyn do sing the song at the play's end, the audience is told directly that the aliens do not understand why humans sing. By paradoxically offering two contradictory alternatives to the pain caused by loss, Congdon succeeds in creating a play that is sure to pose more questions than it answers.

Dramatic Devices

Structuring the play as though it were an alien documentary about humans is a bold dramatic move, and one through which Congdon achieves many narrative and thematic ends. The aliens' voice-overs, and the way they halt and reverse the action when they feel it is necessary, give the play an air of detached irony. This emotional distance allows Congdon to present the essentially tragic material of the human characters' lives in a comic manner. The mock-documentary framework also enhances the way the characters' plights work metaphorically. The aliens' commentary regularly reminds the audience that Cathy and her circle of family and friends are representative examples of humanity. Thus, while the audience is emotionally affected by the story of Cathy and her family, it is also always aware that their struggles are symbolic of larger truths.

The mock-documentary framework also allows Congdon great freedom in the way she arranges the play's scenes. Since, in essence, the pacing of the play is in alien hands, there is no need for a strictly chronological approach. Indeed, time is drastically telescoped in the play, and events that logically must have played out over months or weeks can transpire quickly without Congdon having to continually reestablish proper time. Likewise, Congdon can liberally use abrupt cuts in the action and montagelike sequences without worrying about disrupting the logical continuity of the play. She can, for instance, take Jim from his own kitchen to nearly being hit by a truck with no transition at all. Similarly, she can have Judy, at home, singing a lullaby to her children, and at the same time show the aliens abducting Jerry. It is important to note, however, that Congdon uses these chronological shifts and juxtapositions not only as entertaining and sometimes jarring dramatic devices, but also to reinforce the play's thematic concern with loss. In *Tales of the Lost Formicans*, the world, and the people and things inhabiting it, are literally fleeting.

Congdon bolsters these themes of loss and impermanence with her spare use of scenery and props. While the details of specific productions are up to the director (Congdon has reported once seeing a production in which every object onstage was blue), the play's production notes state that the stage settings should be sparse. Again, this allows Congdon a great deal of freedom. The action can range from kitchen to construction site to nursing home to shopping mall very rapidly with no need for the reconfiguration of scenery. More important, the spare setting reinforces the theme that the physical world is impermanent and constantly changing.

Critical Context

Tales of the Lost Formicans is not only the most widely acclaimed and frequently performed of Congdon's plays; it is also an excellent introduction to her work. It displays, in abundance, all of the hallmarks of her style and examines the major themes common to her work. Her plays, for instance, often focus on contemporary social mores. *Casanova* (pr. 1989, pb. 1991) surveys the history of sexuality, and the short play *New* (pr. 2001) looks at the relationship between the United States and Asia. Her pieces are also distinguished by her mordant humor, which often serves to leaven her take on dark subjects, such as the threat of nuclear holocaust, the subject of *No Mercy* (pb. 1985, pr. 1986). Most important, *Tales of the Lost Formicans* displays Congdon's inventive approach to staging and her experiments with innovative narrative structures.

It is Congdon's creative narrative techniques that have won her the reputation as one of the most significant contemporary American playwrights. Her use of montage, multiple narratives, and nonlinear plots—all fully evident in *Tales of the Lost Formicans*—makes her a quintessentially postmodern writer. Indeed, her work in the late 1980's established her as one of the first important American postmodern dramatists. As such, she served as an important bridge between the avant-garde playwrights who came of age in the 1960's, such as Sam Shepherd and Edward Albee, and more innovative later playwrights such as Tony Kushner and Paula Vogel. Kushner, in fact, has cited *Tales of the Lost Formicans* as a direct influence on his landmark, Pulitzer Prize-winning two-part play *Angels in America* (pr. 1991, 1992; pb. 1992, 1993).

Sources for Further Study

Hussey, Susan. "Constance Congdon: A Playwright Whose Time Has Come." *Organica*, Winter, 1990.

Kushner, Tony. Introduction to *Tales of the Lost Formicans and Other Plays*. New York: Theatre Communications Group, 1994.

Seller, Tom. "Acquisitive Minds." *Theater* 26 (1995): 106-117.

Solomon, Alisa. "Formicans, Call Home." *Village Voice* 35 (May 1, 1990): 116.

Wilde, Lisa. "Trying to Find a Culture: An Interview with Connie Congdon." *Yale Theater* 22, no. 1 (Winter, 1990).

Willingham, Ralph. *Science Fiction and the Theatre: Contributions to the Study of Science Fiction and Fantasy*. Westport, Conn.: Greenwood Press, 1993.

David Keifer

TALLEY'S FOLLY

Author: Lanford Wilson (1937-   )
Type of plot: Social realism
Time of plot: July 4, 1944
Locale: Lebanon, Missouri
First produced: 1979, at the Circle Repertory Company, New York City
First published: 1979

> *Principal characters:*
> MATT FRIEDMAN, an accountant
> SALLY TALLEY, a nurse

The Play

The set consists of an elaborate Victorian boathouse, now gone to ruin, containing a latticework crammed with long-unused fishing equipment. Matt Friedman, forty-two, an accountant from St. Louis, enters and begins to address the audience. Although he mentions that a year ago he visited Sally Talley and spent some time at this very spot, he appears to be more interested in telling the audience that because he is not a "romantic type" of character, the technical elements of theater (lighting, sound, and set) along with the assistance of the audience are required to create the romantic atmosphere for this play. During his monologue he often lapses into seemingly irrelevant digressions that barely conceal his nervousness and volubility. Just when Matt appears completely lost in his whimsical musings, Sally, offstage, yells his name. As if by magic, the houselights dim, the special theatrical effects are added, and the drama begins.

Sally enters. She is thirty-four years old, works as a nurse at a hospital in Springfield, and lives at home with her parents. She complains that his interference with her family has precipitated a crisis she will be forced to resolve. Smatterings of exposition are revealed as they interact. Five months ago Matt had come to the hospital where Sally works and tried to see her; apparently she knew that he was there, but she refused to see him. Sally also notes that she had sent him only one letter in reply to numerous letters on his part. In her letter she had told him clearly that she had no intention of seeing him again.

Matt tries on a pair of old skates he finds stashed in the boathouse. As he simulates skating with Sally, he hums a song and says, "I'm having an old-fashioned skate with my girl." His gambit does not work—Sally responds, "I'm not your girl," and begins to walk away. At that moment, however, fortune smiles on Matt. When he tries to catch up with her, he falls through the floor of the boathouse and is nearly injured.

Now that Matt has Sally's attention again, he tries to coax a favorable response from her by referring to the "affair" the two had last year. He notes that they did see each other seven times in seven days. When Sally again begins to walk away, Matt appeals to her to not run away from this encounter.

Sally admits that she needs to move away from the stifling atmosphere of her parents' house. Matt invites her to consider the possibility that he might be in love with her, and that she might be in love with him. Then he turns to his playful nature and gift of mimicry to ask a series of rhetorical questions about this fascinating woman. He surprises her by referring to conversations he had with the patients at the hospital in Springfield while he waited to see Sally that day back in February; many of them told him that Sally had said she had a "beau."

This moment of intimacy is broken when she sees a spot of blood on his face. When Matt fell while "skating," he apparently scratched himself. Sally becomes the nurse, and as she dabs at his cut, they begin to interact in a more subdued manner. Matt reveals that he learned many details of Sally's past by talking to her Aunt Charlotte. This exposition reveals Sally to have been a free spirit in a conservative family that would have preferred a traditional old maid daughter. Suddenly Sally takes charge and begins to ask questions about Matt's life story. After several playful responses, Matt nervously launches into a strange retelling of a crucial part of his family's history in Europe before World War I. He tells of his family's torture and death at the hands of the French and the Germans because of his father's knowledge of munitions. Matt, then a boy, was smuggled to America with his uncle's family. He concludes that in order to spare a child from ever being lost to similar political machinations, he will never help bring a child into the world.

Matt's story represents an anguished recollection of horrible events, but his telling of the story backfires. Convinced that Aunt Charlotte has shared some secret with Matt, and that Matt has told the story because he feels sorry for her, Sally repudiates him. Matt quickly explains that Aunt Charlotte told him nothing—he told her the story only because she asked him to. Sally calms down, and their conversation drifts away from personal topics.

Finally, Matt sums up his frustration:

> I come down here to tell you I am in love for the only time in my life with a girl who sees the world exactly as I see it. I say to you, I am sorry, Sally, I will not have children, but if there is a life for the two of us, will you have me or not? You scream and yell bloody murder.

One last gambit occurs to him, however, before they leave. He recalls that Aunt Charlotte told him that Sally has a deep dark secret that only Sally can reveal. He probes Sally to discover her secret. She admits that she was "disappointed in love," later adding that she contracted tuberculosis. Then her marriage to the son of a prominent businessman was called off. Matt is not satisfied; he thinks he knows why her marriage was called off—she had an illegitimate child. He presses her relentlessly until she can no longer keep the truth from him. With an emotional outburst, she admits that the tuberculosis caused an infection that rendered her infertile. When her fiancé's family discovered that she could not provide him with an heir, they called off the marriage. Matt responds with sensitivity and love. Relieved that she has revealed her secret, Matt shows Sally that this revelation does not change his feelings for her or their prospects of life together. He does not want a family; she cannot conceive children. What matters is that they can start a life together. They decide to leave for St. Louis that very night. They kiss. Matt turns to the audience and acknowledges that romance has prevailed.

Themes and Meanings

Talley's Folly is a play about the primacy of human relationships and a celebration of romantic love. As Matt says at the opening, "This is a waltz, remember, one-two-three, one-two-three." The audience is cast as willing participants, even advocates, in Matt's ninety-seven-minute wooing of Sally Talley. When the two embrace at the end of the play, the audience realizes that, despite the fragile nature of communication, two people can find a way to form a lasting bond. One key to their union can be found in Sally's family past. Her grandfather built the Victorian boathouse, the "folly" of the play's title. The folly makes no money and does nothing to enhance the status of the Talley family, but the spirit of creativity and spontaneity celebrated by her grandfather's folly casts its spell over the characters (and the audience as well) and sets the stage for Matt's and Sally's love.

The play also incorporates themes about the triumph of individualism over the narrow codes of Old World cultures, and the coming to terms with the end of an era. Matt's immigrant experience has been decidedly atypical. He experienced at firsthand the deadly consequences of European nationalism before World War I. His family's death at the hands of the French and the Germans, who later were enemies in World War I, reflects the insanity of a world in which all nations share complicity for destroying innocent lives. But the brutal reality of his past has not destroyed Matt's spirit. He is a survivor. He is an expert in the affairs of money, he has a playful spirit and loves the inventiveness and spontaneity of language (he loves to mimic Humphrey Bogart), and he is interested in the American landscape.

Sally is much more bound to her culture and to her place than the uprooted Matt has been. Her life had been predicated on serving the goals of the conservative, southern aristocratic culture until her illness took away her usefulness to her family. Matt's love for her affords her an escape from the oppressive judgment of her family and the limited parameters of her life in a traditional male-dominated society.

It is fitting that Sally and Matt come together on July 4, Independence Day. Here are two unlikely patriots. Matt is a pacifist; Sally was fired from teaching Sunday school and believes in unions (not a popular idea in their company town). In other words, both are free thinkers, individuals, and have strong values about honesty, hard work, and the rights of other individuals. Wilson implies that both characters represent American values that should be celebrated on Independence Day.

The couple's interaction occurs at a turning point for American culture. 1944 represents the end of an era (the New Deal and World War II) when Americans were accustomed to shortages, dislocation, and lowered expectations. The future holds economic expansion, adjustment to new values, changes in family relationships, new attitudes in the work place. Matt and Sally will participate in many of these changes, and they will have an opportunity to nurture their own relationship free of the constraints and limitations of the old order.

Dramatic Devices

The play's opening scene presents a number of challenging dramatic devices. When the audience enters the theater and surveys the stage setting, it sees upon the stage a dilapidated Victorian boathouse amid waist-high weeds. Despite the romantic possibilities of the setting, the opposite effect is emphasized at the opening. Lanford Wilson specifies that "all this is seen in a blank white work light; the artificiality of the theatrical set quite apparent. The houselights are up." In other words, most of the magic of the theatrical experience—its ability to transport an audience from one time and place to another—is purposely withheld at the opening of the play.

When Matt enters, the conventions that audiences are accustomed to experiencing in the theater are immediately disrupted. He addresses the audience directly, not as in the conventional monologue, which addresses questions of plot and motivation, but as if he were greeting members of the audience in the lobby before a performance begins. In fact, the first thing he tells the audience is how long the play will last; the audience may well wonder, "Has the play begun?" Wilson wants the audience to understand that it must be an active participant in the overall drama of the play. Matt appears alone before the audience in order to present himself as he is, to gain its confidence, and to exact a promise that the audience will help him generate an atmosphere of romance so that he can win Sally's hand. For his part, he promises to keep the schedule, use the "facilities" of the theater for all they are worth (the special effects of lighting, music, and so on), and to keep Sally onstage until she yields to his proposal.

As soon as Sally's voice is heard offstage, however, Matt the stage manager becomes Matt the character. The transformation is accompanied by the theatrical magic that the audience expects from a romantic play—suddenly the houselights dim, and the illusions of theatrical magic appear: the reflection of a sunset on the river and the sounds of water running and birds singing. The drama begins in earnest, and Matt and Sally begin to dance the elusive "waltz" that Matt refers to at the opening. Each time their dance appears about to end abruptly, some accident or idiosyncratic response reinvigorates the dialogue, and the dance resumes. Meanwhile, the spell cast by their interaction and revelations of character causes the audience to become willing participants in the drama. Matt acknowledges the audience's role when, at the end of the play, he turns to the audience and, as if winking, says, "And so, all's well that ends . . . right on the button. Good night."

Critical Context

Wilson's plays often are characterized by themes derived from experiences in two contrasting worlds: the urban and the rural. In his plays with urban settings, characters live on the edge of existence and are trapped in decaying surroundings. *The Madness of Lady Bright* (pr. 1964, pb. 1967) portrays a woman's descent into madness. *Balm in Gilead* (pr., pb. 1965) portrays a ragged group of the dispossessed who spend time in a small inner-city café. The award-winning *The Hot l Baltimore* (pr., pb. 1973) presents a similar collection of individuals, who live in a decaying hotel near a railroad station.

When Wilson utilizes rural settings, his characters are often so bound up in their hypocritical, guilt-ridden, dysfunctional family relationships that they are blind to the potential beauty and simplicity of the world around them. *The Rimers of Eldritch* (pr. 1966, pb. 1967) examines a town's response to a dark secret, and *The Mound Builders* (pr. 1975, pb. 1976) exposes conflicts between those who would preserve the past and those who would destroy it for the sake of blindly following the god of development. These plays reflect Wilson's ambivalence toward his own Midwestern roots.

Wilson often resolves these tensions by finding hope in the possibilities of life-sustaining human relationships. The relationship between Matt and Sally in *Talley's Folly* exemplifies this hope. This play, which was awarded the Pulitzer Prize in 1980, represents Wilson's ongoing interest in rural Midwestern settings, particularly those of his native Missouri. It is one of three plays that re-creates the lives of the Talley family from Lebanon, Missouri. The Talley family appears initially in *5th of July* (pr., pb. 1978), which portrays events that take place in 1977. In this play Wilson explores themes that also reverberate in *Talley's Folly:* betrayal by members of a family, the narrow-minded and repressive aspects of some Midwestern values, the redeeming quality of human relationships, the life-affirming virtues associated with honesty and hard work, and the special, creative qualities of one family member that balance the iniquities of other family members.

Talley and Son (pr. 1985) adds to the story of the Talley family by focusing on the events that occur while Matt and Sally are discussing their future on that July 4 evening in *Talley's Folly*. The play explores the moral and psychological decline of the Talley family, whose actions are characterized again by betrayal, revenge, and gross materialism.

Wilson's main characters often are misfits or free thinkers, who do not share the narrow-minded values of those in power. Most important, they are individuals. They know what they believe in, and they act on their beliefs. His plays from the late twentieth century include *Eukiah* (pr., pb. 1992), *Redwood Curtain* (pr. 1992, pb. 1993), *Day* (pr., pb. 1996), *A Sense of Place: Or, Virgil Is Still the Frogboy* (pr. 1997, pb. 1999), *Book of Days* (pr. 1998, pb. 2000) and *Rain Dance* (pr. 2000).

Sources for Further Study
Barnett, Gene A. *Lanford Wilson*. Boston: Twayne, 1987.
Busby, Mark. *Lanford Wilson*. Boise, Idaho: Boise State University Press, 1987.
Dasgupta, Gautam. "Lanford Wilson." In *American Playwrights: A Critical Survey*, edited by Bonnie Marranca and Gautam Dasgupta. New York: Drama Book Specialists, 1981.

DiGaetani, John L. "Lanford Wilson." In *A Search for a Postmodern Theater: Interviews with Contemporary Playwrights*. New York: Greenwood Press, 1991.

Gussow, Mel. "Lanford Wilson on Broadway." *Horizon* 23 (May, 1980): 30-36.

Savran, David. "Lanford Wilson." In *In Their Own Words: Contemporary American Playwrights*. New York: Theatre Communications Group, 1988.

Schvey, Henry I. "Images of the Past in the Plays of Lanford Wilson." In *Essays on Contemporary American Drama*, edited by Hedwig Bock. Munich: M. Hueber, 1981.

Wilson, Lanford. "An Interview with Lanford Wilson." Interview by John C. Tibbets. *Journal of Dramatic Theory and Criticism*, Spring, 1991.

Robert E. Yahnke

TANGO

Author: Sławomir Mrożek (1930-   )
Type of plot: Problem play
Time of plot: The mid-twentieth century
Locale: Unspecified
First produced: 1965, at the Jugoslovensko Dramsko Pozorište, Belgrade, Yugoslavia
First published: 1964 (English translation, 1966)

> *Principal characters:*
> ARTHUR, a young man
> STOMIL, his father
> ELEANOR, his mother
> EUGENIA, his grandmother
> EUGENE, his grandfather
> ALA, his fiancé
> EDDIE, a servant

The Play

Tango is set in the living room of the Stomil family. The room is in great disarray: There are piles of drapery everywhere; one of them is used as a bed by Ala. The stage is littered with remnants of the past, such as a faded wedding dress, a baby carriage, and objects dating back to different eras. There is even a coffin in an alcove.

As the play begins, Eugene, Eugenia, and Eddie are interrupted in a furtive game of cards by the arrival of Arthur. The young man, dressed neatly in contrast to the slovenly appearance of the others, upbraids his grandmother for disobeying his ban on card playing and makes her lie down on top of the coffin in the alcove. Arthur is a student who has returned home only to find that his mother is having an affair with Eddie and that the whole family has deteriorated into complete dissolution and inertia. He has made it his task to reform the family and to reinstitute order and moral standards in the Stomil household. Stomil, an avant-garde writer, and his wife, Eleanor, resist Arthur's efforts, pointing out that it was their generation which overthrew all artistic and moral conventions and created a life of freedom for Arthur and his generation.

This very freedom, however, disturbs Arthur: He longs for "an orderly world," a respectable professional career as a doctor, and a conventional marriage. He claims that his parents' nonconformism has deprived him of the right of every young person to rebel against the norms of previous generations. He complains that this nonconformism into which his parents are pushing him "is only a new kind of conformism." Therefore, in order to reassert his right to nonconformism, he will have to reestablish a set of rules and force his family to conform to them.

In act 2, Arthur enlists the help of Eugene for his plan and persuades Ala, his fiancé, that they should have an old-fashioned wedding as an outward sign of the new system of values he wants to create. That would put an end to the promiscuity that followed the abandonment of all rules of moral behavior and shock his family into an acceptance of his intended reestablishment of social and moral conventions. Ala is bored by his philosophizing but is attracted by the idea of a traditional wedding in white. Arthur next attempts to force Stomil, his father, into an act of violence against Eddie, whose affair with Eleanor is known to the whole family, including Stomil. When Arthur's father fails to see what killing Eddie would achieve, Arthur explains to him that it would be an "irrevocable, masterful, classical" act, similar to the actions of great tragedy. Stomil retorts that in the modern world tragedy is no longer possible, only farce. He rejects the revolver Arthur offers him, except to make empty theatrical gestures with it; it is Eugene, the grandfather, claiming to have long waited for this chance, who comes to Arthur's aid and helps him organize the family for the wedding at gunpoint.

The last act presents a changed Stomil family. The room has been tidied and the family members appear in formal dress. Eddie has been promoted to the role of butler. When Ala enters in her white dress and veil, Arthur's plan appears to have succeeded: He has coerced his family to act according to his new forms and can now attempt to instill these formalities with new meaning. Just as the wedding is to begin, however, Arthur returns drunk from his bachelor party, another traditional rite. The liquor has opened his eyes to the fact that there is "no going back, no present, no future." Gloomily he confesses that he has gone about his reforms in a backward manner: "Conventions always spring from an idea," not the other way around. The idea which he will make the basis for his new form of order is absolute power, and he intends to wield this power with the help of Eddie. Eugenia, his grandmother, does not want to be a part of this violent new era; she voluntarily climbs on the coffin and dies. Arthur himself, as it turns out, is not destined to rule: After Ala confesses that she has been unfaithful to him with Eddie on the very morning of their wedding, Arthur, trying to assert his authority, is killed by Eddie, and as the play closes the whole family meekly submits to Eddie's taking command. Eugene dances the tango with the new master of the house; they all will now dance to Eddie's tune.

Themes and Meanings

Tango, like many of Sławomir Mrożek's plays, contains allusions to the political and social situation of Poland in particular and the Western world in general. Like many Polish playwrights, Mrożek was fascinated by the figure of Hamlet and saw the prince of Denmark as a prototype for the modern intellectual. Like Hamlet, Arthur is an intellectual who is faced with a world "out of joint," the disintegration of his family and his country, and who feels compelled to attempt to "set it right." Like Hamlet and all intellectuals, he is inclined to philosophical speculation rather than to determined, forceful action, and so he has only "words, words, words" to put up against the corruption of his environment. Incapable of decisive action, he berates himself for his indecision; instead of taking command to establish a new regime, he nostalgically dreams of the old order and convinces himself that restoring the old forms and ceremonies will also restore the validity of the old ideas. He does not want to acknowledge that these values (personified by his grandmother) have become anachronisms as a result of the nihilistic revolution of his parents' generation. Arthur, a product of this revolution and of the upheavals of the Western world after World War II, longs for a new order, a structure that would give him moral and political guidance, but he has nothing to put up against this lack of order but abstract philosophy and empty formality.

And so, like Hamlet, Arthur will not rule, but will be killed, mainly as a result of his own indecisiveness. There will be a ceremonial funeral with pomp and eulogies, but it is the representative of unthinking force—Eddie, the former servant, an antiintellectual man of action—who will, like Fortinbras, rise to power. He will establish his brand of order, autocratic and based on the force of arms, and the rest of the family will meekly assent to his rule; old hangers-on such as Eugene will do so enthusiastically. Once again, the humane tradition of Europe will prove inadequate, lacking the strength to refuse to dance with a totalitarian regime; paradoxically, the family will dance to the tune of a tango, the dance that symbolized the breaking of all moral traditions to Stomil and his generation.

Here the play's political theme becomes clear. Poland and the Western world are mirrored in the Stomil household. There are the grandparents, senile remnants of *fin de siècle* hedonism, while the parents are representatives of the amoral generation produced by two world wars. Ala, Arthur's fiancé, represents the younger generation, dazed and drifting. Finally, there is Eddie, the proletarian of simple tastes, unburdened by traditions and conventional restraints. He is able to act unscrupulously, filling the power vacuum left by a decadent bourgeoisie and an intelligentsia paralyzed by its incapacity to do more than talk. Mrożek thus evokes Adolf Hitler's rise to power and the ascendancy of fascist and communist tyrants all over the world. *Tango* suggests that unless people create new values from the chaos of the modern era, values that will go beyond reestablishing the old, outdated forms and ceremonies of Western civilization, they will be led a merry dance by the likes of Eddie.

Dramatic Devices

Tango was Mrożek's first full-length, three-act play. Unlike the shorter dramatic pieces of his earlier career, *Tango* makes little use of the formal devices of the Theater of the Absurd. Indeed, the play conforms fully to the conventions of the well-made play by adhering strictly to the unities of time, place, and action and by using a traditional structure of introduction, complication, and resolution. Another conventional dramatic device, absent from Mrożek's early plays, is the use of proper names for his characters; indeed, the name Stomil allows the audience direct associations to Poland. In spite of the specific names, *Tango* is not a psychological play in which the dramatic interest concentrates on the motivations of individual characters. The Stomils and the other denizens of their household are representative characters, quasi-allegorical figures that mirror contemporary European types. In this sense, *Tango* can be viewed as a modern morality play. Beyond the political allegory, there is the existential level: Arthur is a modern Everyman trying to come to grips with an essentially godless world.

Although *Tango* is Mrożek's most conventional play, elements of the modern antiillusionist drama do appear. Most prominent of them is the coffin on which Arthur forces Eugenia to lie as a punishment for her violation of his house rules. It exemplifies Arthur's attempt to bury the past, but even when Eugenia voluntarily climbs on the coffin and dies in the end, nothing is achieved. There is no rebirth after the burial. An additional device of the Theater of the Absurd is the experimental play which Stomil puts on at the end of act 2. To a degree it parallels the play-within-the-play from *Hamlet*, but it also demonstrates that, like the tearing down of all social and moral conventions by Stomil's generation, the discarding of all theatrical conventions by the dramatists of the Theater of the Absurd has left a void.

Critical Context

Tango was an instant success, both in Poland and abroad, and is perhaps the best-known contemporary Polish play. Its obvious allusions to the political situation in Poland contributed to the playwright's exile from his homeland in 1968, as well as to a rediscovery of Polish drama in the Western world. As noted above, *Tango* is one of a large number of Polish plays drawing on William Shakespeare's *Hamlet*; another of these is Stanisław Wyspiański's *Wyzwolenie* (1903; the deliverance, untranslated), which attacks the Polish people (and Polish drama in particular) for an indulgence in lofty rhetoric and a corresponding lack of genuine action. The motif of the tango is taken from Stanisław Ignacy Witkiewicz's last play, *Szewcy* (pr. 1957; *The Shoemakers*, 1968), in which a folk character, instead of doing the traditional Mulch dance in peasant clothes, appears in a tuxedo and does the tango.

As a result of the peculiar political situation of Poland during the latter half of the twentieth century, many contemporary Polish plays reflected on this particular history. Mrożek does not see Poland as a completely singular case but as an extreme example of the consequence of common Western spiritual and political trends. It is this universal appeal that has made *Tango* such a popular play on European stages, allowing audiences all over the world to see themselves reflected in the Stomil family.

Sources for Further Study

Gerould, Daniel. "Mrożek Resisted." In *Slavic Drama: The Question of Innocence. Proceedings*, edited by Andrew Donslov and Richard Sokoluski. Ottawa, Canada: Department of Modern Languages and Literature, 1991.

_____, ed. *Twentieth-Century Polish Avant-Garde Drama: Plays, Scenarios, Critical Documents*. Ithaca, N.Y.: Cornell University Press, 1977.

Kalera, Jozef. "A Concise Guide to Mrożek." *Theatre in Poland* 3 (1990): 8-11.

Kloscowicz, Jan. *Mrożek*. Translated by Christine Cankalski. Warsaw, Poland: Authors Agency and Czytelnik, 1980.

Kott, Jan. *Theatre Notebook, 1947-1967*. Translated by Bodesław Taborski. Garden City, N.Y.: Doubleday, 1968.

Miłosz, Czesław. *The History of Polish Literature*. New York: Macmillan, 1969.

Franz G. Blaha

TEA AND SYMPATHY

Author: Robert Anderson (1917-   )
Type of plot: Social realism
Time of plot: The 1950's
Locale: New England
First produced: 1953, at the Ethel Barrymore Theatre, New York City
First published: 1953

>*Principal characters:*
>TOM LEE, a seventeen-year-old student
>HERBERT LEE, his father
>LAURA REYNOLDS, a former actor
>BILL REYNOLDS, her husband, a housemaster
>LILLY SEARS, the wife of another housemaster
>DAVID HARRIS, a young master
>AL, Tom's roommate

The Play

As the curtain rises on *Tea and Sympathy*, the audience sees a two-room set suggesting security and serenity, the warm and comfortable housemaster's study onstage right, a student's bedroom, a few steps higher, onstage left. As the action begins, young, sensitive Tom Lee is sitting on his bed singing the song "The Joys of Love," while in the study, Laura Reynolds, a casually attired, lovely woman in her mid-twenties, and her friend, Lilly Sears, a flashily dressed woman in her late thirties, are talking idly while Laura sews what is obviously a period costume.

Lilly is unsuccessfully trying to persuade Laura that the boys in this preparatory school are all obsessed with sex; Laura is more inclined to believe that they need understanding and kindness. After Lilly leaves, Tom enters, and it is immediately obvious to the audience, though not to Laura, that he is in love with her. When he asks to take her to an upcoming dance, which her husband the housemaster will not be able to attend, Laura accepts, assuming that Tom simply knows no girls. In this scene, too, the audience learns that the costume that Laura is making is for Tom, who will play the starring role of Lady Teazle in Richard Sheridan's *The School for Scandal* (pr. 1777). Tom confides to Laura that his father, an alumnus of the school, will probably be angered when he learns that Tom is once again playing a woman's role; Tom also hints at some problems with other boys, who have nicknamed him "Grace" simply for his crush on actor Grace Moore. When he cares about someone, Tom admits, he tends to go overboard.

As the act proceeds, the theme of homosexuality is introduced. The young master, David Harris, comes to tell Tom that they were seen bathing together nude and that this indiscretion has cost him his job. In contrast to this episode, which on Tom's part at least was completely innocent, Robert Anderson inserts a brief scene in which Tom's critics display their masculinity by clustering at a window to watch a master's wife nurse her baby. When the housemaster Bill Reynolds enters, anxious to tell Laura the gossip about Tom, it is noticeable that, while he is quick to question Tom's sexuality, he sees nothing peculiar about his own frequent outings with young male students, which are clearly more important to him than vacations with his wife. As the act ends, Tom's father, Herbert Lee, who has heard about the scandal involving his son and Harris, plans a strategy to convince the other boys that Tom is virile and, as a first step, forces Tom to give up his part in the play. Even Laura, Tom's friend and defender, tries to arrange a date for him, and as the curtain falls, the humiliated, guiltless Tom is sobbing alone in his room.

The second act is set two days later. In the first scene, Tom's roommate, Al, is pressured by his father and by his peers to desert Tom. However, he still hopes to save Tom's reputation, and with the best intentions he demonstrates how Tom should change his walk, in order to avoid suspicion of homosexuality, and then persuades Tom to have as a date for the dance the most promiscuous girl in town. Meanwhile, the marital problems of Laura and Bill are intensifying, but when Laura tries to talk to him about their unsatisfactory sexual relationship, Bill changes the subject to Tom, revealing his obsessive hatred of the boy.

The second scene in this act takes place on the night of the dance. It is revealed that Laura, who had overheard Tom's telephone conversation with the notorious Ellie Martin, had gone to look her over. In a tender conversation, Laura tells Tom about her first husband, who became a dead hero in order to prove that he was not a coward. Overwhelmed by his feelings, Tom kisses her; instinctively, she says, "No," and Tom leaves, just as Bill and his mountain-climbing contingent return, defeated by the weather. As the act ends, Bill is reaching toward Laura.

The third act, which takes place the following afternoon, begins with a confrontation between Bill and Tom. Tom is to be expelled from school for being picked up by the police, but the reason has obviously delighted Bill: Unable to perform with Ellie Martin, Tom threatened to kill himself, and Ellie called the police. When Herbert Lee arrives, Bill must repeat the story to him, and Herbert's pleasure in having a wild son turns to disgust with his sexual inadequacy. Furious, Laura insists on a talk with her husband, and, after indicting the masters and the boys who brought Tom to the brink of suicide, she expresses her regret that she had not encouraged Tom to prove himself with her. Real manhood means the courage to be tender and sensitive, she says, claiming that Tom is far more of a man than Bill, whose homophobia may well be disguising his own tendencies. Bill walks out. The marriage is over. As the scene ends, Laura walks into Tom's bedroom, locks the door, and moves into his arms.

Themes and Meanings

In his own introduction to *Tea and Sympathy*, Robert Anderson called it first and foremost a love story. The play began with Tom's love song, expressing his feelings for Laura; proceeded with the gifts of courtship; and concluded with the physical expression of love. The last lines of the play concern love. When in the future Tom speaks of this, his first experience with a woman, Laura admonishes him to "be kind," in other words, to remember the affection that made their sexual union valid.

In contrast, Laura is repulsed by Bill's violent lovemaking. In order to prove his manliness, Bill has forsworn tenderness. Clearly Laura feels as much used as Ellie Martin; thus she can understand Tom's revulsion when he is expected to commit a sexual act with a woman for whom he feels nothing. If there are perverts in *Tea and Sympathy*, Anderson suggests that they are the insecure Bill Reynolds and the immature boys who reassure themselves with Ellie Martin's body.

A second theme in *Tea and Sympathy* involves a specifically American problem. Perhaps owing to their historical proximity to the frontier, it has been noted that Americans tend to define manliness as bragging vulgarity, evidenced in the preoccupation with sports like the mountain climbing that is seen to prove the virility of Bill's young friends, and in the use of women as sexual objects, as in the case of Ellie Martin. As a result, men who, like Tom, are sensitive and thoughtful, who in an older civilization would be considered polished, in the United States are often thought to be effeminate and are even assumed to be homosexuals.

It would be easy to view the play as a plea for freedom in sexual preference. A careful reading, however, does not support that interpretation. As a character, David Harris is not fully realized; the audience is never sure whether he had designs upon Tom. His situation is not the point. Instead, it is Tom Lee's problem that is central; he is accused, convicted, and condemned without evidence; he is the victim of prejudice, for he is prejudged on the basis of false assumptions and circumstantial evidence. Moreover, he is deserted by his peers, by his housemaster, by his father, even seemingly, for a time, by the woman he loves. His heroism is seen in the fact that, in the face of such prejudice, he remains true to his conception of manliness. In the final scene of the play, the three themes are intertwined. Prejudice is defeated; the lovers are united; and Tom's definition of manhood has prevailed.

Dramatic Devices

In *Tea and Sympathy*, the set itself suggests the conflict between two modes of life and two views of love. The set is divided into two areas, the room which belongs to the married couple, the housemaster and his wife, and the room where the student-protagonist lives with his roommate. A hallway at stage left leads to the rooms of the other boys, whose rooms are offstage but whose influence is always present.

As the relationship between Bill and Laura is revealed, it becomes more and more obvious to the audience that the set is a metaphor for their marriage. Their study, too, appears comfortable and pleasant, but, like their relationship, it has been created for the public. Their bedroom is offstage. On the other hand, Tom's bedroom is as exposed as his emotions, brightened by personal touches, which suggest his love of beauty. The Indian prints and the phonograph are not selected to impress anyone but to express his own tastes. The difference between the two rooms is consistent with the difference between Bill and Tom.

The movement of the action between the two rooms suggests the changes which are taking place in the characters. At the beginning of the play, Tom is alone with his love for Laura, and Laura is playing her role of housemaster's wife with a gossipy friend. As the play progresses, Tom comes briefly and formally into the housemaster's area, seeking the conventional tea and sympathy that one would find in a study, except for the moment in act 2, scene 2, when he kisses Laura and then retreats to his room. She does not follow him. Eventually, he is left alone in his bedroom, and after the experience with Ellie Martin, he locks himself in, away from the world. Significantly, at the end of the play, Laura goes into Tom's room, and he is no longer alone.

Bill Reynolds, on the other hand, seems to spend most of his time leaving the room he shares with Laura. His haste to leave is consistent with his haste in intercourse, which Laura describes clearly; at the end of the play, when she angrily unearths his fear of himself, he very nearly strikes her, but then once again he avoids a confrontation by leaving both her and the room in which they have publicly appeared to be husband and wife.

After Bill leaves, it is her movement from one part of the set to the other that reveals her decision between two lives, the public and the private. She leaves the study, which, like Bill, was empty of real love, and goes into the bedroom, where love and Tom are waiting. She is leaving the impersonal, public world for a highly personal, private world. In this way, Anderson's simple divided set serves as a metaphor for the choice that he implies each individual must make between public approval and private integrity.

Critical Context

After a fifteen-year period of apprenticeship, with *Tea and Sympathy* Robert Anderson had a Broadway hit. Still, after its production in 1953 he fell into a long period of relative obscurity. It was not until 1967, with a group of four one-act plays titled *You Know I Can't Hear You When the Water's Running*, that he rose again to general notice. Another successful play and a duo of one-acts followed. Anderson had been writing successful screenplays since his adaptation of *Tea and Sympathy* in 1956, and he was later noted for his adaptation of Richard McKenna's 1962 novel *The Sand Pebbles* in 1966 and for the screen version of his 1968 play, *I Never Sang for My Father* (pr., pb. 1968), which in 1971 won for Anderson the Writers Guild Award for Best Screenplay.

In *Tea and Sympathy*, Anderson introduced the themes that were to be typical in his later works, human isolation and the difficulty in developing relationships between individuals, even between those united by blood or by marriage. The title *I Never Sang for My Father*, for example, suggests the subject of the play, the problems inherent in a father-son relationship, and the guilt that remains after an inevitable failure in the expression of love. *Solitaire/Double Solitaire* (pr. 1971, pb. 1972) consists of two plays which deal specifically with loneliness.

If *Tea and Sympathy* is important because it is Anderson's best-known play, also significant is what it is not. It is a story of a boy who is convicted by his society of being a homosexual solely based on his mannerisms, his cultural interests, and his appeal to a possibly homosexual teacher. In this sense, it is a plea for justice. However, because Tom is not a homosexual, the play is not a plea for tolerance of other sexual preferences; indeed, the most unsympathetic character in the play is probably a latent homosexual, Bill Reynolds. Admittedly, it is this character's dishonesty, even with himself, and his resulting vindictiveness toward Tom that Anderson attacks. In any case, while *Tea and Sympathy*, like Lillian Hellman's *The Children's Hour* (pr., pb. 1934), raised the subject of sexual deviations among teachers and their young students, the focus was on false accusation, and it remained for later playwrights to deal compassionately with homosexuality as a reality.

Sources for Further Study

Anderson, Robert. "Draw Your Own Conclusions." *Theatre Arts* 38 (September, 1954): 32-33.

Bigsby, C. W. E. "Robert Anderson." In *Contemporary Dramatists*. 6th ed. Chicago: St. James, 1999.

Bossier, Gregory. "Writers and Their Work: Robert Anderson." *Dramatist*, Spring, 1998, 4.

Bryer, Jackson R., ed. *The Playwright's Art: Conversations with Contemporary American Dramatists*. New Brunswick, N.J.: Rutgers University Press, 1995.

Clurman, Harold. "Theater." *The Nation* 177 (October 17, 1953): 317-318.

Nesmith, N. "Robert Anderson: A Discussion." *Dramatist*, March/April, 2002, 10.

Newsweek. Review of *Tea and Sympathy*. 42 (October 12, 1953): 84.

Time. Review of *Tea and Sympathy*. 62 (October 12, 1953): 49-50.

Rosemary M. Canfield Reisman

THE TEAHOUSE OF THE AUGUST MOON

Author: John Patrick (John Patrick Goggan, 1905-1995)
Type of plot: Comedy; satire
Time of plot: The late 1940's
Locale: Tobiki, Okinawa, Japan
First produced: 1953, at the Martin Beck Theatre, New York City
First published: 1954

> *Principal characters:*
> SAKINI, an Okinawan interpreter
> COLONEL PURDY, a literal-minded U.S. Army officer
> SERGEANT GREGOVICH, his assistant
> CAPTAIN FISBY, a U.S. Army officer assigned to democratize
>   Tobiki
> CAPTAIN MCLEAN, a psychiatrist
> LOTUS BLOSSOM, an Okinawan geisha

The Play

Sakini, a middle-aged Okinawan man wearing oversized army boots and socks, sets the tone for *The Teahouse of the August Moon* when he greets the audience with typical Oriental formality. After examining the audience curiously, and chewing gum furiously, he stores the gum, resumes his dignified stance, and introduces himself, concluding with a bit of folk wisdom: "Pain makes man think. Thought makes man wise. Wisdom makes life endurable."

Act 1 introduces Colonel Purdy, a U.S. Army officer assigned to democratize Okinawa after World War II, and Sergeant Gregovich, Purdy's assistant. Sakini alternately serves as commentator and actor to establish Purdy's character as a single-minded individual who only knows how to follow orders without question. Captain Fisby, a new aide assigned to Purdy, also arrives. He is in his late twenties, earnest and eager to make a good impression. Fisby has been transferred out of virtually every outfit in the army. Purdy is disappointed over the assignment of this "misfit," but he points out that one must adjust to succeed as a soldier: When he was told to "teach these natives the meaning of Democracy," he accepted the order without question. Fisby, formerly an associate professor of humanities, is handed Plan B for establishing an industry in Tobiki, a plan which anticipates all questions and requires no thinking to implement. He is to build a pentagon-shaped schoolhouse and organize a Women's League for Democratic Action in Tobiki.

Sakini becomes Fisby's interpreter, and they prepare to leave. Fisby salutes smartly and departs; Purdy searches for his adventure magazine. A jeep arrives, piled high with bundles and with an old woman sitting on top. Fisby tells Sakini to get rid of the woman, but Sakini succeeds in convincing Fisby that not only the old woman must stay, but also her daughter, her grandchildren, some goats, and finally an ancient man.

The journey—only four days on foot—takes ten days because the group is repeatedly sidetracked. Fisby cannot say no; he always succumbs to Sakini's intervention on the Okinawans' behalf. Arriving in Tobiki, Fisby holds a formal public meeting and receives various gifts. One gift, a lacquered cup, gives Fisby the idea of a souvenir industry for Tobiki. Then the plan for a school is explained, and, while the people like the idea of education, they want to know more about democracy. Fisby gives an unclear definition, but Sakini cleverly manages to explain things away, and the people applaud Fisby. Fisby initiates elections for public officials, but the people chosen have absolutely no experience in the areas for which they are elected. When he carries out the assignment of organizing the women's league, Miss Higa Jiga is chosen to be the leader. At this point, a geisha girl, Lotus Blossom, is brought to Fisby. At first he vehemently tries to refuse her, but ultimately, as usual, he gives in to the wishes of the Okinawans. Soon, a group of women burst in to complain that Lotus Blossom has been given preferential treatment. A hilarious episode follows in which Fisby is pressured to obtain all kinds of cosmetics and other luxury items like Lotus Blossom has, and the women are appeased.

Lotus Blossom tries to perform as a geisha, but Fisby does not understand her true role and refuses. Finally, Sakini convinces Fisby that a geisha is not the same thing as a prostitute in the United States, and Fisby apologizes to her. A group of people come to ask that a teahouse be built. Being told that there are no provisions for one, Fisby yields to pressure to use the schoolhouse materials for building the teahouse.

A few weeks later, when Colonel Purdy calls Captain Fisby, the audience understands by the end of the conversation that Fisby has not simply adapted to the wants of the Tobiki villagers but has himself become so acculturated that virtually nothing that he set out to do has been carried out according to army regulations. As act 1 ends, Colonel Purdy is sending a psychiatrist to Tobiki to examine Captain Fisby. The psychiatrist, Captain McLean, calls on Fisby, who is dressed Okinawan style and who offers the medical corpsman all the native courtesies. McLean questions Fisby under the guise of doing an ethnological study, and gradually, McLean himself is won over to Fisby's ways, to the utter frustration of Colonel Purdy.

Meanwhile, the plan to develop a souvenir industry fails completely. The American soldiers cannot appreciate that each cup has been handcrafted; they complain that mass-produced cups would take much less time and cost less. It develops, however, that a feasible industry is that of making sweet-potato brandy.

The setting for act 3 is the teahouse, now completed. A celebration is being held, and, lost in concentration, Fisby fails to see Colonel Purdy and Sergeant Gregovich enter. Tobiki is now a thriving, model village, but nothing has been done according to U.S. Army orders. Purdy orders an investigation by Washington bureaucracy and puts Fisby under technical arrest pending court-martial proceedings. Gregovich, however, returns from inspecting the village and congratulates Fisby on his accomplishments. Purdy persists in ordering that the teahouse be torn down and the brandy stills be destroyed. Since Lotus Blossom must leave, she and Fisby go through the imaginary ritual of drinking tea as they take their farewells. Lotus Blossom wants to go to the United States, where, she believes, "Everybody love everybody. Everybody help everybody—that's democracy." Fisby explains that democracy is a system, nothing more, and that the ideal and the reality are not always the same. Sakini, reassigned to Major McEvoy, begs to be allowed to remain with Fisby.

As Fisby is reflecting on what he has learned during his experience at Tobiki, Colonel Purdy appears and asks for Fisby's help in restoring Tobiki—teahouse, brandy stills, and all. Amazed, Fisby learns that after his activities were reported to Washington, some senator decided to use Tobiki as an example of American "get-up-and-go" abroad; he is sending photographers and reporters for magazine coverage. There is mass confusion. Sakini saves the day: He has cleverly managed to keep the barrels intact, and the panels of the teahouse have been hidden away, so that rebuilding takes a matter of minutes. Even Purdy can register approval as he orders a sign naming a main street for his wife and goes with Fisby to the teahouse to have "Twenty Star" strength brandy. As the curtain falls, Sakini concludes with the saying with which he opened the play.

Themes and Meanings

The title *The Teahouse of the August Moon* suggests the central theme of this play. When Fisby asks, "Why an August moon?" Sakini answers that "all moons good but August moon little older—little wiser," a way of saying that, in spite of an initial lack of cross-cultural understanding, it is possible for East and West to learn from each other, given enough time and the willingness to learn.

On the Okinawan side, several important cultural concepts, cloaked in satire and irony, are addressed. Saying one thing and meaning another (*honne* and *tatamae*) is crucial to understanding the Okinawan mind. Thus, when Sakini calls Colonel Purdy a "very wise man" because he can predict the weather, the audience understands that Sakini is, in fact, making fun of Purdy's ignorance of the weather patterns on the island. Language differences that influence ways of thinking are also addressed. Unlike English, the Luchuan dialect has no future tense; thus, when Sakini answers Fisby's question about how long the ride to Tobiki will take by saying, "Oh—not know until we arrive, boss," he is not merely being funny; he is reflecting a cultural difference.

Beneath the humor, the perception of Americans as wasteful is conveyed in a scene in which the jeep that is to take Fisby to Tobiki ends up carrying an old lady, her daughter, her grandchildren, some goats, much baggage, and an old man. To the villagers, it is a wasteful luxury to use the jeep only for Fisby and his staff when many needs can be met with a single trip. In numerous ways, the play conveys the message that causing someone to lose face must be avoided. Though Sakini seems to be manipulative, he also upholds his cultural orientation when he is the go-between to save face with various villagers: The old woman on the jeep is the mayor's grandmother; Fisby must receive gifts before delivering his speech; the loser of a wrestling match is declared winner, though everyone knows better.

Because Fisby does not understand the important concept of *on* (obligation), he interprets as bribery the idea of appointing as village officials those who have given him the best gifts. The precedence of the aesthetic over the pragmatic is demonstrated in the villagers' suggesting that watching the sun set is more important than meeting to learn more about democracy.

The play also speaks to a tendency of Americans to impose their customs on others without understanding the rationale for native ways. Purdy advocates impracticable requirements for the Okinawans regarding laundry. Similarly, issuing one order that will require disobeying another satirizes inept policy-making: Sakini cannot keep his oversized socks pulled up and hurry at the same time. Colonel Purdy is made to look ridiculous in other ways. His ego is deflated when he realizes that Captain Fisby, supposedly the "cream of the Army's geniuses," is in fact a misfit rejected elsewhere. Purdy makes signs for every possible situation, but he looks at a map upside down when he tells Sakini, a native of Tobiki, where it is located.

The theory of democracy is perceived differently by the American and the Okinawan: To the angry townswomen, real democracy would not allow Lotus Blossom to have all kinds of beauty enhancements that they may not also have. The true role of the geisha is not understood by Fisby; he must learn that a prostitute is not an exact counterpart. By the end of the play, misperceptions of both sides have been shared, and the well-meaning, if bungling, efforts of the Americans are complemented by the ability of the Okinawans, with a long history of occupation by foreign forces, to adapt in order to survive.

Dramatic Devices

From the outset of *The Teahouse of the August Moon*, several devices are used to make the audience transfer their thinking to Okinawa after World War II. As the curtain opens, bamboo panels suggest the Asian setting, and, although Sakini has an American face, his costume is sufficiently native for him to be accepted as Okinawan. Moreover, the fact that he is wearing ridiculously oversized army-issue shoes and socks suggests the immediate postwar setting while identifying the play as comic rather than tragic.

Sakini introduces each act by commenting to the audience on Okinawa's record of defeat in the past and on other matters that establish the need for cross-cultural understanding. His use of folk wisdom and pseudophilosophical comments in fragmented English further make clear the bicultural nature of the play, as does the use of stereotypic motions such as bowing and hand clapping. Thus, his commentary functions as the soliloquy does in some plays.

Using something of a reversal of dramatic irony, Sakini more often than not speaks in the guise of sincerity and fact, but because he uses a fallacious line of reasoning, the audience is aware that Sakini is not naïve—quite the contrary—he employs the facade of politeness in order to state what is almost the opposite of his intended meaning. In addition to introductory comments, Sakini makes numerous asides, interpretive and amusing, that allow the audience, throughout the play, to know what he, as a defeated

Okinawan, thinks of his conquerors' customs and ways of thinking, especially those having to do with democracy, government bureaucracy, and the American military forces.

In like manner, the American occupation personnel are made to perform and to react in typical, even stereotypical, American ways. Properties such as Purdy's magazine conform to the stereotype of the mindless enlisted man who does not really have to think as long as he obeys orders from above. The gradual acculturation that is taking place is evidenced from such things as having Captain Fisby put his cricket cage on top of official paperwork, and replacing his uniform with native Okinawan *geta* (wooden sandals) and kimono.

The intervals of time between scenes or acts are logical with reference to what is going on. Several days elapse to allow time for the trip to Tobiki; several weeks pass before Colonel Purdy calls Captain Fisby to receive a progress report; suitable spans of time pass before the villagers return unsuccessfully from trying to sell crafts, and time is allowed for the completion of the teahouse. Sometimes subtle devices are used to convey perceptions of the foreigner about the American. The very fact that Colonel Purdy and Captain McLean (despite his name) are quite fat suggest both the wealth and perhaps the lack of self-discipline often associated with Americans by foreigners. Likewise, the poverty of the Okinawans, by contrast, is easily perceived by the "background of sagging huts" and the fact that the Okinawans are very small.

Critical Context

By the time John Patrick wrote his Pulitzer Prize-winning play *The Teahouse of the August Moon*, based on Vern Sneider's 1951 novel, he was well established as a playwright and screenwriter. His career as a dramatic author was launched with *Hell Freezes Over* (pr. 1935). Patrick's next produced play, *The Willow and I* (pr. 1942, pb. 1943), was much admired but was not very popular. After serving as an ambulance driver with a British unit in Egypt and Syria, he drew from his military experiences to produce, in 1945, *The Hasty Heart* (pr., pb. 1945), a character drama involving a group of soldiers hospitalized behind the front lines. Two years later, Patrick produced a historical drama, *The Story of Mary Surratt* (pr., pb. 1947), which portrayed movingly the vindication of a Mrs. Surratt, who had purportedly taken part in the assassination of Abraham Lincoln and was hanged before her innocence could be established. Moving to other dramatic genres, Patrick produced two light comedies: *The Curious Savage* (pr. 1950), about an eccentric widow who hopes to help people realize foolish dreams by investing her wealth in a Happiness Fund; and *Lo and Behold!* (pr. 1951), which portrays in a fantastic manner the adventures of a Nobel Prize winner who deliberately overeats and consequently dies, only to find himself plagued by a variety of ghosts in the afterworld.

Patrick returned to a military setting in 1953 with *The Teahouse of the August Moon*. In addition to winning the Pulitzer Prize for this play, he was awarded the New York Drama Critics Award and the Tony Award, among others. Several other plays appeared during the next five years: *Good as Gold* (pr. 1957), based on a book by Alfred Toombs; *Juniper and the Pagans* (pr. 1959); *Everybody Loves Opal* (pr. 1961, pb. 1962); and *Love Is a Time of Day* (pr. 1969, pb. 1970). In 1970, a rewritten version of *The Teahouse of the August Moon* appeared, titled *Lovely Ladies, Kind Gentlemen.*

In addition to his plays, a number of Patrick's screenplays have enjoyed considerable popularity. *Three Coins in the Fountain* (1954), *Love Is a Many-Splendored Thing* (1955), *The Teahouse of the August Moon* (1956), *High Society* (1956), *Les Girls* (1957), and *The World of Suzie Wong* (1960) are among the most popular. *Les Girls* received the Screen Guild Award. It has been noted that there is a surprisingly small body of criticism on John Patrick. Reviews abound, however, to acknowledge the variety and the quality of his best work.

Sources for Further Study
Clurman, Harold. Review in *The Nation* 178 (May 15, 1954): 429-430.
Haily, Foster. Review in *New York Times*, August 14, 1955, sec. 2, p. 1.
Matlaw, Myron. "*The Teahouse of the August Moon.*" In *Modern World Drama: An Encyclopedia*. New York: Dutton, 1972.
Moe, Christian H. "John Patrick." In *Contemporary Dramatists*. 4th ed. Chicago: St. James, 1988.
Shipley, Joseph J. *Guide to Great Plays*. Washington, D.C.: Public Affairs Press, 1956.
Sneider, Vern. Review in *New York Times*, October 11, 1953, sec. 2, p. 1.
"*The Teahouse of the August Moon.*" *Theater Arts* 37 (December, 1953): 22-24.

Victoria Price

TEMPTATION

Author: Václav Havel (1936-   )
Type of plot: Social realism
Time of plot: The 1980's
Locale: Soviet Europe
First produced: 1986, at the Burgtheater, Vienna, Austria
First published: Pokoušení, 1986 (English translation, 1988)

Principal characters:
DR. HENRY FOUSTKA, a scientist
FISTULA, an invalid in retirement
THE DIRECTOR
VILMA, a scientist
THE DEPUTY DIRECTOR
MAGGIE, a secretary
DR. LIBUŠE LORENCOVA, a scientist
DR. VILÉM KOTRLÝ, a scientist
DR. ALOIS NEUWIRTH, a scientist

The Play

Temptation begins in a room of a scientific institute. The room serves several functions, creating an "impression of bureaucratic anonymity"; the furnishings and equipment appear to have been assembled by executive whimsy. Lorencova, Kotrlý, and Neuwirth are onstage when the curtain rises, lounging. They call Maggie to bring coffee. Foustka, dressed in black, arrives late for work. The others ask him about his private studies; he pretends ignorance, but Neuwirth insists. The Deputy Director enters with Petruska, who holds his hand throughout the play. After surface pleasantries, the Deputy describes the upcoming garden party. The Director enters and soon explains the need to counter growing mystical tendencies in society. Vilma arrives late, interrupting him; he finishes his remarks with an appeal for Foustka's personal support.

Scene 2 begins with Foustka conducting a ritual that is interrupted by the landlady's knocking at the door of his small, book-lined bachelor room. Foustka covers up his spell, then learns from Mrs. Houbova about his strange, odorous caller. She then sends in Fistula, a small, unflappable vagrant with bad feet. Foustka is first annoyed by the intrusion, then increasingly disturbed as Fistula's conversation suggests that he has special knowledge and supernatural connections. Fistula responds to Foustka's suspicions in several long, articulate speeches, arguing that he is not an agent provocateur but rather a minor spirit who offers himself as the object of a scientific inquiry. As a test of his powers, Fistula volunteers to cause the secretary, Maggie, to fall in love with Foustka at the garden party. Foustka protests, saying that he is faithful to his girlfriend; Fistula wonders if she is faithful in return, then leaves.

Scene 3 takes place in the garden, where the lights first reveal a pair of lovers who exchange intimate thoughts and gestures throughout the scene. Other characters dance in formal dress as Foustka joins Maggie, treating her to a philosophical meditation on the beauty of the cosmos. They are interrupted when Neuwirth asks Maggie to dance; the Director joins Foustka, taking his hand in an appeal for Foustka's opinion of him as a man. This apparent gay proposition is interrupted by the Deputy, who explains that Petruska would like a dance with the Director. Though he declines, they take him off to see a light show designed by Kotrlý. Lorencova explains to Kotrlý that he seeks advancement too blatantly; he is concerned that she may like Neuwirth more than himself. Foustka and Maggie resume their conversation, to which she responds enthusiastically. Kotrlý then interrupts to dance with Maggie; the Director returns to complete his pass, but Foustka uses his plans with Vilma to excuse himself. The Deputy approaches the Director with an invitation for drinks, which is refused. Neuwirth and Lorencova discuss Kotrlý's machinations; he is concerned that she loves Kotrlý, while she is obviously toying with both men. Foustka again resumes his cosmological seduction of Maggie, who declares her love and kisses him passionately. Vilma then appears, coolly interrupting their tryst as the curtain falls.

Vilma's boudoir is revealed in scene 4, where she and Foustka enact a scene of jealous rage. Foustka questions her about a dancer, while she dismisses the dancer's attentions as mere juvenile flattery. Finally, when Foustka threatens violence, Vilma applauds, and it is revealed that the scene was an erotic game. When Foustka confesses that these games test and disturb him, Vilma suggests that he is really only troubled by the recent encounter with the predatory Director. The doorbell rings, and Foustka admits the dancer from the jealousy scene, who delivers flowers and leaves awkwardly. Vilma goes to Foustka, pleading her love with kisses; without batting an eye, he slaps her down and kicks her.

Scene 5 is again the institute, where Foustka and Vilma, sporting her black eye, enter happily. A nervous Maggie delivers coffee as before. The other scientists come in, closely followed by the Deputy, who provides another long-winded but meaningless introduction for the Director. This time the Director approaches Kotrlý with his flirtation, then launches into a speech explaining in highly rhetorical terms the institute's betrayal by a practitioner of black magic, Foustka. When he asks for comments from the others, Maggie comes forward to vouch for Foustka's character and is promptly dismissed from her position. Foustka tries to intervene on her behalf, but in doing so he hurts her feelings and invites the Director's disdain. Foustka, rather than answering the charges, requests a fair, impartial investigation. The Director offers his assurances and approaches Kotrlý again, just as the crying Maggie crosses on her way out. When she closes the door, the chandelier crashes to the floor, and the curtain descends for the intermission.

The second half begins back in Foustka's flat, where Fistula awaits him for scene 6. Foustka expresses his surprise that Fistula has returned, while Fistula compliments him on the success with which he has carried out their projects. Foustka argues that Maggie's love and the other events of the past day were mere coincidence, but Fistula insists on his own role as catalyst until Foustka seems to relent, delivering the title theme in his description of the crimes against Maggie and Vilma as surrenders to temptation. Fistula analyzes this self-blame, describing Foustka's feelings as the "Smichovsky Compensation Syndrome," but Foustka refuses to believe him until Fistula suggests that Vilma has betrayed Foustka to the authorities. When Foustka asks what he should do next, Fistula advises only that he use his cunning in a good cause.

Scene 7, at the institute, opens with the other scientists wondering who will bring them coffee; they scarcely acknowledge Foustka when he enters, only mentioning that Maggie, having attempted suicide, is in a "psycho ward." The Deputy appears as usual for his meaningless rhetorical introduction of the Director, this time on the theme of "truth must prevail." The Director enters, giving Kotrlý the special greeting once reserved for Foustka, while Vilma enters, late again. The Director begins to question Foustka about his hermetic study. When pressed to explain his readings, experiments, and associations with magic, Foustka declares that he was engaged on an independent, undercover project not merely to denounce but to root out and eliminate black magic. The others are so taken aback that only the Deputy recovers; the Director then joins him in accepting Foustka's explanation of his work as ultimately in agreement with the official position of the institute. The Director proposes an appropriate celebration, the conversion of the upcoming garden party into a mock black mass.

Scene 8 returns to Vilma's flat, where Foustka confronts his mistress with Fistula's suggestion that she has betrayed him to the authorities. She denies the accusation, sobbing, and when he sees that he has hurt her, he pretends his questions were only a game. She then rejects him entirely, claiming to have lost respect for him since his deception at the morning hearing. She asks him to go, but Foustka, still fearing betrayal, attacks her and begins to choke her. The doorbell interrupts their struggle, and when Vilma admits the young dancer with his bouquet, Foustka slumps into an armchair, exhausted and disoriented. Vilma makes some excuses for Foustka but asks the dancer to stay.

Scene 9 takes place at Foustka's flat. The landlady warns a pacing Foustka that the suspicious-looking Fistula has returned. She likes Foustka, and does not want him to take chances on such people. Nevertheless, she shows Fistula in, and the two begin to review their arrangement. Foustka is pleased by the way he has manipulated the officials at the institute, while Fistula is annoyed that Foustka has revealed their unspoken agreement to secrecy in their collaboration. Foustka placates Fistula by explaining that he has placed himself in the position of a double agent; he can serve their relationship while throwing the institute off their track. Fistula accepts this explanation but warns Foustka that he must not betray the higher powers on this final chance. When Foustka, pleased with their new understanding, embraces Fistula, the latter leaps backward; Foustka's temperature has dropped to the frigid level of Fistula's in scene 2.

Scene 10 repeats the setting at the institute garden with minor changes. The lovers dance at the back of the scene throughout the proceedings. Foustka is onstage with them at the beginning, dressed as Faust. Lorencova enters with a broom; the Deputy comes out alone, looking for Petruska. The Director, dressed as the devil, enters holding hands with Kotrlý; they discuss fireworks, and Foustka is dismissed when he approaches them.

Vilma and the dancer enter to perform a tango; they are clearly happy together. The Director is stopped by a mysterious secretary, another recurrent piece of business; this man then embraces Lorencova. Maggie enters next, singing Ophelia's song from *Hamlet, Prince of Denmark* (pr. c. 1600-1601). Foustka tries to communicate with her, to no avail, as she quotes Hamlet and the speeches of Foustka from the garden in scene 3. The Director and Kotrlý, having a spat, are interrupted when Neuwirth cries out from some bushes; Petruska has given him a painful love bite. Foustka approaches the Director again, to offer his report, but as he does so, the others begin to circle around him.

The Director denounces Foustka, telling him that he badly underestimated the official organization, then calls Fistula out of hiding to give a report on Foustka. Fistula was a plant, and as Foustka pieces the puzzle together, the circle of others grows and tightens. Fistula explains that Foustka convicted himself through his machinations, by choosing not to recognize any higher authorities; Foustka tried to "play both ends against the middle." Vilma and the dancer perform a violent tango, as Foustka realizes that he was naïve to try to fool the devil. He explains that the real evil is the destructive confidence of a "self-regarding power" that uses science as a guise for its efforts to discredit other kinds of authority. The Director refuses to take Foustka's "banal" moral lesson seriously; his ironic applause soon turns into a general orgy of dance, music, and sulfurous smoke, from which Foustka cannot escape. The stage is finally obscured by smoke. When the fumes clear, a lone fireman appears to begin the curtain call.

Themes and Meanings

Temptation addresses the traditional themes of the Faust myth in the politicized context of Cold-War-era Soviet Europe. The limits of individual human knowledge and power remain prominent in Václav Havel's play, as do secondary themes of love and sincerity, the idea of the spirit, and the price of power. By creating a contemporary context, Havel adds a specific, concrete dimension to the themes that have been treated more universally by writers such as Christopher Marlowe, Johann Wolfgang von Goethe, and the librettists of the grand opera.

Havel's *Temptation* concerns the place of the individual, and of personal ambition, in a political world that is governed by rules that limit freedom of expression. The individual, however clever and insightful, eventually falls victim to frustrated desire when it comes into conflict with some powerful organization. Trapped by the research limitations of an institute devoted to self-confirming hypotheses and the affirmation of conventional wisdom, Foustka seeks escape not in an alternative science but on another plane of existence; with no outlet for his personal desires in the real world, he looks for one in a spiritual realm that probably does not exist at all in the concrete terms of his imaginings. Foustka's revolutionary impulse is displaced into mysticism;

his dissent becomes not an attempt to change the world, but to escape from it. The play's conclusion indicates that such an escape is illusory at best and at worst is self-destructive, impossible. In the real world of political power, no individual in a society can, with impunity, escape from the society of others. Individual knowledge is limited by the inability of one person to comprehend fully the lives of others. Those others cannot control, absolutely, the thoughts of the individual; they can, however, restrict personal choices or cast a member into the margins of social life.

Secondary themes receiving original treatment include the love story; Maggie's attraction, loyalty, and madness seem in retrospect to be quite real, caused by her susceptibility to the individual attraction and eloquence of Foustka. It is Foustka, not Maggie, who doubts the sincere power of love and refuses to accept its spiritual gift. He fails to comprehend the difference between Maggie's inexplicably ethereal devotion and Vilma's self-conscious erotic fictions.

The spiritual element in Havel's play, despite the unmasking of Fistula as an agent provocateur, remains strong. If Maggie's love is real, and the other human affections similarly authentic (the landlady's bond with Foustka for example), then the world is not composed entirely of political and sexual opportunism. Foustka also insists on the reality of evil at the end of the play, though evil is no longer conceived of as a separate spiritual order; rather, evil is the conscious abuse of power in a world where people understand that certain natural laws of justice exist but refuse to observe them.

The price of power in *Temptation* is articulated in unusual terms for a Faust treatment. Typically, Faust pays for his knowledge and pleasure—his power—with his soul. In Havel's play, the lost soul is not Foustka's but the society's. Those who ultimately embrace evil are the political officials, who commit any deception, provoke any response, in order to maintain their positions of power. The price of power remains that of spiritual integrity, yet it is the spiritual integrity of the community, not of the individual, that is lost.

Dramatic Devices

The principal dramatic device is the play's use of a known myth. *Temptation* uses a story with features that are generally known but not completely determined. Consequently, every scene, every element in the play, suggests relations with the story's sophisticated intertext, while Havel's choices are not constricted by a need to adhere to a single version of the myth. Havel's play creates meanings of its own, based on the contemporary context of the story's use, but it also generates meanings in relation to the entire tradition of Faustian works. His Fistula character is typical of the innovative possibilities, for Fistula is neither as spectacular nor as seductive as the typical Mephistopheles character of the myth; conversely, Fistula's insidious qualities help Havel to dramatize the pervasive, apparently innocuous quality of evil in Cold-War-era Soviet life.

The second dramatic device is more characteristic of Havel's work; the play uses repetition as its primary technique for establishing progressive changes. The routines at the office gradually acquire meaning as their variations accrue. The scenes in

Vilma's boudoir are played in reference to previous scenes and games. The Director repeats his attempts to seduce Foustka and Kotrlý. Against the repetitive background of scenes and routines of behavior, key moments are distinct, their differences emphasized by the sameness of their surroundings. The final costume ball could not be appreciated as a transformation, as an admission of spiritual truth, without the earlier garden party, in which evil exists beneath a veneer of bureaucratic intrigue. The repetitive structure also indicates how unlikely Foustka's efforts are to create any significant change in the system of beliefs. The society is as it was in the beginning, and owing to the repetitive structure, the projected life of the world beyond the end of the play promises no significant differences.

Finally, playing against the predictable outlines of the Faust story, Havel deliberately mystifies the surrounding action to increase the play's atmosphere of uncertainty. The institute's precise function is never determined. Fistula's identity remains questionable. Vilma's intentions are not clear, nor is the structure of her fiction and its relation to the dancer. The Director's desires are hinted, not stated; the Deputy's relation to Petruska is never resolved. Foustka's sympathetic earnestness and his structural position as the audience's guide through the play tend to substitute for any concrete information about the hero and his goals. The play maintains a nebulous quality throughout, despite giving the impression that real issues of unquestionable importance are at stake.

Critical Context

Temptation has two primary critical contexts—as a play on the Faust theme and as a play by (and possibly about) Havel. As a Faust play, the work coheres with the myth's emphasis upon the folly of personal intellectual ambition, while remaining sympathetic to the character's desire for truth. *Temptation* also repeats the myth's traditionally dim view of sexual pleasure; it is sex that drives Maggie mad, that inspires Vilma's violent imagination, and that motivates the abuses of men in power. Fortunately, Havel does not partake of the worn "eternal woman" theme but rather comments ironically upon it with the mad Gretchen figure, Maggie-turned-Ophelia.

Havel tells the Faust story more directly than does, for example, Thomas Mann in *Doktor Faustus: Das Leben des deutschen Tonsetzers Adrian Leverkühn, erzählt von einem Freunde* (1947; *Doctor Faustus: The Life of the German Composer Adrian Leverkühn as Told by a Friend*, 1948), yet he shares with Mann an attempt to use the myth to examine the troubled political situation of his country. The sexual politics of *Temptation* bear a clear resemblance to the common "government as brothel" metaphor in contemporary European writing; references to writers such as Jean Genet exist alongside allusions to a specifically Central European body of works: the fireman's reference to the film *Hoří, má panenko* (1967; *The Firemen's Ball*, 1968), by Miloš Forman, Jaroslav Papoušek, and Ivan Passer, and *Požár v suterénu* (pr., pb. 1974; fire in the basement), by Pavel Kohout, or the tango's relation to Sławomir Mrożek's *Tango* (pb. 1964; English translation, 1966). In accord with *Temptation*'s Faustian context, this government is not merely corrupt but essentially evil. In that regard,

Havel's indictment is more firmly based in traditional humanism and is more severe than the satirical writing that was a normal political style in Soviet Europe.

As a play by Havel, *Temptation* has importance as an extension of previous themes and as a personal statement. Havel's first independently written play, *Zahradní slavnost* (pr., pb. 1963; *The Garden Party*, 1969), features an act 2 setting much like the garden scene that transforms into *Temptation*'s Walpurgis Night. The play also echoes the absurd intellectual optimism of the computer scientists in *Ztížená možnost soustředění* (pb. 1968; *The Increased Difficulty of Concentration*, 1969); Foustka even bears some resemblance to the hopelessly entangled hero of that satire. However, *Temptation* also repeats the frustratingly circular power politics of *Spiklenci* (pr. 1974; the conspirators) and the evasive rhetoric of Havel's third Vaněk play, *Protest* (pr. 1978; English translation, 1980).

As with *Largo desolato* (pb. 1985; English translation, 1987), the story tends to inhibit the formal logic to some extent. This is not the first time Havel has used a known story for his plot; his *Žebrácká opera* (pr. 1975; *The Beggar's Opera*, 1976) used John Gay's fable as the basis for a nonmusical play that focuses, like *Temptation*, on the unscrupulous behavior of those in power. The most important difference in *Temptation* is its changed tone. The play is neither particularly humorous nor particularly bitter (as are the post-invasion plays). *Temptation* provides a compelling metaphor for the place of the exceptional individual in a limited society. Neither the hero nor his opponents are completely good or evil, yet their situation seems to be a fair evaluation of the way the philosophy of government in Soviet Europe affected the freedom and creative vision (good or bad) of unusually gifted people.

The play relates, at this individual level, most distinctly to Havel's personal life. The tricks which the institute employs to entrap Foustka are like the tricks documented by Havel in his notes on house arrest, "The Age of Chicanery" (1979). The problems of individual expression, noted in essay form in Havel's "Stories and Totalitarianism," link Foustka to the drama of Havel's own political life in communist-era Eastern Europe. The primary theme, temptation, cuts across the play and Havel's life in two ways. Every time Havel or Foustka is tried, he must decide whether to submit to the temptations—the rewards—of intellectual recantation and political cooperation. If Havel yielded, his ability to work in a theater would be more secure, or he might be allowed to visit the West with a guaranteed permission to return or be allowed any number of other pleasures and privileges. At the same time, he had to resist the added temptation to pursue martyrdom selfishly, to allow his personal difficulties to distract attention from the Czech political issues of freedom and responsible government. Kopriva in *Largo desolato* shows how such a temptation can induce paralysis. Foustka demonstrates how the hero as collaborator ultimately fails, whether collaborating with East or West, the underworld or the political machine, because any such gesture comes at the cost of individuality. As Havel remarked in his comments on *Temptation*, "The truth is not only that which one thinks, but also under what circumstances, to whom, why, and how one says it." At the end of the play, Foustka simply disappears, consumed by the smoke.

Sources for Further Study

Goetz-Stankiewicz, Markéta. *The Silenced Theatre: Czech Playwrights Without a Stage*. Buffalo, N.Y.: University of Toronto Press, 1979.

_____, ed. *The Vaněk Plays: Four Authors, One Character*. Vancouver: University of British Columbia Press, 1987.

Havel, Václav. *Letters to Olga: June 1979-September 1982*. Translated by Paul Wilson. New York: Knopf, 1988.

Keane, John. *Václav Havel: A Political Tragedy in Six Acts*. New York: Harper Basic, 2000.

Kriseova, Eda. *Václav Havel: The Authorized Biography*. Collingdale, Pa.: Diane, 1998.

Mestrovic, Marta. "From Prison, a Playwright Yearns for a Stage." *New York Times*, April 9, 1989, p. H5.

Trensky, Paul I. *Czech Drama Since World War II*. White Plains, N.Y.: M. E. Sharpe, 1978.

Vladislav, Jan, ed. *Václav Havel: Or, Living in Truth*. London: Faber, 1987.

Michael L. Quinn

TERRA NOVA

Author: Ted Tally (1952-   )
Type of plot: Psychological; history; memory play
Time of plot: Winter, 1911-1912
Locale: Antarctica and London
First produced: 1977, at the Yale Repertory Theater, New Haven Connecticut
First published: 1981

> *Principal characters:*
> ROBERT FALCON SCOTT, an English explorer
> ROALD AMUNDSEN, a Norwegian explorer
> KATHLEEN, Scott's wife
> WILSON, a doctor in Scott's expedition team
> BOWERS,
> OATES, and
> EVANS, other members of Scott's expedition team

The Play

The play opens with a bare stage set in the winter of 1912. A series of ten rear-projected slides depict the journey of Robert Falcon Scott's ship, the *Terra Nova*, to Antarctica. A weary Scott sits writing, speaking the words as he writes. Forty-one years old, he has lost the race to the Pole and considers himself a failure. Roald Amundsen, the Norwegian explorer who reached the Pole before Scott, appears throughout the play to both taunt and debate the Englishman. In many ways, Amundsen functions as Scott's conscience, articulating Scott's internal doubts. With the exception of the banquet scene that opens act 2, Amundsen appears only to Scott. Kathleen, Scott's wife, is a compellingly intelligent artist; she also appears only to Scott. This is a memory play, a mixture of the expedition narrative and Scott's last memories.

Amundsen enters and introduces Scott to an audience of Royal Society members, who have gathered to honor the explorers. Scott, although confused as past and present bleed together, explains to the audience the difference between his and Amundsen's strategies and ethics. Scott will train and travel on foot both to and from the Pole, hauling a one-thousand-pound sledge without the aid of dogs. Amundsen will use dogs, slaughtering the animals when they are no longer of use. During this scene, Scott's wife, Kathleen, enters and reveals that she is pregnant with Scott's son. Scott's men, Oates, Bowers, Wilson, and Evans, enter hauling the heavy sledge. Oates is a hardened soldier, Bowers is an optimist, Wilson is a principled doctor, and Evans, the largest and strongest of the men, is the first to show symptoms of physical breakdown. It is the beginning of the last leg of their journey.

Kathleen reenters. She and Scott have been married for two years and have a young son. This scene delineates the differences between Kathleen and Scott. Kathleen's artistic tastes are seemingly in opposition to Scott's withdrawn personality and his obsessive drive to reach the Pole. Their differences, as Ted Tally points out, complement one another. Scott's men enter and set up their tent. It is the seventy-fifth day of the journey, and they are twenty-seven days from the Pole. Their rations are running low and Evans has a deep, unattended gash in his frostbitten hand that is becoming gangrenous. Nevertheless, the men joke in the face of possible death, demonstrating compassion and bravery despite the mounting tension.

Amundsen appears and discusses Scott's progress: Evans is ill, facing snow blindness and eventual madness. When Amundsen advocates leaving Evans, Scott concurs, confronting Evans with the accusation that he has put his own ambitions over the good of the team. As if to highlight Evans's foolishness, Amundsen plants the Norwegian flag at the South Pole, becoming the first human to set foot on the southernmost tip of the globe. Scott and his men also reach the Pole, only to find the Norwegian's artifacts. Scott and his men arrange themselves for a group picture as Scott speaks of the impending end of his life and the end of his heroic dreams of glory. The lights ascend on a rear-projected slide of the men. Amundsen enters and joins the men onstage as they pose. The lights fade, leaving only the slide of the historical photograph of the Scott expedition at the Pole.

Act 2 opens with a hanging chandelier and a lavish dining table. Scott and his men enter and greet each other as if for the first time. This is an imagined reunion in which the lavish food and wine ordered by the men from Amundsen (dressed as a French waiter) represent Scott's desperate yearning for their survival. Amundsen exits, reenters in arctic gear, and helps Scott into his arctic clothing. Scott's men also reenter dressed for the Antarctic. Evans walks with difficulty, his mind beginning to fail.

Kathleen enters. It is her first private meeting with Scott after their introduction. Scott's reveals that he has been a navy man since the age of thirteen and knows little else. He is, Kathleen says, rock hard on the outside but a haunted dreamer inside. Bowers, Wilson, and Oates enter with the sledge, Amundsen perched on top. The men know they have failed and fear the public will turn on them, making the navy look ridiculous. Evans enters as the other men exit. His hands are purple and blackened with blood poisoning. He is raving mad. Scott and his men reenter as Evans convulses, collapses, and dies. In tableau, Scott cradles Evans in his arms. Kathleen enters and asks her husband to say goodnight to their son. Scott cradles the dead Evans, a pictorial metaphor that produces an equivalency between Scott's polar and domestic families.

The next scene is set two weeks after Evans dies. The men are returning from the Pole, forty miles from the relief station. Bowers is snow-blind and Oates limps on gangrenous feet. Although a treacherous storm is forming, Scott will not leave the failing Oates. Against Wilson's wishes, Scott divides the morphine for each man to use for suicide as needed. Scott is about to administer a lethal dose to Oates when the dying man becomes conscious, states that he wishes to die, and staggers off into the blinding storm. As Amundsen points out, this is the central moment in Scott's life. *In extremis*, it is not the race to the Pole that is the true test of his ideals but rather his moral choices in the face of death. He rejects suicide as the easy way out. It is the

141st day of the expedition, and they are only eleven miles from safety but are halted by a blizzard, unable to move. Scott writes to the wives of his men and repeats the words from his journal that opened the play: "The causes of the disaster are these. . . . "

Kathleen enters and is informed of her husband's death. Amundsen, on the opposite side of the stage, tells Scott of the Great War (World War I) and how it has changed the world. Oates and Evans enter in civilian clothing, restored to life. The final dialogue represents a patchwork of Scott's last thoughts. Loving and proud, Kathleen mourns: Amundsen introduces him to the Royal Society. Oates, Bowers, and Amundsen echo the pessimistic words already articulated during the play. As the wind crescendos, Scott abruptly banishes these thoughts and all but Amundsen exit. Alone with Scott, Amundsen delivers a Viking eulogy and exits. Scott, now completely alone, writes the last words in his journal, praising the endurance and courage of his men, a tale that he knows will stir the hearts of all Englishmen.

Themes and Meanings

Literary critic Robert J. Andreach calls *Terra Nova* a spiritual journey, an existential quest that Tally created by altering some aspects of the historical record. For example, Scott used both ponies and dogs during the initial stages of the expedition. When the ponies were no longer of use, they were shot and fed to the dogs. The omission of this fact from the play creates a greater moral opposition between Amundsen's brutal realism and Scott's heroic idealism. In the vast wastes of Antarctica with the race lost, Scott embodies the human condition—a man adrift in a meaningless universe. However, in a land hostile to all life, Scott and his men retain their humanity, and it is this fact, as Amundsen points out, and not the success of their journey that gives meaning to their lives and deaths.

The nineteenth century was the heroic age of exploration, and Scott was a remnant of its adventurers. Through the character of Amundsen, the play examines the relationship between the rhetoric of heroism and the actual experience. By 1912, when Scott's expedition reached its end, one century was dying and another was being born. The cynicism voiced by Amundsen during the play foreshadows the ideological shift from the nineteenth to the twentieth century. Scott's doomed notion of the British ideal of nobility and sportsmanlike ethics is the last gasp of Victorian optimism in a world on the brink of war and moral chaos. The inscription of the Boer War through the character of Oates etches Tally's point in greater clarity. Britain's standing as a world power, achieved through rapid colonialism, reached its height during Queen Victoria's reign. While Scott and his men die in Antarctica, the sun is setting on both the British Empire and the imperialist ethics that made that empire great.

Scott emerges as a tragic hero. Deeply flawed psychologically, withdrawn, unable to connect closely with people, and obsessively ambitious, Scott is also courageous and caring. *Terra Nova* is, above all, a fascinating psychological study of a man consumed by ambition. Because the facts of the expedition are well known, the psychological tension created by Scott's struggles and sacrifice forms the play's core.

Dramatic Devices

This is a memory play that occurs within the mind of one character, and several dramatic devices are employed to keep the narrative coherent. The bare stage allows for easy shifts in time and place. The tent, sledge, dining table, and chandelier, the only large sets employed, are quickly shifted onstage and offstage by the characters. The slides, lighting, and sound effects complement the shifting props, marking transitions between the polar narrative and Scott's internal thoughts. Spotlights separate Kathleen (and often Amundsen) from the central action. The rear screen slides function as visual exposition, giving the audience details of the historical time and place. The scrim also serves as a device for the dramatic use of silhouette. The entrance of the characters into a scene already in progress communicates the fluidity of time and place that marks the entirety of the play. Because the play dramatizes a well-known event, it makes effective use of dramatic irony: The audience's knowledge of history inflects the dialogue of the men who are about to die. Tally maintains a sense of tension through the existential uncertainties that Scott experiences, his relationship to the other characters, and the physical horror of their collective experience.

Critical Context

Ted Tally graduated from Yale College and received his masters of fine arts degree in playwriting from the Yale School of Drama. During the 1970's and most of the 1980's, he honed his playwriting skills in theater. *Terra Nova* was first produced for the Yale Repertory Theatre, winning both an Obie in New York and the *Drama-Logue* award in Los Angeles. The play is loosely based on Scott's journal, which was found along with his frozen body. Regional theaters regularly produce *Terra Nova*, and Tally adapted the play for television in 1984.

Tally is primarily known for his screenwriting. His best-known work is his 1991 screenplay of Thomas Harris's novel, *The Silence of the Lambs* (1988), for which he won an Academy Award for best adapted screenplay. *The Silence of the Lambs*, like *Terra Nova*, articulates the inner psychology of its central character, Federal Bureau of Investigation agent Clarisse, who, like Scott, must come to terms with her own ambition and psychological fears. It is interesting to note that both *The Silence of the Lambs* and *Terra Nova* contain gender issues that suggest possibilities for further exploration. Both Clarisse and Kathleen are intelligent and strong women operating successfully in male-dominated milieus.

Sources for Further Study

Andreach, Robert J. "Tally's *Terra Nova:* From Historical Journals to Existential Journey." *Twentieth Century Literature: A Scholarly and Critical Journal* 35 (1989): 65-73.

Huntford, Roland. *The Last Place on Earth.* New York: Atheneum, 1985.

Tally, Ted. *Terra Nova.* New York: Dramatists Play Service, 1982.

Stephanie Moss

THAT CHAMPIONSHIP SEASON

Author: Jason Miller (1939-2001)

Type of plot: Psychological

Time of plot: 1972

Locale: Lackawanna Valley, Pennsylvania

First produced: 1972, at the New York Shakespeare Festival Public Theatre, New York City

First published: 1972

Principal characters:

> JAMES DALEY, a junior high school principal
>
> TOM DALEY, his younger brother
>
> GEORGE SIKOWSKI, the mayor of the town
>
> PHIL ROMANO, a wealthy businessman in coal strip mining
>
> THE COACH, the architect of the local high school's basketball triumph twenty years earlier
>
> NORMAN SHARMEN, the Jewish candidate for mayor

The Play

The Coach, about sixty years old, has lived in his nostalgia-filled home nearly all of his life. In a ritual that he has continued for several years, he and four of his "boys," as he still calls them, celebrate the twentieth anniversary of their victory in the 1952 Pennsylvania state high school basketball championship. Prominently displayed in the parlor, which provides the sole setting for the play, is the large silver trophy award with the players' names engraved in it.

George, the current mayor of the town and a none-too-bright former insurance salesman, is facing a reelection battle against a popular reform candidate, Norman Sharmen, who is Jewish. Since George won four years earlier with a mere thirty-two votes—thanks to the Coach's spirited support—the mayor expects a difficult campaign. Thus, the get-together is also an occasion to map out campaign strategy and solidify the group's backing. The latter includes the expected financial contribution of Phil, a shady but successful businessman engaged in the toxic practice of open-coal strip mining, a business facilitated by George, who, as mayor, has permitted Phil to have access to lucrative land tracts. Phil seeks release from personal stress by driving his sports car at breakneck speed on the highway and by philandering with various girls and matrons in town, including Marion, George's wife.

The Coach continues to treat his thirty-eight-year-old "boys" as he has done since the championship season, trying to keep alive the old basketball-court spirit. In fact, even though forced into early retirement for hitting an offensive student, the Coach's still uses maxims about striving for excellence, enduring pain, building teamwork, and accepting nothing less than success. Initially the group relives the final ten seconds of the championship game, when, one point behind, the absent fifth player, Martin Roads, scored the winning basket. Martin left town soon after, apparently feeling ashamed and guilty for following the single-minded Coach's order to foul the star black player on the opposing team: Martin was unable to persuade the Coach to return the trophy.

However, soon the magic of the evening is broken as Phil starts to inventory George's blunders as mayor: higher taxes, more unemployment, an unpleasant garbage strike, and worst of all, an incident involving an elephant that George acquired for the town zoo. The elephant turned out to have been ailing and died one month later. It took ten days to figure out how to bury it, at considerable expense.

With George and the Coach out of earshot, James Daley, who feels both frustrated with the sacrifices he has made for his family, including his ailing father, and insignificant, having attained only the position of school principal, now aspires to become George's new school superintendent and eventually to achieve even greater political success. He is George's current campaign manager and takes Phil to task for wavering in his loyalty to George. However, James suggests that with Phil's financial backing he, himself, could run as an alternative candidate against Sharmen.

George, now back, reveals that he holds a trump card. He and the Coach have discovered that Sharmen's uncle, now deceased, was a Hollywood writer blacklisted for invoking the Fifth Amendment during Republican Senator Joseph McCarthy's hearings on communism in the 1950's. Phil laughs this off as outdated and irrelevant. Annoyed with Phil's continued hesitancy about George, James reveals to George the affair Phil is having with his George's wife. George grabs the loaded hair-triggered gun from a rack on the wall and threatens Phil.

In act 2 a calmer George hands over the weapon to the Coach. Phil continues to insist that George cannot win reelection and then accepts James's challenge to call up Sharmen and offer him financial support. Sharmen laughs off both Phil's offer and his suggestion of the alleged communist relative. At this point, Tom rolls down the stairs from the upstairs bathroom, unable to handle all the liquor he has consumed. Even though he is a drifter and an alcoholic, financially supported by his brother James, Tom is the only member of the group outside Martin who clearly recognizes the fraudulent nature of their 1952 victory and the emptiness of their lives.

The Coach then tries to explain to James that for former team-mate George to have a chance at re-election, he has to hire a professional Philadelphia public relations firm rather than use James as campaign manager. James threatens to publicize Phil's affair with the mayor's wife all over town. George gets so upset that, unable to make it to the bathroom, he vomits into the nearest receptacle, the award trophy.

In act 3, after George is taken upstairs and the trophy is cleaned up, the Coach urges them all to keep the faith. He convinces the returning George that he must "pay the price" to keep Phil's financial backing. George reports that he has called his wife, who told him that she had done it all to con campaign money out of Phil. George seems to believe this even though Marion was known to be "fast" in high school. The inebriated Tom repeats that the championship season had been a lie and that they are all whooping cranes en route to extinction.

The Coach now replays the recorded radio narration of the final moments of their championship game, which ends with the roar of the crowd. This exorcises the demons out of the shattered team. They sing the Fillmore High School song, make up, and plan their joint support of George's campaign. The play ends with the team's ritual of having their photographs taken around the silver cup trophy.

Themes and Meanings

That Championship Season is about middle America, its cult of mediocrity, and the way in which it views success. Jason Miller emphasizes that the American Dream has become a nightmare by focusing on the emptiness of the lives of men, who try to preserve their friendships and their egos despite the compromises they have made. The play dramatizes a whole sweep of contemporary life. As the celebratory evening progresses along with the drinking, the players' masks and inhibitions become transparent. Their exposed lives are a metaphor for an America in decay, a point which the Coach continues to emphasize.

Despite the bombastic chatter about the glorious championship game and the desperate efforts, urged by the Coach, to recover the team spirit, it becomes clear that these men are insecure and bewildered, each seeking his own redemption but finding none. Only the alcoholic Tom and the absent Martin seem to understand that the prize was not worth the hateful competition. When the Coach's rallying speech tells them that "lose" is not in their vocabulary because he made them all winners, the audience understands that the opposite is true: They have lost the game of life, which neither their rasping revelations nor their boozy camaraderie can conceal. They cling to the past as the celebration degenerates into a series of brutal confrontations and recriminations over race, ethnicity, religion, and women, as the narrowness and the shabbiness of their empty lives is revealed. In fact, it is their beloved, slogan-slinging Coach who put these bigoted and McCarthyite ideas into their heads, including the belief that winning in sports and life is everything.

Dramatic Devices

The Coach's parlor reeks of nostalgia. The bachelor's faded, old-fashioned living room—the single set in the play—is richly evocative. There is a Tiffany lampshade, a Stromberg-Carlson radio console, and a gun rack on the wall. Framed pictures of distinguished Americans are in evidence, notably those of Presidents Theodore Roosevelt and John F. Kennedy, as well as that of Senator McCarthy, the anti-communist crusader. The large silver trophy is on the table.

The dialogue is fast-paced, sharp, bawdy, and often funny, with its locker-room humor reflecting Jason Miller's gift for language and his sensitivity to the dynamics of character. The numerous racial, ethnic, and anti-Semitic slurs betray a conservative, even reactionary, bent. There is Jew-baiting, communist hunting, and money-shuffling in a town full of bigotry and shady dealings. Miller's grasp of small-town mediocrity and attitudes may stem from his formative years in Scranton, Pennsylvania.

The actors move in and out of the downstairs living room where all the action takes place. Thus, only Tom and George are present at the play's opening as the other characters are away buying fried chicken and more booze for the party. In subsequent scenes, the Coach, who recently endured surgery and suffers sudden pain, and George, upset by the play's sordid revelations, are taken to the bedroom upstairs.

Critical Context

Jason Miller wrote little for the theater since he spent more time as an actor and a poet than as a playwright. Accordingly, he attained his reputation in drama nearly exclusively from the acclaim given to *That Championship Season*, his second full-length play, which won the New York Drama Critics Circle Award, several Tony Awards, and the 1973 Pulitzer Prize in drama.

Miller's themes found in the play can be traced closely to his Roman Catholic background and education (the Jesuit-affiliated University of Scranton, Pennsylvania, and Catholic University of America in Washington, D.C.), his predilection for athletics and sports, and his life in the kind of small mining town featured in the drama. His first but unsuccessful full-length play, *Nobody Hears a Broken Drum* (pr. 1970, pb. 1971), also deals with a Pennsylvania coal town, this time set in the nineteenth century.

That Championship Season follows in the tradition of Arthur Miller's *Death of a Salesman* (pr., pb. 1949) since both works are about individuals who refuse to examine the moral bankruptcy of their lives and their perverted values of competition and success. Eugene O'Neill's *The Iceman Cometh* (pr., pb. 1946) is also similar in its theme about the false promises of a pipe dream that motivates individuals and prevents them from seeing themselves as they really are. In the same vein, Jason Miller's play calls on the strip-all, tell-all realist approaches by playwrights Paddy Chayefsky, Edward Albee, Tennessee Williams, Henrik Ibsen, and Mart Crowley.

Sources for Further Study

Guernsey, Otis L., Jr., ed. *"That Championship Season."* In *The Best Plays of 1971-1972*. New York: Dodd, Mead, 1972.

Kim, Yun-cheol. "Degradation of the American Success Ethic: *Death of a Salesman*, *That Championship Season*, and *Glengarry Glen Ross*." *Journal of English Language and Literature* 37 (Spring, 1991): 233-248.

Miller, Jason. "On the Set: An Interview with Jason Miller." *The New Yorker* 48 (May 20, 1972): 33.

Shelton, Frank W. "Sports and the Competitive Ethic: *Death of a Salesman* and *That Championship Season*." *Ball State University Forum* 20, no. 2 (1979): 17-21.

Simon, John. *"That Championship Season."* *Hudson Review* 25 (1972): 616-625.

Vanderwerken, David L. "'We Owe It All to You, Coach': Teaching *That Championship Season*." *Aethlon: The Journal of Sports Literature* 14 (Fall, 1996): 241-245.

Peter B. Heller

THREE TALL WOMEN

Author: Edward Albee (1928-   )
Type of plot: Absurdist
Time of plot: The 1980's
Locale: An affluent dwelling, presumably in New England
First produced: 1991, at the English Theatre, Vienna, Austria
First published: 1994

> *Principal characters:*
> A, a ninety-two-year-old woman, well dressed but physically and
> mentally compromised
> B, her fifty-two-year-old secretary and caretaker
> C, a twenty-six-year-old female attorney's representative
> THE BOY, a twenty-three-year-old "preppie"

The Play

The action of *Three Tall Women* occurs during two acts set in the bedroom of A, a once-proud woman, who now, at age ninety-two, shows many of the symptoms of Alzheimer's disease or some related illness associated with aging. She is forgetful, suspicious, at times hostile, and given to circular conversations. Joining her in her bedroom are B, her fifty-two-year-old secretary and caretaker, and C, the twenty-six-year-old representative of A's attorney, there to sort out some of A's financial affairs.

A is convinced that people are trying to rob her. She has reached the point when she must dig into her principal to maintain her standard of living. She enhances her income by selling some of her jewelry but she does not live under a dark cloud of abject poverty. When she complains that she is not made of money, C, presumably in a position to know, contests the statement. A still can employ a secretary and a chauffeur, who figure tangentially in her death scene.

The only person onstage besides the three women is a young man, a "preppie." He appears from the shadows early in the second act and sits on A's bed, touching her hand, giving her a peck on the cheek, but saying not a word to her or to any of the others. He is the young Edward Albee, who, in actuality, had a strained relationship with his affluent adoptive mother and who, in real life, arrived in her hospital room only an hour after she died.

The three women in the play are actually a single woman at various stages of life. A is sharp-tongued, often uninhibited in what she says, and defensive, yet at times vulnerable, showing the sort of vulnerability often born of insecurity or fear. B, on the other hand, is level-headed, at times sympathetic. She serves as a buffer between the defensive A and the impatient, often intolerant C, who, through much of the play, demonstrates strenuous denial. A annoys C, who does not mask her annoyance, which is born of her subconscious realization that everyone ages and that, in time, if she lives long enough, she will evolve into A. Several times C points to A condescendingly and vows that she will not become "that," as she impersonally puts it. Although at times she robs A of her very humanity by her statements of denial, C is frightened by her perception of what her future might portend.

During the first act, A is often irrational, her mind wandering, her conversation circular as reflected in some of her speeches: "How couldn't he be thirty years younger than me when I'm thirty years older than he is? He's said it over and over. Every time he comes to see me. What is today?" By the second act, however, A is considerably more rational and lucid. In her long monologue recording her premonition of her own death, her long-term memory is clear, as is often the case with those suffering from senile psychosis.

In a memorable monologue, Albee has A recount exactly the actual circumstances of the death of his own mother, of his arriving in her hospital room one hour after her death, and of his giving her what he identifies as an obligatory kiss on her forehead, strictly for the benefit of those with her when she died, her secretary and chauffeur. In this play, and in this monologue particularly, Albee achieves a personal catharsis that marks a final ending to his strained relationship with his adoptive mother.

Themes and Meanings

Albee, in the play's introduction, acknowledges the drama's autobiographical elements:

> I knew my subject—my adoptive mother, whom I knew from my infancy . . . until her death over sixty years later. . . . I harbor no ill-will toward her; it is true I did not like her much, could not abide her prejudices, her loathings, her paranoias, but I did admire her pride, her sense of self.

Although he says that in her last twenty years almost no one could abide his mother, in the play, he captures the qualities in her that he grudgingly admires, although he does not evade those qualities that he found repugnant.

Although it concentrates on death and dying, *Three Tall Women* is thematically about the inevitable changes that take place in humans as they age. Albee's three women are concerned with what they know, how they know it, and when they knew it. Albee gives each woman a lengthy monologue in which she considers when she was happiest in life. The responses to this question pose another clear question: Do people learn from their experiences?

It is clear that the once hopeful woman C has turned into a cynical, hardened, embittered crone. C represents what A once was, but in her denial that she will ever become like A, one realizes that she is already headed irretrievably in that direction. The intermediate stage, represented by B, hovers between the two extremes, but there is no escaping the inevitability of the sort of change that has transformed C into the old woman whom Albee presents.

The silent son, who appears in the second act, is nonjudgmental. He is present only to witness an event, the death of a mother for whom he has no deep feeling. He reveals through his facial expressions a degree of compassion but no real love for this old woman who lies on her bed in the final hours of her life. Her life has been devoid of love and now is filled with the pervasive self-deprecation that accounts for her cynicism.

There are no winners among the characters in *Three Tall Women*. Time is the only winner, and its booty is an unhappy one. As Albee portrays it, time chips away at one's personhood and robs people of their dignity, passages that are reflected in A's weakened physical condition, in the broken arm that her surgeon wants to amputate, in her incontinence, and in her utter dependence upon others. This once strong woman, who rode horses and managed a household, has now almost reverted to infancy, unable to care for herself. Her suspicions are the product of her fear that she will outlive her resources, although, according to C's comments about A's financial situation, this fear is unrealistic. Her deeper concern is merely her progressive fear of losing her independence. In the end, as A concludes her monologue about what was the happiest moment of her life, she proclaims, "Yes; I know! (*To the audience*) I was talking about . . . what: coming to the end of it, yes. So. There it is. You asked after all. That's the happiest moment. (*A looks to C and B, puts her hand out, takes theirs*) When it's all done. When we stop. When we can stop."

At this point in the play, Albee brings about a catharsis in his audiences and causes those who see the play to sympathize with A, Albee's real-life adoptive mother, Frankie, for whom, according to Albee's own statement, few people had any abiding sympathy. If the play helped Albee achieve a personal catharsis, a peace with a troubled past, it led many people in his audiences to their own similar personal catharses.

Dramatic Devices

The most obvious dramatic device Albee employs in *Three Tall Women* is in assigning mere letters of the alphabet to the three principals in the play, who are never referred to by names. A, B, and C, in descending order of age, are representative of one person, although each has a separate identity—an aged dowager, her secretary and caretaker, and an attorney's assistant. Assigning these women letter designations impersonalizes them. The loss of personhood that results in A's cynicism and defensiveness is emphasized by Albee's decision not to name his characters.

Perhaps the most startling dramatic device Albee uses occurs at the beginning of the second act. B and C are in A's bedroom. A figure in the bed shows every sign of being dead. Before long, however, A emerges from stage left, very much alive. The figure that B and C have been looking at in the bed is a mannequin wearing a death mask that resembles A. The emergent A is more rational than she was in act 1.

Although B and C wear clothing different from what they wore in the first act, A is dressed exactly as she was at the beginning of the play. The change in clothing suggests a passage of time, but the preservation of A's clothing implies that nothing has changed, that A's future remains much as it was in act 1.

The dramatic unity of place here represents the confinement of a once vital woman who has turned into A at age ninety-two. The setting becomes a trap much as the confined setting in Albee's play *Who's Afraid of Virginia Woolf?* (pb., pr. 1962) was a trap. At this point Albee also introduces The Boy into the play, reminiscent of the absent and probably fictional son of George and Martha in *Who's Afraid of Virginia Woolf?* In both instances, audiences learn about these characters indirectly. One never appears; the other, when he appears, does not speak.

Critical Context

When he wrote *Three Tall Women*, Albee's celebrity had faded. The success of such earlier plays as *The Zoo Story* (pr. 1959, pb. 1960), *The Sandbox* (pr., pb. 1960), and his most notable critical triumph, *Who's Afraid of Virginia Woolf?*, was eclipsed by a series of plays that received critical condemnation, notably *Tiny Alice* (pr. 1964, pb. 1965), *A Delicate Balance* (pr., pb. 1966), *Box and Quotations from Chairman Mao Tse-Tung* (pr. 1968, pb. 1969), and *The Lady from Dubuque* (pr., pb. 1980).

As a result of these failures, Albee had difficulty finding anyone willing to produce *Three Tall Women*. Finally, after playwright and director Glyn O'Malley encouraged Albee to submit the play to Vienna's English Theater, the play was accepted for its Vienna premier solely on the basis of the first act. The second act was not yet written and did not exist when Albee flew to Vienna for rehearsals. He finished the play in a hotel room, writing under considerable pressure.

The Vienna premier was promising, although the reviews were mixed. Nevertheless, some American producers, who flew to Vienna to see the play, found it far superior to Albee's work of the prior decades. Although he still failed to find a New York producer willing to bring the play to Broadway, Albee's play generated interest from Lawrence Sacarow, the founder and artistic director of the River Arts Repertory in Woodstock, New York, where it had its first production in the United States. Here it played to packed houses, justifying a one-week extension of the play's run. The drama, although it did not play on Broadway, went on to win a Pulitzer Prize in drama. It redeemed Albee's reputation at a time when it was in need of redemption.

Sources for Further Study

Brustein, Robert. "The Rehabilitation of Edward Albee." *New Republic* 210 (April 4, 1994): 26-28.

Evans, Greg. "Three Tall Women." *Variety* 354 (February 14, 1994): 61-62.

Gussow, Mel. *Edward Albee, a Singular Journey: A Biography.* New York: Simon and Schuster, 1999.

Henry, William A., III. "Albee Is Back." *Time* 147 (February 24, 1994): 64.

Paolucci, Anna. *From Tension to Tonic: The Plays of Edward Albee.* Wilmington, Del.: Griffon House Press, 2000.

Simon, John. "Theater." *New York* 27 (December 19-26, 1994): 128-130.

R. Baird Shuman

THE TIDINGS BROUGHT TO MARY

Author: Paul Claudel (1868-1955)
Type of plot: Verse drama; psychological
Time of plot: The fifteenth century
Locale: France
First produced: 1912, at the Théâtre Malakoff, Paris
First published: L'Annonce faite à Marie, 1912 (English translation, 1916)

> *Principal characters:*
> ANNE VERCORS, a sixty-year-old French landowner
> ELISABETH, his wife
> VIOLAINE, his older daughter
> MARA, his younger daughter
> PIERRE DE CRAON, a master mason
> JACQUES HURY, a foster son of Vercors

The Play

The Tidings Brought to Mary begins with a prologue, set late at night in the large barn at Combernon, the home of the Vercors family. At the back of the barn is a large, heavily bolted door, on which are painted figures of Saint Peter and Saint Paul. Pierre de Craon enters on horseback. Then Violaine Vercors steps out from behind a pillar. Citing the unseemliness of their being alone together at that hour, Pierre urges her to leave, but she refuses, reminding him tauntingly of an earlier occasion when he attacked her with a knife but failed in his attempt on her virtue. Asking her forgiveness, Pierre insists that it was the only time he had ever acted in such a way, and it is clear that Violaine believes him, for she assures him that she has not betrayed his secret.

In the dialogue that follows, Pierre reveals the reason for his year-long absence from Combernon. The day after his attack on Violaine, he had discovered a sign of leprosy. Because his work building churches is so important, he has been permitted to continue, keeping his disease a secret but remaining distant from his workmen. He has come to Combernon to open the door which leads to Monsanvierge, the holy mountain above, where lives an order of nuns. It is Violaine who goes to the heavy door and turns the key for him. She tells Pierre that she will soon be married to the man she loves, Jacques Hury. Pierre admits his own love for her and his bitterness about his affliction, which makes him an outcast. In pity, Violaine kisses him; in the background, her sister, Mara Vercors, watches.

The first act is set in the Vercors kitchen. Anne Vercors is discussing his plans with his wife, Elisabeth Vercors. He wishes to give his daughter Violaine in marriage to Jacques Hury, the poor boy whom he has reared and whom he thinks of as a son. He also intends to make a pilgrimage to Jerusalem. Even though Mara Vercors tells her mother that she loves Jacques desperately and threatens to kill herself if she cannot have him, Anne bestows his daughter Violaine on Jacques.

The second act takes place two weeks later. Anne is gone, and Elisabeth has noticed strange behavior in her older daughter, particularly when she speaks of the forthcoming marriage. Soon the reason for her behavior becomes evident: Violaine tells Jacques that although she loves him, she can never let him touch her. She then shows him the signs of leprosy upon her body. Jacques is furious. With Mara's story of the kiss in his mind, he now believes that Violaine is corrupt. When Mara sees the two, she is overjoyed, for she knows that the marriage will never take place. At the end of the act, Violaine leaves, supposedly to visit Jacques's mother.

Act 3 takes place seven years later. The setting is a forest, where peasants are discussing the road that Pierre has constructed for Charles, now about to be crowned king. Mara enters and inquires for the leper woman. Violaine then appears and guides Mara to her cave. Violaine is now blind. After telling Violaine that Elisabeth is dead and that Anne has not returned, that she is happily married to Jacques and that the farm is doing well, Mara reveals her real reason for coming. She gives Violaine the corpse of her baby and demands that she bring the baby back to life. At Violaine's request, Mara reads the Christmas service, and then the miracle occurs. The baby is alive again, but her black eyes have now changed to blue.

Act 4 takes place a year later in the large kitchen at Combernon. Pierre enters, carrying Violaine, who has been badly injured when a cartload of sand fell on her. Jacques reacts with hostility. When he calls Pierre a leper, Pierre assures Jacques that he is cured; to another question, Pierre admits that Violaine kissed him many years ago, then exits. Coming to consciousness, Violaine tells Jacques that the kiss was innocent. She also tells him that it was she who brought his child back to life. As they talk, Jacques realizes that it was Mara who led Violaine to the sand pit and pushed the cartload of sand on top of her. Pierre returns and carries out the dying woman. Then Anne returns, and Jacques must tell him the tragic story of his two daughters. Offstage, Violaine dies in Anne's arms. In the final section of the play, with the example of Violaine before them, Jacques and Anne manage to forgive Mara for all the evil that she has done, and Pierre plans to set a statue of Violaine on the roof of the church that he is building. At the end of the play, the long-silent bell of Monsanvierge rings once again.

Themes and Meanings

The Tidings Brought to Mary is a play about salvation, which can be achieved only by the way of the Cross. Those who will walk in this way must learn compassion, forgiveness, and self-abnegation. In their sufferings, they must find joy; in death itself, they must rejoice. The aim of life, Paul Claudel believed, is spiritual growth; finally, one must attain perfect subjection to the will of God.

At the beginning of the story, Violaine has simple ambitions: to marry the man she loves and to have his children. Even in the first scene of the play, however, her spiritual qualities are evident. Violaine forgives Pierre for his attack upon her. She denies her own desires by giving up Jacques's ring for the church. Finally, instead of being repelled by Pierre's leprosy, she feels compassion for him and kisses him without a thought of her own danger. It is not surprising that she can accept her own leprosy without anger and that she can forgive Jacques for turning upon her and Mara for causing her death, as she has already forgiven Pierre for a far lesser wrong.

Mara, Jacques, and Pierre illustrate various defects of the soul. Mara's jealousy of her sister causes her to desire Jacques; even when Violaine is leprous and blind, Mara is still in the grips of that old hatred, which drives her to kill Violaine. As Violaine points out, however, Jacques has his own imperfections, which—like Mara's—are the result of a preoccupation with himself and a resulting lack of compassion for others. Jacques reveals his selfishness when he learns of Violaine's disease and his love turns to hatred. If only he had had faith in her, Violaine says as she is dying, she might have been cured by love. The contrast between her tender treatment of Pierre, whom she does not even pretend to love, and Jacques's brusque treatment of her, his betrothed, is obvious. Faced with his own sins, Jacques must forgive Mara, and thus he gains a new spiritual dimension.

Unlike Mara and Jacques, Pierre is by nature spiritual, as Violaine is. Even though in his desire for her he had briefly dreamed of a simple married life, he is essentially a builder of churches, a man of action who will joyfully work for God. It is suffering that he cannot manage, however, whether it results from Violaine's rejection or from his disease. As Violaine tells him, he must learn not only to endure, but also to accept suffering joyfully, as a gift from God. When he does, Pierre is cured of the physical disease, but more significantly, he is spiritually healed. By accepting death, symbolized by leprosy, he attains eternal life.

By her own suffering, her forgiveness, and her acceptance of death-in-life and of death itself, Violaine has far more influence on others than she would have had if, like her father and mother, she had simply led a good but humble life. When the world becomes too busy with its own concerns to remember the demands of God, someone like Violaine is sent to remind it. It is no accident that the play is set during the life of Joan of Arc who, like Violaine, like Christ himself, triumphed over death by submitting to it as the final demand of God.

Dramatic Devices

The Tidings Brought to Mary is a play in which the action is psychological, not physical. Pierre's attack on Violaine took place before the play, and both Mara's attack on her and Violaine's death are described, rather than enacted for the audience. From a visual standpoint, only the scenes in which Violaine reveals the marks of leprosy and in which she revives the baby are truly dramatic. However, even the miracle involving the baby takes place under the shelter of Violaine's cloak.

It is the ebb and flow of emotions, portrayed in poetic dialogue, that give this play its dramatic impact. From the beginning, the dichotomies are established: good and evil, love and hate, compassion and hardness of heart, spirit and flesh, life and death. Instead of good characters in opposition to evil characters, the battle between good and evil is fought in every heart. Thus while in most plays characters such as Mara and Jacques would be punished for their selfishness, in Paul Claudel's drama the Christian substitute for poetic justice is the redemption of those who have been dominated by evil, the penetration of the world by good.

The theme of redemption is reflected dramatically in the intricate exchange of roles between Violaine and Mara. Mara became the wife of Jacques and the mother of his child in Violaine's place. In the miracle scene, however, Violaine seems to have borne the child again and, as the change in eye color suggests, to have become her mother. When Violaine dies, the audience is told that she is buried in Mara's wedding dress, thus in death being perhaps the wife of Jacques or perhaps becoming Mara. In either case, the goodness of Violaine has penetrated the other characters.

Even the settings of Claudel's play have theological implications. The homeliness of the barn and the kitchen, for example, emphasize the fact that human redemption must take place in the ordinary world. Against this background, the songs of angels and the peals of bells from deserted convents, evidencing the existence of a very real invisible world, are even more dramatic than they would be in less-prosaic settings.

Claudel's play is filled with liturgical elements: hymns, homilies, and theological lessons. This pattern can be seen in the climactic scene in which Violaine brings the baby back to life. After a stylized series of questions and answers between the sisters, the bells ring, and Mara reads a series of scriptures and a homily while Violaine prays. Then an angel choir sings, and the baby is reborn under Violaine's cloak. Violaine's role is emphasized by the fact that when the baby emerges, she has milk on her lips and the blue eyes of Violaine instead of the black eyes of her mother. However, even though it would be categorized as a miracle, the scene is as subdued as the mass it imitates. Beneath the liturgy, the action is spiritual: Violaine is in some sense offering her suffering for the life of the child.

When one examines the dramatic techniques of *The Tidings Brought to Mary*, one must conclude that every aspect of the play, from characterization to setting and structure, was based on its theological theme. Instead of hampering the playwright, the domination of theme may well have aided him. Certainly it unified his effort and contributed to his success in what might have seemed an impossible task: to bring the drama of salvation to modern audiences.

Critical Context

The early works of Paul Claudel, produced under the influence of the French Symbolists but already reflecting his religious convictions, were published anonymously during the 1890's but not staged. In 1892, he wrote a play about a character named Violaine, which he later expanded to *The Tidings Brought to Mary*. When it was produced in 1912, it was the first of his plays to be staged, and in its poetic quality and religious theme it set the pattern for his later works.

With *L'Otage* (pb. 1911; *The Hostage*, 1917), Claudel moved to another period of history, the Napoleonic era. As in his previous play, the historical setting is merely the background for a fictional situation. In this play, the heroine protects Pope Pius VII by marrying a villain, thus, like Violaine, sacrificing herself for others.

While this play established Claudel's reputation, his real recognition came in the

1940's, perhaps because his theme spoke to an age which was well aware of the conflict between good and evil and the need for God, and certainly because the directors of the decade felt that his works were worth staging—however difficult the process might be. When *Le Soulier de satin* (pr. 1943; *The Satin Slipper: Or, The Worst Is Not the Surest*, 1931) was produced in 1943, French audiences were enthusiastic about the spectacular staging, as well as about Claudel's poetic power. The complexity of this play is evident; although Claudel described it as a Spanish play taking place over four days, through the visions of its characters *The Satin Slipper* actually ranges through an entire century and moves to Bohemia, Italy, Africa, and America, and then to sea. Again Claudel's emphasis is not on history, but on his theme, the conflict between worldly desires and heavenly aspirations.

Another work which achieved recognition in the 1940's, long after it was written, is *Partage de midi* (pb. 1906; *Break of Noon*, 1960), which was published in a limited edition in 1906 and produced in 1916, but which became well known only after a 1948 production. Again, the setting is semi-historical, but the real conflict is spiritual. Like Pierre, a young man has loved a woman who cannot belong to him. He has never committed himself fully to anything, however, even to her. At the point of death at the hands of Chinese revolutionaries, he comes to understand God's purposes. By suffering and by accepting death, he has at last become fully committed and thus learned to live.

With these productions of the 1940's, Claudel's reputation at last reached the level that it deserved. Critics view him as a great symbolist playwright and rank him, along with T. S. Eliot, as one of the finest religious playwrights of the twentieth century.

Sources for Further Study

Brockett, Oscar G. "Anti-Realist Alternatives." In *Century of Innovation: A History of European and American Theatre and Drama Since 1870*. Englewood Cliffs, N.J.: Prentice-Hall, 1973.

Chiari, Joseph. *The Poetic Drama of Paul Claudel*. 1954. Reprint. New York: Gordian Press, 1969.

Fowlie, Wallace. *Paul Claudel*. London: Bowes and Bowes, 1957.

Gassner, John. "Paul Claudel." In *Masters of the Drama*. 3d ed. New York: Dover, 1954.

Heppenstall, Rayner. "The Playground of Paul Claudel." In *The Double Image: Mutations of Christian Mythology in the Work of Four French Catholic Writers of Today and Yesterday*. London: Secker & Warburg, 1947.

Paliyenko, Adrianna M. *Mis-Reading the Creative Impulse: The Poetic Subject in Rimbaud and Claudel, Restaged*. Carbondale: Southern Illinois University Press, 1997.

"Paul Claudel." In *Guide to French Literature*. Detroit: St. James, 1992.

Rosemary M. Canfield Reisman

TIME AND THE CONWAYS

Author: J. B. Priestley (1894-1984)
Type of plot: Problem play
Time of plot: 1919 and 1938
Locale: Newlingham, England
First produced: 1937, at the Duchess Theatre, London
First published: 1937

> *Principal characters:*
> MRS. CONWAY, a widow
> ALAN CONWAY, her eldest son
> MADGE CONWAY, her daughter, who has intellectual interests
> ROBIN CONWAY, her younger son, his mother's favorite
> HAZEL CONWAY, her daughter, the beauty of the family
> KAY CONWAY, her daughter, who has literary aspirations
> CAROL CONWAY, age sixteen, her youngest child
> JOAN HELFORD, Hazel's friend who marries Robin
> ERNEST BEEVERS, a young businessman who marries Hazel
> GERALD THORNTON, a solicitor

The Play

Time and the Conways opens on an autumn evening in 1919, in a well-to-do home in the manufacturing town of Newlingham, England. A party is heard offstage, but the set is dark. Hazel Conway enters and switches on the light. She is in party dress and carries an armload of props and costumes for charades. She is joined by her sisters and eldest brother, and they begin to rummage through the costumes. Kay Conway enters; it is her twenty-first birthday. She also begins playacting with the charades costumes, and the sisters plan their skits. Mrs. Conway comes in, to plan her part.

The talk turns to an absent brother, Robin, recently demobilized from the Royal Air Force, and to their father's death by drowning. Joan Helford, a friend of Hazel, questions Kay about her writing, which has been unsuccessful: She has burned her last novel. Family members enter and leave throughout as the charades progress offstage. Gerald Thornton enters, arguing politics with Madge Conway. He, too, is being dressed for charades. Ernest Beevers enters: He is an awkward but ambitious man from a lower-class background. He is introduced but is snubbed by Hazel, with whom he is infatuated. He is forced to play charades with the others. Kay reprimands Hazel for being cruel to Beevers, and Hazel responds by poking fun at Kay's ambition to be a writer.

As the last scene for charades is planned, Robin returns home. An emotional reunion ensues between Robin and Mrs. Conway; he is her favorite child. Joan Helford enters, and she and Robin show an obvious interest in each other, which deeply annoys Mrs. Conway. The sisters begin to return to the room, picking up the props and costumes. Mrs. Conway goes out to sing for the guests. Kay is finally left alone on the stage, listening to her mother sing. Attempting to write, she turns off the lights and stares out the window as the curtain drops.

Act 2 opens on the same room, with Kay still seated by the window. When Alan Conway enters and turns on the lights, it is apparent that the act is set in a different time: The room is redecorated, and there is a wireless set onstage. Kay and Alan are middle-aged. They greet each other and discuss Kay's job as a tabloid film journalist in London. Kay reveals that she has given up writing novels and that she has had an unhappy affair with a married man. Alan, somewhat seedy and still a clerk, presents Kay with a gift: It is again her birthday, this time her fortieth.

Joan, who is separated from Robin, arrives followed by Madge, now a headmistress at a girls' school. Madge and Kay begin to spar defensively about their failed careers. Hazel joins them, very well dressed. She is uncomfortable at talk of the possible arrival of her husband, Ernest Beevers. Mrs. Conway enters and takes charge of the company. There is to be a business meeting, and the family is waiting for the arrival of Gerald Thornton, Mrs. Conway's solicitor. Mrs. Conway engages in antagonistic conversation with Kay and Madge. She then presents Kay with a gift, a brooch made of diamonds, once a present from her husband. Gerald and Ernest arrive. Hazel is embarrassed by Ernest's brutal manner with her and fearful of his antagonism toward her family. Mrs. Conway calls the group to order, and Gerald begins to discuss her financial position. Mrs. Conway is revealed to be in financial straits, and Gerald advises that she sell the house and acquire some capital to invest in renovating other properties. The family begins to argue, and Madge accuses her mother of wasting money on her favorite son, Robin.

In the course of arguing and reminiscing, the family discusses the death of Carol Conway sixteen years earlier. Ernest states his conviction that Carol was the best of the Conways. Robin arrives and begins drinking; he receives a warm welcome only from his mother. Gerald tries to remind the family of their mother's precarious financial position, and Hazel asks Ernest to loan her mother the needed capital. Vengefully he refuses, denounces the Conways, and moves to leave. Hazel at first refuses to accompany him, then fearfully gives in. Mrs. Conway slaps Ernest in the face before he leaves. The rest of the family renew their arguing. Gerald, Alan, and Joan depart. Madge reminds her mother of a time when she deliberately ruined Madge's chance for a match with Gerald. Mrs. Conway declares that her once-promising children have amounted to nothing. Family members continue to depart until Alan and Kay are alone. Alan attempts to console the despondent Kay by describing for her a theory of time, according to which one's life is a consistent whole with only a small portion in view at any moment: "Time doesn't destroy anything. It merely moves us on—in this life—from one peephole to the next." He leaves Kay sitting at the window alone as the curtain drops.

Act 3 returns to the setting of act 1, in 1919, as Kay sits by the window listening to her mother sing. Alan enters, and Kay tells him, confusedly, that she has seen something: "I wasn't asleep. But—quite suddenly—I thought I saw . . . we were. . . . Anyhow, you came into it, I think, Alan." The party guests are about to leave, and Kay goes to see them off. Family members and guests begin to enter and leave the stage in succession. Hazel and Ernest discuss his attachment to her; in the course of their conversation she loses her nerve and he begins to dominate her. Madge and Robin enter, arguing about politics. Both begin to argue with—and sneer at—Ernest, leaving him dejected. Carol returns and cheers him up, inviting him to return and play charades.

Gerald and Mrs. Conway enter, talking about finances. The sale of the house is debated and rejected, and Gerald agrees that the Conways' future seems secure. Offstage, Robin announces a game of hide-and-seek. Robin finds Joan, and they kiss and announce their love. The others arrive, led by Carol. Madge is having a spirited political debate with Gerald. Just as he begins to be fascinated by her intensity, Mrs. Conway enters with Hazel and makes fun of Madge, who silently departs. Tea is served, and Robin and Joan announce their engagement. The family happily discuss their prospects for the future, but Kay stops them, crying. She begs Alan to help her: "there's something . . . something . . . you could tell me." Alan promises Kay that one day he will have something to tell her; the lights come down, leaving at first only Kay and Alan and then darkness.

Themes and Meanings

Time and the Conways is a drama about the possible connection between an idea and life. While the opening scenes of the play establish ample potential for plot development—various romances and careers are at their inception—the following two acts reveal that development of story lines is not J. B. Priestley's central concern. Indeed, the play is peculiarly "plotless," focusing as it does on perception rather than action.

The idea that Priestley intends to convey is one he acquired through a considerable amount of reading on time theory, in this case that of the philosopher J. W. Dunne. Dunne's notion of "serial time," expounded in such works as *An Experiment with Time* (1927) and *The Serial Universe* (1934), asserted the possibility of envisioning the future as well as the past. Dunne relied heavily on an interpretation of dreams: In his view, the dreamer represented another observer-self, outside linear time. Thus, in the play, Kay Conway enters such a dream state in act 2: She is both a character within the time of the second act and outside it. Kay is in the same location on the stage at the beginning of each act, and the fact that she alone is never offstage during act 2 shows her double perception: Act 2 is intended to be her vision. The irony that results from the return to the past in act 3 is simply a result of the audience's foreknowledge acquired in act 2: The audience knows precisely how the hopes and plans of the characters will be thwarted. The tragic element in the play, however, comes from Kay's vision of the future and the knowledge she carries with her in the last act. She alone shares the audience's foreknowledge of events.

Where Priestley's play is successful is not in the elucidation of a particular theory—the play can largely be understood without recourse to the writings of Dunne—but in its insistence on the importance of an idea, of order, to life. The relevance of an abstract theory to middle-class English life fascinated Priestley, and in *Time and the Conways* he uses various themes concerned with order and with self-knowledge to drive home his point, and to make the audience aware of multiple meanings in seemingly common, ordinary actions. The charades-playing in act 1 appears to be only a party game, but when the play returns to that time in act 3, the party activities, including the last game of hide-and-seek, are not merely sadly ironic: They serve to underline Priestley's assertion that the world and the self at any one moment are random and fragmentary, and one can observe oneself as a player of a role, or in a game. Only Kay, who has stood outside the moment, can see the potential seriousness of play, and it is she who resists when her mother suggests, "I ought to tell fortunes again—to-night." Priestley's accomplishment in this play is in bestowing metaphysical meaning on the apparently trivial social details of the lives of an unexceptional middle-class English family.

Dramatic Devices

In his examination of the relation between time and life, J. B. Priestley was highly aware of the usefulness of the dramatic form. The drama, relying on illusion, role-playing, and manipulation of a time frame, lends itself easily to an analysis of the nature of perception. In *Time and the Conways*, Priestley made the audience highly aware of the subjective, even unreliable quality of the action onstage. At the opening of the play, the audience is, in effect, backstage, watching family and friends prepare to play their roles. The party itself, which would seem to be the "important" event, is only heard offstage. Throughout the play, significance is removed from what might at first seem important—the party, the plans for the future—and given to the seemingly trivial—the childhood games, the casual remarks.

Priestley's most obvious manipulation of theatrical time appears in act 2, when the action shifts to the future. If Priestley had staged the acts chronologically, the play would remain the story of a family's decline. The resistance to displaying chronological time, however, permits a view not of decline but of the simultaneous knowledge of promise and loss. Act 3 essentially carries on the relationships as they appeared in act 1, but the view of the future that has been granted to Kay and the audience results in a continual summoning of opposites. In act 3, the characters begin to discuss their futures, and Mrs. Conway enthusiastically describes her children's future visits: "with wives and husbands and lovely children of your own . . . enjoying our silly old jokes, sometimes playing the same silly old games, all one big happy family. I can see us all here again—."

The progression of the characters' lives, which usually provides much of the interest of dramatic plots and is therefore desired by the audience, becomes instead something dreaded. The limited, forward impetus of time has been resisted, not only by simple manipulation of the dramatic structure but also by the alteration of audience sensibility that follows. Having seen the outcome of the characters' lives, the audience can no longer be curious about it, and the attention of the audience can thus be focused elsewhere; it is focused, ultimately, on Kay.

Kay's foreknowledge, granted to her in her vision, allies her in the final act with the audience. If Priestley had not made the Kay of act 1 a viewer of the Kay of act 2, then the audience would have remained entirely outside the action onstage. Just as Priestley has given a backstage sense to act 1, however, denying the significance of the party itself and the actual performance of charades, in act 3 the integrity of theatrical performance and its rules is again questioned. Not only is the audience engaged in an activity parallel to Kay's—using the glimpse of the future to judge the "present" moment—but its activity is also an extension of Kay's. The audience observes Kay observing herself, and the theatrical spectator thus becomes a part of the central action of the play. In Priestley's enactment of time theory, theatrical spectatorship becomes a model for the perception of life in time.

Critical Context

Time and the Conways is one of three so-called Time Plays written by J. B. Priestley in the 1930's. *Dangerous Corner* (pr., pb. 1932) and *I Have Been Here Before* (pr., pb. 1937) show the same concern with the possibility of representing an idea using a popular, realistic dramatic form. These plays were written early in Priestley's career as a dramatist; he had already established himself as a novelist and critic, and he would continue to write for the stage into the 1960's. The plays represent both Priestley's early experiments with dramatic form and his lifelong interest in the philosophical possibilities of popular art forms. The Time Plays are among Priestley's most important attempts to domesticate philosophy, to show an abstract significance in the everyday. In these plays, the philosophical matter is provided by the theorists J. W. Dunne and P. D. Ouspensky, whose *New Model of the Universe* (1931) examined the possibility of the recurrence of events in time.

Time and the Conways is the most accomplished of the Time Plays in its dramatic technique. *Dangerous Corner* examines the notion of a division in time, when a seemingly casual comment bears the potential for the concealment or revelation of truth. A group of people at a party are slowly implicated in the death of a friend and relative, and the progress of their conversation can—and does—follow two distinct and opposite paths. The play makes ample use of the mystery at its center, but in this earliest of the Time Plays Priestley has not taken advantage of the theatrical possibilities inherent in his subject. In *I Have Been Here Before*, inspired by Ouspensky's idea of repetition, Priestley is more aware of the dramatic potential of the theory at hand but relies on a character outside the action, the German Görtler, to expound the theory and attempt to break the repetition of tragic events, of adultery and suicide, into which the other characters have fallen. It is only with the creation of Kay Conway that Priestley finds a way to connect theatrical performance with theory.

Sources for Further Study

Cook, Judith. *Priestley.* London: Bloomsbury, 1997.
De Vitis, A. A., and Albert E. Kalson. *J. B. Priestley.* Boston: Twayne, 1980.
Evans, Gareth Lloyd. *J. B. Priestley: The Dramatist.* London: Heinemann, 1964.

Foot, Michael. *William Hazlitt, J. B. Priestley.* Plymouth, England: Northcote House, 1990.

Gray, Dulcie. *J. B. Priestley.* Stroud, England: Sutton, 2000.

Hughes, David. *J. B. Priestley: An Informal Study of His Work.* London: Hart Davis, 1958.

Klein, Holger. *J. B. Priestley's Plays.* Basingstoke, England: Macmillan, 1988.

Priestley, J. B. *The Art of the Dramatist.* London: Heinemann, 1957.

Skloot, Robert. "The Time Plays of J. B. Priestley." *Quarterly Journal of Speech* 56 (December, 1970): 426-431.

Smith, Grover, Jr. "Time Alive: J. W. Dunne and J. B. Priestley." *South Atlantic Quarterly* 56 (April, 1957): 224-233.

Heidi J. Holder

TINY ALICE

Author: Edward Albee (1928-   )
Type of plot: Absurdist
Time of plot: The twentieth century
Locale: United States
First produced: 1964, at the Billy Rose Theatre, New York City
First published: 1965

> *Principal characters:*
> LAWYER, a lawyer in the employ of Miss Alice
> CARDINAL, a cardinal representing the Roman Catholic Church
> JULIAN, a Roman Catholic lay brother, personal secretary to the
>   Cardinal
> BUTLER, a butler in the employ of Miss Alice
> MISS ALICE, a multimillionaire, the representative of Alice

The Play

Tiny Alice opens in the Cardinal's outside garden. Although the Lawyer wishes to discuss business, the Cardinal insists upon recalling their school days, through which the characters establish their mutual antagonism. At the Cardinal's prompting, the Lawyer reveals that his employer, Miss Alice, wishes to give the Church $100 million immediately and the identical sum annually for two decades; the Cardinal's private secretary, Brother Julian, is to finalize the details. The Cardinal agrees to the terms, and the Lawyer exits. The first scene ends with the Cardinal alone onstage talking to his caged cardinals.

In scene 2, in the library of Miss Alice's castle, an imposing model of the mansion dominates the set. Until the Lawyer's entrance, Julian and Butler discuss the workmanship of the model and the mansion itself as well as the coincidence of Butler's name and function being the same. To the Lawyer's questions regarding the six years of his life not covered by the dossier, Julian refuses an answer; he further objects to the Lawyer's antagonism toward the Cardinal. The Lawyer responds that he has learned to distinguish between reality and representation. After the Lawyer's exit, Julian does admit to Butler that during his missing six years he had signed himself into a mental institution because he could not integrate his own perception of God with that of other men. Julian believes that his faith and his sanity are synonymous.

Scene 3, in Miss Alice's tower sitting room, presents the Lawyer and Miss Alice acting out a charade in which Miss Alice appears to be a crotchety, somewhat deaf old woman. Alone with Julian, Miss Alice briefly continues the charade before revealing herself to be an attractive young woman. Miss Alice establishes that Butler was once her lover, that the Lawyer is her current lover (with whom she is bored), and that she is not Catholic. To her query about his absent six years, Julian responds simply that after his faith had abandoned him he institutionalized himself. Nevertheless, Julian is unable to answer with certainty Miss Alice's question regarding his sexual experience. Instead, he graphically describes his hallucinatory period during which he may have had intercourse with a fellow inmate who believed herself to be the Virgin Mary, and who subsequently died of uterine cancer. After responding that she, too, has a secret, Miss Alice returns to the business of her donation. Act 1 ends with the Lawyer and Miss Alice's conspiratorial agreement that nothing indestructible appears to block their plan.

Act 2 begins in the library with the Lawyer's sexual advances to Miss Alice, who with abhorrence catalogs his faults. Butler enters with an analysis of the wine cellar's deteriorating condition. After Julian's entrance, the characters move to a metaphysical discussion of the mansion as a replica of the model and the model as a replica of the mansion. Julian interrupts the quarrel developing between Miss Alice and the Lawyer to point out that the chapel in the model is on fire. Butler, a bewildered Julian, and the Lawyer rush to extinguish the fire in the castle's chapel. Alone, Miss Alice delivers a soliloquy that alternates between prayer and introspection. Julian, still confused, returns to report that the floorboards under the marble altar have given way. Miss Alice and Julian exchange expressions of fear.

The Lawyer and Butler, in the library, open scene 2 with the revelation that Julian and Miss Alice have drawn closer since Julian's move to the mansion. With the Lawyer as the Cardinal and Butler as the Lawyer, the two characters role-play the Lawyer's next visit, disclosing the full conditions of the donation to the Cardinal. Butler suggests that the Cardinal officiate at Julian and Miss Alice's wedding, and the Lawyer enigmatically corrects "*Miss* Alice" to "Alice." The Lawyer and Butler resume the role-playing with Butler now acting as Julian, precariously balancing on the edge of sanity. The Lawyer instructs "Julian" to accept the abstraction that is Alice, "the mouse in the model." The role-playing ended, the Lawyer and Butler resolve to visit the Cardinal. The Lawyer's direct reassurance to the model that Julian will soon belong to it concludes scene 2.

Scene 3, the seduction scene between Miss Alice and Julian in Miss Alice's sitting room, is the turning point of *Tiny Alice*. The two characters have returned from horseback riding. Changing offstage into a black negligee with winged sleeves, Miss Alice recognizes that Julian onstage is describing his childhood riding experiences in repressed sexual terms. As Miss Alice circles and touches him, Julian describes his religio-sexual fantasies of martyrdom. Miss Alice tells Julian three times to marry her but then tells him it is "Alice" who desires his sacrifice. With her back to the audience, Miss Alice enfolds Julian, who kneels as Miss Alice ends act and scene with the direct address that Julian will be Alice's.

Act 3 brings the five characters together in the library after the wedding ceremony. Butler enters first, carrying furniture covers, hurriedly followed by Julian in secular clothing. Julian confides that he feels lost and alone. In need of reassurance, Julian asks if Butler is his friend; Butler answers affirmatively but qualifies it by adding that Julian may not always believe so. Butler then asks Julian if he is indeed dedicated to "reality" rather than "appearance." Julian confirms that he is. As Butler exits to get the champagne, the Cardinal enters and blesses Julian with veiled warnings to accept God's will. When the Lawyer enters, Julian excuses himself to find his wife. The Lawyer verifies the truth of the benefactory agreement in response to the Cardinal's question and reinforces its importance by removing a pistol from the reading table drawer to shoot Julian if he does not acquiesce. Julian enters just before Butler is heard offstage forcing a protesting Miss Alice into the library.

Miss Alice insists that the Lawyer begin the ceremony of Alice. Julian is gradually isolated, both physically and emotionally, by the other characters as Butler serves the champagne—moving first toward, then away from, Julian to serve the other characters first. The Lawyer initiates the toasts, during which Julian's discomfort increases each time Miss Alice's response acknowledges Alice. Rooms in the model light with the Lawyer's toasts. After the Lawyer suggests that the conspirators leave, Miss Alice demands that the Lawyer answer Julian's distressed questions. When the Lawyer's explanation does not clarify the situation, however, Miss Alice explains that she has simply functioned as the representative of Alice, the abstraction in the model. Julian refuses to accept this situation, despite all four characters' urgings, and decides to return to the asylum. Consequently, the Lawyer shoots Julian, who falls in front of the model. The Lawyer offers the Cardinal the briefcase of legal papers documenting the grant. In production, the Cardinal exits with the briefcase; in the published script, the Cardinal refuses the briefcase and exits.

Miss Alice cradles Julian as Butler covers furniture and he and the Lawyer discuss a poem that the Lawyer had written in school. Propping himself against the model, Julian commands Miss Alice to leave, and the Lawyer follows her. Butler remains to kiss Julian on the forehead before exiting. Julian alternates remembrances of a serious boyhood accident with appeals for help to anyone who may be listening behind the closed library door and to God, whom he believes has forgotten him. In midsoliloquy, however, Julian's pleas to God become pleas to Alice, whom he wishes to join him. Even so, Julian is startled to see the lights in the model's chapel extinguish and begin moving toward the library as an almost subliminal heartbeat accompanied by rhythmic breathing that becomes audible first to the audience and then to Julian. The lights descend, and the sounds strengthen. Julian, backed against the model, extends his arms as a shadow slowly darkens the stage. The sounds overwhelm Julian, who accepts Alice/God and dies. Three heartbeats, followed by a brief silence, precede a slow fade; at blackout, the curtain falls.

Themes and Meanings

Tiny Alice is a metaphysical dramatization of the nature and the function of truth and illusion in the individual's search for God and for self-definition. To Edward Albee, it is essential that the seeker address the internal alienation as well as the social dysfunction apparently integral to the process. Julian, the seeker, cannot reconcile his abstract perception of God with humankind's God-image—that is, a God in man's likeness. Therefore, he first questions his own sanity and then the sanity of society.

Critical commentary on both the initial production and the playscript has been divided. Negative production reviews call *Tiny Alice* insignificant, adolescent, unresolved, and incoherent. Positive analyses, however, have been equally eloquent in describing the play as substantial, penetrating, perceptive, and terrifying. Dramatic criticism also reflects a broad range of thematic analyses. *Tiny Alice* has been reduced to a tale of homosexual suicide or of psychotic hallucination. Other critics emphasize its abstract spiritual symbolism as a dramatic consideration of human isolation, a search for salvation, or a confrontation with the reality of death. Albee himself has explained *Tiny Alice* as a simple morality play to be experienced by the unconscious rather than filtered through preconditioned, conscious beliefs. Nevertheless, the majority of published criticism concerns itself with unravelling the dramatic action.

Julian, the protagonist, embodies the fragmentation between the individual and society's institutions as well as that within the individual self. The Cardinal, representative of organized religion, and the Lawyer, symbol of civil authority, sacrifice Julian to attain their ulterior goals. Both rationalize their culpability. Through these two characters, Albee indicts the destructive potential of institutionalized thought and action. Furthermore, as he seeks interaction with his God, Julian initially contributes to his own victimization by creating a delusive wall of religio-sexual hysteria. In the final minutes of *Tiny Alice*, however, Julian is able to relinquish his defense against what he has perceived as God's abandonment. Albee graphically dramatizes that, despite prefabricated functions, each individual is an isolate existing among isolates, subject to self-delusion and the betrayal of others in his search for meaning. Nevertheless, moments of actual communication, person to person and person to God, must occur for the human spirit to survive. A moment of recognition, a rare culmination of an individual's life focus—achieved only when one is willing to give his life for that single moment—is humanity's redemption.

Dramatic Devices

Tiny Alice, a play directed at the unconscious, is replete with techniques designed to keep its audience off balance, unable to operate easily from conventional belief systems. Albee's intensely powerful, compact dialogue (paced by ellipses) mirrors mutable realities through parallel, seemingly unrelated, conversations that intertwine to form a dramatic coherence. Verbal irony underscores the humor of humankind's condition as all five characters deliver lines unexpected for their roles. The Cardinal's and the Lawyer's venomous attacks upon each other in the opening scene immediately set a surprisingly combative tone for two professionals in a business meeting. Miss Alice's charade as a crone is certainly idiosyncratic. Butler's lines are appropriate to his character and to his role as chorus but not to his function as a butler. Julian is uncertain about his actual sexual experiences but is compelling in his bizarre fantasies of martyrdom. In effect, the dialogue is true but startling.

Equally startling are the recurrent covert psychological manipulations for control among the Lawyer, Miss Alice, and Butler. The dramatic ambiguity concerning who is actually dominant shifts too rapidly for resolution, thereby accentuating the theme that the tragedies of the human situation result from humanity's fearful grasping for transient power over others. Consequently, destructive motivations supersede compassion and genuine communication.

Albee's use of dramatic and situational irony reinforces the shifting illusions and realities of *Tiny Alice*. Butler, Miss Alice's former lover, is now her butler. The Lawyer, denigrated by the Cardinal in their youth, now controls the Cardinal's actions but is abhorred by his current lover, Miss Alice. Miss Alice, who once feared growing old, now fears endlessly repeating the same cycle and never aging. Julian, who has dedicated his life in lay service to his abstract God, rejects the abstraction he has married by vowing to return to the asylum. Nevertheless, the audience is aware that he cannot return, that he must be sacrificed to complete the ceremony of Alice. In fact, the audience's involvement in Julian's acceptance of Alice through the movement of lights and the sounds of heartbeats and breathing is itself ironic because the audience is aware of these effects before Julian is; therefore, the audience members themselves become participants in what is either Julian's salvation or his dying hallucination.

Edward Albee's aural and visual symbolism is the crucial dramatic device in *Tiny Alice*. From the characters' discussions of the model and the replica to the Lawyer's use of the word "dimension" in describing the characters' life changes, the ambiguity of reality and illusion is repeatedly examined. Stream-of-consciousness soliloquies by Miss Alice and Julian offer glimpses into the unconscious associations a mind in crisis can create. The model itself is a visual symbol of interchangeable realities (or perhaps the single constant reality) just as Miss Alice, the physical being, is the representative of the real abstraction. Similarly, the foreshadowing of the deteriorated wine cellar and the chapel fire strengthens the later symbolism of Miss Alice and Julian's Pietà—the scene where their pose represents The Virgin Mary mourning the crucified Jesus—as well as that of Butler's lingering kiss of peace.

By the final fade of stage lights, Albee has transformed conventional concrete reality into the reality of the unconscious. Nevertheless, he leaves resolution of the ultimate ambiguity to each individual. Having experienced Julian's faith and his sanity as synonymous, the theater participants must now face the fundamental question: Are they and Julian hopelessly insane, betrayed and abandoned by humankind and God, or have they relinquished themselves to the consummate union?

Critical Context

Tiny Alice is one of Edward Albee's more mystifying dramatic scripts; however, its themes recur in several of his plays. *The Zoo Story* (pr. 1959) dramatizes middle-class complacency in conflict with the desperation of a societal outsider to communicate. *Box and Quotations from Chairman Mao Tse-Tung* (pr. 1968), about apathy as self-destruction and committed action as its remedy, portray human isolation as a direct consequence of passivity in the arts as well as in life. *Listening* (pr., pb. 1977) illustrates both the internal and the interactive alienation effects of not listening.

Moreover, Albee repeats these themes within the context of familial relationships. *The Sandbox* (pr., pb. 1960) and *The American Dream* (pr., pb. 1961) present society's denigration of the aged as well as the pretenses and the sterility of marital relationships most vividly dramatized in *Who's Afraid of Virginia Woolf?* (pr., pb. 1962). *A Delicate Balance* (pr. 1966) demonstrates the effects of a series of crises upon individuals and their relationships. In this script, Albee also investigates the stress caused by balancing one's own needs with those of others. In *Seascape* (pr., pb. 1975), two couples, one human and one fictional intelligent water animals, focus on the necessity of, and the resistance to, change for survival. *The Lady from Dubuque* (pr., pb. 1980) exhibits strains of both *Who's Afraid of Virginia Woolf* and *Tiny Alice* while dealing with relationships of couples to one another in the face of death and intrusive strangers. *All Over* (pr., pb. 1971) also deals with the death experience, but from the perspective of loved ones who recognize the loneliness of the ultimate isolation.

Albee has also crusaded against metaphysical disintegration within other dramatic contexts. *The Death of Bessie Smith* (pr., pb. 1960) portrays death as the consequence of human fear manifested as racial bigotry. *Fam and Yam* (pr., pb. 1960) exhorts the theater world to rejuvenate and to become responsible for itself. *The Man Who Had Three Arms* (pr., pb. 1982) comically satirizes everyone concerned with the lecture circuit: association, agent, speaker, audience, and press, as well as the lecture process itself. Albee functions as a social prophet pointing to the need for committed reform that he believes is necessary for humanity to avoid its own self-created annihilation.

Edward Albee is a controversial experimentalist who resists arbitrary dramatic patterns and who finds imitation stultifying. Although he has won such public accolades as the Pulitzer Prize, the Tony, the New York Drama Critics Circle Award, and the Foreign Press Association Award, critical and audience response has often been both bewildered and bewildering. A significant playwright in the American absurdist theater, Edward Albee does not lead movements; rather, with ingenuity, conviction, and wit, he opens the way for greater experimentation and freedom of dramatic expression.

Sources for Further Study

Amacher, Richard E. "Critics Are Downgrading Audience's Taste and Have Obfuscated Simple *Tiny Alice.*" *Dramatists Guild Quarterly* 2 (Spring, 1963): 9-14.

_____. *Edward Albee*. Rev. ed. Boston: Twayne, 1982.

Bryer, Jackson R., ed. *The Playwright's Art: Conversations with Contemporary American Dramatists*. New Brunswick, N.J.: Rutgers University Press, 1995.

Dukore, Bernard F. "Tiny Albee." *Drama Survey* 5 (Spring, 1966): 60-66.

Kolin, Philip C. *Conversations with Edward Albee*. Jackson: University of Mississippi Press, 1988.

Markus, Thomas B. "*Tiny Alice* and Tragic Catharsis." *Educational Theatre Journal* 17 (October, 1965): 225-233.

Posts, Robert M. "Salvation or Damnation: Death in the Plays of Edward Albee." *American Drama*, Spring, 1993, 32-49.

Rutenberg, Michael E. *Edward Albee: Playwright in Protest*. New York: DBS, 1969.

Kathleen Mills

TOBACCO ROAD

Author: Jack Kirkland (1901(?)-1969)
Type of plot: Social realism
Time of plot: The early 1930's
Locale: Rural Georgia
First produced: 1933, at the Masque Theatre, New York City
First published: 1934

> *Principal characters:*
> JEETER LESTER, a shiftless farmer
> ADA LESTER, his haggard wife
> DUDE LESTER, his lazy son
> ELLIE MAY LESTER, his disfigured daughter
> LOV BENSEY, his frustrated son-in-law
> PEARL, Lov's twelve-year-old wife
> SISTER BESSIE, a country preacher

The Play

   Tobacco Road is set in the backwoods of Georgia, about thirty miles from Augusta. All three acts take place on Jeeter Lester's farm, situated at the end of a tobacco road. The squalid shack and land, once prosperous from tobacco crops, are now completely run-down and everything is in complete ruin. The play opens in late afternoon. Jeeter Lester sits on his dilapidated front porch attempting to patch a worn-out inner tube while his son, Dude, viciously throws a ball against the side of the house. Jeeter yells at Dude, and they begin arguing. Grandma Lester wanders in, gathering up twigs, and Dude taunts her with the ball. Ada, Jeeter's wife, comes out and yells at both men for not hauling wood to Augusta. Ada laments that she is hungry and needs some snuff to calm her stomach pains. Jeeter defends himself throughout the play by telling of his love for the land and his eagerness to plant a new crop, but nothing ever comes of it. Ellie May, Jeeter's passionate daughter, who has a disfiguring harelip, enters, and Ada queries her about Pearl, Ada's favorite child. Pearl married Lov Bensey some months ago and has not returned to the farm since. Jeeter and Ada had seventeen children; only Dude and Ellie May are still at home.

   Moments later, Lov Bensey enters, carrying a gunnysack of turnips. The sight and smell are too much for the hungry Lester clan. Lov complains to Jeeter that Pearl will not share his marriage bed, and he wants her father to force her. Ellie May seductively slithers up to the sexually frustrated Lov, who responds to her advances. Jeeter grabs the turnips and rushes off into the fields while Ada and Grandma Lester drive off a disgusted Lov with their sticks.

   Soon Sister Bessie, a self-styled country preacher, storms in, and after some comic byplay and munching of turnips, she prays that God will forgive Jeeter's wicked ways. During the prayer, Bessie and Dude begin fondling each other. Bessie, a portly forty-year-old widow, announces that she is thinking of marrying again and may choose the sixteen-year-old Dude as her husband. First, however, she must pray; she will announce her decision the next day. Suddenly, Henry Peabody, another shiftless farmer, enters with good news. He reveals that Captain Tim, the land's owner, is arriving from Augusta to give credit once again to the farmers. The act ends on a happy note.

Act 2 opens early the next morning, with Bessie entering excitedly and shouting for Dude. She tells him that her prayers to God were answered and that Dude is to be her next husband. The reluctant Dude quickly changes his mind and agrees when Bessie announces that she will buy a brand-new car with a loud horn as a wedding gift. Ada protests that the family could use some of that money, but Jeeter stops her by explaining that Captain Tim will provide for them. Dude and Bessie leave for the nearby town of Fuller to get a marriage license and the car.

Lov Bensey enters and tells Jeeter and Ada that Pearl has run off and may have gone to Augusta. Lov is desperate and wants to chase her, but Jeeter advises against it. Moments after he leaves, Pearl is spotted and caught by Jeeter. She has stopped by to say good-bye to Ada. Jeeter wants her to go back, but Ada stops him by revealing that Pearl is not really his daughter. Lov later returns but he cannot persuade Pearl to come back with him.

The tension is broken when Bessie and Dude return in their new car—almost new, as Dude enters carrying a dented fender. Bessie, acting as her own minister, marries Dude in the yard with the family as witnesses. She then pulls the unwilling groom into the house to consummate the marriage, while Jeeter, Pearl, and Ellie May look in at the windows. Captain Tim and a banker named George Payne enter. The anticipated extension of credit does not materialize. In fact, Captain Tim announces that he has sold the land to the bank and that everyone must leave the property at once. Jeeter can save his land only if he comes up with one hundred dollars by the next morning. Jeeter persuades the newlyweds to drive some miles away to where his prosperous son, Tom, lives in order to borrow money from him. Act 2 also ends with high hopes.

Act 3 opens at dawn the following morning. Jeeter has slept all night on the porch in anticipation of the money. He learns that Grandma Lester may have died overnight, but he cannot be bothered to deal with her just now. Lov enters with a bag of salt pork for Jeeter and tells his startled father-in-law that he will give him two dollars a week if Pearl comes back. Lov leaves when Ada threatens him.

Bessie and Dude finally arrive, but with no money. Son Tom does not care about his parents' situation. Jeeter starts accusing Bessie and Dude of stealing the money, then remembers Lov's offer. He grabs Pearl, who has just come out, and shouts to Dude and Bessie to bring back Lov. Ada tries to stop them, but she is run over by the offstage automobile. Somehow Ada drags herself back into the yard and begs Jeeter to release Pearl. He refuses, saying that his concern is with the living and his land. Ada bites Jeeter's hand before she dies, and Pearl escapes, presumably to Augusta. Jeeter tells the returning Lov, Dude, and Bessie to dig a grave for Ada. After they leave, he tells Ellie May to run to Lov's house and take Pearl's place. The curtain slowly falls as Jeeter sits all alone by the porch, running the dirt through his fingers, then quietly nodding off.

Themes and Meanings

Tobacco Road is a play with a number of intertwining themes. The most significant one concerns a family's relationship to the land. Jack Kirkland's adaptation of Erskine Caldwell's novel makes it clear that there are basically two types of people in the characters' world—those who stay on the land and those who leave it. Jeeter and Ada have stayed; almost all of their children have left.

Tied directly to this theme is the obsession with the soil and humankind's struggle for the land. Jeeter talks incessantly about the smell of the earth, the joy of planting new crops, and the smoky scent when the broom sedge is burned off. He will do anything to save his land. In fact, the play closes on the powerful image of the defeated farmer sifting the soon-to-be-lost soil through his fingers.

Kirkland also stresses the basic animalism that drives people, particularly the desire for food and sex. Jeeter boasts of the many legitimate and illegitimate children he has sired. Lov lusts after his child-wife Pearl, Ellie May desires Lov, and Bessie wants to bed the adolescent Dude. Even the haggard Ada had a romantic fling with a passing stranger, a liaison which produced Pearl. People must also eat in order to survive. The Lesters are on the verge of starvation. Jeeter sold his twelve-year-old daughter Pearl to Lov for only seven dollars. He steals Lov's sack of turnips in act 1 and food from a neighbor's home in act 2. Jeeter exhibits no sorrow for Grandma Lester's passing and only sees one less mouth to feed.

The need for love in this world becomes apparent. The characters in *Tobacco Road* show no affection for one another. The three marriages depicted are totally loveless and serve the selfish needs of only one spouse. Jeeter and Ada show no tenderness toward each other, Pearl is revulsed by Lov, and Bessie lusts after the ignorant Dude. Almost all Jeeter's many children have left the homestead, and not one has ever returned to visit.

The play is also about silence and the failure to communicate. The isolation of the land and the desolation and barrenness of the fields is further intensified by the lack of communication between the characters themselves and with the outside world. No one ever writes to the Lesters, for example, nor is any mail delivered to them. Pearl does not speak to Lov, and Ada, Jeeter reveals, did not speak to him for many years until he beat her out of the silence.

Tobacco Road portrays a world that is spiritually empty and populated by degenerate rascals such as Jeeter or by self-ordained ministers such as Bessie. The latter talks with God, who supposedly accedes to her every whim, and Jeeter reportedly asks for his blessing although it is never granted. Kirkland makes it clear that these characters are tenacious even if they are deserted by God and humankind.

Dramatic Devices

Tobacco Road employs a number of clever dramatic devices. First, it is deliberately structured like a Greek tragedy. In adapting the novel to the stage, Jack Kirkland wisely rearranged and tightened the dramatic action and limited the characters and locales. He compressed, for example, the time of the book's plot from about two months into less than two consecutive days. Although some episodes in the novel were originally set in nearby Fuller and distant Augusta as well as inside Jeeter's cabin, the playwright employs only the one setting in front of the house throughout the play.

In its simplicity, Jeeter's ramshackle dwelling takes on the importance of a noble Greek site now in ruins. For a chorus, Kirkland employs Grandma Lester as an ancient observer of the passing events. She has seen the fall of the Lester household from its former affluence to its present abject poverty, and now she wanders around as a mute reminder of the family's past glory, a tragic figure felt and seen rather than heard.

Kirkland has eliminated a number of individuals found in the novel and added several new ones for plot purposes. Gone are the amusing scenes involving the brothel owner, the black field hands, the car salesmen in Fuller, and the city hall clerk who issued the marriage license, although the last episode is comically related by Bessie upon her return for the wedding ceremony. Kirkland adds the much-discussed character of Pearl, neighbor Henry Peabody, and two people never mentioned in the book, Captain Tim and banker Payne.

The playwright is not above using titillation as a dramatic device to arouse audience interest. The clumsy, erotic love scene in act 1 between Lov and Ellie May is described fairly graphically in the stage directions, as is the fondling by Bessie and Dude during prayer later. Kirkland also used Ellie May's cleft lip deformity as a visual as well as a symbolic metaphor. Interestingly, in the novel but not in the play, Sister Bessie has no bone or top of her nose and much is made of her grotesque appearance by individuals who meet her.

Kirkland has shown great skill not only in restricting his events, settings, and characters but also in forcing the action into a tighter nucleus as the play progresses, making the episodes much more explosive. *Tobacco Road* is a perfect example of the climactic form of plot construction, and it is to the dramatist's credit that he is able to achieve this from a rambling, often philosophical narrative work.

The playwright's greatest change was in the restructuring of the tragic events which occur at the end of the play. In the novel Grandma Lester, not Ada, is killed by the new car; Jeeter and Ada were also killed by a fire which destroyed their shack. Kirkland, however, has Ada killed instead and links her death to Pearl's freedom, Jeeter's loss of the land he loves, and the final passing of life on the tobacco road.

Critical Context

Tobacco Road is widely regarded by critics as a classic of the American theater. It will never appear on any top-ten list of the great dramas, but no theater history can overlook its important achievement. The play once held the record for the longest-running nonmusical on Broadway, with 3,182 consecutive performances. Jack Kirkland's play ran for seven and a half years at the Masque Theatre, from December 4, 1933, to May 31, 1941. The only other dramatic play to surpass its record was Howard Lindsay and Russel Crouse's adaptation of *Life with Father*, which opened in 1939 and ran for 3,224 performances. *Tobacco Road* was also turned into a much-sanitized film in 1941.

What makes the play's run so remarkable is that it was achieved in spite of uniformly critical reviews. Typical of the negative comments on opening night, for example, is the judgment by Brooks Atkinson, a highly respected drama critic for *The New York Times*, who was deeply offended by the play's language and obscenities and called it "one of the grossest episodes ever put on the stage." *Tobacco Road* almost closed within the first two weeks of its premiere because of this poor reception. However, audiences were drawn to it, and not solely because of its vulgarity and bucolic charm. People were fascinated by Erskine Caldwell's vision of life as seen through the eyes of Georgia Crackers and also by Kirkland's skillful adaptation that captured onstage their tragic, comic, and salacious dimensions.

Despite Kirkland's numerous other plays and adaptations, *Tobacco Road* was his greatest stage success. He was a newspaperman who once worked for the New York *Daily News* before turning to the stage. His first Broadway play, *Frankie and Johnnie*, premiered in 1928 and was followed by *Tobacco Road*. His adaptation of Caldwell's acclaimed *Georgia Boy* (pr. 1945) was an embarrassing failure. Other adaptations included John Steinbeck's *Tortilla Flat* (pr. 1938), Mary Lasswell's *Suds in Your Eye* (pr., pb. 1944), and Nelson Algren's *The Man with the Golden Arm* (pr. 1956). Kirkland also co-authored *I Must Love Somebody* (pr. 1939) with Leyla George.

Tobacco Road remains a favorite play with audiences. Its depiction of one's continual struggle for survival lifts it above the apparent coarseness of character, crudity of language, and lack of moral ethics which permeate the work and gives it a timeless appeal. Critics now recognize it as a powerful social drama about southern poverty and the plight of people who cannot adjust to economic changes.

Sources for Further Study

Bordman, Gerald. *American Theatre: A Chronicle of Comedy and Drama, 1930-1969*. New York: Oxford University Press, 1996.

Caldwell, Erskine. *Conversations with Erskine Caldwell*. Edited by Edwin T. Arnold. Jackson: University Press of Mississippi, 1988.

Cook, Sylvia. *Erskine Caldwell and the Fiction of Poverty: The Flesh and the Spirit*. Baton Rouge: Louisiana State University Press, 1991.

Laufe, Abe. *Anatomy of a Hit: Long Run Plays on Broadway from 1900 to the Present Day*. New York: Hawthorn Books, 1966.

McDonald, Robert L., ed. *The Critical Response to Erskine Caldwell*. Westport, Conn.: Greenwood Press, 1997.

Miller, Jordan Y., and Winifred L. Frazer. *American Drama Between the Wars: A Critical History*. Boston: Twayne, 1991.

Terry Theodore

TONIGHT WE IMPROVISE

Author: Luigi Pirandello (1867-1936)
Type of plot: Surrealist
Time of plot: The early twentieth century
Locale: Theater itself (framing play) and Sicily (inner play)
First produced: 1930, at the Neues Schauspielhaus, Koenigsberg, Germany
First published: Questa sera si recita a soggetto, 1930 (English translation, 1932)

> *Principal characters:*
> DOCTOR HINKFUSS, the director-producer
> THE OLD CHARACTER MAN, who plays Signor Palmiro La Croce
> in the inner play
> THE CHARACTER WOMAN, who plays Signora Ignazia, his wife
> THE LEADING LADY, who plays Mommina, their daughter
> THE LEADING MAN, who plays Rico Verri, a Sicilian, a temporary
> officer in an aviation corps
> THREE ACTRESSES, who play Totina, Dorina, and Nenè, the other
> daughters of Signor and Signora La Croce
> FIVE ACTORS, who play young aviation officers attending the
> daughters

The Play

Tonight We Improvise begins with a lowering of the houselights, the sounds of a squabble behind the curtain, queries from actors planted in the audience, and at length the director's entrance from the lobby. Doctor Hinkfuss, declaring that any play is its director's scenic creation, which, with the help of the audience, brings life to the playwright's art, explains that he will create tableaux in which the actors will enact impromptu Pirandello's Sicilian story of "jealousy of the past." The curtain, raised for the first act, reveals another curtain, from behind which the actors come, costumed, to oppose Hinkfuss's introducing them as actors. Moving in and out of character, the actors provide the exposition: Signora Ignazia La Croce and her daughters, stuck in a traditional Sicilian town, shock the local people with their free, though innocent, pleasures of entertaining young aviation officers (one of whom, Verri, is himself a Sicilian) and of attending and singing melodramatic operas. The actors demand more script; the director demands more poses.

After a five-minute pause, Hinkfuss presents a religious procession of four monks, four young virgins, the Holy Family, and sundry rustics, who parade down the theater aisles into the church on the set of a Sicilian town. Religious music changes to jazz as the lights come up on the town's cabaret, where customers surreptitiously put paper cuckold's horns on Signor Palmiro La Croce's hat as a joke upon the looseness of his household. They also taunt him because he is touched by the crying chanteuse, who reminds him of his daughter Mommina. Outside, the cabaret crowd meets "General

Ignazia," her daughters, and their officer beaux on the march to the theater. The caba-ret tricksters tell Signora Ignazia that they respect her husband but have no respect for her; she calls them low-life ruffians, scoundrels, and wild beasts. Verri and the other officers defend the ladies. The director sends the Signora's party offstage to reappear in a box in the theater audience. Meanwhile, he has a cinema screen and a phonograph set up on the stage. The film, accompanied by recorded music, is the end of the first act of an "old Italian melodrama." The talkative entrance of the tardy La Croce party causes a disturbance, and the audience and the party exchange insults. When the acts of the melodrama and of *Tonight We Improvise* end simultaneously, Doctor Hinkfuss explains that the Signora's party will take intermission in the lobby while he and the stage crew erect the set of an airfield on the open stage.

Act 2 consists of the conversations of the members of Signora Ignazia's party staged synchronously in different parts of the lobby where the audience of *Tonight We Improvise* takes its intermission. Totina and Nenè urge their escorts to take them fly-ing over the town so that they can spit on it. Nardi tells Dorina of her father's foolish devotion to the drunken, weeping cabaret singer, and they tell Totina's group the news. At one side of the lobby, Verri tells Mommina, the most serious sister, that her family's notoriety, specifically her sisters' permissive behavior with the other officers, distresses him. In the guise of protecting her reputation, Verri criticizes Mommina's past behavior as well. Meanwhile, Signora Ignazia, flanked by officers Pometti and Mangini, teases them to give Sicilians lessons in mainland manners but ends by seri-ously stating that she fears the malicious intent underlying the townspeople's insults. The several characters converge and leave the lobby.

Back in the auditorium, the director has set up the scenery for the aviation field. Af-ter giving directions for its lighting, he then decides to cut the scene to have been played there. In an argument with a poet from the orchestra chairs, Hinkfuss insists that poets cannot supply adequate nourishment for the theater, for theater is not merely art, it is life, a momentary "miracle of form in motion." To illustrate, he drops the curtain, brings the houselights up, and asks the returning audience for reports on the conversations in the lobby. The leading man sticks his head out from the curtain to protest a spectator's account of Verri, piano music is heard behind the curtain, and Hinkfuss calls for act 3.

Onstage, in the La Croce drawing room after the melodrama, the couples dance. Si-gnora Ignazia, suffering a toothache, prays before the Madonna. Interrupted by the entrance of Totina masquerading in an officer's uniform, the Signora abandons her rit-ual to direct an impromptu performance of Giuseppe Verdi's *Il trovatore* (1853). Verri orders the revelers out of the house and, as the leading man, criticizes the leading lady for improvising a defense of the revelry. Amid an altercation among the actors and Hinkfuss, the character man protests that no one has given the cue for his entrance and death. Asserting that he cannot perform the death scene, he nevertheless dies as Si-gnor Palmiro, stabbed at the cabaret. Hinkfuss praises the scene, orders a scene of mourning, explains that the stabbing was his idea, not the playwright's, and contrasts his conception of the characters and action with those of the actors, who at this point refuse to go on with the play unless the spectacle-making director leaves them alone. They force him out of the theater and take up the action some ten years after the father's death, by which time Totina has become a successful opera singer and Mommina has married the jealous Verri, who has virtually imprisoned her.

While the actresses dress and make up the leading lady in center stage, the stagehands put up three walls around her to indicate Mommina's confinement. As the character woman narrates, the leading lady and man move into their parts. Verri the husband abuses Mommina for even having memories of her past life. She protests that she never approved of her family's ways. From the dark side of the walls Signora Ignazia and the sisters defend themselves. Learning that Totina is singing *Il trovatore* that night in town, Mommina calls her children, tells them for the first time of her early life, and dies while singing for them the *Il trovatore* gypsy scene that she was singing when her father died. Verri and the family enter to find Mommina, and perhaps the leading lady as well, dead. Hinkfuss breaks the tension by announcing that he has been managing the lights.

Themes and Meanings

Tonight We Improvise is an essay on theater; its most obvious theme is the relative importance of actors and director, action and spectacle, in the making of a play. Though dedicated to director Max Reinhardt, in the pageantry, "scenic creations," and lighting effects of Doctor Hinkfuss, the play satirizes the Reinhardt-like director who lets technical theater control the script. In the scenes of the father's death and Mommina's imprisonment and suffering, the actors show that a drama can be made with only "two boards and a passion." Still, the actors' desire to stick closer to the scenario and to have written dialogue indicates the importance of the playwright's conception and poetry. Hinkfuss's reentry at the end of the play recognizes the value to a theatrical production of both the physical staging and an organizing presence.

The more important art theme, however, is that of the paradox of art: Life's movement finally results in the fixity of death, but art's immutable form lives eternally. Through improvisation, Doctor Hinkfuss tries to escape in temporal theater the "crystallization" of the playwright's literary art.

A broader theme is the paradox of being and seeming; this contrast between appearance and reality is best shown in the Sicilian story that the actors dramatize (although their moving in and out of character and in and out of the audience beautifully illustrates the philosophical concept of multiple planes of reality). In the interior play, the La Croce women, apparently frivolous, are actually competent in women's domestic tasks. Their behavior, though it seems immoral to the Sicilians, is shown in the home scene to be free but innocent. Even their interest in theater and opera, which at first seems to be escapist, becomes in the flux of time the practical means of their economic survival.

A corollary to the paradox of being and seeming is Luigi Pirandello's conception of the multiplicity of personality. The various personalities may be imposed by others, by the passage of time, and by oneself. The Sicilians, including Verri, impose upon

Mommina the quality of looseness that they ascribe to her mother and sisters. To please Verri, she herself assumes a puritanical character, but Verri attributes to her a deep-lying wildness, the appearance of which he must hide by confining her to his home. With the passage of time, Verri's distrust creates in Mommina a spirit of resignation, defeat, and weariness. Then time and external circumstance again reveal another face: When she has learned of her sister's success, Mommina admits having a stifled personality; she says that she is the one who should have become the successful singer. In her swan song she becomes again the person who had loved music and performance and the joys of the gypsy maiden's free life. Mommina's death, the leading lady's participation in it, and, in the intensity of this tragic moment, Hinkfuss's abandoning his plan to end the play with a "bit of farce"—these and the father's earlier identification of the chanteuse's tearful performance with his daughter's genuine sorrow demonstrate Pirandello's ever-present vision of the life of being and seeming as one of intense suffering.

Dramatic Devices

Tonight We Improvise is a paradigmatic theatricalist play. Even before the audience buys its tickets, Pirandello instructed, the first theatricalist device should have begun its work on them: The comedy was to be advertised as an evening of pure improvisation by the actual actors, listed by name, under the management of Doctor Hinkfuss. No author was to be identified. However, every line, every ad-lib, every setting, every lighting effect, every pageant, every tableau is carefully scripted by the author to present the theatricalist vision of multifaceted reality.

A theatricalist playwright can present this vision of all the world as stage by means of any and all manner of stagecraft as long as the level of reality is occasionally jarred. In this play Pirandello does use all. On the naked stage, Hinkfuss constructs a set; the realism of the La Croces' middle-class drawing room is broken both by impressionistic lighting and by the actors' occasionally appearing as themselves; the perspective painting of the Sicilian village is backlighted to show the interior of the cabaret; a film represents the live play that the La Croces attend; the religious procession to the village church reenacts pageantry in everyday life and counterpoints the La Croces' procession to the theater; a symbolist setting implies Mommina's confinement. Whatever the stagecraft, the milieu is always the stage.

As with stagecraft, so also with plot: The theatricalist can use any sort of plot, and Pirandello does so. The La Croce story can be analyzed according to the traditional exposition-complication-resolution. The conflict between the actors and the director is, in the manner of "cerebral theater" and the thesis play, a passionate series of debates, which also includes the director's lengthy lecture on the nature of art. The positions in the debate are illustrated both by the La Croces' story and the actors' and the director's participation in the presentation of it. The leitmotif of Italian opera and Sicilian melodrama, and particularly of *Il trovatore*, creates musical organization: statement-counterstatement-restatement. Also, there is a continuous interweaving of plays within the play.

At least three planes of actuality are apparent in the characters in *Tonight We Improvise:* the characters in the story of the La Croces, the actors as enactments of these characters, and the actors as actors and director. In addition, there are the spectator-characters in the audience. The spectator-characters are stereotypes. All the actors and the characters in the La Croce story, in fact, are based on stock types. The leading man and leading lady, for instance, are opinionated, competitive, and "dramatic"; Verri becomes the macho domineering husband of a Griselda-like Mommina. Doctor Hinkfuss is described in individualizing detail: a big-headed "Tom Thumb of a man" with tiny fingers "as white and as fuzzy as little caterpillars." Hinkfuss is undoubtedly Pirandello's *raisonneur* in his lecture about the relationship of art and life; nevertheless, his appearance might well be an allegorical expression of the playwright's criticism of some directors' egotistic, artificial, and excessive staging practices. However, Pirandello declared that he abjured abstract allegory. Though he conveys many of his messages symbolically in *Tonight We Improvise*, he does it through characters and actors made real by their thought and passion.

Critical Context

Every play of Pirandello, even the folk plays first performed in 1913 and 1916, is about the paradoxical nature of reality and about living as acting. These themes and the suffering and compassion that are both their cause and result he presented perhaps most movingly in *Così è (se vi pare)* (pr. 1917; *It Is So! [If You Think So]*, 1952). Art as an imperfect reflection of life, the values of art, the relationships of the artist to art and life, and the need for synthesis of the two were also lifelong subjects of Pirandello's thought and his plays.

In the period from 1921 to 1928, Pirandello wrote three plays particularly concerned with the relationship of theater to life; these plays made use of the theater itself as setting and of characters in the roles of real-life people and of actors. The first of these, Pirandello's most widely known play, *Sei personaggi in cerca d'autore* (pr., pb. 1921; *Six Characters in Search of an Author*, 1922), treats the impossibility of capturing spontaneous life in art and also the reality and independence of life created by the imagination. Produced in 1922, *Enrico IV* (*Henry IV*, 1923), considered by many Pirandello's finest play, shows both the beauty and the tragedy of real life confined in the repeatable eternity of art.

In the second of his three theater plays, *Ciascuno a suo modo* (pr., pb. 1924; *Each in His Own Way*, 1924), Pirandello presents a *drame à clef* surrounded by a critical audience that includes the people whose personal tragedy the playwright has made into his play. The themes of this play are that art ought to inspire argument, that art can be a "mirror that has somehow gone crazy," and that both art and role-playing can idealize or degrade life.

In *Tonight We Improvise*, written in 1928, the actors, and hence Pirandello, seem to achieve a synthesis of life and art. Nevertheless, in 1930, when it was produced in Germany, where Pirandello had had considerable success, the audience protested its confusion and theatricality. One critic observed with pleasure that the play had at last brought an end to the Pirandello manner. Others have said, however, that *Tonight We Improvise* rounds out what Pirandello began in *Six Characters in Search of an Author,* that in the three theater plays Pirandello pushed drama outside its limits and treated reality on its various fragmentary levels as did other major twentieth century artists from Franz Kafka to Edward Albee. Indeed, Pirandello has been one of the most influential modern dramatists.

Sources for Further Study

Bassanese, Fiora A. *Understanding Luigi Pirandello.* Columbia: University of South Carolina Press, 1997.

Biasin, Gian-Paolo, and Manuela Gieri, eds. *Luigi Pirandello: Contemporary Perspectives.* Toronto: University of Toronto Press, 1999.

Brustein, Robert. "Pirandello's Drama of Revolt." In *The Theatre of Revolt.* Boston: Little, Brown, 1962.

Caesar, Ann H. *Characters and Authors in Luigi Pirandello.* Hyattsville, Md.: Oxford University Press, 1998.

Giudice, Gaspare. *Pirandello: A Biography.* Translated by Alastair Hamilton. London: Oxford University Press, 1975.

Matthaei, Renate. *Luigi Pirandello.* Translated by Simon and Erika Young. New York: F. Ungar, 1973.

Oliver, Roger W. *Dreams of Passion: The Theater of Luigi Pirandello.* New York: New York University Press, 1979.

Paolucci, Anne. *Pirandello's Theater: The Recovery of the Modern Stage for Dramatic Art.* Carbondale: Southern Illinois University Press, 1974.

Sinicropi, Giovanni. "The Later Phase: Toward Myth." In *Pirandello: A Collection of Critical Essays,* edited by Glauco Cambon. Englewood Cliffs, N.J.: Prentice-Hall, 1967.

Pat Ingle Gillis

THE TOOTH OF CRIME

Author: Sam Shepard (Samuel Shepard Rogers, 1943-   )
Type of plot: Musical; allegory
Time of plot: The future
Locale: United States
First produced: 1972, at the Open Space, London
First published: 1974

> *Principal characters:*
> Hoss, a Star Marker (Solo Killer)
> BECKY LOU, a groupie/moll in Hoss's entourage
> STAR-MAN, Hoss's astrologist
> GALACTIC JACK, a disc jockey
> REFEREE, an umpire who monitors play in the game
> CHEYENNE, Hoss's driver
> DOC, Hoss's trainer
> CROW, a Gypsy Marker (Renegade Killer)

The Play

The Tooth of Crime begins with Hoss, a Star Marker, singing a rock song, "The Way Things Are." Images of self-doubt, numbing deadness, betrayal, and the loss of heroes are introduced in the song as "dark, heavy lurking Rock and Roll" reinforces the ominous threat of graphic violence which looms constantly throughout the play. Hoss's song introduces his troubled quest and establishes his hope of becoming firmly established at the peak of the American mythos of stardom. "Sometimes in the blackest night I can see a little light," he sings. "That's the only thing that keeps me rockin'— keeps me rockin'."

His groupie, Becky Lou, enters and discusses their preparations for Hoss's next move in the cross-country "game" that he and other "killers" are playing. Although this game is never fully explained, it appears to be a futuristic combination of the rock and roll music industry and gang warfare. The array of guns she displays and the talk of fast cars attest the thirst for power and speed felt so strongly by the killers. They are all maneuvering for strategic moves which will propel them into the top position of the game, providing them with the tenuous status of a star. Hoss summons his astrologist, Star-Man, who, like Tiresias in Sophocles' *Oedipus Rex*, is asked for advice to rid Hoss of his malaise. Star-Man offers him some sage advice, but Hoss can barely contain his desire for the number-one position and the gold record that comes with it. Hoss wants to go against the rules of the game, but Star-Man cautions him that doing so will risk voiding his play. As Becky Lou reminds him, "You can't go against the code, Hoss." Star-Man elaborates on this risk as he cautions Hoss to restrain his desire and maintain his status as a solo player or risk losing his chance for achieving "something durable, something lasting." He says, "How're you gonna cop an immortal shot if you give up soloing and go into a gang war. They'll rip you up in a night. Sure you'll have a few moments of global glow, maybe even an interplanetary flash. But it won't last, Hoss, it won't last."

Becky Lou attempts to assuage Hoss's doubts once Star-Man leaves, but it is clear while they discuss his position as a "true genius killer" that he is sensing a significant challenge to this position. His next song, "Cold Killer," reaffirms his belief in his ability to attain the rank of top killer as he launches into a rock-patter which displays his expertise in the game.

Hoss's confidence is weakened when his disc jockey, Galactic Jack, enters and assesses Hoss's position in the game. Solo players have taken over and "Gang war is takin' a back seat," he says, which would be good news for Hoss except that another player, Mojo Root Force, has overstepped the boundaries of acceptable play and taken one of Hoss's duly appointed properties. The concept of Gypsy Killers is introduced here as Galactic Jack mentions that they have been altering the game by refusing to play entirely by the rules. This news throws Hoss into turmoil because he begins to feel his age, recognizing that young players are entering the game and could soon depose him. "I got a feeling," he says. "I know they're on their way in and we're going out. We're gettin' old, Jack."

The session with Galactic Jack so disturbs Hoss that he decides to take control of the rapidly deteriorating situation. He summons Cheyenne and tells him "We been suckers to the code for too long now. Now we move outside." Before Hoss can act on his newfound confidence, however, he receives crushing news that Little Willard, a marker of status similar to his own, has been found with a fatal, self-inflicted head wound. As things fall apart all around him, Hoss finds that his reliance on the code has made him vulnerable to new systems of power functioning outside the code—a recognition which challenges everything he believes in (including the game). "Without a code," he laments, "it's just crime."

Becky Lou tries to bolster Hoss's ego, which has been simultaneously strengthened and weakened by news that a Gypsy Marker is rumored to be pursuing him. He recognizes the status associated with being targeted for the fight, since that implies that he might now be ranked as number one in the game; at the same time, however, he senses that his victory against the Gypsy Marker will by no means be easy—or certain. As he evaluates the rapidly changing contours of the game, he develops a growing sense of foreboding. He tries to sharpen his skills at knife fighting, but despite his apparent expertise at bloodying a practice dummy, he senses a change in his abilities. "Something's lacking," he says. "I can't seem to get it up like the other kills. My heart's not in it." Act 1 concludes with Hoss attempting to generate a renewed enthusiasm, but it is clear through his efforts to do so that the upcoming fight is going to bear much significance upon his future as a Star Marker.

Crow, the Gypsy Marker, enters the scene at the beginning of act 2 and immediately creates a threatening impression as a rock and roll punk which produces a strong sense of uneasiness in Hoss. As they assess each other, it is clear that Hoss has fallen behind the game and that new rebel players such as Crow are going to be the next stars. Crow quickly analyzes the distinctive features of Hoss's killer persona, drawing upon rock and roll paradigms to categorize him and thereby identify his weaknesses. As they appraise each other, it is immediately apparent that Hoss is no longer attuned to the newest features of the game. This realization places him at a great disadvantage, which Crow adeptly turns to his favor through calculated verbal jabs at Hoss.

These spoken assaults are preparations for the verbal sparring that constitutes the major action of the second act. Hoss calls for the referee to enter, and the jousting begins. Their form of play involves blows delivered through verbal insults designed to penetrate the field of impersonality they use to protect themselves. From the beginning, Hoss is placed at a disadvantage and even though he manages to catch Crow off-balance at one point, the referee rules that the newcomer has won.

Realizing the need to break free from the old code, Hoss kills the referee and then effaces himself by asking Crow to teach him to be a Gypsy—"Just like you." Crow recognizes Hoss's pathetic condition and humiliates him by giving him some Gypsy lessons which serve only to accentuate Hoss's defeat. In the same manner of suicide employed by Little Willard, Hoss shoots himself in the mouth rather than further degrade himself. In the requiem, the characters discuss Hoss's failure to adjust to the changing game, and the play ends with Crow's song, which expresses his desire to keep "rollin' down" to avoid the stagnation and self-defeat experienced by Hoss.

Themes and Meanings

The issues of conformity, individuality, and self-identity serve as the primary themes developed in *The Tooth of Crime*. Through the aging (at least in rock and roll terms) figure of Hoss, Sam Shepard displays the results of working within a system and conforming one's identity to the system to do so. Hoss has adapted to the restraints of the game so extensively that he has grown to fit the rules. Although he functions as a solo killer, he has remained a pawn in the larger game by voluntarily abrogating his self-responsibility in exchange for the stardom that is granted to those who are willing to make this trade. Hoss's entourage reinforces this abdication of selfhood by acting as parasites who further drain him of self-direction and growth. "I'm not a true Marker no more," Hoss laments; he has become an "industry."

Crow provides a youthful contrast to this conformist. He, unlike Hoss, is not willing to relinquish his identity in order to achieve stardom according to the dictates of the game. Crow remains faithful to himself, offering a model of self-direction that even Hoss grows to envy and wants to emulate at the end of the play. Thus, the triumph of the individual over the conforming system becomes an important theme.

The explorations of their characters during the preparation for the combat and the ensuing duel help to further distinguish the two Markers as they define the perimeters of their identities. Hoss adopts a chameleonlike array of voices as his fighting strategy, illustrating his lack of a firm identity, while Crow maintains a single, largely confident voice. As Crow remarks in summation of Hoss's character at the conclusion,

Hoss "was backed by his own suction, man. Didn't answer to no name but loser." In other words, Hoss fell prey to an oppressive system which kept him from growing as an individual. In effect, he was unable to create a name for himself, thereby earning the only name reserved for those who fail.

The allure of stardom offered to those who will play the game according to the rules is demonstrated through Hoss's actions early in the play as he discusses his motivations and desires with members of his entourage. Hoss has to hold constantly in check his desires to act, those same desires which were partly responsible for his previous attainment of star ranking. As he became a star, however, he also became less and less an individual. Early in the game, Hoss considers this trade-off to be an acceptable arrangement. His opinion changes, however, when the unforeseen shortcomings of the deal begin to surface. The entire play focuses on this exchange of established success for personal identity. Crow demonstrates the harsh and irrevocable consequences of this exchange to Hoss.

Dramatic Devices

A central issue of *The Tooth of Crime* is relayed through the Western-like showdown between Hoss and Crow that is framed in rock and roll imagery. Hoss embodies values of the older, established code of the game. He has prospered by following that code only to find at this point in his life that the rules of the game have changed—and, more important, the game has bypassed him. The game provided the superstructure of his value system; without it, he is set adrift with no remaining ground of assurance. Crow, on the other hand, is the young challenger who typifies the newest manifestation of an ever-changing game. He has adapted to its changes and uses them to his advantage against Hoss, whose role has been diminished, ironically, by the very tradition that the game fostered—the very tradition, moreover, that has helped him to achieve his position as a Star Marker. Crow challenges Hoss's belief in the game, thereby presenting a stronger example of frontier individuality than the rule-bound trappings promoted by the traditional game that has so successfully shackled Hoss.

Sam Shepard uses the duel to illustrate this clash between outdated and updated rules as Hoss quickly founders against his better-equipped opponent. The rock and roll framework for this fight illustrates a characteristic component of Shepard's drama by drawing upon a young and lawless American tradition which has nevertheless changed in a similar fashion. Thus, Hoss is associated with early rock and roll while Crow represents its more current forms.

The codes derived from rock and roll music and Westerns further depict this challenge between the old and the new as Hoss represents the decrepit established power while Crow assumes the role of the progressive young gun who is attempting to make his mark by destroying emblems of the establishment. Killing Hoss is a means for Crow to display the vulnerability of the obsolete values that Hoss represents.

The crises Hoss experiences also demonstrate the extent to which his knowledge of the system is outdated. As he surveys the current state of affairs, he encounters one disappointment after another: Some players are no longer following the rules; he is constrained by "handlers" to the extent that he no longer can act according to his own intuition; the trappings of stardom function only to weigh him down. He has become complacent by following the rules which brought him his fame, and now he is faced with the consequences that attend this complacency.

With an iconography rich in American images of despair, loss, and uncertainty, rock and roll music offers an appropriate medium for the expression of Hoss's feelings as well as those of the other characters who in some way are touched by Hoss's downfall. The songs, which function as modern-day monologues in the play, assist the development of this imagery by allowing the characters to release their thoughts to the gut-wrenching strains of rock and roll music. The combination of a challenge to a power figure, the Western images, and rock and roll metaphors produces an electric mix designed to explore several characteristically American motifs.

Critical Context

Sam Shepard uses elements of rock and roll and Westerns in many of his plays but nowhere with the skillful intensity that is achieved in *The Tooth of Crime*. In this respect, the play is the best representative of Shepard's efforts to fuse and question these characteristics and stands as the epitome of his early attempts in plays of this nature. Because *The Tooth of Crime* helped to launch Shepard's career by being the first to generate extensive critical approbation, it stands as an excellent introduction to his work at its early, arguably more raw stage.

Prior to *The Tooth of Crime*, Shepard had drawn upon an eclectic range of subjects integral to American culture. Thus, the occult and bounty hunters—*Back Bog Beast Bait* (pr. 1971)—mythic figures and film stars—*Mad Dog Blues* (pr., pb. 1971)— cowboys and rock and roll—*Cowboy Mouth* (pr., pb. 1971)—and an alien and a drunk—*The Unseen Hand* (pr. 1969)—populate his early plays. While this bizarre array of stereotypically American subjects continues to appear in his later plays, Shepard displayed a distinct growth toward more domestic concerns toward the end of the 1970's.

This shift records simply another direction in Shepard's attempt to articulate distinctly American concerns, with the family unit being a central issue. The Pulitzer Prize-winning *Buried Child* (pr. 1978), for example, focuses on a family attempting to keep a sordid element of its past buried out of sight in a macabre manner of numbing denial. *True West* (pr. 1980), *Fool for Love* (pr., pb. 1983), and *A Lie of the Mind* (pr. 1985) have demonstrated Shepard's concern with the realistic aspects of home life, drawing upon family relations and love in a manner which distinguishes a move away from his early work toward a more refined approach. His work in film (acting, scriptwriting, and directing) have helped to make him an even more visible figure in the America he has helped to reveal and define, drawing attention to the significant impact he has as a major figure in the theater (and later in film) since his first plays were performed in 1964.

Sources for Further Study

Bottoms, Stephen J. *The Theatre of Sam Shepard: States of Crisis.* Cambridge, England: Cambridge University Press, 1998.

Cohn, Ruby. "The Word Is My Shepard." In *New American Dramatists, 1960-1980.* New York: Grove Press, 1982.

DePose, David J. *Sam Shepard.* New York: Twayne, 1992.

Hart, Lynda. *Sam Shepard's Metaphorical Stages.* Westport, Conn.: Greenwood Press, 1987.

Marranca, Bonnie, ed. *American Dreams: The Imagination of Sam Shepard.* New York: Performing Arts Journal, 1981.

Mottram, Ron. *Inner Landscapes: The Theater of Sam Shepard.* Columbia: University of Missouri Press, 1984.

Oumano, Ellen. *Sam Shepard: The Life and Work of an American Dreamer.* New York: St. Martin's Press, 1986.

Powe, Bruce W. "*The Tooth of Crime:* Sam Shepard's Way with Music." *Modern Drama* 22 (March, 1981): 39-46.

Wade, Leslie A. *Sam Shepard and the American Theatre.* Westport, Conn.: Greenwood Press, 1997.

Scott Simpkins

TOPDOG/UNDERDOG

Author: Suzan-Lori Parks (1964-   )
Type of plot: Social realism
Time of plot: The mid- to late twentieth century
Locale: An unspecified city
First produced: 2001, at the Joseph Papp Public Theater/New York Shakespeare Festival, New York City
First published: 2001

> *Principal characters:*
> LINCOLN, the topdog, a young man who works as an Abraham
>   Lincoln impersonator
> BOOTH "3-CARD," the underdog, Lincoln's younger brother and
>   roommate

The Play

Set in a seedy urban studio apartment, *Topdog/Underdog* explores the relationship between two brothers, Lincoln and Booth, so named as a joke by their father. A former master of the con game three-card monte, Lincoln earns his living by donning whiteface and impersonating Abraham Lincoln in a local arcade, where patrons pay to re-create the former president's assassination with an assortment of cap guns. He has recently been kicked out by his former wife, Cookie, and has moved in with his younger brother, Booth. Nicknamed 3-Card, Booth earns his living by stealing, or "boosting" as he calls it, what he needs. He dreams of becoming a more accomplished and celebrated dealer of three-card monte than his brother. The first half of the play develops this central conflict: Lincoln is content to work at the arcade, earn his paycheck, and take his dose of whiskey, which the brothers affectionately call "med-sin," while Booth dreams of the prestige, the money, and the women that could be his, with Lincoln's help, as a hustler of three-card monte.

Lincoln resists Booth's attempts to draw him back into the world of three-card monte. He left the game when his partner was murdered, and though he resents his position at the arcade, he is glad to earn an honest living and even takes a certain pride in his work. In a scene that is both humorous and foreboding, Lincoln practices his arcade routine with Booth, who suggests that he make the assassination more dramatic. Lincoln experiments with several groans and gestures as Booth pretends to shoot him. In contrast, Booth finds Lincoln's job demeaning and tries repeatedly to persuade Lincoln to pick up the cards so they can work as a team. The siblings take different approaches to their struggle for survival; when Lincoln receives his paychecks, one of the first items in the budget is the bottle of whiskey that takes their minds off their dismal surroundings and their bleak prospects.

In their cramped and dilapidated quarters, Lincoln and Booth relate to each other in primarily combative ways. Though they share lighthearted, even mutually respectful moments, as when Lincoln brings home his paycheck, or when Booth shows Lincoln the new suits that he has boosted from a department store, the brothers exhibit an increasing level of tension in their relationship. Several elements establish the foundation for their conflict and foreshadow an ultimately violent confrontation between the brothers: the details of their family history, remembered differently by each brother; Lincoln's playful but biting sarcasm with regard to Booth's love life; the implication that Booth has betrayed Lincoln with his former wife; and Lincoln's continued refusal through most of the play to teach Booth the secrets of three-card monte. Moreover, the play's central image of a president and his assassin contribute to the uneasiness of the play.

Lincoln returns home in the fifth scene of *Topdog/Underdog* to find Booth expecting a visit from his girlfriend. Lincoln has just lost his job at the arcade and squandered the money from his final paycheck. While he is still hopeful of his girlfriend's imminent arrival, Booth slowly realizes that she has stood him up. In this moment, when both brothers are vulnerable, they begin to discuss their past: the departure of their parents, the $500 left to each brother by their parents, and their efforts to support each other in the wake of their abandonment. "I didnt mind them leaving cause you was there. Thats why Im hooked on us working together," Booth says. "If we could work together it would be like old times." Lincoln finally relents and decides to show Booth the tricks of three-card monte. Encouraged at first, Booth soon discovers that he has much to learn and, when the lesson is over, he storms out of the apartment with his revolver to search for the woman who stood him up. "Thuh world puts its foot in yr face and you dont move," Booth says in response to Lincoln's objections. "You tell thuh world tuh keep on stepping. But Im my own man, Link. I aint you."

Lincoln returns home in the play's final scene with a pocket full of winnings, having made a successful and lucrative return to the streets. Drunk and self-satisfied, Lincoln relents when Booth suggests that they wager money on a game of three-card monte. Lincoln puts up the money he hustled during the previous evening, and Booth wagers his legacy of five hundred dollars, the inheritance that he received from his mother. Overly confident and eager to prove himself the equal of his brother, Booth realizes too late that he has been hustled and picks the wrong card. As Lincoln prepares to open the tied stocking holding Booth's money, Booth reveals that he has killed his girlfriend. Lincoln offers to return his winnings, but Booth flies into a rage and orders him to open the stocking. As Lincoln prepares to cut it open, Booth grabs him from behind and holds a gun to his neck; and after a slight hesitation, he pulls the trigger. "Ima take back my inheritance too," Booth says as he picks up the stocking. "It was mines anyhow. Even when you stole it from me it was still mines cause she gave it to me." He kneels beside the body of his brother and starts to sob, letting the stocking slip to the floor.

Themes and Meanings

The title of Suzan-Lori Parks's Pulitzer Prize-winning drama suggests a fundamental struggle for power between Lincoln (topdog) and Booth (underdog). The brothers have established a successful, though tenuous, symbiosis in their living arrangements at the play's onset. Lincoln supplies the money and Booth provides what material comforts he can successfully steal. As the drama progresses, however, the prospects for their futures bring the siblings into conflict. Booth, the underdog, looks toward a future in the streets as a hustler of three-card monte. In contrast, Lincoln, the topdog, is satisfied with the modest earnings from his job at the arcade and has no wish to return to the streets. The prospective paths of each brother intersect when Lincoln loses his job, and with it the relative stability of the shared household. While Lincoln turns to his skills with the cards, Booth resorts to violence as an outlet for his physical and emotional anguish, first in the killing of his girlfriend, Grace, and finally in his assassination of his brother.

Parks also provides an unusual critique of history in the play. The conflict between Lincoln and Booth is a historical one. They remember their personal histories in different ways. Long-held animosities, buried through the intervening years, are eventually uncovered, compelling Lincoln and Booth to rethink their relationship throughout the play. However, Parks suggests that the conflict being played out between two brothers in a shabby one-room studio is part of a larger historical legacy. On one level, the brothers' names create an obvious connection to history and establish the roles that each brother will occupy. Booth will assassinate his brother just as John Wilkes Booth, an actor, assassinated President Abraham Lincoln in April, 1865. This fact is known, perhaps, from the opening scene of the play. How Booth is driven to fratricide and why he ultimately pulls the trigger provide the substance of the play's dramatic tension. By linking the two brothers to broader historical issues and personages, Parks suggests that their struggle for survival resembles the historical struggle of all African Americans in the face of racial and social inequities.

In the third scene of *Topdog/Underdog*, Booth persuades Lincoln to "go all out" during an impromptu rehearsal of his assassination routine but soon finds the spectacle too realistic. "People like they historical shit in a certain way," Lincoln responds. "They like it to unfold the way they folded it up. Neatly like a book. Not raggedy and bloody and screaming." In *Topdog/Underdog*, as in many of her dramas, Parks challenges the accepted meanings of historical figures and events. Lincoln's daily impersonation of President Lincoln, traditionally thought of by many as the Great Emancipator, is in fact a kind of servitude, a whitewashing of history symbolized perhaps by the whiteface Lincoln uses as a part of his costume. In *Topdog/Underdog* history is ultimately inscrutable, the product of unknown forces whose meaning is constantly being reinterpreted and revised.

Dramatic Devices

Parks sets the tone for the relationship between Lincoln and Booth with their names, suggesting an opposition that will culminate in violence. She further foreshadows a disastrous end throughout the play. In the opening scene, Lincoln returns home in his costume and whiteface, and a startled Booth draws his gun. "You pull that one more time," Booth yells, "I'll shoot you." In scene three, Booth pretends to shoot Lincoln in order to help him practice his routine; but Lincoln's exaggerated death throes disturb him. "Something about it," he explains to Lincoln. "I dunno. It was looking too real or something." The animosity that builds between the brothers, Booth's quick temper and bravado, and the presence of a gun, all signify the likelihood of bloodshed.

Parks also uses the three-card monte game as a central metaphor in the play. The game relies on deception and distraction, and its premise is that one can win only when they are allowed to win. "Cause its thuh first move that separates thuh Player from thuh played," Lincoln explains after he has defeated Booth in the play's final scene. "And thuh first move is to know that there aint no winning." Lincoln understands the nature of the game. In a broader sense, this understanding characterizes Lincoln's approach to life. He is satisfied to reenact the assassination of his namesake for paying customers. In three-card monte, as in life, there is no winning. In contrast, Booth cannot see this principal. He still believes that he can win; when he loses, with his girlfriend Grace, and ultimately with Lincoln, his only recourse is violence.

Critical Context

In her early plays, Parks employed unconventional scenes and characters whose substance seemed more philosophical in nature than representational. *Imperceptible Mutabilities in the Third Kingdom* (pr. 1989, pb. 1995) comprised four separate stories rather than traditional acts to represent various aspects of the African American experience, from the slave era to contemporary times. In *The Death of the Last Black Man in the Whole Entire World* (pr. 1990, pb. 1995), Parks created a cast of unusual characters based on racial stereotypes, such as Black Man with Watermelon and Black Woman with Drumstick, in her examination of historical and current issues of race and identity. In contrast, *Topdog/Underdog* relies on largely conventional characters and a linear plot. While still concerned with the continuum of African American history, Parks creates a more subtle and multidimensional context in which to explore racial and social issues.

In 1989, Parks earned her first Obie Award for best new Off-Broadway play for *Imperceptible Mutabilities in the Third Kingdom*. That year, *The New York Times* named Parks the year's most promising playwright. To these early awards, Parks has added several honors, including prestigious fellowships from the Guggenheim and MacArthur foundations, a second Obie Award for *Venus* (pr. 1996, pb. 1997), and a Pulitzer Prize nomination for her 1999 play *In the Blood* (pr. 1999, pb. 2000). After a highly acclaimed Off-Broadway production of *Topdog/Underdog* in 2001 and the play's opening on Broadway at the Ambassador Theater in 2002, Parks was awarded the Pulitzer Prize in drama, the first such award for an African American woman.

Sources for Further Study

Brustein, Roger. "A Homeboy Godot." *The New Republic* 226 (May 13, 2002): 25.
Bryant, Aaron. "Broadway, Her Way." *New Crisis* 109 (March/April, 2002): 43-45.

Chaudhuri, Una. Review of *Topdog/Underdog*. *Theatre Journal* 54 (May, 2002): 289-291.

Fanger, Iris. "Pulitzer Prize Winner Shakes Off Labels." *Christian Science Monitor*, April 12, 2002.

Parks, Suzan-Lori. *Topdog/Underdog*. New York: Theatre Communications Group, 2001.

Pochoda, Elizabeth. "I See Thuh Black Card." *Nation* 274 (May 27, 2002): 36.

Shenk, Joshua Wolf. "Beyond and Black-and-White Lincoln." *New York Times*, April 7, 2002, p. 25.

Philip Bader

THE TRAGEDY OF KING CHRISTOPHE

Author: Aimé Césaire (1913-   )
Type of plot: History; tragedy
Time of plot: 1806-1820
Locale: Haiti
First produced: 1964, at the Salzburg Festival, Salzburg, Austria
First published: La Tragédie du Roi Christophe, 1963 (English translation, 1964)

> *Principal characters:*
> HENRI CHRISTOPHE, a former slave, cook, and general who is
>   King of Haiti
> MADAME CHRISTOPHE, a former servant, now the queen
> VASTEY, the baron, who is secretary to Christophe
> CORNEILLE BRELLE, the duke of the Cove and first archbishop of
>   the Cape
> MAGNY, the duke of Pleasance and a general
> PÉTION, the president of the republic
> HUGONIN, a parasite, buffoon, and political agent

The Play

The Tragedy of King Christophe begins with a prologue. This prologue takes place at a cockfight, in which earthy peasants bet on two cocks named Christophe and Pétion, the names of the two major protagonists of the play. A commentator apprises the audience of the historical events explaining the conflict between the leader of the northern forces, Christophe, and the leader of the southern French sympathizers, Pétion.

Scene 2 further develops the geographical conflict as Christophe and Pétion come into irresolvable conflict over the necessity of either establishing a republic (Pétion) or creating a kingdom (Christophe). Vastey, Christophe's secretary, urges the crowd to proclaim Christophe king; Christophe, after accepting the call to the throne, immediately warns the Haitians that he will not tolerate their habitual self-indulgence and indolence. Scene 3 supplies some comic relief by showing how the emerging black kingdom is unable to break away from the conventions of the French court which it is trying so desperately to escape. King Christophe is renaming members of his court with titles such as the duke of Pleasance, the duke of Lemonade, and the dukes of Candytown and Marmalade. Vastey explains, quite ironically, how these empty new names define the boundaries of civilization. Christophe then enters to further define the renaming process. He asserts that the French colonizers had stolen their rightful names and that he was obligated to give them new names based on their actual culture.

The next scene shows the actual coronation of King Christophe by archbishop Brelle; however, Christophe snatches the crown out of the archbishop's hands and crowns himself in imitation of Napoleon's action at his coronation, where he snatched the crown from the pope and declared himself the emperor. In the soliloquy concluding the scene, Christophe verbally crowns his people, thus identifying himself with their cause. By scene 5, though, the debilitating effects of the fighting between the north and the south, Christophe and Pétion, are demonstrated in the dying speech of Metellus, whom King Christophe has ordered shot along with the remaining wounded. Metellus delineates the crisis of Haiti: King Christophe is driven by a dream of the "dancing woman" but has come not to build a country but to "stake out" political boundaries instead. The mythic dream has fallen into the political reality of power struggles.

The remaining scenes show King Christophe assuming all the various functions of a reigning monarch as he falls prey to the lures of power and its corrupting potential. He insists that sestets be composed to the national beverage, rum, and that they be taught in every school. He receives letters from such luminaries as Wilberforce, who advises him to be careful with his power; the queen also warns him that his power is threatening to blind him and that he is driving his people beyond reason. She compares him, in keeping with the prevailing botanical metaphors used throughout the play, with the fig tree which grabs hold of the surrounding vegetation and stifles it rather than enabling it to prosper.

The act concludes with King Christophe, the former slave and cook, bitterly denouncing his people for their indolence and perpetual need to do nothing but drink and dance. He calls in his engineer, Martial Besse, to ask him how to build a people, and Besse tells him that they need a patrimony of "energy and pride." King Christophe then resolves to involve his people in such an enterprise by forcing them to build a citadel or monument as a symbol of their identity. His final speech, however, reveals a grandiosity bordering on hubris when he exhorts his people to build this watchtower against the laws of fate, history, and nature itself.

Act 2 shows the beginning of the repressive acts that become vicious atrocities by the end of the act. The peasants complain that they need less pride and more good sense from their king. It is clear that the king's special guards, the Royal Dahomeys, are to enforce new laws such as the prohibition of all voodoo practices, and that all workers are to be treated as members of the military: They must obey orders under penalty of death.

Scenes 2, 3, and 4 show King Christophe intimidating his archbishop and forcing his own children to participate in humiliating acts of propaganda such as waving flags and singing while the peasants build the citadel, which he has named "Sans Souci." The choice of the name further reveals the arrogance of King Christophe since he now obviously thinks of himself as another Frederick the Great of Prussia, whose palace was also called "Sans Souci," or "without care or concern." The citadel has also taken on the characteristics of the biblical Tower of Babel in that it symbolizes an overweening pride and Christophe's accelerating difficulty in communicating with his people.

Along with forbidding any participation in their native voodoo practices, King Christophe is also enforcing new, puritanical repressiveness by forbidding the peasants to cohabit without being married. In a strangely comic scene, the king flushes lovers out of the woods and forces the archbishop to marry them on the spot.

To demonstrate his absolute power, King Christophe continually scans the work through a telescope as the peasant-slaves build the monument on top of a very steep mountain. He catches a sleeping peasant on the mountain and proceeds to have him blasted away with artillery. He concludes the act by two extraordinarily vicious and irrational acts. As he becomes increasingly paranoid, he decides that his archbishop is a potential betrayer and orders him starved to death; the screams of the archbishop close the scene. The other action that demonstrates the hopelessness of King Christophe's situation is that he orders the French ambassador, who has come in peace, to be immediately executed. His final gesture reveals the degree of his arrogance as he exhorts his workers to answer nature's blind violence "with the controlled violence of our lungs" and defiantly shakes his sword at the heavens during a violent storm and warns Saint Peter "not to make war on us!"

As act 1 showed the emergence of a new and hopeful kingdom out of the remains of the French colonization, so act 3 shows the failure of that dream and its collapse into decadence and vain attempts to regain lost ground. Scene 1 opens as the courtiers and ladies are dancing and discussing the new building project, a castle—a congressional palace—which will further drain the little remaining energy that the exhausted peasants possess. Scenes 2, 3, and 4 demonstrate how the ship of state is falling apart and how King Christophe's attempts to replace the old nature deities with the Christian God fail. In fact, it is during one of these scenes at the Church of Lemonade that Christophe experiences a mysterious fall which leaves him virtually paralyzed, a condition that he suspects is a result of the voodoo curse of "Bakula Baka." As the southern republic moves toward capitalism, most of the king's supporters abandon him, and only Hugonin, the buffoon and political agent, remains behind to assist him in his final preparations.

The concluding scenes in act 3 are the most compelling dramatically and rhetorically. Christophe's final speeches resonate with the power and eloquence of the concluding scenes of William Shakespeare's *Macbeth* (pr. 1606) and *King Lear* (pr. c. 1605-1606). He speaks in the language of nature rather than politics; the metaphor changes from an expression of mechanistic power to an identification with the organic animism of the native religions of Haiti. He can finally identify the rhythms of his own body with the rhythms of the movements of nature around him, but it is too late and he knows it. He prepares himself for death, since he knows that his entire project has failed miserably. As Hugonin enters the penultimate scene, drunk and dressed as a decadent French fop, his arrogant speech is interrupted by the pistol shot of King Christophe's suicide. The final scene shows the burial of the king, standing up, in the citadel itself as King Christophe begins the journey that will move him from the status of historical figure to the rank of myth and legend.

Themes and Meanings

The Tragedy of King Christophe is the common story of the rise of an ambitious and hungry young slave and cook to the status of king. Like so many tragic heroes before him, King Christophe, who makes himself king, falls from his high station because of his overweening pride, his tragic flaw. Once Henri Christophe attained his position of power, he forgot the primary reasons for his ambitions: to free his fellow slaves from the tyranny of French colonization and to permit them to be themselves. The story perfectly embodies the principles of classic Greek tragedy since it is the story of the moral decline of a potentially great leader.

On a historical level, the story is part of the history of the island of Haiti. Most of the events actually took place; Henri Christophe did exist and did govern the island from 1811 to 1820. Aimé Césaire chose Haiti because it was the first black country to gain freedom from European domination (1801) and because Christophe was the first black leader who undertook the nearly impossible task of molding an independent black nation. History shows that his methods of building a nation turned cruel when he experienced difficulties in trying to transform the islanders into respectable middle-class European citizens. In unwittingly imposing European, primarily French, strictures on the Haitians, he proceeded to further exacerbate the damage already done to the instinctual lives of the blacks by the departed French. The people rebelled against him in 1820, and he committed suicide.

On a dramatic and philosophical level, however, the play embodies two distinct but interpenetrating tragedies that intersect in the figure of King Christophe. One tragedy cannot be understood fully without understanding its relationship to the other. Césaire delineates the individual tragedy of the main character while simultaneously analyzing the collective tragedy of Haiti itself. In choosing to build Haiti into a kingdom, an anachronism in the nineteenth century, instead of a republic, King Christophe exposes the motivating core of his ambition and, therefore, the reasons that his project could never succeed. Had the French Revolution never taken place and the seeds of democracy never been sown, Christophe's plan may have succeeded. King Christophe takes his place among the many tragic heroes who were born too late and who mistook their desire for power for a nostalgic yearning for the glories of some long-lost Garden of Eden.

Dramatic Devices

The Tragedy of King Christophe does not indulge in any radical theatrical techniques. It is a straightforward three-act play with plenty of colorful spectacle throughout. The major contrasts throughout the play are between the miserable peasant settings and the opulent and overstuffed court scenes. Aimé Césaire has also embedded in the play certain patterns from other literatures that relate it to famous dramas and epics from the past. For example, the hero possesses most of the characteristics of the classical Greek tragic hero including hubris (pride) and hamartia (tragic flaw). Césaire also employs, ironically, some conventions from ancient epics; he presents a cataloging of characters and their new, silly names and ranks rather than the conventional cataloging of weapons and ships that both Homer and Vergil practiced. In this instance, the technique works to satirize the scene and the characters and make them look ridiculous.

Madame Christophe also takes on the role of the Greek chorus in her continuous warnings to her husband to stop flaunting his arrogance and attend to the poverty and agony of his people. The letter from Wilberforce underscores the queen's function by warning him about the same pitfalls of power. Much of the courtly preening and foppish behavior of the king's attendants evokes scenes from both Molière and his English counterparts, the Restoration dramatists, and adds another level of satire that an informed playgoer would undoubtedly detect.

Equally important, however, is the richness of the language Césaire uses throughout the play. He intertwines luxurious Latinate syntax with earthy and sometimes vulgar Haitian French argot which resonates with the rhythms of Arthur Rimbaud, Stéphane Mallarmé, and other French Surrealist poets. The language also possesses the rhetorical power found in lines of Jean Racine, Pierre Corneille, and William Shakespeare.

The most compelling single image in the play is, however, the building of the citadel or watchtower. Indeed, as it reappears throughout the play, it takes on an ominous symbolic dimension and evokes other destructive buildings such as the Tower of Babel, the Egyptian pyramids, and the broken towers of ancient Troy. Césaire's wide literary background enables him not only to tell a story with wit and precision but also to adorn it with sophisticated allusions and literary conventions.

Critical Context

Aimé Césaire's reputation up to the publication of *The Tragedy of King Christophe* was based primarily on his work as a highly respected poet and politician in his native Martinique. His major work up to 1963 was his long poem titled *Cahier d'un retour au pays natal* (1939; *Memorandum on My Martinique*, 1947, also as *Return to My Native Land*, 1968), which had established his literary reputation in both Europe and the United States. In that poem, he articulated the ideals of a term he and another black poet, Léopold Senghor, had invented: "*négritude*." He has, since then, become most consistently associated with that concept, a concept that expresses the pride of black people in the fact of their blackness and urges them to reject assimilation with white, European culture: They should honor and attend to their unique racial roots.

By the early 1960's, however, Césaire wanted to reach a larger audience and turned to the writing of plays that would clearly articulate the concerns of black people using relevant historical and literary models as subjects. His conscious effort to turn away from writing his sometimes highly sophisticated and intellectually challenging poetry to using a more accessible and conventional dramatic structure demonstrated his seriousness in propounding black causes.

The Tragedy of King Christophe was the first drama in a proposed trilogy of plays devoted to the tragedies of famous blacks. His next play was *Une Saison au Congo* (pb. 1966; *A Season in the Congo*, 1968), and it presented the rise and fall of Patrice Lumumba, a revolutionary poet, visionary, and martyr who enabled Africa to move toward independence from its European masters even though he failed to unify his country. The third play in Césaire's trilogy is called *Une Tempête, d'après "La Tempête" de Shakespeare: Adaptation pour un théâtre nègre* (pr., pb. 1969; *The Tem-*

pest, 1974) and is an adaptation of Shakespeare's *The Tempest* (pr. 1611) using Prospero as a model of the white conqueror, the rational man, who opposes Caliban, a symbol of the black instinctual but enslaved man. Ariel becomes a metaphor of the mulatto, a man of science, but equally repressed by the power structure of Prospero.

The writing and producing of these plays has moved this great poet away from the kind of difficult and esoteric poetry that he had previously written, to a serious effort to speak to the agony of his fellow blacks and to find literary and historical models which directly deal with their enslavement and exploitation by European colonization.

Sources for Further Study

Arnold, A. James. "Césaire and Shakespeare: Two Tempests." *Comparative Literature Studies* 30 (Summer, 1978): 236-248.

_____. *Modernism and Negritude: The Poetry and Poetics of Aimé Césaire*, Cambridge, Mass.: Harvard University Press, 1981.

Bailey, Marianne Wichman. *The Ritual Theater of Aimé Césaire: Mythic Structures of the Dramatic Imagination*. Tübingen, Germany: G. Narr, 1992.

Césaire, Aimé. Introduction to *The Collected Poetry of Aimé Césaire*. Edited and translated by Clayton Eshleman and Annette Smith. Berkeley: University of California Press, 1983.

Cohen, Henry. "The Petrified Builder: Césaire's *Roi Christophe*." *Studies in Black Literature* 5 (Winter, 1974): 21-24.

Davis, Gregson. *Aimé Césaire*. Cambridge, England: Cambridge University Press, 1997.

Pallister, Janice L. *Aimé Césaire*. New York: Twayne Publishers, 1991.

Patrick Meanor

THE TRANSFIGURATION OF BENNO BLIMPIE

Author: Albert Innaurato (1948-   )
Type of plot: Expressionist; memory play
Time of plot: 1955-1970
Locale: Italian section of Philadelphia, Pennsylvania
First produced: 1973, at the Eugene O'Neill Theatre Center, Waterford, Connecticut
First published: 1976, in *Yale Theater*

> *Principal characters:*
> BENNO, an obese young man
> MOTHER, his unhappy, abusive mother
> FATHER, his abusive, dissatisfied father
> GIRL, a sexual temptress
> OLD MAN, Benno's grandfather

The Play

The *Transfiguration of Benno Blimpie* is a memory play. The first scene shows the enormously heavy Benno eating alone, locked in a room in the dramatic present time. The other principal characters are revealed one at a time in tableaux. Benno declares to the audience that he is going to eat himself, and the stage is blacked out.

The second scene begins at a neglected city park, quickly moves to Benno's lower-class Italian home, then returns to the park. Benno does not participate in these scenes but remains visible in a simultaneous setting; he and the other actors pretend that he is present to enact these scenes from his childhood. In the park the old man, Benno's grandfather, berates Benno for crushing snails with his feet. At the house, Benno asks his mother for more ice cream—he has eaten seventeen cones—but is told that he is too fat to have more. Between these vignettes, Benno tells short stories about himself. He introduces his father, who plays out a football fantasy. Next, in the park, a girl demands ice cream from the old man, who leaves with Benno. The scene ends with Benno's description of a dream in which he is locked in an oven that burns him when he moves, while people point at him through the oven door.

Scene 3, in the park, shows the old man following the barefoot girl who had asked for the ice cream. He warns her to be more careful walking alone in the park, but she pays no heed and asks him to join her under some shade trees. Benno recites, in a desperate passion, the names of the Great Italian painters, then shines his flashlight to show the old man kissing the girl's feet while she moans.

The next scene shows Benno's parents in the kitchen, squabbling over their meal. His mother begins a long diatribe against the family; when her husband retreats, hiding behind his racing form, she questions his virility and blames him for Benno's monstrosity. Their argument grows more intense until Benno's father slaps his wife, much to the chagrin of the intently watching Benno.

Scene 5 begins with the girl singing alone, while Benno watches from his stool. She then tells of a grotesque dream about eating a chicken. She freezes during a musical transition, and Benno begins a third person monologue about how he came to love painting. He concludes that no matter how beautiful his paintings might be, no matter how sensitive his responses to music, he knows that he is still a monster who will finally consume himself. The girl then resumes her story, describing her brother's wet dream and her hope for more chicken to eat soon.

In scene 6, the girl and the grandfather are lying down together in the park. Benno is chased away by the grandfather he loves so that the old man can touch the girl more intimately. The grandfather promises to give the girl his social security check if she will do what he wants. While they caress each other, Benno is attacked offstage by a gang of boys. His grandfather starts to go help him, but the girl tempts him to remain and take his pleasure.

The next scene returns to the kitchen, where Benno's father prepares a meal while cursing Benno's mother, who has deserted them. Benno's father then begins to criticize him: Why did he not fight back when he was attacked? Why does he spend so much time indoors? As he cooks the eggs, the father mimes a fight that leaves the imaginary opponents broken and bleeding.

Scene 8 again alternates narratives from the girl and Benno. The girl teases her hair and dances while she recounts how her cousin Donny, a sailor, wiped some spilled spaghetti sauce from her dress with his powerful, masculine hands. She freezes, and Benno tells of his return to his old neighborhood at age twenty and explains that his compulsive longing for beauty—in a painting or an image of a pretty girl—is always defeated by his awareness of his own monstrosity. The girl resumes her story, saying that she intentionally spilled the sauce again so that Donny could lick it off; when her parents interrupted them, Donny became ill, proving himself a "sissy." Benno finishes the scene with a description of his plans to lock himself away, blind himself, and offer his poisoned body to the rats—seeing their consumption of his flesh as an act of love.

Scene 9 shifts back to the park, where the old man and the girl drink wine together. The old man endorses his social security check, warns Benno away, and then tries to make love to the girl. Benno returns, and the old man chases him away. The girl tries to push the old man away as he describes how he plans to eat her up, as he did a girl from his youth in Italy. He begins to chase her, and as Benno urges him to stop, she slips away, breaking the wine bottle in order to defend herself. The old man continues to pursue her, and she slashes at him, finally mortally wounding him. As Benno stares silently at his convulsed, dying "Pop-pop," she takes the check and warns Benno to keep quiet.

Benno's mother returns in scene 10, in which the pathetic family prepares to leave for his grandfather's wake. The father leaves first; the mother then delivers a long harangue to Benno about her tragic life, full of lost opportunities and wasted talents. She breaks down, sobbing, while the distraught Benno begs her not for love, but for a cookie.

Scene 11 begins with Benno addressing his sexual past. As he speaks, the now ghostly figure of the old man appears and covers Benno's huge body with a white robe, then draws a butcher's chart on it. Benno's narrative, which is punctuated by abusive voice-overs from his parents, recounts how three older boys at an abandoned schoolyard sexually abused and beat him. Benno describes the moment beyond pain when he felt his soul slip out of his body, into freedom. This moment he calls his transfiguration.

The old man's ghostly figure has finished the chart at the beginning of scene twelve. Benno rises from his stool for the first time in the play, and the other characters watch as he repeats his announcement that he will eat himself to death. As he lowers a meat cleaver onto himself, the lights black out.

Themes and Meanings

The Transfiguration of Benno Blimpie uses almost literally the metaphorical relation of the desire for love (both sexual and familial) and the need for food. Benno's parents' lack of love for him causes him to seek consolation in sweets and family meals. Benno's consequent weight gain, while targeting him for abuse, is successful in the sense that it makes his parents and others notice him. When Benno reaches sexual maturity his frustration increases, which causes him to eat even more. He comes finally to loathe his own flesh, realizing that his weight is a monument to his isolation, a sublimation of his longing for love and beauty. Benno's displacement of desire onto food is so common that it approaches thematic universality, yet his case is so severe that it seems monstrous. The tension between sympathy and revulsion that Benno's obesity evokes provides the primary source of the play's thematic power.

Secondary themes include playwright Albert Innaurato's grotesque treatments of family life, Benno's love of beauty, and his homosexuality. Innaurato's theatrical structure, with Benno absent from the flashback scenes, implies that Benno's grotesque qualities are the products of a grotesque home environment. His parents fight constantly, never showing affection or concern for each other. His grandfather is clearly depraved, his loneliness and fear of death causing him to lose judgment. His mother's disappointments and his father's failures combine to make the family a nightmare version of Sigmund Freud's primal scene.

Benno's love of painting is the play's most contrived element; every other theme derives directly from his environment, and the main tendency of the play is to move inward, toward self-consumption, rather than outward into the world. However, the pain of Benno's experience seems so great that Innaurato's sentimental, romantic treatment of Benno's "artistic interior" provides what may be the play's only consolation. Benno's longing for pleasure is concentrated in a longing for artistic beauty, though the final monologue of scene 11, describing the girl in the red skirt, reveals the bridge between his carnal desires and his passion for images. Paintings do not live, cannot reject the viewer's gaze, and so for Benno they provide a safe haven for his hunger. Art, like food, is another displacement of desire for Benno, who longs to love but is sadly unlovable.

Benno's homosexuality develops credibly, a product of his revulsion toward the young girl who killed his grandfather and his desire to receive (rather than provide) love. However, this homosexuality is far from natural: Benno is a victim of homosexual violence much more than he is someone who chooses this form of sexuality. As love is returned to Benno as hate, so the pleasure he gives his attackers returns to him as pain; his acknowledgement of this transaction inspires his "transfiguration," as well as his subsequent decision to close the cycle by consuming himself.

Dramatic Devices

The Transfiguration of Benno Blimpie uses the familiar devices of narration and flashback to create an aura of tragic inevitability. These traditional devices are augmented by Albert Innaurato's striking use of Benno as a witness to scenes from his past in which the audience and the other characters must imagine his presence. This unusual technique provides a framework in which Benno's objectification of himself (as food) seems to be predicted in the form of the play. Benno's isolation (his weight a monument to his aloneness) is similarly emphasized by his motionless presence on the stool. Benno's watchfulness encourages the audience to watch the other scenes with special care, forcing them to imagine his experience and project his eventual fate.

The fragmentation of the scenes, as well as the theatrical stylization of lighting and set effects, suggests a strong authorial presence that Benno's "memory" cannot fully explain. Innaurato's selection of themes, for example the use of painting, and his ability to create irony and suspense sometimes seems to exceed the possibilities of the hero-as-artist narrative device; Benno's personal style is less subtle than Innaurato's play.

Brevity is the work's hidden strength. Benno is physically static, and much of the action is reported, yet the play is short enough that its progress remains harrowing. Of Innaurato's published work only *Urlicht* (pr. 1971) is shorter, and it is merely a sketch. His other plays tend to spin out of control, especially when they contain elements of the grotesque. *The Transfiguration of Benno Blimpie* is short, but profound and unrelenting.

Critical Context

The Transfiguration of Benno Blimpie is an important work because it explores a problem with self-perception that is as old as the mind-body distinction in human thought. The self-loathing that sickness, disfigurement, or monstrosity can inspire is a great spiritual problem, yet it is one that often goes unnoticed outside of tabloid reports—such as the widely reported case of Walter Hudson, who sequestered himself in Queens, New York, until he became so large that when he fell in a doorframe he was trapped and nearly died. Benno Blimpie's character expands one's sympathy for humanity, helping one to understand the mental anguish of people who seem revolting. *The Transfiguration of Benno Blimpie* takes the psychological reasons for overeating seriously yet the relationship between food and love need not be a tragic one; Juzo Itari's film *Tampopo* (1987) reminds one that the connection of food to sex, love, and desire may take almost any form.

The Transfiguration of Benno Blimpie has special significance in Albert Innaurato's work both as a representative play and as a text with biographical parallels. It was his first play to be produced in New York, and James Coco's performance in the role was widely acclaimed. More than *Gemini* (pr. 1976), which uses realistic conventions, *The Transfiguration of Benno Blimpie* impressed critics with the distinctiveness of Innaurato's voice and perspective. The play uses the Italian neighborhood of Philadelphia of Innaurato's childhood, and it also employs the problems with obesity and homosexuality that Innaurato has had to confront in his own life. Benno's love of painting has a parallel, too, in Innaurato's publicized enjoyment of opera. However, Innaurato reconstituted these biographical elements into original images of unusual power and theatricality, weaving them into an integrated, accessible form.

Later plays have proved disappointing by comparison. The much-praised rewrite of *Coming of Age in Soho* (pb. 1985), for example, in which the central character was changed from a female composer to a gay writer, was interpreted by the director as a gesture of sincerity. Instead of improving that play's quality of observation and artistry, however, the rewrite seems to have aligned it with relatively unexamined biography; references to real life and sincerity have limited uses in fiction. In *Gus and Al* (pr. 1989), Innaurato retains this autobiographical habit, but, by displacing the action into the *fin de siècle* Vienna of Gustav Mahler, he manages to lend a detached charm to his obese hero. Innaurato first achieved notoriety through the self-conscious figure of Benno Blimpie; the play remains so accomplished, in retrospect, that it continues to set the standard that Innaurato's later work struggles to match.

Sources for Further Study

DiGaetani, John Louis. "Albert Innaurato." In *Speaking on Stage: Interviews with Contemporary American Playwrights*, edited by Philip C. Kolin. Tuscaloosa: University of Alabama Press, 1996.

Freedman, Samuel G. "Reshaping a Play to Reveal Its True Nature." *New York Times*, February 24, 1985, sec. 2, p. 1.

Innaurato, Albert. Interview with John DiGaetani. *Studies in American Drama, 1945-Present* 2 (1987): 86-95.

_____. Interview with Mark Katz. *New York Arts Journal* 10 (July/August, 1978): 7-9.

Lester, Elenore. "Innaurato: His Passion for Outcasts Is Finding a Place on Stage." *New York Times*, May 29, 1977, sec. 2, p. 4.

McDaniel, Linda E. "Albert Innaurato." In *American Playwrights Since 1945: A Guide to Scholarship, Criticism, and Performance*, edited by Philip C. Kolin. New York: Greenwood Press, 1989.

Wetzsteon, Ross. "Gay Theatre After Camp: From Ridicule to Revenge." *Village Voice* 22 (April 18, 1977): 87.

Michael L. Quinn

TRANSLATIONS

Author: Brian Friel (1929-   )
Type of plot: Social realism
Time of plot: Summer, 1833
Locale: A hedge-school in the town of Baile Beag in County Donegal, Ireland
First produced: 1980, at the Guildhall, Derry, Ireland
First published: 1981

> *Principal characters:*
> Manus, the crippled son of Hugh O'Donnell
> Jimmy Jack, a sixtyish prodigy in the hedge-school
> Maire, a young woman in the hedge-school
> Hugh, the schoolmaster of the hedge-school
> Owen, the younger son of Hugh, translator for the engineers
> Captain Lancey, the captain of the Royal Engineers
> Lieutenant Yolland, his lieutenant

The Play

Translations opens in the sparsely furnished barn that functions as the hedge-school for the Gaelic-speaking folk of County Donegal. Hugh O'Donnell, the master of the school, arrives from christening a child and is confronted by his student, the strong-willed Maire Chatach, who informs him that "the old language is a barrier to modern progress." One aspect of this "modern progress" is Hugh's news that he has met Captain Lancey of the Royal Engineers, a cartographer assigned the task of mapping the territory in great detail and providing Anglicized names for the various villages and towns.

The appearance of Owen, Hugh's youngest son, brings full circle the conflicts within this play: Owen is now in the employ of Captain Lancey and his assistant Lieutenant Yolland, for whom he translates the Irish the surveyors encounter, but he deliberately blunts the latent military threat of this survey. The first act ends with this confluence of ethnic concerns and languages, and the audience is reminded of the portentous sweet odor that some of the students mentioned to be permeating the countryside: The potato blight is fast approaching.

Act 2 begins *in medias res*, with Owen and Yolland proceeding with their task of converting each toponymy (such as "Cnoc Ban") into an Anglicized form ("Knockban"). Owen assiduously studies the Name-Book, church registry, and other reference books with the large map before him, but Yolland daydreams—"he is at home now." Attempting to make Yolland feel part of the "tribe," Owen tersely tells Yolland that these people can be "decoded." Owen's father is pragmatic and informs Yolland that Gaelic words are but "signals, counters," which are not immortal.

In the second scene of this act, Maire and Yolland joyously flee a dance at Tobair

Vree that same evening for a private interlude. While there are moments of intuitive conversation, in which each unknowingly anticipates the other's words, frustration governs their futile attempts to understand each other. Maire attempts Latin and Yolland tries to raise his voice and enunciate slowly each word. However, their reciprocal affection draws them together as each names a village or area in Gaelic. The subsequent dialogue, though mutually unintelligible, is transcended by their common love.

Tragedy besets the community in act 3. The scene is a rainy day after the dance, and the mood of the hedge-school is one of disruption. Manus, who had been pledged to Maire, has packed and is prepared to leave Baile Beag after having discovered Yolland and Maire in their intimate encounter the night before. Manus's departure troubles Owen because Captain Lancey will assume that Manus has played some part in Yolland's disappearance. Lancey's response to the people of Donegal has been to force Owen to translate his questions and threats of violence if Yolland, who has not been seen since the dance, is not found.

Maire's arrival brings only more questions, and she recalls her last conversation with Yolland. Speaking in fractured Irish, Yolland had told Maire that he would see her "yesterday," meaning "tomorrow." More poignantly, Maire traces a map of England upon the same spot where Owen had previously placed his map of Ireland, and she utters the names of various English villages Yolland had mentioned to her.

The play enters its last moments with the intoxicated entrance of Hugh and Jimmy Jack; both have been at a wake for the baby who was christened just before the action of the play began. Hugh has been informed that the post of master at the new national school, which he had been promised in act 1, has been assigned to a schoolmaster/ bacon-curer from County Cork. Hugh promises to teach English to Maire because he realizes that English is the new language of the tribe. Intermingled with this pragmatic acceptance is Jimmy Jack's confession that he will be married, but not to any mortal: He will marry Pallas Athene, "flashing-eyed Athene," so that he may contend with the loneliness of his existence. Though it is an illusionary marriage of myth and reality, his concern over marrying outside the tribe is a valid one for all the people of County Donegal, who find their "ancient city" conquered by English culture.

Themes and Meanings

By setting the action in a hedge-school, threatened by the establishment of a national school which will conduct all classes in English only, Brian Friel creates a final redoubt for Gaelic culture and the revival of classical languages, which themselves had experienced a decline. Hugh draws just such a comparison between the classics and Irish for Captain Yolland by defining the essence of classical, and implicitly Gaelic, languages, in terms of their etymological and vibrant adherence to a principle innately spiritual ("We like to think we endure around truths immemorially posited"). Hugh's suggestion that the opulence of the Gaelic language provides compensation for the material dearth of the country folk who speak it is the clearest exposition of Friel's intent in the play.

As the play proceeds, Friel depicts a variety of responses to imminent cultural extinction. In the instance of Jimmy Jack, Gaelic and classical myths have merged so inextricably that he resides in a delusional state which, though charming in his blurring of myth and reality, denies him the opportunity for meaningful change and adaptation. Maire's decision to flee the potato blight and learn English is portrayed as a logical step in this time of "modern progress," but it is not passionately embraced by Friel. Captain Yolland's affection for the Gaelic tongue and manners renders him an attractive figure in the play, though his implied death suggests that the barriers of language are not easily surmounted. Owen's duplicitous translations of the English for the Irish invest him with an ambivalence which is itself a prison, as he discovers when he is forced to translate into Gaelic the potential violence to be exacted upon County Donegal by Captain Lancey. Hugh's closing words to Owen sustain his notion that Gaelic myths invigorate a colonized world: "It is not the literal past, the 'facts' of history, that shape us, but images of the past embodied in language." Whether this balance can be maintained under the duress of invasion remains unresolved, and Hugh's quotation from Vergil regarding the *urbs antiqua* (the ancient city) analogically bodes ill for Baile Beag, itself an *urbs antiqua* poised for a heroic fall.

Dramatic Devices

Translations is a fitting title for Brian Friel's play, because it dramatically presents "translation" as a linguistic displacement of one culture by another. To "translate" languages is to carry over or bring across meaning from one culture to another in order to engender a connection or bridge between two entities. Applying this process to the political sphere generates the imperialism and conquest which the play depicts, and the playwright seeks to examine how cultural translation can impede communication just when it promotes quite the opposite goal of understanding. Owen's earlier rendition of Captain Lancey's order to triangulate a survey "to advance the interests of Ireland"—Owen translates it into a mere "map" rather than the military project it is—compromises his integrity as an Irishman and translates him into a traitor to his own people, as his brother Manus seems to imply. His second translation of Lancey's threats of cattle massacre and wholesale eviction of the people because of Yolland's disappearance is a more honest narrative, and it forces Owen to forsake the Anglicized place names and restore the Gaelic originals in order to convey precisely to the country folk Lancey's words.

The play further dramatizes the irony of translation by having all the actors, even the Gaelic speakers of the hedge-school, speak English. The mistranslations and failed communication between Gaelic and English speakers are dramatically evident for the audience, which witnesses both the duplicity of the English project to control the Irish countryside and the tragic distance between Yolland and Maire. The touching scene between Maire and Yolland is made particularly poignant because the audience can hear their dialogue beginning to coalesce as each anticipates the other's thoughts. No translation is needed for their scene, yet their ability to transcend linguistic barriers is a tenuous success, for Yolland's disappearance follows shortly thereafter and shatters the veneer of British benevolence toward the Irish people. The subsequent threats of destruction and eviction are clearly military actions that underscore Ireland's loss of autonomy, and the Anglicizing of Gaelic eponymy is a metaphorical reflection of that oppression.

Friel's decision to scatter fragments of classical words and allusions throughout the play functions to accentuate linguistically the essence of Gaelic existence—its rootedness in the mythologies of the community. Hugh's frequent prompts for etymological derivations are a reflection of the continuity of the entire language and its people. The closing allusion to Carthage suggests that Ireland, like Carthage, must surrender to a conquest which will leave the ruins of its language and culture for future translations.

Critical Context

Translations is representative of the type of regional drama Brian Friel has become renowned for writing: from *Philadelphia, Here I Come!* (pr. 1964) through *Translations*, *The Communication Cord* (pr., pb. 1983), *Dancing at Lughnasa* (pr., pb. 1990), and *Wonderful Tennessee* (pr., pb. 1993). Friel has firmly grounded his plays in the village of Ballybeg in County Donegal. While most of Friel's plays explore the question of Irish existence as defined by the continued presence of British culture and language, *Translations* is viewed as one of his most political works because of its historical perspective. Critics have noted that in the 1970's Friel began to intensify the political dimension of his plays, and *Translations* is the culmination of that process. *Translations* sheds the pathos of Frank Hardy's self-conscious, dramatizing monologues and false miracles in *Faith Healer* (pr. 1979) for a more objective treatment of language as a binding communal force. In part, this shift can be attributed to Friel's work with the Field Day Theatre Group, which he co-founded in 1980 with the Belfastborn actor Stephen Rea, and for which *Translations* was the inaugural play.

In *The Communication Cord*, which Friel considers a thematic extension of *Translations*, a farcical tone replaces the tragic outcome of the earlier play. Tim Gallaher, a university lecturer in linguistics, believes that communication collapses when there is no "shared context" or "agreed code." Tim is a younger modern version of Hugh O'Donnell, who witnesses in *Translations* this diminution in communication and awaits the very modernity Tim is attempting to displace. *Translations* and *The Communication Cord* balance each other in terms of tone, setting, and theme. If *Translations* centers on Ireland's past and its surrender to the future domination by England, *The Communication Cord* harkens back nostalgically to the language which is intrinsically Irish. For Friel and many of his fellow Irish writers, such concerns are inescapable in a world of linguistic and cultural erosion.

Sources for Further Study

Andrews, Elmer. *The Art of Brian Friel: Neither Reality nor Dreams*. New York: St. Martin's Press, 1995.

Dantanus, Ulf. *Brian Friel: The Growth of an Irish Dramatist*. Atlantic Highlands, N.J.: Humanities Press, 1985.

Delaney, Paul, ed. *Brian Friel in Conversation*. Ann Arbor: University of Michigan Press, 1999.

Kearney, Richard. "Friel and the Politics of Language Play." *Massachusetts Review* 28 (1987): 510-515.

_____. "Language Play: Brian Friel and Ireland's Verbal Theatre." *Studies: An Irish Quarterly Review of Literature, Philosophy, and Science* 72 (1983): 20-56.

Kerwin, William, ed. *Brian Friel: A Casebook*. New York: Garland, 1997.

Peacock, Alan J. *The Achievement of Brian Friel*. Hyattsville, Md.: University Press, 1997.

Rollins, Ronald. "Friel's *Translations:* The Ritual of Naming." *Canadian Journal of Irish Studies* 11 (1985): 35-43.

Hardin L. Aasand

TRAVELLING NORTH

Author: David Williamson (1942-   )
Type of plot: Social realism
Time of plot: 1969-1972
Locale: Australia
First produced: 1979, at the Nimrod Theatre, Sydney, Australia
First published: 1980

> *Principal characters:*
> FRANCES, a woman aged about fifty-five
> FRANK, a man of seventy, Frances's lover
> SOPHIE and
> HELEN, Frances's daughters
> SAUL MORGENSTEIN, a doctor
> FREDDY WICKS, a neighbor of Frank and Frances

The Play

Act 1 of *Travelling North* consists of thirteen scenes, act 2 of twenty scenes. The fluid action moves between Melbourne in the southern part of Australia and a tropical area on the Queensland coast, two thousand miles north. Through its use of cinema-like devices, the action not only covers a wide landscape but also probes deeply into varied emotional territories.

The plot revolves around Frances, a woman in her mid-fifties, who falls in love with Frank, a rather dashing seventy-year-old widower. Frances, a survivor of the Depression during the 1930's and a broken marriage, considers her life a failure, believing that she neither gave her two daughters a good home nor fulfilled her own expectations. So when Frank offers romance amid the eternal sunshine of northern Australia's coast, she sets out to claim the happiness that has so long eluded her and for which she has not many years left to seek.

Frank, though, proves to be a difficult man: He is opinionated, authoritative, and demanding. Before long, as her daughters had predicted, he becomes ill, and Frances finds herself acting as a nurse to a crotchety old man obsessed with physical symptoms and medications. In scenes played against a warm, tropical splendor, Frank refuses to accept the truth of his physical degeneration and the chilling reality of his oncoming death. Although trapped in a relationship that has withered, Frances refuses to shirk what she sees as her responsibilities to Frank, an attitude arising from the guilt she still harbors over having failed her daughters when they were young.

The aging lovers' children also figure in the play's action and provide resonance for the hollow lives of their parents. Both of Frances's daughters live in Melbourne and are ostensibly well settled in good homes with successful husbands and happy children. They have benefited from richer days in Australia, following World War II, when more opportunities and a better life became attainable. In spite of the outward changes, though, neither daughter has found much happiness or security, and both draw on their mother for an emotional sustenance that she does not have to give. Frank, on the other hand, is alienated from his son, whom he has not seen for years, and he enjoys only a surface relationship with his daughter. At one point the bitterness the daughter holds over the way Frank treated her mother disrupts the fragile cordiality of their relations.

Set out so factually, the action of the play might call to mind a soap opera. However, such is hardly the case, for each of the numerous scenes—necessarily economical in their development—points up persistent truths about relationships between parent and child, truths about love and living and dying, about unfulfilled ambition and lost dreams. In addition, even though the events cover but two years, the entire lives of the major characters unfold through the dialogue.

The play ends on an indefinite note. The lives of Frances's daughters have worsened: Helen's husband has left her for another woman, and Sophie, who has finally completed her degree, is bitter over a stunted career. Frank has not reunited with his son, nor has he deepened the relationship with his daughter. Then, shortly after Frank and Frances finally get married, Frank dies. According to his directions, the mourners set aside tears, flowers, priests, piety, and headstones for a full magnum of champagne, which they drink while the dead Frank looms in the background. Asked by Frank's doctor and a neighbor what she plans to do, Frances says that she will not return to her family in the southern part of Australia but will go farther north.

Considering that David Williamson uses such an ordinary framework on which to construct a play that deals with issues so large, the work's lack of sentimentality and triteness are especially admirable. It is saved in part from these pitfalls by comedy and satire; the recognizability of its situations also guarantees audience interest. The plot of *Travelling North* gives shape to the triviality of living, then questions what meaning emerges from the myriad ordinary moments that constitute an individual's life.

Themes and Meanings

A celebration of the human spirit lies at the center of *Travelling North*. When Frances announces her decision to travel farther north, the audience cannot help but believe that, in spite of the bleakness of the lives just depicted on the stage, the durability of the human spirit has once more been reaffirmed. The play focuses on life's pettiness: family squabbles, stinginess, hypochondria, jealousy and rivalry, resentment, and personal ambition. The characters, caught as they are in the web of such emotions and situations, believe that the solutions lie in tangibles such as careers, politics, and social acceptance. Frances's announcement that she will continue to travel north, however, constitutes an epiphany for her. Now she intends to set aside the unsatisfactory concrete solutions to life's puzzle in favor of seeking another kind of answer.

Travelling North develops this thematic intent in two major ways. First, the double setting, which blends together on the stage, places the grayness of urban life against the exotic and beckoning tropics where the sun glows in magnificent colors, the more so the farther north one travels. Second, the arts—music, theater, literature—give the characters their greatest satisfaction, far more than that which they derive from human relationships and personal or public success. Classical music, for one thing, dominates the play. In spite of Frances's dreary years of rearing two daughters and struggling to manage financially, she has always found refuge and meaning in music and theater. Frank dies just as he gets ready to listen to a concerto by Antonio Vivaldi.

Although it records the mundane aspects of life, *Travelling North* seeks the extraordinary and tries to find meaning behind the ordinary. Once Frances accepts the quest, she can travel north, thus starting a symbolic journey toward spiritual fulfillment.

Dramatic Devices

Although *Travelling North* is realistic in its presentation of characters, dialogue, and action, the play still has a fragmented air. This quality stems from the short scenes—some of them only a few moments long—that fit together like pieces of a puzzle. Intended to be produced without breaks between the scenes, the play employs a unit setting so that the action can flow from one part of the stage to another. Simple but exact decor and furnishings suggest the locale, whether it be a cottage in Queensland or a home in Melbourne. Lighting plays an important part as well, especially in the exterior scenes. For example, stage directions for the tropical scenes require an "atmosphere" that is "warm and tropical" or full of "light and brightness," whereas those set in the harsher climate of Melbourne are directed to carry a "cold and wintry" atmosphere. At another point, the stage directions say, "We know immediately we are near the tropics by the changes in lighting and scenery."

Like the scenery and lighting, sound effects—especially music—serve as an integral part of the play's overall development. The script calls specifically for the music of Wolfgang Amadeus Mozart, Vivaldi, Franz Schubert, and so on; not simply pretty sounds in the background, the music underscores the characters' emotions and adds subtly to the overall thematic intent.

In addition to utilizing fully the stage's technical possibilities, Williamson shows once again in *Travelling North* his keen sense of dialogue, scene building, and character development. The characters' speech is often witty, always natural, and consistently appropriate. Each scene, even the very short ones, builds to a climax and connects the previous bit of human experience to the next fragment, so that the action heads almost breathlessly toward its denouement. While the characters do not seem to be given much time to establish their identity, they manage to do so through the concentrated dialogue and responses allowed them, no matter how brief their appearance in a particular situation.

The dramatic technique of *Travelling North* is rich and varied, making full use of both the technical and literary devices available to the playwright. As is the case with any good play, *Travelling North* gains its highest expression when performed and all the effects blend together. The play has been turned into a successful film, for which David Williamson wrote the script. Although able to create the all-important atmosphere more easily, the film lacks the sheer originality of the stage production with its mosaic effect. The adaptation of film technique to the stage lends *Travelling North* a special quality that can be realized only through the magic of the living theater. There all the fragments meld together to explore what it means to "go travelling further north."

Critical Context

David Williamson is first and foremost an Australian dramatist who, as he himself said about his work, records the life of his particular "tribe," which happens to be ordinary, modern, urban Australians. However, as Williamson noted in an interview, the best of that "tribal writing" transcends the particular tribe and becomes universal. To an extent, *Travelling North* does so more effectively than some of Williamson's other plays, which often depend on the Australian context so fully that they at times remain somewhat inaccessible to audiences abroad.

Travelling North also marks a change in Williamson's dramatic technique. In the past his work reflected the dictates of the well-made play, the action unfolding through fully developed scenes played out in a single set, rather than through fragments moving back and forth in a variety of locales. This technique, with which he experimented so successfully in *Travelling North*, he puts to use as well in his next two plays, *The Perfectionist* (pr. 1982) and *Emerald City* (pr. 1987). Williamson rounded out the twentieth century with a number of well-received plays, including *Money and Friends* (pr., pb. 1992), *Brilliant Lies* (pr., pb. 1993), *Dead White Males* (pr., pb. 1995), and *Corporate Vibes* (pr., pb. 1999).

Critics have noted that *Travelling North* is Williamson's most "religious" play in that it addresses matters far more spiritual than a particular tribe's social and political affairs. While an earlier work such as *Don's Party* (pr. 1971) concerns itself with social mores and inherently Australian political matters, *Travelling North* looks at life more fully, examines emotions and relationships more deeply, and tackles questions that are in no way peculiarly Australian but that are posed by all members of the human tribe.

Sources for Further Study

Fitzpatrick, Peter. *Williamson*. North Ryde, Australia: Methuen, 1987.

Kiernan, Brian. "Comic-Satiric-Realism: David Williamson's Plays Since *The Department*." *Southerly* 46 (March, 1986): 3-18.

_____. *David Williamson: A Writer's Career*. Sydney, Australia: Currency, 1996.

McCallum, John. "A New Map of Australia: The Plays of David Williamson." *Australian Literary Studies* 11 (May, 1984): 342-354.

Moe, Christian H. "David Williamson." In *Contemporary Dramatists*. 6th ed. Detroit: St. James, 1999.

Parsons, Philip. "This World and the Next." *London Magazine* 20 (August/September, 1980): 121-126.

Robert L. Ross

TRAVESTIES

Author: Tom Stoppard (Tomas Straussler, 1937-   )
Type of plot: Problem play; memory play
Time of plot: 1917-1918, remembered in the 1970's
Locale: Zurich, Switzerland
First produced: 1974, at the Aldwych Theatre, London
First published: 1975

Principal characters:
  HENRY CARR, as Young Carr, a British Consular official in his
    twenties and, as Old Carr, about age eighty
  TRISTAN TZARA, the Romanian Dadaist
  JAMES JOYCE, the Irish writer, at age thirty-six
  LENIN (VLADIMIR ILYICH ULYANOV), the Russian revolutionary,
    at age forty-seven
  BENNETT, Carr's butler/valet
  GWENDOLEN CARR, Henry's sister, Joyce's secretary
  CECILY CARUTHERS, a librarian and follower of Lenin, about age
    twenty-two and, as Old Mrs. Carr, about age eighty
  NADYA (NADEZHDA KRUPSKAYA), Lenin's wife, at age forty-
    eight

The Play
  Travesties opens in the Zurich Public Library in 1917. Among tall bookcases,
James Joyce and Gwendolen work on *Ulysses* (1922), Lenin writes, and Tzara cuts up
words he has written and randomly rearranges them. As he declaims the resulting
poem, librarian Cecily enters and tries to quiet him. Both women leave, accidentally
(and obviously) switching folders of Lenin's and Joyce's work. Nadya brings Lenin
news of the revolution in St. Petersburg, they converse in Russian, and eventually all
leave.
  The scene changes to Carr's room, with Old Carr perhaps playing a downstage piano to cover the set change. He recalls his days in the Consular office and acidly comments on Joyce and a production of Oscar Wilde's *The Importance of Being Earnest:
A Trivial Comedy for Serious People* (pr. 1895) that Joyce helped manage. From this
point on, some of the lines, names, and action will recall Wilde's play. Old Carr's 170-
line monologue shifts to Lenin, then to Dada. He is obviously rambling and occasionally inaccurate. Suddenly he removes hat, dressing gown, and large carpet slippers
and becomes the dapper Young Carr. Bennett enters and the conversation moves errat-
ically to a series of comments on the war, Tzara, and the Russian Revolution. Bennett,
with more facts and more intelligence, bets on Lenin.

Tzara enters, speaking with a Romanian accent, followed by Joyce and Gwendolen. The dialogue becomes a rapid series of limericks as the characters meet each other and Joyce asks for money. Gwen, Tzara, and Joyce leave, but Tzara returns, without accent, and a travesty of Wilde's dialogue ensues. The discussion shifts to the war, which Carr remembers in terms of trousers ruined in the trenches. Tzara leads the conversation to the Dadaist concept of art controlled by chance, but Carr returns it to the war. The lights dim, then raise, and Tzara's entrance is played a third time, with the conversation again focusing on art.

Since all the dialogue is controlled by Old Carr's memory, there are many jumps rather than a logical completion of any train of thought. Carr and Tzara talk of Joyce and *Ulysses*, of Cecily and her devotion to Lenin's cause, of Tzara's interest in Gwendolen, and of the relationship between art and labor. Tzara's ranting is interrupted by the reentry of Joyce and Gwendolen. Joyce offers Carr the part of Algernon in an amateur production of *The Importance of Being Earnest*. The costumes interest Carr, and he and Joyce exit to look over the play. Tzara offers Gwen a Dadaist rearrangement of William Shakespeare's eighteenth sonnet and eventually slips into a parody on the proposal scene from *The Importance of Being Earnest*. Gwendolen leaves to tell Carr of the proposal, while Joyce enters, grabs Tzara's hat, and leaves.

Joyce quickly returns, covered with bits of sonnet that were in the hat, and discusses Dadaism with Tzara. During the discussion, Joyce pulls various things out of the hat while countering Tzara's statements. He finally produces a rabbit, then leaves. Tzara joins Gwendolen offstage while Old Carr returns to reminisce about the lawsuit against Joyce that he lost. He recounts a dream in which he tried to shame Joyce by asking what he did in the war, only to be answered, "I wrote *Ulysses*."

The much shorter second act opens in the library, the set now including Cecily's desk or counter, on which people occasionally stand to make speeches. Cecily, spotlighted, waits downstage for the audience to return from the intermission so she can begin her lecture on Marxism, communism, Lenin, and Russian history. (Tom Stoppard's stage directions allow for cuts but specify that the lecture must start by the time Cecily talks of the war and the Lenins' arrival in Switzerland.) Lights come up, and Lenin and Nadya repeat the Russian conversation from act 1 while Cecily translates.

Tzara had earlier used the name Jack, so Carr enters into a parody of Wilde's plot, presenting himself to Cecily as Tristan. The scene now mixes Carr's repeated luncheon invitations to Cecily, details of Lenin's plans to travel in disguise to Russia, and discussions of art's relation to society and of the war as economic opportunism.

Cecily perceives that subconsciously Carr is more interested in her underwear than her arguments. Stoppard suggests that she here climb onto the desk, under colored lights, with "The Stripper" playing softly as she continues lecturing. With lights back to normal, Carr declares his love and they disappear behind the desk as Nadya enters to tell the audience about further plans to get Lenin to Russia. Tzara returns, and Nadya's narrative is interwoven with a travesty of Wilde's third-act meeting between Algernon and Jack. The sound of a train announces Lenin's departure just as Carr decides he should be stopped.

Everyone else leaves, and Lenin returns, climbs on the desk, and lectures on the writer and socialism. His statements are eventually intercut with Nadya's comments on his literary and musical tastes. Ludwig van Beethoven's "Appassionata" sonata covers a set change to Carr's room, where Gwendolen and Cecily speak in a parody of the music-hall song "Mr. Gallagher and Mr. Shean" as they drink tea and chat about events so far in the play. They argue over their claims to Tzara until Carr arrives, followed by Tzara, and is identified by Gwendolen. Both women berate the men for their deceptions and exit.

Bennett tells the men about critical responses to the production of *The Importance of Being Earnest*. Joyce enters, and the argument over money for tickets sold and the cost of Algernon's trousers is recapitulated. Joyce discovers that part of his *Ulysses* manuscript is missing. When the switch of folders in act 1 is resolved and the manuscript restored, the men and women embrace. Carr and Cecily dance off and, as Tzara and Gwendolen leave, return as the old Carrs. She corrects his recollections: He never met Lenin; the production of Wilde's play took place in 1918, not 1917; Bennett was the British Consul. Carr ends the play with a bumbling remark on the desirability of being an artist or a revolutionary.

Themes and Meanings

Travesties is primarily about revolution in politics and art, and the role of the artist. At times the discussion of art becomes philosophical in tone as Tzara advances the Dadaist concept that chance rules all. Carr, by contrast, believes that the artist is someone special, although he resents that a bit. Lenin is primarily interested in the way art can serve revolution. He and Cecily see it generally in practical terms. Joyce, conversely, thinks of art for art's sake, regards himself as a shaper of material, and considers his work a high calling. Interwoven with these discussions are comments on World War I, which was raging in Europe while Joyce, Lenin, Tzara, Carr, and Nadya were in neutral Switzerland.

Although they were in Zurich at about the same time, Lenin, Tzara, and Joyce may never have met. Carr and Joyce did in fact go to court in a dispute over expenses for the production of *The Importance of Being Earnest*. Juxtaposing the four men is Stoppard's device for testing various arguments against each other: Joyce was revolutionizing the novel with *Ulysses*; Tzara and other Dadaists were trying to revolutionize all art; Lenin would soon help revolutionize Russia. Stoppard creates various combinations of figures and lets them speak their own words or his version of what they might have said. Lenin is more distant and does not argue with the others, but one of Stoppard's creations, Cecily, voices his views on social revolution and engages Tzara and Carr in debate.

Carr, although a real person, is given a special character and purpose. In the arguments he represents the conservative Edwardian English attitude. He utters clichés about duty and honor and saving Belgium from the Germans and cannot begin to understand the various revolutionary viewpoints, although he supports freedom of expression. His statements act as catalysts, making Joyce and Tzara argue more passionately. As Old Carr, he shapes what the audience sees and hears, so that later speeches and statements are inserted into 1917 scenes. In addition, his faulty memory and limited intellect make the recollections disorganized, so that arguments often break off before they are completed.

The contrast of the seriousness of Lenin, the zaniness of Tzara, the satiric self-centeredness of Joyce, and the conservatism of Carr help to engage the audience in comparing their statements, as well as responding to the speakers. The swirl of ideas is also kept going by occasionally adopting Wilde's witty, aphoristic style and by interspersing arguments with afternoon tea, formal calls, and Carr's personal recollection of trench warfare.

Dramatic Devices

Travesties is a "memory play," controlled by Old Carr's erratic and inaccurate recollections. Old Carr (in the mid-1970's) inhabits exactly the same room in Zurich that Young Carr does. The library sometimes becomes a place for political lectures and at other times functions realistically as a library, depending on how Carr is remembering events. Frequently there are repeated attempts to start a dialogue or present an entrance; each start lets conversation and action go in a slightly different direction. Lighting is occasionally used to signal Old Carr's mental lapses. Lights dim, then come back up as the conversation starts over.

There is very little physical action. Tzara breaks some crockery; Carr and Cecily disappear behind the desk; Old Carr becomes young by removing some clothes; Cecily may move a bit to "The Stripper." Almost nothing is made of the exchange of the folders containing Joyce's and Lenin's work. One of the theatrically best scenes is Joyce's series of magic tricks with Tzara's hat. Most of the action is mental, and consists of heated arguments. Occasionally, there are long monologues.

The title suggests an important device—the travesty or parody. The speeches of Joyce and Lenin are in the two men's sharply contrasting styles; this can be seen if one reads part of *Ulysses* and some of Lenin's writings. Joyce was also fond of limericks, and part of a scene is done in that form. The main takeoff is of *The Importance of Being Earnest*. Stoppard's two creations, Gwendolen and Cecily, are named after Wilde's heroines. Many lines are quoted or paralleled. Some scenes, such as Tzara's proposal or the women's argument, recall Wilde's originals. The actual production of Wilde's play in Zurich keeps intruding into recollections of major events.

Old Cecily Carr tries to correct some major errors in Carr's memories at the end. Trivia, such as Joyce's misrecorded middle name, and major points, such as Carr's slanted opinion of Joyce, plus the intermingling of fictitious and real people help create a shifting surface that is intellectually challenging.

Critical Context

Almost a decade before he wrote *Travesties*, Stoppard achieved major theatrical success with *Rosencrantz and Guildenstern Are Dead* (pr. 1966), raising existential questions about taking action as he focused on the two young men whom Hamlet sends to their deaths in William Shakespeare's play. *Jumpers* (pr., pb. 1972) carried philosophical arguments further as Stoppard's Professor George Moore twists the logical system of the real G. E. Moore while practicing for a debate that may secure for him a university chair. In a more extreme juxtaposition of diverse elements than that in *Travesties*, Moore's wife verges on a breakdown as she watches a moon landing, sings, and is surrounded by a troupe of acrobats celebrating a radical political victory.

In *The Real Inspector Hound* (pr., pb. 1968) Stoppard explored the problem of reality's relation to fiction by pulling drama critics into the play they are reviewing. The mystery, a parody of Agatha Christie, is solved after the critics become victims. In *Hapgood* (pr., pb. 1988), a confusing tale of spy and counterspy, he again mixed an intellectual debate (on Heisenberg's Uncertainty Principle) with parody.

Occasionally, Stoppard has written more naturalistically, as in *Night and Day* (pr., pb. 1978), in which he examines journalistic ethics against an African setting, or *The Real Thing* (pr., pb. 1982), where he debates the nature of love. Generally, however, Stoppard seems to prefer to mix intellectual references to literature, philosophy, and art with mechanically controlled plays that are based on some trick—as in *Travesties*, where everything is filtered through Old Carr's mind. Some critics have seen such devices as brilliant, while others have complained of the lack of plot and of indulgence in words and monologues for their own sake. All see Stoppard as a master of ideas who presents an intellectual challenge to his audiences.

Sources for Further Study

Anchetta, Richard A. *Tom Stoppard: An Analytical Study of His Plays*. Chicago: Advent, 1991.

Bigsby, C. W. E. *Tom Stoppard*. Harlow, England: Longman, 1976.

Cahn, Victor L. *Beyond Absurdity: The Plays of Tom Stoppard*. Rutherford, N.J.: Fairleigh Dickinson University Press, 1979.

Dean, Joan Fitzpatrick. *Tom Stoppard: Comedy as a Moral Matrix*. Columbia: University of Missouri Press, 1981.

Gabbard, Paquet Lucina. *The Stoppard Plays*. Troy, N.Y.: Whitston, 1982.

Gitzen, Julian. "Tom Stoppard: Chaos in Perspective." *Southern Humanities Review* 10 (1976): 143-152.

Gussow, Mel. *Conversations with Stoppard*. New York: Grove-Atlantic, 1996.

Harty, John. *Tom Stoppard: A Casebook*. New York: Garland, 1987.

Hayman, Ronald. *Tom Stoppard*. London: Heinemann, 1977.

Londre, Felicia Hardison. "Tom Stoppard." In *Contemporary Dramatists*. 6th ed. Detroit: St. James, 1999.

Whitaker, Thomas. *Tom Stoppard*. New York: Grove Press, 1984.

Frances A. Shirley

THE TREE CLIMBER

Author: Tawfiq al-Hakim (1898-1987)
Type of plot: Absurdist
Time of plot: The early 1960's
Locale: al-Zaytun, on the northern outskirts of Cairo, Egypt
First produced: c. 1961, at the Masrah al-jayb, Cairo
First published: Ya tali' al-shajarah, 1962 (English translation, 1966)

> *Principal characters:*
> THE DETECTIVE, a policeman sent to investigate Bihana's
>   disappearance
> THE MAIDSERVANT, a gossiping woman who feeds the detective's
>   suspicions
> BIHANA, a woman of about sixty
> BAHADIR EFENDI, her husband, a retired railway inspector
> THE ASSISTANT TICKET INSPECTOR, an inefficient railway worker
>   who angers Bahadir Efendi
> THE DERVISH, a mysterious person who insinuates that Bahadir
>   Efendi has killed his wife

The Play

The peculiar convolutions of a plot which transmutes mysteries into unanswerable riddles are set forth in the initial dialogue, in which a police detective, in questioning a household maid, is apprised of some unusual domestic concerns. A woman has disappeared while she was on a shopping trip, even though habitually she has gone on errands of that sort to buy yarn for the dress of her daughter, who, during a previous marriage, was aborted forty years ago. Her present husband, Bahadir Efendi, who retired from railway work five years before, spends much of his time in their garden with Lady Green (Shaykhah Khadra'), a lizard which he claims has maintained a sanctuary in an orange tree; however, the maid has never seen any indication that such an animal has ever existed. The elderly couple hardly have anything to do with each other, according to the maid; as if to demonstrate her point, even as she is talking to the detective, the wife appears suddenly at the window of the house and calls out to her husband; when he responds, they launch into a series of statements that virtually seem to be parallel monologues. Each one's thoughts are turned around to suit the other's preoccupations. What to the husband is the growth of the orange tree, to the wife is the growth of her unborn daughter; as Bahadir Efendi muses upon green foliage, his wife interjects her fond thoughts about the child's green dress that she has constantly been knitting.

When the detective summons the husband, he is surprised to hear Bahadir Efendi announce that something completely out of the ordinary has taken place: The venerable lizard which has lived in the garden for nine years inexplicably has disappeared. As the questioning proceeds, matters take a new turn when Bahadir Efendi admits to contemplating the murder of his wife, and then, after a few bizarre and befuddling exchanges, he divulges that her body has been buried at the foot of the orange tree; however, when the detective proposes that they dig there, the husband protests that any injury to its roots would be tantamount to a blow against his person. Then he suggests that perhaps she has not been killed after all.

When the husband holds forth on his past work as a railway inspector, they are spirited away to a train coach. Bahadir Efendi, after upbraiding an assistant inspector who has been, he claims, lax in his duties, comes upon a mysterious dervish who proffers his birth certificate in place of a ticket and then points out that, since at present he does nothing, and he will do nothing if he is imprisoned, there is nothing to be gained from instituting proceedings against him. Nevertheless, as the inspector and the detective look on in astonishment, the dervish produces ten valid tickets out of empty air. In an oracular fashion, the dervish maintains that either the husband has killed his wife, or he has not yet killed her; for a motive, the detective suggests that Bahadir needed her body as nourishment for the tree.

As the second act opens, the detective is seen supervising efforts to unearth the wife's body; this operation is suspended once Bihana appears and—in a state of some amazement—asks the investigator what is happening. For her part, she can make little sense indeed out of the investigator's account of police actions in this case; she maintains that Bahadir Efendi would hardly have any reason to kill her since they have remained an affectionate couple and have never seriously disagreed about anything. Somewhat ominously, Bihana points out that because of their reliance on suspicion and circumstantial evidence the police would have kept Bahadir in prison, and, had she not returned at this time, quite possibly he would have faced charges arising from her supposed disappearance. When the husband comes on the scene again, he embraces Bihana; then, after some scattered comments about her daughter and his tree, the husband announces that his beloved lizard has returned.

For Bahadir, his wife's recent whereabouts still present a conundrum, in that he has not seen her for three days; whenever one has been present the other has been absent, and they have been together since the police inquiry began. Doubts and uncertainty like those that have clouded others' dealings with Bahadir Efendi now are directed against his wife; dark suppositions suddenly seem possible, and her assertions that she was somewhere do not assuage her husband's mounting and morbid curiosity. He names fifty-seven separate sorts of places, asking her one by one whether she was in any of them; each time she answers "No," without any explanation. Later he inquires whether she thought of staying away, or whether she did not think of staying away, and in both instances as well she responds "No." Infuriated by her apparent evasions, he seizes her by the throat and shakes her; as she still will not answer, his agitation gets the better of him, and he throttles her until apparently she is dead.

When Bahadir Efendi, distraught and remorseful, realizes what he has done, he calls the detective, who, proceeding on his earlier assumptions, concludes that the wife has disappeared again and urges Bahadir not to become disturbed. As he prepares to bury the body, Bahadir suddenly is confronted with the dervish, who, instead of offering to bear witness against the husband, poses another puzzle for him: If the tree cannot smell its own flowers, see its own colors, or eat its own fruit, then it seems consigned to an existence that, from its own standpoint, is futile. However, the dervish has asserted that it actually can bear four fruits in season and is the sort of tree for which no name yet exists. If scientists later investigate its secrets the body of Bihana certainly will be discovered and Bahadir will return to prison. Captivated nevertheless by the thought of his association with this wondrous tree, Bahadir goes back into the garden; in the place of his wife, who somehow has taken leave of them once more, he finds the body of Lady Green, the lizard he has regarded as his peculiar benefactor.

Themes and Meanings

When ordinary distinctions between appearance and reality seem to founder on semantic confusion, and any dealings with others appear to be fraught with misunderstandings, basic problems of human relations seem cast in high relief. Each of the characters has a specific and distinctive point of view which seems grounded in certain presumptions that limit or indeed exclude any comprehension of different situations—even where the interpretation of ostensibly mundane facts is concerned. Bihana and Bahadir Efendi, in particular, do not carry on conversations so much as they engage in tangential discourses in which certain images or thoughts may coincide. When the same sounds or colors may call to mind the wife's missing daughter or the husband's tree, there will be a temporary conjunction of ideas which then will cause one or the other to embark on a fixed course.

As the extent to which their own preoccupations have affected relations with each other becomes clear, it may be observed as well that each has become devoted to some imagined or anthropomorphic being—whether a garden-dwelling lizard or a child who was never born—that has displaced the wife's attentions toward the husband and the husband's regard for the wife. In encounters of another sort, once the detective has become convinced that any disappearance means murder, his questions of the accused man seem to lead ineluctably to this conclusion, until the husband, to prevent any digging around his beloved tree, maintains first that Bihana has not been buried there and then that he has not actually killed her. The detective protests that there is a lack of understanding between them, whereupon the husband contends that they share no mutual understanding about understanding. Similarly, many of the wife's statements appear to be internally consistent (at least until the end), but what she says cannot be reconciled with the preconceived notions that others have formed. Reasoning sometimes seems to proceed backward from premises that may be plausible to some but are seriously mistaken to others.

For that matter, the reader or playgoer is not necessarily much better informed; during the initial investigations, there is from the standpoint of the audience little to distinguish one supposition from another, and some queries remain unanswered throughout. It never is determined where Bihana actually was during the three days of her disappearance, and other matters remain no less murky for viewers or readers than they are for actual participants in the drama. At the end, it is by no means clear what has happened to the wife's body, if indeed she even was killed once and for all. Although Tawfiq al-Hakim does not really advance any form of outright solipsism, the notion that facts and perceptions cannot be distinguished from the subjective bases of knowledge and ideas is raised implicitly throughout this work. The question of whether logical reasoning also follows a course which is specific to each individual is also considered. In another light, it is hinted that words and objects may be confounded; by referring to some person or some entity in a certain way, habits of speech eventually seem to impose certain qualities and attributes upon the referent. In an extreme form, through this transposition of functions, it may appear that speaking of an object may call it into being; some of the dervish's sleight of hand seems to be accomplished in this way, and indeed the entry and disappearance of certain characters appear to follow particular invocations of their names.

Dramatic Devices

Although the philosophical issues posed by Tawfiq al-Hakim in this work may seem perplexing, if not daunting, there are some indications that the playwright did not mean them to be taken too seriously. To be sure, the presentation of weightier issues is supported by a certain number of specific devices which create an atmosphere that is suitable for unnatural events. The stage directions call for no sets and no fixed props; the players are to bring accessories such as tables and chairs with them. Evidently other effects, such as those suggesting a railroad car, are to be conveyed obliquely by inference from the dialogue and deportment of the characters. Some individuals remain unseen by the audience; the man hired to dig in Bahadir Efendi's garden, for example, remains offstage while he does his work. The playwright has also arranged it so that, with only a few exceptions, at any time only two characters will be speaking to each other; in effect, it is left to the audience to decide which one has the greater credibility. Thus the impression of multiple illusions, where inexplicable events follow one another, is heightened by some of the limitations that the author purposely has imposed. It would not, however, appear to be a difficult work to perform, and indeed since it first appeared, productions have been staged both in the original version and in translation.

Part of the appeal of *The Tree Climber* lies in its use of playful motifs drawn from regional folklore, which leaven some of the more abstruse passages in the work. The title was taken from a children's nonsense song, and ostensibly refers to Bahadir Efendi's green lizard. In keeping with the wife's concern about her unborn daughter, she sometimes sings verses that are used at the parties which traditionally are given to celebrate the seventh day after the birth of an infant. At certain times, and notably at the end, the sounds tend to merge and resemble each other. Some representational forms have been likened to those from the Arabian Nights tales and other classical works, in which magic, soothsaying, and mysterious appearances and absences were freely utilized. Thus a certain number of whimsical and lighthearted touches may be found where Tawfiq al-Hakim has combined ideas and material from several sources.

Critical Context

Since his student years in Paris, between 1925 and 1928, Tawfiq al-Hakim traveled in Europe on various occasions, and when *The Tree Climber* was published, he referred to the influence the Theater of the Absurd had exerted on him, particularly after a lengthy stay in France in 1959 and 1960. Among those he cited as important predecessors in this sense were Samuel Beckett and Eugène Ionesco. Nevertheless, al-Hakim preferred to designate his particular conception as irrationalist, and he has maintained, though not to the satisfaction of some critics, that his ideas in this regard should be considered a distinct formulation in their own right. Although it may be contended perhaps that during various stages of al-Hakim's career, Western drama has provided inspiration for certain works, it should also be noted that his own efforts have manifested distinctive features which have set forth some of the themes and techniques that were recast in *The Tree Climber*. His early work *Shahrazad* (pb. 1934; partial English translation, 1944) supplied the author's own ending to a work which represented in effect a continuation of the Arabian Nights. Some of al-Hakim's other plays have employed jinn and other fabled beings to achieve unusual, seemingly magical resolutions of problems which were handled in an ironic mode.

In somewhat flippant sketches, such as *Himari qala li* (pb. 1945; short plays, one translated as *The Donkey Market*, 1981) and *Kullu shay' fi mahallihi* (pb. 1966; *Not a Thing Out of Place*, 1973), the notion of a talking donkey produces a number of passages where philosophy and nonsense each appear to be allotted their due. Those who have regarded some of al-Hakim's works specifically as absurdist would include in this category *al-Ta'am li-kull fam* (pb. 1963; *Food for the Millions*, 1984), in which mysterious stains on the wall of an apartment seem to evoke images of murder and family intrigue; the shapes that form appear to perform a shadow play of their own, which has particular meanings for different characters. Another well-known work which may be interpreted in several ways is *Masir sursar* (pb. 1966; *Fate of a Cockroach*, 1973), which presents quarrels over precedence between an insect king and his queen that very much resemble any wife's squabbles with her husband; however, first one and then the other becomes fascinated with the struggles of a stranded cockroach—until the household cook drowns the poor creature and the insect and his wife begin arguing again. By such means, al-Hakim's combinations of comic and bizarre conceptions have given proof of his great versatility in handling various forms of drama.

Sources for Further Study

Audebert, C. F. "Al-Hakim's *Ya tali' al-shajara* and Folk Art." *Journal of Arabic Literature* 9 (1978): 138-149.

Badawi, Muhammad Mustafa. "A Passion for Experimentation: The Novels and Plays of Tawfiq al-Hakim." *Third World Quarterly* 10, no. 2 (1988): 949-960.

_____. "Tawfiq al-Hakim." In *Modern Arabic Drama in Egypt*. Cambridge, Mass.: Cambridge University Press, 1987.

Cachia, Pierre. "Idealism and Ideology: The Case of Tawfiq al-Hakim." *Journal of the American Oriental Society* 100, no. 3 (1980): 225-235.

Gella, Julius. "Marginal Comment on Tawfiq al-Hakim's Symbolic-Intellectual Drama *Ya taliʿ al-shajara*." *Graecolatina et Orientalia* 7/8 (1975/1976): 251-264.

Long, Richard. *Tawfiq al-Hakim: Playwright of Egypt*. London: Ithaca Press, 1979.

Starkey, Paul. *From the Ivory Tower: A Critical Analysis of Tawfiq Al-Hakim*. Atlantic Highlands, N.J.: Ithaca Press, 1998.

_____. "Philosophical Themes in Tawfiq al-Hakim's Drama." *Journal of Arabic Literature* 8 (1977): 136-152.

J. R. Broadus

TRIFLES

Author: Susan Glaspell (1876-1948)
Type of plot: Mystery and detective
Time of plot: The early twentieth century
Locale: A family farmhouse in the American Midwest
First produced: 1916, at the Wharf Theatre, Provincetown, Massachusetts
First published: 1917

Principal characters:
>GEORGE HENDERSON, the county attorney, a young man investigating John Wright's murder
>MR. PETERS, the middle-aged sheriff and local representative of the law
>MRS. PETERS, his middle-aged wife
>MR. HALE, a middle-aged neighbor of the Wrights who discovers the crime
>MRS. HALE, his wife

The Play

Trifles tells the story of two investigations into the murder of John Wright. The male characters carry on the official investigation while the female characters carry on their own unofficial investigation.

The play opens when its five characters enter the kitchen of the Wright farmhouse. The county attorney takes charge of the investigation, guiding the sheriff and Mr. Hale in recounting their roles in the discovery of the crime. Mr. Hale tells how he came to the house to ask John Wright about sharing the cost of a phone line, only to find Mrs. Wright sitting in a rocker. When he asks to speak with her husband, Mrs. Wright says that he cannot speak with Mr. Hale because he is dead. Mr. Hale investigates and finds that Wright has been hanged. After commenting on Mrs. Wright's poor housekeeping in ways that irritate the women present, the county attorney leads the men upstairs so he can search the scene of the crime for a motive.

The women are left alone. While gathering some household goods to make Mrs. Wright feel more at ease in jail, they discuss Minnie Wright, her childhood as Minnie Foster, her life with John Wright, and the quilt that she was making when she was taken to jail. The men reenter briefly, then leave. The women discuss the state of the Wright household before Mr. Wright's death. In the process, they communicate how greatly Mrs. Wright had changed over the years and how depressing her life with John Wright had been. The women express sympathy over what the kitchen disarray would mean emotionally to Mrs. Wright and how much of an intrusion it was for her to have all of these outsiders searching through her goods. The women discover Mrs. Wright's pet bird. It has been killed, and Mrs. Wright had hidden it in her sewing box.

The women's eyes meet, but they do not speak directly about the bird. When she hears the men returning again, Mrs. Hale hides the dead bird.

Once the men have left again, the women discuss past pains and losses that parallel those that Mrs. Wright has suffered. A boy killed Mrs. Peters's kitten when she was a child, and she was childless for a time, like Mrs. Wright. The women express a shared sense of responsibility for her isolation and suggest that they were criminally negligent to allow her to be entirely alone. Just before the men reenter, Mrs. Peters suggests that they are getting too upset over a dead bird.

The county attorney summarizes the case as he enters and indicates that the entire case is clear except for a missing motive. As the investigation ends, the sheriff asks the attorney if he needs to inspect the things the women are taking to Mrs. Wright in jail. The county attorney dismisses this jokingly, suggesting that there is no need because the sheriff's wife, Mrs. Peters, is essentially married to the law. When the men leave the room to check one last detail, the women's eyes meet again. Mrs. Peters tries to hide the box containing the dead bird in the bag of quilt pieces she is taking to Mrs. Wright, but it does not fit. Mrs. Hale hides the box in her coat pocket. When the men reenter, the women have one last chance to share this clue with them. They do not, and the play closes.

Themes and Meanings

Though its plot focuses on a single moral choice, that of Mrs. Hale and Mrs. Peters deciding whether or not to expose why Mrs. Wright killed her husband, *Trifles* is thematically complex. It addresses the abiding issue of justice and contemporary issues of gender and identity politics. Susan Glaspell's power comes from the way she interweaves these issues until they are impossible to separate. When they enter the farmhouse, Mrs. Hale and Mrs. Peters are there as wives, adjunct to their husbands' roles in society. However, through the process of attempting to help another woman by gathering items from her household that might comfort her in jail, they learn to identify themselves first as women and only secondarily as wives. Each woman recognizes her own life in Mrs. Wright's suffering, and each comes to see that given the wrong circumstances, she, too, would have killed the man that so damaged her. These women symbolize all women, and this growing awareness suggests the possibility of personal transformation that decades later emerged in feminist consciousness-raising groups. When they decide to hide the evidence of Mrs. Wright's motive for the murder, the two women are condoning the crime, or declaring that it is not a crime, but justice for the suffering that John Wright inflicted on his wife.

This stance creates a tremendous moral dilemma. The ideal of justice is that a truly just society is impartial. All the male characters are blind to what is going on and are even condescending to the women. The county attorney is the worst example of this. He is so certain that he knows what the situation entails that he will not even let other characters finish speaking. Yet, he and all the male characters cannot see the truth that is literally right in front of their faces. Mr. Hale and the sheriff cannot see that the women they live with are keeping something from them. This suggests that the entire concept of justice is flawed. Either there are different justices for different groups, according to their experience of the world, or, worse, there are different realities, invisible to those who do not share them. The choice to hide a dead bird may symbolize the death knell for the Western political system: How can a fair and functioning society be constructed in such circumstances? At the very least, the play casts doubt on all existing legal structures unless the female perspective is integrated.

Dramatic Devices

In *De poetica* (c. 334-323 B.C.E.; *Poetics*, 1705), Aristotle's treatise on drama, he argued that a tragedy should consist of a single action, completed in one place and taking no longer than one day. *Trifles* follows these rules perfectly, taking place in a single room and far less time than one day. However, *Trifles* is more a social criticism than tragedy. Glaspell uses a variety of dramatic devices to critique her society. There are no formal scene breaks in *Trifles*. Instead, the entrances and exits of the male characters define the play. Each time the men leave, the women exchange private information; each time they enter, the men force or prevent crucial decisions. This action controls the pace of the play and symbolizes how men run women's lives, controlling and silencing them as John Wright silenced his wife.

The many doubles in *Trifles* create a symbolic structure. Mr. Hale is accompanied by his wife; the sheriff is accompanied by his wife, Mrs. Peters. The county attorney is there because another pairing, Mr. and Mrs. Wright, was disrupted, indicating that the law must step in when the symbolic foundations of society breaks down. To underscore this point, the county attorney looks for a way to speak for Mrs. Wright, who refuses to speak for herself, and who is, indeed, completely absent from the play, making her invisibility to the social order literal. The final doubling is between Mrs. Wright and her bird. The bird symbolizes Mrs. Wright, a beautiful creature who loved to sing. When her husband killed it, it was as if she had been killed, and she killed him in turn.

Glaspell adapts a technique from German expressionist drama, referring to the male characters primarily by their social roles. Yet, Glaspell gives this casting an ironic twist by giving the characters names that reveal who they really are. Mr. Hale is hale and hearty; Mr. Peters, whose name means "rock," is a sheriff, or a foundation of society. These names fit far less well for the women. Minnie Foster was out of place as a foster child, and the man she marries, John Wright, is anything but Mr. Right. Irony runs through the dialogue as well. During the play's climax, the women discuss how Mrs. Wright killed her husband, but the men assume the women are still discussing housework. This is the final example of the "trifles" that give the play its ironic title.

Critical Context

Susan Glaspell was part of a group of artists and thinkers devoted to a broad range of progressive causes, such as feminism, socialism, Darwinism, and legal reform. She and her husband, George Cram Cook, founded the Provincetown Players, a theater group committed to transforming American theater from mere entertainment into an artistic medium in which serious social issues could be treated realistically. The group was crucial in establishing American drama. In addition to Glaspell's work, the Players produced work by Edna St. Vincent Millay and Eugene O'Neill. Glaspell wrote several plays for the company, but *Trifles* is the best known and helped introduce the use of expressionist technique to the American stage.

Trifles is also important for its place in Glaspell's individual career and for its place in American theater history. While writing for newspapers in her native Iowa, Susan Glaspell covered a murder trial in which a wife killed her husband. This trial became the basis not only of *Trifles*, but also of *A Jury of Her Peers* (1927), the story version of the play. Clearly, this story haunted Glaspell, and understanding this play is central to understanding Glaspell's career as a dramatist. Her deep involvement in the play's topic led her to play Mrs. Hale (her husband played Mr. Hale) in the original production.

Trifles demonstrated that the emerging popular genre of detective fiction could be used for higher artistic aims. Glaspell achieved this in part by the technical perfection of the play: *Trifles* is one of the classics of the one-act form. It is economically written, something not always true of Glaspell's later work, even of *Alison's House* (pr., pb. 1930), the play that earned for Glaspell the 1931 Pulitzer Prize. *Trifles* also introduces a technique that Glaspell reuses in other plays: The pivotal character never appears onstage. *Trifles* is the first major work of feminist theater written by an American playwright. It was well known when it was first performed, playing successfully throughout the United States and Europe, but was not performed as often during the middle of the twentieth century. Some critics argue that this absence indicates the way that women have traditionally been eclipsed on the American stage. However, with the emergence of a feminist consciousness late in the twentieth century, *Trifles* once again received the attention it so richly deserves.

Sources for Further Study

Ben-Zvi, Linda, ed. *Susan Glaspell: Essays on Her Theater and Fiction.* Ann Arbor: University of Michigan Press, 1995.

Glaspell, Susan. *"Lifted Masks" and Other Works.* Edited by Eric S. Rabkin. Ann Arbor: University of Michigan Press, 1993.

Ozieblo, Barbara. "Rebellion and Rejection: The Plays of Susan Glaspell." In *Modern American Drama: The Female Canon.* Cranbury, N.J.: Associated University Presses, 1990.

Shafer, Yvonne. *American Women Playwrights, 1900-1950.* New York: Peter Lang, 1995.

Waterman, Arthur E. *Susan Glaspell.* New York: Twayne, 1966.

Greg Beatty

THE TRIP TO BOUNTIFUL

Author: Horton Foote (1916-   )
Type of plot: Domestic realism
Time of plot: The early 1950's
Locale: Houston, Harrison, and Bountiful, Texas
First produced: 1953, at Henry Miller's Theatre, New York City
First published: 1954

Principal characters:

LUDIE WATTS, an accountant in Houston
MRS. WATTS, his elderly mother
JESSIE MAE, his wife
THELMA, a young woman Mrs. Watts meets in the Houston bus station
THE SHERIFF, the lawman who escorts Mrs. Watts to Bountiful from Harrison
TWO HOUSTON TICKET MEN, agents in the Houston bus station
HARRISON TICKET MAN, the agent in the Harrison bus station

The Play

The Trip to Bountiful opens in a neat and sparsely furnished three-room apartment in Houston, where Ludie Watts and his wife, Jessie Mae, are lying in their bed. Ludie quietly moves into the living room, where his mother is rocking in a chair and humming an old hymn. When she speaks to him, her first three words are "Don't be afraid"—words that are in accord with the bracing message of the hymn of comfort.

As Ludie and his mother chat quietly in their country dialect, clamorous traffic noises from the urban street outside create a sense of incongruity. Mrs. Watts tells Ludie that she has never been able to sleep when the moon is full and reminds him of a night long ago in their home in Bountiful when she took him for a walk under a full moon. Ludie initially claims not to remember that night but near the end of the play admits that he does remember it. Her words indicate the contrast between that night in Bountiful, when she comforted him and dismissed his childish fear of death, and the present moonlit night in a cheap apartment in Houston. When Ludie complains about not having a yard, his mother sings a few lines of a song he liked as a child and offers to fix him hot milk. The nostalgic moment is suddenly interrupted by a loud traffic noise that awakens Jessie Mae, who goes to the kitchen and begins quarreling with Mrs. Watts. Ludie, who evidently loves his wife despite her shrewish disposition, returns to the living room and gently asks his mother to apologize to Jessie Mae. Without argument, his mother does so. Jessie Mae is concerned that Mrs. Watts's pension check has not arrived and evidently needs it to pay for her own frequent visits to beauty shops, movie houses, and drugstores. However, Mrs. Watts finds her check and hides it in her nightgown.

In the bedroom, Ludie discusses with Jessie Mae his mother's attempts to run away to what Jessie Mae calls "that old town" and tells Jessie Mae that he plans to ask for a raise the next day. When she falls asleep, he returns to the living room, where his mother tells him she wants to go home. He explains that he can only make a living in Houston and goes back to bed. His mother then packs her suitcase and hides it.

The following morning finds Mrs. Watts asleep in her chair. As she awakens, Ludie prepares for work, and Jessie Mae again asks about her check and sends her mother-in-law down to the mailbox to see if it has come. After Jessie Mae calls her beauty shop to make an appointment, she notices that Mrs. Watts is pale, but Mrs. Watts assures her that nothing is wrong. After Jessie Mae goes out, Mrs. Watts takes her hat, coat, and suitcase and leaves the apartment.

The second act opens in the Houston bus terminal, where Mrs. Watts enters the ticket line to buy a ticket to Bountiful. However, the agent tells her that she must buy a ticket to Harrison, a town near Bountiful, leaving her slightly confused. In the waiting room, she sits next to a young woman named Thelma, whom she asks to watch her bag as she paces the room. Suddenly, she retrieves her bag and dashes toward the rest room, as Ludie enters the station, followed shortly by a furious Jessie Mae. When Ludie spots his mother's handkerchief on the floor, he gets Thelma to admit to having seen his mother earlier. Ludie and Jessie Mae return home to wait for Mrs. Watts, but Ludie says that he will only wait one hour at home before setting out in pursuit of his mother.

The next scene opens inside a moving bus, in which Mrs. Watts is sitting next to Thelma, who is going to her parents' home to stay while her husband is abroad on military duty. Mrs. Watts tries to raise the younger woman's spirits by quoting from a biblical Psalm but is unsuccessful. She goes on to reminisce about the good old days in Bountiful and tells Thelma about her problems with her daughter-in-law. Gradually, the two women confide their feelings to each other. When Thelma talks about her deep love for her husband, Mrs. Watts surprisingly responds that she never loved her own husband. Instead, she always loved a man named Ray John Murray, whose father prevented their marriage.

The next scene opens in the Harrison bus station, where Thelma asks the ticket agent how Mrs. Watts can get to Bountiful. The puzzled agent tells her that no one has lived in Bountiful since the last resident, Mrs. Callie Davis, recently died. Mrs. Watts—who told Thelma that she planned to stay with her childhood friend Callie Davis—is stunned by this news. Nevertheless, she resolves to continue with her plan to go home. As she prepares to sleep on a station bench, she discovers she has left her purse on the bus. With Thelma's help, however, she arranges with the ticket agent to have her purse sent back from the next stop. She tells Thelma that if her daughter had lived, "I would have wanted her to be just like you."

After Thelma boards a bus for her home town, Mrs. Watts asks the ticket agent about old acquaintances in Harrison, only to learn that they are all dead or forgotten.

Finally, she makes up a bed on a bench, the ticket agent turns out the lights, and Mrs. Watts goes to sleep on the bench while the agent dozes in his office. The local sheriff enters the station and tells the ticket agent that the Houston police have asked him to hold Mrs. Watts until her son arrives. However, he cannot bring himself to awaken her, so he goes out to call Houston. While he is gone, Mrs. Watts wakes up and learns from the agent what is going on. She tries to flee from the station, but the agent blocks her way. When the sheriff returns, she begs him to let her visit her old home. The scene ends with her struggling and whispering, "Bountiful . . . Bountiful. . . ."

The third act opens early the next morning, with the sheriff and Mrs. Watts in front of her old home, which is now dilapidated. Their conversation reveals that Mrs. Watts has seen a doctor and that the sheriff has taken it upon himself to drive her to her old home and to wait there for Ludie and Jessie Mae. As Mrs. Watts enters the house, the lights go down.

When the lights return, the sheriff tells Mrs. Watts that her son has arrived. Ludie thanks him as he leaves. When Mrs. Watts apologizes to Ludie for causing him trouble, he tells her that he will probably get the raise he requested. As they reminisce, Ludie admits that he lied earlier in saying that he did not remember their moonlit walk when he was a small child. "It doesn't do any good to remember," he says, as Jessie Mae begins honking the car horn. After Mrs. Watts begs Ludie one final time to be allowed to stay at the old place, she realizes the pain she is causing him and decides to accept what must be.

When Jessie Mae joins Ludie and his mother, she informs Mrs. Watts of a list of rules she has drawn up for the old woman's behavior. Mrs. Watts readily agrees to abide by all of them. However, when Jessie Mae again demands the pension check, Ludie asserts himself for the first time in the play, reminding his wife that she has given her word to live in peace with his mother. Mrs. Watts hands her the check anyway, and, surprisingly, Jessie Mae puts it in Mrs. Watts's purse.

As the three prepare to go back to the car Ludie has borrowed, Mrs. Watts falls behind the others. When she is alone, she sifts dirt through her fingers and says goodbye to Bountiful.

Themes and Meanings

This play resembles other Horton Foote plays in that it reminds the audience of the extraordinariness of ordinary human existence. Foote resembles the novelist William Faulkner in his conviction that fundamental truths can be found and expressed by means of a fictionalization of one's intimate experience of a region. He also brings to mind Aristotle, for Mrs. Watts's recognition of the unnecessary suffering of her son brings about the reversal of her misery as she realizes that she can act to diminish his pain. Her immediate sense of recovered strength and dignity amounts to a transformation.

The idea that wisdom comes through suffering is ancient, but this theme is as fundamental in Foote's plays as in ancient Greek tragedies. It is the agony of Mrs. Watts's disappointment in the Harrison bus station, echoed somewhat more mildly in her final outburst to Ludie at the old house, that makes it possible for her to comprehend and manage her disappointment. She renounces her dreams as she returns to the self-sacrificing role of loving mother, a woman who realizes she now has the strength to do what she must do and tolerate what she must tolerate in the final days of her life.

This play develops some of the significant conflicts familiar to any person of rural background who has moved to the city. The abandonment of the natural world for the artificial world can stress or distort human nature itself, and Mrs. Watts and Ludie feel that stress and distortion intensely. Jessie Mae, however, a selfish parasite, finds it highly comfortable to exploit the conscientiousness of her gentle husband and the excellent housekeeping and cooking of her "crazy" mother-in-law.

The play also sets forth conflicts between the relatively young and the old. Jessie Mae is contemptuous of the old. In her selfish view of the world, she only tolerates Mrs. Watts because of the latter's pension checks. She hates the hymns Mrs. Watts sings because spirituality means nothing to her. For Jessie Mae, a higher reality can be found in Hollywood films and movie magazines—the psychological equivalent of her favorite physical sustenance, Coca Cola and ice cream.

A final theme is that of compassion and redemption. Hurt as she is by her husband's departure overseas, Thelma does everything in her power to help Mrs. Watts on her journey. The sheriff, who at first seems resolved to do things by the book, takes pity on Mrs. Watts and drives her out to her old place. Their conversation reveals considerable compassion. The most intellectually intense moment of the play is that quiet moment of recognition when Mrs. Watts understands the intensity of her son's suffering and renounces her own dreams at the same moment he is developing new inner strength himself. Even Jessie Mae finally seems somewhat favorably affected by Ludie's quietly growing strength.

Dramatic Devices

The most significant dramatic device is Mrs. Watts's journey itself, along with the recurring hymn "There's Not a Friend Like the Lowly Jesus." On several previous occasions, Mrs. Watts tried to escape from her son's apartment, but this time she is successful, at least for a while. The incompetence she exhibits, partly because of her deteriorating faculties and partly because she clings to a lost past, make it clear that in any ordinary sense she has no business taking off alone for Bountiful. She keeps her pension check hidden throughout the play but when the play closes, her check has not yet been cashed, although it has set off a number of minor panic attacks. When she tries to escape the urban nightmare of Houston for the rural atmosphere of a romanticized past, she succeeds in some measure, only to find that that past, like her old house, is falling apart. Although the farms and old buildings are disappearing, she finds abiding human compassion and consideration in her chance encounters with Thelma and the sheriff.

The old hymn itself expresses a paradox. Sung as it was by churchgoers within the ceremonies of the rural church, it touches on the fundamental isolation of individuals and the necessity of their depending upon Jesus instead of other humans. Clearly, this hymn has sustained Mrs. Watts in her struggle against both the tyranny of Jessie Mae and the good-natured, loving ineffectuality of Ludie. A Christian reading of the play might well assert that in the moment of Mrs. Watts's recognition of her son's suffering she finds it possible to emulate the founder of her faith.

Critical Context

Horton Foote originally wrote *The Trip to Bountiful* for a 1953 broadcast of the *Philco Television Playhouse*, an early television program that presented live sixty-minute plays. The part of Mrs. Watts was played by Lillian Gish. When Foote later adapted the drama for the stage, it was produced in New York. He also wrote the screenplay for the film version in 1985. His screenplay was nominated for an Academy Award, and Geraldine Page, who played Mrs. Watts, won an Oscar as best actress.

The author of more than sixty plays, Foote has won Academy Awards for his adapted screenplay of *To Kill a Mockingbird* (1962) and for his original screenplay for *Tender Mercies* (1983). His play *The Young Man from Atlanta* (pr., pb. 1995) won a Pulitzer Prize. His only novel, *The Chase*, came out in 1956. In 1999, he published *Farewell: A Memoir of a Texas Childhood*, which was followed in 2001 by a sequel, *Beginnings: A Memoir*. In 2001, at the age of eighty-five, Foote saw his play *The Carpetbagger's Children* in its premiere performance in Houston.

Sources for Further Study

Briley, Rebecca. *You Can Go Home Again: The Focus on Family in the Works of Horton Foote*. New York: Peter Lang, 1993.

Moore, Barbara, and David G. Yellin, eds. *Horton Foote's Three Trips to Bountiful*. Dallas: Southern Methodist University Press, 1993.

Porter, Laurin R. "An Interview with Horton Foote." *Studies in American Drama, 1945-Present* 6, no. 2 (1991): 177-194.

Wood, Gerald C. *Horton Foote: A Casebook*. New York: Garland, 1998.

_____. *Horton Foote and the Theater of Intimacy*. Baton Rouge: Louisiana State University Press, 1999.

Robert W. Haynes

TROUBLE IN MIND

Author: Alice Childress (1916-1994)
Type of plot: Social realism
Time of plot: The 1950's
Locale: New York City
First produced: 1955, at the Greenwich Mews Theater, New York City
First published: 1971, in *Black Theater*

> *Principal characters:*
> WILETTA MAYER,
> MILLIE DAVIS, and
> SHELDON FORRESTER, veteran actors
> JOHN NEVINS and
> JUDY SEARS, novice actors
> AL MANNERS, a theatrical director

The Play

Trouble in Mind is set on a Broadway stage as the characters rehearse "Chaos in Belleville," a play written, directed, and produced by whites which is saturated with stereotypes of African Americans who respond to oppression with subservience. Act 1 opens with Wiletta Mayer, a middle-aged veteran actor, accepting accolades from the doorman, who recognizes her from past performances. Wiletta is joined by John Nevins, a novice actor. Wiletta admires John, particularly when she discovers that he is the son of her girlhood friend. Sensing John's eagerness to excel in the theater and to please the director, Wiletta takes it upon herself to coach John in the art of deception. She gives him advice on how to survive and succeed on the American stage, which popularizes stereotypes of African Americans. Wiletta admonishes John to do his very best to anticipate the white director's wishes and moods. She tells him that he must laugh, cry, or shuffle on demand in order to keep a part in a play and to earn a pittance. She boldly informs him that he must play the Uncle Tom, the servile black person who flatters whites in order to secure favors. She says that twenty years in the theater have taught her that any demonstration of assertiveness on the part of a black actor may result in unemployment. When John proudly asserts that he intends to succeed in the theater without compromising his integrity, Wiletta essentially tells him that he is a fool and abandons her efforts to serve as his mentor.

The two actors are joined by Millie Davis, a thirty-five-year-old black actor who has become disillusioned by the Aunt Jemima roles she has had to play. While Millie is flaunting her mink coat and boasting that her husband really does not want her to work, Judy Sears and Sheldon Forrester enter. Judy, a young white actor who has recently been graduated from Yale University, is optimistic that the American stage will embrace women. Sheldon, an elderly black actor who is accustomed to settling for any role he can get, wants all other black actors to make as few disturbances as possible about characterization.

While the group waits for the director to arrive, the black actors speak freely about the plight of African Americans both on and off the American stage. They discuss causes of racial unrest, including the Little Rock school desegregation incident and the protests in Montgomery, Alabama (the play is set during the 1950's). Wiletta and Millie tease each other about the limiting roles, as either mammies or ladies of the evening, they have played. They remind each other that they have played every flower (Gardenia, Magnolia, Chrysanthemum, Petunia) and every jewel (Crystal, Pearl, Opal, Ruby). Sheldon, afraid that the whites will overhear the two malcontents, cautions them to keep quiet and allow him to put food on his table.

Tension mounts when the director, Al Manners, arrives—praising the script for its brilliant portrayal of African Americans. Scenes which Manners interprets as realistic, Wiletta, Millie, and Judy find offensive and completely unnatural. Wiletta, the most vocal of the three, offers suggestions that would present the black person as he is and not as whites perceive him to be. Sensing Wiletta's hostility, Manners instructs her to deliver specified lines and begins to badger her about her character's motivation. Manners forces Wiletta into a word-association game, presumably to make her understand the importance of motivation when delivering lines. What results is an epiphany for Wiletta, wherein she realizes that she has degraded herself—and all African Americans—by accepting stereotypical roles. Act 1 ends with Wiletta announcing that she wants to be the best actor she can be without having to demean herself.

Act 2 of *Trouble in Mind* opens with a full-blown rehearsal of "Chaos in Belleville," a play which centers on whites in an imaginary town who form a mob to lynch a young, poor, southern black man, Job, because he dared to vote. The more Wiletta reads, the more irritated she becomes with the gross inaccuracies in characterization. She disrupts the group by asking for script changes, particularly a rewriting of the climactic scene, in which the parents of Job chastise him for not knowing his place, refuse to help him escape, pray for God's help, and tell him to give himself up to the law for safekeeping. She vehemently argues that these poor African Americans are inaccurately portrayed as being too underprivileged and uneducated to come to the aid of their son, who will meet certain death. She begs Manners to try to persuade the playwright at least to allow Job, since it seems he must die, to be killed while running away or to be dragged out of the house with his parents battling to the very end. Manners, angered by Wiletta's dissatisfaction, tells her to stick to acting and to leave the writing to the author and the interpretation to the director.

When Wiletta refuses to be silenced, Manners tells her that since no one in the cast has seen a lynching, each must imagine one, as did the playwright. Sheldon, however, vividly recalls a real lynching which left him silently screaming. Manners, embarrassed and infuriated, remains unwilling to request script changes and insults Wiletta by telling her that she thinks that she knows more about black life than does the author. Wiletta truly forgets her place and shouts to Manners that he is racist.

A break is immediately called, during which Wiletta recants her earlier advice to John. She tells him that she was a fool to tell him to cater to white directors in order to secure degrading roles. John, who during the course of the rehearsal has internalized Wiletta's advice and has become a carbon copy of Al Manners, ignores Wiletta and moves closer, spiritually and physically, to Judy. He looks to Judy and Manners for positive reinforcement. Wiletta, however, helps to recover John from Manners's influence by asking Manners if he would send his son out to be lynched. Manners tells the cast that neither Job nor John can be compared to his son because they have nothing in common with his son. John is humiliated, realizing that Manners sees him as inferior. Manners retreats offstage, leaving the cast to wonder if they will be fired.

The play ends with the cast being told that rehearsal will resume the next day and that they can expect a call. Wiletta announces that she probably will not be called but that she will appear anyway and force Manners to fire her. They play ends with Wiletta, alone with the doorman, reciting Psalm 133, a fulfillment of her dream of doing something grand in the theater.

Themes and Meanings

Trouble in Mind is about the shoddy treatment that African Americans and white women receive both on and off the American stage, which becomes symbolic of society at large. It is also a satiric drama about white writers, producers, and directors, who, because they are unfamiliar with black life and culture, uphold inaccurate portraits. Alice Childress suggests that African Americans must strive for integrity in the theater by refusing to accept roles that depict them as selfless, subservient, exotic, or dehumanized creatures. Wiletta and Millie, in their roles as docile servants whose primary function in "Chaos in Belleville" is to sing and to pray, exemplify the stereotypes which dominated the stage of the 1950's and which come under attack by Childress.

Trouble in Mind deals with the obstacles that many black actors face when they choose the theater as a career. Wiletta reminds the cast that Broadway shows are wholly owned and controlled by white men, who also create and manipulate the images of African Americans. The harnesses worn by black actors in the theater parallel the limitations placed upon African Americans in society, such as segregated housing, schooling, and transportation.

In defense of theater executives, Al Manners comments that the stereotypes of African Americans which reach the stage are perpetuated because such images make a play commercially successful. He explains that the American public is not ready to be told the unadulterated truth about African Americans and that theater executives will not raise a hundred thousand dollars unless a play has the potential to be successful.

On another level, *Trouble in Mind* pokes fun at the cutthroat competition for the few roles offered to African Americans. Childress demonstrates the conflicts black actors engage in as they insult one another and flatter white directors in order to secure these demeaning parts. Sheldon is accustomed to making compromises. He needs to feed his family and exchanges what Wiletta terms dignity for small, degrading parts in plays. While Wiletta and Millie fling barbs at Sheldon for his refusal to demand script changes, Sheldon lashes out by telling them that the reason African Americans cannot get jobs in the theater is that someone is always complaining about unfair treatment. He is grateful to have work and wishes the other African Americans would be satisfied as well. Childress demonstrates that the bickering among the African Americans only hurts their chances of pressuring theater executives to present more accurate images of African Americans.

Not only did Childress hold up the American theater as racist, but she also claimed that it is sexist. The women in the cast are treated with obvious condescension. When Millie offers suggestions about interpretation, Manners tells her that he loves the fabulous way that she dresses or that she is beautiful in order to silence her. When Wiletta disagrees with the images of African Americans, he tells her that she is totally out of her element. Judy, however, becomes Manners's scapegoat. He openly abuses her verbally and physically. Almost immediately after Judy boasts that she is a graduate of the Yale University drama program, Manners begins to victimize her. Apparently intimidated by Judy's credentials—and perhaps insecure about his own abilities—Manners shouts at her, orders her around, forcefully grabs her by the shoulders to direct her to various stage positions, silences her with a wave of his hand, and talks to her in baby talk—none of which he does to any of the male cast members. Manners's behavior toward Judy, Wiletta, and Millie clearly demonstrates Childress's notion that women in the American theater of the 1950's were treated as immature stepchildren.

Dramatic Devices

The main ideas of *Trouble in Mind* are conveyed through Alice Childress's manipulation of metadrama—drama about drama. The play-within-the-play is constructed so that its performance is set apart from the main action, with the cast of the primary play recognizing the existence of the inner play—the cast members of *Trouble in Mind* know that they have come together to rehearse the play "Chaos in Belleville." Childress links the inner world of the secondary play, "Chaos in Belleville," to the inner world of the primary play, *Trouble in Mind*, both of which mirror the outer world as one laden with racism, sexism, and poverty.

The world of "Chaos in Belleville" is one in which poor African Americans are lynched for trying to exercise their rights. The characters in "Chaos in Belleville," which is set shortly after the end of slavery, are depicted as poor, dejected, submissive people who relinquish any semblance of power in favor of protection from the law. Similarly, in the world of *Trouble in Mind*, African Americans discuss segregated housing and schools, racial violence, boycottings, riots, and stereotypical theatrical roles. Like the house servants in "Chaos in Belleville," John and Sheldon are docile and obsequious. All the characters, during the course of rehearsal, alternate back and forth so frequently between the primary and the secondary play that it becomes difficult for the audience to separate the drama from the metadrama. The characters are able to break and resume character so smoothly because the issues in both plays are the same: the presumptuousness of white liberals and racial and gender stereotyping.

The worlds of the primary play and the secondary play are meshed largely through humor. When Al Manners runs around waving his hands to silence the cast (particularly Wiletta), the audience recognizes his redundance, as his very presence and manners stifle the characters. The exaggerated force that he uses to keep them quiet seems ludicrous. Manners's behavior toward Judy is equally ridiculous. When she cannot recall the various stage directions, Manners rushes to her and pulls her quickly around the stage as he shouts out the positions. Whenever Judy offers suggestions, Manners sarcastically shouts that "Yale" should please keep quiet. Manners's insistence on belittling Judy implies his belief that women do not belong on the American stage.

Childress suggests that just as women, black and white, were unwelcome on the stage, so were black men who wished to play serious roles. She magnifies the limitations placed upon black men in the theater by depicting Sheldon as a man who is content to secure any part in a play. He grins and shuffles on cue, and Childress holds him up as an object of scorn. As much as he ingratiates himself to Manners, he alienates himself from Wiletta and Millie. He tells them that it is no myth that "colored women" wake up in the morning eager to fight. The humor, alternating between light and sardonic, propels the play along even as it reminds the audience that Childress believed that very little is truly humorous about the conditions of African Americans and women in America.

Critical Context

Trouble in Mind, like other plays by Alice Childress including *Florence* (pr. 1949), *Wedding Band: A Love/Hate Story in Black and White* (pr. 1966), *Mojo: A Black Love Story* (pr. 1970), *Wine in the Wilderness* (pr. 1969), *When the Rattlesnake Sounds* (pb. 1975), *Sea Island Song* (pr. 1977), and *Moms* (pr. 1987), seeks to illuminate the condition of poor women for whom the act of living is sheer heroism. Her characters generally include domestic workers, washerwomen, seamstresses, and the unemployed, as well as dancers, artists, and teachers. Childress portrays emotionally mutilated heroines who are morally strong, sometimes vulnerable, but resilient. She portrays these women honestly as they fight daily battles not simply to survive but to survive whole.

Childress's experiences as a poor Harlem, New York City, resident shaped her attitudes about society. She came to the theater with the aim of telling unvarnished truths about America. *Trouble in Mind* cemented her career in the theater. Running for ninety-one performances, *Trouble in Mind* won for Childress the Obie Award for the best original Off-Broadway play of the 1955-1956 season. The first black woman to win an Obie, Childress is the only woman playwright in the United States whose plays have been written, produced, and published consistently since 1950. Having had plays produced in New York City, across the United States, and in Europe, Childress bequeathed a legacy to the American theater that is monumental.

Alice Childress wrote plays that incorporate the liturgy of the black church, traditional music, African mythology, folklore, and fantasy. She won acclaim by writing sociopolitical, romantic, biographical, historical, and feminist plays. Striving to find new and dynamic ways of expressing old themes in a historically conservative theater,

Childress also opened the door for other black playwrights, such as Lorraine Hansberry (*A Raisin in the Sun*, pr., pb. 1959) and Ntozake Shange (*for colored girls who have considered suicide/ when the rainbow is enuf*, pr. 1976), to make advances in the theater.

Alice Childress's intense and microscopic examination of life matches such great dramatists as Anton Chekhov, August Strindberg, Jean Anouilh, Sholom Aleichem, Sean O'Casey, Noël Coward, Tennessee Williams, and the Nobel Prize-winning African dramatist Wole Soyinka. *Trouble in Mind*, like the plays of many great American dramatists, depicts society both as it is and as it should be. *Trouble in Mind* has made an indelible mark on American theater because it addresses the struggles of the downtrodden and yet offers hope.

Sources for Further Study

Abramson, Doris E. *Negro Playwrights in the American Theatre, 1925-1959*. New York: Columbia University Press, 1969.

Brown-Guillory, Elizabeth. "Alice Childress: A Pioneering Spirit." *SAGE: A Scholarly Journal on Black Women* 4 (Spring, 1987): 66-68.

_____. *Their Place on the Stage: Black Women Playwrights in America*. New York: Greenwood Press, 1988.

Jennings, La Vinia Delois. *Alice Childress*. New York: Twayne, 1995.

Turner, Darwin T. "Alice Childress." In *Contemporary Dramatists*. 4th ed. Chicago: St. James, 1988.

Elizabeth Brown-Guillory

TRUE WEST

Author: Sam Shepard (Samuel Shepard Rogers, 1943-   )
Type of plot: Realism
Time of plot: The 1980's
Locale: A suburb forty miles east of Los Angeles
First produced: 1980, at the Magic Theatre, San Francisco
First published: 1981, in *Seven Plays*

Principal characters:
AUSTIN, a suburbanite scriptwriter in his early thirties
LEE, his older brother, in his early forties
SAUL KIMMER, a Hollywood producer
MOM, Austin and Lee's mother, a woman in her early sixties

The Play

True West opens at night with both brothers in their mother's kitchen, where all the action of the play will occur over three days. Crickets and occasional barks of coyotes can be heard. Austin, in charge of the house while their mother is vacationing in Alaska, tries to write at the kitchen table; Lee, having arrived unexpectedly after living for three months in the desert, drinks beer and talks. The brothers are opposites in dress and demeanor: While Austin, dressed in a cardigan and jeans, is the neat suburbanite, Lee, in soiled second-hand remnants, conveys the menace of a desperate loner.

They have not seen each other in five years and are awkward and tense. This tension grows when they discuss their father, a mysterious character who lives in the desert, and is further fueled when Lee mocks Austin for writing television scripts. When Austin asks how long Lee intends to stay at the mother's house, he says that his stay depends on how successful his burglaries are in the neighborhood. He further frightens Austin by asking for his car in order to case the area. Austin refuses to give Lee the car but tries to help him by offering money and a place with his family up north. Lee attacks Austin for insulting him with such a handout. After a pause, Lee calms down and recounts his success with dogs trained for fighting. He rejects Austin's offer by saying that the north is too cold and then leaves.

The next morning Lee returns from his nocturnal walk through the neighborhood and tells Austin how the area has changed for the worse with development. Both brothers remember their youthful escapades in the area's foothills, but Lee breaks their nostalgia with a description of a house that he cased. Austin, apprehensive, asks Lee if he ever grew lonely while living in the desert. He answers mysteriously by saying that Austin never really knew him. Austin changes the subject by announcing that Saul Kimmer, his producer, is coming to visit shortly and that he would appreciate Lee's absence. Lee bribes Austin into giving him the car keys to leave. Reluctantly, Austin does, and as Lee exits, he announces that he has a story to sell the producer as well.

The next scene opens in the middle of Austin's conversation with Kimmer, a loudly dressed Hollywood producer. Lee enters with a stolen television and announces his regret at returning too soon. When Austin tells Kimmer that Lee has lived in the desert, Kimmer thinks of Palm Springs and starts to discuss golf. Playing along with the misunderstanding, Lee talks Kimmer into a golf game the next morning at which Lee will relate his idea for a Western. Kimmer, not quite sure what to make of Lee but intimidated by him, agrees to the golf date and leaves. Austin, astounded by Lee's actions, asks for his car keys back; Lee just smiles.

That night, Lee dictates his story sketch to Austin, who types it perfunctorily. As Lee becomes more serious about the story, Austin becomes more skeptical of its plausibility, finally stopping his typing and dismissing Lee's tale as contrived. Lee warns Austin that he has his car keys and will return them only after Austin finishes helping him. Austin's fear of Lee grows, and Lee aggravates it by reminding Austin that most murders occur between family members. Lee then softens, gives the car keys to Austin, and says that selling this story could change his life. He goes on to admit that he envies Austin's middle-class life; Austin, surprised, confesses his envy for Lee's independence. With this truth out, the brothers now work together on the story line. When Lee asks again for the car keys, Austin reluctantly gives them to him.

In act 2 the brothers' situations are reversed. During golf, Lee has successfully sold his story to Kimmer at the expense of Austin's script. When Kimmer arrives and calls Lee's story a true Western, Austin argues that there is no West any more, only freeways and Safeways—the subjects of his stories. Austin's frustration drives him to drink, which makes him not only less frightened of Lee but also, ironically, more like him. That night Lee is writing at the typewriter while Austin taunts him by claiming that he can steal toasters better than Lee can write. By morning, Lee is smashing the typewriter with a golf club while Austin proudly polishes a row of toasters that he has stolen during the night. Lee recognizes that he really needs Austin's help to write, and angrily pulls out all the kitchen drawers and, finally, the telephone off the wall. Amid the debris, Austin calmly makes a large pile of toast and asks Lee if he could accompany him into the desert. Thinking that Austin is ridiculing him, Lee smashes Austin's pile of toast. However, Lee soon realizes Austin's changed attitude and makes a deal with him: Austin will write the script, and Lee will take him into the desert.

The last scene of the play opens at midday with the brothers working well together on the script. Mom's unexpected return from Alaska disrupts them. She has returned because she misses her plants, now thoroughly wilted and dead; she shows little concern over the destroyed kitchen or even for her sons. Lee realizes that his wish to join this middle-class world is insane and decides to go back to the desert alone. Austin, angry that Lee will not take him, grabs the telephone cord and throttles Lee with it. As they struggle, the mother claims not to recognize anything and leaves. When Lee appears to be dead, Austin releases the cord and tries to get to the door. Lee, however, springs up and blocks his exit. The lights fade to moonlight as the two brothers "square off to each other, keeping a distance between them."

Themes and Meanings

While at its heart *True West* portrays the classic philosophical problem of distinguishing illusion from reality, it extends this theme to the dilemma the artist encounters in creating art that is true to life. Both thematic concerns are centered on the brothers' struggle to write a real Western story.

The play opens with the brothers' disagreeing on where the real West is. In essence, they are arguing over reality and illusion. Lee, the idealist, maintains that the West has been "wiped out" by development, while Austin, the pragmatist, accepts the West as the land of freeways and Safeways. However, both brothers fail to recognize the inevitable change occurring in their idealized childhood West and in themselves as well even as it occurs in the play. While Lee wishes for Austin's pragmatic world, Austin begins to idealize Lee's desert life. He says to Lee that "there's nothing real down here" for him, but Lee punctures Austin's ideal West: "Do you actually think I chose to live out in the middle a' nowhere? Do ya'? Ya' think it's some kinda philosophical decision I took or somethin'?" The brothers' conflict suggests a paradoxical definition of reality as an uneasy combination of illusion and experience, producing the myths which are necessary for psychic survival.

The brothers' reversal of roles in act 2 reflects the inner conflict of the artist as a divided self. Each brother represents one requisite side of the artist's creativity: Lee, emotive, Dionysian; Austin, rational, Apollonian. As Kimmer says, each brother needs the other to create. However, each brother sees the other's strengths not as complementing but as replacing his own. Their struggle delineates the difficult, if not impossible task of harmonizing emotion and intellect in the creation of art, since by nature each side seeks to dominate the other. Only after the brothers exchange roles, climaxing in the humorous scene with the stolen toasters, do they recognize their need for this union.

The image of the brothers circling in the devastated kitchen offers a provocative but inconclusive ending. Some critics have suggested that this disturbing final scene reflects Sam Shepard's view of life as an endless struggle between illusion and reality, passion and reason; to be true, art must portray this struggle without a neat resolution.

Dramatic Devices

The setting allows the audience to accept *True West* as a realistic drama as well as a fable about art. Located forty miles east of Los Angeles, the setting is a meeting point for the modern West and the primitive one, represented by the desert, foothills, and the constant background sounds of crickets and coyotes. For Shepard, the coyotes become metaphors for the conflict between illusions and reality. Lee tells Austin that coyotes, icons of the mythic Wild West, have, in fact, become suburban pests. The desert also symbolizes the disparity between reality and illusion. Lee calls it empty; Austin sees it as more real than his urban environment. In the climactic fight scene myths and reality merge: The coyotes bark loudly, and the kitchen set dissolves into "a vast desertlike landscape" to reflect the brothers' confusion.

The kitchen represents this blend of reality and illusion. While it resembles the usual set of realistic "kitchen" dramas that deal with domestic conflicts, the kitchen—with its plastic grass carpet and potted plants—also emblematizes the artificiality created by the mother's attempts to make her ideal West real. Lee's description of another kitchen he spied, in an ersatz hacienda, underscores this symbolism. The domestic conflict occurring in the brothers' kitchen is more mythic than realistic, recalling the archetypal contest between Cain and Abel. In Shepard's fable, however, the father embodies a West idealized in films and pulp novels that attracts because of its escapism. Both parents, their namelessness befitting their mythic status, represent the allure and danger of accepting myths as reality. At the end, Mom ignores the vivid reality of the brothers' struggle to declare that she can find nothing real in the house anymore.

More symbolically, the brothers' film stories portray the artist's divided self. Lee's ideal Western, the film *Lonely Are the Brave*, identifies him with the artist's emotional side that wants to create illusion and myth; Austin's story of his father's teeth makes him the artist's rational half that wants realism. Each story is incomplete in depicting reality, however; one is too maudlin and the other too rationally cool.

The play's role as a fable on art is most obviously revealed in its title, which Shepard borrowed from the defunct magazine *True West*. The magazine supposedly told true stories of the West, but was also inadvertently creating myths for its readers. So too, the brothers' fight over whose story is more true cannot be resolved, since both stories abstract reality and create myths that are partially true. The closing scene with the brothers forever frozen in struggle not too subtly hints that the only true story of the West is the play itself.

Critical Context

True West is the second of a series of plays, starting with *Curse of the Starving Class* (pb. 1976), that break from Sam Shepard's earlier nonrepresentational works such as *The Tooth of Crime* (pr. 1972). Structured in a representational form, these plays draw upon autobiographical material for their naturalistic plots involving domestic conflicts. The settings are either rural middle America (where Shepard was born), as for *Buried Child* (pr. 1978) and *A Lie of the Mind* (pr. 1985), or the Southwest (where Shepard grew up), as for *Curse of the Starving Class*, *Fool for Love* (pr. 1983), and *True West*. Character types and images reappear in these plays: a distant father in conflict with a dominating mother (resembling Shepard's parents) and children dislocated by their parents' sometimes mysterious behavior, and references to coyotes and barren land that evoke ambiguous interpretations.

Shepard employs his trademark technique of character transformation in these plays to represent divided characters whose struggles reflect his perennial concerns: critiquing American myths and portraying the artist's inner conflict in creating art. *True West*, in particular, has provoked much critical comment in response to its rendition of these themes. While some critics find the play troubling for its inconclusiveness, others find it a rich work full of provocative interpretations.

Sources for Further Study

Demastes, W. W. "Understanding Sam Shepard's Realism." *Contemporary Drama* 21 (Fall, 1987): 229-248.

Graham, Laura K. *Sam Shepard: Theme, Image, and the Director.* New York: Lang, 1995.

Hart, Lynda. *Sam Shepard's Metaphorical Stages.* Westport, Conn.: Greenwood Press, 1987.

Marranca, Bonnie, ed. *American Dreams: The Imagination of Sam Shepard.* New York: Performing Arts Journal, 1981.

Mottram, Ron. *Inner Landscapes: The Theater of Sam Shepard.* Columbia: University of Missouri Press, 1984.

Orbison, T. "Mythic Levels in Shepard's *True West.*" *Modern Drama* 27 (December, 1984): 506-519.

Oumano, Ellen. *Sam Shepard: The Life and Work of an American Dreamer.* New York: St. Martin's Press, 1986.

Wade, Leslie A. *Sam Shepard and the American Theatre.* Westport, Conn.: Greenwood Press, 1997.

Wilcox, Leonard, ed. *Rereading Shepard.* Basingstoke, England: Macmillan, 1993.

Zinman, T. S. "Sam Shepard and Super-Realism." *Modern Drama* 29 (September, 1986): 423-430.

Richard Stoner

TWENTY-SEVEN WAGONS FULL OF COTTON
A Mississippi Delta Comedy

Author: Tennessee Williams (1911-1983)
Type of plot: Grotesque; tragicomedy
Time of plot: The 1940's
Locale: Blue Mountain, Mississippi
First produced: 1955, at Tulane University, New Orleans, Louisiana
First published: 1945

> *Principal characters:*
> JAKE MEIGHAN, a cotton-gin owner
> FLORA MEIGHAN, his wife
> SILVA VICARRO, the superintendent of the Syndicate Plantation

The Play

Twenty-seven Wagons Full of Cotton, a one-act play in three scenes, begins and ends on that most southern of domestic architectural features, the front porch. The setting is Blue Mountain, Mississippi. Tennessee Williams, through detailed staging, requires enough appurtenances so that "the effect is not unlike a doll's house."

The play opens in early evening. The audience first sees Jake Meighan, "a fat man of sixty," scurrying offstage with a can of coal oil as dogs bark in the distance. As he drives away, his wife, Flora, emerges from the house onto the porch in search of her white kid purse. The bovine Flora cries after her husband as "a cow moos in the distance with the same inflection." At this point a distant explosion sounds, and various voices speculate about the noise. As Jake returns, Flora learns that the Syndicate Plantation has caught fire.

Flora berates Jake for leaving her with no Coca-Cola in the house, but Jake soon establishes his male dominance by treating his wife roughly. At this point it becomes apparent that theirs is something of a sadomasochistic relationship. He hurts her, and she seems to enjoy it. Jake had departed abruptly in order to blow up the Syndicate's cotton gin so that he could profit from ginning the extra cotton. With considerable effort Jake fashions his alibi—he never, he repeats to Flora, left the front porch that evening. Flora's reluctance to absorb Jake's alibi suggests her stupidity and establishes her childlike innocence.

Scene 2 opens the same afternoon with Silva Vicarro, the superintendent of the Syndicate Plantation, joining Jake and Flora at their residence. Vicarro, a "rather small and wiry man of dark Latin looks," contrasts with his beefy neighbors; he represents a recurring Williams character, the outsider. Jake, having exploded Vicarro's cotton gin, assures his Latin neighbor that he will find a way to gin his cotton for him.

He introduces his wife to Vicarro and teases her about her weight while admitting that he prefers "a woman not large but tremendous." After embarrassing Flora about her corpulence, Jake exits in order to gin Vicarro's cotton. Jake's absence allows Flora and Silva the opportunity to become better acquainted. Vicarro immediately begins flirting with Flora while seeking information about his ruined gin. Vicarro knows, or at least senses, that Jake has destroyed his cotton gin; he ironically taunts Flora about Jake's "good-neighbor policy," which Jake explains as "you do me a good turn an' I'll do you a good one." Vicarro clearly intends to reciprocate. His suspicions about arson are confirmed when Flora spoils her husband's alibi. Silva's knowledge motivates his revenge, which is to abuse and violate his adversary's wife. Initially Flora resists Silva's advances but soon succumbs, the scene ending with the two entering the house as "the gin pumps slowly and steadily across the road."

The final scene takes place that evening about nine o'clock. The front porch is empty but bathed in "a full September moon of almost garish intensity." Flora emerges; "her appearance is ravaged." Her eyes contain "a vacant limpidity," and her lips are set sensually apart. Dark streaks on her shoulders and arms indicate that Vicarro has whipped her with his riding crop. Even though she has been raped and whipped, the stage directions suggest that the experience has not been altogether unpleasant. Jake ambles up, ironically singing to himself, "By the light of the silvery moon." He then brags about the work he has done, ginning twenty-seven wagons full of cotton, as Flora says, "You're not the only one's—done a big day's—work." Without stating why, Flora tells Jake what a mistake it was to "fool with th' Syndicate Plantation." Their ensuing conversation is characterized by Flora's double entendres, which never penetrate the oblivious Jake. She says to Jake, "maybe you don't understand th' good-neighbor—policy," and announces that Vicarro is "gonna let you do a-a-lll his ginnin'—fo' him!" The play ends as Flora, with a "smiling and ravaged face," sings "Rock-a-bye Baby" while cradling her white kid purse, suggesting that Vicarro has impregnated her.

Themes and Meanings

Twenty-seven Wagons Full of Cotton presents a curious mixture of thematic elements. On one hand, it is a play about moral misdeeds and poetic justice. It also analyzes an unstable marriage and unhealthy emotional relationships. Tennessee Williams accomplishes the former by representing the South through the characters of Jake and Flora, who are depicted as boorish southern rustics. Jake, dishonest and malicious, naïvely assumes that only opportunistic profit will result from his blowing up the gin. Although the "foreigner's" gin has been burned, his retaliation by raping Flora leads audiences to feel little sympathy for his role of the helpless outsider. Jake may stand for the violent masculinity of the South, but his failure to recognize his cuckoldry at the play's end leaves him emasculated and vulnerable.

Williams's tone regarding the brutal sexuality should be seen as nonjudgmental. Flora virtually seems to thrive on abuse; her resistance to both Jake's and Vicarro's treatment is meek. Williams's drama occasionally focuses on the bestial, violent nature of relationships, and some of his work, like the short story "Desire and the Black

Masseur," depicts sadomasochism in very erotic terms. Whether such relationships are autobiographically inspired has been the source of incessant speculation. Perhaps Williams is simply acknowledging that what seems repugnant for some is pleasurable for others.

The other idea—of the alien confronting the power structure—appears throughout Williams's drama. Unlike other outsiders, however, Vicarro seems triumphant at the play's end. Granted, he has lost his gin, but he has abused his adversary's wife, impregnated her, and made her happy in the process. Whether Flora will leave Jake (or indeed be invited to do so) is unresolved, but retribution has been enacted, and Jake is the only one oblivious.

Although Flora may actually enjoy abuse, there is a pathos in her predicament that should not escape a close reader or sympathetic theater-goer. Those who receive gratification from being mistreated harbor a twisted view of what constitutes need. Flora's "ravaged" appearance at the play's end, combined with her somewhat deranged frame of mind, suggest that she is not mentally equipped to realize what would be best for her: keeping her distance from such abusive men.

Dramatic Devices

Twenty-seven Wagons Full of Cotton combines two dominant motifs, psychological regression and sadomasochistic behavior, to produce a strange, haunting portrait of dependence, greed, and deviance. Every image associated with Flora suggests her childishness and stupidity. To begin with, she lives in a cottage that resembles a dollhouse. Most of Jake's conversation is sprinkled with the word "baby." A particularly infantile conversation that occurs in the first scene is illustrative of this motif:

> JAKE: (*huskily*) Tha's my swee' baby girl.
> FLORA: Mmmmm! Hurt! Hurt!
> JAKE: Hurt?
> FLORA: Mmmm! Hurt!

This dialogue continues for several lines, with Jake both caressing and harming Flora. Jake describes Flora as a "baby doll" when talking with Vicarro. In her conversation with Vicarro after her husband leaves, Flora forgets her husband's alibi and thus reveals his complicity. Several other bits of dialogue illustrate Flora's dim-wittedness, and additional images, such as her clutching her white kid purse, are designed to reveal her childish dependency. At the end of the play, Flora tells Jake, "I'm not—Baby. Mama! Ma! That's—me. . . . " This revelation seems to say more about her prenatal condition than about any intellectual maturation.

Flora's childish bearing is juxtaposed to her dependence on physical abuse. She finds pleasure in being mistreated by both her husband and neighbor. Jake alternately hurts her and fondles her. Vicarro arrives holding a riding crop and uses it on Flora. All of her denials of finding pleasure in brutality are at best feeble, and her giddy, detached air at the play's conclusion indicates that she harbors pleasant memories of her afternoon with the Latin disciplinarian. Such behavior presents the theatergoer with the choice of either feeling sorry for Flora or being repulsed by her. Again, Tennessee Williams appears content to let the audience decide.

Another motif is a variation of quid pro quo, what Jake calls the "good-neighbor policy." The term is loaded with irony whenever it is used to describe good turns. Jake does Vicarro a "favor" by ginning his cotton for him, and Vicarro returns the favor by abusing and impregnating his wife. In this story of lust and greed, Williams perverts neighborly altruism to a game of one-upmanship, and Vicarro is clearly the victor.

Critical Context

Twenty-seven Wagons Full of Cotton is the title play in an edition of thirteen short dramatic pieces, most of which are set in the South. In terms of quality the collection is uneven, but it does contain some of Tennessee Williams's best one-act plays, such as *The Last of My Solid Gold Watches* (pb. 1946). Most of his main characters are temporal misfits who dwell in the past to avoid confronting the miserable reality of their present existence. *Twenty-seven Wagons Full of Cotton* deals with such displacement; it falls into a particular genre of southern writing, the grotesque.

The grotesque synthesizes the comic and the tragic and characterizes by way of exaggeration. Flannery O'Connor said of the grotesque, "Whenever I'm asked why Southern writers particularly have a penchant for writing about freaks, I say it is because we are still able to recognize one." This play presents three "freaks." Jake is a beefy, bumbling opportunist who deals with problems the only way he knows how—through violence. Vicarro, with dark features, high-laced boots, and a riding crop, is something of a satanic figure bent on sadistic revenge. Flora, of almost cartoon proportions, exists in a state of puerile regression. By living in her fantasy world of the past, she becomes easy prey to abusive men such as Jake and Vicarro. In other words, her defense mechanism (regression) becomes the very tool of her destruction, as is often the case. Rather than confronting the sorry state of their marriage, a relationship in which Flora exists as chattel, she retreats to the more comfortable condition of infancy. Vicarro and Jake both sense her weakness and take full advantage, each in his own sadistic way.

In *Twenty-seven Wagons Full of Cotton* Williams offers a rather disturbing story of greed, lust, and violence set in familiar territory—the Mississippi Delta. He called this play a comedy. There is much to laugh at in this short drama—Jake's bumbling entrepreneurial scheme, Vicarro's cunning retribution, and Flora's infantile utterings—but given the greed and sexual deviance that motivate the characters, the humor is ultimately black.

Sources for Further Study

Bloom, Harold. *Tennessee Williams*. Broomall, Pa.: Chelsea House, 1999.

Boxill, Roger. *Tennessee Williams*. New York: St. Martin's Press, 1987.

Crandele, George W. *The Critical Response to Tennessee Williams*. Westport, Conn.: Greenwood Press, 1996.

Falk, Signi. *Tennessee Williams*. Boston: Twayne, 1978.

Griffin, Alice. *Understanding Tennessee Williams*. Columbia: University of South Carolina Press, 1994.

Gunn, Drewey Wayne. *Tennessee Williams: A Bibliography*. 2d ed. Metuchen, N.J.: Scarecrow Press, 1991.

Kolin, Philip G. *Tennessee Williams: A Guide to Research and Performance*. Westport, Conn.: Greenwood Press, 1998.

Spoto, Donald. *The Kindness of Strangers: The Life of Tennessee Williams*. Boston: Little, Brown, 1985.

Weales, Gerald. *Tennessee Williams*. Minneapolis: University of Minnesota Press, 1985.

Robert Bray

TWO FOR THE SEESAW

Author: William Gibson (1914-   )
Type of plot: Tragicomedy
Time of plot: The late 1950's
Locale: New York City
First produced: 1958, at the Booth Theatre, New York City
First published: 1959, in *The Seesaw Log*

Principal characters:
JERRY RYAN, an attorney from Nebraska
GITTEL MOSCA, a former dancer

The Play

At the start of *Two for the Seesaw*, the contiguous spaces onstage, each representing a room belonging to one of the two main characters, contrast sharply, foreshadowing the insurmountable differences between Jerry and Gittel. His space is drab and disorderly; it has the feel of a temporary stopover. Hers is crowded but cozy; it has the look of a permanent abode. Using the excuse of wanting to buy a used icebox (refrigerator) from her, Jerry telephones Gittel, and although she tells him that she has given the box away, Jerry asks her out for dinner and a show. From the outset, it is clear that both characters have problems: Gittel, as Jerry tells her, is a "born victim," whereas Jerry constantly berates himself for his sly way of asking for handouts without acknowledging that fact.

When they return to Gittel's at the end of the evening (in scene 2), Jerry tells her that he is an unemployed attorney (since his Nebraska license does not allow him to practice law in New York). He also says that he is married but has left his home because his wife is divorcing him to marry someone else, and, last, that it is his birthday. Gittel tells him that she is divorced, that she makes her scanty living by sewing dance costumes because she cannot afford a dance studio, and, most important, that she has an ulcer which periodically hemorrhages. Gittel decides to break her rule of not sleeping with anyone on a first date and asks Jerry to stay; however, he decides to avoid "a handout" and leaves while she is getting ready for bed.

Scene 3 begins at five o'clock the next morning with Jerry telephoning Gittel, assuring her that he did not leave because she was unattractive and offering to bring over an ice bag to forestall bleeding after she has a tooth extracted—his way of letting her know that he cares about her welfare. Then, as she settles back in bed, Jerry reads aloud the telegram he has received from Nebraska: "I called to say happy birthday you stinker don't shut me out God help both of us but will you remember I love you I do Tess."

Act 2 begins a month later. Jerry's room has been transformed in what the playwright describes as "the peasant style of Gittel's garb," and the result is pleasantly warm. As Jerry enters, Gittel is getting their dinner on the table, complete with candles and wine, and the feeling is that these two have come together happily. Jerry has good news: He has been to see an attorney friend who has given him a job preparing briefs. Now he is ready and anxious to financially back Gittel's dance studio. With Gittel's bright announcement that Jerry's wife has telephoned and will call back, however, there is a definite change of mood. As the conversation goes on, Gittel suggests that Jerry "study up" and take the New York bar examination, and she senses that his reluctance to do so may mean that he does not intend to remain in New York permanently.

Finally, the telephone rings; Jerry refuses to answer, and when Gittel picks it up, he is furious. It is not Tess, however, but Gittel's dance partner, Larry, calling to talk about the dance studio. Misunderstanding Jerry's reluctance to talk to his wife, Gittel says, "What did that bitch do to you?" and is surprised at Jerry's response: "Bitch? Married me, helped put me through law school. Stood by me in pinches. Loved me, if anyone did or could. She was never a bitch, don't call her that again." At this point, Gittel accuses Jerry of running away and suggests that he talk to Tess and face facts, which in turn evokes his evaluation of Gittel. He tells her that she is "on the edge of a nightmare" and all alone, that she always gives, never makes her needs known, never makes a real claim on anyone; she is always used rather than cared for. As their exchange escalates, so that Gittel is in tears, the phone rings again, and this time Jerry answers it.

His conversation with Tess is very revealing: He does not want to be friends with her and her fiancé; he has a job, he has a girl, and he is beginning a new life. His final statement, however, costs both him and Gittel dearly. He says, shakily: "I'm not unfeeling, I don't want to be haunted either; my God, you made a choice, get your hand out of my bowels!" The scene closes when Jerry asks Gittel to need him for something, if only to rent the studio, and Gittel agrees, but she says softly, "I'll never hear you tell me that I got a hand inside you."

Scene 2 takes place some weeks later. Jerry is in his room, surrounded by legal papers, talking to his boss on the telephone, and the audience learns that he is contemplating taking the bar examination, with Frank as sponsor. Gittel is in her room on the telephone with her friend Sophie; from her conversation, all seems to be going well with Jerry. However, he makes a call to his former father-in-law because of concern for Tess, who now seems to be devastated since learning that Jerry has a girl, and when he tells this to Gittel, she breaks their dinner date.

The final scene of act 2 takes place late on a Saturday night several months later. Gittel enters alone, drunk, and dials her doctor, leaving an urgent request for him to call her. Jerry then enters and immediately confronts her with an accusation. He had been to a party at Frank's (Gittel had not been included in the invitation), and when he went to pick her up at Sophie's, he had seen her leaving with a man and followed them, watching outside the man's basement apartment for an hour, drawing unpleasant conclusions. There are harsh words on both sides, but what finally comes out of the fray is that Gittel has realized that she is not a dancer, while Jerry has concluded that he cannot ask his former father-in-law for the documents he would need to enter law practice without taking the bar examination. Furthermore, Gittel knows that he has been calling Tess; his defense is that she has now decided not to remarry and is "having a very rough time." Finally, Gittel tells Jerry that he shortchanges people, which he acknowledges, saying, "You mean I want a—complete surrender. And don't give one."

It is an epiphany for Jerry, seeing himself as he was with Tess and as he is with Gittel, and he finally tells Gittel that she is wonderful as she is. He starts to leave, but comes back when she tells him that all she did in Jake's basement was to faint, because her ulcer is bleeding, and that she is very frightened. She says she did not want to "trap him" with her illness, but he insists that she needs him now, and she admits that she does. The act ends as he is calling her doctor.

At the beginning of act 3, Jerry's room looks unused because he has moved into Gittel's to take care of her. She is really enjoying the unaccustomed care she is getting, but, more significantly, she is afraid that when she has fully recovered, Jerry will leave. He assures her that he is not cramming for the bar in order to leave New York, and Gittel is somewhat reassured when she learns that he is giving up his room.

Scene 2 finds both characters in Jerry's room, packing his things for his final move to Gittel's. There is a sense of something unspoken between them. Jerry has passed the bar, and Gittel now plans to take shorthand and act as his secretary, and she actually asks him to marry her. He tells her it is not possible until the divorce from Tess becomes final, but as she is packing, Gittel comes across the final divorce decree. Incensed that he had not told her, Gittel asks him if he has told Tess about the hemorrhage. Jerry admits that he has, explaining that Tess needed him and he had to explain to her why he could not come. At this point, Gittel asks him point-blank if he will ever marry her, and when he admits that he will not—that he still loves Tess and considers that a lifetime promise—Gittel decides that she will let him go, that she will not accept a half-commitment, from a man who cannot even say "I love you" but who is willing only to be around in case she needs him.

The final scene is a short telephone conversation between Jerry and Gittel, during which each tells the other how the "affair" has helped them to grow into better human beings. Jerry will not return to his father-in-law's office; he will begin an independent life, but he vows that he will not shortchange Tess. Gittel, too, has learned to value herself more. At the very end of their conversation, Gittel says, "I love you, Jerry! Long as you live I want you to remember the last thing you heard out of me was I love you!" Jerry answers, "I love you too, Gittel."

Themes and Meanings

Two for the Seesaw tries to show that even though two people are ill-suited to spend their lives together, their fleeting but intimate contact gives them new insights which will improve their separate lives in the future. Most of the original reviewers concentrated on Henry Fonda, who played Jerry Ryan, and were even more laudatory about the young actor, Anne Bancroft, who played Gittel. Interestingly, when a musical adaptation called *Seesaw* appeared on Broadway in 1973 (fifteen years after the original play), with much of the original dialogue intact, many reviewers noted some of the factors which weighted the seesaw in favor of the white Anglo-Saxon Protestant (WASP) Jerry Ryan and against the Jewish Gittel Mosca. Presumably having gone through the 1960's, they felt freer to critique the play on this basis.

From the beginning, Gittel's New York accent contrasts with Jerry's cultured speech. She is shown as a lovable loser; he is pictured as a man temporarily confused but an eventual winner. Jerry makes jokes which Gittel does not understand because she takes everything literally. For example, there is an interchange between them at their first meeting. She asks Jerry what state he is from and he answers, "Nebraska," after which Gittel says, "Nebraska. That's somewhere way out in California, isn't it?" Gittel is not aware of the patronizing tone of Jerry's reply: "I think it's Nevada that's in California."

In the course of the play, Gittel confesses that she has made only one long-distance call in her life; later, when she talks to her friend Sophie, she says, "Take him home to meet Momma? He'll leave New York in a balloon . . . he plays *golf* for instance. I never knew anybody personally who played golf." Overall, she seems more like a country girl than a woman of nearly thirty, born and bred in New York. Presumably the character is drawn this way to contrast with Jerry's unseen wife, Tess. There is more than a suggestion of stereotype, however, which may add to the humor but which has some serious flaws.

In the last scene of act 2, Jerry's attack on Gittel because he thinks she has slept with Jake (the man in the basement) is quite cruel. Gittel counterattacks by telling him that he is only half with her, that he has only been using her to prove something to Tess. Thus the seesaw momentarily tips in each direction. However, at the end of the play, it is Gittel, alone in her room, who is taking down her dance photographs, signifying that she knows that she is not a dancer or choreographer but only a woman on the fringe. Jerry, on the other hand, is able to go back to Nebraska, his career, and Tess on his terms. Gittel tells him that she has learned to look for a caring man, that she will no longer be the "victim." Jerry tells her that "after the verb to love, to help is the sweetest in the tongue."

It would seem that although Gittel might have learned to place a higher value on her worth after her affair with Jerry, it is he who is on the more positive side of the balances, while Gittel is left alone. The playwright suggests that she is tough—at one point Jerry calls her "a street fighter"—and that she will survive, and the audience can see her innate goodness, so that she is possibly a more sympathetic character than Jerry. Nevertheless, there is more than a suggestion in the play that Jerry's decision to return to his world is the best course of action, and this denouement does carry negative implications.

Dramatic Devices

In addition to a split set, William Gibson has illustrated his title by having the two characters in an almost constant state of flux—first one is up and the other down; then in the next scene, the situation is reversed. As a means of emphasizing the comic aspects of the play, there is an almost constant effort to contrast the social backgrounds of the two protagonists, frequently by making Gittel unable to understand the subtleties of Jerry's conversation, while at the same time giving her lines which supposedly typify a Bronx-born, first-generation Jewish girl. Gittel is a "free spirit," as audiences would have understood that term in 1958, and everything from her gaminelike appearance to her New York accent is meant to convey that impression.

As might be expected in a two-character play, the telephones of both Jerry and Gittel act almost as additional characters. Jerry's reluctance to talk to Tess and then his many calls to Nebraska, as well as his conversations with his attorney friend, Frank, are mandatory expository devices. Gittel's conversations with her unseen friend, Sophie, serve the same purpose. These conversations via telephone also serve to let the audience know what the characters are thinking about their lives and their relationship when they are not face-to-face. Ultimately, the end of the affair between Jerry and Gittel takes place over the telephone.

Gittel's illness itself could be considered a dramatic device because it provides Jerry with a reason for taking care of her. Even in the first scene of act 2, when Gittel has made dinner for them, he tries to keep her from eating fried potatoes— a "no-no" for someone with an ulcer. Later, when she has had too much to drink, he is concerned about the effect on her ulcer. Still later, after she has had the hemorrhage, it provides the motivation for his moving to Gittel's. Her reluctance to "trap" him because she is in need of his succor adds dimension to her character. She may no longer be a "victim" in the original sense, but despite Jerry's assurances that she can call him if she needs him in the future, it is highly unlikely that she will telephone Nebraska the next time her ulcer acts up.

Critical Context

William Gibson (he also used the pseudonym William Mass) wrote some one-act plays and *Dinny and the Witches: A Frolic on Grave Matters* (pr. 1948), published a book of poetry, and wrote a novel, *The Cobweb* (1954), but it was *The Miracle Worker* (pr. 1957), written as a television script for *Playhouse 90*, which really launched his career. As he writes in his preface to the published edition of *Dinny and the Witches* and the stage play *The Miracle Worker* (pr. 1959), he based the television script on letters written by Anne Sullivan that appear in the appendix to Helen Keller's autobiography. When he adapted it for a 1959 Broadway production, it won the Tony Award for best play.

Before this time, however, *Two for the Seesaw* (originally written, but not published, under the title "After the Verb to Love") had been accepted and successfully produced. Gibson believed that the tribulations involved in production were quite dreadful, and so he wrote *The Seesaw Log* (1959) as a narrative of the play's journey from conception to its birth on Broadway, sparing none of the details of the difficult delivery. It is noteworthy that Gibson was particularly resentful of Henry Fonda's insistence (as a well-known Hollywood star) on enlarging his role, which may have some bearing on the final characterization of Jerry Ryan.

With two commercial successes to his credit, Gibson was given the opportunity to do *Dinny and the Witches* Off-Broadway in 1961, but it did not enjoy a long run. Gibson also worked on the musical adaptation of Clifford Odets's *Golden Boy* in 1964, when Odets was dying of cancer. The emphasis shifted when the protagonist was made a black man, thus raising the issue of race; the play starred Sammy Davis, Jr., as the musician turned prizefighter, and it was a popular success. *A Cry of Players* (pr. 1948), a period drama about the rebellion of a young Elizabethan (presumably William Shakespeare) against the pettiness of his society, found little favor with the critics.

During the 1960's, Gibson also wrote screenplays including *The Miracle Worker* (1962) and *A Cry of Players* (1969). He also wrote a book, *A Mass for the Dead* (1968), dealing with his early life but concentrating mainly on his parents. Then came the musical *Seesaw* (1973), with music by Cy Coleman, lyrics by Dorothy Fields, and direction and choreography by Michael Bennett.

The fifteen years between 1958 and 1973 were years of significant change in American society, a fact which becomes apparent when comparing the original with the musical version. For example, in the latter, when Jerry telephones Gittel before their first date, she is trying to remember him, since she had given her number to many men at a party the night before. She finally identifies him as "the WASP with the white shirt and narrow tie!" In the first play, Jerry does not stay at Gittel's after their first evening; in *Seesaw*, he does. Despite the changes made to bring the script into line with the mores of the 1970's, however, in this version, too, Jerry goes back to his life, and Gittel is left with hers. The theme of the play remains as it was: Two people from very different worlds can never find permanent happiness together. The seesaw cannot be balanced.

In 1984, Gibson wrote *Handy Dandy*, which was produced the same year, though not on Broadway, a play about the dangers of the nuclear age and the necessity of protest. That same year, his musical *Raggedy Ann and Andy* did open on Broadway but was not very successful.

Sources for Further Study

James, T. F. "Millionaire Class of Young Writers." *Cosmopolitan*, August, 1958, 42.

Moe, Christian H. "William Gibson." In *Contemporary Dramatists*. 6th ed. Detroit: St. James, 1999.

"On The Seesaw." *The New Yorker* 33 (February 15, 1958): 23-24.

Plummer, William, and Maria Wilhelm. "An Activist and Her Playwright Husband Address the Nuclear Peril with His Words and Her Deeds." *People* 24 (October 14, 1985): 65-66.

Saturday Review. Review of *Two for the Seesaw*. 42 (November 7, 1959): 28.

Time. Review of *Two for the Seesaw*. November 2, 1959, 30.

Edythe M. McGovern

UBU ROI

Author: Alfred Jarry (1873-1907)
Type of plot: Absurdist
Time of plot: Unspecified
Locale: An imaginary Poland
First produced: 1896, at the Théâtre de l'Œuvre, Paris
First published: 1896 (English translation, 1951)

> *Principal characters:*
> PÈRE UBU, the former king of Aragon
> MÈRE UBU, his wife
> CAPTAIN BORDURE, their confederate
> KING WENCESLAS, the king of Poland
> PRINCE BOURGELAS, his son

The Play

Ubu Roi ("Ubu the king") begins as a Punch-and-Judy show, with the Ubus—Mère and Père Ubu—trading accusations, insults, and threats. Mère upbraids her husband, the former king of Aragon, who is now content to be a captain of dragoons and confidential officer to Wenceslas, king of Poland. He is at first appalled by her suggestion to overthrow the king, but when she says that as monarch he will have a new umbrella and "a great big cloak," Ubu yields to temptation and becomes, in Mère's view, "a real man." Together they enlist the aid of Captain Bordure, offering him the Dukedom of Lithuania and "a magnificent meal" that includes "cauliflower à la shittr" and a lavatory brush. Summoned by the king, the cowardly Ubu immediately begins to confess the plot, putting all the blame on Bordure and Mère Ubu, only to realize that the king wishes to make him the Count of Sandomir, for which honor Ubu absurdly repays the king with a toy whistle.

Even the king's fourteen-year-old son Bourgelas knows "what an ass that Père Ubu is"; the kindly but myopic king does not. Back at the Ubu residence, the conspirators meet to work out their plan. All reject as "beastly" Ubu's suggestion that they poison the king but agree that splitting him open with a sword, as Bordure suggests, is quite "noble and gallant." Standing before Mère Ubu (who substitutes for the requisite priest) the conspirators swear to fight "gallantly," and then, in a parody of William Shakespeare's *Julius Caesar* (pr. c. 1599-1600), fall upon the deceived king, assassinating him and two of his sons, and winning the Polish army to their side. Bourgelas, having fled to the mountains, is visited by the ghosts of his ancestors, who charge him with avenging his father's murder.

Meanwhile, as the new king, Ubu reluctantly heeds his wife's and Bordure's advice and distributes food and money to the people in order to win their support. He then kills three hundred nobles, appropriates their property and titles, and, after murdering five hundred magistrates, enacts new tax laws that will enable him to take the rest of the country's wealth. He also reneges on his promise to Bordure, who is imprisoned but escapes to Russia. The Czar sees Bordure for what he is, a traitor and an opportunist, but nevertheless agrees to help him overthrow Ubu. As Poland continues to suffer under his tyranny, Ubu occupies himself, Nero-fashion, by inventing systems "to bring good weather and exorcise rain" until Mère Ubu explains how dire his situation is. Ubu "weeps and sobs" for himself but finally agrees to wage war, as his wife urges. Refusing to pay his soldiers and looking "like an armed pumpkin," Ubu goes to war as Mère Ubu plays the part of the good bourgeois wife seeing her husband off to work: "Adieu, Père Ubu. Be sure to kill the Czar." Then she turns to more important matters: stealing the royal treasure for herself.

At the front, Ubu, as incompetent as he is gluttonous, decides to eat rather than prepare for the Czar's attack. Although shot by a Russian soldier, Ubu cuts his assailant to pieces. Shot at a second time, Ubu believes himself mortally wounded, but, upon learning from Bordure that the charge was only a blank, Ubu recovers and tears his former ally to pieces as well. His army routed, Ubu manages to escape to a cave with two of his Palotins, Pile and Lotice. When a huge bear attacks Lotice, Ubu climbs out of harm's way to recite the Lord's Prayer, while Pile struggles to save his companion. Referring to himself by the royal "we" (*nous*), Ubu tells his shaken and disgusted Palotins, "We did not hesitate to climb on to a higher rock so that our prayers would have less distance to travel to reach the heavens." Still lazy and fearful, he will not even help prepare the bear for supper. That night, Pile and Lotice debate whether to stay with their king or abandon him; under cover of darkness, and with Ubu asleep, they leave.

As the fifth and final act begins, Mère Ubu enters the cave, offers a reprise of all that has befallen her, and only then realizes that her husband is there, talking to himself in his sleep. Claiming to be the archangel Gabriel, she orders Ubu to forgive his wife, but dawn breaks, and Ubu literally sees through her ruse and in Grand Guignol fashion "begins to tear her to pieces." The fight expands when Bourgelas and his men enter the cave, followed shortly after by Ubu's Palotins, inexplicably returned. The Ubus and their party escape, however, and are last seen aboard a ship, passing Hamlet's Elsinore Castle, cheerfully making their way home (either to Spain or to France), with Père Ubu saying, "Ah, gentlemen! However beautiful [Germany] may be, it can never equal Poland. If there weren't any Poland, there wouldn't be any Poles!"

Themes and Meanings

The title character of *Ubu Roi* is, in critic Martin Esslin's words,

> a savage caricature of a stupid, selfish bourgeois seen through the cruel eyes of a schoolboy, but this Rabelaisian character, with his Falstaffian greed and cowardice, is more than mere social satire. He is a terrifying image of the animal nature of man, his cruelty and ruthlessness.

The play's setting is a wholly imaginary Poland, a land which in its history has literally been torn to pieces, partitioned out of existence, a nowhere that Alfred Jarry's telling makes an any- or everywhere, just as his palindromic hero becomes a modern Everyman, as ridiculous and empty as the oaths he likes to utter: "shittr," "gadzookers," "by my green candle." Based upon Jarry's physics teacher, Félix Hébert, at the Lycée of Rennes, a man as unjust and incompetent as he was physically absurd, Ubu appears as a grotesque, nearly hairless figure, an enormous belly surmounted by a pear-shaped head, the very embodiment of the bourgeoisie that Jarry despised for their stupidity, avarice, and moral posturing. Utterly egocentric and entirely cash-minded, Ubu is exactly what the play's other characters call him: swine, idiot, imbecile, oaf, coward, ass, creature, beast, blockhead, villain, and, above all, traitor and (as suggested by the title's echo of Sophocles' *Oidipous Tyrannos*, c. 429 B.C.E.; in French, *Oedipe roi*) tyrant. Gluttony is the outward sign of his avaricious nature; additionally, his avarice is coupled with that inertness of mind and spirit that his physical bulk connotes. He is on one hand the embodiment of sloth and simple-minded self-satisfaction, unwilling to do anything but be what he is, a machine for ingesting and growing fat; yet, on the other hand, he is marked by his ever-increasing appetite for food and wealth.

In the depths of his gluttonous self, the folds of his fat, Ubu alone exists; all others are merely things, commodities, to be used or consumed and then discarded. "But look here, Père Ubu," his wife admonishes him, "what sort of a king do you think you are, you kill everyone." Ubu's brutality is part of a larger problem, his inability to consider anyone other than himself. He has no feelings, no conscience, and (as Roger Shattuck has noted) no "insight into his own monstrosity." Ubu's obtuseness exceeds his obesity. Chased by the Czar, he cries out with all apparent sincerity, "This madman is chasing me! What have I done. . . ." Any wrongs he has committed, he claims, were not done "on purpose" and are not his fault. Ubu's language proves no closer to reality than he himself is, and it is this discrepancy between word and world that Jarry exploits so well. His aim, however, is not merely to be humorous. "Ubu's speeches were not meant to be full of witticisms," Jarry has pointed out, "but of stupid remarks, uttered with all the authority of the Ape."

Jarry repeatedly punctures the emptiness of bourgeois language (and with it bourgeois morality), as in the conspirators' concern over exactly how "to kill a king properly." Jarry largely accomplishes this aim by inverting words and meanings, turning gallantry, for example, into treachery and human dignity into bestiality. Jarry has named the characters significantly: Some of the names are scatological puns— Bordure has been translated as "Macnure," Bourgelas as "Buggerlas." Further, Mère and Père Ubu ("ma and pa") not only are childless, but also are the very antithesis of idealized bourgeois parents. Jarry also turns the material he has borrowed from the tragedies of Sophocles and Shakespeare upside down, transforming them into Rabelaisian farce. For the tragic dignity of humanity, Jarry substitutes greed and gluttony and a world in which good exists only in the most attenuated form and certainly does not triumph. "Your kindness knows no bounds," Ubu says to King Wenceslas, then adds in an aside, "Yes, but . . . you won't be any the less slaughtered, you know." Ubu is not an exception; he is the very type of bourgeois man. Ubu, his wife, Bordure, and even the Poles are all driven by self-interest in a plot in which treachery and duplicity are the norm, and where understanding, justice, fidelity, and compassion (of, for example, the magistrates and Bourgelas) are clearly the exceptions. *Ubu Roi* is a truly disturbing work. As Barbara Wright has claimed, "it shamelessly displays what civilization tries hard to hide, and that is more than lavatory brushes and schoolboy swearwords, it is an aspect of truth."

Dramatic Devices

Ubu Roi is a play in which the lavatory brush replaces the scepter, and in which the first word, *merde* ("shit," childishly but deliberately misspelled *merdre*), declares Jarry's intent, *épater les bourgeois*. The play is an assault on the audience and theater of the *belle époque*. Viewed against a backdrop of labor unrest, anarchist attacks on the political system, bourgeois smugness, and late nineteenth century French theater, with its emphasis on the well-made play, its star system, its commitment to theater as entertainment, and its preservation of the status quo, it becomes clear how revolutionary a work *Ubu Roi* actually is.

In subject and treatment, content and form, Jarry designed his play to subvert the audience's assumptions and expectations about both theater and humankind. He conceived the play as a funhouse mirror in which the viewer would be able to see an exaggerated image of "its ignoble other self." Not surprisingly, Jarry described the theatergoing public in Ubu-like terms as "a mass—inert, obtuse, and passive—that . . . need to be shaken up from time to time." Jarry shakes his audience up by offering them a carnival theater of exaggeration and grotesquerie rather than either the pseudo-realistic clichés of the era's popular plays or the naturalistic dramas that Émile Zola had been demanding. *Ubu Roi* innovatively suggests the stylized naïveté of Jarry's friend, the painter Henri Rousseau, as well as the primitivism of Paul Gauguin, but mixed with a certain expressionistic brutality and childlike perversity.

Jarry's most startling and important innovation involves his having conceived the play not simply as a funhouse mirror but as a puppet play. Dispensing entirely with the dramatic unities of time, place, and action, Jarry chose to let his title character loose, so to speak. Neither Ubu nor any of the others are "characters" in any traditional sense; they are caricatures, abstract and depersonalized, played by actors whom Jarry directed to suppress all traces of their own individuality and whom for a time Jarry wanted attached to strings (an idea as interesting as it is impracticable when dealing with actors rather than puppets).

The actors were to appear onstage either wearing masks or as if wearing masks, to speak in a distinctive monotone, and to employ the simplest and, therefore (according to Jarry), the most universal gestures. Possessing no psychological depth whatsoever, the figures appear cartoonish in word, deed, and costume. Indeed, the very logic of the play follows that of the cartoon and puppet show—a character may die in one scene yet return quite alive in the next; not surprisingly, *Ubu Roi* was several times staged by Jarry as a puppet play and was later turned into an animated cartoon by Geoff Dunbar (which aired on the BBC in 1978). Clearly, the frequent and sudden shifts in time and place contribute to the play's cartoonish, anti-illusionistic effect, especially since these shifts are not indicated by any change in the set.

The play is acted out against either a plain backdrop or one painted so as to suggest simultaneously a discordancy of scenes: indoors and out, city and country (Jarry, Pierre Bonnard, Édouard Vuillard, Paul Sérusier, and Henri de Toulouse-Lautrec all had a hand in the painting of the original backdrop, and other prominent painters have been connected with later productions: Max Ernst in 1937; David Hockney, 1966; and Joan Miró, 1981). In keeping with the play's essential antirealism and anti-illusionism, Jarry wanted all scenery to be kept to the barest possible minimum and whatever scenery was necessary to be treated as props. If a window is needed, for example, one will be brought onstage, used, and then removed, all in full view of the audience. As in a puppet show, changes in setting are indicated by placards posted onstage. The frequency of these changes contributes to the play's irrealism and, given the large cast of characters and equally large number of scenes (thirty-three in five acts), its surprising continuity.

This continuity of action, which has been likened to cinematic montage, parallels Jarry's belief in the continuity of all life, including waking and sleeping, reality and hallucination, the rational and the irrational. Jarry used these and other innovative techniques in order to shock his audience out of their accustomed modes of perceiving a world that had been made to conform to bourgeois conceptions by showing them an exaggerated version of themselves. Although some have held that the riot that occurred on opening night evidences the public's failure to understand *Ubu Roi*, Jarry himself, a little perversely perhaps, believed otherwise—the public "resented it because they understood it too well."

Critical Context

Ubu Roi is not Jarry's only work; he also wrote poems and novels as well as other plays. It is, however, the work on which his reputation largely rests and to which he devoted much of his brief career. Its history goes back to the play *Les Polanaise* (the Poles), which Jarry either wrote or collaborated on in 1888 while still at the lycée. Numerous versions followed, including one in book form in July, 1896, which received favorable notices. The play itself was performed five months later, on December 9 and 10, at Aurélien-Marie Lugne-Poë's Théâtre de l'Œuvre, and thanks to the riots which occurred (and which Jarry may have helped orchestrate), *Ubu Roi* became a *succès de scandale*. Although it was never again performed during Jarry's lifetime, Jarry continued to revise, plunder, and publish parts, versions, and spin-offs, including two new puppet plays and a sequel, *Ubu enchaîné* (pb. 1900; *Ubu Enchained*, 1953), named after Aeschylus's *Prometheus desmōtēs* (c. 450 B.C.E.; *Prometheus Bound*), in which Ubu seeks his same goals by adopting precisely the opposite course—becoming a slave rather than a king. The two have often been performed together; *Ubu Cocu* (pb. 1944; *Ubu Cuckolded*, 1953), the earliest of the three Ubu plays and also the most scatological and least coherent, has very rarely been performed.

Perhaps the most disconcerting result of the two December performances was the diminutive author's own subsequent metamorphosis into his huge Ubu, thus breaking down the barrier separating author from character, life from art, and sanity from madness. Although some have interpreted this transformation as a sign of the pain Jarry felt upon seeing his play rejected, others have offered a quite different explanation. It was, they claim, Jarry's way of "showing his contempt for the cruelty and stupidity of the universe by making his own life a poem of incoherence and absurdity." Jarry was not the only one influenced by *Ubu Roi.* Just as he had been influenced by the Symbolists (especially Stéphane Mallarmé), he in turn had a pronounced effect on avant-garde writers, painters, composers, and movements that were to follow: Surrealism, Dadaism, Futurism, Fauvism, Theater of the Absurd, Guillaume Apollinaire, Eugène Ionesco, René Clair, Raymond Queneau, Jacques Prevert, Erik Satie, Jean Cocteau, Pablo Picasso, and Samuel Beckett.

Sources for Further Study
Beaumont, Keith S. *Alfred Jarry: A Critical and Biographical Study.* New York: St. Martin's Press, 1985.
Esslin, Martin. *The Theatre of the Absurd.* 3d ed. London: Methuen, 2001.
LaBelle, Maurice Marc. *Alfred Jarry: Nihilism and the Theater of the Absurd.* New York: New York University Press, 1980.
Remshardt, Rolf Erik. "King Ubu and Scenes from *Macbeth.*" *Theatre Journal* 46 (May, 1994): 262-267.
Schumacher, Claude. *Alfred Jarry and Guillaume Apollinaire.* New York: Grove Press, 1985.
Shattuck, Roger. *The Banquet Years; The Arts in France, 1885-1918: Alfred Jarry, Henri Rousseau, Erik Satie, Guillaume Apollinaire.* London: Faber and Faber, 1958.
Stillman, Linda Klieger. *Alfred Jarry.* Boston: Twayne, 1983.

Robert A. Morace

VIENNA: LUSTHAUS

Author: Martha Clarke (1944-   )
Type of plot: Surrealist
Time of plot: The late nineteenth century
Locale: Vienna
First produced: 1986, at St. Clement's Church, New York City
First published: 1987, in *The Drama Review*

> *Principal characters:*
> SOLDIERS,
> LOVERS,
> SKATERS,
> DANCERS, and
> MODELS, portrayed by an ensemble of eleven actors and six
>   musicians

The Play

Vienna: Lusthaus is a series of forty-four dreamlike vignettes which sometimes overlap, sometimes occur simultaneously, and sometimes fade in and out of one another. As the performance begins, a pool of light reveals a couple slowly waltzing in center stage. A crowd begins to gather while a man and a woman converse. The man recounts the surrealistic scene that ensued when an acquaintance named Leonard flew across the seats in the opera, put his hand in the man's mouth, and pulled out two of his teeth. The crowd exits, leaving a soldier alone onstage. In a movement sequence, he makes a gradual transformation from man to horse. He lowers his body to all fours before galloping offstage.

A couple waltzes across the stage. Two women, one in a dress and the other in a man's suit, begin a slow waltz, stop, and hesitantly begin to remove their jackets. The room comes to full light when a young man begins to tell a story about his Aunt Cissi. Women in white undergarments gather in a doorway. As they approach the man on the bench, he becomes flustered while describing his aunt's clothing. The women laugh and wave to him as he makes his hurried exit. A harpist plays a lush melody as the six women form a line.

The women sit or kneel on the floor as one describes a sexual encounter with a man in India several thousand years ago. An older actor begins to sing in German; two women sit on the piano bench and kiss. One tells of her mother who, carrying an armful of flowers one day, forgets to hold the banister, walks through an open window, and falls to her death. The soldier from the beginning of the piece approaches her. He grooms her like a horse, then the couple ride off as horse and rider.

In the next sequence, the older woman watches a younger woman in a lyrical movement phrase while a bearded man recounts the story of how he and his daughter watched a fountain from their hotel balcony. The water, he recalls, suddenly shot up in the air and directly into his daughter's face. When he attempted to deflect the water, a woman called out from the hotel ballroom to let the girl get wet: "Otherwise what's the point of life?"

A couple waltzes in. They caress in a tender, impassioned *pas de deux* while the older woman watches. She slips into the younger woman's place so that when the man turns he embraces the older woman instead. Two nude women sit downstage right on a white sheet, their clothes scattered about them. They perform a symmetrical movement phrase, arching their backs and rolling their heads sensuously, as a violinist plays a brisk waltz. The music stops; the lights shift to illuminate the figures of a nude man and woman in a doorway. They begin a slow, sustained embrace, then exit as a man in a top hat enters and a nude man walks to upstage center. The man in the hat tells of the miracle he witnessed while standing along the banks of the Danube. He describes the sudden swelling of the river, which overflows its banks, and an ensuing rainstorm which drenches one bank but does not fall at all on the other side, leaving it in radiant sunlight. While he speaks, the nude man falls to the floor in agonized, contracted movements.

A half-dressed soldier enters with a young girl. He sits on the bench; she sits stiffly on his lap. He manipulates her arms and legs to accommodate his caresses. She remains expressionless, moving woodenly to the positions he desires, as though she is a doll. Throughout this sequence an accordion player and clarinetist play a brisk, dissonant song. The soldier carries the girl off when the song ends.

A soldier and a woman stand side by side. They both speak parts of the same story, but out of synchronization. They retell the opening story about Leonard. Each asks why he would want to do that—is he a Jew? The only answer is that so much of life is unaccountable these days. Each speaker then tells of stopping a young girl on a staircase to chastise her for a taunting remark she had made. Each recalls how he or she then began sexually molesting the child.

In the next scene, a young woman catalogs her many dislikes in time with a jaunty melody. A couple ride through, and three women dance across upstage. This cheerful scene quickly fades. In a pool of white light center stage, a man wearing white long underwear and a woman's black shoes on his hands performs both parts of a sexual encounter. In the next sequence, a woman stands while a man lies at her feet, his head beneath her dress; she then sits on his face. Meanwhile a very properly dressed young woman unbuttons the jacket, vest, and shirt of an older man. They embrace and sit on the bench. The lights go out. When they come back up, a woman wearing only black stockings and black shoes sits on the bench posing coyly. She stands, exposing her carefully shaven pubic hair, and exits.

Then a woman in a black dress lies on the floor. At her feet, a soldier explores her body with the tip of his whip. Another man recites a list of his erotic conquests or rapes and the number of times he was with each woman. While he recites his list, the woman rolls onto her face and tries to crawl toward center stage. The soldier watches her while another young woman dances across the back of the stage. Then the soldier begins slowly removing his clothes. The young woman struggles with her jacket, but runs offstage. The soldier sits on a chair; his hands become like hooves as he struggles to unbutton his pants and remove his boots. This sequence is very tense and is accompanied by the plucking of violin strings.

At the end of this scene, the older woman reenters carrying a lantern and speaking in German. Snow begins to fall and the violin plays a sweet melody. Couples in winter clothing move as if they are skating; others waltz. A woman tells the story of her mother who woke up early one morning in pain and announced that she was going to jump out the window because she did not want to live anymore. A man tells of his Aunt Alexandra who was convinced that a large sofa was lodged in her head, making it impossible for her to leave the house. The women and soldiers skate or dance offstage, except the last speaker, who describes seeing a black and white butterfly on a green leaf. He explains that the butterfly did not move at his waving hand because it thought it was safely camouflaged even though it was really completely exposed.

The old woman reappears, drawing circles in the continually falling snow. Two soldiers march onto the stage; they fall into the snow face first, continuing to mark time with their boots. Their legs quiver; they stand and exit. A couple waltzes across the stage to the sound of the marching boots and a violin. The older man in the top hat reenters. He describes being unable to choke a gigantic rat he found in his room one night. He says he thought it was some kind of Greek fate, to be left forever trying to choke a rat.

A center pool of light comes up on a soldier lying with his bandaged head in a woman's lap. She embraces him, but his body is lifeless. She begins to shake him; she rises and repeatedly hoists his body from the floor and bangs it down again. Eventually she stops. Skaters sail by as the snow continues to fall. The dead soldier asks the man in the top hat about how to tell when a person has been shot. The two discuss the physical transformation of death. The soldier asks what colors a body passes through in death. The other man answers light pink, red, light blue, dark blue, purple-red. The old woman crosses again with her cane. The pale lights fade out while the harp softly fades out to silence.

Themes and Meanings

In *Vienna: Lusthaus*, Martha Clarke explores love and death in various manifestations. Clarke's images of eroticism and decadence are filtered through memories and dreams to describe the link between sex and destruction and the slow degeneration of life in *fin de siècle* Vienna. The two themes are effortlessly and inextricably intertwined. A young woman remembers her beautiful mother with arms full of flowers on a summer day walking through their house and falling to her death. Couples waltz and skate to the sweet strains of Johann Strauss while a woman recounts her mother's announcement that because she is in so much pain she is going to kill herself.

Scenes of seduction and pleasure are juxtaposed with scenes of sexual dominance and cruelty or with another character's subconscious sexual yearnings. The characters' repressed desires and fantasies are revealed, thereby liberating these men and women from the strict mores of their society. A young woman sits tense and un-moving on a much older man's lap. When she stands to exit, a nude woman steps from behind the man to take the girl's place. The story of the sexual encounter with the young girl on the staircase, told simultaneously by a man and a woman, suggests devi-ant sexual behavior as well as fantasy. The insinuation of child molestation and rape takes on lesbian overtones in the woman's recounting of the scene. In *Vienna: Lust-haus*, men and women are driven by their desires, and almost all the characters seem capable of satisfying their lusts. The nineteenth century romantic notion of love has been replaced by seduction and sex to attain power; yet these desires are overshad-owed by war and death.

Soldiers march, fall, and lie in the snow. A man speaks of "natural selection" which will eventually obliterate the black and white butterfly whose color cannot camou-flage it. Another describes his futile attempt to choke a large rat in his apartment. An older woman appears in scenes which depict her sexual desires as incongruous with her aging body. Because of her age, she is often placed outside the authority of the sexuality that drives the others; her presence is a constant reminder of their morality.

The third subtheme of memory and dreams underlies the structure of the work it-self. The images and characters, as well as the incomplete stories and memories they describe, reflect the incongruity and illogic that characterize the structure of dreams. The associative rather than narrative organization of these images creates openings and ambiguities in the textual framework of *Vienna: Lusthaus* which must then be filled by the spectator's own associations.

Dramatic Devices

Martha Clarke uses nudity as a dramatic device in *Vienna: Lusthaus*. Sometimes the actors turn shyly from the audience's gaze and other times coldly face them as if they were voyeurs. Scenes of seduction and sexual passion are played alternately by women in layers of frilly, white Victorian underwear with men in full uniform, by nude women with clothed men, and by nude couples. The women in their lacy cami-soles and petticoats are sometimes beautiful partners in acts of love and sometimes powerless victims of rape or incest. Nude women appear as objects of sexual conquest in some scenes, while in others they use their erotic presence to exert power over men or one another. Additionally, Clarke contrasts nude figures with clothed figures in scenes that simultaneously suggest beautiful and horrible images. In one scene, a gen-tleman in formal evening wear and a top hat describes the miracle of rain falling on only one side of a riverbank and speaks of his own awareness of witnessing this beau-tiful event. Meanwhile, the man who had transformed himself into a horse in the first scene stands nude upstage, gradually writhing in agony until he falls lifelessly on the floor. This kind of fragmentary juxtaposition of stage figures illustrates the relation-ship between man and animal, between pleasure and pain.

Another important device in *Vienna: Lusthaus* is the use of an ensemble rather than a cast of actors who portray specific characters. This allows the actors to change roles from scene to scene in the non-narrative framework of the performance. The speaking performers deliver their fantastic tales candidly; those who do not speak instill their movements with the same ingenuousness. This performance attitude further skews the logic of the text and movement. The use of an ensemble suggests that the themes are representative of all experience rather than peculiar to any particular "character" within the performance.

Clarke's choice of the collage structure serves to layer the images and meanings; her use of cross-fading and blending lyrical scenes and illogical scenes dramatizes the dream form. A scene often begins only to be interrupted by a new movement sequence or a completely different monologue. Condensation and displacement of these fragmented images is then mirrored in text and choreography. The text, by Charles L. Mee, Jr., is largely composed of the writings of Sigmund Freud and Marcel Proust, observations from Mee's own dreams, and phrases from conversations that might have been overheard in old Vienna. While most of the text is written as reminiscences spoken in monologue, the actors sound as if they are retelling dreams. In an early scene, a young man begins to talk about his Aunt Cissi's obsession with her youthful beauty, but his musings are interrupted when a young woman is taken by a sudden memory of a sexual encounter with a man in India several thousand years ago. The flow of action and text is seamless; the delivery of the spoken text has the candor and clarity of dreams retold in a formal, clinical setting.

Clarke's use of movement is the real substance of the work. Since more than half the scenes are wordless, Clarke uses movement to describe the same surrealistic structure of scenes and to link images with text. A man transforms into a galloping horse. A man enacts both parts of a sexual encounter. Soldiers march to their deaths, and women undress and kiss, pose coyly, or waltz and skate. The scenes collect Clarke's ideas about sex, war, love, and fate, and culminate in the final scene of a woman embracing the body of a dying soldier under falling snow. While the movement sequence of this scene is violent and horrible, Clarke manages to blend pain with beauty in the subsequent dispassionate dialogue which asks and answers the soldier's questions about the body passing through death.

Critical Context

Vienna: Lusthaus focuses on the daily activities, thoughts, and fantasies of *fin de siècle* Vienna, a city inhabited by Sigmund Freud, Gustav Klimt, Gustav Mahler, and Johann Strauss, as well as Adolf Hitler. This historical period has been the subject of numerous books and major museum exhibits, such as New York's Museum of Modern Art's "Vienna 1900: Art, Architecture, and Design." A revival of interest in art nouveau and a nostalgia for the humanistic values and beauty of the nineteenth century surround Martha Clarke's work. She says her inspiration for this piece was derived in part from her observations at a 1984 exhibition in Venice about late nineteenth, early twentieth century Vienna titled "Dream and Reality."

Clarke's synthesis of text, music, dance, visual environment, and *mise-en-scène* is similar to the work of German choreographer/director Pina Bausch and theatrical directors Richard Foreman, Robert Wilson, and Peter Brook. This total theater, or "theater of images," allows these artist to create thematically complex, multilayered performance art. Clarke's work is distinguished by her characteristic use of detailed movement sequences to further explore the themes of the text. *Vienna: Lusthaus* is Clarke's second major performance work. Some of the extraordinary movement sequences in this piece reflect the choreographic influence of her seven years with Pilobolus Dance Theater. With this company she collaborated on such works as *Monkshood's Farewell* (pr. 1974) and *Untitled* (pr. 1975). The addition of collaborator Mee's spoken text for *Vienna: Lusthaus* brings another dimension to Clarke's already rich, disturbing works. Her earlier work, *The Garden of Earthly Delights* (pr. 1984), and later works such as *The Hunger Artist* (pr. 1987) and *Miracolo d'Amore* (pr. 1988) similarly synthesize dance, gesture, design, and spoken or sung text. Each of these pieces demonstrates Clarke's unique vision in her articulate use of the human body. In *Vienna: Lusthaus*, Clarke is able to evoke both the beauty and the underlying decadence that signaled the city's gradual decay and destruction.

Sources for Further Study

Acocella, Joan Ross. "Body and Soul: A Review of Martha Clarke's *Vienna: Lusthaus.*" *Dance Magazine* 60 (August, 1986): 40-45.

Clarke, Martha. "A Conversation with Martha Clarke." Interview with Elizabeth Kendall and Don Daniels. *Ballet Review* 12 (Winter, 1985): 15-25.

_____. "Images from the Id." Interview with Arthur Bartow. *American Theatre* 5 (June, 1988): 10-17, 55-57.

Martin, Carol. Review in *Performing Arts Journal* 10, no. 2 (1986): 88-90.

Mee, Charles L., and Amanda Smith. "Martha Clarke's *Vienna: Lusthaus.*" *Drama Review* 31 (Fall, 1987): 42-58.

Sadler, Geoff. "Martha Clarke." In *Contemporary Dramatists*. 6th ed. Detroit: St. James, 1999.

Schorske, Carl. *Fin-de-Siècle Vienna: Politics and Culture.* New York: Knopf, 1981.

Diane Quinn

VOLUNTEERS

Author: Brian Friel (1929-   )
Type of plot: Political
Time of plot: The 1970's
Locale: Ireland
First produced: 1975, at the Abbey Theatre, Dublin, Ireland
First published: 1979

> *Principal characters:*
> GEORGE, the site supervisor
> MR. WILSON, the guard
> DES, an archaeology student
> KNOX,
> BUTT,
> SMILER,
> KEENEY, and
> PYNE, the prisoners who volunteer to work on the archaeological
> excavation

The Play

Volunteers is set on an archaeological site in the middle of an Irish city, presumably Dublin, in the mid-1970's. A parking garage and some houses have been razed to allow construction of a luxury hotel, complete with underground swimming pool. Workers have removed layers of Georgian cellars and Norman debris to reveal the foundations of a tenth century Viking house. These foundations and a Viking skeleton the workers have named Leif are the dominant features of the set, which remains unchanged throughout the play.

Because of the archaeological value of the discoveries, hotel construction has been temporarily halted to allow fuller study. Funding for the project, however, has been exhausted, and the task is being completed by the volunteers of the title—five prisoners on daily parole. These prisoners' offenses, though revealed only in broad outlines, have resulted from a frustrating Irish mix of political and economic disfranchisement, so that they are neither clearly criminals nor clearly political prisoners. Shortly after the play begins, they are delivered to the site by Wilson, an obtuse guard (a former officer in the British army) who leaves immediately to spend the rest of the day observing his daughter's music examination.

On the site, the prisoners are supervised by Des, an archaeology student fond of Marxist clichés, and by George, an indifferent bureaucrat who proudly displays a thirteenth century jug he has pieced together out of 593 fragments. The fragments were discovered by Smiler, a volunteer whose only crime was civil disobedience but who has' been beaten by the police into a state of childlike dependence on his friends.

Keeney, the closest thing to a leader of the volunteers, is a cynical joker with a fondness for limericks and a sardonic dislike of pretense.

As the play begins, it is to be the last day of the dig, and it is revealed that the prisoners, by volunteering, have completely isolated themselves. The other prisoners resent cooperation in any form with the government which has interned so many and have refused to speak to the volunteers since the project began five months ago. Old friends outside the prison have similarly ostracized the volunteers, who now have only one another to talk to. It is that companionship, the guard Wilson correctly realizes, which they will miss the most when the dig is over.

The volunteers settle in for another typical day on the site—playing practical jokes on one another, speculating about why Leif's skeleton has a hole in the skull and a noose around the neck, and mercilessly parodying the school tours and American tourists who regularly visit the site. When Des arrives, he learns that the dig is at an end but that the prisoners have not yet been told. Insisting that the site director has been bought off by speculators and is ending the dig only because he has already "looted enough for another coffee-table book," Des calls the volunteers together to announce the site's closure and to vow support for them in "whatever protest you think fit." He then rushes off to protest the end of the dig to museum authorities.

Meanwhile, Smiler has wandered off the site. Convinced that he cannot take care of himself in the "outside" world, George is encouraged by the prisoners to call and report Smiler's disappearance; they hope he will be captured and returned to safety. Keeney, however, stops them. The night before, he announces, he learned that the other internees plan to execute the volunteers for their cooperation with authorities. Keeney argues persuasively that Smiler would stand even less chance of survival inside the prison than he will outside. As the curtain falls, Keeney is polling the others on their feelings, which are now clearly against allowing George to report Smiler's escape.

When act 2 opens, the volunteers are cleaning up the site, but the lines of authority are plainly reversed. Keeney is in charge, and George is reduced to spluttered threats that he will tell Wilson about their interference with the escape report. As the volunteers recognize their entrapment between enemies inside the prison and enemies outside, their joking becomes almost frantic. Sensing that they have nothing left to lose, they emphasize their new resistance to authority by playing keep-away with George's precious reconstituted jug, quitting only when they decide that the jug rightfully belongs to Leif, at whose feet they deposit it. The mixture of humor and serious debate continues as each volunteer creates a story explaining why Leif has a hole in his skull—each story an ironic echo of the teller's own history.

Des returns, having readily agreed to end the dig since he himself is assured of continuing work assessing the artifacts. Keeney mocks Des's abandonment of Marxist principles, telling him that the volunteers have written a letter of protest to the paper, quoting Des freely. Into the middle of this increasingly tense atmosphere walks Smiler, whose desire to get away has not been able to dominate his need for the care and direction provided by the other prisoners. Butt, Smiler's closest friend, deliberately drops George's jug, fragmenting it beyond repair. As a gesture of respect, the volunteers cover Leif with a tarp and conduct a burial service of sorts, before leaving him to final burial by the cement mixer. Wilson returns (pathetically uncertain how the English examiner had reacted to his daughter's playing) to take the volunteers back to prison and almost certain death. Keeney delivers a closing limerick which bitterly summarizes the world's view of the volunteers as worthless. The volunteers exit with Wilson. Left alone on the stage, George removes the tarpaulin from Leif's skeleton and folds it as the lights go down.

Themes and Meanings

The entrapment of the prisoners in *Volunteers*—caught by historical, political, economic, and personal forces—reflects the entrapment of all Irish people and, by extension, of all humans at all times. Brian Friel's play about the very public issue of the Irish troubles has a very private focus, recognizing the complexity of factors which shape both public and private action.

As the volunteers excavate layers of history—Georgian, Norman, Viking—they reveal the forces which have made Ireland. They also help to shape the Irish future, in this case represented by a luxury hotel. As Keeney insists in his parody of a visiting schoolteacher, however, "the more we learn about our ancestors . . . the more we discover about ourselves. . . . So that what we are all engaged in here is really a thrilling voyage in *self*-discovery." The volunteers cannot excavate their country's history without discovering their own personal histories; they cannot shape their country's future without shaping their own futures. What they discover is that nation and individuals are both trapped by forces difficult to sort and evaluate. They are no more certain how and why Leif died than they are about what determined their own opposition to authority. The precise date of the foundations they are excavating turns out to be as uncertain as their reasons for volunteering. The difficulty of putting the pottery fragments together reflects the difficulty with which they restructure their lives—and both jug and lives are easily shattered.

The stories that the prisoners create to explain Leif explain their own experiences as well. Each offers a specific, convincing reason for the hole in the skull and the noose around the neck. It hardly matters that the stories cannot all be true, since their major function is not to reveal reality but to create explanations. That these explanations are largely fabricated does not blunt the necessity for their comforting existence. People need "the protection of the myth" and its implication that their experiences are understandable.

The prisoners' myths share a focus on tribal warfare. Each myth explains Leif in part by creating a situation which pits brother against brother, family against family, in bitter and unrelenting conflict. It is the contemporary Irish (and the contemporary human) situation in tenth century Viking dress. *Volunteers* illustrates what Friel once described as "life repeating itself and surviving," and the play poses central questions about history: Does the past shape the present by providing a pattern for it? Or does the present shape the past by imposing a pattern on it?

Volunteers reveals a tangle of imprisoning forces. The volunteers are trapped by a political history which puts those, such as Wilson, who have cooperated with the British, in positions of authority while simultaneously leaving them subject to the judgments of such Englishmen as the music examiner. (The play's title, *Volunteers*, is a reflection of the Irish Volunteers who fought in the Easter Rebellion of 1916.) They are trapped by economic forces which theoretical Marxists such as Des cannot break through, by the indifference of petit bourgeois (represented by George), and by their own need to create myths which shape and explain experience by oversimplifying it. Above all, they are trapped by habitual tribal warfare: Ostracized by those who ought to support them, the volunteers cannot even keep from fighting among themselves.

Given this welter of conflicting chains, Keeney maintains his sanity by mocking the authorities, American tourists, Irish schoolteachers, Marxist ideologues, his fellow volunteers, and himself. It is behavior which Friel describes elsewhere as "defensive flippancy."

Dramatic Devices

The set of *Volunteers* emphasizes the play's themes of entrapment and isolation. Simultaneously a construction and an excavation site, the area of the dig is fifteen feet below ground and shielded from the life of the surrounding city by sheets of corrugated iron that make it impossible to look in or out. The prisoners, literally and symbolically beneath the surface, dig into their own and the city's pasts. The supervisor's office perched halfway up the wall of the excavation reflects the hierarchical nature of this society. The tips of television antennas and the fact that it will soon be the location of a high-rise hotel emphasize the commercial nature of contemporary Ireland, set to destroy its varied past in favor of a graceless commercial present. The set reflects the enclosed nature of Irish society, the enclosed nature of the volunteers' experiences, and the enclosed nature of the Irish minds (including the prisoners' minds) which produced this situation.

The relative bareness of the set adds importance to a number of symbolic props, most notably the skeleton of Leif and the jug which has been glued together out of fragments. At the end of the play, when the jug has been smashed, and when George folds the tarp with which the prisoners have sought to provide a minimum of protection and dignity for the skeleton, the audience is given powerful visual reinforcement for two of the play's major themes: the difficulty of reconstituting or understanding the past and the indifferent contemporary commercialism which unthinkingly prefers saving an item of minimal value to providing a measure of dignity to people and to the past.

The names of characters also function symbolically in this play. George and Mr. Wilson, the two supervisors, have appropriately British names. Des, the theoretical Marxist, has a traditional Irish name. The prisoners' names, however, are colorful, unlikely, and often ironic reflections of their reality. Keeney, for example, reminds the audience that this mocking character is using his keen wit as a means of mourning (keening) the lives and the world he sees around him. Smiler, Knox, Pyne, Butt—the names eloquently reflect Brian Friel's assessment of the prisoners' characters and situation.

The play's mixture of comic high jinks and serious social commentary is a dramatic technique of which Friel has made skillful use in a number of plays. The audience is rocked with laughter at the prisoners' mocking, playful attitude. Keeney's limericks, barbed and bawdy, suggest an almost music-hall atmosphere, similar to the atmosphere which Friel creates with songs in other plays. However, the humor has a sharp edge and cuts close to painful social issues, so that ultimately *Volunteers* is not only a serious play but a bitter play as well. It is the essence of Friel's realism to refuse to separate artificially the comic and tragic aspects of his world.

Critical Context

Volunteers is one of a number of Brian Friel plays which address the contemporary Irish situation. Like other Irish writers, he is caught in what Irish poet Seamus Heaney has called "the quarrel between free, creative imagination, and the constraints of religious, political, and domestic obligation." Friel has most often dealt with social, political, and economic problems as they affect the lives of ordinary people. His first widely popular play, *Philadelphia, Here I Come!* (pr. 1964), examines why one young Irishman becomes part of the vast wave of emigration. *The Freedom of the City* (pr. 1973) uses actual events in the northern city of Derry to assess the impact of denial of civil rights on three ordinary residents. With *Volunteers*, Friel moves south, where he again uses historical events as the loose basis for an imaginative assessment of the impact of public events on private lives. In part, *Volunteers* is Friel's insistence that the Irish "troubles" are not simply a northern phenomenon. The Viking references also link this play to similar material in the poetry of Heaney, to whom *Volunteers* is dedicated.

In *Translations* (pr. 1980), nineteenth century lovers are destroyed by the conflicting demands of their tribes. *Making History* (pr. 1988) continues what Declan Kiberd has called Friel's "search for a usable past," a search which often focuses on "the cries of those caught up in the fury of lived histories." Friel often modifies historical facts to fit dramatic necessity, but his works demonstrate a commitment to drama which opens dialogue on important issues.

Friel's commitment to social dialogue is also evident in his involvement, since 1980, in Field Day, an Irish company which he co-founded and which has taken as its mission the participation in anything that might further discussion and lessen tension and violence. Field Day produces plays, publishes pamphlets, and has compiled a comprehensive anthology of Irish writing designed to "show how the various groups, sects and races which have intermingled in Ireland have produced a literature which is unique to them and an achievement which makes manifest what they have in common." In his effort to create drama which will further social dialogue, Friel frequently uses innovative dramatic techniques, but his restless experimentation is less obvious in *Volunteers* than elsewhere.

The thematic concern with the past, the mixture of mythmaking and verbal play with a straight realistic plot line, and the concern with the interplay of public and personal events mark Friel as working in the mainstream of contemporary Irish drama, along with playwrights such as Frank McGuinness and Stewart Parker, with whom he has worked closely on several projects.

Sources for Further Study

Andrews, Elmer. *The Art of Brian Friel: Neither Reality nor Dreams*. New York: St. Martin's Press, 1995.

Dantanus, Ulf. *Brian Friel: The Growth of an Irish Dramatist*. Atlantic Highlands, N.J.: Humanities Press, 1985.

Delaney, Paul, ed. *Brian Friel in Conversation*. Ann Arbor: University of Michigan Press, 1999.

Kearney, Richard. "Friel and the Politics of Language Play." *Massachusetts Review* 28 (Autumn, 1987): 510-515.

Kerwin, William, ed. *Brian Friel: A Casebook*. New York: Garland, 1997.

Maxwell, D. E. S. "The Honour of Naming: Samuel Beckett and Brian Friel." In *A Critical History of Modern Irish Drama, 1891-1980*. New York: Cambridge University Press, 1984.

Peacock, Alan J. *The Achievement of Brian Friel*. Hyattsville, Md.: University Press, 1997.

Helen Lojek

A VOYAGE ROUND MY FATHER

Author: John Mortimer (1923-   )
Type of plot: Psychological; memory play
Time of plot: The 1930's-1960's
Locale: England
First produced: 1970, at the Greenwich Theatre, London
First published: 1971

> *Principal characters:*
> FATHER, a barrister blinded in an accident and prone to rages
> MOTHER, his patiently enduring wife
> BOY and
> SON, a character who is played by two separate actors, one as a
>   boy and one as an adult
> ELIZABETH, the son's wife

The Play

A Voyage Round My Father opens in a family garden. A father, blind and in his six-ties, asks his grown son to describe the flowers and earwig traps. The son, turning to the audience, recalls that his father was a barrister who went to the London law courts but returned each day "to the safety of the dahlias, the ritual of the evening earwig hunt," hiding among the flowers from the few visitors who came to call. The action re-verts to the past, and the son as a young boy enters with a young girl who teaches him to whistle, the first of two such initiation scenes. The next retrospective vignette shows the father on a ladder pruning trees. The adult son relates: "He hit his head on the branch of a tree and the retinas left the balls of his eyes." Though the father became blind, nobody referred to the affliction because he "had a great disinclination to men-tion anything unpleasant." This concern is ironic, though, because the father is an iconoclastic curmudgeon who is insensitive to his doting wife and cold to his admir-ing son.

When the time arrives for the boy to go away to school, the father is discouraging: "All education's perfectly useless. But it fills in the *time!*" Schoolmasters, he says, have "second rate minds" and life is "a closed book" to them. At school, the boy has a headmaster who wants to be called Noah (and tells the boys they are animals) and teachers who suffer from World War I shell shock and battle fatigue. Among the boy's classmates is Reigate, and they exchange fantasy portraits of their parents who, "it was obvious, needed a quick coating of romance." When Reigate visits the boy's home, he is surprised that the parents get along and that the mother is sober. While there, the boys put on a play ("something to keep you from thinking of your great un-happiness," Reigate tells the bewildered mother) about two World War I subalterns.

The next dramatic interlude, the leave-taking ceremonies at the school, has "Noah" warning the boys about the dangers of sex but so obtusely that they are not at all enlightened. In a subsequent discussion with his son, the father says of sex: "The whole business has been over-estimated by the poets." By now a mature young man (he "lights a cigarette with careless expertise"), the son is encouraged to go into law—so he will have spare time for writing, according to his father. The law, he says, does not require brilliance, only common sense and "relatively clean finger nails." The father, says the son, regards the law as "a small mechanical toy which might occupy half an hour on a rainy afternoon." However, the father is an eminently successful barrister, even after he becomes blind; a vignette shows the blind man performing his singular courtroom act in a divorce case. The next scene has the father and son walking arm in arm, the son describing the countryside (painting verbal pictures for his father) and telling him that Misses Baker and Cox, local bookshop owners, may get him a war job helping to make government propaganda films. The act ends with the men coming upon these two women sunbathing—and embracing and kissing. The father, blind to this sight, has the last word in the act ("We saw a good deal—of the monstrous persistence of Nature.") but is unaware of the unwitting irony of his comment.

The second act begins on a film production set, where the son's primary responsibilities are to fetch snacks for the crew and to maintain silence during takes. When he fails at this role, he is moved to the writer's department, where he meets Elizabeth, a scriptwriter who is supporting her husband and children. The son confesses that he is quitting films to enter the law, and by the next scene the son has been at the bar for nine months, Elizabeth has been divorced from her husband, and the two are planning to wed. The father tries to dissuade his son for economic reasons and then attempts the same approach with Elizabeth, but he meets his match with her. The son announces: "In that case his advocacy failed. In time he became reconciled to me as a husband for his daughter-in-law."

Financial problems soon bear down upon the son; busy though he is with divorce cases, he sees little money, for a clerk in the firm (his father's) collects the fees and dispenses payments in a quixotically parsimonious manner. Thus the son goes to the Free Legal Centre to make extra money and at the same time starts to write plays, though the father warns him to "hold hard on the law" and instructs him on the importance of timing in cross-examinations. The ensuing episode has the son in court attempting to emulate his father, but he fails laughably. In the next scene, however, the family celebrates his success in a major domestic case. Elizabeth questions its propriety, since the victor did not deserve to win, but the son says, "*I* won." She concludes that he is getting more like his father every day, a man who plays games and makes jokes but takes nothing seriously. The son says to the audience about his father, "He had no message . . . no belief. He was the advocate who can take the side that comes to him first and always discover words to anger his opponent." After an interlude in which the father regales his grandchildren with stories, the last episode of the play focuses upon the deterioration of the garden in tandem with the dying of the father. The play ends with the son speaking to the audience: "I'd been told of all the things you're meant to feel. Sudden freedom, growing up, the end of dependence, the step into the sunlight when no one is taller than you and you're in no one else's shadow. I know what I felt. Lonely."

Themes and Meanings

A Voyage Round My Father is John Mortimer's memoir of growing up in a middle-class English household dominated by a dictatorial blind father. Autobiographical though the work is, its playwright-*raisonneur* mainly is objective about the people and experiences he recalls. Unlike the narrators of such similar (American) plays as Tennessee Williams's *The Glass Menagerie* (pr. 1944) and Robert Anderson's *I Never Sang for My Father* (pr., pb. 1968), the son of *A Voyage Round My Father* is not striving for psychological purgation.

Whereas Williams's and Anderson's narrators are haunted by the past, Mortimer's merely retells it. The title of the play, however, calls attention to the peculiarly distant and unemotional relationship between son and father. The boy never could get as close to the older man as he wanted, and not only because of the father's blindness. Rather, because the father treated life as a game, he created an impenetrable emotional barrier between himself and everyone else. It is easy to understand how the onset of blindness in his middle years and his refusal to acknowledge the affliction could have led to his desire for social isolation and a retreat to the sanctuary of his garden. Even his long-suffering wife, on whom he is totally dependent, seems to be nothing more to him than his servant. She selflessly caters to all of his whims and demands but gets no sign of warmth, affection, or even appreciation in return. Further, though the father gives his son advice over the years about such matters as education, sex, careers, the law, and marriage, he presents everything in a tone of annoyance, contempt, or satiric disparagement. The son, therefore, never can be wholly certain as to how seriously the father intends his advice to be taken.

Despite all of this, in the last lines of the play—when the son shares with the audience his reactions to his father's death—Mortimer makes clear that he wants the work to be considered an act of love, something he felt compelled to write. This passage and the episode in which the two men are walking arm in arm across the countryside are the most revealing in the play. They reveal that notwithstanding the father's coldness toward his family and his self-absorption to the point that he forecloses any meaningful involvement with others, the father-son relationship was a symbiotic one. At the same time, the son's life with his father was a voyage *round* him and not *with* him because the son always had to give his father a wide berth and stay a safe distance from him.

In addition to its primary thematic concern, the play explores other social matters. For example, Mortimer takes critical aim at English preparatory school education and dramatizes the ineptness of its leadership and instruction. He also treats the legal establishment and the practice of law with irreverence, dismissing the belief that there is much of a moral or ethical foundation to the profession and suggesting that it is out of touch with society. Mortimer focuses his analytical and critical skills upon the family, the law, and education, and he dramatizes the decline of these three pillars of English society between the 1930's and the 1960's.

Dramatic Devices

A Voyage Round My Father comprises a series of episodes that are unified by the reflective narrator who bridges past and present and by the chronological order in which they are presented. It is a memory play whose narrator recalls the past of which he was a part. In the course of the two acts, he participates in the retrospective action (as boy and as man) and frequently steps out of it to speak directly to the audience. Despite the fact that this inclusive drama of two lives covers so many years, the play is not at all diffuse. Instead of being divided into separate scenes, the episodes flow into one another and move back and forth between past and present, with the son/narrator providing a distinctive point of view and functioning as the unifying force.

The memory play, which *A Voyage Round My Father* is, is more common to the American theater than to the English stage; two examples are Williams's *The Glass Menagerie* and Anderson's *I Never Sang for My Father.* These American dramas, however, are fundamentally products of their playwrights' imaginations, and autobiographical elements are highly stylized. John Mortimer's work, though, is only slightly fictionalized autobiography. In short, it is a personal essay in dramatic form. Mortimer has changed some details, but the two acts of the play are composed mainly of situations and events that directly parallel the past as he has recorded it in his autobiography, *Clinging to the Wreckage: A Part of Life* (1982). Although the main characters of the play—the father, the son, and the mother—are unnamed, there is no suggestion of universality or Everyman about any of them: They are the Mortimers as the playwright sees them.

The staging is not entirely realistic. The fluidity of the action, with various episodes flowing into one another, also precludes a fully representational setting. Therefore, Mortimer's text calls for a bare stage with a table, some chairs, and a bench. There also are bits of foliage to suggest a garden and flowerpots inverted on sticks to serve as the earwig traps about which the father had such a fixation. Changes of lighting help to convey different places, as does the son as narrator. At the start of the second act, the episode on the propaganda film set, Mortimer calls for an unusual juxtaposition of make-believe and reality. He wants a projection on a backdrop to suggest the sky, a radar installation, and an observation post, and he also asks that the backstage theater personnel come onstage to act as film technicians and cameramen.

Finally, the second act opens with a character singing an obscene ditty, and occasionally elsewhere in the play either the father sings or music from a radio is heard in the background. Mortimer has said that in the theater it is easier to establish a period or time with music than in any other way. In such other works as the stage play *Collaborators* (pr., pb. 1973) and the television serial *Paradise Postponed* (1986), he uses music for the same purpose.

Critical Context

A Voyage Round My Father is only one of John Mortimer's works with significant autobiographical elements, though they are most prominent and least fictionalized in it. For example, members of the legal profession are present in the plays *The Dock*

Brief (pr. 1957 as a radio play and televised; staged 1958), *Two Stars for Comfort* (pr., pb. 1962), and *The Judge* (pr., pb. 1967); the radio and television play *Edwin* (pr. 1982 and 1984, respectively); the novel *Like Men Betrayed* (1953); and the Rumpole of the Bailey stories and television dramatizations (1975-1987). Writers are prominent in *Paradise Postponed* (the 1985 novel and 1986 television series), the novel *Charade* (1947), and the play *Collaborators*, whose main character is a barrister who also writes radio plays and film scripts.

In all of his plays and novels, even the early one-act stage pieces that are little more than whimsies, Mortimer deftly manages situations and presents characters who are believable even when they are largely stereotypes. Further, in almost all of his work he reflects a Dickensian humanism, the sense that one should feel sorry for the less fortunate. In contrast with his father, the son in *A Voyage Round My Father* sometimes reveals himself as a sensitive man with a social conscience. There is an unheroic quality about the son, which is a common characteristic of Mortimer's protagonists. The father exemplifies traits that he shares with others in Mortimer's works: He is a lonely man who cannot communicate with others but who retains enough of his illusions to survive and even to prevail.

Mortimer's social conscience and his interest in the problem of communication between people link him to other English playwrights who emerged in the 1950's. Whereas most of his contemporaries' works deals with the working class, however, Mortimer's plays focus upon the English middle class in decline. In addition, unlike such fellow dramatists as Harold Pinter and N. F. Simpson, Mortimer is a traditionalist in terms of form. His plays do not break new ground but are close to Chekhovian and pre-1950 English stage practice. Thus, among his stage works, the introspective memory play *A Voyage Round My Father* stands apart from the rest; it is his major achievement in the theater.

Sources for Further Study

Hayman, Ronald. *British Theatre Since 1955: A Reassessment*. New York: Oxford University Press, 1979.

Morley, Sheridan. "Brisk Business at the Bar." *Times* (London), January 4, 1982.

Mortimer, John. *Character Parts*. London: Viking, 1986.

_____. *Clinging to the Wreckage: A Part of Life*. New Haven, Conn.: Tichnor and Fields, 1982.

_____. *Murderers and Other Friends: Another Part of Life*. New York: Viking, 1994.

Smith, Christopher. "John Mortimer." In *Contemporary Dramatists*. 6th ed. Detroit: St. James, 1999.

Taylor, John Russell. *The Angry Theatre: New British Drama*. Rev. ed. New York: Hill and Wang, 1969.

Wardle, Irving. Review in *The Times* (London), November 27, 1970.

Gerald H. Strauss

VOYAGE TO TOMORROW

Author: Tawfiq al-Hakim (1898-1987)
Type of plot: Science fiction
Time of plot: The late 1950's and 309 years later
Locale: Earth and an unknown distant planet
First published: Rihlah ila al-ghad, 1957 (English translation, 1984)

> *Principal characters:*
> THE FIRST CONVICT, a doctor convicted of murder
> THE PRISON DOCTOR, the doctor who listens to the first convict's
> troubles
> THE WARDEN, a man who helps to save the convicts' lives
> THE REPRESENTATIVE, a man from an agency conducting space
> experiments
> THE SECOND CONVICT, an engineer who committed four murders
> THE FIRST CONVICT'S WIFE, a woman who used her second
> husband to kill her first and then schemes to have him
> disposed of also
> THE BLONDE, a cold and cynical woman
> THE BRUNETTE, a partisan who believes in human emotions

The Play

This ironic and suspenseful study of crime and romantic attachment in the space age begins with a single convict speaking to himself in solitary confinement. The prisoner speculates bitterly about the unhappy secrets which he may take with him to the gallows, for he has been sentenced to die in the next day or two. The guard brings in the prison doctor to see him, and as they discuss his case, the convict maintains that, though he has confessed to murder, during his trial he came to believe that he was betrayed and placed in a false position. As a young and somewhat idealistic physician, he had been impelled to kill a woman's husband when the man was portrayed to him as a vicious and insensitive brute who had a host of girlfriends on the side; he was goaded into murder for the woman's sake, and after they were married she testified on his behalf when he was brought to trial. During the proceedings, however, he became convinced that his wife actually had been scheming with a young lawyer to implicate him more seriously, much as she managed to convince the court of her selfless loyalty to the condemned man.

The convict, who at one time was so swept away by infatuation that he could kill a man for the sake of his beloved, is troubled still by conflicting impulses prompted by lingering affection and the desire for vengeance. He does not actually see his wife in person, however, for the warden brings in the representative of a scientific agency who has been authorized to make an unusual offer. Final preparations have been made to launch a manned spaceflight which will travel beyond the outer reaches of the solar system; the chances that any astronaut could return safely, however, have been estimated at one in one hundred. Ordinary volunteers can hardly be considered, but the government has been willing to waive execution of the convict should he agree to participate. The prisoner seizes this opportunity with alacrity, and as the second act begins he finds himself in a cylindrical chamber inside a space vessel.

To accompany the prisoner, a second convict has been selected who originally had been an engineer and an atomic scientist. As they watch the earth recede in the distance they are informed, by an announcer at ground control, that in the next three minutes, when they reach a distance of five million miles, communication will no longer be possible; as a realization of their chasmic isolation from all that has been familiar sweeps over them, each man is brought to express a deeply felt regret at having brought upon himself this new and unusual form of banishment. When the second convict learns that a woman was behind his companion's crime, he discloses that he killed four women in succession and was discovered only when a fifth attempt inexplicably failed. Unlike the first convict, his motivations combined mercenary and altruistic interests to an odd extent; he had arranged to inherit large sums from his victims in order to provide money for engineering projects that would have benefited many people.

The first convict has some open misgivings about this variety of murder for gain, however, and it is by no means certain that feelings about their guilt have abated even in the dark void of empty space; at least where the first convict is concerned, earth's morality, law, and customs still cast a troubled shadow over his conscience. Just as they seem forever lost in space—and indeed they speculate that they have approached the speed of light when the dial on the ship's instrument panel presses against its frame—they are apparently drawn into the gravitational field of a distant planet. When they reach this strange metallic body, they find it surprising that even in falling they have suffered no real ill effects.

The third act shows some unusual discoveries which are made in the course of their preliminary investigations. There appear to be no trees or bodies of water on this strange new world, and for that matter, though the sky is a brilliant turquoise hue, there is practically no atmosphere; the convicts seem to subsist on electrical currents; moreover, communication by charged particles supplies access to the other's thoughts without the need for conventional speech. By a concentrated effort of mind, the first convict is able to summon forth images of his wife, which appear in space as though they were broadcast on a screen; when she begins speaking to her husband, however, he recoils in anguish and horror. It pains him still that such a beautiful woman could have schemed at his destruction. Neither convict wishes to remain on this barren, bleak outpost, where no activity beyond mere existence seems possible. It does not seem likely, however, that they will find an easy death in a land where electromagnetic impulses appear to support life in ways they had not believed possible. They manage somehow to repair their rocket and set forth again in the direction from which they had come.

The convicts soon return to earth, and the fourth act brings some realization that life under a regime where material wants and physical infirmities have been all but eliminated may not be so desirable as might be thought. After awakening from a prolonged sleep, the first convict is met by a blonde woman who informs him that 309 years have passed since their original flight into space; as the result of traveling at the speed of light, however, a much shorter period of time has elapsed within the space vessel.

The convict learns that in this future world people age relatively slowly, and often they live for several centuries. Medical needs have been met to such an extent that many doctors do not need to work; food can be obtained by synthetic means from commonly available substances. Money is a concept known only to those versed in ancient history, while mechanical work is done primarily by automatic devices. Evidently shortly after the convicts departed a limited nuclear war took place, and since that time the world has been divided not by nations or military camps, but by two parties. The blonde woman, who is from the first group, is practical, efficient, and not very sentimental; she will let either convict kiss her as long as he does not take up too much time.

Another secretary, a brunette woman, is a partisan of a minority faction which believes that progress achieved by technocratic means should not be allowed to stifle expressions of human love and creativity. The first convict, who already has begun to doubt that happiness is possible in a world of enforced idleness, is immediately attracted to her. On the other hand, the blonde woman is of a suspicious disposition and has a penchant for eavesdropping; she regards any utterances of discontent as conspiratorial if not revolutionary. When a security man is summoned to separate the brunette from the others, the first convict begins to wrestle with the guard and threatens to kill him; then, as the convict is taken away, he kisses the brunette before going off to prison once more for the sake of a woman.

Themes and Meanings

Questions of enduring values during an age of scientific advances and material prosperity seem to be posed on several levels in this work. Motivations for murder and degrees of guilt may be different for particular individuals, but the comparative effects do not appear to be diminished by traversing immense distances or through the passage of several centuries. Other forms of attachment and repulsion that originally seemed fixed in particular points of space and time also have a lasting quality, which the first convict realizes when he calls forth the image of his wife from a distant planet many light-years away. At other times, when the two convicts discuss such matters between themselves, differences of temperament and indeed of values emerge.

The first convict is of an impulsive, ardent, and romantic disposition, whose fatal flaw it was to be carried away by his longings and his urges; the other man, who claims that his companion disdains him, is of a calculating and utilitarian bent, and he is inclined not so much to justify his actions as to insist that in his way the first convict has been culpable as well. Their contrasting outlooks seem reflected in the differing attitudes of two ages, and no doubt it is significant that the first convict finds it difficult to accept the moral premises of an advanced technological world, whereas for his fellow prisoner such a future society seems more congenial. On a more general plane it would appear that science and human values are by no means easily compatible here, and that any attempt to promote unbridled progress without regard for deeper concerns can only produce a social order where people carry on an existence that is bereft of any purpose or higher aspirations.

In addition to questions of scientific means and social ends, there are interesting reflections on the notion of punishment, which concern not merely whether it is made to fit the crime but also how differing situations may lead to a similar effect: In the face of otherwise certain execution, the condemned men eagerly grasp at any opportunity to prolong their lives, but their exile to a bleak and forbidding part of the cosmos leads them to contemplate death in a much different light. Indeed, on the unknown planet the great difficulties they would encounter in any effort at self-destruction provoke some dismay and fear. Although the eternal promptings of hope in any form originally led the convicts to enlist in this hazardous project of space exploration, such later circumstances, which are far from life-threatening, lead them to consider measures as drastic as those upon which the state had originally decided. After they return to earth, it is learned that, even under a regime which has brought about abundance and leisure on an unprecedented scale, many people commit suicide rather than resign themselves to an essentially shallow and uninteresting way of life. Thus, for the convicts, the instincts which held life dear are tempered by a growing awareness that other values may make this existence worthwhile; like any unanswerable dilemma, this issue is posed and then left unresolved at the end.

A further concern, which in various ways has appeared in other works by Tawfiq al-Hakim, is the perennial conflict between men and women; here it is instructive to note that two female characters (out of only three) act to tempt an unwary protagonist into incriminating or unacceptable situations. Both the first convict's wife and the blonde secretary from the future world are outwardly attractive but are also underhanded and hypocritical; in this respect, women seem not to have changed from one age to another. Indeed only the brunette's sympathetic and selfless attentions seem to justify the first prisoner's conviction that love may be a sufficient justification for desperate deeds. While some open affection on her part would seem necessary to support the first convict's belief that a life devoid of romantic interests would be meaningless, it may be pointed out as well that the second convict, who has few compunctions about murdering women, seems at the end to have established a genuinely friendly relationship with the cynical blonde secretary.

Dramatic Devices

The imaginative and distinctive settings of this work perhaps would make it difficult to produce in a conventional manner, at least for a theater audience. It has not, in fact, ever been produced. A number of unusual props and special effects would be required to simulate the sights and impressions of spaceflight. The author's instructions refer to a rocket interior complete with its instrument panel and radar equipment; it would further be necessary to devise a screen upon which the first convict is able to see his wife. Other materials would also be required to show the landscape of the unknown planet of act 3, which is described as a metallic spheroid with sheer forbidding mountains that is situated against an unearthly blue-green background.

For the fourth act, additional props would have to be used to create the salon in the dwelling house of the new age, which has semiluminous walls and is decorated with curtains; the author suggests that, because they belong to a future world, such fixtures cannot be described exactly in advance. At various times throughout, other small machines to suggest sophisticated telephone, radio, and video equipment are called for; for that matter, certain interlocutors, such as a ground control monitor and a government official, are heard but not seen. Thus the actual surroundings which are important for the author's purpose have been set down to convey an appropriate sense of place; it is quite possible that the complexity of such arrangements has discouraged actual stage productions. On the other hand, while it often has been maintained that Tawfiq al-Hakim's plays have been meant to be read as much as to be performed, here the dramatic situation and dialogue probably could be interpreted to advantage by live actors.

Although there are a certain number of philosophical excuses, and some critics have found fault with the play's construction and length, there are a number of sequences which produce dramatic tension and uncertainty as unexpected events affect the fate of the two convicts. Further interest is added by details about the prisoners' past lives, which are supplied at suitable intervals. Moreover, while it has also been contended by some observers that al-Hakim's characters are not particularly memorable—those who are featured in certain works could as easily be utilized in others—the figures who appear in this work are well suited to convey the ideas the author has set forth. Indeed, it is the response of certain individuals to unusual and seemingly paradoxical turns of events that directs interest to this play's outcome.

Critical Context

Among the numerous types of plays Tawfiq al-Hakim has written, affinities with works of several sorts, from different periods of his career, may be found. In his important and controversial drama *Ahl al-kahf* (pb. 1933; partial translation, *The People of the Cave*, 1955-1957), which is based upon the biblical story of the Seven Sleepers of Ephesus, in its Koranic version, the device of prolonged time lapse is used to ponder problems of hope and resurrection during earlier historical periods; in that work, refugees from Roman religious persecution undergo a miraculous sleep of 309 years before succumbing to despair at the prospects of life in a different age. There, as in *Voyage to Tomorrow*, the ironic convergence of themes across a period of several centuries is skillfully developed.

Other early works also present violent death arising from infatuation and troubled relations between men and women. Later efforts have considered scientific development in a speculative vein while posing problems of political power and the destiny of individuals in the nuclear age. *Li'bat al-mawt* (pb. 1957), for example, concerns attempts to sustain a scientist's love affair despite the effects of radiation sickness, while *Ashwak al-salam* (pb. 1957) explores the need for international reconciliation in view of the threats to world peace posed by atomic weapons. Other variations of the theme of crime and guilt were explored in *al-Wartah* (pb. 1966; *Incrimination*, 1984), where evidence which, it appears, would point to one culprit is revealed instead to implicate a law professor who has been investigating a murder. The conflict between science and nature brought about by the exploration of space has been considered from a somewhat playful standpoint in *Ahl al-qamar* (pb. 1969; *Poet on the Moon*, 1984). For that matter, even as he turned to writing on religious subjects during the final years of his life, in his last play al-Hakim utilized the Faust legend in order to depict the opposition faith has encountered from scientific and socialist dogmas.

Sources for Further Study

Badawi, Muhammad Mustafa. "Tawfiq al-Hakim." In *Modern Arabic Drama in Egypt*. Cambridge, Mass.: Cambridge University Press, 1987.

Cachia, Pierre. "Idealism and Ideology: The Case of Tawfiq al-Hakim." *Journal of the American Oriental Society* 100, no. 3 (1980): 225-235.

Hammouda, Abdel-Aziz. "Modern Egyptian Theatre: Three Major Dramatists." *World Literature Today* 53 (1979): 601-605.

Hutchins, William M. "The Theology of Tawfiq al-Hakim: An Exposition with Examples." *Muslim World* 78, nos. 3/4 (1988): 243-279.

Long, Richard. *Tawfiq al-Hakim: Playwright of Egypt*. London: Ithaca Press, 1979.

J. R. Broadus

A WALK IN THE WOODS

Author: Lee Blessing (1949-   )
Type of plot: Political
Time of plot: The 1980's
Locale: Outskirts of Geneva, Switzerland, in a pleasant wooded area
First produced: 1987, at the Yale Repertory Theater, New Haven, Connecticut
First published: 1988

Principal characters:
ANDREY BOTVINNIK, a fifty-seven-year-old Soviet career
diplomat
JOHN HONEYMAN, a forty-five-year-old American negotiator

The Play

A Walk in the Woods is the story of an impossible friendship, one that grows between an earnest young American arms negotiator and his more cynical Soviet counterpart during their private walks together over a period of many months. It is also the story of two nations attempting to avert a nuclear holocaust in spite of the political and economic forces that seem to be pushing them relentlessly toward it.

The conflict between these two contrasting elements of the play, the public and the private, the political and the personal, is established in the first of the play's four scenes, during which the novice American negotiator, Honeyman, repeatedly refuses the more experienced Botvinnik's offer of friendship.

His rebuff is not due to any personal hostility based on Cold War rivalry. On the contrary, he comes to the table full of enthusiasm and high hopes for a rapid and successful conclusion to the talks, replacing a more experienced negotiator named McIntyre, whose personal inflexibility was a source of irritation to Botvinnik. "We negotiated for two years, and he never changed his position," complains Botvinnik. "The American position changed . . . " objects Honeyman, to which the Russian responds: "No, no—*his* position. Sitting there, at the table. He always sat straight up. For two years he never relaxed."

Honeyman appears in the opening scene to be cut from the same stiff cloth as McIntyre, and much of the play revolves around Botvinnik's attempts to break through his bureaucratic exterior and find the man within, while Honeyman struggles to hammer out an agreement on arms reduction.

The second scene opens, two months later, with the two men on another of what has become a regular series of walks: Botvinnik's pursuit of an informal relationship between the two negotiators seems to have succeeded. Yet, the essential conflict of the first scene reemerges with greater intensity when Honeyman begins pressing Botvinnik for some movement, any movement, in the Soviets' position before the upcoming American presidential election. Botvinnik agrees on one condition: that the two men have a "frivolous" conversation.

Honeyman awkwardly slips into a discussion of space weapons technology before finally declaring: "Well . . . let's see. OK, um—I hate brown suits." Botvinnik is disappointed with the attempt, noting that "There's a difference between trivial and boring." In spite of this failure, however, the act concludes with Botvinnik's promise to push his government toward a gesture of compromise prior to the American election.

The second act opens in late winter, with the two men chasing a rabbit through the woods, in much the same way that Botvinnik recalls doing as a young boy in Leningrad, before the war. This somewhat comical moment illustrates the two men's growing friendship but is also symbolic of their seemingly fruitless pursuit of a meaningful agreement between their two countries. Botvinnik tells Honeyman that his government has rejected the latest proposal, not due to any real objections, but because it is "too good."

Honeyman will not be deterred, however. He has learned enough about the politics of arms negotiations from his counterpart to know that "a new name, a few insignificant points altered" may be all it takes to save the proposal, and the scene ends with the two returning together to meet the waiting reporters, "Because we don't often do that, and they will be confused."

The final scene of the play takes place in early spring, after the rejection of Honeyman's revised proposal, this time by his own government. The wooden idealist of the play's opening scenes has become a more disillusioned creature of flesh and blood, as demonstrated by Honeyman's retelling of an incident earlier that day in which he was nearly arrested for littering. Botvinnik responds to his counterpart's anecdote by asking his favorite color; he wants to buy him a tie.

The reason for this gesture is made clear when the Soviet announces that he is leaving and will soon be replaced by a new negotiator. Their relationship has come full circle. Soon Honeyman will find himself playing the role of the wiser, older man, struggling to transform a less experienced antagonist into a friend.

Themes and Meanings

A political play of ideas, *A Walk in the Woods* is so full of profound political commentary and timely social relevance that one might expect such mundane elements as plot and character to be mere scaffolding on which to hang the more important message of the play. However, the primary theme of the play is not the danger of nuclear weapons or the horror of war, but the importance of friendship, a friendship depicted through the mundane elements of plot and character.

The negotiations in which Botvinnik and Honeyman are involved come to no conclusion during the course of the play. A presidential election takes place between acts, but there is no real change in the international political situation. The conflict around which the play revolves is, instead, the personal one between two men, one seeking friendship, the other seeking to maintain a more formal relationship. However, as Botvinnik proclaims, "Formality is simply anger with its hair combed."

Honeyman initially objects to wasting time by taking a walk in the woods. "Making friends is a fine thing, but not on someone else's time, so to speak." Honeyman believes that talking must have a point. Yet, talking *is* the point. As Honeyman himself eventually comes to understand, "We have to start with the bare fact that there *are* two of us here." In talking to one another, both sides find recognition: "We look across the table, and we see ourselves." "The talks will go on for hundreds of years," laments Botvinnik at the conclusion of the play. Then adds, "if we are lucky."

The play's political message is articulated often through the course of the play, generally through the interplay of Botvinnik's cynicism and Honeyman's idealism. "Man," says Botvinnik, "is an animal who must fulfill every potential. Even the potential to kill himself." Honeyman counters by arguing that "man has the potential to become a whole new animal. One that trusts instead of fears. One that agrees when it makes sense to agree. That finds the way to live, because life has become for him—has *finally* become—a sacred thing." Honeyman defends his considerably more idealistic view by asserting that, in the age of nuclear weapons, "Idealism is no longer a choice for mankind. It's a necessity."

Botvinnik points out that the rapid pace of technological development will inevitably undermine any treaty the two can devise. "Look at the money, time, and energy our governments put into making ready for war," he exclaims. "What do we put into making ready for peace? You and me. That's all." In the face of this impossible race against technological progress, Botvinnik is tempted to abandon any real effort at a treaty and to work instead to maintain the appearance of good intentions: "If we have never agreed to a treaty, then when a new technology comes along, we are simply two nations who are trying to make a treaty, but who must remain prepared for war. It creates a much better impression." Even in Botvinnik's lighthearted moments, as when he is blaming the failure of the negotiations on the comfort and security of Switzerland, where the talks take place, he displays his dark view of human nature: "We should put the table at the bottom of a missile silo. Then we would negotiate." Ultimately, however, the play's political message is conveyed most clearly not through these aphoristic utterances but through a growing friendship between an individual Soviet and an individual American.

Dramatic Devices

A Walk in the Woods is a very simple play, requiring only two actors and one set. Every scene takes place in the same "pleasant woods" outside Geneva. Such classical unity of place is offset, however, by the fact that each of the play's four scenes is separated from the others by a period of several months. In fact, each scene takes place in a different season, beginning in late summer and ending in early spring. This simple device illustrates not only the passage of time but also the dramatic arc of the ongoing conversation between the two protagonists. Summer fades into winter as Honeyman's initial hopes fade into bitterness and despair. Yet, the play concludes not in the coldest depths of winter, but with the renewal of hope promised by the earliest days of spring.

The cycle of the seasons also reflects the changing relationship between the two protagonists. Botvinnik begins as the mature mentor to Honeyman's naïvely optimistic newcomer, but in the second act the American assumes a more clear-eyed maturity, while the Russian moves toward retirement. The contrast between these two characters, and the development of their relationship over the course of the play, is a key element of the drama.

Another important dramatic device in *A Walk in the Woods* is paradox due, in part, to the paradoxical nature of the subject matter. The principle of "mutual assured destruction" on which the concept of nuclear deterrence is based dictates that each side must maintain a massive nuclear arsenal in order that neither side will ever have to use it. The United States and the Soviet Union discuss arms control not because they have already ended their political rivalry, but because each still sees the other as a military threat. Botvinnik and Honeyman thus have the opportunity to become friends only because their countries regard one another as enemies.

Botvinnik is especially aware of the paradoxical nature of their situation. Rather than allowing it to confound him, however, he seems to thrive on it. In the opening scene, Botvinnik plays with paradox by agreeing with Honeyman's position regarding friendship:

> HONEYMAN: You agree?
> BOTVINNIK: Yes
> HONEYMAN: That we shouldn't be friends?
> BOTVINNIK: Yes
> HONEYMAN: That's not what you said before.
> BOTVINNIK: But then I didn't know your view. Now I do, and I want to agree with you.
> HONEYMAN: You want to agree with me.
> BOTVINNIK: Yes.
> HONEYMAN: Why?
> BOTVINNIK: Because you are my friend.

Even at the play's conclusion Botvinnik continues to express himself through paradox. In his final assessment of their apparently futile efforts, he laments: "Our time together, John, has been a very great failure. *But*—a successful one."

Critical Context

Following its world premiere at the Yale Repertory Theatre, *A Walk in the Woods* had its West Coast premiere at La Jolla Playhouse in 1987, winning the American Theater Critics Association's award for best play. It opened on Broadway on February 28, 1988, and received Tony Award nominations for best play and best actor (for Robert Prosky as Botvinnik).

In *A Walk in the Woods* Lee Blessing takes a well-known historical incident and reshapes it to reflect his own political observations and dramatic interests. During deadlocked arms reductions talks in Geneva in the summer of 1982, negotiators Yuli A. Kvitsinsky and Paul H. Nitze stepped away from the table and took a stroll in a nearby park, returning with an unprecedented new proposal, one which was ultimately rejected by the hardliners of both sides.

Throughout his career, Blessing has continued to draw upon historical characters and events for dramatic purposes, using the theater to reexamine social issues and public policy in more than one dozen different plays. *Cobb* (pr. 1989, pb. 1991) presents the life of legendary baseball player Ty Cobb in all its complexity, including the racism that relegated the "Black Cobb," baseball player Oscar Charleston, to the Negro leagues. *Patient A* (pr., pb. 1993) examines the case of Kimberly Bergalis, the first known instance of HIV (human immunodeficiency virus) transmission from a health care worker to a patient. *Two Rooms* (pr. 1988, pb. 1990) explores the various ways in which terrorism is exploited, by all sides, for political purposes. It was the success of *A Walk in the Woods* that set the stage for Blessing's continued exploration of the intersection of politics and drama.

Sources for Further Study

Blessing, Lee. "Accidents in a Moral Universe." *American Theater* 18 (October, 2001): 10-11.

_____. "An Interview with Lee Blessing." Interview by Joseph G. Rice. *American Drama* 2 (Fall, 1992): 84-100.

Henry, William A. Review of *A Walk in the Woods*. *Time* 129 (March 9, 1987): 88.

Sauvage, Leo. Review of *A Walk in the Woods*. *The New Leader* 71 (March 21, 1988): 23.

Edgar V. McKnight

THE WATER HEN
A Spherical Tragedy in Three Acts

Author: Stanisław Ignacy Witkiewicz (1885-1939)
Type of plot: Absurdist
Time of plot: Unspecified
Locale: Unspecified
First produced: 1922, at the Słowacki Theater, Cracow, Poland
First published: Kurka wodna, 1962 (English translation, 1968, in *The Madman and the Nun, and Other Plays*)

Principal characters:
 ALBERT WAŁPOR, a retired skipper of a merchant ship
 EDGAR WAŁPOR, Albert's good-looking, if inept, son
 TADZIO, a boy who is supposedly Edgar's son
 LADY ALICE, DUCHESS OF NEVERMORE, a beautiful blonde
  woman who falls in love with Edgar
 ELIZABETH GUTZIE-VIRGELING (THE WATER HEN), Edgar's
  confidante, and later Tadzio's beloved
 RICHARD DE KORBOWA-KORBOWSKI (TOM HOOZEY), sometimes
  called "the scoundrel," he is devoted to Alice

The Play

The play begins with the Water Hen scolding Edgar Wałpor for not shooting her promptly. They have discussed the whole matter and decided on this course of action, but Edgar has trouble taking aim and firing. He dreads the consequences—no one to talk to—and believes that she is only using him to accomplish her purpose. She replies that he is being cowardly and that this is his opportunity to perform a unique deed. Finally convinced by her argument, Edgar does in fact shoot her dead.

Edgar is not sure he has achieved anything by this death. It is rather all of a piece with his feelings that his life has had no meaning and that he is without convictions—even though he is pressed by Tadzio to explain the significance of death. Edgar is not willing to acknowledge Tadzio as his son and suggests that he is not even sure of his own existence.

Edgar's father, Albert, is not at all surprised to learn of the Water Hen's death, and he does not believe that it makes much difference in the total scheme of things. Still, a killing is an impressive event, Albert admits, and he concedes that his son may yet make something important of his life. Edgar, meanwhile, falls under the spell of Lady Alice, the Duchess of Nevermore, whose husband, Edgar, has just died, and who is slavishly served by the scoundrel Korbowski (also her lover), who resembles Edgar Wałpor. The relationships between characters becomes even more complicated when

Lady Alice reveals that her dead husband Edgar was an intimate of the Water Hen and was much affected by her letters to him. Except for Korbowski's disturbing presence, Edgar feels (by the end of act 1) that he has created a family for himself by adopting Tadzio (perhaps the Water Hen's son) and marrying Alice, his friend's wife.

However, at the beginning of act 2, Tadzio confesses to Alice that he forgets why Edgar is his father. As usual in this play, no relationship, no idea, remains intact. Alice counsels Tadzio that it does not make much difference—that it does no good to question why things are as they are. There are no answers.

Korbowski spends much of act 2 berating Alice for her life with Edgar, who in Korbowski's eyes is weak and a poor replacement for her dead husband. Alice does not care for these personal reflections, for she has her mind on a new business: the Theosophical Jam Company. Amassing capital is more important to her than probing human emotions. Why should Korbowski care about Edgar so long as no sex is involved, she asks him.

Then the Water Hen returns. Edgar is amazed but almost immediately accuses her of lying when she refuses to acknowledge Tadzio as her son. Still feeling like a nonentity, Edgar withdraws with the Water Hen just after Alice acknowledges that the Water Hen was the only woman her dead husband ever loved. Again Edgar Wałpor's father is not surprised at this turn of events, and the Water Hen suspects that nothing has really changed as the result of her death. Still, Edgar insists that he has suffered, and to prove his point submits to the physical agony of a torture machine—as though it would somehow demonstrate the reality of his feelings.

Like Edgar, Alice feels she must also come to grips with the influence of the Water Hen on her life. Although she has admitted her dead husband's love for the Water Hen, she now dismisses it as a figment of his imagination—a point the Water Hen seems to sanction when she admits that she lies about everything, and that, in fact, she does not exist. Thrown together by their desperate desire to believe in love and in the harmony of human relationships, Alice promises to love Edgar even as he ends act 2 dreading the meaninglessness of life—except for those who are the magnificent liars and can make something great out of it.

Act 3 takes place ten years later. Tadzio is twenty and much taken with the Water Hen, who is now beautiful and sensuous. Even Albert Wałpor is surprised when he comes upon Tadzio and the Water Hen enveloped in a violent embrace. Edgar and Tadzio quarrel over Tadzio's declaration that he loves the Water Hen and wants to marry her. Edgar once again takes aim and shoots the Water Hen, even though she confesses she was only trying to make Edgar jealous. The Water Hen dead once again, Alice tries to take responsibility when the detectives arrive, but Edgar regards the death as the culminating event that ties him even more strongly to life—an outcome he thwarts by shooting himself. Outside, the shots and the commotion of a revolution can be heard. Inside, Albert Wałpor sits placidly playing cards, predicting that his card-playing colleagues will have no problem getting jobs in the new government. The play ends with one of the cardplayers indicating he will "pass."

Themes and Meanings

The Water Hen is a play about the arbitrariness of life and of theatrical conventions. Stanisław Ignacy Witkiewicz is at pains to undermine notions of chronology, of plot development, and of the stability of human character. His characters are confused about life and death and about the extent to which they can have any influence on their lives or on the lives of others. Neither life nor art, in his view, comes to a tidy conclusion. The conflicts between human beings and within families are not resolved as they often are at the end of plays. Thus the arguments between Edgar and his father, Albert, are continued in the relationship between Edgar and his son. Alice's concern with the Water Hen, who won her dead husband away from her, is repeated in her concern that Edgar Wałpor, too, will go off with the Water Hen.

In most plays, the death of a major character changes the plot, and a revolution means a new beginning, but in *The Water Hen* several characters suggest that nothing really changes and there is no such thing as a new life. For example, Edgar speaks of living "another life"—but not a new life. However, the play implies that people go on behaving as though real change is possible. Subtitling his play a "spherical tragedy," Witkiewicz is at pains to demonstrate that people actually move in a circle and keep repeating themselves. That is why the Water Hen has to die twice and why Tadzio must become obsessed with her just as his father was.

If *The Water Hen* is not gloomy, it is because its characters are still capable of acting as though human behavior might make a difference. Edgar Wałpor's father is impressed that his son has actually pulled the trigger. There remains the possibility that human actions might lead to something new, even though Albert does not expect the revolution that takes place at the end of the play to amount to much.

There are many references in the play to art and to lying. The two are connected in the sense that art is a construct, a figment of the imagination, that can imbue life with significance. If Albert has some hope that either Edgar or Tadzio will become an artist, he bases that hope on the fact that the artist can create meaning where none existed before, and that is a kind of lying, a substitution of the imagination for reality. The Water Hen epitomizes this point of view when she claims that she is a liar and that she does not really exist. This characterization precisely defines the position of art, Witkiewicz implies, which is entirely invented and yet all the more desirous because it has a purpose that life itself does not contain. Realistic plays, then, are a contradiction in terms, since there is no reality, no truth, outside the play to which the play corresponds. There is only the play—arbitrary and true to its own principles.

Dramatic Devices

The character of the Water Hen is itself a dramatic device. It is Witkiewicz's parody of Henrik Ibsen's great realistic and symbolic play *Vildanden* (pb. 1884; *The Wild Duck*, 1891). In Ibsen's play, the wild duck, which is shot, is a symbol of human emotions, which are also destroyed. By changing the symbol to a water hen, Witkiewicz not only indulges his sense of humor—reducing the pretensions of art to a rather prosaic symbol—but also calls attention to the tricks of art, to the way art embellishes life and makes it seem more significant than it actually is. Witkiewicz is not so much against this symbol-making as he is dedicated to showing it for what it is—not a reflection of life's meaning but a substitute for the absence of meaning. Thus in act 3 of *The Water Hen*, the Water Hen is transformed from a pretty but not sensuous woman into an irresistible sexual object. Art has, in other words, triumphed over the reality of what the Water Hen was in the first two acts. This is laughable, even absurd, but such is the power of art.

Since the human personality is not solid or individual, Witkiewicz delights in giving different characters the same name or giving a single character several names. Thus, both of Alice's husbands are named Edgar, and Richard de Korbowa-Korbowski is referred to as the scoundrel and Tom Hoozey. He also resembles Edgar Wałpor, even though he is his romantic, demoniac opposite. The Water Hen is also identified as Elizabeth Gutzie-Virgeling. In Polish, her name, Elzbieta Flake-Prawacka, is a combination of the words *flaki* (tripe) and *prawiczka* (virgin), a fittingly humorous name for a woman who is a bizarre combination of the down-to-earth (the guts of things) and the unbesmirched ideal.

In general, Witkiewicz's dramatic devices are designed to undermine the logical, rational, and linear development of traditional realistic plays. When the Water Hen appears at the beginning of act 3 after a ten-year absence, Tadzio's servant, Jan, announces, "Sir, the lady who was here ten years ago wishes to speak to you." The figure of the Lamplighter, who accuses Edgar Wałpor of playing dumb, of refusing to recognize his own function as a dramatic device, is also the playwright's way of calling attention to theatricality. The theater shines a light on life—as does the Lamplighter in act 1, when his lantern makes a pattern of "eight concentric beams of intense green light." Art, Witkiewicz implies, is a self-defining, circular way of giving life a form.

Critical Context

Stanisław Ignacy Witkiewicz was a philosopher, painter, novelist, and aesthetician as well as a playwright. In one of his most important essays, he elaborated the concept of "pure form," a term that is referred to in *The Water Hen*, generally acknowledged as one of his greatest plays. Witkiewicz believes that plays should be as visual as paintings, that they should not be narratives but pictures, images of existence such as the one the Lamplighter creates with his lantern. Existence cannot be grasped rationally or logically; it can only be represented as form, which can be pure in the sense that it does not argue a message—that is, it does not come to some conclusion about the nature of things. The theater, in other words, is not a comment on life; the theater is, rather, its own world and constitutes its own shape. The Water Hen, for example, can come back to life because the return, the repetition of things, is essential to the form of the play. Thus the theater creates its own sense of order and its own rules.

Witkiewicz grew up in a world shaped by war and revolution. His own father, a distinguished artist, argued for precisely the kind of realism that his son rejected. Like one of his own characters, Witkiewicz even invented a name for himself, Witkacy, and lived a rather eccentric existence which demonstrated that he would not be bound by the strictures of his society. He was skeptical of humankind's ability to order the world, and put all of his energies into the creation of art. He is one of the most important playwrights of the twentieth century, anticipating the absurdist drama of Samuel Beckett and others while expressing a peculiarly Polish sense of the futility of history. He committed suicide in 1939 shortly after German and Russian armies invaded Poland.

Sources for Further Study

Gerould, Daniel C. *Witkacy: Stanisław Ignacy Witkiewicz as an Imaginative Writer.* Seattle: University of Washington Press, 1981.

_____, ed. and trans. *The Witkiewicz Reader.* Evanston, Ill.: Northwestern University Press, 1992.

Gerould, Daniel C., and C. S. Durer. Introduction to *The Madman and the Nun, and Other Plays.* Seattle: University of Washington Press, 1968.

Miłosz, Czesław. "The Pill of Murti-Bing." In *The Captive Mind*, translated by Jane Zielonko. 1953. Rev. ed. New York: Octagon Books, 1981.

_____. "S. I. Witkiewicz, a Polish Writer for Today." *Tri-Quarterly* 9 (Spring, 1967): 143-154.

Puzyna, Kostanty. "The Prism of the Absurd." *Polish Perspectives* 7 (June, 1963): 34-44.

Tarn, Adam. "Plays." *Polish Perspectives* 8 (October, 1965): 8.

Toeplitz, Krzysztof. "Avant-Garde with Tradition." *Poland* 4 (April, 1965): 28-31.

Carl Rollyson

THE WEIR

Author: Conor McPherson (1971-   )
Type of plot: Comedy
Time of plot: The late twentieth century
Locale: Rural northwest Ireland
First produced: 1997, at the Royal Court Theatre Upstairs, London, England
First published: 1997

> *Principal characters:*
> JACK, a garage owner in his fifties
> BRENDAN, a farmer and bar owner in his thirties
> JIM, a man who works for Jack, in his forties
> FINBAR, a local entrepreneur in his late forties
> VALERIE, a woman in her thirties new to town

The Play

The Weir depicts an evening at a small bar located on a farm in rural Ireland where the proprietor, three other local men, and a woman new to the area meet, drink, and tell stories. The banter consists of friendly local talk and gossip that is uneventful in itself, but overall reveals the characters' isolation and the figurative ghosts that haunt them.

The play opens as Jack, a customer clearly familiar with the bar, comes in and, in the absence of the proprietor, helps himself to a drink. Brendan then enters carrying peat for the fire to warm them on the windy and chilly night, and they chat about their day. The talk is familiar and friendly, about drinking, the weather, whether Brendan will give in to his sisters' pressure to sell some of the farmland, Jack's luck at betting on the horses, and to gossip about Finbar. Jack has heard that Finbar sold the Nealon house, which had sat empty for several years, to a young woman from Dublin, and that he would bring her by the bar that night to meet everyone. Jack especially expresses disapproval of Finbar's showing the woman around. He feels Finbar will make them, two single men, look desperate by comparison. Though their language is full of profanity, it is not aggressive, and even suggests a certain decorum: A married man should not be going around with another woman. Rather, they are two single men to whom the mention of a young woman new to town is particularly interesting.

Jim enters and talks of driving his elderly mother to visit her sister, and he and Jack talk about work they will do the next day. The talk again turns to Finbar and the woman, identified by Jim as nice looking. They speculate about the nature of that relationship, whether Brendan would sell or rent the land for tourists' caravans, and the beginning of the tourist season. Joking about keeping out the chill, they pour more drinks, and Jack offers cigarettes.

Finbar and Valerie enter, and Finbar introduces Valerie to the men. The men tease

Finbar about his financial investments and about the inheritance his father, Big Finbar, left him. Finbar takes this with humor, saying they are jealous that he made his fortune in town, while they "stayed out here on the bog" in the country. Jack jokes that this expansive, somewhat arrogant side of Finbar is the "one [that] comes out at night." The sexual tension already identified in the single men's jealousy, though unthreatening, increases as Jack and Brendan especially challenge Finbar's fitness for Valerie. They identify the old photographs on the wall for Valerie's sake: the weir; Big Finbar; Brendan's father, Paddy Byrne; Jack at age seven; and a view of the town of Carrick from the field Brendan says he will not sell. Brendan explains that the scenic part, which is popular with tourists, is associated with the faeries of folklore. Brendan points out a ring of trees, a fort, and the ruins of a once important abbey. They turn to telling old stories about the faery road that runs under the house into which Valerie has moved.

Most of the remainder of the play is made up of the recounting of and responses to five stories that become increasingly serious and personal: the first three, faery or ghost stories told by Jack, Finbar and Jim; the fourth, the story of Valerie's daughter's death; and the fifth, Jack's story about his past. The first story is about mysterious knocking on the door of the Nealon house; the second concerns the apparition of a woman summoned through a Ouija board; and the third tells about the ghost of a dead child molester seeking the grave of his victim. The fourth story, Valerie's true story of her young daughter's death by drowning one year earlier, abruptly changes the mood of the group, who express their sympathy and support. After this story, Finbar and Jim leave. The last story is Jack's, told to Brendan and Valerie, in which he confesses his selfishness toward a woman he once loved and the deep regret and loneliness he has felt ever since. The play ends as they leave the bar and Brendan closes it, joking that maybe they would be willing to visit with the tourists after all, and "stay with the company and the bright lights."

Themes and Meanings

The overriding themes of the play are the power of the past, both historic and personal, the fragility of life, and loneliness. The past is engaged in many ways, through references to aging parents, old or dead neighbors, past loves, and the vehicle of the ghost stories, several of which concern the faeries of Irish myth. By integrating references to the local faery lore, McPherson sets up a contrast between a romantic, pagan Ireland and contemporary life, yet also connects the faeries with the lost spirits and ghosts of the stories and to the haunted existences of Valerie and Jack.

The weir of the title—referring to a local dam built in 1951 to regulate water and generate power—functions as the major symbol in the play, linking the past and the changes of the twentieth century to the natural world, as well as providing a figurative barrier between the old world of folklore and contemporary life. The opening of the weir is a significant moment in the history of the region; Jack mentions that "when the weir was going up," the mysterious knocking in the Nealon house, which had stopped after a priest's blessing, returned, suggesting that the spirits objected to the weir. According to local legend, the faeries traveled the faery road to the beach to bathe, and thus the modern weir can be seen as a barrier between the past and present, and between tradition, modern pragmatism, and development. Traditionally, a weir is a fence made of sticks or wattles built across streams or rivers that trap fish and other animals by acting as a sieve, and Jack recalls how, when the modern weir went up, it gathered "a fierce load of dead birds all in the hedge." While the traditional weir is essentially an agricultural tool, the modern weir controls water for power, and its effect on the natural world is pictured as fierce and absolute.

Valerie's daughter's death by drowning in a pool rather than in a natural body of water and Valerie's fear that her daughter is somehow a lost spirit unable to find her way home, points as much to the unromantic reality of death and grief as it does to the idea of wandering faeries, ghosts, and spirits. Extending this to the theme of a romantic Irish past, McPherson has Brendan and Jack both clinging to habit and routine, wary of change but deeply isolated as well. Finbar teases them about staying "out on the bog'" in the country; they resist leaving the past as it is manifested through place. Brendan loves the view from the hill but later admits it is lonely. Jack, after confessing his poor treatment of a lover and his consequent loneliness, admits that there is not a morning that he does not wake up thinking of her. He quickly adds, "We'll all be ghosts soon enough." What began as a night of curiosity about checking out the new single woman in town has become a night of soul-searching and connection between isolated people that far outweighs any sexual concerns. The play becomes an exorcism of Jack's lost soul through storytelling and provides a view of the fragile emotional balances people maintain.

Dramatic Devices

The play happens in real time, taking about one hundred minutes in performance, and thus the audience essentially is eavesdropping on the characters' conversation, as though they were customers in the bar. The dialogue is informal, easygoing, comic, and arguably a bit quaint, as some reviewers found the play an exercise in Irish picturesque. It is, however, very realistic, rhythmic, and natural, easily engaging the audience through generally likable if imperfect characters. While much of the dialogue between stories may seem like aimless banter, it provides glimpses of each character's private thoughts. Since the play is essentially one act without action, the only changes onstage are the characters' entrances and momentary exits that alter the dynamics between them. For example, Valerie's visit to the ladies' room after hearing the third ghost story allows the men to argue, then decide not to tell more stories that might upset or frighten her, thus increasing the tension and irony of their own fear and horror when they later hear Valerie's story. Like any evening full of storytelling, drink, and lonely characters, the play moves from light comedy to intriguing mystery about what frailties each of the characters is trying to hide, to deeply poignant silences. The final movement of the play occurs when Jack, the most world-weary figure, unveils his own sorrows and, in sharing them with Brendan and Valerie, allows them to drop their masks and speak honestly, gently, and as kindred wandering spirits.

Critical Context

In addition to *The Weir*, for which he won the 1999 Olivier Award for Best New Play and the 1997 Evening Standard Award for Most Promising New Playwright, McPherson has authored the plays *Rum and Vodka* (pr. 1992), *The Good Thief* (pr. 1994), *St. Nicholas* (pb. 1997), and *A Dublin Carol* (pb. 1999, pr. 2000). He also adapted *This Lime Tree Bower* (pb. 1996) as the screenplay *Saltwater* (2000), and wrote the screenplay *I Went Down* (1997).

Reviews have been very positive about McPherson as a member of a new generation of Irish dramatists who are arguably less political and more universal than the previous generation. McPherson's greatest gifts are in characterization and dialogue, and in combining humor, irony, and even tragedy in plays that are poignant and moving. His plays depend less on action than on the engagement and discovery of emotionally complex and isolated people. His works have been extremely well received in London, and especially in American cities with large Irish American communities.

Sources for Further Study

Adam, Michelle. "A Stage for the Irish." *World of Hibernia* 6 (Summer, 2000): 70.

Brantley, Ben. "Dark Yarns Casting Light." *New York Times*, April 2, 1999, p. E1.

McPherson, Conor. "Late Nights and Proclamations." *American Theatre* 16 (April, 1999): 45-46.

Renner, Pamela. "Haunts of the Very Irish." *American Theatre* 15 (July/August, 1998): 16-19.

"The Weir Breaks on Broadway." *World of Hibernia* 5 (Summer, 1999): 13.

Patricia Gately

WHAT PRICE GLORY?

Authors: Maxwell Anderson (1888-1959) and Laurence Stallings (1894-1968)
Type of plot: Realism; war
Time of plot: World War I
Locale: French countryside
First produced: 1924, at the Plymouth Theatre, New York City
First published: 1926, in *Three American Plays*

> *Principal characters:*
> FIRST SERGEANT QUIRT, the company's first sergeant
> CAPTAIN FLAGG, the company commander
> LIEUTENANT ALDRICH, second in command
> CHARMAINE DE LA COGNAC, a young French woman

The Play

What Price Glory? begins in a French farmhouse serving as a U.S. Marine head-quarters in World War I. Three enlisted men, Gowdy, Kiper, and Lipinsky, are cynically discussing their motivations for volunteering for duty in France. Sergeant Quirt then appears, announcing that he is "the new top soldier here," and abruptly dismisses Kiper and Gowdy. After receiving a briefing from Lipinsky, the company clerk, on the sad state of the company, Quirt "briskly" leaves headquarters to find Captain Flagg, the company commander.

Flagg, however, enters soon after Quirt exits. Charmaine, described as a "drab," follows closely at his heels. She is distraught over the possibility that Flagg might leave her. He takes her by the shoulders and assures her that he will come back; it will only be "eight days in Paris." Private Lewisohn then enters, reports in, and tells Flagg that he has lost his identification tags. The captain quickly dismisses him but asks Kiper to get him a new tag because "the God-forsaken fool's dying from grief away from mother." Quirt then reenters. During the course of their conversation, which primarily involves Flagg's description of the merits of his company, the captain reveals that he was a corporal under Quirt in China. Even more revealing is the fact that a woman evidently was involved in their quarrel, which continued when Quirt first served under Flagg in Cuba. Quirt is then introduced to Flagg's platoon leaders: Lieutenants Aldrich, Moore, Schmidt, and Sockel, who knows Quirt from Cuba. With a quick farewell, Flagg departs with his company, leaving Quirt alone with a cup of dice until Charmaine enters. He asks her for a date; she quickly refuses until Lipinsky and Gowdy bring in a rowdy Irishman. Quirt, after repeatedly telling Mulcahy to "pipe down," dispatches the recalcitrant with a blow to the jaw. The scene ends with Quirt and Charmaine kissing.

Scene 2 opens with the news that Flagg has been imprisoned for ten days on an attempted manslaughter charge, brought against him while he was in a drunken fit. He enters, still inebriated, and discovers Cognac Pete, Charmaine's father, waiting outside; he claims someone has taken advantage of his daughter. Flagg, assuming that he himself is the culprit, asks, through Moore, who acts as an interpreter, "how much he wants." Cognac Pete, in a rage, demands five hundred francs and that the man in question marry his daughter. To Flagg's obvious surprise, Pete points to Quirt. Flagg acts quickly; he orders Quirt to marry Charmaine and surrender two-thirds of his pay to Pete, reminding his senior noncommissioned officer (NCO) that an Army court-martial would not look favorably upon a "hayshaker." Before Quirt can put up much resistance, a runner brings an order for the company to move out within the hour. A general enters and explains the impending operation to Flagg: Hold a village on the line, capture a German officer for intelligence purposes, and penetrate the enemy lines to post propaganda leaflets. As the first act ends, Quirt plays his trump card: He refuses to serve unless he can do it as a single man. Flagg, pressed for time, agrees, leaving Charmaine a single woman with a soldier's allotment.

Act 2 begins in a wine cellar in the besieged town. Spike and Kiper, disheveled, are sleeping. Gowdy, a pharmacist's mate, and Quirt enter, followed by Flagg, who supports the wounded Aldrich. Soon after Aldrich is given a dose of morphine, Lieutenant Moore enters in a distressed state, a victim of shell shock. Two fresh officers enter the cellar as replacements. Flagg quickly dispatches one of them, Lundstrom, to the lines as a replacement platoon leader. As soon as Lundstrom leaves, Quirt reenters the cellar, limping with a leg wound he received from a German sniper. Flagg and the other new platoon leader, Cunningham, make plans to capture a German officer in an abandoned railroad station. Suddenly, there are grenade explosions and shouts: A German attack on the cellar has failed. Act 2 ends with Flagg manhandling a German officer prisoner and the appearance of Private Lewisohn, who was mortally wounded in the attack.

Act 3 opens back at Cognac Pete's tavern, two days later. Quirt enters in a major's blouse that hides his hospital pajamas. Charmaine appears and becomes distraught when she sees that Quirt is injured; embarrassed at his dress, he leaves to find a suitable uniform. Flagg enters and, in a revealing conversation with Charmaine, expresses his fatigue and disgust over the war. Quirt then reappears, and in an argument exacerbated by liquor, the two agree to play blackjack; Flagg reveals the stakes: six cards under 21 and Quirt can shoot his commander. Quirt, however, is dealt a king and immediately upsets the game and the candles, pitching the room into darkness. Flagg empties his automatic wildly into the night.

Charmaine enters the tavern; apologetically, Flagg professes his love for her. Lipinsky then arrives with the news that the battalion has been ordered to the front. Flagg reluctantly parts company with Charmaine and exits. Quirt, from a upper floor stairway, asks Flagg to wait for him as the curtain falls.

Themes and Meanings

What Price Glory? depicts war in its brutal, bloody reality; yet, through Maxwell Anderson and Laurence Stallings's characters, the play ends on a romantic note. Thus, the play becomes a realistic appraisal of the romance inherent in armed conflict.

Even for modern playgoers, the play is rough, violent, and brutal. All the characters in Captain Flagg's company have long abandoned any sense of the nobility of soldiering; the war has become senseless, meaningless, and mundane. This lack of control over their lives compels them, in their few hours of independence, to abandon any sense of morality and virtue. They use profanity without hesitation; they drink to excess; they womanize without any consideration of feminine virtue. However, when the call to battle is sounded, they quickly and unhesitantly respond.

Contemporary reviews of *What Price Glory?* have gone so far as to call this human reaction to war tragic. Thus, Laurence Stallings and Maxwell Anderson see the most important aspect of war as not the carnage and the destruction itself but the senseless reaction that human beings have to the brutality of war. In essence, the authors have made war a symbol for the anarchy and senselessness of human existence. The entire battle in which Captain Flagg's company engages in act 2 could have been avoided, they later learn. All the fury of armed conflict thus becomes action without purpose.

It would seem that this radical (for its time) indictment of war would put *What Price Glory?* under the category of "revolutionary drama." Many critics, however, find it to be an example of a classical play. There is no advocacy of change in *What Price Glory?* In effect, the play is an example of drama as art in that the ultimate goal is to display human life accurately. The moral assumptions upon which Anderson and Stallings constructed their characters were accepted by post-World War I American society; thus, *What Price Glory?* is not a revelation, but an affirmation of the attitudes and perceptions that were already firmly in place in the audience.

Critics have mentioned the naturalistic theme found in the play, specifically in act 2. The environment has overwhelmed the beleaguered company; Lieutenant Moore, in particular, seems on the verge of a nervous breakdown. The pharmacist's mate looks upon the horrible scene with callous indifference. However, there is a glimmer of hope; a ray of compassion appears in, of all characters, Flagg, as he comforts his troubled lieutenant. The audience is compelled to ask themselves, however, if it really is compassion or, in fact, a sense of duty to his subordinates that compels Flagg to act so seemingly out of character.

Dramatic Devices

Without a doubt, the most powerful artistic device employed in *What Price Glory?* is the provocative language. In fact, the play's first director, Arthur Hopkins, added a note to the playbill, justifying Laurence Stallings's and Maxwell Anderson's use of obscenities:

> The speech of men under arms is universally and consistently interlarded with profanity. Oaths mean nothing to a soldier save a means to obtain emphasis. . . . The authors of *What Price Glory?* have attempted to reproduce this mannerism along with other general atmosphere they believe to be true. . . . The audience is asked to bear with certain expletives which, under other circumstances, might be used for melodramatic effect, but herein are employed because the mood and truth of the play demand their employment.

This profanity has an extra bite to it: The characters use it to describe things traditionally treated with at least some degree of reverence. The valor of the profession of arms, the sanctity of death, the glory of the human soul, and even the virtue of a beautiful woman are not immune to the vile barbs of Flagg's company. No man is protected from the war's brutality; even the most pious young soldier must find an outlet for the pressures of the violence around him.

Anderson and Stallings also employ more typical dramatic devices. The play is constructed in three acts; acts 1 and 2 basically serve to depict the common marine of the war; no one character is revealed in enough depth to display a unique and distinct personality. Quirt and Flagg's relationship is revealed, as well as their mutual desire for Charmaine, but neither characteristic can be seen as unique to these men; all the soldiers are womanizers. Act 3 is much the same; the soldiers have returned from battle as profane and as brutal as ever and, even more significantly, still ready to leap back into action.

It is in act 3, in a scene placed between the stereotypical depictions, that Flagg, Quirt, and a few of the minor characters acquire some sense of personality. In the dismal wine cellar of a bombed-out French house, the tragedy of *What Price Glory?* unfolds. The "bloody naturalism" of the scene brings out the compassion of these men and, eventually, their cynicism. Dramatic juxtaposition allows the audience to see the brutality of war and its effect on the men; their profanity seems somehow justified. The audience's reactions are further affected by Quirt's and Flagg's quick acquiescence to return to battle. Anderson and Stallings make no comment on the situation; they sought to depict war realistically in the play, not to discuss it morally or philosophically. The viewer may draw his own conclusion if he wishes, but the realistic writer must consider his mission complete if the audience has the tools with which to make the decision.

Critical Context

Maxwell Anderson and Laurence Stallings blazed new dramatic trails when *What Price Glory?* premiered in 1924. Postwar cynicism was at its height; America had had enough of the "glory" of war. The play's depiction of the ugly truth of war and its effect on humankind was an instant success, playing for 435 performances. Certainly the timeliness of the production contributed to its popularity: Finally, the experience of the soldier could be truthfully and realistically portrayed. Anderson and Stallings wrote *What Price Glory?* not to advocate, criticize, or satirize any political, social, or cultural institution or group; instead, they responded to the public's demand for reality, for a glimpse into the American Expeditionary Force as it truly was. This shift in American attitudes had not been recognized by the authors of the time, at least not in the realm of drama. (Thomas Boyd's *Through the Wheat*, 1923, makes a strong argument for an awareness in fiction, at least.)

One might expect that veterans of the "war to end all wars" would look upon any realistic portrayal of their experiences favorably. However, many top-ranking U.S. Navy and Marine Corps officers objected to what they saw as stereotypes in the play, specifically in the characters' frequent use of profanity. Stallings based Flagg upon an officer he had met in the war who had commanded an American company at the bloody battle of Belleau Voop; the subject, however, vehemently denied any connection between himself and Flagg's violent swaggering.

The key to the success of *What Price Glory?* lies in its realistic portrayal of the human tragedy of war. If that realistic portrayal must use crude language to be accurate and true, then the author must not hesitate to employ it. Such a rejection of the societal contrivances normally found in early twentieth century drama made *What Price Glory?* the unique and provocative play that it was in 1924—and has continued to be.

Sources for Further Study

Anderson, Maxwell. *Dramatist in America: Letters of Maxwell Anderson, 1912-1958*. Edited by Laurence G. Avery. Chapel Hill: University of North Carolina Press, 1977.

Bailey, Mabel Driscoll. *Maxwell Anderson: The Playwright as Prophet*. New York: Abelard-Schuman, 1957.

Brittain, John T. *Laurence Stallings*. Edited by Sylvie E. Brown. New York: Twayne, 1975.

Hazelton, Nancy J., and Kenneth Kravs, eds. *Maxwell Anderson on the New York Stage*. San Jose, Calif.: Library Research, 1991.

Horn, Barbara L. *Maxwell Anderson: A Research and Production Sourcebook*. Westport, Conn.: Greenwood Press, 1996.

Krutch, Joseph Wood. *The American Drama Since 1918: An Informal History*. New York: G. Braziller, 1957.

Shivers, Alfred S. *The Life of Maxwell Anderson*. New York: Stein and Day, 1983.

Richard S. Keating

WHEN YOU COMIN' BACK, RED RYDER?

Author: Mark Medoff (1940-   )
Type of plot: Social realism
Time of plot: The late 1960's
Locale: Southern New Mexico
First produced: 1973, at the Circle Repertory Theatre Company, New York City
First published: 1974

Principal characters:
STEPHEN, a nineteen-year-old night counterman at Foster's Diner
ANGEL, a waitress at the diner
LYLE, an owner of a gas station
CLARK, the franchise owner of the diner
CLARISSE, a successful concert violinist
RICHARD, her husband, a businessman
TEDDY, a Vietnam War veteran and drug smuggler
CHERYL, Teddy's twenty-year-old girlfriend

The Play

It is early morning in Foster's Diner, in New Mexico, when the curtain goes up on *When You Comin' Back, Red Ryder?* Two of the protagonists are enacting a daily ritual: Young Stephen Ryder is reading the morning newspaper, picking his teeth, and showing a 1950's macho attitude as Angel, the chubby waitress, cleans up and tries to engage him in conversation. They are at cross-purposes; she wants him to stay in the dusty outpost, hoping that in time he will recognize her female charms, he wants to get out and make a success of himself in the big world. His distant goal is to be a waiter in a tuxedo and own a Corvette Sting Ray "the color of money." She quarrels with his insistence on being called "Red," arguing that it does not make sense since his hair is brown. He insists that "when I was a kid I had red hair." He identifies with the cowboy hero Red Ryder, with whom he shares a last name. The routine continues as, in turn, Clark, the owner of the franchise, and Lyle, who owns the adjacent gas station and motel, make their entrances, doing and saying their usual things. Lyle is a man in his early sixties. He has a slight disability that forces him to walk with a crutch, and he has designs on the waitress Angel even though she is probably forty years his junior.

Emerging from one of Lyle's motel rooms to descend on the diner are two symbols of big cities and life in the fast lane, Richard and Clarisse Ethredge. He is a successful businessman, and she is an equally successful concert violinist. She carries a violin case containing a Guarnerius violin. There is an aura about them of self-confidence and success. They settle in to have breakfast and listen to the idle, if somewhat hostile, chatter of the locals.

With the arrival of Teddy and Cheryl, a feeling of unease and danger enters the forlorn and dusty diner. Teddy is a forceful man in his early thirties, dressed in an army fatigue jacket; he switches back and forth between being jocular and quietly threatening. For much of the play, he affects a broad Western accent. Cheryl is pretty, slightly scared, and braless—the last causes some helpless staring by Stephen and Lyle.

The tenor of the action has changed. Where before Teddy's arrival there was a feeling of constantly shifting focus and lazy morning activity, there is now a decided power center: Teddy. He forces all present to focus their attention on him and, under the guise of jovial horseplay, intrudes brutally into their lives and dreams. He is quick to recognize the tangled tensions of sex and attraction between Angel, Lyle, and Stephen. He also immediately creates a strange rapport, with undercurrents of both threat and mutual attraction, with Clarisse Ethredge. The discrepancy between the nickname Stephen has chosen for himself and the way he looks is not wasted on Teddy. He finds it both hilarious and thought-provoking that Stephen is mired in an image of himself that makes him identify with a defunct cowboy hero. Teddy forces Richard Ethredge to ruminate with him about the demise of their boyhood heroes and the values they stood for.

Teddy and Cheryl have stopped to get gas and to get a new generator for their van. A combination of threat and good old boy jocularity convinces Lyle to procure the generator despite the fact that it is Sunday. Teddy carefully instructs Lyle not to put the generator into the van—he will do it himself. Lyle wants to be helpful, however, and opens the hood of the van only to discover the drugs Teddy is smuggling into the United States from Mexico. Suddenly the atmosphere in the diner changes from being vaguely unpleasant to being actually threatening. Teddy demands money from the Ethredges and reveals that he has stolen their car keys. The first act ends with a showdown between Richard Ethredge and Teddy. Richard refuses to give Teddy money and moves to leave the diner and call the police even as Teddy points a gun at him. Teddy shoots him as the stage goes black.

In the second act, Teddy, having pinpointed the relationships and dreams of the other characters in the first, forces them to face reality. He shows Stephen, in a cruel game of cowboys and horses, that he is a wimp—not the hero he has dreamt himself to be, and he shows Angel that her dream of marrying Stephen is impossible. Her best, and only, hope is Lyle the cripple (the owner of the town's only color television). He also forces Richard, who was only superficially wounded by the gunshot at the end of act 1, to realize—with Clarisse watching in fascination— that he is not the man he—and she—had imagined him to be. Certainly, he is no match for Teddy. The power relations between the Ethredges at the end of the play have shifted to her advantage. The audience gets the feeling that their marriage is doomed, based on their new insights about each other.

The act is a whirlwind of action as Teddy, his imagination and emotions ignited by the ruminations about Red Ryder and other Western heroes, forces the other characters to participate in his own version of therapy theater: first "the lone rider returns to his girlfriend," then a steamy dance. Curiously, Teddy himself is perhaps the one who is most affected by the proceedings. He comes face to face with his own dreams and loss of values. As the action escalates he becomes more and more frantic and violent, terrifying the others and driving himself to a point of abject desperation. He steals three hundred dollars from Richard, ties everybody up, and stomps out, leaving a disillusioned group—including Cheryl—behind.

When Clark, the franchisee, arrives and frees the captives, they are no longer the people they were when the audience first met them. Stephen asks Clarisse Ethredge to give him a lift out of town, and she agrees—over the protests of Richard. Lyle is quietly triumphant to see his rival for Angel's affections disappear, as Angel is set to accept the inevitable: Lyle and his color television.

Themes and Meanings

At the heart of *When You Comin' Back, Red Ryder?* is a sense of despair at the loss of dreams and heroes. The two protagonists, Stephen and Teddy, are both locked in the myths of machismo and heroism of the 1940's and 1950's. Whereas Teddy has had his myths and ideals shattered by his sojourn in Vietnam and by a subsequent slide into criminality, however, Stephen stubbornly dresses and acts the role of the cowboy hero—even as *his* reality refutes the myth almost as much as that of Teddy.

Another theme is the schism between perceived reality and the real world. All the characters of Mark Medoff's play have constructed personal myths that only selectively allow the bright light of reality to shine in. Teddy, the violent catalyst, forces each of them, himself included, to compare their personal scripts of their lives with reality. They all come out stripped of illusions and, perhaps, wiser.

For Medoff, in this, as in several of his other plays, the central conflict is between the ideals and myths of boyhood, symbolized by the heroes of cowboy epics such as Red Ryder, and the adult reality of the 1970's: an unjust war in Vietnam, the Richard Nixon scandal, and the decline of America as a symbol of freedom and justice. As Teddy says, "Goddamn, where did all those people get to so fast? Where the hell's goddamn Tim Holt, Jim? Johnny Mack and the Durango Kid? Lash LaRue. Jesus Christ, somebody pulled a fast one."

Medoff unites a group of people who, on the surface, are fairly ordinary Americans, who are somehow representative. Under normal circumstances neither the audience nor the characters themselves would have become aware of the distance between their personal universes and misconceptions and the real world they live in. These people, however, are confronted with a man who has not only the capacity to see through them but also has the gumption and the desire to break down the wall between the private and public universes. The process is painful, and the characters resist. They do not want their dreams to be destroyed; they do not want to live in a world where they have no myths. Teddy, however, has no mercy. He has had his own dreams and ideals brutally and abruptly rendered, and he, and perhaps playwright Medoff, believe that only when people see themselves and the world as they really are can they begin to do something about their situations.

Dramatic Devices

The dramatic prescription used in *When You Comin' Back, Red Ryder?* is common enough in the theater: A group of people's normal lives and routines are destroyed by an outside catalyst who then forces them to face themselves as they really are. The immediate model for the play is Robert E. Sherwood's *The Petrified Forest* (pr., pb. 1935), which is also set in a diner somewhere in middle America; it deals with people who dream and create myths about themselves until the firebomb of a violent criminal on the run drops into their midst, pushing them to sort out reality and myth.

In *When You Comin' Back, Red Ryder?*, Medoff establishes a routine reality and a small group of characters whose myths, dreams, and illusions are bared for all to see. Once the audience has familiarized themselves with these characters and perhaps begun to care for them, the playwright introduces a troubled man whose own dreams and illusions are buried and forgotten in the memories of a person he can probably no longer believe he once was. The mixture of the dreaming innocents and the man whose dreams have died proves chemically unstable. Trying to understand where his own dreams and myths died, Teddy forces the other characters to face the schism between myth and reality in their lives.

Medoff also very consciously plays with a dramatic device from the cowboy movie genre, the strong, silent stranger who rides into town and solves all the problems, only to saddle up and ride off again into the sunset having changed everybody's lives. Not only is the author conscious of this mesh of myth and style, he lets his antihero, Teddy, be conscious of it too. Once he has sized up the situation in the diner and the relationships between the individuals he finds there, Teddy amuses himself by playing his own perverse variation on the theme of "Teddy, the Lone Rider."

From the moment Teddy enters, there is also a measure of mystery to the play. Is Teddy really dangerous, or is he merely a hick with a sick sense of humor? Richard Ethredge, for one, gambles on the latter and loses. The audience does not know what to make of Teddy until the moment when he pulls out the gun and shoots Richard. He is ambiguous for the duration of the first act, which gives the play a mixture of comedy and serious drama. The first act, particularly, is very humorous and exciting because of Teddy's vicious and slightly demented humor and his superior intelligence. In the second act, the play increasingly becomes a frightening nightmare for the characters as well as the audience. Teddy loses control, and there is a constant sense that he may, before he leaves, do something really awful.

Critical Context

A recurrent theme in Mark Medoff's oeuvre is the discrepancy between the heroic and innocent dreams of childhood and adult reality. Besides *When You Comin' Back, Red Ryder?*, this same conflict is central to *The Kramer* (pr. 1972) and, especially, *The Majestic Kid* (pr. 1965). The device is perhaps most obvious in *The Majestic Kid*, where Medoff introduces as a character in the play the cowboy hero the Laredo Kid. The Kid can only be seen by the protagonist of the play, Aaron Weiss, who himself throughout the play tries to conform to the macho image of his boyhood heroic projection of himself as the Majestic Kid. The Laredo Kid is a fleshing out of subconscious processes in Aaron's mind as he faces various situations and challenges. The conflict is that the cowboy heroes and their ideals, if they ever had live models, belong in the 1940's and 1950's. In Medoff's plays, they are like dinosaurs trying to pass as twentieth century animals: They simply do not belong. Aaron is a modern, sensitive man, full of angst and possessing a healthy respect for women. He cannot fill out the heroic shadow of his childhood ideal, nor can he see how this awkward, oversized piece—the cowboy hero—could ever fit into the puzzle of a modern, sleek world.

Another recurrent element in Medoff's works is the violent outsider who tries to come to grips with a world with which he somehow is about to lose contact. Teddy in *When You Comin' Back, Red Ryder?* has counterparts in other Medoff plays such as *The Kramer, The Hands of Its Enemy* (pr. 1984), *The Wager* (pr. 1967), and, in a slightly different way, *Children of a Lesser God* (pr. 1979). The outsider who has no real ties to reality himself, who is adrift in a world whose values he no longer understands, becomes a catalyst for other characters who, to all appearances, are well anchored in a world and reality they do understand. The confrontation always produces sparks and a heightened—although not necessarily happy—perception of reality.

Most of all, Medoff's plays try to come to grips with a modern world where traditional values and morality are outmoded, where greed, ambition, and egotism are becoming the accepted ideals. Medoff always operates with characters who are encapsulated in a separate universe that they try to make impregnable to attacks from reality. He then confronts his dreamers with people whose dreams have been destroyed and who, in turn, have been destroyed by their loss. The real world lies somewhere in between, in a vacuum between myth and destruction.

Sources for Further Study
Adams, Elizabeth. "Mark Medoff." In *Contemporary Dramatists*. 6th ed. Detroit: St. James, 1999.
Erben, Rudolf. "The Western Holdup Play: The Pilgrimage Continues." *Western American Literature*, February, 1989, 311-322.
Gladstein, Mimi. "An Interview with Mark Medoff." *Studies in American Drama, 1945-Present*, 1993, 61-83.
_____. "Mark Medoff." In *Speaking on Stage: Interviews with Contemporary American Playwrights*, edited by Philip C. Kolin and Colby Kullman. Tuscaloosa: University of Alabama Press, 1996.
Medoff, Mark. "In Praise of Teachers." *New York Times Magazine*, November 9, 1986, 72.
The Nation. Review. November 26, 1973, 572.
The New Yorker. Review. December 17, 1973, 99.
Stasio, Marilyn. "Mark Medoff: At Home on the Range." *New York Times*, November 27, 1988, p. H7.

Per Schelde

WHERE HAS TOMMY FLOWERS GONE?

Author: Terrence McNally (1939-   )
Type of plot: Satire
Time of plot: 1971
Locale: New York City
First produced: 1971, at the Yale Repertory Theatre, New Haven, Connecticut
First published: 1972

> *Principal characters:*
> TOMMY FLOWERS, a thirty-year-old dropout and urban guerrilla
> BEN DELIGHT, a has-been stage actor
> NEDDA LEMON, an aspiring cellist and fugitive from suburbia
> ARNOLD, Tommy's sheepdog

The Play

Where Has Tommy Flowers Gone? opens with Tommy's address to the audience in which he introduces himself by thanking all the people who have made him the free-loading, shoplifting, wittily charming scourge of convention that he is. Walt Disney and Tonto, the Wolf Man and Chuck Berry, Ma and Pa Kettle, Fidel Castro and Thomas Jefferson ("who said something about God forbid we should ever be twenty years without a rebellion")—to these and other unlikely figures he dedicates the act.

Having been presented with this rebel's pedigree, the audience, in the first of many flashbacks and loosely associated episodes, is whisked away to St. Petersburg, Florida, 1952, to one of Tommy's early run-ins with authority. When asked on a civics test to list the ten most admired men in the United States, Tommy writes "Holden Caulfield," J. D. Salinger's fictional protagonist in *Catcher in the Rye* (1951), ten times, an act for which he predictably receives an F grade. The combined forces of parents and principal make him recant and produce the acceptable list of establishment icons; however, Tommy emerges feeling Holden's righteous disgust at these "phonies," longing to be off in Times Square with his fictional idol, smoking Lucky cigarettes and pining over Jan Moody. By the time he does escape the confines of St. Petersburg for what he insists on calling the Big Apple, he is a confirmed malcontent, pitted against the tyrannical power of officialdom, plotting to blow up the country and start over again. As he explains, "We can blow it up nice or we can blow it up tough. What I'm doing now is nice." The pattern of Tommy's defiance has been established, but so far his anarchic assaults on authority have remained a kind of playful sniping.

The scene changes to the streets of New York City, where Tommy and Ben Delight are panhandling, lamenting the increased competition from "fake Buddhist monks" on their corner, rehearsing the moral collapse of the United States, and extolling the value of traveling light (Tommy carries only a toothbrush, change of shorts, autographed photo of James Dean, and a nun's habit). Ben, an old actor who claims he spent his career in Paul Muni's shadow, has never seen or heard of James Dean, but he is one of the few people to have witnessed Tommy's disastrous one-line performance in the "humorless, pedantic, philosophically sophomoric, cliché-ridden and plagiarized" play *Kumquat*. Ben's amused recital of this embarrassing failure catapults Tommy into a savage attack on Ben as an old, impotent loser, an insult he just as quickly withdraws and tries to smooth over by promising Ben new clothes from Bloomingdale's. Tommy flags a cab, lights a joint, and blithely ignores the cab fare when they alight in front of the department store.

The lights come up on a row of pay toilets in the ladies' room of Bloomingdale's. Behind one of the doors, Tommy is singing "Shenandoah." Standing up and looking down into the adjoining booth, he sees Nedda Lemon, who comes charging out brandishing her cello case. Tommy promptly discovers that it is full of shoplifted goods, but since he is busy stealing a handful of items himself, the two of them sit down to smoke a relaxing joint, something Nedda admits she probably needs.

A cellist who has fled the suburbs for New York City and the promise of a musical career, Nedda complains that she has found instead a mean, cold city which offers at best the prospect of being booked "to play the Lord's Prayer at somebody's Bar Mitzvah in Brooklyn." As Tommy invites himself, Ben, and Arnold down to her place in the Village, he artfully dons his nun's habit and, routing another authority figure, sweeps them past the Bloomingdale's police officer who has been called to investigate the chaos in the ladies' room. Before leaving, however, Tommy gets control of the public address system and announces to terrified shoppers that a bomb has been placed in the store. When the lights come up on Tommy shedding his nun's habit, he assures the audience that he has not really planted a bomb. He is still playing it "nice," but that applies since nice has been fun—so far.

Act 2 opens with a Twentieth Century Fox fanfare and Tommy in a blonde wig as Marilyn Monroe, another American casualty, singing "Happy Birthday" and answering questions from the grave about her new man, Kay (as she calls him) Guevara. The scene then shifts to a supermarket, where Tommy, Ben, and Nedda are serenely but craftily stealing food. Tommy seems happy with his life, its carefree anarchic days and quiet evenings at home, Nedda playing the cello and Ben reading *Variety* with Arnold at his feet. However, Tommy has not been domesticated: When the others are gone, he brings out the cigar-box bomb he has been making—instructions supplied by the U.S. Army Corps of Engineers—and settles down to work while watching the news on television.

In an instant replay of the news, Tommy appears as ten-year-old Puerto Rican Rachel Gomez, the "mentally retarded, leukemia-stricken, Fight for Sight poster girl" in whose name the numbingly condescending and racist First Lady is dedicating a treatment center. The First Lady's saccharine pieties are cast in grim counterpoint to Rachel's horrifying tale of barrio life and her hard-edged, utterly knowing performance of "Clavelitos," capped by a defiant shout of "Vinceremos" and a bouquet that explodes in the First Lady's face. There are fireworks in earnest now.

Tommy and Nedda next appear in a Howard Johnson's, celebrating her first job (a wedding in Newark) and the fact that he actually intends to pay for a meal—he has the money, he says, from selling his body to a faded and desperate film queen. Having stolen the silverware and catsup, however, Tommy schemes to get away with the meal too, and in the end he manages to have the two of them thrown out without having to pay. While Tommy applauds his victory, Nedda expresses her doubts about continuing in this way. She questions whether Tommy really loves her—whether he even can love her—and has begun to nurse fantasies about pipe-smoking doctors, suburbs, station wagons, and stability. She returns to the restaurant to pay the check, only to be arrested. With Nedda incarcerated and Ben now sick and dying in Bellevue, Tommy and Arnold are on their own again. However, even Arnold wanders off (soliloquizing) when Tommy leaves him to follow a mindless but sexy seventeen-year-old California high school student back to her hotel room.

Bounced from the hotel in his jockey shorts soon after, Tommy rushes in with the only thing he has left: the red shopping bag containing his bomb. It is a cold and rainy night; Ben is dead, Nedda is locked up, and Arnold is gone. Tommy calls for Nedda at the detention center but gets only a foul and abusive response and a prodding from a police officer to move on. Retreating to a telephone booth, he makes himself up in his *Kumquat* role and, chanting to himself that his so-called antisocial aggression is really a love for the world, he takes out his bomb and wires it. When the policeman returns to chase him away, Tommy leaves the bomb in the telephone booth and runs off thumbing his nose at it all. As the lights fade, the sound of ticking grows louder until there is an enormously loud explosion, and the lights come up on a bare stage.

Themes and Meanings

Where Has Tommy Flowers Gone? presents, in a kaleidoscopic range of scenes and tonalities, one young man's rebellion against a materialistic, oppressively regulated world, a world fiercely intolerant of any deviation from the norm and dedicated to the systematic elimination of individual self-expression. An antihero both charming and terrifying, Tommy Flowers careens through the play's two acts in an exuberant one-man assault on the soggy American pieties, stifling conventions, and assorted forces of conformity that he has faced as a boy in the 1950's and as a young adult in the more confusing, volatile 1960's. His only rule is unruliness.

Like one of his heroes, Holden Caulfield, Tommy has a keen sense of the phony, and he rages against the fraudulent wherever he finds it: in supermarkets, on film screens, in family living rooms. He hates advertising for its prostitution of literature to sell Lorna Doon cookies; he loathes star chasers, geriatric groupies, and movie magazines for their reduction of life to lurid tabloid headlines; he despises the suburban family for its complacent celebration of therapists and orthopedists and color television. So he hurls his defiance at an unforgiving world, joyously taking drugs, engaging in sex at any opportunity, shoplifting everything from radios to recordings of Beethoven symphonies. "America's a rich country; it can afford me," he cries, stuffing some more lamb chops down his trousers. Ironically, he feeds off the society he condemns.

There are real high jinx here; however, even if it is sung with gleeful, full-throated abandon, Tommy's protest is genuine. He sees himself as an outsider, a James Dean who celebrates his alienation and warms himself with his fiery nonconformity. The bomb he carries around New York City is his threat to the entrenched authority of the state, the family, the school, the church. He's having fun, but the purely verbal fireworks with which he cons and cajoles people seem poised at any moment to turn into the real thing. In the end, they do.

To many readers and viewers, Terrence McNally has created in Tommy Flowers a contemporary rogue, a social outcast who functions as the innocent eye through which is seen the corruption of failing American institutions; others, however, think less of the eponymous hero, seeing not an uncompromising rebel forced to go underground when life above is all disillusionment and hypocrisy, but rather, as the critic Jack Kroll says, "a maudlin little stinkpot, his ringlets dripping with self-indulgence, who blows and sets his fuse because old people die, because his girl . . . doesn't want to play any more, because a cop has told him to quit loitering." However, it is difficult not to feel some kind of sympathy for Tommy. McNally has fashioned not simply a discontented confidence artist but an individual who cries out for the very thing he so relentlessly seeks to destroy. In creating his surrogate family in Ben, Nedda, and Arnold, Tommy admits his need for a small community to validate his revolutionary attempts to pull down the larger community which he feels thwarts his individualism. It is this family of which he is deprived in his final refusal to reconcile himself with authority; he emerges a lonely figure, running through a blasted cityscape, shouting his name to a world that does not want to recognize him.

Dramatic Devices

Where Has Tommy Flowers Gone? makes no attempt at dramatic realism. The action is wildly episodic in structure, with abrupt scene changes, flashbacks to the past, fantasy sequences in the present, madcap monologues, and frequent direct addresses to the audience. Terrence McNally makes use of Brechtian techniques, demanding that the audience admit to the theatricality of the play, its presentational rather than representational quality. He refuses to allow the audience the comfort of escaping into a re-created reality, insisting instead that they face up to the provocative, often assaultive images the play presents. Nevertheless, McNally is artful enough to provide the dramatic texture and depth of character that Brecht rarely supplies. The loosely connected episodes may suggest the chaotic, disjunctive nature of contemporary life and defy traditional notions of comprehensible motive, action, and character, but McNally is canny enough to provide the dramatic texture and depth of character that Bertolt Brecht often does not supply, so that in spite of the discontinuous plot, audiences feel neither confused nor bludgeoned with ideas. McNally is careful to mix opaque incidents or surreal scenes (the Marilyn Monroe opening of act 2 or the fantasy with Tommy and James Dean in act 1, for example) with extended and dramatically developed scenes (Tommy and Nedda at Bloomingdale's).

In an introductory production note to the play, McNally suggests that the staging should be extremely fluid, almost cinematic, and that scenery should be kept to a min-imum. He seems to want the scenes to flow into one another even though the connec-tions are anything but smoothly logical. In various early productions, directors have chosen to use slides (projecting onto several screens) or even filmed sequences to con-vey the shifting locales. Whether the rapid changes are effected by projections or blackouts, the entire play is held together and informed by its rich comic sense, a physical and verbal humor that is sassy and quick-hitting. McNally gives his charac-ters nimble, witty dialogue, at times almost epigrammatic; they revel in clever allu-sions to films, theatrical in-jokes, outrageous puns. This sort of backstage gossip is thematically telling. Both Ben and Tommy are failed but stagestruck actors; Ben reads *Variety* religiously, and Tommy never stops acting. He lies and charms his way through life, putting on a new persona with disturbing ease. His identity is fluid in a world that will not tolerate fluidity; in his schizophrenic assumption of roles and his self-absorbed, operatic enactment of them, he can be both the means of the play's sat-ire and one of its objects.

Critical Context

Where Has Tommy Flowers Gone? shares with other Terrence McNally plays of the 1960's and 1970's the witty yet pointed satiric tone of protest against a society that threatens individual freedom. In a clutch of plays that combine rambunctiously amus-ing surfaces and darkly disturbing depths, he creates a stylish but barbed satire that ex-plores the problematic relations between the communal and the individual. By means of an array of misfit heroes, he skewers his characteristic targets (conventional moral-ity, the Vietnam War, intolerance for nonconformity and eccentricity, governmental blindness, and authoritarian brutality) with an anger that is searing even when cheeky and high-spirited.

Next (pr. 1967) takes on the dehumanized absurdity of induction into the military, a process that turns a mild, middle-aged man into a sadistic, pompous parody of the very bureaucratic forces that threaten him. It is also the theme of *Witness* (pr. 1968), a play which shows again the pernicious effects of an individual's being subjected to an intense dose of the normative: It can turn one into a desensitized assassin. In *Bringing It All Back Home* (pr. 1969), McNally presents an American family (eroded by drugs, promiscuous sex, patriarchal power, and mindless television watching) as it confronts both the return home of the elder son, a soldier killed in Vietnam, and the television crew that comes to film the family's reaction for a jaded national audience. Madness, undiagnosed and untreated, clearly looms on the American landscape; in *Bad Habits: Ravenswood and Dunelawn* (pr. 1971), McNally focuses on this directly. *Bad Habits* links two one-act plays set in different sanatoriums and shows the effects on inmates' habits of two different forms of treatment. Though both approaches to patients' prob-lems are presented hilariously, it is clear that the repressive method at Dunelawn—attempting to eliminate all vices—is the road to genuine madness while the form of therapy at Ravenswood—allowing everyone to have what he or she wants—is the way to produce healthy, well-adjusted individuals.

With his popular play *The Ritz* (pr. 1975), McNally turned in the direction of farce and toward more personal rather than broadly social issues, placing greater emphasis on those qualities of rapid pace, campy wit, overtly homosexual characters and situations, and theatrical self-reference. In *It's Only a Play* (pr. 1986), McNally addresses directly the business of being a playwright and scores nonstop laughter with an unrelenting series of one-liners that resonate with real-life Broadway personalities: the critics, performers, and producers that plague a dramatist's life. In *The Lisbon Traviata* (pr. 1985), McNally's well-known love for opera gets full play in a portrayal of the violent breakup of two men, lovers and impassioned opera enthusiasts. The dialogue glitters with opera arcana and bitchy put-downs as the plot moves toward a final aria worthy of one character's favorite diva, Maria Callas, a character who makes another appearance in McNally's *Master Class* (pr., pb. 1995). McNally's late twentieth century plays wed the emotional exuberance and wicked satire of his earlier plays to a lyrical abandon and linguistic virtuosity that makes him seem to many theatergoers one of the most amusing and penetrating of American dramatists. His plays and adaptations in the 1990's, including *Love! Valor! Compassion!* (pr. 1994), *Ragtime* (pr. 1996), and *The Full Monty* (pr. 2000), were spirited productions and earned several Tony nominations and awards.

Sources for Further Study

Ballet, Arthur. "Terrence McNally." In *Contemporary Dramatists*. 6th ed. Detroit: St. James, 1999.
Clurman, Harold. Review in *The Nation*, October 25, 1971, 410-411.
Kalem, T. E. "Holden Caulfield's Return." *Time*, October 18, 1971, 80.
Kroll, Jack. "Please Omit Flowers." *Newsweek*, October 18, 1971, 108.
Oliver, Edith. Review in *The New Yorker*. October 18, 1971, 101.
Zinman, Toby, ed. *Terrence McNally: A Casebook*. New York: Garland, 1997.

Thomas J. Campbell

WHY MARRY?

Author: Jesse Lynch Williams (1871-1929)
Type of plot: Satire; women's
Time of plot: The early twentieth century
Locale: A country estate
First produced: 1917, at the Astor Theater, New York City
First published: 1914, as *And So They Were Married*

> *Principal characters:*
> JOHN, a wealthy industrialist
> LUCY, his wife
> JEAN, his youngest sister, a socialite
> HELEN, his eldest sister, a scientist
> ERNEST, a scientist courting Helen
> REX, a wealthy playboy courting Jean
> UNCLE EVERETT, a wise judge
> THEODORE, a poor clergyman cousin

The Play

This three-act play occurs entirely on John's well-furnished estate. It is the story of five couples who represent five divergent views of marriage. The primary couple, Ernest and Helen, form the center of the play's action. They represent options other than marriage for two people to express their love and respect for one another. They enjoy each other's company, share in each other's professional work, and are both ready to commit emotionally to each other, yet they feel no great compulsion to formalize their bond with a legal contract. Ernest is a famous scientist whose medical research has saved thousands of lives. Helen is a brilliant scientist in her own right and her assistance to Ernest has been a primary factor in his success and renown. They view each other as equals in all things. The characters' exchanges—Helen and Ernest's discussions of the pros and cons of marriage and their coy shyness about declaring their love, and John's machinations to force Helen and Ernest either apart or into marriage—give the play an objective. John's interest in the pair stems from his desire to see his sister, Helen, marry a monied man instead of a poor scientist. His primary leverage is his position as a trustee in the institute that employs Ernest. John alternates between trying to lure Ernest to Paris, where his research can go forward, but with the stipulation that Helen remains behind, to threatening to fire Ernest and leaving him without visible means of support, should he persist in courting Helen.

A further complication is that John is likewise determined to marry off his other sister, Jean, to Rex, a womanizer whose wealth and family connections make the pairing a better business deal than an emotionally satisfying match. Rex and Jean do feel an occasional and fleeting passion for each other, but both are mature enough to know that their desire is a poor foundation for marriage. Nevertheless, they are willing to consider marriage for the sake of appeasing the expectations of their families.

John sees himself as the prototypical man-of-the-house, accustomed to making the decisions for his two sisters, Helen and Jean, as well as for his wife, Lucy. He and Lucy have, to his belief, a perfect marriage. He provides the money and she provides a clean and well-ordered house, a totally traditional arrangement within the parameters of what society expects. He has bought and paid for everything in his life, including his wife, but Lucy is miserable, suffering in silence under John's bullying. During the course of the play, Lucy asks John for a divorce.

The Judge, Uncle Everett, has been married for twenty-five years to Julia, who is offstage for the duration of the play. To all observers, Everett and Julia have a perfect marriage, but she is in Reno filing for a divorce because, as Everett explains it, "She likes her beefsteak well done; I like mine underdone. . . . She loves the opera and hates the theater; I love the theater and hate the opera."

The fifth couple is Theodore, the impoverished clergyman and his wife, Mary, who is also offstage for the duration of the play. She is convalescing at a sanitorium for undisclosed reasons, but the fact that she has had to care for five children under extreme financial privation is hinted to be a factor. They represent couples who stay together through sickness and poverty according to the highest ideals of faith.

Themes and Meanings

Why Marry? addresses the issues of a specific time and place. A tremendous social upheaval was occurring in the United States in 1917 concerning the role of women. The vernacular of the day termed this conflict the "New Woman" versus the "True Woman." Helen represents the New Woman. She is well educated and independent; she does not require a man in her life to provide her with money, career direction, or emotional fulfillment. She is free to enter the workplace and to find her own way.

Lucy is given the role of the True Woman. Her lot is to remain at home in a subservient role to her husband. She is expected to sacrifice her emotional needs to his material comfort. Love between husband and wife is nice, but the union is more of a financial and legal arrangement. Divorce is not an option for the True Woman.

Jean is poised on the brink of one role or the other. If she marries Rex, her fate will be sealed as a True Woman, trapped in a loveless marriage, but bought and paid for in the best capitalist tradition. If she defies John and declines the union with Rex, she has a chance to find love on her own terms as a New Woman.

The odd factor in this play is the relationship between Uncle Everett and Julia. They are getting divorced becausen after twenty-five years of marriage, they have finally discovered that neither of them wants to be married. From the beginning of their relationship, each has sacrificed for the other with concessions of their own desires, not because it was expected of them by society but because they thought the other spouse wanted the concession. More often than not, they would later discover that the concession was unnecessary, that they had mistaken what the other spouse wanted and behaved contrarily to what the other spouse desired. As Uncle Everett gets daily telegrams from Aunt Julia, it becomes evident that their love is deep and their commitment is real. They agree to divorce because each thinks it is what the other wants.

Dramatic Devices

Why Marry? is in the tradition of George Bernard Shaw, with an emphasis on dialogue and repartee and with little concern for developing a plot. Neither is there a clear-cut antagonist or protagonist, nor does anything actually happen onstage that would require physical movement (except for the opening scene of Rex forcing his affections on Jean over her protests). There is a type of climax as Uncle Everett tricks Helen and Ernest into declaring their love for each other in the presence of witnesses, then surprisingly produces a license and declares them man and wife.

The set is simple and basic, acting as the terrace of a country house. The only changes necessary are lighting shifts to indicate different times of day.

As a Shavian drama—one that follows in the vein of those written by George Bernard Shaw—*Why Marry?* values the stage as a platform for the communication of ideas: It confronts the audience with issues of social and political importance, aiming to stimulate not just the hearts but also the minds of New York's theatergoers. One of the major innovations of Shavian drama was the unusually large role given to thought and debate enlivened with a love of wordplay and paradox. The success or failure of such plays depends on the facility with which such ideas are presented and incorporated into a smooth flow of dialogue. The danger is for the characters to pontificate and wax overly didactic. *Why Marry?* successfully escapes these dangers by remaining always lighthearted and somewhat sardonic.

Critical Context

Why Marry? has a secure place in history as the first drama to be awarded the Pulitzer Prize. The play began as prose, but Williams decided on a dramatic format and published it in 1914 as *And So They Were Married* through Charles Scribner's Sons. It took three years before Broadway would produce it because, Williams once noted, it was written ahead of its time. It ran for 120 performances at New York's Astor Theater and was made into a silent film in 1924.

Why Marry? addresses a host of issues brought on by the early twentieth century's feminist movement. The movement was fueled not only by suffrage but also by the gradual need of the United States' nascent industrial economy, which was in need of a type of worker who did not require tremendous upper-body strength. Between 1900 and 1920, the percentage of American women employed in clerical and sales positions rose dramatically, as did the number of women enrolled in public colleges and universities. The debates that stemmed from this empowered generation of women saturated the newspapers, journals, novels, movies, and dramas of the day: Would the New Women stay at home to become wives and mothers? With financial independence, could emotional independence be far behind? Once women had been freed from their dependencies, what was to become of society? Images of the New Woman were legion: Caricatures of women as cigarette-smoking, bicycle-riding, bob-haired flappers whose bloomers are exposed were among the images ingrained in Americans' consciousness.

Along with addressing the concerns of this new feminism, Williams managed to incorporate into his play a great deal of discussion about economic equity. Time and again, the problems of social institutions are interwoven with the disparity of pay between men and women as well as between the creative and healing professions versus that of industry. In the play, John and Uncle Everett have the following exchange regarding scientists' meager two-thousand-dollar-a-year income:

> JUDGE: Well, why not give the young man a raise?
>
> JOHN: Oh, that's not a bad salary for scientists, college professors, and that sort of thing. Why, even the head of the institute himself gets less than the superintendent of my mills. No future in science.
>
> JUDGE: Perfectly practical. . . . The superintendent of John's mills saves the company thousands of dollars. These bacteriologists merely save the nation thousands of babies. All our laws, written and unwritten, value private property above human life. I'm a distinguished jurist and I always render my decisions accordingly.

The issues addressed by *Why Marry?* remain uncannily modern even today. Yet at the same time, the attitudes espoused by even the most enlightened of its characters are rooted in an unsettling worldview that would be intolerable in a contemporary setting. The opening scene between Rex and Jean is nothing less than a sexual assault. She says "no" repeatedly and is ignored. Rex only stops after they are interrupted by Lucy, and the entire incident is brushed aside. Jean is flippant and later confides to her sister that at first Rex's kisses were distasteful but, after a while, she began to enjoy them. This play provides stark evidence that American society has made advances, but it also acts as a subtle reminder about how much more remains to be done.

Sources for Further Study

Chothia, Jean, ed. *The New Woman and Other Emancipated Woman Plays*. New York: Oxford University Press, 2001.

Marks, Patricia. *Bicycles, Bangs, and Bloomers: The New Woman in the Popular Press*. Lexington: University Press of Kentucky, 1990.

Murphy, Brenda. *American Realism and American Drama*. Cambridge, England: Cambridge University Press, 1987.

Newlin, Keith, ed. *American Plays of the New Woman*. Chicago: Ivan R. Dee, 2000.

Richardson, Angelique, and Chris Willis, eds. *The New Woman in Fiction and in Fact: Fin de Siècle Feminisms*. New York: Palgrave/St. Martin's, 2000.

Wilmeth, Don, and Christopher Bigsby, eds. *The Cambridge History of American Theatre, Volume II, 1870-1945*. Cambridge, England: Cambridge University Press, 2000.

Tony A. Markham

WIELOPOLE/WIELOPOLE
An Exercise in Theatre

Author: Tadeusz Kantor (1915-1990)
Type of plot: Psychological
Time of plot: Post-World War II
Locale: Poland
First produced: 1980, at the Teatro Regional Toscano, Florence, Italy
First published: Wielopole, Wielopole, 1984 (English translation, 1990)

Principal characters:
UNCLE JÓZEF (THE PRIEST)
GRANDMA KATARZYNA
HELKA, the author's mother
MARIAN (RECRUIT I), the author's father
AUNTIE MAŃKA
YOU KNOW WHO
THE LITTLE RABBI
AUNTIE JÓZKA
UNCLE KAROL
UNCLE OLEK
UNCLE STAŚ, a deportee
ADAŚ (RECRUIT II)
WIDOW OF THE TOWN PHOTOGRAPHER
RECRUIT III
RECRUIT IV
RECRUIT V
RECRUIT VI
RECRUIT VII
RECRUIT VIII

The Play

At the beginning of *Wielopole, Wielopole*, the audience finds itself in what Tadeusz Kantor has described as the "poor room of my childhood" which forms the *mise en scène* of the majority of his original works. The playwright himself, although never appearing in his works as an actor, sits on the stage—as himself—and lends direction to the action.

Act 1 of the play is titled "The Wedding." The ceremony with which the play opens, however, is rather funereal: The Priest—Kantor's great-uncle—is lying on his death-bed. The family gathers itself around the dying man for a group portrait. The widow-photographer, however, turns her daguerreotype machine on a group of soldiers standing in the corner. As she begins to take their picture—with a demented laugh—her camera turns itself into a machine gun, and she proceeds to "shoot" at the platoon. The soldiers, who had before this moved around somewhat, freeze completely.

With the exit of the widow-photographer, the Priest rises from his deathbed to perform a marriage ceremony in which Kantor's father—also in uniform—and mother are wed. In his notes, Kantor calls this a "posthumous" wedding, and indeed, the actors are wooden, lifeless in repeating their vows.

Act 2, "Degradation," begins with a spooling action in which the family repeatedly move in and out of the "room." It seems as if they have not been in this locale for some time, as the twins Uncle Karol and Uncle Olek (once the "moving in and out" has been completed) quibble over the arrangement of furniture and people in the room, desirous of setting everything up "as it was then."

Mannequins as well as actors populate the stage in act 2. People are "doubled" just as the action of the play repeats itself: The playwright's father, Marian, whose wedding has just been reenacted in act 1, returns from the war front, to the general amazement of the family. Another long-lost relative who "returns" at this juncture is Uncle Staś, an officer in the Austrian army taken captive by the Russians and released in 1921. An artist, he returns now with a violin-box on his shoulder, which, when cranked, plays a Christmas carol from a scherzo by Frédéric Chopin.

The family turns on Marian, whom they accuse of abandoning and insulting Helka, the playwright's mother. Then, in a curious reversal, the family decides that since Marian has insulted Helka, they should follow suit. Thus takes shape the curious "degradation" scene which parodies the Palm Sunday litany. "Crucify Him! Crucify Him!" jeer the family, as Helka is degraded beneath a cross on wheels. The dead soldiers get into the act as well, tossing the mannequin-double of Helka high in the air and finally leaving it sprawled on the floor. The widow-photographer makes an appearance here in the person of Pilate, washing her hands with a dirty rag over the limp dummy. The act closes with the repeated wedding of Helka and Marian.

Act 3, "Crucifixion," begins in an almost clownish atmosphere, in which the twin uncles perform an absurd ritual of dressing and undressing themselves; while one dresses, the other undresses, and so on. The atmosphere changes shortly into one of impending doom as "possessed" Auntie Mańka begins to spit out fragments of Scripture. Through the doors, which open and close thrice in this act, the audience sees "Child-Soldiers" at an unusual game: They are busy nailing the effigy of the Priest to the wheeled cross. Meanwhile, uncles Olek and Karol set up three empty chairs in the middle of the room for no apparent purpose. Auntie Mańka now returns in a military uniform. After a short slapstick routine carried out by the uncles (in which they fail to achieve the desired result), Karol, Olek, and Mańka decide to arrange a "field tribunal" in which the Priest—and his mannequin—will appear as the accused. The crime they are accused of is "repetition."

The "real" priest, when discovered, will be the one to bear the weight of punishment, as it is he who is guilty of having a copy made of an "original" fashioned by God. The cross is brought in, and the Priest is made to carry it until he falls beneath its weight. Then it is raised on Helka's shoulders, and she carries it until she falls. Finally, little Adaś is made to bear the cross—in the end, he climbs up upon it. The family leaves the room sounding the wooden clappers—the "Wooden Bells of Death"— which in the Roman Catholic Church replace bells during Holy Week. The Priest carefully takes Adaś down from the cross, lays him upon the ground, and smoothes out his clothes. Adaś awakes and hurriedly exits, looking behind him. The Priest goes to sit at the foot of the cross, sorrowful; Kantor takes him by the hand and leads him offstage.

In act 4, "Adaś Goes to the Front," news reaches the family that the boy has been called to the colors. Each has his own opinion of the matter, some judging it good, some bad. In the next scenes, the audience discerns that time "has slipped foward": Adaś has fallen in battle, and the Priest carries in his gun and satchel—all that remains of him. Then the slanted, wheeled cross makes another appearance: The Priest wheels it about like a bicycle, with Adaś strapped to one side of it. The back wall opens to reveal a large number of recruits in a train heading east. The Priest carefully removes Adaś from the cross and flings his body into the boxcar. A quick handful of dirt tossed his way and an abbreviated requiem bring the act to a close.

Act 5, "The Last Supper," begins with the Priest laid out on his deathbed once again. The bed has two sides; with a crank, it can be turned over to reveal the Priest's mannequin. This is done over and over, the divided family fighting over which of the priests was their dearly beloved relative. Finally the Priest is given burial when the soldiers enter again, dragging the cross. The largest of them raises the cross on his shoulder (upon the cross is nailed the Priest-mannequin) and leads the rest in a circular march around the stage; the real Priest hurries after his double. Then the Little Rabbi enters and performs a "tingle-tangle" song of mourning, for which he is shot by the soldiers (again an event occurring out of temporal sequence—a "negative from later times").

The play ends with a rushed-together representation of Leonardo da Vinci's painting *The Last Supper*. Psalms, a loud march, and the mechanical strains from Uncle Staś's music box mix and rise over the scene. The actors slowly leave the stage; there remains only the Priest lying on the floor. The Little Rabbi comes in and leads him off. Kantor carefully folds the white tablecloth which has lain on *The Last Supper*'s long table, puts it beneath his arm, and leaves.

Themes and Meanings

Since drama is a living, syncretic art, which unites the expressive capabilities of the word, visual gesture, tempo, and even architecture, any summary of a play is doomed to be at best incomplete, at worst misleading. The problem is especially apparent when one turns to the dramas of Tadeusz Kantor. This dramatist, who was also a noted avant-garde painter, constructed his plays as visual canvases, in which sparsity of language and suggestive visual theatrics combine in a powerful, distilled alloy to effect the message the playwright wished to convey to his audience. A summary of a play by Tadeusz Kantor is about as effective as a verbal summary of a Flemish painting. Nevertheless, such a summary may provide insight into the philosophical underpinnings of Kantor's drama.

Critics often refer to Kantor's plays as "séances," following the subtitle of his first play, *Umarła klasa* (pr. 1975; *The Dead Class*, 1979). Deceased personages populate Kantor's stage. Their constant shuffling back and forth between their shadowy existence and the life-experience of the audience (the only "live" people in the theater, according to Kantor) is indicative of the playwright's distinctive conception of drama. In his plays, Kantor sought to evoke the interpenetration of the world of the living and the world of the dead. In the disjointed action of Kantor's theater, there is a curious, constant ebb and flow from one world into the other. For Kantor, the world of life is one's present state, where one is today. The world of the dead is memory, and the people preserved in it are the ghosts of that "other world" which constantly barge in on the living, usually haphazardly, often awkwardly, always urgently.

The very personal theater of Tadeusz Kantor, then, is an attempt to dramatize visually the intricate workings of memory. The "poor room of my childhood," elsewhere termed "the poor room of our imagination," can be seen as the artist's mind, through which flutter figures and events from the past. This explains the discontinuities in *Wielopole, Wielopole*, as well as the repetitions, which, at first glance, may seem to be redundant. Kantor did for theater what James Joyce did for the novel: He visualized the unpredictable processes of free association.

However, it would be unjust to say that Kantor "only" mapped the kaleidoscopic scenes of one's semiconscious reveries. He also showed how one passes judgment on people or events in memory, poeticizing them by interweaving particular memories with the large cultural and artistic heritage which affords people the archetypal signifying material with which they assign people and things a classifying meaning. For example, in *Wielopole, Wielopole*, Kantor does not simply rue the hard lot of his family, spun out in all directions by the centrifuge of history; he infuses it with a strong pathos by superimposing upon it themes from the Passion of Christ. To be sure, the Passion has lost all of its grandeur in *Wielopole, Wielopole*—all that remains is its great pain and pathos. There are no great, salvific messages to be drawn from the "Passion" of the family in Kantor's drama (as might be found in the works of the Polish Romantics, who were enamored of messianism); what is inescapable is their helplessness, made even more pathetic by their smallness, their generality.

Dramatic Devices

The first obvious dramatic device in *Wielopole, Wielopole* is the role of the playwright himself. Kantor's presence onstage—as himself, not as an actor—sympathizing with and to a certain extent directing his characters, suggests that the audience is somehow able to gaze into his mind as he sits engrossed in thought and "see what is going on in his head" in a very real sense.

The camera is a very important instrument, as far as Kantor is concerned. In taking a picture, one is freezing time. Freezing time is death. Thus, the primitive camera of the widow-photographer becomes a machine gun, an instrument of death which will people the world of memory with its negatives and prints. Indeed, Kantor elsewhere speaks of memory as a file of photographic negatives. Totally unrelated memories, distant from one another in space and time, mix themselves up in the mind (and on Kantor's stage) like photographic negatives placed one on top of the other. In *Wielopole, Wielopole* this accounts for the drastic shifts of time, such as Adaś's death and that of the Little Rabbi, which have apparently little to do with the train of thought going on presently, yet are summoned forth by the mysterious workings of mental association.

The Christian imagery in the play is obvious. Most striking in this connection is the final scene of the drama, when Kantor "strips the altar" as does the priest on Holy Thursday. However, whereas the Passion Week ends in triumph for Christ, in this play there is no Resurrection—or, if there is, it is a very dubious one indeed.

Critical Context

Tadeusz Kantor first gained recognition as an innovative director and radical theorist of drama. Like his compatriot Jerzy Grotowski, Kantor sought to infuse the modern theater with the primitive power of drama's origins. Kantor theorized that drama began when "someone stepped out of the circle of communal customs and religious ritual, communal ceremonies and ludic celebrations and made the hazardous decision to Break Away from the cult community." Modern drama, Kantor asserted, "must recapture the Original Force of the Trauma caused by the moment when Man (the viewer) was faced for the first time by Man (the Actor)." It is of the essence of drama as Kantor conceived of it to be heretical, subversive, indecent.

In part at least, such attitudes reflect the influence of Stanisław Ignacy Witkiewicz. In fact, until his first production of an original work, *The Dead Class*, Kantor was best known in Poland as a renowned producer of "Witkacy's" own brand of absurdist theater. However, Kantor's preoccupation with self-study was foreign to the earlier dramatist, and his unsettling approach to the supernatural (which, in the modern age, perhaps unfortunately, has come to be equated with the unconscious) placed him in the tradition of Polish "Monumental Theater," which stretches from Adam Mickiewicz to Stanisław Wyspiański and Leon Schiller. Still, Kantor was such a unique personage— a theatrical legend in his own time—that it is easier to use him as the critical context for modern Polish theater than it is to find the context which can encompass such an extraordinary talent as his.

Sources for Further Study

Gerould, Daniel. "Tadeusz Kantor (1915-): A Visual Artist Works Magic on the Polish Stage." *Performing Arts Journal* 4, no. 3 (1979): 28-38.

Jenkins, R. "Ring Master in a Circus of Dreams." *American Theatre* 2 (March, 1986): 4-11.

Kantor, Tadeusz. *A Journey Through Other Spaces: Essays and Manifestos, 1944-1990*. Edited and translated by Michael Kobiałka. Berkeley: University of California Press, 1993.

Kłossowicz, Jon. "Tadeusz Kantor's Journey." *Drama Review* 30 (Fall, 1986): 98-114.

Kobiałka, Michal. "Kantor—Candor: An Interview with Tadeusz Kantor." *Stages* 6, no. 6 (1986): 6-37.

Kott, Jan. "The Theatre of Essence: Kantor and Brook." *Theatre* 3 (Summer/Fall, 1983): 55-58.

Mikłaszewski, Krzysztof. *Encounters with Tadeusz Kantor.* Edited and translated by George Hyde. London: Routledge, 2002.

Charles S. Kraszewski

WINGS

Author: Arthur Kopit (1937-   )
Type of plot: Expressionist
Time of plot: The 1970's
Locale: A hospital and a convalescent hospital
First produced: 1977, as a radio play; 1978, at the Yale Repertory Theatre,
    New Haven, Connecticut
First published: 1978

> *Principal characters:*
> MRS. EMILY STILSON, a woman suffering a stroke
> AMY, her physical therapist

The Play

Wings is an attempt to portray the world as it appears to a person who has just suffered a stroke. Spoken thoughts, recorded voices, and fragmented images all help to create the chaotic perceptions of the leading character's mind. The "Prelude" to *Wings* begins with a simple picture: a cozy armchair in a pool of light with the sound of a clock ticking in the darkness. The lights fade, and when they return an elderly woman, Emily Stilson, is sitting in the armchair reading a book. The ticking sound is louder than before. Suddenly, Mrs. Stilson looks up and a portion of the setting disappears into the darkness. She tries to continue reading, and the clock skips a beat. The clock stops, and Mrs. Stilson drops her books and stares into space. The lights go to black.

Next a collage of images and sounds fills the stage. These consist of the images that Mrs. Stilson perceives, the sounds that surround her, and the words she thinks and speaks. The author clearly states that the particular order of these images and sounds will be developed in rehearsal. Visual images include dazzling whiteness, explosions of color, mirrors, and partial glimpses of doctors, nurses, and hospital equipment. The sounds include wind, random city noises, a siren "altered to resemble a woman screaming," incomprehensible questions, and endless echoing. At the same time, Mrs. Stilson's voice is heard questioning, reacting to her visions, describing her physical sensations, and attempting to determine a rational order.

The chaos fades to reveal Mrs. Stilson in a chair surrounded by darkness. Act 1, "Catastrophe," depicts her struggle to overcome the effects of the stroke. She struggles with her sense of isolation and her inability to identify clearly the sounds and images that surround her. In broken speech interspersed with moments of clarity and some totally incomprehensible series of words, she attempts to create order out of the chaos. Gradually the outside world begins to take form, and Mrs. Stilson exclaims, "Oh my God! Now I understand! THEY'VE GOT ME!"

In a series of short scenes, Mrs. Stilson gradually is able to piece together some sense of her world, although speech is still impossible and information is presented too randomly and rapidly for her to discern clear meanings. Struggling to explain her condition and her surroundings, she comes to the conclusion that she was flying a plane and crashed.

A doctor appears to work with Mrs. Stilson, asking her simple questions that she answers with a puzzling combination of correct answers and total nonsense. She begins to think that people are deliberately misleading her, and she becomes aware that her speech is muddled. "Everything I speak is wronged. SOMETHING HAS BEEN DONE TO ME!" In a moment of rage she briefly speaks with total clarity.

A therapist, Amy, begins to work with her. Mrs. Stilson can now manage to communicate, although sentences are still oddly organized and words sometimes escape her. Amy urges her to talk about the past, and Mrs. Stilson remembers a time when she flew planes and walked on the wings. In a dream, she remembers those days and is surprised to find herself in tears.

Act 2, subtitled "Exploration," begins in the recreation room of a rehabilitation center. Mrs. Stilson enters and struggles to maintain a line of thought through the interruptions of the outside stimuli. Amy is still with her, but now Mrs. Stilson is more aware of her own condition and begins to doubt if she will improve much. She wanders through a maze of passageways, encountering a series of voices ranging from intellectual, scientific discussions to simple questions and answers. This section concludes with a single musical tone as Mrs. Stilson recognizes that everyone there is just like her. Mrs. Stilson is introduced to some other patients in a group therapy situation. Each of them is at a different stage of progress, and Mrs. Stilson becomes aware of the work it will take to improve. For the first time, she acknowledges thoughts of death.

Further therapy with Amy provides more improvement. Mrs. Stilson relates an adventure in which her son came to visit and took her out to see airplanes. She tells of sitting in the cockpit of the plane and having her hands know how to fly without any conscious awareness on her part. She says that she was crying "and then all at once— it remembered everything!" After a long pause, she adds "But now it doesn't."

Mrs. Stilson's improvement is matched by a growing rapport with Amy, and the two women share moments of laughter as well as the struggle. One day, as they share a quiet moment outside, Mrs. Stilson tells of a dream in which a person—she does not know if it was a man or woman—came over to her bed and whispered "Emily . . . we're glad you changed your mind," and then left. At that point, she claims, she left her body, floating on the ceiling and looking down on herself lying in the bed.

Abruptly, Amy recedes into the darkness and Mrs. Stilson recognizes that she is somewhere else. In fact, she is in a plane. She asks herself, "Is it . . . remembering?" She concludes that "No . . . no, I'm simply there again!" She is flying a plane, and she is lost. She sees faint lights below and drops down searching for a place to land. She finds a tiny town, totally deserted. She circles, knowing that fuel is short and that she may crash. She circles, afraid to leave and go back into empty blackness. She knows she must leave and pulls the nose up with great effort and finds herself in the dark, and not even scared. "God, but it was wonderful! Awful scary sometimes, though!"

Amy appears in the distance calling for Emily. A sudden sound is heard, Mrs.

Stilson gasps, and Amy disappears. Mrs. Stilson pauses, says, "Thank you," and the lights go to black.

Themes and Meanings

Wings is essentially a study of the disruption of a normal human life as the consequence of a stroke. Beyond this obvious theme, however, Arthur Kopit's play explores more universal concerns including the power of language, the isolation of the individual, and the meaning of "self."

The entire structure of the play is designed to allow the audience to experience to some degree the disorientation that Mrs. Stilson feels and thus identify with the pain and anguish of the disabled. The use of darkness as an isolating factor, the inability to distinguish external stimuli, the failure of memory, and the inadequacy of speech to express one's ideas all contribute to Mrs. Stilson's isolation and her inability to control her own life. It is Mrs. Stilson's struggle against these unnameable and thus unknowable forces that forms the central action of the play.

This struggle is not an easy one. From a fear of total loss of self, even to the point of physical fragmentation ("Where's my arm? I don't have an arm! What's an arm?"), through periods of feeling like a victim and a prisoner in an alien world, Mrs. Stilson grasps at moments that allow her to verify her own existence. At the beginning of act 1 she can say "I am still intact," and by the end of that act she realizes that *she* has changed, not the external world ("I can't make it do it like it used to").

She experiences "dream" or "memory" moments when she is freed from her condition because "no one talks here" and thus gains further faith in a self that does not rely on language. She gains some temporary relief from her awareness that there are others who are "just like me." Such relief is not satisfactory, however, and she begins to think that death might be a better alternative. Temporary breakthroughs, such as the episode in the airplane, are as painful as they are rewarding, for they reveal the temporary nature of such clarity and integration of self even more clearly. Her final step is an acceptance not only of her condition, but also of her own death.

This struggle has universal implications as well, for Mrs. Stilson's condition can be viewed as an analogy to modern life. The experience of isolation—of not fully being able to comprehend or organize the external world—and of the failure of language to bridge the gaps that isolate individuals from one another is all a part of existence. Kopit's play is not totally negative, however, for underneath the struggle and the pain is the recognition that human beings are more than their limited vocabularies can express. They all share the knowledge that words cannot fully convey their experience; they may function as the legs of their minds, but not as the wings of their soul.

Dramatic Devices

Wings employs a wide range of dramatic devices to portray the inner experience of the leading character. The structure of the play is fluid, with no clear demarcation between scenes. It allows the audience to experience Mrs. Stilson's temporal and physical world, in which time is no longer linear and in which space is no longer discrete.

She moves without warning forward and backward in time and "discovers" herself in a different space rather than consciously moving from place to place. At the same time, the play maintains its cohesiveness by projecting a fundamental sense of progression. There is a forward movement in time, but it is not a direct path. At the same time, Arthur Kopit does not allow the play to become random or structureless. He interweaves some scenes that are traditional representational drama with people interacting in normal ways while time and space remain discrete. Such scenes occur with more regularity as the play progresses, paralleling Mrs. Stilson's recovery.

Much of the play's effectiveness is accomplished through the use of set, lighting, and sound. Kopit describes the set as a system of black scrim panels that move silently and easily to create featureless corridors. Some are mirrored to multiply and refract images. These panels serve at times to surround Mrs. Stilson in a black void. At other times, characters appear behind the panels, clearly separated from Mrs. Stilson's world. Alternatively, the panels can open to provide a sense of being outdoors. The silent speed and ease is essential in maintaining the fluidity of time and space the play requires. Kopit's use of these devices is clearly demonstrated near the end of act 1. A doctor and nurse appear behind the screens, separated from Mrs. Stilson and yet acting as though they were directly beside her. While the doctor and nurse struggle to calm the "physical" presence which the audience cannot see, the audience views the "inner" Mrs. Stilson in front of the screens.

Lighting is used dramatically in the opening scene in which Mrs. Stilson's chair is separated by a void of darkness from the table which would normally sit next to it, thus emphasizing her separation from the physical world. Lighting also allows objects and people to appear and disappear as they move in and out of Mrs. Stilson's consciousness. A symbolic use of light is seen in the presence of a cool, blue light to indicate Mrs. Stilson's "dream" or "memory" episodes.

Sound is used to produce a further sense of Mrs. Stilson's fragmented perception. At one point, a "cacophony of sounds heard from all around, both live and from the speakers" is used to convey Mrs. Stilson's impressions as she is moved through the hospital. At other times, music, single tones, the sound of bells, and a sound of "something flapping rapidly" are used to indicate fleeting impressions and awarenesses. All elements are well integrated with the spoken dialogue. Far more than most plays, however, *Wings* is dependent on the full range of theatrical tools, and the use of each element is essential to the production.

Critical Context

Arthur Kopit has generally been considered a part of the Theater of the Absurd movement from his first commercial success, *Oh Dad, Poor Dad, Mama's Hung You in the Closet and I'm Feelin' So Sad: A Pseudoclassical Tragifarce in a Bastard French Tradition* (pr., pb. 1960). In the final moment of the play, Madame Rosepettle enters the bedroom to find that her son, Jonathan, has just killed the young woman who attempted to seduce him as he lay draped over his father's corpse. Surveying this chaos, she asks "What is the meaning of this?" The impossibility of any reasonable answer is precisely the absurdist's point.

The failure of language as a means of communication is introduced in the character of Jonathan, who cannot speak without stammering. This issue is taken to an extreme in *The Day the Whores Come out to Play Tennis* (pr., pb. 1965) as a group of men aimlessly debate methods of getting rid of the women who have taken over the tennis courts of their country club. Finally, in *Wings*, Mrs. Stilson questions the very structure and validity of language.

The question of personal identity or authenticity is pursued in *Chamber Music* (pb. 1965). A group of women incarcerated in an insane asylum meet to take action to curb a series of hostile incidents. In the cast list, the women are identified only by external qualities, and the question of personal identity is further complicated by the fact that each woman has chosen to role-play a historical heroine. In *Indians* (pr. 1968), William Cody struggles to distinguish himself from his professional identity as Buffalo Bill, and Sitting Bull fears that he has become the white man's image of him. *Indians* also addresses this issue on a national scale. Kopit questions basic American myths of altruism, moral superiority, and technological prowess by showing that those very qualities were used to justify the destruction of the Native Americans. Although early reviews do not mention it, later critical studies have noted the direct analogy to the American experience in Vietnam.

Kopit's determined aversion to representational drama corroborates his perception of the stage as a place for exaggeration and grotesquery. He is influenced by Brechtian concepts in which the aim is to alienate the audience to the degree that they will not identify with the characters but will be forced to consider the issues or ideas.

Although Kopit utilizes many techniques that have been labeled "absurdist," it is essential that such a tag not place arbitrary boundaries on his work. Although he shares some elements of absurdist thought, Kopit's plays do not accept the negativity or passivity that so often characterize absurdist drama. As in the case of Mrs. Stilson, there is a base recognition of personal identity, an acceptance of personal responsibility, and a positive movement toward integration and understanding.

Sources for Further Study

Auerbach, Doris. *Sam Shepard, Arthur Kopit and the Off-Broadway Theater.* Boston: Twayne, 1982.

Kopit, Arthur. "The Vital Matter of Environment." *Theatre Arts* 45 (April, 1961): 12-13.

Myers, Norman J. "Two Kinds of Alaska: Pinter and Kopit Journey Through Another Realism." *Pinter Review*, 1992-1993, 11-19.

Rose, Carol. "Killing Pain in the End Beds." In *Plays of Impasse.* Princeton, N.J.: Princeton University Press, 1983.

Secrest, Meryle. "'Out West' with Kopit." *Washington Post*, April 20, 1969, p. K1.

Weales, Gerald. "Arthur Kopit." In *Contemporary Dramatists.* 6th ed. Detroit: St. James, 1999.

John C. Watson

THE WINSLOW BOY

Author: Terence Rattigan (1911-1977)
Type of plot: Problem play
Time of plot: Shortly before the outbreak of World War I
Locale: The drawing room of a home in Courtfield Gardens, South Kensington, London
First produced: 1946, at the Lyric Theater, London
First published: 1946

> *Principal characters:*
> ARTHUR WINSLOW, head of the household, a retired businessman about sixty years old, formerly employed by the Westminster Bank
> GRACE WINSLOW, about fifty years old, Arthur's wife and mother of Dickie, Catherine, and Ronnie
> RONNIE WINSLOW, their son, a cadet at the Royal Navy School, Osborne
> RICHARD "DICKIE" WINSLOW, Ronnie's older brother, an undergraduate at Oxford
> CATHERINE WINSLOW, Ronnie's older sister, about thirty years old
> VIOLET, a housekeeper for the Winslow family
> JOHN WATHERSTONE, about thirty years old, Catherine's suitor
> DESMOND CURRY, the Winslow family solicitor, also interested in Catherine
> SIR ROBERT MORTON, a prominent solicitor who defends Ronnie Winslow

The Play

Act 1 opens in a drawing room of a home in Courtfield Gardens in South Kensington, London, in July, during a year not long before the outbreak of World War I in 1914. Ronnie Winslow, a cadet at the Royal Navy School at Osborne, returns unexpectedly from his school on a Sunday and is greeted by Violet, the family's housekeeper. Ronnie is obviously depressed. His parents, Arthur and Grace Winslow, his brother Dickie, and sister Catherine are attending church services but return home shortly. Unaware that Ronnie has returned home, the other members of the family discuss Dickie's lack of seriousness in his studies at Oxford. Arthur compares Dickie unfavorably with his younger brother's intellectual achievements at Osborne; Dickie is defensive in refuting these statements. The conversation turns to Catherine's pending engagement to John Watherstone, a subaltern in the British army; the Winslows support Catherine's decision to marry John. They express concern over the impact of the news on Catherine's other suitor, Desmond Curry.

The conversation is interrupted when Grace sees someone hiding in the garden; the doorbell rings and John Watherstone enters. After giving directions to Catherine on how to signal them at the appropriate time, Arthur greets John to discuss his proposal to Catherine. Surprisingly, Arthur knows the details of John's salary and his monthly allowance from his father. Arthur then reviews the details of his own financial affairs and announces that he intends to provide Catherine with a dowry of twelve hundred fifty pounds. As the family discusses the engagement, Ronnie Winslow is noticed in the garden; the family learns that Ronnie has been expelled from Osborne for stealing a postal order. Arthur confronts his son, who denies the theft. Act 1 closes with Arthur placing a phone call to the Royal Naval College, Osborne.

Act 2 opens six months later in the family drawing room with Catherine and Dickie having a conversation, when the daily newspaper arrives with two letters to the editor on the case of the Osborne cadet. By this time Arthur's efforts to vindicate his son's denial have become a public issue. While some indicate support for the government's position that this matter is much about nothing, there is considerable criticism of the Royal Navy's initial handling of the case and allegations of a conspiracy designed to save face for those involved in the decision. The conversation between Catherine and Dickie reflects the feminist issues of the period when Catherine hears them refer to what is appropriate for a woman to say. The conversation is interrupted when Arthur arrives, and while his spirits are good, the struggle in support of Ronnie has taken a toll on Arthur's health. After confronting Dickie about his lack of academic progress at Oxford, Arthur announces that he will no longer be able to support him for another year and that Dickie needs to get a job. The cost of the case and the prospect of retaining Sir Robert Morton have drained the Winslow family finances.

Ronnie returns from school with accounts of his recent successes and appears to be oblivious about the impact of the case on his father's health and the family's finances. Catherine indicates her dislike for Sir Robert Morton, but Arthur asserts that the fortunes of the family are in his capable hands. Sir Robert Morton arrives at the Winslow home and meets Catherine; immediately, Sir Robert and Catherine are engaged in an animated conversation about the case and each other's interests.

The last and most important section of this act consists of a conversation between Ronnie and Sir Robert Morton. In response to a lengthy series of pointed questions, which amount to an interrogation, Ronnie provides Morton with a detailed account of the incident and the subsequent developments. This second act closes with Sir Robert Morton informing Arthur that he will take the case because it is obvious that Ronnie is innocent.

Act 3 opens nine months later in the drawing room of the Winslow home. Arthur is reading an account of a debate in the House of Commons, where the Admiralty was forced to respond to questions concerning its procedures in handling the case and where Arthur's request for a Petition of Right was being considered. Advocates for the Winslows argued that the House of Commons should "Let Right be Done," the focus for justice in this case. Sir Robert Morton provides Arthur with a report on the progress of the case. In addition to the details, it is evident that Sir Robert and Catherine are interested in each other.

Sir Robert advances a new strategy intended to result in action from the Director of Public Prosecutions, but Arthur is inclined to give up the case because of the many sacrifices that have been made. Catherine reveals that John Watherstone's father sent a letter to Arthur stating that the attack on the Admiralty in the Commons was a disgrace and implying that the engagement may be terminated. Catherine maintains that, even if Colonel Watherstone's threat includes ending John's allowance, they would be able to survive as a married couple.

Shortly, John Watherstone arrives and is visibly upset over his father's threat to end his allowance to thwart the wedding. John and Catherine discuss the case and its impact on their relationship; she learns that he is more concerned with his allowance than justice and appears to agree with his father. A telephone call to Sir Robert provides information on a new development; unexpectedly, the debate on the Winslow case has resumed in the Commons and the Admiralty has agreed reluctantly to endorse the Petition of Right, advancing the case to a trial. Without question, Catherine supports continuing the case. The act closes with John Watherstone departing in a rage.

Act 4 opens in the Winslow drawing room in June, four months later. Dickie has arrived for the closing of the trial. The press and interested onlookers have besieged the Winslow home. The dense family solicitor, Desmond Curry, who has been providing minor assistance to Sir Robert, arrives and proposes to Catherine. Arthur urges his daughter to reject the proposal. As Arthur and Catherine discuss Desmond and John Watherstone's upcoming marriage to someone else, news arrives that the court has decided that Ronnie Winslow was innocent and that Arthur Winslow's effort for the Petition of Right was vindicated. The act closes with a conversation between Catherine and Sir Robert in which they demonstrate that they both possess intelligence and wit and suggest that they will have contact in the future.

Themes and Meanings

The Winslow Boy was based on a famous case involving George Archer-Shee, a student at the Royal Navy College at Osborne in 1908. He was accused of stealing a five-shilling postal money order and was expelled immediately. Outraged, his father, Martin Archer-Shee, was determined to vindicate his son and the family name and initiated a legal battle that was considered in the House of Commons and the Court of the King's Bench. After his expulsion from Osborne, George Archer-Shee returned to Stonyhurst College, where he had previously been enrolled. The focal point of this case was the Archer-Shee argument that the British military as an arm of the Crown could not be sued. The plaintiffs had to obtain a special dispensation from the king that stated "Let Right Be Done," so that the case could be advanced; contemporaries viewed it as a conflict between justice and the rights of office. By October, 1910, Archer-Shee had been vindicated and received an apology from the First Lord of the Admiralty and damages of seven thousand pounds. During the two years of the Archer-Shee case, it was widely reported and discussed in the press. While the Archer-Shee family prevailed, the experience took a toll on the family. Martin suffered severe stress and died in 1913, and George worked for an American firm on Wall Street between 1912 and 1914, joined the British Army as a lieutenant after the outbreak of World War I in August 1914, and was in killed in action in October, 1914.

Terence Rattigan wrote *The Winslow Boy* immediately following the close of World War II. Most of his colleagues urged him to avoid writing such a play; they argued that audiences would be bored with it. Nonetheless, Rattigan was intrigued by the issue of "right" and pursued his project. The resulting play develops the theme of justice and the impact of its pursuit on an upper-middle-class family. Family loyalty, persistence in pursuing the truth, and human frailties are the essential themes in the play's subtext.

Dramatic Devices

Rattigan maintained that plays should be focused on people and not on artificially construed plots. In *The Winslow Boy* Rattigan retained a few of the developments from the Archer-Shee case: the prolonged struggle for a trial, the actual case history, and the interview of Ronnie by the solicitor at home. The remainder was created for dramatic effect, including Catherine's relationships and the hardships of the case on the family. Rattigan was criticized for sentimentality and for producing a rather boring play. These critics failed to recognize that Rattigan's success with *The Winslow Boy* was achieved by his craft in developing a classic tale of the conflict between individuals and the state and about the triumph of "right." In a turbulent age of mass culture and big government, a determined family prevailed because they were "right." Perhaps the most surprising dramatic device that Rattigan employed was his avoidance of any trial scene and his sustaining the central plot developments within the Winslows' drawing room.

Critical Context

Terence Rattigan emerged as a writer of comedy and light plays in Britain during the 1930's. His most significant play during the pre-World War II era was *French Without Tears* (pr. 1936, pb. 1937). During World War II, Rattigan wrote a series of pro-British plays in support of the war effort: *Love in Idleness* (pr. 1944, pb. 1945) and *Flare Path* (pr., pb. 1942) were representative of his works during the early 1940's. As the war closed, Rattigan became interested in writing a screen script based on the Archer-Shee case. The result was *The Winslow Boy*, which paved the way for Rattigan's acceptance as a serious playwright.

The Winslow Boy captured the interests of critics and the public and proved to be a turning point in Rattigan's career: It opened to acclaim in both London and New York. In 1948 a film adaptation of *The Winslow Boy* was produced. In 1999, playwright David Mamet produced another film version of *The Winslow Boy* starring Nigel Hawthorne, Jeremy Northam, Rebecca Pidgeon, and Gemma Jones. While some critics charged Rattigan with pandering to "middle-class standards," others applauded his craftsmanship as a master of the "problem play." In the last three decades of his life, Rattigan wrote a series of acclaimed plays: *Playbill: The Browning Version and Harlequinade* (pr. 1948, pb. 1949), *Separate Tables: Table by the Window and Table Number Seven* (pr. 1954, pb. 1955), *Ross* (pr., pb. 1960), *A Bequest to the Nation* (pr., pb. 1970), *In Praise of Love* (pb. 1973, pr. 1974), and *Cause Célèbre* (pr. 1977, pb. 1978).

Sources for Further Study

Darlow, Michael. *Terence Rattigan: The Man and His Work.* Rev. ed. London: Quartet Books, 2000.

O'Connor, Sean. *Straight Acting: Popular Gay Drama from Wilde to Rattigan.* London: Cassell, 1998.

Rusinko, Susan. *Terence Rattigan.* Boston: Twayne, 1983.

Wansell, Geoffrey. *Terence Rattigan.* New York: St. Martin's Press, 1997.

Young, Bertram A. *The Rattigan Version: Sir Terence Rattigan and the Theatre of Character.* New York: Atheneum, 1988.

William T. Walker

WIT

Author: Margaret Edson (1961-   )
Type of plot: Social realism
Time of plot: The 1990's
Locale: A university hospital in the United States
First produced: 1995, at the South Coast Repertory Second Stage Theater, Costa Mesa, California
First published: 1999

Principal characters:
VIVIAN BEARING, a professor of English
HARVEY KELEKIAN, the chief of oncology at the university hospital
JASON POSNER, a clinical fellow at the university hospital
SUSIE MONAHAN, a nurse in the cancer inpatient unit
E. M. ASHFORD, a retired professor of English
MR. BEARING, Vivian's father

The Play

Wit dramatizes the last days of a renowned professor of English, who is dying of ovarian cancer. As the play opens, Vivian Bearing, a noted scholar specializing in the study of Metaphysical poet John Donne's holy sonnets, is alone onstage in hospital garb, attached to an IV pole. Her opening lines and many others thereafter are addressed directly to the audience, to whom she describes her reactions as she learns of the progress of her disease. Her physician, Harvey Kelekian, a renowned oncologist, enters and, in an exchange that Vivian can hardly follow, suggests a series of strong and potentially painful chemical injections to arrest her cancer. Although she agrees to the procedure, it is clear that she and Kelekian have a strained relationship. He proposes treatment because "it will make a significant contribution to our research," while she accepts treatment to show her independence and toughness.

The scene shifts back in time to Vivian's undergraduate years, when she was the protégé of the great English scholar E. M. Ashford. While Vivian looks up to Ashford as the model of a strong woman, Ashford seems interested only in sharpening Vivian's focus on literary study. Lecturing her on the requirements of word choice, punctuation, and wordplay, Ashford teaches Vivian that to succeed in academe, one must master the arcane knowledge and specialized vocabulary that will be accepted by academic peers.

Back in the present, Vivian undergoes a series of medical tests conducted by technicians, who understand only the rote procedures of medical care. She discovers that the clinical fellow working with Kelekian at the hospital is Jason Posner, a former undergraduate in her Metaphysical poetry class. Jason subjects her to a grueling inquiry into family and medical history and eventually conducts a physical examination that Vivian finds particularly degrading, as it is performed by a former student.

The central scenes of the drama display Vivian's deteriorating condition. She is repeatedly poked and prodded not only by physicians but also by interns, who see her as a classic case study in the invidious effects of disease. Despite the efforts of the medical staff and of her nurse, Susie Monahan, the cancer resists treatment and continues to spread throughout her body. At the same time, Vivian explains to the audience how her confinement in the hospital has made her aware of her isolated existence as a professor. The joy she has taken in explicating Donne's works has been earned at the expense of friendships.

In a key scene that gives the audience insight into her character, Vivian describes "the very hour of the very day" when she knew "words would be my life's work." In a flashback, she recalls her fifth birthday, when, while reading a fable to her father, she became enamored of the word "soporific." What the audience notices is the interplay between father and daughter: The enthusiasm of the child, who discovers how words convey both action and feeling, is contrasted with the restraint of the adult, who gently leads her to awareness but refrains from expressing a shared feeling of joy in her discovery.

As Vivian falls further into the grip of the disease, she struggles to recapture some sense of the dignity and power she experienced in her own milieu, the university classroom. To demonstrate her power in that realm, she lectures the audience on Donne's "Holy Sonnet V," reciting the textual history of the poem, citing important modern criticism, and explaining the interplay between God and the speaker. In the midst of the imaginary lecture, however, she is whisked away for more tests, becoming once again a pawn in the hands of hospital staff.

Following her tests, in a conversation with Jason, Vivian finally glimpses what has been wrong with her life as a scholar. Jason is intent on gathering data for his research and seems unaffected by the knowledge that his patient and former teacher will soon die. "Do you ever miss people?" she asks him. While he says he does, his behavior makes it clear that he is merely humoring her to keep her stable for further medical analysis. Immediately thereafter, Vivian imagines herself talking to her students about Donne's poetry. Her unflinching demands on them demonstrate that she has treated them as Professor Ashford, Doctor Kelekian, and Jason now treat her.

The nurse Susie interrupts Vivian's reverie to discuss the hospital's policy regarding resuscitation in case of the failure of major organs. Vivian opts not to be resuscitated, and Susie marks "DNR" (do not resuscitate) on her chart. While heavily sedated, Vivian experiences a final flashback: She is visited by Professor Ashford, who, instead of talking of literature, climbs into bed and reads to her the same fable that Vivian read to her father when she was five years old.

When Vivian's vital signs fail, Jason ignores the DNR notation on her chart and calls in a team to try to keep her alive. Only when hospital personnel force him to rescind the order does he back away, disappointed that he may not be able to continue his research. As the staff cleans up the room following the pronouncement of death,

Vivian rises from her hospital bed, raises her arms, and disrobes, the light bathing her as a sign that she is moving from this world to the next.

Themes and Meanings

By drawing parallels between the world of academe and the world of medicine, Margaret Edson demonstrates that there are many ways for professionals to isolate inadvertently those they purport to serve. Clearly, hospital patients, no matter what their status in society, are lost amid the corridors of machinery, operating suites, and examination rooms. Further, patients are unable to comprehend some of the most basic information about their condition; the language that is clear to physicians evokes terror in those unable to break the code. What is important to note, however, is that Edson intends her viewers to see that all who are caught up in matters of self-interest are cutting themselves off from others, weaving a cocoon of isolation that will eventually choke off their own humanity.

It may be easy to see *Wit* as an indictment of the medical profession. The doctors who treat Vivian consider her more an object for scientific study than a human being facing the inevitability of her own death. Repeatedly, Kelekian and Posner stress the importance of their treatments as a means of gathering data for their research. Both treat Vivian with condescension and occasional disdain. Neither seems to have time to comfort her or allay her fears.

A careful review reveals, however, that it is not simply the medical profession that Edson criticizes. Vivian and her mentor, E. M. Ashford, are as arrogant with their students as the doctors are with their patients. Undergraduates seem to be impediments to the intellectual happiness of the faculty, and only when one of the students displays some promise does he or she merit grudging attention. At one point in the play, Kelekian has slight praise for his protégé, Jason. Similarly, in an early scene, Ashford acknowledges that Vivian has the potential to ascend to the professoriat but only if she applies herself to study at the expense of all other activities.

Edson stresses that knowledge without human relationships is sterile and ultimately deadly. Good relationships involve the recognition of personal dignity, the willingness to understand others, and the ability to extend forgiveness. At the beginning of the play, Vivian possesses great personal dignity but little understanding of others and virtually no ability to forgive others' mistakes. From the first scene, however, she is presented in a degraded state, wandering the hospital corridors in flimsy robes, a baseball cap covering her bald head. Although she is apprehensive even in the first scene, she is unable to engage in serious conversation with anyone because she insists on playing on the meaning of words, seeing double entendres and allusions even in the most sobering analyses of her condition. She discovers, much to her dismay, that she is unable to communicate directly with the hospital staff because their precise vocabulary is as arcane as that of her favorite Metaphysical poet.

Because *Wit* is the story of a strong-willed, powerful woman having to face her own death, the play also rivets one's attention on the value of life itself. Although Vivian is quite capable of achieving success on her own terms and without help in the academic world, she is unable to control events at the hospital. The movement from the vexation to the helplessness that she feels as death approaches suggests that there are forces over which even the most powerful men and women can exercise no control.

Dramatic Devices

Written to be staged without scene breaks or an intermission, *Wit* displays the inexorable progress of the protagonist toward a death that she is powerless to prevent. Though the action cuts back and forth between past and present, there is always a sense of inevitability created by the dialogue and transitions from initial scenes involving exploratory diagnosis to the final, hectic scene in which the hospital staff tries to resuscitate Vivian.

Edson also makes excellent use of flashbacks, moving the action from the present back to key periods in Vivian's life to illustrate why she became isolated and where she missed opportunities to demonstrate her humanity. In this fashion, *Wit* resembles Arthur Miller's *Death of a Salesman* (pr., pb. 1949), a play that skillfully melds past and present to dramatize the tragic end of the life of the protagonist, Willie Loman.

Edson herself has said on more than one occasion that the play presents the tragedy of isolation in modern society. The concept of "wit" serves as the principal device for dramatizing that sense of isolation. The eighteenth century man of letters, Samuel Johnson, gave the term its modern literary definition: "a combination of dissimilar images, or discovery of occult resemblances in things apparently unlike." The specific kind of wit practiced by John Donne and his contemporaries among the Metaphysical poets informs Edson's critique of modern society. Taking two highly specialized professions, medicine and literary studies, she demonstrates how professionals caught up in their work not only develop a coded language almost impervious to outsiders but also frequently behave with disdain toward those not possessing the specialized knowledge that they have mastered.

The play is an extended exercise in metaphysical wit, constantly comparing two dissimilar professions: one highly regarded by the general public, one usually perceived as ephemeral and of little use to mainstream society. What Edson demonstrates in *Wit* is that there are more similarities than differences between the practice of medicine and the practice of literary study. Both, when raised to the level of an intellectual game, actually harm society by devaluing personal relationships. The pedantry in Vivian's insistence that students understand the significance of Donne's use of a comma rather than a semicolon in the final line of his sonnet "Death Be Not Proud" shares chilling similarities with the inhumane conversations among research physicians and their interns at the bedside of dying patients.

Critical Context

As drama, *Wit* approaches the form of Shakespearean tragedy, appearing at times to be comedic but moving inevitably toward its predetermined end. It is not Vivian Bearing's death that makes the play tragic, however, but her failure to realize, until it is too late, how much of her life she has wasted in pursuing knowledge at the expense of personal relationships. This particularly modern theme resonates with audiences because modern American society has placed such emphasis on professional accomplishment as a means of establishing self-worth.

Wit won the 1999 Pulitzer Prize in drama, the New York Drama Critics Award, the Lucille Lortel Award, the Drama Desk Award, and the Outer Critics' Circle Award. It is Edson's first play, and she stated to numerous reviewers and reporters that she would not pursue a career as a dramatist and would remain a kindergarten teacher. Nevertheless, the critical acclaim that met the production when it first debuted in California, the consistent praise it received from New York critics, and the continuing interest further productions generated in cities across the country suggest that the play strikes a chord with playgoers that will give *Wit* staying power on the American stage.

Sources for Further Study

Iannone, Carol. "Donne Undone." *First Things: The Journal of Religion and Public Life* 100 (February, 2000): 12-14.

Kanfer, Stefan. "Leaps of Faith." *New Leader* 81 (October 5-October 19, 1998): 22-23.

Philip, Abraham, MD. "*Wit:* A Play." *JAMA* 283 (June 28, 2000): 3261.

Simon, John. "Well Done." *New York* 31 (September 28, 1998): 78-79.

Sulmasy, Daniel P. "At Wit's End: Dignity, Forgiveness, and the Care of the Dying." *Journal of General Internal Medicine* 16 (2001): 335-338.

Laurence W. Mazzeno

THE WOMEN

Author: Clare Boothe Luce (1903-1987)
Type of plot: Satire; women's
Time of plot: The 1930's
Locale: New York City and Reno, Nevada
First produced: 1936, at the Ethel Barrymore Theatre, New York City
First published: 1937

>   *Principal characters:*
>   MARY HAINES, a society wife and mother
>   SYLVIA FOWLER, a society wife and malicious gossip
>   EDITH POTTER, a pregnant society wife
>   NANCY BLAKE, a professional writer
>   LITTLE MARY, the daughter of Mary and Stephen Haines
>   MRS. MOREHEAD, Mary Haines's mother
>   CRYSTAL ALLEN, Stephen Haines's mistress
>   PEGGY DAY, a recently married society girl
>   COUNTESS DE LAGE, an aging society woman
>   JANE, Mary's Irish American maid
>   MAGGIE, Mary's cook
>   MIRIAM, a flashy young woman involved with Sylvia's husband

The Play

The first act of this two-act play, presented in seven scenes, shows the destruction of Mary Haines's marriage. When the curtain opens, Mary is absent. Four women sit playing bridge, smoking and gossiping as Sylvia Fowler complains about her husband. He expects her to stay home and keep house despite their wealth and servants. The other players include the young Peggy; Nancy, a writer; and Edith, a colorless and sloppy woman unhappily pregnant. When Edith leaves the room, Sylvia tells the others of Edith's husband's unfaithfulness. Sylvia has also heard that Stephen Haines has a mistress. By the end of the scene, Sylvia plans to take Mary to the beauty shop, where Mary will hear about her husband. The second scene takes place in that shop. Nancy, a professional woman whose next book, she later suggests, will be titled *Gone with the Ice-Man* or *Sex Has No Place in the Home*, tries to convince Mary that appearance does not matter if a man loves a woman, but Mary accepts the superficial values of her other friends. She stays, and a manicurist, making conversation, reveals Stephen's affair with Crystal Allen. In the third scene, in Mary's sitting room, her mother, Mrs. Morehead, tries to persuade her to ignore the affair. Mrs. Morehead whisks her daughter off to Bermuda.

In the fourth scene, two months later, Mary has returned and meets Crystal in a dressmaker's shop. Sylvia, upset by Mary's acceptance of the situation, hints that

Crystal will alienate the affections of Mary's children. This is pure malice: In a later scene, it is obvious that Crystal wants nothing to do with the Haines children. Sylvia's suggestion, however, causes Mary to ignore her mother's advice and to confront Crystal. Sylvia keeps Mary's friends informed, and, in scene 5, in a beauty shop, Edith reveals that she told a newspaper gossip columnist about the Haines's marriage. She claims to have forgotten she was talking with a gossip columnist. The affair now is made public, and Mary feels compelled to confront Stephen. In scene 6, Mary's maid, an Irish American girl, Jane, and the new cook, Maggie, discuss the confrontation during which Mary felt it necessary to ask for a divorce. Marriage, Maggie points out, exists for the family, not for the pleasure of husband and wife. By scene 7, however, Mary is packed to leave for Reno, Nevada, then the only American city where divorces could be obtained easily and relatively quickly. She does not want a divorce, but, thanks to her friends and the values of her social world, she feels she must obtain one.

The second act, made up of five scenes, begins in the room where Edith is recovering from childbirth. She complains of her misery. Her nurse cannot persuade Edith to refrain from smoking while nursing, so Edith carelessly drips cigarette ash onto the head of her newborn. Peggy enters to explain that she and her husband are getting a divorce and that Howard Fowler has thrown the unfaithful Sylvia out of the house. In the second scene, the women meet again in Reno, where they are joined by the Countess de Lage, who is looking for a fourth husband although two of her earlier husbands have tried to murder her. Miriam, a flashy young girl, advises the countess to take her current boyfriend Buck to Hollywood and make him a star. Sylvia enters, complaining about her abandonment, but a gossip column reveals that her husband will marry Miriam. Sylvia physically attacks Miriam. Mary throws out Sylvia. Peggy has announced that she is pregnant, so Mary calls Peggy's husband and sends Peggy back to New York. When Stephen calls Mary, she is prepared to admit the divorce is an error, but it is too late. He is to marry Crystal the next day.

The last three scenes take place back in New York. The first is set in Crystal's trashily decorated bathroom, where she is talking on the phone to Buck, her lover and the countess's new husband. She also makes plans for Stephen, whether Stephen likes the plans or not, and tries to force Little Mary into a show of affection. Instead, the child criticizes Crystal's vulgar taste and reveals Stephen's increasing dissatisfaction. Sylvia, prowling in Crystal's bedroom, finds a key to the apartment where Crystal meets her lover, recognizing the key because Sylvia and her own lover met at the same place.

The fourth scene takes place in Mary's bedroom. It has been two years since Mary and her friends have gone Reno, and they have just returned from an anniversary dinner. The other women want to go on to a nightclub, but Mary, who, to the despair even of her mother, is still mourning the loss of Stephen, refuses to go out until Little Mary enters and reveals that Crystal is having an affair with Buck and that Stephen is unhappy. Mary gets out of bed and dresses, and the final scene takes place in the women's lounge of the Casino Roof nightclub. The countess is hysterical, having discovered that Buck is unfaithful. Mary tricks Crystal into revealing that she is Buck's lover. Ignoring what they themselves have done, Crystal and Sylvia both scold Mary for underhanded behavior, but Mary has finally taken her life into her own hands. She bares her bright red, clawlike fingernails at them and goes out to reclaim Stephen as the play ends.

Themes and Meanings

Of the forty-four women's roles in *The Women* (no men appear onstage), Broadway critics focused on those of the upper-class characters. Critics often still assume that the play attacks women in general, despite Clare Boothe Luce's repeated insistence that she intended to attack only self-obsessed, parasitic women of wealth, such as Sylvia and Edith, who demand perpetual pleasure and romance and disclaim any form of responsibility. Even Mary Haines, who has found satisfaction in her roles as wife and mother, abandons her values when she is swayed by the opinions of her peers. When she confronts Stephen, both she and Stephen speak in the trite language of magazine fiction and Hollywood films. Neither wants a divorce: Both merely behave in the way their world expects.

The object of Luce's satire is made clear through the minor characters, who comment, in increasingly strident voices, on the stupidity of their social betters. They variously express contempt, bitterness, resignation, wry amusement, and anger. Maggie, Mary's cook, for example, talks about marriage as family centered, not pleasure centered. The nurse in Edith's hospital room explodes at Edith's complaints, contrasting her easy delivery with those of poor women who deliver without comfort and return immediately to work. Two women from Stephen's office visit Mary on business and, left alone, bitterly describe what single life is like on a woman's wages, at that time generally far below the wages of men. A Reno maid is resigned to her life, although she is physically abused by her husband. The cigarette girl, in the play's final scene, would like to marry, but she and her boyfriend cannot afford marriage. She is thinking about becoming a communist. These voices often directly criticize the behavior of the wealthy women while elsewhere, they simply reveal the contrast between frivolous, privileged lives and those of the vast majority of women.

While these ordinary women are generally patronized or ignored by the society women during the course of the play, the Reno scene contains an episode emphasizing that the difference between these social classes is a matter of wealth and luck, not personal quality. When Sylvia realizes that her former husband will marry the flashy Miriam, she assaults Miriam, even biting her. When Mary breaks up the fight, Sylvia shatters breakables against the wall, thus revealing a spirit as common as any on the streets. To emphasize this point, in a 1966 revision, Luce changed the ending. In the last scene of the 1966 version, Mary leaves the women's lounge of the nightclub to reclaim Stephen, but, as the curtain falls, Miriam is preparing to physically attack Sylvia, who backs away. The curtain falls, then rises again to show the two women pulling each other's hair.

Dramatic Devices

Luce was an admirer of Irish playwright George Bernard Shaw, even visiting Shaw at his home in England. Shaw's *Candida: A Mystery* (pr. 1897, pb. 1898) was among her favorite plays, and Mary, in her warmth, home-centered values, and sympathy for others, strongly resembles Shaw's heroine. While Candida's marriage is threatened by a young artist who wants to save the heroine from the boring life of middle-class marriage, in Luce's play the enemies of marriage are more impersonal. Sylvia, Edith, and Crystal resemble the figures of a medieval morality play. Sylvia embodies the traditional sin of envy: Discontented with herself, her husband, and her life, she enviously tries to destroy the happiness of others. Edith is a figure for laziness, traditionally called sloth: Her unwanted pregnancies, her inadvertent talk with the gossip columnist, and her sloppy appearance and behavior betray a person who cannot exert herself to care about others. Crystal embodies greed. The helpless anger of the poor is made understandable through many of the minor characters, but Crystal wants more than just survival; she wants wealth, pleasure, lovers, and to see the last of Little Mary. The minor characters who share their hardships and misery constitute a traditional dramatic chorus.

Critical Context

The original production was not favorably reviewed by New York critics, who generally focused on the upper-class characters. Most found the play unpleasant. Nonetheless, the play ran for 657 performances, commanding record attendance from audiences. This was followed by a twenty-city tour, frequent revivals, and film and television productions. Viewers, unlike the critics, apparently recognized the social satire. In real life, Luce acted out the beliefs expressed in the play. Born out of wedlock, to a poor letter copier and an unsuccessful piano salesman, Luce could have settled into the role of pampered wife after her marriage to wealthy alcoholic George Tuttle Brokaw or her second marriage to *Time* magazine publisher Harry R. Luce. Instead, although her first divorce settlement made it unnecessary for her to work, she worked for *Vogue* and *Vanity Fair* magazines, and continued her career after her second marriage.

By the time of her death, Luce had written other plays and Hollywood scenarios, served as a war correspondent during World War II, entered Congress as a liberal Republican (in 1944, she was considered a possible vice-presidential candidate), and served as a U.S. ambassador to Italy. Her life registered her contempt for women preoccupied with personal pleasures. This contempt for a leisured and irresponsible class is depicted, in lighter tone, in stories published as *Stuffed Shirts* (1933) and, with deepening earnestness, in such anti-fascist plays as *Kiss the Boys Goodbye* (pr. 1938, pb. 1939), in which southern aristocracy is specifically associated with Nazism.

Sources for Further Study

Fearnow, Mark. *Clare Boothe Luce: A Research and Production Sourcebook.* Westport, Conn.: Greenwood Press, 1995.

Lyons, Joseph. *Clare Boothe Luce.* New York: Chelsea House, 1989.

Martin, Ralph G. *Henry and Clare: An Intimate Portrait of the Luces.* New York: G. P. Putnam, 1991.

Morris, Sylvia Jukes. *Rage for Fame: The Ascent of Clare Boothe Luce.* New York: Random House, 1997.

Shadegg, Stephen. *Clare Boothe Luce: A Biography.* New York: Simon and Schuster, 1970.

Weintraub, Rodelle, ed. "The Gift of Imagination: An Interview with Clare Boothe Luce." In *Fabian Feminist: Bernard Shaw and Women.* University Park: Pennsylvania State University Press, 1977.

Betty Richardson

THE WOODS

Author: David Mamet (1947-　　)
Type of plot: Psychological
Time of plot: The 1970's
Locale: A summer cottage in the woods
First produced: 1977, at the St. Nicholas Theater Company, Chicago, Illinois
First published: 1979

Principal characters:
RUTH, a woman approximately twenty-five years old
NICK, a man, also about twenty-five

The Play

Scene 1 of the conversational *The Woods* opens at dusk with the play's two characters, Ruth and Nick, seated on the porch of Nick's summer cottage in the woods,
where the two lovers have come for a weekend getaway. Ruth, animated by the atmosphere and encouraged by Nick's "Tell me," comments on the environment's natural
denizens: seagulls, herons, and crickets. She talks about the ozone layer, pirates, and
bears, noting, "We don't have to be afraid. Because we have each other."

The less talkative Nick, who is not afraid, is nevertheless angered by her "understanding." He barely listens to what has become nonstop commentary, soliloquies
punctuated with clichélike truisms such as "nothing lasts forever" and "things change."
He wants her affection more than her conversation. At her persistence, he relates for
her his father's story of accidentally falling into a hole "during the War" and ironically
finding the man he had been sent to search for. Suddenly, Ruth stops listening. She
wants Nick to take her inside the cottage and make love to her, adding that she bought
him a present. Nick agreeably promises to finish his story as the two go inside.

At the beginning of scene 2, night has fallen, and Ruth, who has had trouble sleeping, is sitting on the porch. Nick joins her, verbalizing that he is upset because his
watch has stopped and he does not know the time. He is also worried about the oncoming rain and cold. Ruth soothes his whining by telling her Granma's story, which
has the elements of a children's fairy tale: a new moon to see by, wolves, bears, and
small children who lose their way in the woods. The story reminds Ruth that she lost
her beloved Granma's bracelet by carelessly dropping it into the lake. Nick likens that
incident to his father's accidental fall into the hole. This seemingly aimless conversation continues until "Nicky" rushes Ruth into lovemaking. She tells him that if he
were a man, he would treat her better. He tells her that she talks too much. Nick does
not accept her present (a gold bracelet engraved "Nicholas. I will always love you.
Ruth") and hints that he has brought others to the cottage. "Nothing lasts forever,"
quotes a sadder and wiser Ruth, who decides she will go home on the next bus. She
adds, as she goes in to pack, "Many things go on. We have to learn from things."

Scene 3 occurs the next morning. Nicky does not want to "do" anything, and he does not want Ruth to leave, so he talks of herons and the like. Ruth still thinks that Nick does not love but only wants her, and she challenges his manhood with "You make this manly stuff up." He retaliates, "You're nothing honey." Physical violence ensues. Ruth lunges with the oar that was used to steer a now-rotting boat, and a threatened Nick knocks her down, which indicates to Ruth that Nick does not like women. Then a stunning reversal occurs: Nick's fear at being left alone and not knowing himself forces him to admit, while she slaps some sense into him, that he loves her. She denies this assertion but calms him down as she retells the story of the lost children in the woods.

Themes and Meanings

The Woods is, like other Mamet works, a play in which the characters delve into their backgrounds to achieve a limited self-understanding. On one hand, this effect is accomplished through a simple, minimalistic two-character play that conforms to the classical demands of setting, time, and action. Its plot revolves around two characters who, in addition to being afraid to be alone with themselves, have great difficulty being with and communicating with each other. Their basic fears, which they try to hide, cause them to alienate each other as much out of a sense of self-preservation as from mistrust and misunderstanding.

On the other hand, the play has multiple meanings as deep as the hole that Nick's father fell into and as elusive and slippery, perhaps, as the shimmering golden bracelet that falls out of reach. The play can be seen both as a classical retreat into the pastoral mode and as a metaphorical dramatization of a naturalistic fairy tale. When Ruth and Nick go to the cottage in the woods to get away from the civilization of the city, the natural environment forces them to come to terms with their more primitive instincts. (Nick tells the story of a savage bear that returned to bury itself under the cottage, which was placed upon the bear's den.) Through the retelling of their forebears' stories, they search for meaning that simultaneously shows them to themselves and entraps them therein.

The play's ending is rich in the same multilevel ambiguity seen throughout. Although Ruth does not mean to stay, and probably should not stay, she does so, at least temporarily, at his request—validating her pessimistic foreknowledge about relationships in the 1970's, "We pick the people that we know are bad for us. We do that all the time."

Dramatic Devices

Within the device of Nick and Ruth's storytelling, Mamet uses repetitive dialogue, as he does in all of his plays, to underline and dramatize a search for meaning. When Ruth looks up to the great firmament, her usual sureness crumbles. She is unable to find an answer in the configuration of the heavens, unable to give meaning to a new story or find similarity in an old one. Her repetition underlines her confusion, rather than adding clarity:

> RUTH: The lightning doesn't look like anything. Do you know what I mean?
> NICK: No.
> RUTH: The lightning doesn't "look" like anything. Do you know what I mean?
> NICK: No

The impact of this inability to communicate is heightened by the nonproductive repet-itiveness.

The play runs the risk of being produced as a static "play of ideas." Mamet, ironi-cally, introduces physical violence at the very moment his characters admit they care, dramatically emphasizing the characters' fear of loving and being loved. The play-wright presents the "rape" scene in full view of the audience. Although Ruth says no, Nick forces her, not even allowing her to go inside to get lubrication or birth-control protection ("some stuff"). Nick, therefore, becomes an unsympathetic character who uses brute strength to get what he wants. The audience sees Ruth treated as an object, and empathy for his lonely plight is lost.

Mamet further brings out their animalistic qualities by having Ruth repeat the shrill and caustic sound of the migratory birds. "Caw, caw, caw. And Winter comes and they go somewhere else." Mamet enhances the whys and wherefores of this deteriorating relationship with the imagery of decay: the rotting boat, the musty raincoat, the damp-ness, and the chill that will not go away. No panacea—neither mercurochrome nor as-pirin—can relieve the pain already caused. A special poignancy in this modern-day winter's tale is achieved when Ruth realizes that Nick wanted the very same things from Ruth that she desperately wanted to give to him.

Critical Context

One can readily see the influence of Anton Chekhov, specifically of *Chayka* (pr. 1896; *The Seagull*, 1909), on Mamet's early work, *The Woods*. Both plays include natural imagery as symbols for the process of decay. The storytelling motif is used by Mamet much as Chekhov uses the play-within-the-play, which the characters see as a fictive quasi reality. Nick becomes the bear who cannot speak, much as Nina becomes the tossed-aside seagull.

One can also trace the development of Mamet's storytelling device in *The Woods* from that of his short, one-scene *Dark Pony* (pr. 1977), in which a tender father tells a favorite story to lull his daughter to sleep. *Dark Pony* was published as a companion piece to the more dramatic (and more hopeful) *Reunion* (pr. 1976), in which a differ-ent father tells a story to try to explain himself to his daughter. In *Reunion*, as in *The Woods*, the characters seem able and willing to set aside their differences, if only for the moment, out of their need and loneliness. In addition, Bernie gives Carol a brace-let as a token of his love in *Reunion*, much as Ruth gives one to Nick. *The Woods*, therefore, can be seen as a beneficiary of earlier plays and as a springboard for the de-velopment of later ones, specifically *Speed-the-Plow* (pr., pb. 1988), which has as a subplot the same major theme, how to "know oneself," and is also structured with a neoclassical unity of time, space, and action. Ruth recognizes that people are afraid to be alone and afraid to die. Her love is giving, curative, and maternal; yet she needs to feel loved to be secure. Nick needs her to smother his aloneness. He does not love her; nevertheless, they "go on," with Ruth lulling Nick's fears by telling him a story.

Sources for Further Study

Bigsby, C. W. E. *David Mamet*. New York: Methuen, 1985.

_____. Introduction to *Beyond Broadway*. Vol. 3 in *A Critical Introduction to Twentieth-Century American Drama*. New York: Cambridge University Press, 1985.

Carroll, Dennis. *David Mamet*. New York: St. Martin's Press, 1987.

Christiansen, Richard, "David Mamet." *Contemporary Dramatists*. 6th ed. Detroit: St. James, 1999.

Dean, Anne. *David Mamet: Language as Dramatic Action*. Teaneck, N.J.: Fairleigh Dickinson University Press, 1990.

Friedman, Samuel G. "The Gritty Eloquence of David Mamet." *New York Times Magazine*, April 21, 1985, 32-38.

Kane, Leslie, ed. *David Mamet: A Casebook*. New York: Garland, 1991.

Lahr, John. "David Mamet." In *Show and Tell: New Yorker Profiles*. Woodstock, New York: Overlook Press, 2000.

Marjorie J. Oberlander

WORDS AND MUSIC

Author: Samuel Beckett (1906-1989)
Type of plot: Absurdist
Time of plot: Unspecified
Locale: Unspecified
First produced: 1962, BBC Third Programme, London
First published: 1962, in *Evergreen Review*

Principal characters:
WORDS
MUSIC
CROAK, their "Lord"

The Play

The plot of Samuel Beckett's radio play *Words and Music* is at once dismayingly simple in its minimalist reductiveness and disturbingly complex in the ways in which the play's basic components are combined. The play opens with only two of its three characters present. While Music (comprising a small orchestra) tunes up, Words breaks in rather peremptorily to rehearse his speech on one of Beckett's favorite subjects, Sloth. As soon becomes clear, the relationship between Words and Music is antagonistic; each implores, loathes, interrupts, and seeks to gain ascendancy over the other until they hear the sound of Croak, in his bedroom slippers, approaching from the distance. Croak arrives as lord and peacemaker, addressing Words and Music as "my comforts," "my balms," and more familiarly, and comically, as Joe and Bob, whom he advises to be "friends."

After rhetorically begging their forgiveness for his being late and then offering some vague fragments of explanation ("on stairs," "in tower"), Croak considers their theme for the evening. After some thought, he decides on love. With only one exception, Croak expresses himself elliptically by means of sighs, groans, single words, short (usually two-word) phrases, and by thumping his club. Called on first, Words responds by repeating the same speech he had been rehearsing at the very beginning of the play, substituting "love" for "sloth" wherever necessary. Neither Croak's sigh nor his thumping dissuades Words from continuing until Croak thumps his club a second time and calls for Bob (Music). Even then Words only falters; he does not stop until Croak summons Music more forcefully: "Bob!" Only then does Words cease, and Music begin, playing "as before." Croak, perhaps displeased by Words's incessant protestations and pleadings, demands that Music play more loudly, which Music does, thereby drowning out Words but also losing his own earlier expressiveness.

At this point there is a pause which signals that the play's first cycle is over and the next about to begin, repeating the first in general outline though not in all particulars. Croak's gentle summons, "Joe sweet," evokes more words from Words, which in turn evoke more groans from Croak until Croak stops Words and again calls on Music. (As before, he issues his summons twice, first gently, "Bob dear," then more insistently and effectively, a simple "Bob!"). Again Music plays, and again Words protests ("no," "please"), all leading to the inevitable pause. The second cycle differs from the first in two important if not entirely obvious ways. One is that Words's protestations are less audible than before; the other and more important difference is that Words is not merely repeating the speech he had rehearsed earlier. His speech now is delivered hesitantly; the numerous pauses suggest that the words here are improvised rather than repeated. Neither these changes nor Music's playing satisfies the still-anguished Croak. Having heard how little "love" has to offer, he changes the subject to "age."

The ensuing third cycle is much shorter than the previous two. Words now appears to be truly at a loss and as a result quickly gets the thump. Music fares no better, and Croak, displeased and still demanding, orders them to perform "together . . . Together, dogs!" Each improvises and in turn follows the other's lead as best he can as individually and together they try to please their imperious master. Then, with Words "trying to sing" and Music willing to accompany, they compose a quite passable poem, to which Croak responds with something other than his characteristic groan, repeating the enigmatic phrase "the face" five times. Neither their success nor Croak's memory lasts, however. Music and Words begin to bicker anew, yet despite his own faltering (evidenced by frequent pauses and ellipses) and despite Croak's renewed groans, Words perseveres and evokes an even more emotional response from his lordly audience, the name "Lily!" His endeavor nearly comes to an abrupt end when Music interrupts Words's highly descriptive (but also remarkably vague and hackneyed) narrative with an "irrepressible burst of spreading and subsiding music."

In keeping with the tenor of the entire play, Beckett makes no attempt to explain why the outburst is "irrepressible." Is it Music's own emotionally charged response to Words's words or his victory over his antagonist? Either way, Music's "triumph and conclusion" proves short-lived. Words, still persevering (and far more patient than earlier), resumes his tale. Again he falters, but Music quickly picks up the lead, discreetly offering a tune to which Words tentatively adapts his phrases, each growing more confident as they proceed, until finally together they compose a second poem:

> Then down a little way
> Through the trash
> Towards where . . .
> All dark no begging
> No giving no words
> No sense no need . . .
> Through the scum
> Down a little way
> To whence one glimpse
> Of that wellhead.

The poem over, Words is "shocked," though whether by this uncharacteristic harmony of Words and Music or by Croak's own ambiguous response—letting his club fall, he shuffles haltingly away, presumably back to the tower "whence" he came—remains unclear. More surprising still is Music's "Brief rude retort" to Words's imploring (but also Croak-like) "Bob," followed by Words's again Croak-like command, "Bob!," which Music does obediently heed, supplying a reprise of earlier musical phrases which Music then repeats "as before or only very slightly varied." The play ends with neither Words nor Music but instead with yet another pause, followed by Words's wordless but yet again Croak-like "Deep sigh."

Themes and Meanings

A. Alvarez has described *Words and Music* as "a brilliant, witty, and utterly original dramatization of the labor and frustrations of creation, the poet alternately bullying and despairing, his instruments inept, unwieldy; then the final letdown when there is nothing more to be done. It also illustrates vividly that split between the music the poet hears in his head and the leaden words at his command, and the slow, unwilling process of disciplining and refining these two elements until they finally chime together in a single work of art." This is a plausible, even perceptive, and in a way remarkably comprehensive reading of Beckett's brief but puzzling play, but it is also decidedly partial, for although *Words and Music* may be read as an allegorical representation of the creative process, as Alvarez, a poet as well as a critic, maintains, it cannot be said to be only that.

Despite its brevity, *Words and Music* is, as all Beckett's imaginative writings are, to be thought of less as the means by which the author expresses or transmits a certain content than as a machine for generating meanings, for provoking responses from its bewildered audience of listeners and readers. Something surely happens in *Words and Music*—or at least seems to happen—but exactly what it is is impossible to say. Like its characters, its audience may well prefer that "something" not be "nothing." Meaning nothing itself, *Words and Music* can mean anything and everything; it can accommodate those partial readings it invites yet resists.

This multiplicity of interpretive possibilities derives in large measure from Beckett's willingness to divorce form from content, emphasizing the one while very nearly eliminating the other altogether. "It is the shape that matters," Beckett once said of a sentence of which he is particularly fond, and one can learn much about the effect *Words and Music* has on its audience (and therefore about its meanings) by looking at its shape. Here is a play based on repetition rather than progression, permutation rather than elaboration or development. It is a drama of stasis ending in closure and involving abstract voices rather than realistic characters.

If the medium is the message, as media observer Marshall McLuhan has claimed, then the message of *Words and Music* is its "medium of pure audition" (Hugh Kenner's apt phrase). Kenner's description nicely sums up the futility of the characters' efforts, the endlessness of a performance that must always be penultimate. The languages they employ—verbal and musical—prove similarly ineffectual. However, although communication is always impossible in Beckett's world, the need of characters and author alike to go on performing—speaking and playing—remains. Words and music may convey no meanings, but they do exist, if not as vehicles then as pure forms, in and for themselves, and they do evoke responses. Read along conventional lines, the play may seem to be about Sloth, Age, and Love. Such a reading is, like Alvarez's, plausible but partial, for the fact that Words uses these subjects interchangeably, freely substituting any one for any other, turns attention away from their referents to the words themselves—to, that is, language and humanity's relationship to it.

The play circles around a number of vaguely related ideas, images, and situations. Language (speaking and playing) is the most pervasive; imploring, pleading, inviting, accompanying, submitting, dominating, trying, failing, and repeating are others. Together they contribute to the play's movement away from the intolerable burden of endless performance, of meaningless existence, and toward the release to be found in the stasis of a final and perfect performance, or of death. Words and Music long to be released (presumably by Croak) from having to speak and to play. That is, they long to be released from the burden of having to be what they are (the one words, the other music) and released too from consciousness of self (incomplete, dependent, unsatisfied, and unsatisfying) and of the other, especially of the tyrant other they serve, Croak, who appears to be driven by an identical longing which, paradoxically, only his tormentors can fulfill. The poem heard near the end sums up the nature of their quest well: through trash and darkness, beyond words and need, to "one glimpse of that wellhead," to, that is, one glimpse of the very source of life itself in the perfect wordlessness of nothing, free at last of their own desperate need to speak, which is to be.

Dramatic Devices

Words and Music belongs to the Theater of the Absurd. Its preoccupation with the existentialist theme of the pain and anguish of having to live in an absurd world is reinforced by the manner in which Beckett presents his material: the isolation and cartoonishness of the characters, the antirealism of the setting, the nonrational language and the circular plot. The play's characters simply "are." They have no past and no future; they exist in an endlessly repeatable present and solely in terms of the words by which they are designated. The play's setting is similarly rendered: placeless, timeless, and meaningless—a nonplace or, given Croak's slippers, a dreamscape, the perfect setting for Beckett's existential nightmare.

The dialogue is equally barren, a collection of croaks, groans, individual words, and brief verbal and musical phrases (the latter composed by John Beckett, the author's cousin). The pauses do not so much punctuate or even interrupt the play's various sounds as call attention to that overwhelming silence or void against and within which Croak, Words, and Music play their parts. This existential silence, figured in the pause, becomes a character in its own right, a palpable and disconcerting presence. Beckett treats words and music in similar fashion: They are not so much allegorized as foregrounded, treated not as the means to meaning but as an object in space, not as tools used by the characters but as characters themselves. Beckett used music in a number of his earlier plays, including the radio plays *All That Fall* (pr., pb. 1957) and *Embers* (pr., pb. 1959), but in *Words and Music* and in his next radio play,

Cascando (pr., pb. 1963), music emerges from the background to assume a new status. No longer merely a means for heightening the dramatic effect—as in melodrama—it emerges in dialogue with language, each qualifying as well as clarifying the essential nature of the other.

The fact that *Words and Music* is a radio play is also significant, for as Martin Esslin has pointed out, "Beckett's preoccupation with the process of human consciousness as an incessant verbal flow . . . here found its logical culmination, one which only radio could provide." Writing for radio enabled Beckett to focus more intensively on language than ever before, to equate it with character and to emphasize it as sound, or noise, and to give it its own autonomous existence by freeing it from the need for a physical speaker. Instead of a human character, Beckett offers a disembodied voice, the essence of humanity, which exists solely in the imagination of its audience rather than as a character on a realistic stage. In this way Beckett strips away all that is superfluous—body, social trappings, and so forth—in order to focus on the human figure as at once absurd and tragic, a mere word away from not existing at all.

Critical Context

Although Beckett claims to have written his plays solely as diversions and only when he found himself blocked in the writing of the novels he contends are far more important, his dramatic pieces form an integral rather than subordinate part of his aesthetic achievement. This was already clear to others at least as early as 1969, the year he was awarded the Nobel Prize in Literature for having produced a "body of work that, in new forms of fiction and the theatre, has transmuted the destitution of modern man into his exultation." The indisputable originality of Beckett's plays and fictions involves his willingness to explore and perfect the formal means by which the "destitution" that he has placed at the very center of his art can be depicted. As he wrote in his 1931 study of Proust, "The artistic tendency is not expansive, but a contraction. . . . And art is the apotheosis of solitude. There is no communication because there are no vehicles of communication." Beckett has progressively narrowed and intensified his focus in a steadily contractive movement toward a static, nonrational discourse, toward a single permuted image, toward a distilled or attenuated form barren of content—thus, the typically Beckettian movement toward brevity, indeed toward the ultimate diminishment that is "nothing" itself. From the relative fullness of his earliest plays, Beckett turned to other, less conventional means, especially radio. *All That Fall*, his first radio play, is fairly conventional. *Embers* and *Words and Music*, on the other hand, show how quickly Beckett began to exploit radio's possibilities for reducing drama to a question of voice, to making voice the very basis of humankind's identity, and to making the audience wholly dependent on what the voice says is real. As Henry says in *Embers*, "I mention it [that the sound that is heard is the sound of the sea] because the sound is so strange, so unlike the sound of the sea, that if you didn't see what it was you wouldn't know what it was," as indeed the play's audience does not know because it does not "see"; it hears only, and what it hears are sounds that may not exist at all outside Henry's solipsistic imagination.

Such sounds generally exist in their most basic or most abstract and attenuated forms, as, for example, the sound of the sea or of dying embers in *Embers* or words, music, and croaks in *Words and Music*. This obsessive interest in the purity and ambiguity of the voice results in the brilliantly involuted monologue *Company*, a prose work published in 1980 and performed on radio the same year. Although *Embers*, *Words and Music*, and even *Company* may be approached in the context of existentialist philosophy and absurdist drama, they also attest Beckett's emergence as an acknowledged leader of the postmodern movement. His interest in radio and television, fiction and film, mime and music evidences his preoccupation with technique as its own end; it suggests a turning away from the existentialist context in which he has most often been interpreted (and which he always felt confining) and a turning toward a typically postmodern interest in purely verbal, structural, and technical matters.

Sources for Further Study

Abbot, H. Porter. *Beckett Writing Beckett: The Author in the Autograph*. Ithaca, N.Y.: Cornell University Press, 1996.

Alvarez, A. *Samuel Beckett*. New York: Viking, 1973.

Andonian, Cathleen. *The Critical Response to Samuel Beckett*. Westport, Conn.: Greenwood Press, 1998.

Astro, Alan. *Understanding Samuel Beckett*. Columbia: University of South Carolina Press, 1990.

Ben-Zvi, Linda. *Samuel Beckett*. Boston: Twayne, 1986.

Cohn, Ruby. *Just Play: Beckett's Theater*. Princeton, N.J.: Princeton University Press, 1980.

Esslin, Martin. "Samuel Beckett and the Art of Broadcasting." *Encounter* 45 (September, 1975): 38-46.

_____. *The Theatre of the Absurd*. 3d ed. London: Methuen, 2001.

Gordon, Lois. *The World of Samuel Beckett*. New Haven, Conn.: Yale University Press, 1996.

Gussow, Mel. *Conversations with and About Beckett*. New York: Grove-Atlantic, 1996.

Homan, Sidney, ed. *Beckett's Theaters: Interpretations for Performance*. Lewisburg, Pa.: Bucknell University Press, 1984.

Kenner, Hugh. *A Reader's Guide to Samuel Beckett*. Syracuse, N.Y.: Syracuse University Press, 1996.

McCarthy, Patrick A., ed. *Critical Essays on Samuel Beckett*. Boston: G. K. Hall, 1986.

Robert A. Morace

THE WORDS UPON THE WINDOW-PANE

Author: William Butler Yeats (1865-1939)
Type of plot: Naturalistic
Time of plot: The 1920's
Locale: Dublin, Ireland
First produced: November 7, 1930, at the Abbey Theatre, Dublin, Ireland
First published: 1934

Principal characters:
DR. TRENCH, an elderly scholar
MISS MACKENNA, the secretary of the Dublin Spiritualists'
    Association
JOHN CORBET, a graduate student at the University of Cambridge
CORNELIUS PATTERSON, a gambler
ABRAHAM JOHNSON, an evangelist
MRS. MALLET, an experienced spiritualist
MRS. HENDERSON, a medium

The Play

The action of *The Words upon the Window-Pane* takes place in the parlor of a now-seedy Dublin boardinghouse that has an illustrious history. Built in the eighteenth century and originally owned by friends of Jonathan Swift, the house has had as its occupants two celebrated Irish patriots, as well as Esther Johnson (1681-1728), Swift's "Stella."

As the one-act play opens, guests are arriving for a séance, to be conducted by Mrs. Henderson, a medium who has journeyed from London at the invitation of the Dublin Spiritualists' Association. The participants are greeted by Dr. Trench, the Association's president, and Miss Mackenna, its secretary. The first arrival is John Corbet, a doctoral candidate at the University of Cambridge who is writing a thesis on the relationship between Swift and Stella. Corbet declares his skepticism of spiritualism, and Dr. Trench responds by relating the story of his own early disbelief until his conversion during a séance much like that which is about to take place. Trench explains to Corbet that Mrs. Henderson will act as a medium for the voices of the dead; he cautions Corbet, however, that a "hostile influence" has disrupted Mrs. Henderson's past séance.

Trench is interrupted by the arrival of Cornelius Patterson, a gambler, whose interest in spiritualism is chiefly to learn whether horse races are run in the life after death. Switching topics, Trench tells Corbet the history of the house and points out the lines from one of Stella's poems, incised on the glass of the parlor's window. While Corbet attempts to read the now faintly cut lines in the dim light, Abraham Johnson enters. Johnson, an itinerant preacher, is anxious to rid the séance of its hostile influence by reciting the rite of exorcism, but he is dissuaded by Dr. Trench.

Corbet now recognizes the poem cut into the glass—four lines written by Stella for Swift's fifty-fourth birthday:

> You taught how I might youth prolong
> By knowing what is right and wrong,
> How from my heart to bring supplies
> Of lustre to my fading eyes.

Trench and Corbet discuss Swift's dual tragedy, his inability to return the love offered him by both Stella and "Vanessa" (Esther Vanhomrigh, 1690-1723), and the destruction of his political hopes, embodied in an ideal order mirroring the Roman senate of Brutus and Cato.

Mrs. Mallet enters. She tells Corbet that her motive for attending the séances is to contact her drowned husband. When Mrs. Mallet describes the appearance of her husband in a previous séance, gasping and struggling for breath, Dr. Trench explains that in addition to their death the spirits often relive "some passionate or tragic moment of life." With the arrival of Mrs. Henderson, the séance begins.

Mrs. Henderson passes into a trance in which she speaks through Lulu, a child who is her spirit "control." As Lulu, Mrs. Henderson is about to contact the spirit of Mrs. Mallet's husband, when she is possessed by the hostile spirit, who chastises an unnamed woman for her jealousy. He angrily reminds her of the means by which he has raised her from ignorance. The woman replies, addressing her accuser as "Jonathan." Trench and Corbet realize that Mrs. Henderson is acting as a medium for the unhappy spirits of Swift and Vanessa.

A lengthy dialogue between Vanessa and Swift, related through Mrs. Henderson, follows. Vanessa counters Swift's accusations by describing her loyalty and passion. If Swift and Stella are not married, she asks, what other obstacle can come between them? Swift alludes darkly to a disease of the blood "that no child must inherit," but Vanessa offers her own health and strength as surety for the well-being of the child they might have. As the dialogue continues, however, it becomes apparent that the true stumbling block to their marriage is Swift's intellectual arrogance, against which Vanessa poses her enlivening passion. As Vanessa leaves Swift to his solitude, Mrs. Henderson, possessed by Swift's spirit, beats upon the locked parlor door.

Mrs. Henderson sinks into her chair, exhausted, and the sitters prepare to end the séance. Suddenly the spirit of Swift returns, now speaking to Stella. He praises her poem, in which she exalts their intellectual love. Swift asserts that women who are able to love "according to the soul" possess greater happiness than those who experience bodily love. He then recites the poem, and Corbet recognizes it as the work from which the lines incised on the window glass are taken. After prophesying that Stella will "close [his] eyes in death," Swift vanishes and Mrs. Henderson wakes.

The participants begin to leave, each laying down money for Mrs. Henderson as he departs. John Corbet remains behind. Although he denies his belief in her mediumistic talents, he praises Mrs. Henderson's abilities as an "accomplished actress and scholar." He is now convinced that the medium has revealed the long-standing mystery of Swift's celibacy: The writer's genius enabled him to foresee the debasement of the modern world—thus his repugnance, through his own posterity, toward adding to the "collapse."

However, Mrs. Henderson claims to be ignorant of Swift; Corbet's speech is nonsense to her. She describes the loathsome appearance of the evil spirit whom she has called up; his clothes are filthy, his face broken out in boils. Corbet tells her that she has seen Swift in old age, after the onset of madness. After Corbet leaves, Mrs. Henderson is left alone. As she slowly goes about making a cup of tea, the spirit of Swift weaves in and out of her trance, raving.

Themes and Meanings

In *The Words upon the Window-Pane*, William Butler Yeats returns to a theme that dominates his poetry and plays: the mysterious layering of the past within the present, specifically as the history of Ireland is embodied in the lives of contemporary men and women. Incorporated in this dominant theme are other significant motifs having to do with Yeats's own struggle with old age and the poet's attempt to come to terms with the relationship between reason and passion.

The play's setting, the mundane Dublin boardinghouse, represents at once commonplace, ordinary life and the absurd and trivial existence of modern Ireland. Several of the characters reinforce this sense of the coarseness of contemporary life: The third-rate horseplayer, Patterson; the slightly crazed evangelist, Johnson; and even Mrs. Henderson, the medium, are inane, petit bourgeois personalities who symbolize the tawdriness of modern humanity. Against this frayed backdrop peopled by unexceptional characters erupts a mystery that bears out Yeats's belief that moments of "passionate intensity" remain vital past death.

Swift's tragedy, his denial of the women who loved him and the failure of his ideal commonwealth, contains a reality so powerful that it sweeps aside the spurious appearances which constitute the lives of those attending the séance. However, although the living are deeply moved by the reenactment of that tragedy, they are baffled by it, and leave the séance puzzled, or, like Corbet, they misinterpret what they have seen and heard. For Yeats, this is as it must be; as citizens of the twentieth century, the play's characters are blind to the spirit which dwells in history. Their perspective has shrunk to the small scope of their own petty needs and self-obsessions.

In contrast, Swift's agony overshadows them: The clarity with which he confronts his torment brings his death to life and casts the existences of the living into a kind of netherworld. Swift's denial of Stella and Vanessa assumes significance precisely because it is so closely tied to his denial of humanity. As Corbet tells Mrs. Henderson, Swift "was the chief representative of the intellect of his epoch," a paradigm of reason "free at last from superstition." He foresaw that the modern world would bring the "collapse" of reason; he prophesied just such a collection of ill-thought-out, sordid worldviews as the living guests bring with them to the séance. Swift's horror of the future, however, is by no means abstract. His disgust takes palpable form, the fathering of children. "Am I," he asks Vanessa, "to add another to the healthy rascaldom and knavery of the world?"

It is, then, Swift's unified sensibility—his merging of personal emotion and social consciousness—that makes him a tragic figure. Like that of all such figures, his tragedy arises from the transcendence of a purely individual grief and the embodiment of his personal situation in the wider disaster of history. Corbet comes closest among the living to grasping this truth, but he diminishes what he might have learned from Swift's ghostly appearance by placing it in the context of his own scholarly ambition.

Toward the end of his exchange with Stella, Swift prays that he "may leave to posterity nothing but this intellect that came to [him] from heaven." These lines echo corollary themes in Yeats's poems of this period, such as "Sailing to Byzantium" (1927) and "The Circus Animals' Desertion" (1939). Faced with what he viewed as Ireland's political failure and his own increasing self-doubt in old age, Yeats dreamed of a kind of apotheosis where he might find "monuments of unageing intellect."

Swift's own doubts, which he expresses in the subsequent dialogue with Stella, are redeemed by her poem, the words upon the window-pane. She says of his old age that "a beauteous mind repairs/ The loss of chang'd or falling hairs;/ How wit and virtue from within/ Can spread a smoothness o'er the skin." Against the obtuse self-preoccupation of the séance participants, who symbolize degraded modern Ireland, Yeats poses Swift's, and his own, belief in a historically and bodily transcendent reason metamorphosed through spirit.

Dramatic Devices

The most striking dramatic element in *The Words upon the Window-Pane* is the play's joining of naturalistic setting and characterization with a supernatural central action more in keeping with the fantasy of Yeats's earlier dramatic work. The characters verge on being the stock figures of Irish melodrama—the bragging gambler, the motherly Mrs. Mallet, the deranged fundamentalist preacher. The play's locale, too, is reminiscent of early twentieth century naturalism. Thus, characters and setting frame the supernatural action of the drama.

Yeats turns the conventions of naturalism against naturalism's usual intent—to portray human beings as victims of historical and economic fate. The passionate interchanges between the disembodied spirits of Swift and Vanessa, and Swift and Stella, come to assume more emotional reality than the "real," tangible existences of the living characters who witness this reenactment of long-dead events. In a sense, the social determinism of naturalist theater molds the lives of the living characters while, at the same time, the heroic dead finally escape it. The undisguised irony here is that those who might be supposed to have some control over their social roles, the living, are helpless before them, and those who can only reenact their lives on earth triumph over their circumstances.

The one-act structure, from which Yeats rarely departed, is well calculated to reinforce the significance of isolated human actions. Early in the play, Dr. Trench comments that "some spirits . . . go over and over some painful thought, except that where they are thought is reality." Trench's remark is a clear instance of another dramatic irony: For Yeats, thought is also the only reality, and Trench's "living" reality is only counterfeit. The absence of a longer, three-act structure frees Yeats from the necessity of the sort of character development that would lend significance to his living characters, thereby diminishing the importance of the spirits' sole, passionate action.

That the séance participants act as spectators to the play's central action is an additional strength of the one-act format. Once again, the interchanges among the dead gain reality at the expense of the living. Trench, Corbet, and the others fall naturally into the roles of passive witnesses to history, a role, Yeats believes, into which people of the modern era are all cast. Moreover, as the "real" audience watches the characters onstage becoming an audience for past events that they do not understand, the playgoers are given the opportunity of making sense of the interaction between past and present, the living and the dead.

Critical Context

The Words upon the Window-Pane is without question the least typical of Yeats's plays, at least in apparent structure. In some respects, the work seems more akin to Sean O'Casey's gritty Irish realism or George Bernard Shaw's ironic exposure of contemporary self-deceptions. However, all the authentic Yeatsian dramatic elements are also present: the fascination with the supernatural, the obsessive concern with Irish history, and the mystery of human mortality, the play's Nō-like structure centering on an overwhelming pivotal event.

The play is also one of Yeats's most autobiographical, at least in terms of the drama's basic premise, the séance. Yeats had attended many such séances and other spiritualistic encounters and had during the 1920's composed *A Vision*, a mystical work based on his wife's gift for automatic writing. He brings to the plot, then, his intimate and realistic knowledge of the kinds of people—sincere mystics and opportunistic cynics—who participate in séances; at the same time, the action of the play depends on Yeats's actual belief in the ability of the living to contact the dead.

The concern with Swift's old age, as well as his emblematic status as a member of the Anglo-Irish gentry, also reflects Yeats's image of himself during these last years of his life. Increasingly disillusioned with both the wider failures of Western society and the more specific collapse of Irish independence, Yeats had begun to divorce himself from the folk heritage that was so powerful an element in his earlier poetry and plays. In place of the Celtic bard, who had been his model for three decades, Yeats substituted Swift, with whom he felt particular kinship. From Yeats's perspective, Swift, too, was an outsider in Ireland—an intellectual, a non-Catholic, a cosmopolite. Like Swift in old age, the aging Yeats had begun to revile the disintegration of his own body.

In general, critics believe that the play's success lies in Yeats's imaginative recreation of Swift the man, rather than in the poet's elevation of Swift's eighteenth century ideals of civic republicanism and classical learning. Perhaps because the play's structure is so unlike Yeats's other dramatic work, audiences otherwise sympathetic to Yeats have found this play difficult going. The play's tone is unquestionably grim, and the rather desperate theme is not lightened by the fascinating symbolism and physical grace of the Cuchulain cycle (*On Baile's Strand*, pr. 1904; *The Golden Helmet*, pr., pb. 1908; *At the Hawk's Well*, pr. 1916; *The Only Jealousy of Emer*, pb. 1919; *The Death of Cuchulain*, pb. 1939) or the dance plays (*Four Plays for Dancers*, pb. 1921). Nevertheless, critics and audiences have admired this experiment in naturalism, and have thought the play to be an untypical, but still striking, success.

Sources for Further Study

Archibald, Douglas N. M. *Yeats.* Ann Arbor, Mich.: Book Demand, 1983.

Brown, Terence. *The Life of William Butler Yeats: A Critical Biography.* Oxford, England: Blackwell, 1999.

Dorn, Karen. *Players and Painted Stage: The Theatre of W. B. Yeats.* Totowa, N.J.: Barnes and Noble Books, 1984.

Harper, George Mills. *The Mingling of Heaven and Earth: Yeats's Theory of Theatre.* Atlantic Highlands, N.J.: Humanities Press, 1975.

Knowland, A. S. *W. B. Yeats: Dramatist of Vision.* Totowa, N.J.: Barnes and Noble Books, 1983.

Moore, John Rees. *Masks of Love and Death: Yeats as Dramatist.* Ithaca, New York: Cornell University Press, 1971.

Nathan, Leonard E. *The Tragic Drama of William Butler Yeats.* New York: Columbia University Press, 1965.

Rajan, Balachandra. *W. B. Yeats: A Critical Introduction.* 2d ed. London: Hutchinson, 1969.

Skelton, Robin, and Ann Saddlemyer, eds. *The World of W. B. Yeats.* Seattle: University of Washington Press, 1967.

Watanabe, Nancy. *A Beloved Image: The Drama of W. B. Yeats, 1865-1939.* Lanham, Md.: University Press of America, 1995.

John Steven Childs

THE WORKHOUSE WARD

Authors: Lady Augusta Gregory (1852-1932) and Douglas Hyde (1860-1949)
Type of plot: Comedy
Time of plot: c. 1900
Locale: A ward in Cloon Workhouse, Ireland
First produced: 1908, at the Abbey Theatre, Dublin, Ireland
First published: 1909

Principal characters:
MIKE MCINERNEY and
MICHAEL MISKELL, old paupers
MRS. DONOHUE, a countrywoman

The Play

In *The Workhouse Ward*, Mike McInerney and Michael Miskell, former neighbors, are confined to neighboring beds in an Irish poorhouse. The old men are alone during most of this twenty-minute comedy, the other inmates having gone to Mass, and the action is limited almost entirely to talk. As the play opens, they trade extravagant physical complaints in a rich Kiltartan dialect, moving quickly to invective and a rehearsal of all the quarrels they have had with each other during nearly seventy years of living side by side. Each blames the other for his present poverty, having spent his money building barriers and protecting his property to no avail; Michael's pigs still ate Mike's gooseberries, and Mike's dogs still attacked Michael. Each impugns the other's ancestry and boasts of his own, as measured by the number of generations buried at the Seven Churches or the screeching of the banshee at the death of a family member. They reveal a history of lawsuits and petty grievances, they bemoan the fact that they are doomed to spend the rest of their lives "chained" together in this place, and they wish each other dead. Mike McInerney's exclamation is typical of both men:

> And I say, and I would kiss the book on it, I to have one request only to be granted, and I leaving it in my will, it is what I would request, nine furrows of the field, nine ridges of the hills, nine waves of the ocean to be put between your grave and my own grave the time we will be laid in the ground!

At this point, a countrywoman enters and identifies herself as Honor Donohue, the recently widowed sister of Mike McInerney, whom she has not seen in five years. She brings her dead husband's "good frieze coat . . . and a hat in the fashion" and an invitation to Mike to come and share her "wide lovely house" and "a few acres of grassland." Mike eagerly agrees to join her in what has become in his vivid imagination the promised land:

The goat and the kid are there, the sheep and the lamb are there, the cow does be running and she coming to be milked. Ploughing and seed sowing, blossom at Christmas time, the cuckoo speaking through the dark days of the year! . . . Age will go from me and I will be young again. Geese and turkeys for the hundreds and drink for the whole world!

Michael Miskell, however, is distressed at this threat of desertion by his ancient antagonist: "All that I am craving is the talk. There to be no one at all to say out to whatever thought might be rising in my innate mind!" The specter of the loss of this particular type of intimacy moves Mike McInerney. He pleads with his sister to take both of them, but she indignantly rejects the suggestion; she wants no stranger, and even less does she want an old quarrelsome neighbor. Mike refuses to stir without Michael, and Mrs. Donohue leaves angrily. As the play closes, the two men return to their mutual invective, hurling pillows, mugs, and prayerbooks at each other.

Themes and Meanings

The Workhouse Ward is, on the surface, a slight play intended primarily for entertainment. Several reviewers dismissed it as farce when it was first produced, and Lady Augusta Gregory herself modestly stressed her motive in writing this and similar "peasant comedies" as a response to the need of the Abbey Theatre for brief, easily staged, crowd-pleasing plays to serve as curtain raisers or to put on at the end of verse plays. However, as Lady Gregory said, "farce is comedy with character left out"—in this play, character is brought in, expressed in language which implies a sense of community, however skewed, a need for intimacy, a connectedness with the land and with tradition, and a fertile mythmaking imagination. The theme of the play lies in this rich and complex vision of the Irish people.

Such a vision was part of the author's purpose. At this point in the history of the Abbey Theatre, Lady Gregory and William Butler Yeats sent a notice to aspiring playwrights reading, in part, "A play to be suitable for performance at the Abbey should contain some criticism of life, founded on the experience or personal observation of the writer, or some vision of life, of Irish life by preference, important from its beauty or from some excellence of style. . . . For art [is concerned] with realities of emotion and character that become self-evident when made vivid to the imagination." *The Workhouse Ward*, though brief, fulfills this purpose admirably, and it does so primarily through the reverberations of the language.

Lady Gregory, along with Yeats and others involved in the Irish Literary Movement, had a vision of Ireland which she wanted to impress upon those who did not share it and to reinforce in those who did. Her aim was, broadly, to restore the ancient dignity of Irish life, to rescue the old legends and folktales from oblivion, to reassert a sense of sacredness in the mundane, to recover pride in rural traditions, and in general to resist British obliteration of Irish culture. One way these purposes found expression was in her interest in Gaelic, which she learned only after persistent effort and never well enough to write fluently, though well enough to understand and translate. For her, Gaelic embodied a deep sense of national identity. Specific projects included collecting stories about and poetry by the last Irish bard, Raftery, as well as collecting and translating Gaelic legends. She could not write in Gaelic, however, nor was Gaelic understood by a wide audience, so she developed her Kiltartan dialect, a version shaped for dramatic dialogue of the Gaelic-influenced speech of the common people she had lived among since childhood. Before her use of this speech, it had been considered vulgar and inartistic; she displayed its beauty and made it acceptable as literature.

This Kiltartan dialect is the language of *The Workhouse Ward*, and conveys in its texture a sense of the community from which it springs, a community reflecting Lady Gregory's view of the Irish. It is a timeless language steeped in the land and the small farms, in family pride, and in folklore. It is a language strongly differentiated from standard English, as the culture of its speakers is proudly resistant to English-imposed customs. Its effective use requires skill and practice, and becomes an end in itself; the men's quarrel is a game that gives great pleasure. After one trenchant volley, Mike McInerney asks, "Now, have you anything to say?" and Michael Miskell replies, "I have everything to say, if I had but the time to say it!" Ultimately, it is the visionary language of bardic poetry; Mike McInerney's evocation of the paradise he will enjoy at his sister's house echoes the language of the poet Raftery describing the community where he was born, as translated by Lady Gregory in *Poets and Dreamers* (1903): "And if I were standing in the middle of my people, age would go from me, and I would be young again."

These profound implications lurking in the language of the play made Lady Gregory annoyed with those who complained that her depiction of the peasants made them appear ridiculous, or displayed an aristocrat's amusement at their quaint country ways, or reproduced the detested image of the stage Irishman. Indeed, those critics seemed to be answered by the great popularity of her comedies with Abbey Theatre audiences, and particularly with the people in the "pit," where the less prosperous playgoers sat. They saw not aristocratic condescension but vitality and affection, not the stage Irishman but Irish characters rooted in local reality and in universal human nature.

Still, her love for her country was not without astringency. She wrote of the play, "I sometimes think the two scolding paupers are a symbol of ourselves in Ireland— 'it is better to be quarrelling than to be lonesome.'" Mike McInerney and Michael Miskell, with their rich language, their agile imaginations, their fear of loneliness, their deep-seated pride, and their addiction to quarreling, embody Lady Gregory's view of Ireland.

Dramatic Devices

The most characteristic device in *The Workhouse Ward*, other than the dramatic language discussed above, is its economy of means. The play has been deliberately pared to its essentials: three characters; a spare set consisting of two beds, two blankets, and a night stand; and a swift, efficient development of character and situation. Writing the play encouraged the refinement of these qualities.

The Workhouse Ward was adapted from *Teać na mBocht* or *The Poorhouse* (pb. 1903), a Gaelic play by Douglas Hyde based on a lengthy scenario by Lady Gregory, which in turn grew out of her charitable visits to Gort Workhouse near her estate at Coole Park. *The Poorhouse* had five characters as well as several offstage voices representing other inmates of the ward, and somewhat looser dialogue; according to Lady Gregory, it "did not go very well. It seemed to ravel out into loose ends" and was not popular with the actors or the audience.

When the Abbey Theatre needed a new, easily produced play, Lady Gregory rewrote *The Poorhouse* for three actors, recasting the dialogue and tightening the structure. In her version, the old men emerge cleanly, without wasted words; their characters are bolder and more forceful, and Mike's rejection of his sister's offer is more resonant. The play is swift, concentrated, and delicately balanced. With a few brief speeches, Lady Gregory creates the world of the old men, almost hermetically sealed in its exclusivity; as soon as this world is established, it is breached by Honor Donohue, bringing news of a reality which will destroy their imaginative construct. Within minutes, her reality has been incorporated into their construct and then rejected as unnecessary and destructive. No word or motion is wasted.

The bare set was practical, given the limited physical resources of the Abbey; symbolic, since it evoked the material deprivation of the characters and the extent to which a good frieze coat and a couple of acres of land represent paradise; and dramatically effective, as it fixes the audience's attention on character and language. The small cast stresses the mutual interdependence and the complementary effect of the men.

Lady Gregory's stagecraft was influenced by the practices of Molière, two of whose plays—*Le Médecim malgré lui* (pr., pb. 1666; *The Doctor in Spite of Himself*, 1672) and *Les Fourberies de Scapin* (pr., pb. 1671; *The Cheats of Scapin*, 1701)—she had translated for the Abbey stage by this time with decided success. Like Molière, she discarded the superfluous and constructed a brisk duel of words which could lead unexpectedly to a burst of eloquence, and like him she was drawn to comic irony. Lady Gregory was pleased with the result of this experiment in tight dramatic construction and accepted the challenge to apply this technique to most of her succeeding plays.

Critical Context

For the student of drama, Lady Gregory's major significance is as cofounder of the Abbey Theatre, with William Butler Yeats and Edward Martyn, and as its continuing godmother, providing direction, ongoing supervision, money, political support, even costumes and food—and plays. Though she had previously written in several other genres, she began writing plays only in her fifties to fit specific needs at the Abbey and to promote specific nationalistic aims. These parameters should not suggest that her plays are mechanical, merely utilitarian, or thesis-driven; on the contrary, once she discovered this form she found both a talent and a desire for drama itself, and quickly became the most prolific of the Abbey dramatists. The spoken language and the interaction with a notoriously responsive audience brought out her genius. She loved the challenge of appealing to a popular audience, and said that if she had not had the Abbey, she would have been drawn to the music halls of England.

The Workhouse Ward assumes its first importance in this context; it is representative of the one-act plays she wrote during the Abbey's first six years, plays whose popularity helped build an audience, whose brilliance inspired a number of imitations, whose view of the Irish people had a political effect, and whose roots in actual life helped move the Abbey toward a broad-based realism rather than a more esoteric mythic drama.

Her work in general is also valued for its influence on the dramaturgy of Yeats, John Millington Synge, Sean O'Casey, and others. Although they are certainly not imitators of Lady Gregory, all of them were influenced by her handling of language and tight dramatic structure. The practice she gained in writing one-acts—*Spreading the News* (pr. 1904), *Hyacinth Halvey* (pr., pb. 1906), *The Jackdaw* (pr. 1907), *The Rising of the Moon* (pb. 1904), and *The Gaol Gate* (pr. 1906), as well as *The Workhouse Ward*—also contributed to her own success in three-act comedies, tragedies, and folk-history plays.

Aside from its importance to the Abbey and to the Irish Literary Movement, *The Workhouse Ward* and others of Lady Gregory's one-acts have been important in the little theater movement in the United States and Europe, both creating interest and providing material. Although they lose some degree of resonance when translated or performed out of their cultural contexts, they are nevertheless effective, popular, and easily produced.

Sources for Further Study
Adams, Hazard. *Lady Gregory*. Lewisburg, Pa.: Bucknell University Press, 1973.
Ellis-Fermor, Una. *The Irish Dramatic Movement*. 2d ed. London: Methuen, 1967.
Fay, Gerard. *The Abbey Theatre: Cradle of Genius*. New York: Macmillan, 1958.
Kohfeldt, Mary Lou. *Lady Gregory: The Woman Behind the Irish Renaissance*. New York: Atheneum, 1985.
Kopper, Edward A. *Lady Isabella Persse Gregory*. Boston: Twayne, 1976.
Mikhail, E. H. *Lady Gregory: Annotated Bibliography of Criticism*. Troy, N.Y.: Whitston, 1982.
_____. *Lady Gregory: Interviews and Recollections*. Totowa, N.J.: Rowman and Littlefield, 1977.
Saddlemyer, Ann, and Colin Smythe, eds. *Lady Gregory, Fifty Years After*. Totowa, N.J.: Barnes and Noble, 1987.

Caroline L. Cherry

WOZA ALBERT!

Authors: Mbongeni Ngema (1955-   ), Percy Mtwa, and Barney Simon (1932-1995)
Type of plot: Satire; political
Time of plot: The 1980's
Locale: Johannesburg, South Africa
First produced: 1981, at the Market Theatre, Johannesburg, South Africa
First published: 1983

> *Principal characters:*
> PERCY MTWA and
> MBONGENI NGEMA, coauthors of the play who, as themselves,
>   play different characters within it
> MORENA, the black Savior, voice only
> INTERVIEWER, a person reporting on Morena's impending arrival,
>   voice only

The Play

Woza Albert! is a twenty-six-scene, quick-action play, whose succession of vignettes of black life during South Africa's apartheid period shows the absurdity of racial oppression. It also illuminates the logic of a plot in which South Africans seek the return of a savior, Morena, who fulfills the biblical prophecy that Jesus Christ will return. The play's title means "Rise Albert," referring to the deceased leader of the African National Congress (ANC) and Nobel Peace Prize winner Albert Luthuli and symbolizing biblical prophecies that the dead will rise to join Jesus Christ when he is resurrected. At the conclusion of the play, Morena goes to the cemetery to raise Luthuli from the dead (as Jesus miraculously raised Lazarus in the New Testament) and to summon other prominent past leaders, including Robert Sobukwe, Lilian Ngoyi, and Steven Biko, to rise and make South Africa a "heaven on earth" for blacks by addressing the atrocities of apartheid.

The stage for *Woza Albert!* is sparsely set with two tea chests and a suspended wooden plank with nails that hold the ragged clothes that the actors use for character transformations. The actors wear pink clown noses held with elastic bands around their necks for use in scenes in which they portray white characters.

Brief chronological scenes reveal a thematic unity as the two characters demonstrate the types of relationships and encounters that exist within South African society. For example, in the opening scene, a policeman interrogates a South African entertainer about the expiration of his passbook, a permit that allows him to work and move about freely. The injustice of the episode is clear, but scene 2 confirms that such an offense leads to jail time for the offender. The successive scenes demonstrate South Africans' reduced quality of life and their desires for freedom and personhood as the actors transform themselves from prison inmates, who debate the merits of protest strategies versus religious perseverance, to train-hoppers, who debate religion and the possibilities of Morena returning.

Beginning in scene 7 the characters interview international figures, such as Cuban leader Fidel Castro, as well as local South Africans about their thoughts and expectations regarding Morena's possible visit to South Africa. These interviews mock modern media and television strategies of sensationalizing events for the sake of ratings, but as the characters transform into local South Africans, they reinforce the hopes and desires of an oppressed body of people. Mbongeni Ngema and Percy Mtwa adeptly reconstruct daily interactions that one would encounter in Johannesburg by dramatizing conversations with a young meat-vendor, who sells rotten meat; an old woman, who searches garbage cans for food; a barber, who works in an open-air market with only a chair and old clippers; and a fragile, toothless old man, who shares a historical narrative in order to emphasize that Morena will be slaughtered if he chooses to come to South Africa.

The foreboding seriousness of the old man's prophecy has a limited effect as the next set of scenes comically portrays the national and international, media-frenzied, Hollywood-style anticipation of Morena's arrival on a jumbo jet. "Film-makers" get full coverage of Morena's arrival, only to discover that the man they thought was Morena is merely a simple man, Mr. Smith, who is visiting his great-aunt Matilda.

With different motives, all levels of South African society begin to anticipate Morena's arrival, but no group anticipates the Savior's arrival more than African men struggling to find work, keep work, and receive money in order to meet the needs of their families. Ngema and Mtwa perform the most elaborate action of the play in scenes 16 and 18, when they scathingly demonstrate the exact nature of their day-to-day oppression by a system that has no regard for their human needs, their freedoms, their wives, or their children.

Inevitably, Morena arrives and, true to the play's biblical context, performs modern miracles, is betrayed and crucified, rises on the third day and resurrects South Africa's past heroes, and triumphantly shows that the human spirit of South Africans will survive. The ritual repetition of a freedom song in the final scene signifies celebration: "Our Lord is calling./ He's calling for the bones of the dead to join together./ He's raising up the black heroes./ He calls to them."

Themes and Meanings

Woza Albert! has been criticized for doing too much in too little space, likely because the play addresses oppression, labor, survival, separation of families between South African homelands and the cities, poverty and homelessness, police brutality, and political imprisonment. However, the play addresses three key themes that have the most meaningful implications for theatergoers. Resisting oppression with religious faith is an important theme of the play. This theme takes on ironic undertones because, in a society where there is such institutionalized racism and systematic oppression, it seems hypocritical that the Afrikaner government is a self-proclaimed Christian nation. Thus, the metaphor of the Savior's return is complex and appropriate for the type of satire that Ngema, Mtwa, and Barney Simon created for the stage.

Fantasizing a biblical prophecy in South Africa is ironic because all Morena's miracles relate to the mundane yet politicized struggles of South Africans. The play challenges people's definitions of fantasy by testing the apartheid government's commitment to Christianity and their anticipation and treatment of a black Savior. In scene 18, when Morena is betrayed and caught, Morena, like Jesus at the crucifixion, prays, "Forgive them, they do not know what they are doing," but his follower insists, "They know! They know!," a striking blow to the Christian morality that Afrikaners claim to have.

The play also questions to what extent freedom is a fantasy. The answer, for those who believe the promises of Christianity, is that freedom is not a fantasy because the Bible and the Savior have promised that it is possible for justice to reign on earth just as it does in heaven. In scene 22 the prisoners at Robben Island are perplexed with the fact that they, as prisoners, were given Bibles since the New Testament emphasizes freedom through a belief in the Savior.

The second coming of Christ, who is portrayed by the black Morena, internationalizes the apartheid struggle as a globally noteworthy situation and highlights another theme: Although the international media are readily willing to cover Jesus's return, the same media do not mobilize to demonstrate apartheid's atrocities to the world. This discrepancy indicts the international world for not helping South Africans gain freedom from apartheid. Numerous international newspapers and periodicals are mentioned for converging on Robben Island to get interviews with the soldiers guarding Morena. In addition, the mass media, including "pressmen, radiomen, South African television, [and] international television," were waiting for Morena upon his arrival at the airport in Johannesburg in order to get a good story.

The final theme of the play is the pressing need for South African black leadership. At the time the play was written, most leaders were either imprisoned or deceased. The one free leader, Bishop Desmond Tutu, is mentioned as one of the first people with whom Morena meets upon his arrival. The playwrights also refer to Nelson Mandela's imprisonment on Robben Island, although the text mentions him only as "the agitator imprisoned on the Island." Ngema and Mtwa give scathing commentary on so-called black leaders who act as "puppets" for the apartheid regime. The fact that Morena, a black Jesus, performs nonsupernatural "miracles" for South Africans is perhaps the true irony of the play. It suggests that ordinary men could also do these "feats" and that apartheid is so oppressive that the attainment of basic human rights requires supernatural power. Morena's resurrection of Luthuli, Sobukwe, Ngoyi, and Biko, among others, is a symbolic resurrection that becomes a call for new leaders to forge their way into the political struggle against apartheid in the tradition of these fallen heroes.

Dramatic Devices

Woza Albert! creatively makes use of satire and humor as a way of balancing sharp political commentary. The quick scene changes and the two-man, revue-style cast to cover more than one dozen different characterizations prevent the audience from being overwhelmed. The most visible prop, the clown nose used to designate white male characters, symbolizes the buffoonery, absurdity, and cowardice of the apartheid regime. Having the principal characters perform a multitude of roles under their real names gives the play a reality check and reminds audiences that these actor-playwrights have firsthand knowledge of the absurdity that they dramatize. In addition, many of the lines and words in the play are spoken in both Zulu and Afrikanns. The dramatic text provides translations.

The performers make use of mime, dance, music, song, and an impressive athleticism that sustains the energy of this ninety-minute, no-intermission play. Biblical symbolism grounds much of Morena's action throughout the play. He is asked to perform miracles comparable to those of Jesus and with which audiences are likely to be familiar. In scene 18, there is an archetypal Judas figure whose dramatic betrayal is identical to the biblical betrayal, except for the fact that Morena confronts his Judas face-to-face. The audience is also challenged to identify other biblical symbolism, such as an instance when Morena is hungry and thirsty but is offered only salt and vinegar-flavored potato chips and a cola drink. This is similar to Jesus being given vinegar, instead of water, when he requested a drink at his crucifixion.

Another dramatic convention is the characters' use of monologue to convey the words and actions of Morena during most of the play. This strategy implies that the action involves three characters, rather than the two men that audiences actually see. Morena is not characterized with his own voice until the final scene of the play. This use of monologue to permit virtual conversation between two actual characters and one virtual character is also used to present an invisible interviewer, who canvasses South Africans about the blessings and miracles they seek from the Savior.

Critical Context

Woza Albert! is regarded as South Africa's finest example of social theater, and the collaboration between Ngema and Mtwa, two black playwrights, and Simon, a white producer, was a significant relationship that crossed the color barrier. Theater served as a vehicle for educating white audiences about the horrors of apartheid and became a vehicle for black self-expression during this period when other, more direct forms of social criticism were banned. After *Woza Albert!* Mtwa continued to present the political realities of South African life in his play *Bopha!* (1986), which dramatized the conflicts between two brothers who have different interpretations of their functions as black policemen serving the white South African government. Simon's innovative Market Theatre continued to thrive, even after his death in 1995. Ngema went on to receive international acclaim for *Asinamali* (pr. 1983) and for *Sarafina* (pr. 1987).

Revolutionary anti-apartheid theater emerged in 1973 after the premier of Athol Fugard's play, *The Island* (pb. 1974), making plays such as *Woza Albert!* and Ngema's *Sarafina* and *Asinamali* possible. While the authorities attempted to ban such protest theater, the playwrights insisted that instead of being defined as protest theater, their art should instead be viewed as a celebration of surviving their life experiences. It is ironic that upon Mandela's release from Robben Island in 1990, the international media behaved similarly to the way in which Mtwa, Ngema, and Simon envisioned they would upon Morena's return. Mandela's freedom made several plays in the political protest genre irrelevant with their lines demanding that Mandela be released, but the end of apartheid and Mandela's release signaled a new era in which playwrights have the freedom to address concerns and social aspirations.

Sources for Further Study

Fuchs, Anne. "Re-Creation: One Aspect of Oral Tradition in the Theatre in South Africa." *Commonwealth Essays and Studies* 9 (Spring, 1987): 32-40.

Jenkins, Ron. "South African Political Clowning: Laughter and Resistance to Apartheid." In *Fools and Jesters in Literature, Art, and History: A Bio-bibliographical Sourcebook*, edited by Vicki K. Janik. Westport, Conn.: Greenwood Press, 1998.

Ngaboh-Smart, Francis. "The Politics of Black Identity: *Slave Ship* and *Woza Albert!*" *Journal of African Cultural Studies* 12 (December, 1999): 167-185.

Tompkins, Joanne. "Dressing Up/Dressing Down: Cultural Transvestism in Postcolonial Drama." In *The Body in the Library*, edited by Leigh Dale and Simon Ryan. Amsterdam: Rodopi, 1998.

Christel N. Temple

YANKEE DAWG YOU DIE

Author: Philip Kan Gotanda (1949-   )
Type of plot: Social realism
Time of plot: End of the twentieth century
Locale: Hollywood, California
First produced: 1987, at the Berkeley Repertory Theatre, Berkeley, California
First published: 1991

Principal characters:
> VINCENT CHANG, a successful actor of Japanese descent in his sixties
> BRADLEY YAMASHITA, an actor of Japanese descent in his late twenties

The Play

Yankee Dawg You Die begins and ends with Vincent Chang and Bradley Yamashita, two Asian American actors of different generations, in a private conversation on the balcony of a Hollywood Hills home while an entertainment industry party takes place inside. Nine scenes in two acts reveal one year of their relationship during which they move from initially feeling their differences acutely to their growing awareness of their similarities as actors, as American-born men of Japanese descent, and as humans full of powerful ambitions and abiding insecurities.

In the first scene the two men are strangers isolated on the balcony just as they are marginalized in the entertainment industry. Although allied by gender, profession, and dreams of success in the star system, they are divided by age, work experience, historical circumstance, and personal competitiveness. Meeting in auditions and in acting classes in the months that follow, Vincent and Bradley discuss their careers, the limited and stereotypical roles available to them, and their frustrations, accomplishments, and strategies for success. They learn each other's life secrets and, through conversations that often move in rhythms of revelation, insult, and apology, develop a bond of respect and affection. Woven into their conversations are dreamlike interludes that represent their inner feelings and their past and present roles in film and theater.

In the five scenes of act 1, the established star, Vincent Chang, reveals details of his decades-long career as a Hollywood actor, including the fact that he dropped his Japanese name and changed the shape of his nose in response to extreme racial prejudices in American society during and after World War II. Though generally limited to roles like that of Sergeant Moto, a gross 1940's stereotype of a Japanese soldier, his talent was recognized nonetheless by an Academy Award nomination for best supporting actor. Vincent's recollections of his career provide glimpses into the history of Asians in the American entertainment industry during the 1940's and 1950's. He moved from the "chop suey" vaudeville circuit to years of one-dimensional minor roles as menacing soldiers and obsequious houseboys and waiters, to the status of a leading man, who nevertheless is not allowed to kiss the female star.

In contrast, as a member of the newer generation of Asian American actors working in local theater, Bradley Yamashita is a politically correct idealist, who scorns Vincent's decisions to accept roles no matter how degrading they are. As the scenes unfold, Vincent and Bradley enact shifting roles of father and son, teacher and pupil, until eventually they become professional colleagues, confidants, and mutual supporters. Act 1 culminates in their collaboration in a workshop production of a political drama called *Godzilla* at a local Asian American theater. There they gain freedom to explore Asian experiences and traditions albeit at the price of exclusion from mainstream theater and culture.

Although act 2 begins with Vincent coaching Bradley for a Shakespearean role, its scenes are dominated by their mutual rage at mainstream exclusion and their painful career reversals. Bradley is rejected by his high-powered agent and is reassigned to an Asian agent. Vincent rehearses one line for a tiny role, this time as a North Vietnamese general—yet another version of the Sergeant Moto character. In the play's climax, scene 3 of act 2, Vincent declares that in Bradley, he sees himself. He identifies with Bradley's search for personal identity and fulfilling work, and he also sees that Bradley must struggle with the forces of discrimination just as he did thirty-five years earlier. Though the two men reverse their positions as the play ends, with Vincent acting in local Asian theater and Bradley compromising his ideals by taking a stereotypical commercial role, their careers suggest that little has changed for Asians in an American culture that continues to exclude non-Europeans from power with limited opportunities.

Themes and Meanings

Vincent's first speech as Sergeant Moto in interlude 1 evokes the "evil empire" and the gross distortions of Asian character by American propaganda during World War II. Moto's speech and the trite image of the vicious Japanese soldier are repeated with variations throughout the play, but Sergeant Moto breaks the stereotype by directly questioning Americans about their inability to truly see and hear him. Moto's appeal to be seen and heard—to be recognized as a human being—resonates in every scene.

The play also suggests, through the personal and professional struggles of Vincent and Bradley, that being identified as Asian American can cause one to be unseen and unheard. Philip Kan Gotanda suggests that being identified as a minority in the United States can be an unsatisfactory and limiting designation, perhaps just as debilitating as racist film stereotypes like Sergeant Moto. Both Vincent and Bradley are painfully aware that "Asian American" implies otherness, not American, or worse, less than American. The term "Asian" is itself a confusing conflation of many cultures—Japanese, Chinese, Vietnamese, Korean, and Indian, among others, and this conflation erases individual character and personal history. In the play, the shared experiences of Vincent and Bradley serve to criticize recent decades of American history and indict one-dimensional depictions of people of color, which persist in contemporary media and continue to exclude minorities from many entertainment arenas.

The two characters' lives represent not only the struggle of each to find meaningful work in his chosen profession but also the struggle of each to build a coherent personal identity in a society that subtly implies that color makes one "less than" or "other than" American. The term emphasizes difference even for those like Chang or Yamashita, born in the United States to families who have lived in the country for generations. Both men recount experiences that reveal their dual identity as a source of confusion and pain. How can one who has never been to Japan, cannot speak Japanese, and knows little of Japanese culture or traditions think of himself not as American but as Japanese American? How can one be proud of one's ancestry when it is used to exclude one from full acknowledgment as a human being?

Both actors wear many professional, public, and private faces in the play. They gaze upon and consume each other's performances and experiences. In seeing themselves in each other, they achieve the first step of being seen and heard by other Americans, perhaps taking the first step in social transformation. Bradley's initial condescension and his ideological disapproval of aspects of Vincent's career fade, and in the last scene, the two men stand together on the Hollywood balcony, this time as equals united in their star gazing, united in their continuing search for success among the roles in the entertainment industry. At the play's end, Vincent and Bradley look to the North Star as a symbol for guidance in life. Their new appreciation of each other suggests the value in celebrating the small personal, professional, and social victories, and their new bond implies a strong affirmation of the collective quest of Asian Americans to be seen and heard in American culture.

Dramatic Devices

The seven interludes of private reflection and glimpses of theatrical roles, which are incorporated into the play's nine realistic scenes, comment upon and dramatically contrast the exchanges between Vincent and Bradley. Like the entertainments integrated into traditional morality plays, these interludes operate as flashbacks or flashforwards and reflect conscious or unconscious experiences, all of which add depth and complexity to the play's characterizations and themes. The repetitious and varied racial stereotypes, seen by the audience in the past roles of Vincent and Bradley, constitute a cumulative critique of contemporary society. The faces and voices of Vincent and Bradley shown in the interludes contribute fluid, surreal depth to their portraits, an aspect further highlighted by minimalist staging, with shifting key words and thematic images projected upon abstract backdrops resembling traditional paper shoji screens.

The realistic drama begins and ends with Vincent and Bradley looking first at the real Hollywood stars partying nearby. However, the play also begins and ends with the image of the two men gazing upward at the North Star, a universal emblem of guidance. This symbolic scene affirms the possibility that the distortions and mazes of day-to-day struggle can be navigated if one's gaze is kept on the larger picture, the whole of human experience. Thus microcosmic and macrocosmic perspectives in the conventional scenes of the drama resonate with one another to suggest the possibility of finding a positive path into the future.

Critical Context

Philip Kan Gotanda established his national reputation with a series of realistic plays focused primarily on struggles within Japanese American families. These works included a trilogy of plays created during the 1980's, each of which showed the same Nisei family from the perspective of a different family member. Gotanda's focus on the professional lives of Asian American actors and the discrimination in the Hollywood entertainment industry in *Yankee Dawg You Die* appealed to broader audiences, and since the 1990's, the play has been produced not only in Asian American theaters but also in larger venues across the country. In addition to his successes in theater, he has also written, directed, and performed in award-winning independent films. Gotanda ranks among the most important pioneers of Asian American theater, finding a niche among notable literary figures such as Frank Chin, David Henry Hwang, and Velina Hasu Houston.

Yankee Dawg You Die continues to be performed and read for its exploration of the power of racial and gender stereotypes in contemporary lives as well as its examination of the power of the entertainment industry to perpetuate or fracture such fixed images. The play's glimpses into the history of Asians in film and theater offer opportunities to research and discuss American social change during the twentieth century.

Sources for Further Study

Fichandler, Zelda. "Casting for a Different Truth." *American Theatre* 5 (May, 1998): 18-23.

Kurahashi, Yuko. *Asian American Culture on Stage: The History of the East West Players*. New York: Garland, 1999.

Moy, James S. "David Henry Hwang's *M. Butterfly* and Philip Kan Gotanda's *Yankee Dawg You Die:* Repositioning Chinese American Marginality on the American Stage." *Theatre Journal* 42 (March, 1990): 48-56.

Shimakawa, Karen. "Asians in America: Millennial Approaches to Asian Pacific American Performance." *Journal of Asian American Studies* 3 (2000): 283-297.

Swanson, Meg, with Robin Murray. *Playwrights of Color*. Yarmouth, Maine: Intercultural Press, 1999.

Virginia M. Crane

THE YEAR OF THE DRAGON

Author: Frank Chin (1940-   )
Type of plot: Social realism
Time of plot: A Chinese New Year in the 1970's
Locale: San Francisco's Chinatown
First produced: 1974, at the American Place Theatre, New York City
First published: 1981, in *"The Chickencoop Chinaman" and "The Year of the Dragon": Two Plays by Frank Chin*

Principal characters:
FRED ENG, a Chinese American travel agent and tour guide
PA, Fred's father
CHINA MAMA, Pa's Chinese wife
MA, Pa's American wife
SIS (MATTIE), Fred's sister
ROSS, Mattie's husband
JOHNNY, Fred's brother

The Play

Act 1 begins with forty-year-old Fred Eng addressing a tour group in San Francisco's Chinatown during celebrations for the Chinese New Year. Using a stereotypical Chinese American accent, he identifies himself as Chinatown's best guide for a tour of the district's exotic sights. He tells the tourists they make him feel good and he likes them. After his spiel, however, the cursing under his breath reveals his contempt for this work.

In the next scene, Fred's sister Mattie (called "Sis" by family members) and her white husband, Ross, arrive at the Eng family apartment. The newlywed couple has traveled to the city from Boston to visit Sis's terminally ill father (Pa) and promote Sis's Chinese American cookbook—one of the projects of the couple's company, Mama Fu Fu, Inc. Ma, Sis's mother, only makes a slight reference to a seemingly unmovable Chinese woman—China Mama—who sits next to her luggage. This peasant woman had married Pa in China during the early 1930's, but an immigration law prohibited her from coming to the United States with her husband. Without a wife in this country, Pa married Ma—who was then a fifteen-year-old American who risked losing her citizenship by marrying a Chinese alien.

Sis appears uncomfortable in the presence of China Mama and, after a fourteen-year-long absence, seems to regret returning to a place which forces her to acknowledge her ethnic identity. Later, she confesses her distaste for the Chinatown inhabitants, whom she characterizes as "[r]ats, goodie goods, cowards, cry babies, failures, [and] nice Charlie Chans." In contrast, Ross relishes the opportunity to be in America's most famous Chinatown and have a look at first hand at a culture that he had avidly studied for many years.

After a long day of impersonating the happy Chinatown tour guide for people he despises, Fred is (not surprisingly) hostile to his brother-in-law, who unabashedly admits that he tells his wife he seems more Chinese than she does. Despite Sis's warnings, Ross appears to be oblivious to Fred's attitude toward him. Instead, he continues to anger his brother-in-law with his insensitive cultural remarks. Nevertheless, Fred realizes that Ross is still the husband of his beloved sister; further, the couple's business, in which Fred has a sizable investment, may one day provide him with a means of escaping his family's tourist business once his father has died. Moreover, he hopes that Sis and Ross might take his delinquent teenage brother, Johnny, back to Boston with them. In the East, Fred believes, Johnny would have a chance to avoid the bleak and desperate fate of the youth's hoodlum friends by obtaining a college education.

Pa comes home and promptly shows that he has little regard for Fred's ambitions. The elderly man reveals that China Mama is Fred's natural mother. He had sent for the woman at this time because he was sure that he would die this year—the year of the dragon. Pa expects Fred to continue working in the tourist business and add China Mama to the family members he has to support.

Pa fails to realize this new obligation has further strained his relationship with his son. At one time, Fred aspired to be a writer and had actually seen one of his works published. When Pa's illness was diagnosed, however, Pa asked Fred to leave college to run the family tourism business. Fred put his own dreams on hold as he met the familial responsibilities his father could no longer keep. Ironically, Pa seemed ashamed of Fred's success, because his son did not have a college degree or hold a more prestigious position. This became painfully evident when Fred realized his father had ceased to acknowledge their relationship in the presence of eminent Chinatown citizens.

After Johnny arrives to make the family complete, Pa announces that he has been named as the year's honorary Mayor of Chinatown and will deliver a speech during the New Year festivities. Pa insults Fred, a former English major, by asking his white son-in-law to correct the text of his speech for the proper use of the English language. In celebration of his appointment as mayor, he exuberantly dances until his overexertion causes him to collapse. Dutifully, Fred tends to his father as the sickly man coughs blood and defecates.

In the drama's climactic scene in act 2, Pa practices his mayor's speech against the festive sounds of the New Year's parade outside his home. In a joke written by Ross as a parody of 1930's film character Charlie Chan, Pa introduces Fred as his "Number One son [who] allaw time, saying 'Gee Pop!'" The telling of his joke, based on a disparaging stereotype, makes Fred aware of how much dignity the family had already lost. To salvage their last bit of integrity, Fred promises his father that he will not leave Chinatown if Pa will order Johnny and Ma to move to the East. When Pa refuses to do so, Fred will no longer acknowledge himself as his son. The conflict erupts into violence as Pa continuously strikes his passive son until the elder man collapses and dies.

At the play's end, Fred—dressed in a white suit—"appears to be a shrunken Charlie Chan, an image of death." His tour guide spiel has become bitter and hateful. He now describes Chinatown as a despairing and depressing place. He admits that tourists will not feel comfortable eating here and confesses he too knows "the feeling . . . BAD FEELING."

Themes and Meanings

In *The Year of the Dragon*, Frank Chin shows the detrimental effects that ethnic myths can have on a people. The Eng family attempts to exploit these myths for their own financial gain. For this end, however, they must pay a high price—the loss of their dignity. The Eng family have supported themselves by pandering to the expectations of tourists who have come to see the realization of myths about Chinese Americans. As guides, Fred and Johnny intentionally bastardize the English language and emphasize those features of Chinatown—exotic foods, strange sights, and alien social customs—which fit its stereotypical image. Although Sis criticizes her family's business, she too uses the popular image of Chinatown for her own gain. She perpetuates the myth in her Mama Fu Fu cookbook because she recognizes that the image can enhance sales.

The perpetuation of these myths takes its toll on the family. Knowing the tourism business perpetuates a sham, Johnny readily accepts the company of those involved in illegal activities because he can see little difference in the moral standards of the two enterprises. Sis shows a lack of ethnic pride and self-esteem by having married a man who, despite his cultural studies, displays an ignorance of her heritage and tends to exacerbate those conflicts which are tearing apart the family. Pa enjoys the financial rewards of the tourism business, yet he will not publicly acknowledge his eldest son because their enterprise is not one in which many Chinatown citizens take pride. When he finally decides to recognize Fred, it is within a humiliating context in which the stereotypical images of Charlie Chan and his "Number One Son" supplant the true relationship between Pa and his eldest son.

Fred has become accustomed to wearing the mask of the happy tour guide and removing it after working hours. However, the longer he remains in the business, the more difficult it becomes for him to separate his identities. His own aspirations become less important to him and, instead, he attempts to improve the prospects of other family members. To save the integrity of the family, Fred recognizes that Pa still commands enough respect from family members to be able to change the course of their lives. If Pa would acknowledge each member as an individual and encourage him to renounce the myths which bind them in shameful employment, then the family may have an opportunity to create lives of which they can be proud. When Pa refuses to allow such a change to occur, he condemns his family to a despondent life controlled by destructive cultural myths.

Dramatic Devices

Frank Chin uses various dramatic devices to reveal the deterioration of the Eng family resulting from the influence of cultural myths. Through a series of monologues interspersed throughout the play, changes in Fred's character as the tourist guide effectively mirror the degeneration of the Engs. Initially, Fred seems able to separate his contempt for his work from his spiel. He dons the mask of the happy tour guide and finds an outlet for his disdain by cursing under his breath after he has finished his pitch. Fred cannot continue to withstand the destructive pressures of the cultural myths, however, which have already weakened the integrity of his family. Each successive tourist spiel becomes more tinged with cynicism and more flagrant in its pandering to the stereotypical images sought by the tourists. At play's end, after the family has lost its last shred of dignity, the spiritual death of the Engs is reflected in the supplanting of Fred's character with that of a stereotype. Devoid of any semblance of his former self and dressed in white like Charlie Chan, this final image of Fred creates within the audience an unforgettable portrait of a man lacking a sense of self-esteem or hope for the future.

As effective as these monologues is the use of the festive sounds of the New Year's parade as a striking contrast to the clash of wills between father and son during the play's climactic scene. By themselves, the joyful sounds of celebration punctuated by remarks from the parade's cheerful commentator would create an atmosphere of fun and merriment. In this scene, however, the activity serves to emphasize the disparity in the mood between the festivities and the bitter conflict within the Eng home which will lead to the destruction of that family. Using a broader perspective, the scene illustrates how the festive mask worn by Chinatown during such celebrations functions to hide serious internal problems which are causing its social structure to deteriorate.

Other dramatic devices also serve to expose problems within the Eng family. The play uses overlapping dialogue to show that family members are often more interested in giving their own opinions than fully listening to and considering the concerns of others. At several points during the drama, a lack of communication is also exhibited when two or more topics of conversation are discussed simultaneously while the characters seem unaware of what the others are talking about. After Pa collapses in act 1, the lighting of incense before the photographs of deceased Eng relatives suggests an expectation of death by family members. In act 2, the lighting of more incense, and its lingering smell, serves as a morbid reminder of a dreadful prediction that will be fulfilled at play's end.

Critical Context

When Frank Chin's drama *The Chickencoop Chinaman* (pr. 1972) was first produced, it was the first serious play by an Asian American given the opportunity to be produced on the professional stage in New York. *The Year of the Dragon* also enjoyed a professional production and a much wider audience when the Public Broadcasting Service (PBS) televised the play in its "Theatre in America" series in 1975. Through his writings and lectures, Chin has undoubtedly inspired more Asian Americans to use the theater as a vehicle for the depiction of their lives and experiences.

The Year of the Dragon challenges the romanticized portrait of Chinatown previously presented in novels, films, and the theater. Several times in the play, Chin makes disparaging references to a popular novel, *Flower Drum Song* (1957), by C. Y. Lee, which later was adapted into a Broadway musical (pr. 1958) and film (1961). For Chin, works such as *Flower Drum Song* foster a superficial, idealized image of Chinatown and its inhabitants. While characters in these works are sometimes shown to be affected by racial discrimination, the works tend not to treat seriously the lasting and debilitating effects of discriminatory practices.

In contrast, *The Year of the Dragon* presents a more complex, although despairing view of the experience of Chinese Americans. Chin's characters strive to make the American Dream a reality by catering to the cultural myths created by the general public. Though financially successful, they find themselves unable to withstand the degenerating effects of the stereotypes they had adopted for monetary gains. Moreover, in both this drama and *The Chickencoop Chinaman*, Chin calls attention to the plight of the Chinese American who lacks a sense of identity or role models on which to pattern himself. The dramatist appears to be telling his audience that without self-understanding, the American citizen of Chinese descent will never truly feel a part of the American mainstream.

Sources for Further Study
Chu, Patricia P. "Tripmaster Monkey, Frank Chin and the Chinese Heroic Tradition." *Arizona Quarterly: A Journal of American Literature, Culture, and Theory*, Autumn, 1997, 117-139.
Kim, Elaine H. *Asian American Literature: An Introduction to the Writings and Their Social Context*. Philadelphia: Temple University Press, 1982.
_____. "Frank Chin: The Chinatown Cowboy and His Backtalk." *Midwest Quarterly* 20 (Autumn, 1978): 78-91.
Kroll, Jack. *"Primary Color."* *Newsweek*, June 19, 1972, 55.
Li, David Leiwei. "The Production of Chinese American Tradition: Displacing American Orientalist Discourse." In *Reading the Literatures of Asian America*, edited by Shirley Geok Lim and Amy Ling. Philadelphia: Temple University Press, 1992.
McDonald, Dorothy Ritsuko. Introduction to *"The Chickencoop Chinaman" and "The Year of the Dragon": Two Plays by Frank Chin*. Seattle: University of Washington Press, 1981.
Wong, William. "Chinatown Viewed from Within." *Wall Street Journal*, June 19, 1972, p. 14.

Addell Austin

YOU CAN'T TAKE IT WITH YOU

Authors: George S. Kaufman (1889-1961) and Moss Hart (1904-1961)
Type of plot: Farce
Time of plot: 1936
Locale: New York City
First produced: 1936, at the Booth Theater, New York City
First published: 1937

Principal characters:

PENELOPE "PENNY" VANDERHOF SYCAMORE, a mother in her
  mid-fifties

ESSIE SYCAMORE CARMICHAEL, her daughter, a dancer and candy
  maker

ED CARMICHAEL, Essie's husband, a xylophonist and printer

PAUL SYCAMORE, Penny's husband, a fireworks maker

GRANDPA MARTIN VANDERHOF, the person around whom the
  family revolves

ALICE SYCAMORE, a nearly normal younger daughter of Penny
  and Paul

ANTHONY "TONY" KIRBY, JR., Alice's boyfriend

MR. DE PINNA, a former iceman who has been in the house for
  eight years

RHEBA, the maid

DONALD, Rheba's boyfriend

BORIS KOLENKHOV, a ballet teacher and wrestler

MR. KIRBY, Tony's father, a powerful businessman

MRS. KIRBY, Tony's mother, a conventional woman

The Play

You Can't Take It with You opens with Penny Vanderhof Sycamore typing at a play
in the living room of a house near Columbia University. She is working on her elev-
enth play in the eight years since a typewriter arrived at the house, quite by accident;
in this household, the delivery of a typewriter is enough to begin a literary career.
Essie Carmichael enters from making candy in the kitchen, and the nonstop action begins. While Essie practices dancing, Penny tries to extricate her heroine from the
monastery in which she has spent the last six years. At times, she wonders aloud
whether to return to sculpture. Mr. Sycamore and Mr. De Pinna arrive from making
fireworks in the basement; they plan a grand display including balloons. Ed Carmichael begins playing the xylophone. When Donald arrives to visit Rheba, he brings
flies for Grandpa's snakes. Ed plans to print some sayings from Trotsky to package
with Essie's next batch of candy.

Grandpa Vanderhof, still spry at age seventy-five, has just attended a graduation at Columbia University. When Alice arrives home, she seems very different from the other inhabitants. While Alice talks about her boyfriend and boss, a government man makes inquiries about Grandpa's back taxes. Grandpa has not been paying taxes; indeed, he has been doing whatever pleases him since he walked away from his job thirty-five years ago. Grandpa buried an unnamed milkman as a Vanderhof when he died eight years before the time of the play. Now when mail comes for Grandpa, no one thinks to give it to him. Having seen none of the government's letters, he does not know that the government wants back taxes. Tony visits Alice to meet the family. Kolenkhov begins a dance lesson with Essie. At any slight lull in the action, a new set of fireworks booms out of the basement. The absurdities continue in the second scene. Alice explains to Tony that her family is not normal; various members of the household readily demonstrate that fact. Nevertheless, Tony plans to marry Alice.

In act 2, Grandpa brings a drunken actor home to help Penny with her play. Alice announces that she has invited the Kirbys to dinner. As the family makes grand plans for the dinner, the Kirbys arrive a night early. Grandpa explains something of his philosophy to Mr. Kirby. He does what pleases him rather than conforming to what the world requires for success. He points out that he does not need bicarbonate and that he enjoys freedom from taxes and business worries.

Kolenkhov shows that he is also a wrestler by throwing Mr. Kirby to the floor. Before a second dinner is ready, Mrs. Kirby starts their exit by pleading a headache. While Penny tries to invite the Kirbys to return the next night, Alice tells Tony that that would not work. Before the Kirbys can leave, FBI men stop everything and arrest everyone, including the Kirbys. They are investigating the printed sayings that Ed has put in Essie's candy packages. Grandpa explains that Ed just likes to print words that sound nice. The agents also discover the gunpowder from the illegal fireworks operation in the basement, and they lead Mr. De Pinna from the cellar. Before they leave for the jail, Mr. De Pinna's pipe (left in the basement during the commotion) sets off the whole year's supply of fireworks. The second act ends in mayhem.

Like the first two acts, the third contains frantic activity and fast-paced dialogue. Donald reads the news account of the night in jail. Rheba explains Mrs. Kirby's reaction to a stripteaser who sang a stripping song while Mrs. Kirby was being searched. Rheba regrets that no party will use the party food. Every piece of the fireworks has exploded. Alice will not return to work and is ready to leave everything behind. Kolenkhov brings the Grand Duchess Olga Katrina, now a waitress in New York, to visit, and she fixes her special blintzes for dinner. Tony tries to keep Alice from leaving. Mr. Kirby comes to find Tony. Before he can rescue Tony, he finds himself discussing life and happiness with Grandpa Vanderhof; Grandpa points out that Mr. Kirby worries himself to make more money although he has all he can use. He concludes, "you can't take it with you." His philosophy is simple: Enjoy life by doing what one wants and avoiding doing things merely to please others or to make money. Tony reminds his father of his youth when he tried to run away from business, but Mr. Kirby retorts that he is thankful that his father knocked those ideas out of him. Tony points out that he still has a saxophone in the back of his closet. He adds that he intended to bring his parents on the wrong night; he wanted them to see a real family.

Grandpa suggests that most people would not be willing to settle for what they eventually get; Mr. Kirby agrees to eat the duchess's blintzes; the United States government even apologizes for trying to collect taxes from a man who has officially been dead for eight years. Grandpa offers a simple grace:

> Well, Sir, here we are again. . . . Things seem to be going along fine. Alice is going to marry Tony. . . . Of course the fireworks blew up, but that was Mr. De Pinna's fault not Yours. We've all got our health and as far as anything else is concerned we'll leave that to You. Thank you.

Everyone begins talking in different directions once again.

Themes and Meanings

You Can't Take It with You is a situational farce that reflects its time. It presents a reaction to the struggles that filled the minds of Americans during the Great Depression. The title indicates one theme of the play: Accumulation of wealth is useless when it goes beyond immediate happiness. Whatever one accumulates cannot be taken beyond the grave. If gaining wealth (or achieving other success) is done for others, then it does not bring happiness. Rather, the good life consists in doing what one wants to do instead of what is considered normal or reasonable. After this premise is accepted, the actions become logical extensions of the characters.

The skimpy plot revolves around the love relationship between Alice and Tony, but the household revolves around Grandpa. Grandpa is the center of the thematic development of acting to give oneself happiness. Grandpa and his followers seek personal fulfillment, even when their desires lead to activity that most consider meaningless. Grandpa himself collects snakes and attends commencement exercises. Thirty-five years before the time of the play, he had decided to leave his job on the spur of the moment. He rejects the joyless pursuit of money and power. Penny writes plays and attempts to sculpt Mr. De Pinna as a Greek discus thrower. Essie dances and makes candy; at least the candy making shows some profit. Ed prints things that sound good and plays the xylophone. Paul Sycamore makes fireworks and generally accepts anyone for what he or she is. Mr. De Pinna formerly delivered ice and now helps make fireworks, from which there is an occasional profit. Kolenkhov ostensibly visits to teach Essie ballet but really comes to get a good meal and sometimes to exercise his wrestling skills. By the end of the play, Mr. Kirby joins the free spirits for dinner. The film version, which won the Academy Award for Best Picture of 1938, emphasizes the conversion of Mr. Kirby, by having him play a harmonica duet with Grandpa. Only Mrs. Kirby has not escaped the bonds of success.

The conventional love story centers on Alice and Tony, who accepts the eccentricities of her family. Some have found the love interest the only portion of the play that is dull and essentially humorless, while others, including Hollywood, have found it the part that ensures the play's being a comedy. Tony, the son of a wealthy family, falls in love with his typist, the daughter of the Sycamore family of inspired bedlam. The only way that boy can keep girl in this play is for him to convince her that his father accepts the premises of her family. Since what Alice really wants is to marry Tony, the idea of the upcoming marriage fulfills Grandpa's philosophy of acting to enjoy oneself. Tony and Alice are set for their version of the good life. The play becomes farce with some slight purpose, but its major meaning is sheer entertainment. With the multiple action taking place, the play presents laughs and escape throughout.

Dramatic Devices

You Can't Take It with You presents the audience with a variety of action. Snakes, a typewriter, a saxophone, a xylophone, and dancing all abound. Offstage are the basement with its fireworks manufacture and the kitchen with its candy making and meal preparation. Any lull in the onstage action is sure to start fireworks from the basement. The dialogue is typical of George S. Kaufman and Moss Hart. Grandpa argues that he should not pay the income tax by asking what the government would do with the money. He continues, "What do I get for my money? If I go into Macy's and buy something, there it *is*—I see it. What's the Government give me?" After listening to the agent's list of things that government supplies, Grandpa decides that he might pay seventy-five dollars. The dialogue leaps from subject to subject, its logic apparent only to the characters themselves. As Essie asks Ed to remember the music he just played on his xylophone, Penny interjects, "Ed, dear. Why don't you and Essie have a baby?" Ed and Essie answer, but Penny is already back working with her manuscripts.

A rickety card table used for typing, cages for snakes, a xylophone, and the dining table fill the set; the family really lives in this room. Entrances are timed for comedic effect. Immediately after Alice asks that a nice dinner be planned for Tony's parents on the next evening, the Kirbys show up in full evening dress. As the Kirbys start to leave, the government agents arrive and arrest everyone. While Mr. Sycamore stalls Alice's request for a taxi, Tony arrives to intervene. Exits also offer grounds for comedy. The tax agent starts to leave after threatening Grandpa, only to be warned to watch out for the snakes and then to be frightened by an explosion from the basement. He literally jumps out of the room. Penny's word association game is filled with words that embarrass Alice: potatoes, bathroom, lust, honeymoon, sex.

The action on the crowded set includes Essie dancing through conversations, Kolenkhov throwing Mr. Kirby to the floor in a wrestling demonstration, and the pompous entrance and attempted exit of Mr. and Mrs. Kirby. Sound effects range from Penny typing and Ed printing to the music of Ed's xylophone and the frequent explosions of the fireworks from the basement.

The hobbies chosen by each of the characters help to build the characterization. Each of the images created by the hobbies indicates how far the Vanderhof family departs from the accepted norm in its pursuit of true happiness. Money, success, and power have no place in their activities. The Kirbys, in contrast, choose hobbies that are fashionable for the rich and powerful: Mr. Kirby raises orchids, and Mrs. Kirby pursues spiritualism. Alice explains to Tony, "Your mother believes in spiritualism because it's fashionable, and your father raises orchids because he can afford to. My mother writes plays because eight years ago a typewriter was delivered here by mistake."

Critical Context

You Can't Take It with You is one of six plays, two musicals, and one one-act written by the team of George S. Kaufman and Moss Hart. Best known of the other plays are *Once in a Lifetime* (pr., pb. 1930), *The Man Who Came to Dinner* (pr., pb. 1939), and *George Washington Slept Here* (pr., pb. 1940). Kaufman and Hart were the most successful collaborators of their generation. Despite a few topical references to the contemporary scene, *You Can't Take It with You* wears well. Some revivals change the topical references; others allow them to provide historical authenticity.

You Can't Take It with You reflects the Depression era from which it comes. The madcap farce of antimaterialism opened in December of 1936. By February, 1937, its seats were selling four months in advance. It was not until the heat waves of July and August that there were empty seats, and even then they had been sold. Its initial run included 837 performances. The combination of the notion of seeking happiness by pursuing activities for their own sake and the delightful spectacle of the Vanderhofs penetrating the pomposity of the Kirbys perfectly fit the needs of late Depression-era audiences. It was selected as the Pulitzer Prize winner for the best play of 1937.

The main idea that the good life comes from doing what one wants to do rather than what others consider reasonable or even normal serves as a sound comic base. When pushed to farce, it becomes an entertaining tale of a madcap family juxtaposed with a staid family from the successful social world of American business. Despite their unmethodical actions, the Vanderhofs do seem to offer sense. They urge members of the audience to seek their own paths rather than to conform to the ways of their society. They may be mad, but they are lovable. These eccentrics provide a form of almost sensible insanity; when contrasted to the power-crazed successes of their day, they seem both happier and more sensible. *You Can't Take It with You* provides both entertainment and insight into the mindset of the Depression era as it warns against taking standard ideas of success too seriously.

Sources for Further Study

Brown, John Mason. "The Sensible Insanities of *You Can't Take It with You.*" In *Two on the Aisle: Ten Years of the American Theatre in Performance*. New York: W. W. Norton, 1938.

Goldstein, Malcolm. *George S. Kaufman: His Life, His Theater.* New York: Oxford University Press, 1979.

Gould, Jean. "Some Clever Collaborators: George S. Kaufman and Moss Hart." In *Modern American Playwrights*. New York: Dodd, Mead, 1966.

Harriman, Margaret Case. "Hi-yo Platinum! Moss Hart." In *Take Them Up Tenderly: A Collection of Profiles*. New York: A. A. Knopf, 1945.

Hart, Moss. *Act One: An Autobiography.* 3d ed. New York: St. Martin's Press, 1989.

Mason, Jeffrey D. *Wisecracks: The Farces of George S. Kaufman.* Ann Arbor: University of Michigan Research Press, 1988.

Mason, Richard. "The Comic Theater of Moss Hart: Persistence of a Formula." *Theater Annual* 23 (1968): 60-87.

Meredith, Scott. *George S. Kaufman and His Friends.* Garden City, N.Y.: Doubleday, 1974.

Pollack, Rhoda-Gale. *George S. Kaufman.* Boston: Twayne, 1988.

Teichmann, Howard. *George S. Kaufman: An Intimate Portrait.* New York: Atheneum, 1972.

David B. Merrell

THE YOUNG MAN FROM ATLANTA

Author: Horton Foote (1916-   )
Type of plot: Domestic realism
Time of plot: Spring, 1950
Locale: Houston, Texas
First produced: 1995, at the Kampo Cultural Center, New York City
First published: 1995

> *Principal characters:*
> WILL KIDDER, a businessman
> LILY DALE KIDDER, his wife, a homemaker
> PETE DAVENPORT, Lily Dale's stepfather
> RANDY CARTER, a former roommate of Will's son and the play's
>   title character
> CARSON, Pete's great-nephew
> TED CLEVELAND, JR., head of Will's company
> TOM JACKSON, Will's young colleague and friend
> CLARA, the Kidders' African American maid
> ETTA DORIS, formerly the Kidders' maid

The Play

The Young Man from Atlanta is set in Houston, Texas, in the spring of 1950. The first of its six scenes takes place in the office of the wholesale grocery company where Will Kidder, who is sixty-four, has worked since he was in his early twenties. The setting of the remaining five scenes is the den of Will's expensive new home.

The play begins with Will at his desk, taking a final look at his house plans. As Will explains to his fellow worker Tom Jackson, his house is tangible proof of his deepest conviction: that whatever his background, a man with a gift for competition will always succeed. Will seems untroubled by the fact that building the house has wiped out his savings or by his recent discovery that he has developed heart trouble. He has even come to terms with the death of his son Bill, which Will is certain was not an accident but suicide. The title character of the play is Bill's former roommate, Randy Carter. Will confides to Tom that he suspects Randy's motives and has forbidden his wife, Lily Dale, to have any further communication with him. Clearly Will believes in himself, in his future, and in his ability to deal with whatever life brings him. Before the scene ends, however, his confidence is shattered. Will is fired by Ted Cleveland, Jr., the son of the man with whom Will built the business. Cleveland tells Will that he is no longer effective. For the good of the business, he must be replaced by a younger man, Will's protégé Tom Jackson.

In the scene that follows, Will experiences one disappointment after another. At first he is sure that he can start his own business. However, the bankers he thought were his friends are less than cordial. Although Lily Dale's stepfather Pete Davenport will help, Will needs far more than Pete has available. When Will asks Lily Dale for a loan from her savings account, into which she had deposited the money he gave her each Christmas, she has to admit that she has given almost all of her funds to Randy, primarily because he kept assuring her that her son, Bill, was a good, religious man. Lily Dale's revelation causes Will to fly into a fury and precipitates a heart attack.

In the third scene, which takes place one week later, Will is recovering. However, his relationship with Lily Dale is so strained that they cannot even discuss what looks like a very grim future. Nevertheless, Will still has enough pride to tear up a check from Ted. Meanwhile, another young man from Atlanta has appeared, Pete's great-nephew Carson. He soon has Pete charmed into paying for his mother's operation and his own college education, as well as for an excursion to Atlanta, where, it appears, Carson had known both Bill and Randy.

The play ends with Will and Lily Dale reconciled. Though Will is still not well, he plans to take advantage of Ted's offer of a lower-level job, while, despite her age, Lily Dale may start teaching music again. Will's discovery that his son gave his roommate every cent he had has intensified his suspicions about their relationship, but Lily Dale still chooses to believe in the young man from Atlanta and in the version of her son that he provides for her.

Themes and Meanings

The Young Man from Atlanta is a play that pits the wisdom of this world against a higher standard. In the end, the characters whose only principle is self-interest are shown as the real losers, while those who hold to their values triumph over adversity.

It is interesting that those characters who seem to lack moral standards are all relatively young. The title character takes advantage of a mother's grief in order to extract money from her. Pete's great-nephew is no better; in fact, he uses similar hard-luck stories to pry Pete loose from his Houston family and from his money. One suspects that the only true statement Randy makes in the course of the play is that Carson has a bad character. Ted Cleveland, Jr., is also unprincipled. He does not value Will's past achievements or his proven loyalty. Instead, he dismisses him, assuming that a younger man will do better, despite the fact that everything Tom knows he has learned from Will. Tom himself feels some twinges of guilt about taking Will's job, but not enough to argue with Ted.

Will's dead son, too, exhibits a lack of moral fiber. Though he may have been a hero in wartime, he lacks the courage to face the fact that his roommate or sexual partner is taking advantage of him, perhaps blackmailing him. He must have known that his suicide would devastate his parents, but he flees from life just the same.

By contrast, the older characters in the play all hold to their old-fashioned values. Ignoring Lily Dale's insensitivity, as shown in her foolish comments about the Disappointment Club, both Clara and Etta Doris demonstrate their capacity for compassion when they sympathize with Lily Dale and reassure her that God will sustain her. Lily Dale and Pete, too, are kindly souls. It is their generosity of spirit, however, that makes it so easy for the two young men to part them from their money.

Although at first he is shown to be as smug and boastful as a Greek tragic hero, Will Kidder, too, becomes more admirable in adversity. Though, unlike his wife, he cannot find the answers he seeks in religion, like her he does accept the fact that one has no real control over his or her fate. All anyone can do, he finds, is to respond appropriately. When he asks Lily Dale and Pete for money and later, when he agrees to take whatever job Ted offers, Will demonstrates a new humility. When he forgives Lily Dale and even lets her keep her illusions about her son, Will shows his new understanding of what love means. Like a tragic hero, Will has become a far wiser man, and a better person, than he was at the beginning of the play.

Dramatic Devices

The Young Man from Atlanta has simple, realistic sets. The first scene takes place in the office where Will works; it is functional but not luxurious. The other scenes take place in the den of the Kidders' new home, a room that is described as well furnished but rather impersonal. Most of the time, the dialogue is just as sparse as the sets, and even when Will is boasting or Lily is reminiscing, one has a feeling that the actual words are inconsequential, like a musical accompaniment to the real action. Like the language, the movements of the actors exhibit a high degree of restraint. They walk in, talk, and walk out. There are no grand gestures. This simplicity is consistent with Foote's intention: to present what seems like a slice of life, leaving the audience to find the underlying themes by paying attention to the hints the playwright has provided.

One of the most unusual devices employed by Foote is his use of an invisible but extremely important title character. The "young man from Atlanta" is in Houston throughout the play, attempting to reach Will or Lily Dale by phone or appearing at their home, only to be turned away by the maid. In the final scene, Lily Dale confesses to her husband that despite his objections, she has seen Randy once more; despite her pleas, Will refuses to see him. Though he never appears onstage, Randy is as important to the play as if he were actually present. He is the most menacing figure in the play, though it is not clear what he has done or exactly who he is. In Will's eyes, he remains a menace, and even more so because Lily Dale continues to see him as the medium through whom she can maintain contact with her deceased son. Like Will, the audience has to live with the mystery of what may or may not have happened in the past and with the certainty that the "young man from Atlanta" will continue to be a sinister presence in the Kidders' future life.

Critical Context

Over his half-century career, Horton Foote has written some fifty plays, along with numerous successful scripts for radio, television, and film. Two of his screenplays brought him Academy Awards: his adaptation of Harper Lee's *To Kill a Mockingbird* (1962) and his original screenplay *Tender Mercies* (1983). In 1995, Foote won a Pulitzer Prize for his play *The Young Man from Atlanta*. However, though Foote is ranked among the finest American dramatists, his plays are not as well known as his films. Generally his plays have been produced at small theaters well away from Broadway;

sometimes they have not even made it to New York. *The Young Man from Atlanta* was produced by an Off-Off-Broadway company and, according to a *New York Times* editorial writer, it was seen by only seventeen hundred people over its four-week run.

Negative reviews of *The Young Man from Atlanta* suggest why Foote's dramas are less popular than they deserve to be. The play was called uninspired, insubstantial, and undramatic. However, other reviewers noted that, although Foote's middle-class southerners are too well mannered to make scenes or to voice their frustrations in profanity, their sufferings are just as intense as those of the undisciplined characters so often seen in contemporary theater. As his admirers point out, Foote is a realist. The substance of his plays is life as it is lived by millions of Americans. His characters work hard, lose their jobs, worry about money, quarrel with their spouses and forgive them, love and lose their children, face illness and death, and, sometimes with the aid of religion and sometimes with only the vague hope of something better, still find the strength to go on.

In its style, its subject matter, and its themes, *The Young Man from Atlanta* resembles Foote's other plays. It is true that the setting is Houston, rather than the small fictional town called Harrison or Richmond, which is based on Foote's native Wharton, Texas. Harrison/Richmond was the setting of most of Foote's earlier works, including the nine-cycle play *The Orphans' Home* (pr. 1977-1997, pb. 1987-1989), in which Will, Lily Dale, and Pete all appeared. Clearly when they moved to Houston, these characters all brought with them their small-town customs and their old-fashioned values. For fifty years, Foote's plays have revealed his abiding belief that one can find stability in a changing world only in such old-fashioned principles as honor, loyalty, courage, family, and faith.

Sources for Further Study

Briley, Rebecca Luttrell. *You Can Go Home Again: The Focus on Family in the Works of Horton Foote*. New York: Peter Lang, 1993.

Gallagher, Michael. "Horton Foote: Defying Heraclitus in Texas." *Southern Literary Journal* 32 (Fall, 1999): 77-80.

Wall, James M. "The World of Horton Foote: Home, Family, Religion." *Christian Century* 114 (February 19, 1997): 179-180.

Wood, Gerald C. *Horton Foote and the Theater of Intimacy*. Baton Rouge: Louisiana State University Press, 1999.

_____. "Old Beginnings and Roads to Home: Horton Foote and Mythic Realism." *Christianity and Literature* 45 (Spring/Summer, 1996): 359-372.

_____. "The Physical Hunger for the Spiritual: Southern Religious Experience in the Plays of Horton Foote." In *The World Is Our Home: Society and Culture in Contemporary Southern Writing*, edited by Jeffrey J. Folks and Nancy Summer Folks. Lexington: University Press of Kentucky, 2000.

_____, ed. *Horton Foote: A Casebook*. New York: Garland, 1998.

Rosemary M. Canfield Reisman

CHRONOLOGICAL LIST OF TITLES

This index lists all the plays covered in *Masterplots II: Drama Series, Revised* in order of the earliest dates they were produced or published. (Most plays were produced before they were published. See the articles on the individual plays for fuller production and publication details.)

1937   *The Lost Colony* (Paul Green)
         Susan and God (Rachel Crothers)
         Time and the Conways (J. B. Priestley)

1938   *The Corn Is Green* (Emlyn Williams)
         Ivona, Princess of Burgundia (Witold Gombrowicz)
         Restless Heart (Jean Anouilh)

1939   *Morning's at Seven* (Paul Osborn)
         The Philadelphia Story (Philip Barry)

1942   *As the Crow Flies* (Austin Clarke)
         Red Roses for Me (Sean O'Casey)

1943   *The Good Woman of Setzuan* (Bertolt Brecht)

1944   *Caligula* (Albert Camus)
         Harvey (Mary Chase)

1945   *The Hasty Heart* (John Patrick)

1946   *The Chinese Wall* (Max Frisch)
         An Inspector Calls (J. B. Priestley)
         The Winslow Boy (Terence Rattigan)

1947   *Summer and Smoke* (Tennessee Williams)

1948   *Anne of the Thousand Days* (Maxwell Anderson)
         The Caucasian Chalk Circle (Bertolt Brecht)
         The Marriage (Witold Gombrowicz)
         Mister Roberts (Thomas Heggen and Joshua Logan)

1949   *The Big Knife* (Clifford Odets)
         Cock-a-Doodle Dandy (Sean O'Casey)
         Deathwatch (Jean Genet)
         Romulus the Great (Friedrich Dürrenmatt)
         South Pacific (Oscar Hammerstein II and Joshua Logan)

1950   *Come Back, Little Sheba* (William Inge)
         The Rose Tattoo (Tennessee Williams)

1951   *The Lesson* (Eugène Ionesco)
         A Penny for a Song (John Whiting)

1952   *The Chairs* (Eugène Ionesco)
         A Moon for the Misbegotten (Eugene O'Neill)

1953   *Camino Real* (Tennessee Williams)
         Picnic (William Inge)
         Tea and Sympathy (Robert Anderson)

Purlie Victorious (Ossie Davis)
The Screens (Jean Genet)
Song of a Goat (John Pepper Clark-Bekederemo)
The Tree Climber (Tawfiq al-Hakim)

1962   *The Black Hermit* (Ngugi wa Thiong'o)
Exit the King (Eugène Ionesco)
Funnyhouse of a Negro (Adrienne Kennedy)
The Physicists (Friedrich Dürrenmatt)
The Subject Was Roses (Frank D. Gilroy)
Words and Music (Samuel Beckett)

1963   *Barefoot in the Park* (Neil Simon)
The Deputy (Rolf Hochhuth)
The Garden Party (Václav Havel)
In White America (Martin B. Duberman)
A Severed Head (Iris Murdoch and J. B. Priestley)
The Tragedy of King Christophe (Aimé Césaire)

1964   *After the Fall* (Arthur Miller)
Benito Cereno (Robert Lowell)
Blues for Mister Charlie (James Baldwin)
Entertaining Mr. Sloane (Joe Orton)
Inadmissible Evidence (John Osborne)
Incident at Vichy (Arthur Miller)
Philadelphia, Here I Come! (Brian Friel)
The Royal Hunt of the Sun (Peter Shaffer)
The Sign in Sidney Brustein's Window (Lorraine Hansberry)
Tiny Alice (Edward Albee)

1965   *The Effect of Gamma Rays on Man-in-the-Moon Marigolds*
        (Paul Zindel)
The Homecoming (Harold Pinter)
Keep Tightly Closed in a Cool Dry Place (Megan Terry)
Loot (Joe Orton)
The Memorandum (Václav Havel)
The Road (Wole Soyinka)
Saved (Edward Bond)
Tango (Sławomir Mrożek)

1966   *America Hurrah* (Jean-Claude van Itallie)
Offending the Audience (Peter Handke)
Operetta (Witold Gombrowicz)
A Rat's Mass (Adrienne Kennedy)
The Rimers of Eldritch (Lanford Wilson)

1973   *Da* (Hugh Leonard)
             The Freedom of the City (Brian Friel)
             The Hot l Baltimore (Lanford Wilson)
             The Last Meeting of the Knights of the White Magnolia (Preston
                 Jones)
             The Norman Conquests (Alan Ayckbourn)
             The Transfiguration of Benno Blimpie (Albert Innaurato)
             When You Comin' Back, Red Ryder? (Mark Medoff)

1974   *Buchanan Dying* (John Updike)
             The Floating World (John Romeril)
             Geography of a Horse Dreamer (Sam Shepard)
             Lu Ann Hampton Laverty Oberlander (Preston Jones)
             The Oldest Living Graduate (Preston Jones)
             Sexual Perversity in Chicago (David Mamet)
             Short Eyes (Miguel Piñero)
             Travesties (Tom Stoppard)
             The Year of the Dragon (Frank Chin)

1975   *American Buffalo* (David Mamet)
             A Chorus Line (James Kirkwood, Nicholas Dante, and Michael
                 Bennett)
             The Dead Class (Tadeusz Kantor)
             The Mound Builders (Lanford Wilson)
             Otherwise Engaged (Simon Gray)
             Seascape (Edward Albee)
             The Shadow Box (Michael Cristofer)
             Volunteers (Brian Friel)

1976   *Curse of the Starving Class* (Sam Shepard)
             Dirty Linen and *New-Found-Land* (Tom Stoppard)
             Einstein on the Beach (Robert Wilson and Philip Glass)
             Gemini (Albert Innaurato)
             Streamers (David Rabe)

1977   *Childe Byron* (Romulus Linney)
             Cold Storage (Ronald Ribman)
             The Elephant Man (Bernard Pomerance)
             Fefu and Her Friends (Maria Irene Fornes)
             Getting Out (Marsha Norman)
             I Will Marry When I Want (Ngugi wa Thiong'o with Ngugi wa Mirii)
             A Photograph (Ntozake Shange)
             Terra Nova (Ted Tally)
             Wings (Arthur Kopit)
             The Woods (David Mamet)

Ma Rainey's Black Bottom (August Wilson)
The Road to Mecca (Athol Fugard)

1985   *Aunt Dan and Lemon* (Wallace Shawn)
        Lend Me a Tenor (Ken Ludwig)
        Les Liaisons Dangereuses (Christopher Hampton)
        A Lie of the Mind (Sam Shepard)
        Pravda (Howard Brenton and David Hare)
        Sand Mountain (Romulus Linney)
        The Search for Signs of Intelligent Life in the Universe (Jane
            Wagner)

1986   *The Colored Museum* (George C. Wolfe)
        Green Card (JoAnne Akalaitis)
        "I Don't Have to Show You No Stinking Badges!" (Luis Miguel
            Valdez)
        Joe Turner's Come and Gone (August Wilson)
        Temptation (Václav Havel)
        Vienna: Lusthaus (Martha Clarke)

1987   *Driving Miss Daisy* (Alfred Uhry)
        The Piano Lesson (August Wilson)
        Serious Money (Caryl Churchill)
        The Stick Wife (Darrah Cloud)
        A Walk in the Woods (Lee Blessing)
        Yankee Dawg You Die (Philip Kan Gotanda)

1988   *Hapgood* (Tom Stoppard)
        M. Butterfly (David Henry Hwang)
        Our Country's Good (Timberlake Wertenbaker)
        Speed-the-Plow (David Mamet)
        Tales of the Lost Formicans (Constance S. Congdon)

1989   *The Gospel at Colonus* (Lee Breuer)

1990   *Death and the Maiden* (Ariel Dorfman)
        The Grapes of Wrath (Frank Galati)

1991   *The Kentucky Cycle* (Robert Schenkkan)
        Lost in Yonkers (Neil Simon)
        The Madness of George III (Alan Bennett)
        The Ride Down Mt. Morgan (Arthur Miller)
        The Substance of Fire (Jon Robin Baitz)
        Three Tall Women (Edward Albee)

1993   *Keely and Du* (Jane Martin)

SCREEN ADAPTATIONS OF PLAYS IN
MASTERPLOTS II: DRAMA SERIES, REVISED

The best chance that many people have to see actual performances of the plays covered in these volumes is on screen. This appendix lists about 185 English-language screen adaptations of nearly 150 of the plays covered in this set. Productions are listed by their own titles, which in most cases match those of the plays. Cross-references are also provided from plays to films whose titles are changed.

All these productions were made for theatrical release except the television plays denoted as "TV." All are American productions unless otherwise noted. It should be kept in mind that the faithfulness of screen adaptations to their source material varies greatly. Older films and television plays tend to follow their original sources more closely than more recent productions, but this tendency cannot be taken as a rule.

The entries below include years of original release, approximate running times in minutes, nationalities of production (other than U.S.), directors' names, and samplings of cast member names. The latter are provided to help in identifying individual films. Character names that follow actors' names in parentheses are taken from the film and television production credits and may differ from the original names used in the plays. Asterisks indicate productions that were available on videotape or DVD in 2003, according to the Internet Movie Database (http://imdb.com). It may be worthwhile to check library collections for copies of other titles that are out of print in video formats.

*About Last Night . . . (1986; adapted from *Sexual Perversity in Chicago*; 113 min.) *Dir.:* Edward Zwick. *Cast:* Rob Lowe (Danny), James Belushi (Bernie), Demi Moore (Debbie), Elizabeth Perkins (Joan).

Absurd Person Singular (British TV, 1985) *Dir.:* Michael A. Simpson. *Cast:* Nicky Henson (Sidney Hopcroft), Maureen Lipman (Jane Hopcroft), Michael Gambon (Geoffrey Jackson), Cheryl Campbell (Eva Jackson).

The Accidental Death of an Anarchist (British TV, 1983) *Dir.:* Alan Horrox, Gavin Richards. *Cast:* Gavin Richards (The Loony), John Surman (Inspector Bertozzo), Jim Bywater (Inspector Pissani), Clive Russell (Superintendent).

The Adding Machine (1969; 100 min.) *Dir.:* Jerome Epstein. *Cast:* Milo O'Shea (Zero), Phyllis Diller (Mrs. Zero), Billie Whitelaw (Daisy Devore), Carol Cleveland (Judy).

After the Fall (TV, 1974; 128 min.) *Dir.:* Gilbert Cates. *Cast:* Christopher Plummer (Quentin), Bibi Andersson (Holga), Mariclare Costello (Louise), Faye Dunaway (Maggie).

*Agnes of God (1985; 98 min.) *Dir.:* Norman Jewison. *Cast:* Jane Fonda (Doctor Margaret Livingston), Anne Bancroft (Mother Miriam Ruth), Meg Tilly (Sister Agnes).

***Amadeus** (1984; 160 min.) *Dir.:* Miloš Forman. *Cast:* F. Murray Abraham (Antonio Salieri), Tom Hulce (Wolfgang Amadeus Mozart), Elizabeth Berridge (Constanze Mozart), Jeffrey Jones (Emperor Joseph II).

***American Buffalo** (1996; 88 min.) *Dir.:* Michael Corrente. *Cast:* Dennis Franz (Don "Donny" Dubrow), Sean Nelson (Bob "Bobby"), Dustin Hoffman (Walt "Teach" Teacher).

***Anne of the Thousand Days** (British, 1969; 145 min.) *Dir.:* Charles Jarrott. *Cast:* Geneviève Bujold (Anne Boleyn), Richard Burton (King Henry VIII), Anthony Quayle (Cardinal Wolsey), John Colicos (Thomas Cromwell).

***Awake and Sing!** (TV, 1972; 120 min.) *Dir.:* Robert Hopkins, Norman Lloyd. *Cast:* Ruth Storey (Bessie), Milton Selzer (Myron), Robert Lipton (Ralph), Felicia Farr (Hennie).

***The Balcony** (1963; 84 min.) *Dir.:* Joseph Strick. *Cast:* Jeff Corey (The Bishop), Shelley Winters (Madame Irma), Peter Brocco (The Judge).

***Barefoot in the Park** (1967; 104 min.) *Dir.:* Gene Saks. *Cast:* Jane Fonda (Corie Bratter), Robert Redford (Paul Bratter), Mildred Natwick (Mrs. Ethel Banks), Charles Boyer (Victor Velasco).

Barefoot in the Park (TV, 1981) *Cast:* Bess Armstrong (Corie Bratter), Richard Thomas (Paul Bratter), Barbara Barrie (Mrs. Banks), Hans Conried (Victor Velasco).

***The Best Man** (1964; 102 min.) *Dir.:* Franklin J. Schaffner. *Cast:* Henry Fonda (William Russell), Margaret Leighton (Alice Russell), Kevin McCarthy (Dick Jensen), Cliff Robertson (Joe Cantwell).

Betrayal (British, 1983; 95 min.) *Dir.:* David Hugh Jones. *Cast:* Patricia Hodge (Emma), Jeremy Irons (Jerry), Ben Kingsley (Robert).

***Beyond the Horizon** (TV, 1975; 90 min.) *Dir.:* Rick Hauser, Michael Kahn. *Cast:* Richard Backus (Robert Mayo), Maria Tucci (Ruth Atkins), Geraldine Fitzgerald (Mrs. Atkins).

***The Big Knife** (1955; 111 min.) *Dir.:* Robert Aldrich. *Cast:* Jack Palance (Charles Castle), Ida Lupino (Marion Castle), Paul Langton (Buddy Bliss), Jean Hagen (Mrs. Connie Bliss).

***Biloxi Blues** (1988; 106 min.) *Dir.:* Mike Nichols. *Cast:* Matthew Broderick (Eugene Morris Jerome), Corey Parker (Arnold Epstein), Matt Mulhern (Joseph Wykowski), Markus Flanagan (Selridge).

***The Blue Bird** (1940; 88 min.) *Dir.:* Walter Lang. *Cast:* Johnny Russell (Tyltyl), Shirley Temple (Mytyl), Russell Hicks (Daddy Tyl), Spring Byington (Mummy Tyl).

The Blue Bird (U.S./Soviet Union, 1976; 99 min.) *Dir.:* George Cukor. *Cast:* Todd Lookinland (Tyltyl), Patsy Kensit (Mytyl), Elizabeth Taylor (Queen of Light/Mother/Witch/Maternal Love).

Boesman and Lena (South Africa, 1974) *Dir.:* Ross Devenish. *Cast:* Athol Fugard (Boesman), Yvonne Bryceland (Lena).

The Boys in the Band (1970; 118 min.) *Dir.:* William Friedkin. *Cast:* Kenneth Nelson (Michael), Frederick Combs (Donald), Cliff Gorman (Emory), Keith Prentice (Larry).

*****Brighton Beach Memoirs** (1986; 108 min.) *Dir.:* Gene Saks. *Cast:* Jonathan Silverman (Eugene Morris Jerome), Blythe Danner (Kate), Bob Dishy (Jack), Judith Ivey (Blanche).

*****Buffalo Bill and the Indians, or Sitting Bull's History Lesson** (1976; adapted from *Indians*; 123 min.) *Dir.:* Robert Altman. *Cast:* Paul Newman (William F. "Buffalo Bill" Cody), Geraldine Chaplin (Annie Oakley), Frank Kaquitts (Sitting Bull).

Butley (British/Canadian, 1974; 94 min.) *Dir.:* Harold Pinter. *Cast:* Alan Bates (Ben Butley), Richard O'Callaghan (Joey Keyston), Susan Engel (Anne Butley), Jessica Tandy (Edna Shaft).

Camino Real. See **Ten Blocks on the Camino Real**.

Caucasian Chalk Circle (British TV, 1973) *Cast:* Patrick Magee, Leo McKern, Robert Powell, Jack Thaw.

The Caucasian Chalk Circle (British, 1997; 178 min.) *Cast:* Simon McBurney (Azdak).

*****The Ceremony of Innocence** (TV, 1972; 88 min.) *Dir.:* Ken Rockefeller, Arthur Allan Seidelman. *Cast:* Richard Kiley (King Ethelred), James Broderick, Larry Gates, Robert Gerringer.

Chicken Soup with Barley (British TV, 1966) *Dir.:* Charles Jarrott. *Cast:* Margery Mason, Stanley Meadows, Clive Revill, Stella Tanner.

*****A Chorus Line** (1985; 113 min.) *Dir.:* Richard Attenborough. *Cast:* Michael Douglas (Zach), Terrence Mann (Larry), Audrey Landers (Val), Vicki Frederick (Sheila).

The Colored Museum (TV, 1991; 90 min.) *Dir.:* Andrew Carl Wilk, George C. Wolfe. *Cast:* Danitra Vance (Miss Pat), Linda Hopkins (Aunt Ethel), Victor Love (The Guy), Kevin Jackson (Junie Robinson).

*****Come Back, Little Sheba** (1952; 99 min.) *Dir.:* Daniel Mann. *Cast:* Burt Lancaster (Doc Delaney), Shirley Booth (Lola Delaney), Terry Moore (Marie Buckholder), Richard Jaeckel (Turk Fisher).

Come Back, Little Sheba (TV, 1977) *Dir.:* Silvio Narizzano. *Cast:* Laurence Olivier (Doc Delaney), Joanne Woodward (Lola Delaney), Carrie Fisher (Marie), Nicholas Campbell (Turk).

*****The Connection** (1961; 110 min.) *Dir.:* Shirley Clarke. *Cast:* Carl Lee (Cowboy), Warren Finnerty (Leach), Jerome Raphael (Solly), Garry Goodrow (Ernie).

The Contractor (British TV, 1974; 75 min.) *Dir.:* Barry Davis. *Cast:* Joseph Maher (Fitzpatrick), Kevin O'Connor (Glendenning), Michael Finn, Reid Shelton.

Copenhagen (British TV, 2002) *Dir.:* Howard Davies. *Cast:* Daniel Craig (Werner Heisenberg), Stephen Rea (Niels Bohr), Francesca Annis (Margrethe Bohr).

***The Corn Is Green** (1945; 115 min.) *Dir.:* Irving Rapper. *Cast:* Bette Davis (Miss Lilly Moffat), John Dall (Morgan Evans), Mildred Dunnock (Miss Ronberry), Rhys Williams (Mr. Jones).

***The Corn Is Green** (TV, 1979; 93 min.) *Dir.:* George Cukor. *Cast:* Katharine Hepburn (Lilly C. Moffat), Ian Saynor (Morgan Evans), Anna Massey (Miss Ronberry), Artro Morris (John Goronwy Jones).

***Curse of the Starving Class** (1994; 102 min.) *Dir.:* J. Michael McClary. *Cast:* Henry Thomas (Wesley Tate), Kristin Fiorella (Emma Tate), Kathy Bates (Ella Tate), James Woods (Weston Tate).

***Da** (1988; 102 min.) *Dir.:* Matt Clark. *Cast:* Martin Sheen (Charlie), Barnard Hughes (Da), William Hickey (Drumm).

***Dangerous Liaisons** (U.S./British, 1988; adapted from *Les Liaisons Dangereuses*; 119 min.) *Dir.:* Stephen Frears. *Cast:* Glenn Close (Marquise de Merteuil), Swoosie Kurtz (Madame de Volanges), Uma Thurman (Cécile de Volanges), John Malkovich (Valmont).

***A Day in the Death of Joe Egg** (British, 1972) *Dir.:* Peter Medak. *Cast:* Alan Bates (Bri), Janet Suzman (Sheila), Peter Bowles (Freddie), Sheila Gish (Pam).

***Death and the Maiden** (British/U.S./France, 1994; 103 min.) *Dir.:* Roman Polanski. *Cast:* Sigourney Weaver (Paulina Escobar), Stuart Wilson (Gerardo Escobar), Ben Kingsley (Dr. Roberto Miranda).

Deathwatch (1967; 88 min.) *Dir.:* Vic Morrow. *Cast:* Michael Forest (Greeneyes), Paul Mazursky (Maurice), Leonard Nimoy (Jules LaFranc).

Design for Living (1933; 90 min.) *Dir.:* Ernst Lubitsch. *Cast:* Miriam Hopkins (Gilda), Fredric March (Tom Chambers), Gary Cooper (George Curtis), Edward Everett Horton (Max Plunkett).

Design for Living (British TV, 1979) *Cast:* Rula Lenska (Gilda Farrell), Dandy Nichols (Housekeeper).

***The Devils** (British, 1971; 111 min.) *Dir.:* Ken Russell. *Cast:* Oliver Reed (Urbain Grandier), Vanessa Redgrave (Sister Jeanne), Georgina Hale (Philippe).

***The Diary of Anne Frank** (1959; 180 min.) *Dir.:* George Stevens. *Cast:* Joseph Schildkraut (Otto Frank), Gusti Huber (Mrs. Edith Frank), Millie Perkins (Anne Frank), Diane Baker (Margot Frank).

The Diary of Anne Frank (TV, 1967; 124 min.) *Dir.:* Alex Segal. *Cast:* Diana Davila (Anne), Max von Sydow (Otto Frank), Donald Pleasence (Mr. Dusseli).

The Diary of Anne Frank (TV, 1980; 109 min.) *Dir.:* Boris Sagal. *Cast:* Melissa Gilbert (Anne), Maximilian Schell (Otto Frank), Joan Plowright (Mrs. Frank), Melora Marshall (Margot Frank).

***Dinner with Friends** (TV, 2001; 94 min.) *Dir.:* Norman Jewison. *Cast:* Dennis Quaid (Gabe), Andie MacDowell (Karen), Greg Kinnear (Tom).

***The Dresser** (British, 1983; 118 min.) *Dir.:* Peter Yates. *Cast:* Tom Courtenay (Norman), Albert Finney (Sir), Zena Walker (Her Ladyship), Eileen Atkins (Madge).

***Driving Miss Daisy** (1989; 99 min.) *Dir.:* Bruce Beresford. *Cast:* Jessica Tandy (Daisy Werthan), Morgan Freeman (Hoke Colburn), Dan Aykroyd (Boolie Werthan).

Eden End (British TV, 1951) *Cast:* Jack Allen, Peter Cushing (Charles Appleby), Rachel Gurney, Julien Mitchell.

The Effect of Gamma Rays on Man-in-the-Moon Marigolds (1972) *Dir.:* Paul Newman. *Cast:* Joanne Woodward (Beatrice), Roberta Wallach (Ruth), Judith Lowry (Nanny), Ellen Dano (Janice Vickery).

The Elephant Man (TV, 1982; 90 min.) *Dir.:* Jack Hofsiss. *Cast:* Kevin Conway (Frederick Treves), Richard Clarke (Carr Gomm), Philip Anglim (John Merrick), Christopher Hewett (Ross).

***The Entertainer** (British, 1960; 96 min.) *Dir.:* Tony Richardson. *Cast:* Roger Livesey (Billy Rice), Laurence Olivier (Archie Rice), Brenda De Banzie (Phoebe Rice), Alan Bates (Frank Rice).

The Entertainer (TV, 1976; 105 min.) *Dir.:* Donald Wrye. *Cast:* Ray Bolger (Billy Rice), Jack Lemmon (Archie Rice), Sada Thompson (Phoebe Rice), Michael Cristofer (Frank).

Entertaining Mr. Sloane (British/Austrian, 1970; 94 min.) *Dir.:* Douglas Hickox. *Cast:* Beryl Reid (Kath), Peter McEnery (Mr. Sloane), Alan Webb (Kemp), Harry Andrews (Ed).

***Execution of Justice** (TV, 1999; 98 min.) *Dir.:* Leon Ichaso. *Cast:* Timothy Daly (Dan White), Jonathan Higgins (Doug Schmidt), Khalil Kain (Sister Boom Boom), Shannon Hile (Dianne Feinstein).

A Flea in Her Ear (British TV, 1967) *Cast:* Peter Cellier, Edward Hardwicke, Anthony Hopkins.

A Flea in Her Ear (U.S./France, 1968; 94 min.) *Dir.:* Jacques Charon. *Cast:* Rex Harrison (Victor Chandebisse), Georges Descrières (Don Carlos de Castilian), Isla Blair (Antoinette).

French Without Tears (1939; 86 min.) *Dir.:* Anthony Asquith. *Cast:* Kenneth Morgan (Kenneth Lake), Guy Middleton (Brian Curtis), Ray Milland (Alan Howard), Jim Gérald (Maingot).

French Without Tears (British TV, 1976) *Cast:* Anthony Andrews, Nicola Pagett.

***Getting Out** (TV, 1994; 100 min.) *Dir.:* John Korty. *Cast:* Rebecca De Mornay (Arlene Holsclaw), Amy Dott (Young Arlie), Ellen Burstyn (Arlie's Mother), Robert Knepper (Carl).

Gone Are the Days! (1963, adapted from *Purlie Victorious*; 99 min.) *Dir.:* Nicholas Webster. *Cast:* Ossie Davis (Reverend Purlie Victorious Judson), Ruby Dee (Lutiebelle Gussie Mae Jenkins), Hilda Haynes (Missy Judson), Godfrey Cambridge (Gitlow Judson).

The Grapes of Wrath (TV, 1991; 142 min.) *Dir.:* Kirk Browning, Frank Galati. *Cast:* Gary Sinise (Tom Joad), Robert Breuler (Pa Joad), Lois Smith (Ma Joad), Sally Murphy (Rose of Sharon).

***The Great White Hope** (1970; 103 min.) *Dir.:* Martin Ritt. *Cast:* James Earl Jones (Jack Jefferson), Joel Fluellen (Tick), Lou Gilbert (Goldie), Jane Alexander (Eleanor).

***The Green Pastures** (1936; 93 min.) *Dir.:* Marc Connelly, William Keighley. *Cast:* George Reed (Mr. Deshee), Oscar Polk (Gabriel), Rex Ingram (Adam), Myrtle Anderson (Eve).

The Green Pastures (TV, 1957) *Dir.:* George Schaefer. *Cast:* William Warfield (De Lawd), Earle Hyman (Adam).

Hands Around. See **Ronde, La**.

Happy Days (TV, 1980) *Dir.:* David Heeley. *Cast:* Irene Worth (Winnie), George Voskovec (Willie).

***Happy Days** (Irish TV, 2000; 79 min.) *Dir.:* Patricia Rozema. *Cast:* Rosaleen Linehan (Winnie), Richard Johnson (Willie).

***Harvey** (1950; 104 min.) *Dir.:* Henry Koster. *Cast:* James Stewart (Elwood P. Dowd), Victoria Horne (Myrtle Mae Simmons), Josephine Hull (Veta Louise Simmons), Peggy Dow (Miss Kelly).

Harvey (TV, 1972) *Dir.:* Fielder Cook. *Cast:* James Stewart (Elwood P. Dowd), Marian Hailey (Myrtle Mae Simmons), Helen Hayes (Veta Louise Simmons), Madeline Kahn (Nurse Ruth Kelly).

Harvey (TV, 1996) *Dir.:* George Schaefer. *Cast:* Harry Anderson (Elwood P. Dowd), Swoosie Kurtz (Veta Simmons), Jim O'Heir (Wilson).

***The Hasty Heart** (British, 1949; 102 min.) *Dir.:* Vincent Sherman. *Cast:* Ronald Reagan (Yank), John Sherman (Digger), Orlando Martins (Blossom), Howard Marion-Crawford (Tommy).

***The Hasty Heart** (TV, 1983) *Dir.:* Martin M. Speer. *Cast:* Perry King (Yank), Cheryl Ladd (Margaret), Jesse Ferguson, Gregory Harrison.

***High Society** (1956; adapted from *The Philadelphia Story*; 107 min.) *Dir.:* Charles Walters. *Cast:* Grace Kelly (Tracy Samantha Lord), Sidney Blackmer (Seth Lord).

The Homecoming (U.S./British, 1973; 111 min.) *Dir.:* Peter Hall. *Cast:* Paul Rogers (Max), Cyril Cusack (Sam), Michael Jayston (Teddy), Vivien Merchant (Ruth).

***Hurlyburly** (1998; 122 min.) *Dir.:* Anthony Drazan. *Cast:* Sean Penn (Eddie), Chazz Palminteri (Phil), Kevin Spacey (Mickey), Garry Shandling (Artie).

Idiot's Delight (1939; 107 min.) *Dir.:* Clarence Brown. *Cast:* Clark Gable (Harry Van), Norma Shearer (Irene Fellara), Edward Arnold (Achille Weber), Burgess Meredith (Quillery).

Inadmissible Evidence (British, 1968; 94 min.) *Dir.:* Anthony Page. *Cast:* Nicol Williamson (Bill Maitland), Peter Sallis (Hudson), David Valla (Jones), Jill Bennett (Liz).

***Incident at Vichy** (TV, 1973; 72 min.) *Dir.:* Stacy Keach. *Cast:* Allen Garfield (Lebeau), Bert Freed (Marchand), Rene Auberjonois (Monceau).

Indians. See **Buffalo Bill and the Indians, or Sitting Bull's History Lesson**.

***Inherit the Wind** (1960; 128 min.) *Dir.:* Stanley Kramer. *Cast:* Fredric March (Matthew Harrison Brady), Spencer Tracy (Henry Drummond), Elliott Reid (Tom Davenport), Gene Kelly (E. K. Hornbeck).

Inherit the Wind (TV, 1965; 90 min.) *Dir.:* George Schaefer. *Cast:* Ed Begley (Matthew Harrison Brady), Melvyn Douglas (Henry Drummond).

Inherit the Wind (TV, 1988; 96 min.) *Dir.:* David Greene. *Cast:* Kirk Douglas (Matthew Harrison Brady), Jason Robards (Henry Drummond), Josh Clark (Davenport), Darren McGavin (Hornbeck).

Inherit the Wind (TV, 1999; 127 min.) *Dir.:* Daniel Petrie. *Cast:* George C. Scott (Matthew Harrison Brady), Jack Lemmon (Henry Drummond), Brad Greenquist (Tom Davenport), Beau Bridges (E. K. Hornbeck).

An Inspector Calls (British, 1954; 75 min.) *Dir.:* Guy Hamilton. *Cast:* Arthur Young (Arthur Birling), Olga Lindo (Sybil Birling), Eileen Moore (Sheila Birling), Bryan Forbes (Eric Birling).

The Kitchen (British, 1961; 76 min.) *Dir.:* James Hill. *Cast:* Carl Möhner (Peter), Mary Yeomans (Monica), Gertan Klauber (Gaston), Scott Finch (Hans).

La Ronde. See **Ronde, La**.

***Last of the Red Hot Lovers** (1972; 98 min.) *Dir.:* Gene Saks. *Cast:* Alan Arkin (Barney Cashman), Sally Kellerman (Elaine), Paula Prentiss (Bobbi Michele), Renée Taylor (Jeanette).

The Laundromat (TV, 1985; 59 min.) *Dir.:* Robert Altman. *Cast:* Carol Burnett (Alberta Johnson), Amy Madigan (Deedee Johnson).

Lear (British, 1982) *Cast:* Bob Peck (Lear).

Les Liaisons Dangereuses. See **Dangerous Liaisons**.

Loot (British, 1970; 101 min.) *Dir.:* Silvio Narizzano. *Cast:* Milo O'Shea (Mr. McLeavy), Lee Remick (Fay), Roy Holder (Hal), Hywel Bennett (Dennis).

***Lost in Yonkers** (1993; 114 min.) *Dir.:* Martha Coolidge. *Cast:* Irene Worth (Grandma Kurnitz), Mercedes Ruehl (Bella Kurnitz), Richard Dreyfuss (Uncle Louie), Susan Merson (Gert).

Luther (British TV, 1965) *Dir.:* Alan Cooke. *Cast:* Geoffrey Bayldon, Alec McCowen.

Luther (British/Canadian, 1973; 110 min.) *Dir.:* Guy Green. *Cast:* Stacy Keach (Martin Luther), Patrick Magee (Hans), Judi Dench (Katherine), Maurice Denham (Johann Von Staupitz).

***M. Butterfly** (1993; 101 min.) *Dir.:* David Cronenberg. *Cast:* Jeremy Irons (Rene Gallimard), John Lone (Song Liling).

The Madness of George III. See **The Madness of King George**.

***The Madness of King George** (British, 1994; 107 min.; adapted from *The Madness of George III*) *Dir.:* Nicholas Hytner. *Cast:* Nigel Hawthorne (George III), Helen Mirren (Queen Charlotte), Rupert Everett (Prince of Wales), Julian Wadham (Pitt).

***The Matchmaker** (1958; 101 min.) *Dir.:* Joseph Anthony. *Cast:* Paul Ford (Horace Vandergelder), Shirley Booth (Dolly Gallagher Levi), Anthony Perkins (Cornelius Hackl), Robert Morse (Barnaby Tucker).

***Mister Roberts** (1955; 123 min.) *Dir.:* John Ford Mervyn LeRoy. *Cast:* Henry Fonda (Lieutenant Doug A. Roberts), William Powell (Doc), James Cagney (Captain Morton), Jack Lemmon (Ensign Frank Thurlowe Pulver).

Mister Roberts (TV, 1984; 100 min.) *Dir.:* Melvin Bernhardt. *Cast:* Robert Hays (Lieutenant Doug Roberts), Howard Hesseman (Doc), Charles Durning (The Captain), Kevin Bacon (Ensign Frank Pulver).

***A Moon for the Misbegotten** (TV, 1975) *Dir.:* José Quintero, Gordon Rigsby. *Cast:* Colleen Dewhurst (Josie Hogan), Ed Flanders (Phil Hogan), Jason Robards (James Tyrone, Jr.).

The Mound Builders (TV, 1976) *Dir.:* Ken Campbell, Marshall W. Mason. *Cast:* Brad Dourif (Chad Jasker), Trish Hawkins (Jean), Tanya Berezin.

Mrs. Warren's Profession (West Germany, 1960; 103 min.) *Dir.:* Akos Von Rathony. *Cast:* Lilli Palmer (Mrs. Warren), Johanna Matz (Vivie), O. E. Hasse (Sir Crofts), Rudolf Vogel (Samuel Gardner).

Mrs. Warren's Profession (British TV, 1972) *Dir.:* Herbert Wise. *Cast:* Coral Browne (Mrs. Warren), Derek Godfrey, James Grout, Richard Pearson.

***My Dinner with André** (1981; 110 min.) *Dir.:* Louis Malle. *Cast:* Wallace Shawn (Wally), André Gregory (André).

Night Must Fall (British, 1964; 101 min.) *Dir.:* Karel Reisz. *Cast:* Susan Hampshire (Olivia), Albert Finney (Danny), Mona Washbourne (Mrs. Bramson), Sheila Hancock (Dora).

***The Norman Conquests** (British TV, 1978; three parts: 93 min., 120 min., and 120 min.) *Dir.:* Herbert Wise. *Cast:* Tom Conti (Norman), Fiona Walker (Ruth), Richard Briers (Reg), Penelope Keith (Sarah).

***The Old Maid** (1939; 95 min.) *Dir.:* Edmund Goulding. *Cast:* Miriam Hopkins (Delia Lovell Ralston), Bette Davis (Charlotte Lovell), Donald Crisp (Doctor Lanskell), James Stephenson (James Ralston).

The Oldest Living Graduate (TV, 1980) *Dir.:* Jack Hofsiss. *Cast:* Henry Fonda (Colonel J. C. Kincaid), George Grizzard (Floyd Kincaid), Cloris Leachman (Maureen), John Lithgow (Clarence).

Once in a Lifetime (1932; 91 min.) *Dir.:* Russell Mack. *Cast:* Russell Hopton (Jerry Hyland), Aline MacMahon (May Daniels), Jack Oakie (George Lewis), Sidney Fox (Susan Walker).

Painting Churches. See **The Portrait**.

***The Petrified Forest** (1936; 83 min.) *Dir.:* Archie Mayo. *Cast:* Leslie Howard (Alan Squier), Porter Hall (Jason Maple), Bette Davis (Gabrielle "Gabby" Maple), Humphrey Bogart (Duke Mantee).

***The Philadelphia Story** (1940; 112 min.) *Dir.:* George Cukor. *Cast:* Katharine Hepburn (Tracy Samantha Lord), Mary Nash (Margaret Lord), John Halliday (Seth Lord), Virginia Weidler (Dinah Lord). See also **High Society**.

***The Piano Lesson** (TV, 1995) *Dir.:* Lloyd Richards. *Cast:* Charles Dutton (Boy Willie), Alfre Woodard (Berniece), Carl Gordon (Doaker), Courtney B. Vance (Lymon).

***Picnic** (1955; 115 min.) *Dir.:* Joshua Logan. *Cast:* William Holden (Hal Carter), Kim Novak (Madge Owens), Susan Strasberg (Millie Owens), Betty Field (Flo Owens).

Picnic (TV, 1986) *Dir.:* Marshall W. Mason. *Cast:* Gregory Harrison (Hal Carter), Jennifer Jason Leigh (Madge Owens), Dana Hill (Millie Owens), Rue McClanahan (Flo Owens).

Picnic (TV, 2000; 100 min.) *Dir.:* Ivan Passer. *Cast:* Josh Brolin (Hal Carter), Gretchen Mol (Madge Owens), Chad Morgan (Millie Owens), Bonnie Bedelia (Flo Owens).

***Plenty** (British/U.S., 1985; 121 min.) *Dir.:* Fred Schepisi. *Cast:* Charles Dance (Raymond Brock), Meryl Streep (Susan Traherne), Tracey Ullman (Alice Park), Sam Neill (Lazar).

***The Portrait** (TV, 1993; adapted from *Painting Churches*) *Dir.:* Arthur Penn. *Cast:* Lauren Bacall (Fanny Church), Gregory Peck (Gardner Church), Cecilia Peck (Margaret Church).

The Price (U.S./British TV, 1971) *Dir.:* Fielder Cook. *Cast:* George C. Scott (Victor Franz), Colleen Dewhurst (Mrs. Franz), David Burns (Mr. Solomon), Barry Sullivan (Walter Franz).

Purlie Victorious. See **Gone Are the Days!**

The Quare Fellow (British, 1962; 85 min.) *Dir.:* Arthur Dreifuss. *Cast:* Walter Macken (Regan), Patrick McGoohan (Thomas Crimmin), Hilton Edwards (Holy Healey).

Reckless (1995; 100 min.) *Dir.:* Norman René. *Cast:* Mia Farrow (Rachel), Tony Goldwyn (Tom), Scott Glenn (Lloyd), Mary-Louise Parker (Pooty).

The Removalists (Australia, 1975; 93 min.) *Dir.:* Tom Jeffrey. *Cast:* Peter Cummins (Sergeant Dan Simmonds), John Hargreaves (Constable Neville Ross), Kate Fitzpatrick (Kate Mason), Jacki Weaver (Fiona Carter).

***The Rimers of Eldritch** (TV, 1974; 88 min.) *Cast:* Rue McClanahan (Cora Groves), Susan Sarandon (Patsy), Frances Sternhagen (Wilma Atkins).

***The River Niger** (1976; 105 min.) *Dir.:* Krishna Shah. *Cast:* James Earl Jones (Johnny Williams), Cicely Tyson (Mattie Williams), Hilda Haynes (Wilhelmina Geneva Brown), Louis Gossett, Jr. (Dr. Dudley Stanton).

The Road to Mecca (South Africa, 1992) *Dir.:* Athol Fugard, Peter Goldsmid. *Cast:* Yvonne Bryceland (Miss Helen), Kathy Bates (Elsa Barlow), Athol Fugard (Rev. Marius Byleveld).

***La Ronde** (France, 1950; adapted from *Hands Around*; 95 min.) *Dir.:* Max Ophüls. *Cast:* Simone Signoret (Leocadie), Serge Reggiani (Franz), Simone Simon (Maid), Daniel Gélin (Alfred).

La Ronde (France, 1964; adapted from *Hands Around*; 110 min.) *Dir.:* Roger Vadim. *Cast:* Marie Dubois (La fille), Claude Giraud (Georges), Anna Karina (Rose), Jean-Claude Brialy (Alfred).

***The Rose Tattoo** (1955; 117 min.) *Dir.:* Daniel Mann. *Cast:* Anna Magnani (Serafina Delle Rose), Marisa Pavan (Rosa Delle Rose), Mimi Aguglia (Assunta), Virginia Grey (Estelle Hohengarten).

***The Royal Hunt of the Sun** (U.S./British, 1969) *Dir.:* Irving Lerner. *Cast:* Robert Shaw (Francisco Pizarro), Nigel Davenport (De Soto), Michael Craig (Estete).

***The Ruling Class** (British, 1972; 154 min.) *Dir.:* Peter Medak. *Cast:* Peter O'Toole (Jack Arnold Alexander Tancred Gurney), William Mervyn (Sir Charles Gurney), Coral Browne (Lady Claire Gurney), James Villiers (Dinsdale).

***The Search for Signs of Intelligent Life in the Universe** (1991; 120 min.) *Dir.:* John Bailey. *Cast:* Lily Tomlin (Lily).

A Severed Head (British, 1970; 98 min.) *Dir.:* Dick Clement. *Cast:* Ian Holm (Martin Lynch-Gibbon), Jennie Linden (Georgie Hands), Lee Remick (Antonia Lynch-Gibbon), Richard Attenborough (Palmer Anderson).

Sexual Perversity in Chicago. See **About Last Night . . .**

The Shadow Box (TV, 1980) *Dir.:* Paul Newman. *Cast:* James Broderick (Joe), Valerie Harper (Maggie), Christopher Plummer (Brian), Ben Masters (Mark).

Shadow of a Gunman (British TV, 1995) *Dir.:* Nye Heron. *Cast:* Kenneth Branagh (Donal Davoren), Bronagh Gallagher (Minnie Powell), Stephen Rea (Seumus Shields).

Short Eyes (1977; 100 min.) *Dir.:* Robert M. Young. *Cast:* Tito Goya (Cupcakes), Shawn Elliott (Paco), Nathan George (Ice), Don Blakely (El Raheen).

***The Show Off** (1926; 82 min.) *Dir.:* Malcolm St. Clair. *Cast:* Louise Brooks (Clara), Claire McDowell (Mom Fisher), Lois Wilson (Amy Fisher Piper), Ford Sterling (Audrey Piper).

The Show-Off (1934; 77 min.) *Dir.:* Charles Reisner. *Cast:* Lois Wilson (Clara Harling), Clara Blandick (Mrs. Fisher), Madge Evans (Amy Fisher Piper), Spencer Tracy (J. Aubrey Piper).

***The Show-Off** (1946; 83 min.) *Dir.:* Harry Beaumont. *Cast:* Jacqueline White (Clara Harlin), Marjorie Main (Mrs. Fisher), Marilyn Maxwell (Amy Fisher Piper), Red Skelton (J. Aubrey Piper).

Sister Mary Explains It All (TV, 2001; adapted from *Sister Mary Ignatius Explains It All for You*; 77 min.) *Dir.:* Marshall Brickman. *Cast:* Diane Keaton (Sister Mary Ignatius), Max Morrow (Thomas), Jennifer Tilly (Philomena Rostovich).

Sister Mary Ignatius Explains It All for You. See **Sister Mary Explains It All**.

*****Sleuth** (British, 1972; 138 min.) *Dir.:* Joseph L. Mankiewicz. *Cast:* Laurence Olivier (Andrew Wyke), Michael Caine (Milo Tindle).

*****A Soldier's Play** (1984; 98 min.) *Dir.:* Norman Jewison. *Cast:* Adolph Caesar (Sgt. Waters), Howard E. Rollins, Jr. (Capt. Davenport), David Alan Grier (Cpl. Cobb), Denzel Washington (Pfc. Peterson).

*****South Pacific** (1958; 151 min.) *Dir.:* Joshua Logan. *Cast:* Mitzi Gaynor (Ensign Nellie Forbush), Rossano Brazzi (Emile de Becque), John Kerr (Lt. Joseph Cable), Juanita Hall (Bloody Mary).

*****South Pacific** (TV, 2001; 129 min.) *Dir.:* Richard Pearce. *Cast:* Glenn Close (Nellie Forbush), Rade Serbedzija (Emile de Becque), Harry Connick, Jr. (Lt. Joseph Cable), Lori Tan Chinn (Bloody Mary).

Speed the Plow (1999) *Cast:* David Kaye (Bobby Gould).

*****Streamers** (1983; 118 min.) *Dir.:* Robert Altman. *Cast:* Albert Macklin (Martin), Mitchell Lichtenstein (Richie), Michael Wright (Carlyle), Matthew Modine (Billy), David Alan Grier (Roger).

*****The Subject Was Roses** (1968) *Dir.:* Ulu Grosbard. *Cast:* Jack Albertson (John Cleary), Patricia Neal (Nettie Cleary), Martin Sheen (Timmy Cleary).

*****The Substance of Fire** (1996; 97 min.) *Dir.:* Daniel J. Sullivan. *Cast:* Ron Rifkin (Isaac Geldhard), Tony Goldwyn (Aaron Geldhart), Timothy Hutton (Martin Geldhart), Sarah Jessica Parker (Sarah Geldhart).

*****subUrbia** (1996; 121 min.) *Dir.:* Richard Linklater. *Cast:* Nicky Katt (Timmy), Steve Zahn (Buff), Giovanni Ribisi (Jeff), Samia Shoaib (Pakeesa Chaldi).

*****Summer and Smoke** (1961; 118 min.) *Dir.:* Peter Glenville. *Cast:* Malcolm Atterbury (Rev. Winemiller), Una Merkel (Mrs. Winemiller), Geraldine Page (Alma Winemiller), Laurence Harvey (John Buchanan, Jr.)

Summer and Smoke (British TV, 1972) *Cast:* Lee Remick (Alma Winemiller), John Buchanan (David Hedison), Barry Morse.

Summer of the Seventeenth Doll (U.S./British/Australia, 1959; 93 min.) *Dir.:* Leslie Norman. *Cast:* Anne Baxter (Olive), Angela Lansbury (Pearl), John Mills (Barney), Ernest Borgnine (Roo).

*****Sunrise at Campobello** (1960; 144 min.) *Dir.:* Vincent J. Donehue. *Cast:* Ralph Bellamy (Franklin Delano Roosevelt), Greer Garson (Eleanor Roosevelt), Zina Bethune (Anna Roosevelt), Robin Warga (Franklin Roosevelt, Jr.)

*****Susan and God** (1940; 115 min.) *Dir.:* George Cukor. *Cast:* Joan Crawford (Susan Trexel), Fredric March (Barry Trexel), Rita Quigley (Blossom Trexel), Rose Hobart (Irene Burroughs).

*****Sweet Bird of Youth** (1962; 120 min.) *Dir.:* Richard Brooks. *Cast:* Paul Newman (Chance Wayne), Geraldine Page (Princess Kosmonopolis), Ed Begley (Boss Finley), Rip Torn (Tom Junior).

*Sweet Bird of Youth (TV, 1989; 95 min.) *Dir.:* Nicolas Roeg. *Cast:* Mark Harmon (Chance Wayne), Elizabeth Taylor (Alexandra Del Lago), Rip Torn (Boss Finley), Kevin Geer (Tom Junior).

*Tea and Sympathy (1956; 122 min.) *Dir.:* Vincente Minnelli. *Cast:* John Kerr (Tom Robinson Lee), Edward Andrews (Herb Lee), Deborah Kerr (Laura Reynolds), Leif Erickson (Bill Reynolds).

*The Teahouse of the August Moon (1956; 115 min.) *Dir.:* Daniel Mann. *Cast:* Marlon Brando (Sakini), Paul Ford (Colonel Wainwright Purdy III), Glenn Ford (Captain Fisby), Eddie Albert (Captain McLean).

*Ten Blocks on the Camino Real (TV, 1966) *Dir.:* Jack Landau. *Cast:* Albert Dekker (Mr. Gutman), Martin Sheen (Kilroy), Hurd Hatfield (Jacques Casanova), Lotte Lenya (The Gypsy).

That Championship Season (1982; 110 min.) *Dir.:* Jason Miller. *Cast:* Stacy Keach (James Daley), Martin Sheen (Tom Daley), Bruce Dern (George Sitkowski), Paul Sorvino (Phil Romano).

*That Championship Season (TV, 1999; 130 min.) *Dir.:* Paul Sorvino. *Cast:* Terry Kinney (James Daley), Gary Sinise (Tom Daley), Tony Shalhoub (George Sitkowski), Vincent D'Onofrio (Phil Romano).

Tobacco Road (1941; 84 min.) *Dir.:* John Ford. *Cast:* Charley Grapewin (Jeeter Lester), Elizabeth Patterson (Ada Lester), William Tracy (Dude Lester), Gene Tierney (Ellie May Lester).

Travelling North (Australia, 1987; 96 min.) *Dir.:* Carl Schultz. *Cast:* Julia Blake (Frances), Leo McKern (Frank), Diane Craig (Sophie), Michele Fawdon (Helen).

Travesties (TV, 1977) *Cast:* Martin Benrath, Nikolaus Paryla, Klaus Guth, Kurt Meisel.

The Trip to Bountiful (TV, 1953; adapted from *A Trip to Bountiful*) *Dir.:* Vincent J. Donehue. *Cast:* John Beal (Ludie Watts), Lillian Gish (Carrie Watts), Eileen Heckart (Jessie Mae Watts), Eva Marie Saint (Thelma).

*The Trip to Bountiful (1985; 108 min.) *Dir.:* Peter Masterson. *Cast:* John Heard (Ludie Watts), Geraldine Page (Mrs. Watts), Carlin Glynn (Jessie Mae), Rebecca De Mornay (Thelma).

True West (TV, 1984; 110 min.) *Dir.:* Allan A. Goldstein. *Cast:* Gary Sinise (Austin), John Malkovich (Lee), Sam Schacht (Saul), Margaret Thomson (Mom).

True West (TV, 2002; 107 min.) *Cast:* Chad Smith (Austin), Bruce Willis (Lee), Andrew Alburger (Saul Kimmer), Danielle Kennedy (Mom).

Twenty-seven Wagons Full of Cotton (1990) *Dir.:* Don Scardino. *Cast:* Peter Boyle (Jake), Lesley Ann Warren (Flora), Ray Sharkey (Silva).

*Two for the Seesaw (1962; 119 min.) *Dir.:* Robert Wise. *Cast:* Robert Mitchum (Jerry Ryan), Shirley MacLaine (Gittel Mosca).

*A Voyage Round My Father (British TV, 1982; 90 min.) *Dir.:* Alvin Rakoff. *Cast:* Laurence Olivier (Clifford Mortimer), Alan Bates (John Mortimer), Elizabeth Sellars (Mother), Jane Asher (Elizabeth).

When You Comin' Back, Red Ryder? (1979; 113 min.) *Dir.:* Milton Katselas. *Cast:* Marjoe Gortner (Teddy), Hal Linden (Richard Ethredge), Lee Grant (Clarisse Ethredge), Peter Firth (Stephen Ryder), Pat Hingle (Lyle Striker).

*The Winslow Boy (British, 1948; 117 min.) *Dir.:* Anthony Asquith. *Cast:* Cedric Hardwicke (Arthur Winslow), Marie Lohr (Grace Winslow), Neil North (Ronnie Winslow), Jack Watling (Dickie Winslow).

The Winslow Boy (TV, 1958) *Dir.:* Alex Segal. *Cast:* Fredric March (Arthur Winslow), Florence Eldridge (Grace Winslow), Rex Thompson (Ronnie Winslow), John Warner (Dickie).

*The Winslow Boy (1999; 104 min.) *Dir.:* David Mamet. *Cast:* Nigel Hawthorne (Arthur Winslow), Gemma Jones (Grace Winslow), Guy Edwards (Ronald Arthur "Ronnie" Winslow), Matthew Pidgeon (Dickie Winslow).

*Wit (U.S./British TV, 2001; 98 min.) *Dir.:* Mike Nichols. *Cast:* Emma Thompson (Vivian Bearing), Christopher Lloyd (Dr. Kelekian), Jonathan M. Woodward (Jason Posner), Audra McDonald (Susie Monahan).

*The Women (1939; 131 min.) *Dir.:* George Cukor. *Cast:* Norma Shearer (Mrs. Stephen Haines [Mary]), Rosalind Russell (Mrs. Howard Fowler [Sylvia]), Phyllis Povah (Mrs. Phelps Potter [Edith]), Florence Nash (Nancy Blake).

Words upon the Window Pane (Ireland, 1994; 98 min.) *Dir.:* Mary McGuckian. *Cast:* Ian Richardson (Dr. Trench), Geraldine Chaplin (Miss McKenna), John Lynch (John Corbet), Donal Donnelly (Cornelius Patterson).

The Year of the Dragon (TV, 1975; 89 min.) *Dir.:* Portman Paget. *Cast:* George Takei (Fred Eng), Pat Suzuki.

*You Can't Take It with You (1938; 126 min.) *Dir.:* Frank Capra. *Cast:* Spring Byington (Penny Sycamore), Ann Miller (Essie Carmichael), Dub Taylor (Ed Carmichael), Samuel S. Hinds (Paul Sycamore).

You Can't Take It with You (TV, 1979; 97 min.) *Dir.:* Paul Bogart. *Cast:* Jean Stapleton (Penny Sycamore), Beth Howland (Essie Carmichael), Paul Sand (Ed Carmichael), Eugene Roche (Paul Sycamore).

*You Can't Take It with You (TV, 1984; 116 min.) *Dir.:* Kirk Browning, Ellis Rabb. *Cast:* Elizabeth Wilson (Penny Sycamore), Carole Androsky (Essie Carmichael), Christopher Foster (Ed Carmichael), Jack Dodson (Paul Sycamore).

PLAY TITLES IN
MASTERPLOTS, REVISED SECOND EDITION

The plays listed here are covered in Salem Press's twelve-volume *Masterplots, Revised Second Edition* (1996). Some of these titles were covered in the first edition of *Masterplots II: Drama Series*; however, none of these titles is covered in *Masterplots II: Drama Series, Revised Edition*.

Abraham and Isaac—Unknown
Acharnians, The—Aristophanes
Admirable Crichton, The—Sir James M. Barrie
Affected Young Ladies, The—Molière
Ajax—Sophocles
Alcestis—Euripides
Alchemist, The—Ben Jonson
All Fools—George Chapman
All for Love—John Dryden
All My Sons—Arthur Miller
All That Fall—Samuel Beckett
All's Well That Ends Well—William Shakespeare
Amphitryon—Plautus
Amphitryon 38—Jean Giraudoux
Andria—Terence
Andromache—Euripides
Andromache—Jean Baptiste Racine
Angels in America—Tony Kushner
Anna Christie—Eugene O'Neill
Antigone—Jean Anouilh
Antigone—Sophocles
Antony and Cleopatra—William Shakespeare
Arbitration, The—Menander
Arms and the Man—George Bernard Shaw
As You Like It—William Shakespeare

Baal—Bertolt Brecht
Bacchae, The—Euripides
Back to Methuselah—George Bernard Shaw
Bald Soprano, The—Eugène Ionesco
Barber of Seville, The—Pierre-Augustin Caron de Beaumarchais

Bartholomew Fair—Ben Jonson
Beaux' Stratagem, The—George Farquhar
Beaver Coat, The—Gerhart Hauptmann
Becket—Jean Anouilh
Bedbug, The—Vladimir Mayakovsky
Beggar's Opera, The—John Gay
Bérénice—Jean Baptiste Racine
Birds, The—Aristophanes
Birthday Party, The—Harold Pinter
Blithe Spirit—Noël Coward
Blood Wedding—Federico García Lorca
Boris Godunov—Alexander Pushkin
Braggart Soldier, The—Plautus
Brand—Henrik Ibsen
Break of Noon—Paul Claudel
Britannicus—Jean Baptiste Racine
Broken Jug, The—Heinrich von Kleist
Brothers, The—Terence
Browning Version, The—Terence Rattigan
Bus Stop—William Inge
Bussy d'Ambois—George Chapman

Caesar and Cleopatra—George Bernard Shaw
Cain—Lord Byron
Camille—Alexandre Dumas, *fils*
Candida—George Bernard Shaw
Captives, The—Plautus
Caretaker, The—Harold Pinter
Cat on a Hot Tin Roof—Tennessee Williams
Catiline—Ben Jonson
Cenci, The—Percy Bysshe Shelley
Chairs, The—Eugène Ionesco
Changeling, The—Thomas Middleton and William Rowley

Cherokee Night, The—Lynn Riggs
Cherry Orchard, The—Anton Chekhov
Chickencoop Chinaman, The—Frank Chin
Children of a Lesser God—Mark Medoff
Children of Herakles, The—Euripides
Children's Hour, The—Lillian Hellman
Cid, The—Pierre Corneille
Cinna—Pierre Corneille
Clouds, The—Aristophanes
Cocktail Party, The—T. S. Eliot
Comedy of Errors, The—William
    Shakespeare
Comus—John Milton
Confidential Clerk, The—T. S. Eliot
Conscious Lovers, The—Richard Steele
Coriolanus—William Shakespeare
Countess Cathleen, The—William Butler
    Yeats
Country Wife, The—William Wycherley
Courtesan, The—Pietro Aretino
Crimes of the Heart—Beth Henley
Critic, The—Richard Brinsley Sheridan
Crucible, The—Arthur Miller
Cyclops—Euripides
Cymbeline—William Shakespeare
Cyrano de Bergerac—Edmond Rostand

Dance of Death, The—August Strindberg
Dancing at Lughnasa—Brian Friel
Danton's Death—Georg Büchner
Death and the King's Horseman—Wole
    Soyinka
Death of a Salesman—Arthur Miller
Death of Empedocles, The—Friedrich
    Hölderlin
Deirdre—William Butler Yeats
Deirdre of the Sorrows—John Millington
    Synge
Delicate Balance, A—Edward Albee
Desire Under the Elms—Eugene O'Neill
Devotion of the Cross, The—Pedro Calderón
    de la Barca
Dining Room, The—A. R. Gurney, Jr.
Doctor Faustus—Christopher Marlowe
Doll's House, A—Henrik Ibsen

Don Carlos, Infante of Spain—Friedrich
    Schiller
Don Juan Tenorio—José Zorrilla
Double-Dealer, The—William Congreve
Duchess of Malfi, The—John Webster
Dumb Waiter, The—Harold Pinter
Dutchman—Amiri Baraka
Dynasts, The—Thomas Hardy

Eastward Ho!—George Chapman, with Ben
    Jonson and John Marston
Edward II—Christopher Marlowe
Egmont—Johann Wolfgang von Goethe
Elder Statesman, The—T. S. Eliot
Electra—Euripides
Electra—Hugo von Hofmannsthal
Electra—Sophocles
Emilia Galotti—Gotthold Ephraim Lessing
Emperor Jones, The—Eugene O'Neill
Endgame—Samuel Beckett
Endymion—John Lyly
Enemy of the People, An—Henrik Ibsen
Epicæne: Or, The Silent Woman—Ben Jonson
Equus—Peter Shaffer
Eunuch, The—Terence
Every Man in His Humour—Ben Jonson
Every Man out of His Humour—Ben Jonson
Everyman—Unknown
Exiles—James Joyce

Faithful Shepherdess, The—John Fletcher
Fake Astrologer, The—Pedro Calderón de la
    Barca
Family Reunion, The—T. S. Eliot
Father, The—August Strindberg
Fences—August Wilson
Firebugs, The—Max Frisch
Flies, The—Jean-Paul Sartre
Fool for Love—Sam Shepard
*for colored girls who have considered
    suicide/ when the rainbow is enuf*—
    Ntozake Shange
Foreign Girl, The—Florencio Sánchez
Friar Bacon and Friar Bungay—Robert
    Greene
Frogs, The—Aristophanes

Galileo—Bertolt Brecht
Gardener's Dog, The—Lope de Vega Carpio
Ghost Sonata, The—August Strindberg
Ghosts—Henrik Ibsen
Glass Menagerie, The—Tennessee Williams
Glengarry Glen Ross—David Mamet
Golden Boy—Clifford Odets
Gorboduc—Thomas Norton and Thomas
　Sackville
Great Galeoto, The—José Echegaray y
　Eizaguirre
Green Grow the Lilacs—Lynn Riggs

Hairy Ape, The—Eugene O'Neill
Hamlet, Prince of Denmark—William
　Shakespeare
Heartbreak House—George Bernard Shaw
Hedda Gabler—Henrik Ibsen
Heidi Chronicles, The—Wendy Wasserstein
Helen—Euripides
Henry IV—Luigi Pirandello
Henry IV, Part I—William Shakespeare
Henry IV, Part II—William Shakespeare
Henry V—William Shakespeare
Henry VI, Part I—William Shakespeare
Henry VI, Part II—William Shakespeare
Henry VI, Part III—William Shakespeare
Henry VIII—William Shakespeare, with
　John Fletcher
Hippolytus—Euripides
H.M.S. Pinafore—W. S. Gilbert
Horace—Pierre Corneille
House of Blue Leaves, The—John Guare
Hyde Park—James Shirley
Hypochondriac, The—Molière

Iceman Cometh, The—Eugene O'Neill
Ignes de Castro—Antonio Ferreira
Importance of Being Earnest, The—Oscar
　Wilde
Inspector General, The—Nikolai Gogol
Intruder, The—Maurice Maeterlinck
Iolanthe—W. S. Gilbert
Ion—Euripides
Iphigenia in Aulis—Euripides
Iphigenia in Tauris—Euripides

J. B.—Archibald MacLeish
Jew of Malta, The—Christopher Marlowe
Julius Caesar—William Shakespeare
Juno and the Paycock—Sean O'Casey

King and No King, A—Francis Beaumont
　and John Fletcher
King Johan—John Bale
King John—William Shakespeare
King Lear—William Shakespeare
King, the Greatest Alcalde, The—Lope de
　Vega Carpio
Knight of the Burning Pestle, The—Francis
　Beaumont
Knights, The—Aristophanes
Krapp's Last Tape—Samuel Beckett

Lady from the Sea, The—Henrik Ibsen
Lady Windermere's Fan—Oscar Wilde
Lady's Not for Burning, The—Christopher
　Fry
Largo Desolato—Václav Havel
Liar, The—Pierre Corneille
Life Is a Dream—Pedro Calderón de la
　Barca
Liliom—Ferenc Molnár
Little Clay Cart, The—Unknown
Little Foxes, The—Lillian Hellman
Long Day's Journey into Night—Eugene
　O'Neill
Look Back in Anger—John Osborne
Love for Love—William Congreve
Love in a Wood—William Wycherley
Love Suicides at Sonezaki, The—
　Chikamatsu Monzaemon
Love's Labour's Lost—William Shakespeare
Lower Depths, The—Maxim Gorky
Lute, The—Gao Ming
Lysistrata—Aristophanes

Macbeth—William Shakespeare
Madwoman of Chaillot, The—Jean
　Giraudoux
Maid of Honour, The—Philip Massinger
Maids, The—Jean Genet

Maid's Tragedy, The—Francis Beaumont and John Fletcher
Major Barbara—George Bernard Shaw
Malcontent, The—John Marston
Man and Superman—George Bernard Shaw
Man for All Seasons, A—Robert Bolt
Man of Mode, The—Sir George Etherege
Man Who Came to Dinner, The—George S. Kaufman and Moss Hart
Manfred—Lord Byron
Marat/Sade—Peter Weiss
Maria Magdalena—Friedrich Hebbel
Marriage à la Mode—John Dryden
Marriage of Figaro, The—Pierre-Augustin Caron de Beaumarchais
Master Builder, The—Henrik Ibsen
MASTER HAROLD . . . and the Boys—Athol Fugard
Mayor of Zalamea, The—Pedro Calderón de la Barca
Measure for Measure—William Shakespeare
Medea—Euripides
Menaechmi, The—Plautus
Merchant of Venice, The—William Shakespeare
Merry Wives of Windsor, The—William Shakespeare
Mid-Channel—Arthur Wing Pinero
Midsummer Night's Dream, A—William Shakespeare
Mikado, The—W. S. Gilbert
Miracle Worker, The—William Gibson
Misanthrope, The—Molière
Miser, The—Molière
Miss Julie—August Strindberg
Mistress of the Inn, The—Carlo Goldoni
Mithridates—Jean Baptiste Racine
Month in the Country, A—Ivan Turgenev
Mother Courage and Her Children—Bertolt Brecht
Mourning Becomes Electra—Eugene O'Neill
Mousetrap, The—Agatha Christie
Mrs. Dane's Defence—Henry Arthur Jones

Much Ado About Nothing—William Shakespeare
Murder in the Cathedral—T. S. Eliot

Nathan the Wise—Gotthold Ephraim Lessing
New Way to Pay Old Debts, A—Philip Massinger
Night of the Iguana, The—Tennessee Williams
'night, Mother—Marsha Norman
No Exit—Jean-Paul Sartre
No Trifling with Love—Alfred de Musset
Normal Heart, The—Larry Kramer

Odd Couple, The—Neil Simon
Oedipus at Colonus—Sophocles
Oedipus Tyrannus—Sophocles
Old Bachelor, The—William Congreve
Old Fortunatus—Thomas Dekker
Old Wives' Tale, The—George Peele
Oresteia, The—Aeschylus
Orfeo—Poliziano
Orpheus—Jean Cocteau
Othello—William Shakespeare
Our Town—Thornton Wilder

Passion Flower, The—Jacinto Benavente y Martínez
Patience—W. S. Gilbert
Peace—Aristophanes
Peer Gynt—Henrik Ibsen
Pelléas and Mélisande—Maurice Maeterlinck
Pericles, Prince of Tyre—William Shakespeare
Persians, The—Aeschylus
Peter Pan—Sir James M. Barrie
Phaedra—Jean Baptiste Racine
Philaster—Francis Beaumont and John Fletcher
Philoctetes—Sophocles
Phoenician Women, The—Euripides
Phormio—Terence
Pillars of Society, The—Henrik Ibsen
Pirates of Penzance, The—W. S. Gilbert
Plain-Dealer, The—William Wycherley

MASTERPLOTS II

DRAMA SERIES
REVISED EDITION

TITLE INDEX

TITLE INDEX

AUTHOR INDEX

AUTHOR INDEX

TYPE OF PLOT INDEX

ABSURDIST

American Dream, The (Albee) I-48
Balcony, The (Genet) I-95
Caligula (Camus) I-234
Chairs, The (Ionesco) I-260
Deathwatch (Genet) I-410
Embers (Beckett) II-501
Exit the King (Ionesco) II-525
Fefu and Her Friends (Fornes) II-546
Goat, The (Albee) II-615
Happy Days (Beckett) II-681
Indian Wants the Bronx, The (Horovitz)
  II-776
Ivona, Princess of Burgundia
  (Gombrowicz) II-802

Keep Tightly Closed in a Cool Dry Place
  (Terry) II-839
Killer, The (Ionesco) II-853
Lesson, The (Ionesco) II-902
Loot (Orton) III-939
Marriage, The (Gombrowicz) III-1008
Police, The (Mrożek) III-1206
Three Tall Women (Albee) IV-1557
Tiny Alice (Albee) IV-1572
Tree Climber, The (al-Hakim) IV-1625
Ubu Roi (Jarry) IV-1662
Water Hen, The (Witkiewicz) IV-1696
Words and Music (Beckett) IV-1755